W9-BWP-652

RESERVED BOOK

WITHDRAWN
University Libraries
University of Memphis

UOM MAIN LIBR
DATE DUE
10 14 02

THE
ARCHITECTURE
OF AMERICA

THE ARCHITECTURE OF AMERICA

A Social and Cultural History

by JOHN Ely BURCHARD

and ALBERT BUSH-BROWN

WITH PHOTOGRAPHS

An Atlantic Monthly Press Book

LITTLE, BROWN AND COMPANY · BOSTON · TORONTO

COPYRIGHT © 1961 BY JOHN BURCHARD AND ALBERT BUSH-BROWN

ALL RIGHTS RESERVED. NO PART OF THIS BOOK MAY BE REPRO-
DUCED IN ANY FORM WITHOUT PERMISSION IN WRITING FROM THE
PUBLISHER, EXCEPT BY A REVIEWER WHO MAY QUOTE BRIEF PAS-
SAGES IN A REVIEW TO BE PRINTED IN A MAGAZINE OR NEWSPAPER.

LIBRARY OF CONGRESS CATALOG CARD NO. 61–5736

SECOND PRINTING

The authors wish to thank the following for permission to reprint material
from published books and magazines:

Architectural Record for R. H. Shreve's "The Economic Design of Office
Buildings," published in Vol. LXVII, 1930.

Cornell University Press for Edward Chase Kirkland's DREAM AND
THOUGHT IN THE BUSINESS COMMUNITY, 1860-1900.

Dodd, Mead & Company for Fabian Franklin's THE LIFE OF DANIEL COIT
GILMAN.

Duell, Sloan & Pearce, Inc., for FRANK LLOYD WRIGHT ON ARCHITECTURE,
edited by Frederick Gutheim, copyright 1941 by Duell, Sloan & Pearce.

Harvard University Press for Loeb Classical Library Edition of PROCOPIUS.

Houghton Mifflin Company for AUTOBIOGRAPHY OF ANDREW CARNEGIE and
THE EDUCATION OF HENRY ADAMS.

Hoyle, Doran & Berry for Ralph Adams Cram's MY LIFE IN ARCHITEC-
TURE.

Massachusetts Historical Society for "The Atkinson Papers" as quoted in
Edward Chase Kirkland's DREAM AND THOUGHT IN THE BUSINESS COMMU-
NITY, 1860-1900.

Oxford University Press, Inc., for Talbot Hamlin's GREEK REVIVAL ARCHI-
TECTURE IN AMERICA.

Studio Books, London, for Bruno Taut's MODERN ARCHITECTURE.

ATLANTIC–LITTLE, BROWN BOOKS
ARE PUBLISHED BY
LITTLE, BROWN AND COMPANY
IN ASSOCIATION WITH
THE ATLANTIC MONTHLY PRESS

*Published simultaneously in Canada
by Little, Brown & Company (Canada) Limited*

PRINTED IN THE UNITED STATES OF AMERICA

For MARJORIE *and* FRANCES

131891   NA
705
B8

It is not because I wish to make a display of skill, nor through any confidence in my eloquence, nor because I pride myself on my personal knowledge of many lands, that I have set about writing this record; for indeed I had no grounds for venturing so bold an intention. Yet the thought has many times occurred to me, how many and how great are the benefits which are wont to accrue to states through History, which transmits to future generations the memory of those who have gone before, and resists the steady effort of time to bury events in oblivion; and while it incites to virtue those who from time to time may read it by the praise it bestows, it constantly assails vice by repelling its influence. Wherefore our concern must be solely this — that all the deeds of the past shall be clearly set forth, and by what man, whosoever he might be, they were wrought. And this, I believe, is not an impossible task, even for a lisping and thin-voiced tongue.

— PROCOPIUS OF CAESAREA, Volume VII, *Buildings*, Ii
(translated by H. B. Dewing)

I suppose, if Lacedaemon were to become desolate, and the temples and the foundations of the public buildings were left, that as time went on there would be a strong disposition with posterity to refuse to accept her fame as true evidence of her power. . . . But if Athens were to suffer the same misfortune, I suppose that any inference from the appearance presented to the eye would make her power to have been twice as great as it is.

— THUCYDIDES, *The History of the Peloponnesian War*, I, 10
(translated by Sir R. W. Livingstone)

Foreword

A GOOD FIVE YEARS BEFORE THE CENTENNIAL CELE-
bration of The American Institute of Architects in 1957, it was
suggested that a fitting, if not essential, by-product of the celebration would be publication of a history of the Institute's first hundred
years. The proposal seemed not without merit. After some search of
the records, it was found, however, that the history of an organization,
even that of The American Institute of Architects, was not exactly apt
to titillate the public and, at best, would interest the membership but
slightly. It seemed scarcely a subject for a major endeavor. It then occurred to the Executive Director that instead of a history of the Institute,
it would be well for the A.I.A. to publish a book on American architecture during the Institute's lifetime. The book, he felt, should relate more
to the impact of our changing society on the profession and the resulting
architecture, than construe a tenuous, if flattering, premise that things
happened the other way around. In other words, he asked for a scholarly treatise — one which would call for skill.

The Committee on the Centennial Celebration enthusiastically
adopted the proposal. The Chairman, Alexander Robinson, III, appointed a subcommittee under the chairmanship of Dean Wurster, who,
with his customary foresight and enthusiasm, persuaded Dean John E.
Burchard of the School of Humanities and Social Studies, Massachusetts
Institute of Technology, to undertake the task. Subsequently, Professor
Albert Bush-Brown of M.I.T. was enlisted as co-author.

As it turned out, it was impossible to even ask that a work of such
magnitude, demanding such staggering amounts and depth of research,
be completed, let alone printed, in time for the A.I.A. Centennial in
1957. It was therefore agreed that it would be better to have the job
done well than hurriedly.

This decision was wise, for the authors have succeeded far beyond the anticipations of anyone to produce a book which should and will, I think, prove to be *the* major work on American architecture of the past century.

The American Institute of Architects is proud to lend its name and sponsorship to this work.

> Edmund R. Purves, FAIA
> Executive Director
> The American Institute of Architects

The Octagon
Washington, D. C.
September 1960

Contents

The Nature of Architecture

ARCHITECTURE IS A SOCIAL ART. ANY ART, IT MAY BE argued, must serve some social purpose but the demands upon architecture are clear. They impose limitations on the architect which are not inevitably imposed on the painter or sculptor.

A building of high artistic merit, measured solely in visual terms, is architecture even if it is badly built or if it performs its practical functions indifferently. With these defects it will not of course be fine architecture. On the other hand, a building which serves practical functions well and is eminently durable but lacks art is not architecture at all.

Architecture cannot be too ephemeral. A stage set, no matter how convincing, is not architecture; a tent is not architecture either, though both may have architectural qualities. Buildings of plaster, intended only to last through a summer's exposition, are not architecture. But such butterflies have often had important influence on later architecture, and a few have survived their first purpose and become permanent parts of the community.

Architecture then requires three things. A building must serve the social needs for which it is built. The materials and the structure must be firm and suitably durable. And then there is the art.

These three conditions for architecture have been stated by many critics in many times and in many ways. The best-known expression is probably that of Sir Henry Wotton. It comes from 1624 when he published a paraphrase of a ten-volume treatise on architecture by a mediocre Augustan architect, Marcus Vitruvius Pollio. This asserted that architecture must embrace firmness, commodity and delight. No society has valued all three equally, but even if they are all coveted the full demands of utility and structure and art cannot often be met in a single building. Architecture as a social art is doomed to the imperfection that is at once its limitation and its glory.

The examination and understanding of architecture require the study of how buildings have or have not worked for the society that built them, how they have employed materials and structural principles, and how they can be measured as art. Some of the understanding can come from the intellect; some is sensuous, even intuitive. Before we face the all-important question of how artistic quality can be assessed with reasonable objectivity, we should understand how society works on its architecture; and then how the architecture works on it.

I

SOCIETY DETERMINES THE PURPOSES OF ITS BUILDINGS AND WHICH OF those purposes it values most highly; it defines the uses of the buildings; it prescribes the materials and techniques that are available; it sets the price it is willing to pay for architecture in competition with other things it wants and this includes how much, if anything, extra it will pay for beauty transcending utility; it restricts the scope of architecture through laws of safety and health; it affects the architects' views of tradition and innovation; it determines the levels of skill that it will accept or demand.

Architecture in turn acts as a catalyst to influence uses and taste; it may provide symbols; it may reinforce conservatism or encourage a people to be adventurous; it can improve society but it does not always do this; it can lead to some extent but most of the time it will be led. Since buildings are commissioned primarily by those in power, architecture is more limited in its revolutionary capacity than painting or poetry or the polemic and didactic literatures. The revolutionary architect is more likely to be revolutionary with his forms than with his ideas about a reconstructed society; or, at any rate, this will be so for his buildings. Thus, quite aside from their quality as formal design, buildings are also documents that divulge what the men in power were like who built them, when they were built, and why.

However much a Western architect of today might yearn to build a Hagia Sophia, he could not find the opportunity; for the powerful Justinian, Emperor of the Byzantines and Manifestation of Christ, has no modern Western counterpart. Nor will we see another pyramid like that of Gizeh unless the world again practices a cult of physical immortality in a state of slave builders or unless some Egyptian dictator seeks like Mussolini to reconstruct a theatrical reminiscence from a great past. If the skyline of a medieval town is dominated by a cathedral, if most other buildings are lower and less well built, then that relation tells us what medieval society valued. If a jagged skyline of skyscraper office buildings dwarfs the churches and schools, then we have a sign of the aspirations of a society whose dreams are unracked by medieval visions of the Apocalypse and the Last Judgment.

The exotic lamaseries of Tibet do not appear in the Swiss Alps; the sensitive Katsura Palace in Japan, a response to a civilized imperial life, would not have served Diamond Jim Brady. Minarets where muezzins cry at sundown; Britain's Houses of Parliament; Broadway at Forty-fourth Street: all these are signs of the inexorable necessity that every society will cast an architectural image of itself.

Without glass, metal frames, and panel construction, New York's Lever House would be impossible. Without modern cements and steels and mathematics, Pier Luigi Nervi could not span his colossal Italian spaces. However great their aspirations to build wider and higher naves, Gothic architects were limited by their stereotomy, as they learned by the several collapses of audacious Beauvais. Technological possibilities have occasionally been anticipated by prescient architects with designs requiring materials and techniques not yet generally available. More frequently, what is possible and practical limits architectural imagination to forms that utilize the materials, techniques, and shapes acceptable to society and easily supplied by it.

Sometimes societies have been profligate or generous about architecture; at other times austere and frugal. The posture was influential. What is called economical depends upon what is demanded. Even Hagia Sophia was economical in terms of the Byzantine insistence upon placing a celestial and mortuary symbol, the dome, above each tomb of Christ, the altar. Even though earthquakes threatened, Justinian decreed these expensive and unstable symbolic forms; symbolism overweighed expense or risk. A design that fails to provide full emotional and physical performance is not economical, however cheap. Indeed, cheapness has never been a criterion of great building, however much it has seemed important in times of austerity or to a congenitally frugal people.

Not all societies have been willing to pay a premium price for beauty or permanence. Mining and drilling and manufacturing societies have not been noted for beautiful or permanent architecture. Commercial societies like that of America's twentieth century have learned to exploit architecture as the supreme advertisement. Monarchies and dictatorships have loved monuments, while necrologic permanence was the enduring objective of Egyptian architects. But the nomadic Hebrew cared little for resting his mobile Ark of the Covenant beneath a stable architectural tradition, and the Japanese periodically rebuild some of their wooden temples; the ceremonial act of rehousing their gods within traditional forms has more value to them than anything gained through permanence or innovation.

Laws restrict the scope of architecture. Modern building codes prohibit some interesting architectural possibilities. The fire hazards risked with large panes of glass in stair towers have forced architects to use smaller ones even when the resultant scale has failed to harmonize with that of the building. Social restrictions sometimes eliminate architectural wonders, like the elegant open spiral staircase which no longer appears in public buildings because its narrow treads and open well are dangerous and safety is more esteemed than elegance. Other overriding social necessities such as those brought about by war may limit architecture by setting priorities on materials. Where prices for materials are high and prices for men are low, architectural results may be different than when the opposite relation exists. Sometimes the economy of a society results in architectural irony; a rich nation can no longer afford the handsome marble used in the Lincoln Memorial even if the shipment from quarries high in Colorado is only to the adjacent Air Force Academy, which finds it more practical to import from remote Georgia. The owners of the pure white stone of Colorado now prefer to grind, bag and ship it as fertilizer.

Sometimes people find the original mood of an important old building incompatible with their new beliefs. During the sixteenth and seventeenth centuries Protestants in northern Europe were often iconoclasts; they hacked away at Catholic churches of Gothic times, knocking heads from statues, removing stained glass, replacing altars with Communion tables, inserting tall pulpits, filling naves with pews where congregations could receive Communion. Economic obsolescence fosters demolition. So do changes in land use. Some of America's finest buildings have been victims of that sort of change. Taxation may accelerate decentralization, causing people to abandon old and expensive properties within cities. Not all this demolition is regrettable; it makes way for something new, perhaps even better; but it also wrecks valuable things, and how much of this wreckage is tolerated or encouraged is in itself an indication of the value society places on its architecture and on the tangible evidences of its past.

The architect's views of tradition and innovation are influenced by the views of his fellow citizens. Today's cult of originality often avoids repeating anything that can be recognized as having ever been done before. We forget how new this idea is. Neither the Greek nor the medieval man valued originality so much as competence; he perfected traditional types of art, even transcribing what was read to him from manuscripts. His occasional deviations were not flights of idiosyncrasy so much as provincial usages or errors. Some recent buildings, notably the tall ones, seem to have been advancing towards perfected types, but uniqueness, self-conscious innovation, characterizes even them. Other buildings have been flagrant flights of innovation. Modern society rewards novelty more readily than it does perfection. The fact that innovation is usefully rampant in, for example, the design of aircraft does not necessarily prove that it is equally important or even desirable for architecture.

Architects will not easily gain support for the exciting space, for sculpture and painting, or for the plan that reserves part of a skyscraper's site for a public garden, unless society comprehends and wants them enough to be anxious to pay for them. Like the other arts, architecture may be jostled and scuffed in the mass-consumer market, losing its loftiness and refinement at the hands of indifferent buyers and all-too-enterprising hucksters. An architect cannot easily maintain high standards for a society that is content with artlessness or which willingly accepts tools that have been nicked by vulgarity. The aesthetic of a nation is largely determined by the taste of its citizens and not by the talent of its artists. Architects will not long seek perfection for compatriots who admire the nondescript, the copied, the merely utilitarian or the banal, as they did at the end of the Hellenistic or Byzantine times. In times of transition architectural leadership is possible; in frozen times it is not.

Society prescribes what architecture may express. In a period of concentration upon low-cost housing and slum clearance, the architect who is inclined towards social liberalism fares better than one whose training has prepared him to be suspicious of social reform and to prefer to design palaces for a few rich, even reactionary, patrons. A twist in political objectives may throw the balance another way. Still, though society may propose, the architect will dispose; for architecture is not different from any other creative activity. It prospers only when the architect has enthusiasm for what he is doing, and is thus at its best when the artist and the society are in agreement.

Society must sometimes yield the leadership to architecture. Taste is a joint effort. If anything about art is securely true, it is that fashion changes. Architecture itself has often served as the catalyst. One new skyscraper attracts others to its vicinity; one admirable building raises the architectural quality of others that follow it. Each new experimen-

tal building changes taste and makes further innovation more acceptable. Society here often, indeed usually, acts as a retarder. It seldom in-
spires greatness and only tentatively accepts the daring or difficult.

Architecture provides symbols for society but it does not invent them,
for symbols come from the roots and the soil, not from the mind. They
do not spring full-panoplied, but grow. Functional forms like the tall
slab and funnel-shaped auditorium of the United Nations headquarters
may become signs after they are built and much later might be symbols.
Nonutilitarian forms are sometimes assigned religious or political meanings, as when, after 1825, men associated Christianity and democracy
with historical types of architecture. Such symbolism has often led to
flagrant scene-painting in which the more literary aspects of buildings
gained precedence over organization of useful and well-constructed
spaces and masses. Many symbols arise from strictly functional or structural requirements like the transept of the Gothic church, which was first
provided not to make the plan into a symbolic cross but to accommodate more people of the upper classes near the altar. They may attain
the status of symbols later, even after they have lost their utilitarian
significance. Thus the transept may be retained even in a democratic
and Protestant church where the cruciform symbol, now become literary, is more valued than the current inconvenience is disliked. The unified symbolic form subordinates the use that attended its birth; it
achieves a freedom that overpowers utilitarian demands so that the
Gothic cathedral or Greek temple remains a formal attainment quite
oblivious to physical comfort or efficiency. Such a symbol then acquires
social power.

Architecture may broadcast the general philosophical bias of a society.
To a Renaissance man a formal garden was nature at its best, not rude
and unkempt and spoiled by the irregularities of knolls, winding
streams, natural trees, and clouds; but orderly, organized by a man who
believed that supreme nature contained perfect geometrical forms like
the sphere, arranged on axes and circles, proportioned arithmetically,
and placed in exact balance. He projected this notion of perfection
upon his gardens and architecture and cities. To such a man, gardens
like those of picturesque Stowe in England or Central Park in New
York would have seemed chaotic. But they did not seem so to the
nineteenth-century man whose rustic landscapes were filled with contrived accidental variation, surprising vistas, and highly individualized
trees and plants. His gardens reflected a view of primeval nature, un-
molested by man, and if nature was perchance too orderly he would set
about artificially to create a "natural" disorder.

Such contrasting views are not invented by architects. They are

learned from poets and artists and scientists. Nor do architects fashion
a metaphysical scheme and then seek spaces and masses to embody it.
Rather, each age seems to enjoy a few vividly characterized metaphors
of space. These reflect not only a contemporary aesthetic but the metaphysical system that underlies it. Often those metaphors are legacies
from the past lagging the current thought. The Parthenon was more
conservative than Sophocles. Thus, today, in an era when scientific naturalism or at least agnosticism prevails among leading intellectuals,
many architects still cling to theology or romanticism; and they consciously thwart the dehumanization they see in stringent mechanism.
Once adopted, such a point of view affects the kinds of architecture a
designer creates. His buildings will most frequently be striking affirma-
tions of prevailing opinion; or occasionally the architect may use a
building as a rejection of the common view or a warning that the view
should be changed. This opportunity, however, comes to few architects
and is grasped by fewer. Thus only a few buildings are polemics.

Architecture's role in shaping history is not easy to discern; for a
building exists only because society has previously defined the need for
it. What might be causative is already at work in society, and we cannot
claim that architecture alone is entirely responsible for a given social
result. Still, unless architecture benefited and often changed society,
buildings would not have profound effects. Architectural symbols set
the image of a Lincoln or a government or a city. Errors in siting and
planning may cause businesses to collapse, and the client may not deserve the whole responsibility; an attractive shopping center is responsive to decentralization but also accelerates it; the Grand Central Terminal at New York seems to draw clusters of new office buildings but
an Empire State Building does not — yet each may establish the character of a section of a city. The architecture of a street may define
whether it will be a fine area or a slum, if only for a while.

Churchill understood all this when he persuaded Parliament to rebuild its bombed-out House of Commons along traditional lines despite manifest inconveniences in the transaction of parliamentary business. Those regions of Europe where Gothic and baroque churches
attained supreme expression consistently resisted the advance of Protes-
tantism as the Gothic plans opposed alteration and preserved the aesthetic of older liturgies. Where, as in the United States, there was no
one great religious architectural tradition, there have been enormous
variations in the interpretation and practice of Christian worship. People possessing a great architecture are not so apt to exchange it for
something new, particularly when they run the risk of not obtaining
something better. They cling to their architecture and to the ideas ex-

pressed by it. As Churchill said, "We shape our buildings and after-wards our buildings shape us."

We must not draw the wrong inference from the fact that architecture does have social consequences. A building is not great architecture simply because it evokes responses and affects society. The Empire State Building was never great architecture, though it may have briefly been one of the greatest nerve centers of American commerce; the Pentagon is not great architecture even though it may be a very convenient head-quarters for the Department of Defense. The Statue of Liberty may suggest ideas that deserve the highest approbation, but it is not im-plicitly beautiful thereby. Conversely, the Temple at Karnak is no less beautiful because it is the handiwork of a succession of despotic slave-driving Pharaohs.

We are led astray, also, if we infer that great art always improves so-ciety. Following Ruskin, many have believed that a moral or democratic architecture will make a society moral or democratic. But excellent ar-chitecture cannot be proved to have inspired better moral or more democratic behavior. The Pazzi consummated their conspiracy against the de' Medici within the cathedral at Florence; Thomas à Becket met his fate in Canterbury Cathedral. Architectural Paris has served, in-differently, Empire and Republic, Commune and Vichy. The theater has often capitalized upon the shortcomings of inadequate stages; the performances in Palladio's great theater at Vicenza are not necessarily the best. Let us not claim too much for architecture. Families living in architecturally undistinguished houses may be abundantly happy, while a pleasure dome may be the seat of despair. No doubt, progressive ideas about elementary school education have been aided by recent school architecture, but architecture remains only an instrument of education, not the teacher, and fine new school buildings do not guarantee that Negroes will be tolerantly and well educated in Virginia. The sky-scraper helped centralize businesses, and separated them from the sources of production and distribution; but it did not originate cen-tralization, which began before the appropriate architecture and its es-sential technical partners were fully accepted. In all these, architecture assisted society to move along new lines or even accelerated the move-ment; but it did not create the new directions nor generate the will be-hind them.

Architecture is thus a powerful historical document and it is a pleas-ure to study it for this purpose alone. An understanding of the historical and social environment in which a building was made will add much to the total enjoyment of the building as a building. But all this process is highly intellectual. It will not explain architecture.

2

ON THE OTHER HAND, THE AESTHETIC VIRTUE OF A MAGNIFICENT BUILDING can be sensed without any knowledge of its history at all. This is a physical sense. It also is not without standards of measurement and is certainly not wholly subjective; but it cannot rely on the intellect alone. It depends upon the impressions the building produces of its firmness, its commodity, and its delight.

One does not need to be able to analyze a truss to see when it is fitting for its purpose. The refinement of a great groin vault and the coarseness of a crude one will be apparent to a sensitive person who could not begin to wrestle with the stereotomy that produced them. The quality of a brick wall, whether the bricks are fine bricks, the workmanship careful, can be appraised, as a generality, with little sophistication. Firmness does, of course, rest on sound, even brilliant, engineering, on the knowing application of theory and practice, but when it has been achieved it should be possible to recognize it, once one has learned not to take it for granted.

The assessment of commodity requires knowledge of another kind. One cannot understand whether the Gothic cathedral is commodious if he has no idea what is supposed to happen in it. To this extent the appreciation of commodity is intellectual; one needs to measure the achievement of specific purpose against what the purpose is. But again there are other elements of commodity which transcend specific purpose. In a well-designed building, the way you enter, the way you come naturally to the important spaces without signs, without threading a maze, the way you find important corridors or elevators, all these can be sensed almost independently of the purpose. This element of commodity, known technically as the circulation, should always be crystal clear. If it is not, the building lacks commodity, no matter how impressive it may be in other ways. A truly commodious building seems to work with a certain inevitability. It does not prompt you easily to conjectures as to how it might have worked better.

Thus finally we come to the indispensable ingredient, delight, sensuous delight, augmented by the intellect but elusive to intellectual analysis.

Before a building appeals to the intellect it will have appealed to the senses. The sense of architecture does not require the taste buds and only rarely the nose. The ears are more important. A bell or a fountain may affect our impression of space. People need some spaces where sounds are clear, some where silence is supreme and privacy secure, some which are dominated by resonance. Touch also accentuates architectural sensation. We can increase our sense of space by walking. Touching with our hands, we learn the texture of materials. A pool or shaded court may produce more than relief from heat and humidity; we feel temperature, sun and shadow and the movement of air, and these modify our sensations of space.

But more than any of these, the eye must be satisfied. It seeks fine space, appropriate furnishings, appealing changes of level, and convincing ways of entering and leaving. It relishes well-formed masses and eloquent surfaces. Colors and patterns of light are important; so are exquisite small details or the synchronized work of painters and sculptors and craftsmen. The architect must decide what light will do: whether it will illuminate, cast shadows, create mood, stimulate movement, or arrest activity as the rose window at Chartres does. He must decide when a space shall use color *fortissimo* and when *pianissimo* and when not at all; when he shall enrich with ornament and when leave bare; when textures shall be rough, when smooth, when neutral; when to bring a colleague from painting or sculpture into a full collaboration and when to reject all these more personal arts.

Water, too, is an element of architecture in its protean capacity to be ice, liquid, and steam, to be musical or still, to cascade or reflect. In fine architecture all of these will be controlled and led to a climax. Problems as common as that of bringing water down from the roof will receive poetic answers rather than obscure or perfunctory solutions. Snow and moonlight, sunshine and rain — these surround and enrich even the meanest building if the architect will only allow them.

The foremost principle of this visual experience of architecture is that it is three-dimensional and physical. Photographs have made us familiar with particular aspects of a few famous buildings, always from the same viewpoint, but we must never forget that there are many points of view for any significant building and that they cannot all be assumed simultaneously, even in the memory.

There is no substitute whatever for the first-hand physical experience. Buildings are made by men for men, and their size in relation to a man, the limitations they impose or the freedoms they propose, cannot be suggested in anything more than a meager way by photographs or motion pictures or anything short of the three-dimensional full-scale encounter.

Great architecture offers not only external visual satisfactions of mass, form, or detail which can be sensed much as monumental sculpture can

be sensed. Almost always it also insists that you enter and be enveloped
by it so you must meet a great building in two fundamentally different
space situations, one where you are outside it and one where it is outside you. If you have not given the interior of a building an opportunity for the embrace, you do not really know the building. This embrace, too, can be experienced only progressively through time.

The visual pleasures of architecture depend on two quite different
experiences. The more important one, which we call the experience of
composition, or *design*, results from the arrangement of the elements
that make up a work of art, and particularly from its spaces, masses, and
planes. While design affords the first and fundamental experience of
architecture, secondary pleasures depend upon the observer's interpretation of the mood and meaning of the building. The source of this experience we call *expression*.

As we create or analyze architecture, we have difficulty separating design from expression. The building involves both; the separation is an
abstraction, useful for analysis, untruthful to experience. Many architects and critics assert that architectural enjoyment stems almost entirely from design; others implore us to concentrate upon expression.
The historical fact is that architecture has been richest when excellent
design and meaningful expression have been joined. Let us examine
the lesser experience first.

Different buildings induce different moods. Some seem to dampen
informal conversation and lighthearted or frivolous action. Others ridi-
cule pomp and circumstance as clearly as the African hut mocked the
Englishman's dinner jacket. The delicate, even fragile, lines of the Taj
Mahal, dedicated by an Eastern prince to the memory of his favorite
wife, are totally different from those of the warlike fortress, the Palazzo
Vecchio, which bristles with Florentine belligerence. The stately emotions find ready expression in architecture but so do the serene ones.
Heroism resounds from the brick wall of Ludwig Mies van der Rohe's
Liebknecht Monument at Berlin, faith from the vaults at Amiens. At
Versailles, the vain Louis continues his *lever* and *coucher* before sycophantic courtiers; the Ca' d'Oro flirts with the canals of Venice. Less
lasting emotions seldom appear: anger almost never, humor rarely.
Their life is local and ephemeral, while architecture seldom is either. But
gaiety can be captured in theaters and restaurants, and a Louis XV
boudoir speaks of the delicate, sometimes subtle, intimacies of the eighteenth century.

Beyond these direct expressions are those brought to us by sentiment,
memory — they may come from our devotion to God, to the state, to

the family, to youth, to history. They may be literary. They may be fantasy or fairy-tale. No one can quite remove them from his assessment of a building.

The expressiveness of a building is bound then to be somewhat personal since it builds on the accumulated experience of the viewer. It is often quite subjective, depending on how the building affects us, whether we are tired or rested, responsive or callous to its messages. Subjective interpretations account for the fact that one may like or dislike a building whether its architecture is bad or good. Personal likes and dislikes in architecture are thus inevitable as in all the other arts; they are not undesirable. But they should not be confused with the absolute merit of what is liked or disliked. Thus it is reasonable to say of a piece of good architecture that you dislike it; but unreasonable to call it bad merely because you dislike it. Whether it is good or bad transcends personal like and dislike and is subject to reasonably objective determination.

Architectural beauty, thus understood, is not a matter of pleasantness and certainly not of sweetness, for the beautiful may be delicate or strong, refined or crude, receptive or forbidding. To please is not the only aim of art or architecture. It may sadden, frighten, even horrify, as well as lift up, console, or reassure. If the architect prompts us to return, if he has established a definite and consistent organization of space and mass, then he has fashioned a beautiful thing, whose beauty transcends hasty pleasure or displeasure, transient like and dislike.

We may quit whatever is beautiful at this point, satisfied by the enjoyment of axes sensed, invitations half accepted, directions vaguely followed. Or we may inquire into the experience to obtain more objective understanding of the building. Dissecting the building, defining its spaces and masses, studying their transitions, need not destroy the experience as though we were pulling the petals from a flower. Instead, it may enrich it. That is the guerdon of the professional architect or critic. His eye is alert to the proportions of a space, the sources of light, the rhythm of structural members, how one moves from space to space, where one feels pressed and congested, where expansive and free, where one is arrested by a vista or a wall, the experiences of color and texture, the elegance or charm of detail or ornament. These are dividends that do not have to be restricted to the professional.

3

THE MAJOR IMPACT OF ARCHITECTURE IS MADE THROUGH ITS SPACE AND
mass. Necessarily, the architectural imagination works with geometric
shapes. In the long run, unless he seeks amorphism, the architect is
limited to a few basic shapes, separately or in combination. There are
the primary, elementary forms: the pyramid at Gizeh; the cylinder of the
tower at Pisa; the parallelepiped of the Palazzo Strozzi; the half-cylinder,
laid horizontally, of the granaries of the Ramesseum at Thebes; the
sphere of Vaudoyer's House of a Cosmopolite; the half-sphere or dome
of the igloo; the ellipse of the Colosseum; the parabola of the vaults of
Freyssinet's hangar at Orly; the cones of Indian wigwams and of the
shielings at Jura in Scotland; the beehive domes of the trulli at Albero-
bello; the triangular prisms of the roof of San Antonio at Padua; the octagonal prisms of San Vitale at Ravenna. An elementary shape such as
that of a cylinder may define a whole building; reduced, it may be
the base for a dome; reduced still farther, a column or shaft or even just
ornament. Elementary shapes may be combined in manifold ways:
the cylinder and hemisphere of the Pantheon, or the parallelepipeds and
intersecting half-cylinders of the Basilica of Constantine at Rome. Other
shapes are doubly curved and highly irregular. Some, like those of San
Carlo alle Quattro Fontane in Rome, or the chapel at Ronchamp by Le
Corbusier, are spaces of enormous complexity that defy simple description.

The varied combinations of masses mold complicated spaces, modify
them, pinch them, make them seem to flow plastically until space itself is the material that seems to have been carved and modeled. The
cathedral at Amiens achieves such plasticity. Seeing it, we realize that
space is the medium of architecture. The masses of a great building are
merely the negative or positive imprints of space, which billow inside
them, pressing St. Peter's dome outward, cascading down the stairs in
Michelangelo's Laurentian Library at Florence, rebounding from the
sculptural revetments of the dome of Santa Chiara at Bra.

While the kinds of space are theoretically unlimited, the geometry that
is preferred for use at any one time has never been unrestricted. Some
geometric forms, like vortices, are difficult to construct, require special
and expensive manufacture, and may not be very useful if made, no
matter how much curiosity they might arouse. Others, like helices, may
be interesting as sculpture but of little use as architecture. Some, like the
pyramid and sphere, are hard to combine happily. Some plane figures,

like the triangle, circle, and rectangle — which appear together in the west façades of Gothic cathedrals — pose difficult problems of interrelation that even Gothic architects did not always resolve well. The problem of wedding hemispheric domes to rectangular or square plans found no structurally or aesthetically satisfactory solution before the Byzantines joined them at the corners by pendentives approximating spherical triangles. Technology frequently limits the architect's geometric vocabulary. It was not ready to permit a Roman to suspend or cantilever his aqueducts across the deep gorges. It forced a Byzantine to make his domes more hemispherical after earthquakes had unsettled the flat one on Hagia Sophia.

Still the most severe limitations upon geometric imagination are set by architects' predilections for certain forms. Each age has space-metaphors it seems to prefer. The Moslem liked the cube topped by a bulbous dome; the eighteenth-century classicists enjoyed the cylinder set on a parallelepiped; the twentieth-century West is intrigued by the glazed parallelepiped raised on stilts; the Egyptian preferred the spaceless pyramid; the Japanese, the piled pyramids of a pagoda or the interpenetrating rectangles of their houses. Each of these has a distinctive silhouette and their spaces are expressive indices to the society that built them. If we see a sphere, we know immediately that it is not Egyptian or Greek or Roman or Gothic or Renaissance. If we see an onion-shaped roof we think at once of Russia. If we see a series of parallelepipeds piled up for many stories, we know we are observing either an Assyrian ziggurat or a Mayan pyramid or a twentieth-century skyscraper. The space-metaphor that obsessed many Italian architects of the sixteenth century is visible in Michelangelo's west face of St. Peter's at Rome. His undulating masses enclose unique spaces; whenever you see them you may be certain they stem from Italian work of the sixteenth century.

The various space-metaphors are the primary indices of style. There are many kinds of style. There is, for instance, a basic continuity in the architecture of Western civilization that distinguishes it from Eastern and primitive buildings. The West has had a long predilection for the parallelepiped and the boxlike space defined by walls or colonnades leading to a single focus at the end of a central axis.

Style may be less than civilization-wide. It may be the designator of a period of history, like the Gothic. The Churrigueresque of Spain is almost exclusively national. The English Gothic is a national version of a period style. The *détente* sculpture of sixteenth-century Lorraine is solely regional. Style may be local, even comprising the work of a single school, like that of the followers of Palladio around Vicenza. At its most individual, style may be completely personal, as was that of the Spanish architect Antonio Gaudi, and personal style may change radically so that there have been recognizable stylistic breaks in the careers of many architects. Style is a hallmark — the imprint of imagination on material. Wherever two or more buildings have recognizable affinities in their spaces and masses, then the similarities constitute stylistic features. They designate common origin in a civilization, period of history, nation, region, locality, or possibly even the same hand. Styles are so distinctive as to enable historians to ascertain the provenance of unfamiliar objects with surprising accuracy. Even careful revivals of archeological styles or the cleverest fakes usually contain noticeable give-aways. Style, therefore, expresses provenance.

Climate and landscape affect style. Some designers believe that the form of a building should reflect the terrain on which it stands, others that a region or a locality rather than a particular piece of terrain should determine a local or regional style. Regionalism is the natural state of primitive architectures; they depend upon local materials and traditional ways of gaining the air, sun, and outlook a building should have. They are slow to change, and physical and tribal barriers inhibit stimuli for change. Development of any widely admired style, classic or not, tends to destroy regionalism. Perhaps the most destructive agent is technology. Advances in communication, standardization of materials, mass marketing, and techniques for controlling environment — all beat upon provincial enclaves of regional expression. The universal forms developed from technology have often been gladly embraced by some architects; but others, faced with increasing sameness, have bolted towards an extreme, even a self-conscious, regionalism.

Functional need and its expressions are determinants of stylistic form. They are the sources of the pleasure afforded by the sight of something perfectly fitted for its task. It is like the joy of the carpenter in his tools, the engineer in his locomotive, the sailor in his ship. We sense it in many bridges, airplanes, dams, and instruments. This functional satisfaction is important, but it has misled some men into believing that it is the only source of architectural excellence. They try to persuade us that forms should exactly reflect their structure or their efficient plans. This ignores the fact that a chief function of architecture is to be a work of art. Is the form of the Parthenon less beautiful because it was inefficient in its use of structure and materials, in its wasteful use of space? Is it less beautiful to one who does not know how the Greeks worshiped there? Was it less beautiful when the Turks stored powder in it? Is it less beautiful now that its ruins serve no practical purpose save that of swelling Athenian coffers with tourist money? Physical performance is a determinant of form, but not the only one, not always even the most important one. Mere excellence in physical or social functioning does not guarantee beauty.

Again there is pleasure in noticing firm construction, neat assembly, careful finishing by consummate workmanship. Following the gossamer of the Golden Gate or George Washington Bridges, sensing the tensions and compressions, we see a marvelous counterpoint of weight and support, spring and leap. Many structures have no such thrill, are no more than wooden boxes or piano wires. But a hammerbeam truss arched above a dining hall, the visible skeleton of a skyscraper, a giant reinforced-concrete cantilever or thin-shelled canopy, a tetrahedral dome — these may be poetic. Whether one believes that structure should be exhibited, as the early Gothic architect did, or covered, as the Renaissance architect often did, it is not wise to follow those who insist that excellent design can occur only when forms emerge from the "honest" expression of structure. Mere skill and boldness in engineering may produce beauty, but does not assure us of it.

Throughout history there have been great changes in structural capacities from the simple wall, through the narrow spans of Egyptian and Greek stone posts and lintels, the wide-spanning arches, domes, and barrel vaults of the Romans, the counterbalanced forces of pinnacle, rib, and buttress that let the light into the Gothic naves, to the slender structures of steel, the almost limitless span of the steel arched truss, the thrustless reinforced-concrete vaults, the thin, continuous, compoundly curved shells and the geodesic domes of today. All have been designators of style.

Some architects would add still another determinant of style, the nature of materials. The characteristics of stone inhibited the Greek builder from enclosing enormous spaces by his trabeated construction. The Gothic builder could not have obtained colored light without opening the walls by bracing his stone rib-vaults with flying buttresses. Some architects, like Palladio, created forms that might have been built in any number of different materials. Others, like Frank Lloyd Wright, have insisted that forms be uniquely suited to materials so that wood continues to look like wood, glass like glass. When we see a material superbly worked we may be enchanted by what a craftsman has uncovered or enriched; but, again, we must not be led to the *non sequitur* that form must be limited to a direct or unimaginative expression of the nature of materials.

The axioms about style are subjective, however pontifically critics and architects announce them. The popular notions about "honesty" of structure, faithfulness to materials, and expression of use are all debatable shibboleths. Palladio and Michelangelo created great designs without accepting any of them. There are even romantic ideas that a building must express "the spirit of the times," the personality of the client, the temper of the architect, the building's site and regional terrain, its national origin, its age — especially modernity — and technology. Each of these dogmas has its proponents. All of them are important indicators of style and expression in some time. But not one of them was believed by excellent architects of the Gothic, classic, Renaissance or academic periods, who recognized that a building may express all these things without being great architecture. They assumed that an architect could not help but express his age, the materials and the use of the building; but they never made the error of believing that expression, alone, especially the self-conscious kind, made a building a work of art. Changes in style reflect mere changes in hypotheses, not in the bases for quality judgments.

But even these hypotheses are somewhat less subjective than might be supposed. Each reflects a viewpoint about architecture that is related to schemes for understanding the world. Recent architects, like recent scientists and philosophers, have tended to subscribe to one of several fundamental views of nature. These dispose them toward well-defined space-metaphors that are compatible with their hypotheses about style.

One of the oldest interpretations is the view that the universe contains and the mind knows certain perfect shapes or forms and that most natural things are lesser, imperfect approximations of them. That view, called formalism, has been the philosophy traditionally ascribed to Platonists, and it tends to be the viewpoint of geometers who have preferences for certain interesting shapes like spheres, prisms, or hyperbolic paraboloids. According to that view, purity of form is marred by contact with brute, unrefined material. Its follower cares little for the nature of materials, terrain, use, structure, or individuality of the client. These are unimportant to him because they tend to obscure and damage purity of form. He seeks universality within the form he regards as perfect, as the Renaissance architects Palladio and Bramante did. He rejects axioms regarding materials and site in favor of qualities of measure and precision like those of the Villa Capra or Versailles, where particular location, materials, structure, and client are obscured behind a geometry so rigorous that trees and gardens must be clipped to conform.

Opposed to formalism are the many versions of romanticism, where the individuality of particular materials, sites, plants, and structural systems is cherished and emphasized. In marked opposition to the formal garden, the romantic "Strawberry Hill" of Horace Walpole and

Marie Antoinette's *Petit Hameau* at Versailles featured the unique and particular in rustic nature. Even the use of "primitive" architecture like the Gothic or a provincial idiom was intended to recall less civilized times. Confronting a gnarled and burned tree stump or a cataract or a Chinese pagoda within a romantic garden, the imagination was titillated by sublime contrasts to formal sophistication. Those contrasts were valued not because they contained formal perfection but because their expressive power provoked awe or longing or horror and stimulated dreams and excitement. Design capitalized upon accidents in materials, much as it has in recent work by the regional architects of California; structural exhibitionism, variegated light, close adaptation to sites now fascinated architects. The expressed whims of clients and architects, mindful of their own age, frequently were directed towards modernity, nationalism, or Christianity. The temple ruins they built in their gardens kept them alert to time, the destroyer of perfect form.

Still a third hypothesis of style sees the universe as an organization of masses that operate uniformly and universally in accordance with laws that can be described mathematically. Regarding the universe as a well-working machine, the mechanists tend to devalue individual differences in favor of universal forms and laws. They favor machined forms that are calibrated exactly, finished highly. They value functional and efficient planning, and they regard frank exposure of structure as a moral virtue. Recent advocates of this view, like Walter Gropius, tend to ally themselves with modernism and particularly with modern social and industrial problems and the products of machines. They are frequently interested in ways of manufacturing standardized materials that can be used internationally and rationally, irrespective of site or client, to solve the large social problems of housing and education. In their quest for universal forms, the extreme mechanists resemble the formalists, and the two views are sometimes combined as they are in Mies van der Rohe. Le Corbusier, on the other hand, is a fine example of mechanist and romanticist, sometimes romantically exaggerating the machine and often stating primitive or irrational contrasts to it.

A fourth point of view that has fired the imagination of architects is organicism, a belief that the universe resembles the organization of a plant or animal, rather than a machine. This view has natural alliances with all three preceding ones. It shares with romanticism a belief in highly individualized living things which are uniquely adapted to their particular environment. It shares with mechanism the belief that physical laws describe the actions of inert bodies and that structure should be visible. It has less that resembles formalism, but its emphasis upon the primacy of organic forms is similar. The organicists suggest that evolu-

Athens, Acropolis

ALL PHOTOGRAPHS IN THIS SECTION BY G. E. KIDDER SMITH

Athens, Parthenon from Propylea

Athens, Parthenon
and view of Athens

Athens, Erechtheum
from Parthenon

Chartres, town and Cathedral

Chartres, Cathedral,
southwest buttresses

Chartres, Cathedral, southwest buttresses, detail

Chartres, Cathedral, interior of nave

Venice, St. Mark's Square, with Basilica of St. Mark, Campanile, and Doge's Palace

Vicenza, Villa Capra, ca. 1550, Palladio, arch.

Maser, Villa Barbaro, ca. 1570, Palladio, arch.

tionary theory, including adaptation and natural selection, gives hints as to how buildings should be organized. Hence they insist that buildings be adapted to their environment, both physical and social, to their sites, uses, materials, authors, even to the nation in which they stand. Frank Lloyd Wright's organicist thesis that form must change with changing conditions is anathema to formalists and mechanists or any who believe in the universality of particular geometric forms. The extreme formalist might even assert, as Matthew Nowicki did, that function must remain subordinate to form.

Few artists accept any one of these metaphysical notions fully or exclusively. They pick up snatches from them and they rightly point out that these bases for stylistic axioms are ultimately matters of expression; they have nothing to do with quality in art. Artists, therefore, rove freely among them but the greater artists are perhaps the more doctrinaire. Certainly they have the firmer convictions. They cling to larger portions of whole, consistent interpretations and consequently are led towards the intellectual, religious, and social commitments that are their consequences. The types of building an architect designs well, his style, the space-metaphors that are characteristically his, are deeply affected by his beliefs, and vice versa. In many times one or another theory has been supreme. Today they are competing and this is not the least of our confusions.

All of these subjective ideas about expression, circling around style, furnish material for most of the interesting architectural debates you are likely to hear. They are inevitable in the development of art, but they are challengeable. Even if they were uncontestable, such ideas would not guarantee quality. It is to John Ruskin's everlasting credit that he awoke an architecturally indifferent public to the possibility that styles may have different meanings, but his notion that Gothic was morally good and Renaissance bad confused aesthetic and ethical judgments. The latter were irrelevant, even untrue.

4

BECAUSE BITTER AND SUBJECTIVE ARGUMENTS ABOUT STYLE ARE NOT only possible but even inevitable, it is easy to be trapped into thinking that all aesthetic judgments are subjective and therefore that any man's opinion is as good as another's. This conclusion misinterprets the obvious fact that taste changes; it ignores the remarkable consistency of trained critical judgment. Even though many once thought Puvis de Chavannes and Paul Chenavard were the best nineteenth-century painters, no informed critic mentions them in the same breath with Rembrandt, Titian, Velasquez and Rubens. Were many critics to make individual lists of the fifty greatest buildings in the West before 1900, most of the choices would be unanimous and independent of the individual critic's predilection for classic or Gothic or Renaissance or baroque style. The Parthenons, the Karnaks, the cathedrals of Chartres and Amiens, the Versailles palaces, the Villa Capras would be there. The Paul Revere Houses, the Wayside Inns, the Monticellos would not. Why?

Is it not because we are now speaking of excellence of a kind that excludes many things well revered and cherished for other reasons? When you understand the range of possible architectural expression you must exclude buildings that are merely social documents or the scene of historic events, like the courthouse in Appomattox, or sentimental reminiscence, like John C. Calhoun's house in the South Carolina hills. If you do not understand this excellence you may include none of the great buildings. But the ignorant provide no meaningful tribunal. The judgment of experts, artists and students has been generally agreed about noncontemporary buildings in spite of all changes in taste or style or expression; they have consistently called certain buildings "masterpieces" and have judged others accordingly.

What, then, are the objective criteria of quality? The fundamental ones are criteria of unity, of balance, of rhythm, of scale. These have been necessary in all the great periods of architecture. They are the primary ingredients of *quality,* which refers to *design,* not to style. Style is the product of a time, the expression of what a people considered choice. Design refers to the organization of architectural elements — mass, space and plane — independent of their style. Two buildings in the same style may be differently valued as to their quality as compositions, while two buildings in different styles may both be fine compositions.

Unity insists that a work of art must be consistent with itself. Nothing patently extraneous can appear. Insert a bit of Mondriaan into a Titian, stop the action in *Henry* V by an interlude of Sartre's prose, or a ballet by Jerome Robbins. You may create something humorous or annoying; you may even heighten the action and deepen the effect by an insertion that artfully points up the contrast you intend. But the original mood of the Titian or of *Henry* V disappears as fully as when Duchamp satirized the *Mona Lisa* by adding a mustache and goatee. Great art sets a dominant theme and sustains it; it may be eminently self-consistent or it may be filled with jarring oppositions and surprising violations so that it disquiets and provokes.

Unity in architecture is easily noticed when the building has a very simple plan and is made up of one dominant shape such as the pryamid or the obelisk, the Greek temple or the great ellipse of the Roman Colosseum. But few modern buildings can be made with one overriding all-enveloping simple form. Thus unity is more often achieved by blending various compatible parts, even by skillfully combining apparently discordant features. The former is the classical sort of unity which was greatly enjoyed by Renaissance and baroque artists who often crowned a building by a single element, the dome, while lesser parts were subordinated in diminishing hierarchy. A contrasting sort of unity appears where spaces and masses struggle against integration, rebel and break loose as each element strives to dominate, shouting the incongruities of vigorous contrasts in form, texture and scale. Here are new principles of design equally productive of consistency by a unity with a different premise.

If the purpose is to create something beautiful of a serene and pleasing sort, then anything that disturbs balanced, singly dominated unity must be avoided. The building, then, must be one undivided thing and so perceivable in the first instance. Reasons of utility or symbolism may require combinations of incompatible shapes, which appear as dualities, warring with each other. Equivocation between two strongly self-contained shapes may be resolved. There is the classic method of dividing a façade so an even number of solids will force resolution in the central odd space, as in the Parthenon. But now be wary! Design depends on purpose. Duality may be a good thing; it may serve to reduce the apparent size of an object and thereby enable a large building to stand harmoniously within a small environment; it may also prevent an object from seeming to be complete in itself, making it intentionally disunified except as it is related through spaces to other buildings in a composition. Thus unity, the fundamental feature of a work of art, may be accomplished by principles that require positive and negative applications according to the purpose intended.

Equilibrium or balance — one of the chief aspects of unity — is also dependent on purpose. Any part of a composition may be unbalanced and generate thrusts and directions that are not self-contained. A single flying buttesss at Amiens appears in balance only in relation to the full cross-section of the nave. There are many kinds of balance. The classical sort is symmetrical disposition of solids and voids on an axis. Frequently, programs suggest asymmetrical compositions and then visual inequalities are inevitable unless the program is distorted. They can be controlled by establishing an eccentric focus where various masses and voids find a resolution of their axes and apparent weights. Symmetrical buildings like the Villa Capra offer no problem; but unless Chartres or Notre Dame at Paris is viewed either as a planar detail, like the west façade, or from the east end with the towers crowning the foreshortened mass, the result seems to lack unity.

Phrasing too is a means for achieving unity. Unless the rhythms established by masses and spaces are begun, ended, and phrased, they are not effective. A completely unpunctuated wall may serve to define a space that has little climax or termination, but most buildings require punctuation. A corner offers one of the most difficult problems in design; it does not suffice merely to butt two sides together. Top and bottom terminals are equally important. Where a building leaves the ground it needs special attention. Its conclusion against the sky requires distinctive modification of form, not a mere cessation of the rhythm and pattern of the middle stories. All the decisive and telling moments occur when the building changes its statement; those transitional periods are masterfully emphasized and enriched by great architects, ignored or crudely handled by others. Beginnings, joinings, departures, and conclusions — these are the places where the inept designer fails to make his geometry become architecture.

Unity alone does not guarantee quality. A simple and completely unified form like a pyramid may fail because it is inappropriate in size or because it rises too high on an inadequate base or squats too low on an overly adequate one. Though some proportions such as that of the Golden Rectangle are generally pleasing, they will not work everywhere; at the same time we tend to reject proportions which exaggerate one dimension with respect to the others. Proportion is an arithmetic relationship between the dimensions of a space or mass. A room may have bad proportions because they are unsuited to its purpose, but even if its proportions are acceptable at the utilitarian level of hearing and seeing, some relations are psychologically more pleasurable than others. Within these larger elements, moreover, the rhythm of the lesser elements, like windows and furnishings, will be disturbing unless their proportions are related to the spaces in which they stand. A sense of proportion is indispensable to an architect, who must always be mindful of how color, light, texture, and sound alter spaces, apparently changing the actual dimensions.

Yet, a building may have a well-proportioned unity and still fail of quality if it is out of scale. Scale, too, is related to purpose. A whole building may be out of scale with its purpose. Monumentality in a house may destroy the sense of domesticity. A puny building may deny a lofty purpose. A portion of a building may be badly scaled in either of two ways. It may actually be too small or too large for the remainder of the building. It will be equally misscaled if it is the proper size but *appears* to be too small or too large. The relationship between one element and another without regard to actual dimensions establishes an order of magnitude for the major components of a building. This is radically different from scale as defined by the mensurate size an element has or seems to have relative to other objects whose size we know — for example, men. Both kinds of scale are found in the Egyptian pyramids, for instance, where the individual steps have a fixed absolute scale. But what the actual size of those steps is, we cannot determine until we learn the pyramid's relative scale by observing the size of details closely or see a man dwarfed by the blocks of stone in a step. Dramatic results can be obtained, as in St. Peter's at Rome, by aggrandizing relative scale of steps and columns past all expectations. The absolute scale needed in buildings where crowds assemble is larger than that required in houses, and their relative scale must be adjusted from the colossal sizes to the requirements of the crowd acting corporately or individually.

Ornament provides one of the means for giving scale to buildings. The decoration of a building may serve no other function than to enrich its walls and its skyline, or it may reduce the scale of a large module to that of a smaller screen. The function of ornament has not often been so neglected as in the modern period, when architects have forgotten that ways of resisting wind, draining water from roofs, controlling sun, or removing bad air and smoke all provide excellent opportunities for enriching building form. Too often the inexorable logic of pure geometric form has blinded designers to the visual excitement of the colorful brick patterns in the Doge's Palace, the weird gargoyles at Notre Dame, the buttress scrolls at Santa Maria della Salute in Venice, the wood carving at Urnes in Norway. Walls, fences, stairs, fire escapes too often became drab utilitarian devices instead of having the scale-giving function or poetic enrichment that they might provide.

Unless the architect has achieved unity, good proportion, and adequate scale for the major elements of his building, he can never repair the disaster by polishing the details. Mediocre architects constantly forget this and try to impose interesting internal rhythms or decoration in a vain hope. But though the subordinate elements of a design cannot supply what is missing, they can destroy the unity, proportion and scale implicit in the main masses and spaces. Windows, doors, pilasters, moldings, decorative details, painting, sculpture and furniture can obliterate fundamental quality if they are incoherent, badly proportioned, indiffer-

ent to the major proportions, out of scale with each other or the major
elements, or so obtrusive that they distract attention from the main at-
traction, which should always be the building.

For purposes of simplicity we have spoken throughout as though
architecture were definable in terms of single buildings. But a city, too,
has architecture and the urban architecture is not a simple summation
of the good and bad qualities of its individual buildings. A building's
environment, its site, and its neighbors are important aspects of architectural enjoyment. Spaces between buildings are frequently more important than the buildings themselves. Some of the quadrangles at Oxford
or the Piazza di San Marco in Venice or the Göteplatsan in Göteborg or the interlocking squares of Verona are examples of excellent
outdoor spaces that are beautiful even though some of the buildings
that form them are nondescript or fractious. It is not enough, nor even
necessary, that all the buildings be works of art in themselves; their
whole context is the true unit of design.

This frequently requires that individual buildings be asymmetrical,
not self-centered, modest, almost walls, rather than monumental sculptures, to the end that the spaces may be fully enjoyable. In such spaces,
certain types of building that serve communal uses tend to dominate
their environment, like the Senate of the Campidoglio in Rome or
San Marco in Venice. Others, intended for more private and personal
use, tend to remain subordinate to the spaces among them. Such a hierarchy of importance depends upon a society's sense of decorum. But if
architects have so often failed of quality in their separate enterprises and
if architectural geniuses have so often insisted on parading their personal
competence, it is not surprising that overall quality has come to but a
few cities. For the city as a whole, political problems and problems of
competing interest and problems of economics seem to be almost overwhelming. But unless they are solved cities will no longer have civic
beauty, for civic beauty cannot arise simply from the haphazard accumulation of individual buildings even if each building were, miracu-
lously, to be individually excellent.

5

As WE LOOK AT BUILDINGS AND SQUARES AND CITIES ANYWHERE, WE CAN
then bring some impersonal standards of judgment to bear upon them.
It is particularly helpful to bring them to the familiar things, even the
loved things, of our own land. Necessarily, the standards you bring to
bear in assessing the architecture of modern America must not be differ-

ent from those by which you measure that of any past. You will want to
judge its capacity for expression, its quality as form; but you will also
want to ask two further questions. First you may wish to think about the
pervasive architectural landscape with its modest houses, stores and
offices and ask whether they live up to the quality of some other folk
architectures. Next you may ask of a few monumental and public buildings whether they will stand the test of being considered alongside two
great and sophisticated architectural achievements of the past, the Greek
temple and the Gothic cathedral.

When we move back towards the past, behind the Abbot Suger, behind Pericles, behind Sargon, behind Cheops, we still find an "anonymous" folk architecture. We can find it today in a forest of Borneo, on a
mountain of the Cameroons, on the Amazon in Brazil, here living its
ancient life; we can find it half living such a life in the upper coves of the
valleys of Switzerland, clinging to the tops of the Norwegian fiords, co-
existing with a sophisticated architecture in the highlands of Tibet,
wasting away in technological America. Perhaps it is doomed in all the
world of industry; but it has been more durable in the Old World than
in the New, which overvalues change as a good in itself. It has served
simple human purposes, first as the dwelling for people, sometimes collectively, sometimes privately; second as the storehouse for grains or
domestic animals or tools; later as the simplest possible shrine or holy
place. It is usually an architecture of the farm or the village. It does not
often survive the city. It is better where it takes root and lasts than
where it is always moving on; so the Russians, the Norse, the Swiss and
the Tibetans have developed more elegant log cabins than ever graced
the American frontier. It does not have to consist entirely of ancient
motifs; the elevators of the rural American Midwestern towns or the
metal storage silos of a Grain Administration can become a part of it;
before anyone consciously made architecture for industry there were architecturally excellent anonymous warehouses and mills.

Not every primitive or simple and rural people has made such an architecture. The noble savage can make ugly work as well as wonderful
work; Americans who did well by New England did badly by the prairie
later. The amazing thing about the work is that so many primitive and
rural peoples have achieved it, in so many different ways; that it has
been durable in so many places, often continuing while the fashions of
men's greater buildings have come and gone.

Whether it is the Breton village and farm, the pine-tree-shaped, carved
stave church of the Norwegian Middle Ages, the simple Shaker stone
house, the white New England town, the regional character is always
owed to the fact that the buildings were produced by an art that was

communal, not specialized, dependent upon a common and accepted experience which the builders did not try to refine much, to change much; above all, one on which they did not seek to impress their own special personalities. Thus the art is communal, continuing, but in no sense spontaneous. It is a clear response to a common history, to a common environment, and to a common assessment of what is desirable. It uses local materials, it accommodates itself to the local climate, it fits sympathetically into the local landscape and it takes care of the local custom. It has one other thing in common: it is very conservative.

If we make a tour of Europe from the Arctic Circle as it crosses Scandinavia to the heel of Italy, we will see a panorama of different and quite sophisticated, certainly not primitive but nevertheless anonymous architectural representations of local life. We will become aware of differences that seem national or racial and of others that are functions of mountains or of plains rather than of political boundaries. From an architecture of wood we will pass to an architecture of brick and stucco and in the end an architecture of stone. Generally, the roofs are steeply pitched in the North to shed the snow and they flatten as the sun goes higher. In the coldest regions windows and doors are small to keep out the unfriendly wind, in the Middle North they open up to catch what sun there is, and when the sun is hot and a menace more than a caress the walls grow thick, the windows small, so that the interior is dark and cool. The house of the North centers on the interior and the hearth where the logs burn; the house of the South invites you outdoors into the atrium or the patio. All these things were worked out long ago as a result of differences in climate and differences in the way of life.

Decisions were taken, consciously or subconsciously. One was to build usually for individual families and not for families living communally. At most a common wall might be shared by adjacent village houses. This was not an inevitable decision. In Indonesia some peasant communities have long houses for many families, others have separate buildings. The Iroquois and the Indians of Puget Sound built communal long houses, while the Penobscots and others built singly. But the choice was an important one for the West; it conditioned not only the interior arrangements but the scale of the buildings. Another choice was of equal consequence, the choice of the rectangular plan. That choice was not inevitable, either. Circular buildings are common enough throughout the world. The Mongolian yurt is circular; the Ba Vendas and other African tribes erect low circular walls of sticks and mud and cover them with curved roofs. Sometimes conical roofs are taken all the way to the ground to serve as walls. We know this form in the tipis of the plains Indians but less portable structures have also been made so.

The snow igloo is a half sphere. Sometimes an oval plan has replaced the circle or the rectangle. Some Greek houses, we know, were elliptical. There have been repeated efforts to reintroduce the circular form, to replace the rectangle, but they have almost always been proposed by self-conscious seekers for new solutions. Though such experiments have often been admired by critics and publishers, they have not made their way with the people.

Choices of form were still possible. All the variations were meant to provide a single room or at most two rooms for family living, to protect the family while it was asleep, to keep it sheltered against inclement weather, to permit cooking in climates where cooking was difficult out of doors. Little more was asked. Some were designed to be portable but again the West soon disclaimed the advantages of obvious nomadism for the advantages of the semipermanent abode. For primitive people who could not learn how to keep a site from exhausting itself, the buildings were intended to remain until the soil was exhausted and then would be left while the people moved on; and this was a pattern for many Western miners and pioneers as well. It was only the growing civilizations that learned at the same time to build for permanence and to value change, thereby posing themselves an almost impossible dilemma.

The peasant types could be damaged by time and the elements; they could be damaged by change and by the possibilities of technology. In recent years it has become technologically possible to overcome climatic differences. With more leisure we have sought more outdoors life, even in the North. Thus we have been able — and, alas, all too often we have wanted — to transfer the appearance of the house of one climate and soil and weather to a different land and climate. A Swiss chalet on the desert, a Mexican patio in a Vermont winter, a Cape Cod cottage in Florida are diminished by their surroundings; their falsity damages the surroundings too but we build them almost every day.

But the anonymous types were as much damaged by self-conscious refinement as by transferral to unnatural environments. Sometimes they found a way to accommodate themselves to slow change, to build for greater permanence, to enlarge the conveniences, to make the beauty more formal. They were not always more beautiful thereby, but when the development was slow and natural they were not necessarily less so and they could become more elegant, more versatile. The New England house of the eighteenth century stood at the end of such a development reaching back at least to the cruck houses of the early Saxons. It could be damaged only by over-rapid change, by carelessness and neglect, by efforts to improve it in ways that brought no improvement, much as an African hut is destroyed when sheet iron replaces the thatch roof. It passed its prime when owners demanded too many things of it, when it wasted away under heedless hands on the prairie, or when self-conscious minds tried to push it where it could not go or tried to resurrect its simplicity for days that were no longer simple. The critic of American architecture may regret our failure to develop and preserve a handsome "anonymous" architecture. Or he may glory in the fact that American civilization was too vital to age gracefully.

6

WHILE AMERICA'S MAIN STREETS AND BROADWAYS INVITE SPECULATION upon the quality of a society's folk architecture, some of her buildings may suggest comparisons with the great architectural inheritances from the Western past, especially the Greek and Gothic. What is required in society to produce a great architecture? What may that architecture be expected to express in the way of national character and aspirations?

Most of the great monuments of the world are products of wealth, power, purpose, and urbanization, based on earlier anonymous forms and expressed in the same greater terms. Few of the great works of architecture can be found outside of cities despite their rural genesis; most of the notable exceptions are temples or shrines, sometimes set outside the city or even remote from it but nonetheless products of the urban culture. The buildings were in one way or another symbols of power or at least of discipline and wealth, power of the monarch in a palace, power of the state in a governmental hall, in a temple the power of the gods or God or the power of a church, which was not always the same thing. When buildings of power rose to the level of great art, more than power was inevitably involved; there was also belief and agreement, even love.

The Athenians, for example, did not think in servile terms. Thucydides prized civic character above civic beauty, but beauty still stood high with the Athenians, higher for example than mere wealth though lower than the spirit it exhibited. The prideful example was the Parthenon. Built on a terrain of barren, earthquake-riven mountains of marble, facing a blue and ubiquitous sea, it was made for a climate of alternating tempest, steady winds, capricious flood and snow and a short summer. It was an architecture to stand on brown hills, to go with anemones and olives, aloes and conifers. It was an architecture for a people who came near to hibernating in the winter but filled the spring and summer and fall to the brim with outdoor life and much talk. It stood against a sky which was almost always filled with clouds but seldom, save in the rainy season, leaden or overcast, a vibrant, bracing, clear sky, sending down a light that was always mobile and sharp like the Greek temper. It was a temple to suit the spirit of restless traders and seafarers who were seldom serene and never quite predictable.

They were a people dedicated to the *polis*, a dedication which cannot be understood in the simplest terms of mere patriotism or acceptance of civic duty. They were dedicated to the principle of "nothing too much," and to a belief in *arete* which a horse could have as well as a man, that is, a capacity for giving the utmost performance within one's possibilities.

The temple was for a people who held an ironic view of the capricious conduct of their all-too-human gods. It was set on the strongest hill, which most other Greek cities would have used for a fortress. It was approached by a winding and unspectacular path which the Romans later converted into a monumental way.

Reaching the top, you entered the sacred precinct through another important architectural monument, the Propylaea. And here you found yourself in some confusion. For the sacred precinct was not dedicated solely to the goddess patroness. Her temple did dominate the layout but her statues were not the largest. And there were also minor temples for other deities, treasuries, covered colonnades with historical paintings, votive monuments to heroes, to winners of games who were close to heroes in the Greek eye, even to sufficiently generous donors. It is a restless idea to us, a strange mixture of the sacred and the profane.

Nor was the Parthenon the only important building on the Acropolis; many would value the Erechtheum as highly. But it was the main building. And what was it for? For the simple purpose of providing a great central hall or *naos* in which there would be a votive statue of the goddess Athena, another room for her treasure, and an exterior which would provide a suitable backdrop for ceremonies before the outdoor altar.

The Parthenon is not very large. Its base is just over a hundred feet wide and just under two hundred and thirty feet long. It had only two rooms. Its colonnade is not the greatest nor the most elaborate of the classic peristyles. It struggles with anachronistic triglyphs over the columns, vestiges of the ends of wooden beams no longer used. To a consistent modern ideologue the Parthenon may therefore not even have been "honest" architecture. It was not full of innovations, either. All it had done was to use much earlier innovations and reduce them to a moment of perfection — perfection of proportion, subtlety of entasis on the columns and curvature of the bases, elegance of flutings on the columns, brilliancy of carving of the metopes between the triglyphs, brilliance in solving the problem of the *naos* whose columnar scale must not be permitted to compete with the scale of the statue itself, equal bril-

liance in solving the difficult sculptural problem of the cramped triangular pediment, great accommodation to the color, the light and the sky.

If you sense even a little of the Parthenon you will not attempt to
adapt it for the purposes of a bank, a state house, a college secret or
debating society. If you know Greek society well you may ask if any
building could typify the world of Themistocles, Pericles, Cleon, Alci-
biades, Nicias and Socrates, and whether the Parthenon does. This may
lead to skeptical inquiry about architecture as history.

But there is a further simpler message from the Parthenon. It does not
proclaim a nationalistic architecture. There were no more deadly rivals
in the days of its building than the Ionian state of Athens and the Dorian
state of Sparta. Yet the Parthenon and the Propylaea were Dorian, not
Ionian. The Athenians could not permit themselves the absurdity of demanding an "Athenian" architecture.

Does this mean that the Athenians were supranational? Not at all.
They were as nationalistic as a people ever could be. But they were also
sensible. They knew that nationalism applied to architecture was an
irrelevancy. Irrelevancy is something they seldom permitted themselves.

The Parthenon has one more thing to say. We know about Ictinus
and Callikrates because they were its architects, and not the other way
around. In fact, we really do not care much about the lives or words of
Ictinus and Callikrates. We care about the Parthenon. That is the way it
should be.

Sixteen hundred years and almost as many miles from the gulfs of
Greece another great architecture arose on the plains of the Île de
France. It was a different land, flat or slightly rolling, generously fertile.
The seas of wheat washed the feet of Chartres, the road to Bourges
passed across a protective fen. You could see a cathedral spire miles
away. The sun hung low over the long winter's snow; the spring was
dripping wet; the summer was hot and dry; the fall was a nostalgic
brown when peat burned and pigs rooted for truffles among the oaks
and beeches. The long slants of the sun cast stronger shadows from
vertical buttresses than from horizontal cornices. Buildings needed
larger windows to gather light from the duller sky; roofs had to be steep
to slip the heavy snow. Most of all, the religion was different.

Gothic buildings were made of stone and glass. There was no Pen-
telic marble. Weather and sky would not have admired it or treated it
well had there been any. There were no special quays to receive the
products of an empire. Abbot Suger was a man who never spared expense for his Abbey Church at St. Denis. He had seen and admired the
Baths of Diocletian in Rome. He sent emissaries far and wide to hunt
for comparable stones, but in the end had to settle for the local quarry

of nearby Pontoise. You might carry stone from Caen on a river barge but that was about all. Even then, it would be no more than a fine-grained limestone. Glass could come a little farther overland, reach across the hundred-mile radius of the Île de France from a vitrine center like Chartres.

You brought the stone and the glass for a single purpose, the glorification of God. This does not mean that medieval France did not contain as many contradictions as classic Greece. Chivalrous knights used the torture; Crusaders looted for personal gain. Holy men sold indulgences. Scholarly historians could believe that whatever they could not learn by research they could fill in by faith. The growing trade was beset by brigandage. The word of a Moorish infidel was often more to be trusted than that of a Christian merchant or prince. The loyalties of the feudal system, aimed up and down, still permitted hard exploitation of serfs, nowhere more than in the monasteries. The Virgin was adored as a model of chastity; but though the conventions of courtly love may have been modeled after the Virgin, the practice was all too human. The church took every advantage of the people's love for color and pageantry, and preached asceticism at the same time; an argument on this question between Bernard of Clairvaux and Abbot Suger of St. Denis was not abnormal.

The central objective was a transcendent God, not man; the will was not governed by reflective reason but by ecstatic faith. Greek art might bar infinitude, Gothic art could be content with nothing less. It sought it all the time in soaring vaults, dissolving spires. The Greek virtues remained, but there were three others, faith, hope, and one greater than these, the love of God. That was the Gothic virtue, par excellence. The cathedral was its greatest emblem.

It was an age of hierarchy. The structure, the façades, the iconography of the cathedrals were hierarchical. After you have picked the thirteenth century apart as much as you may, you will still find it a period of amazing unity. The cathedral was in art what the Crusade was in politics and the *Summa* in theology, a servant of this unity. The actual organization of the building emphasized and stated over and over again the Thomist principles of totality, articulation and interrelation. For those who could not comprehend this and met the cathedral on a simpler level it was uncomfortable or awe-inspiring as often as affectionate. It served for the jubilant public celebration of a major Mass and for the silent prayers and tears of a single mourner. It was both mysterious and intimate. Its sculpture and glass provided doctrine and simple counsel. It was part of you, and you could make yourself part of it.

The iconography had standardized symbols that everyone understood. The artist was not encouraged to make up his own private symbols to bewilder the eye of an observer, for bewilderment was not sought; he was not expected to put shoes on the feet of Christ or bestow an aureole or nimbus where it did not belong, or add to or subtract from the number of apostles because he personally thought it would yield a more interesting composition. The art was a kind of sacred writing, and a complicated one; yet the artists accepted all these limitations and produced one of the greatest arts — perhaps a hint to the unhappy, rebellious and "independent" painters and sculptors of today.

The Gothic cathedral does not have one supreme exemplar to compare with the Parthenon. There are those who think the finest Gothic buildings were not even built in France. But in France are some of the greatest. Though you might choose Amiens for its loftiness, Laon for its scholarship, Paris for its strength, Chartres for its humanity, Bourges for its ambulatory and west-front sculpture, Rheims for its history, none is perfect. The classic Gothic cathedral has to be defined differently. The general principles of how to build and what to put on were so well accepted that the simplest of plans would suffice for the masons. Thereafter, however, a good deal of extemporizing went on within the accepted framework. The classicism set a limitation of structural method, a limitation of what the main parts should be; a demand of an architectural sort that established plan, elevations, structure and the Thomism of the building; and a demand of iconography that concerned the sculpture and the stained glass.

The cathedrals can send us the same three messages as the Parthenon. First you must not overdo the notion that they are a total representation of a society which it is oversimplification to call unified, or insist that the cathedral of Chartres fully expressed and satisfied the whole range of medieval sentiments and aspirations. Skepticism has to admit that architecture is a clouded mirror of history. Like the Greek, Gothic development was international; the principles came first, the regional or national variations afterwards. The idea of the Middle Ages was supranational, but the competition between kings and nations was intense. There cannot be a successful and persistent international architecture merely as a matter of fashion. There must be an international purpose.

So we see that it is meaningless to speak of a French architecture, or a German architecture, an Italian architecture or an English architecture. The Gothic architectures of the different nations are more alike than are the architectures of two different periods in the same nation. These countries have gone through many periods of architectural history. They have lived through times when there was one or another international bond. These bonds and purposes have generated international styles like Gothic. Then the people of the nations have put their particular imprints on the general agreement. To speak of French or English or German architecture is meaningless. The terms have no generic quality. To speak of Gothic or Renaissance or baroque architecture does have a generic meaning. It becomes more precise when we combine the two, into French Gothic or German baroque; still more so if we use regional terms like Provençal, Norman, North German. But there is no doubt that the national and regional discriminations are the lesser.

Gothic cathedrals echo the other message of the Parthenon. Sometimes, though not often, we know the names of the master masons who are called their architects. We never have to measure the worth of Chartres or Bourges by the worth of their architects, by reading their comments, by knowing how they lived or whether they opposed their times, were ignored and abused or simply great, well-rewarded and happy conformists.

Greek architecture, usually as modified by the Romans and the men of the Renaissance, and Gothic architecture, usually as modified by the English and imperfectly understood, have been the two dominating historical teachers of later Western architecture. Almost every effort to revive past styles has worked from one or the other. They almost certainly represent the greatest two architectural achievements of Western men. Their works were built at moments of great arrival, at moments of crystallization of great societies, societies not in transition but standing at their peaks, unaware of the brinks of disaster on which they stood. The structures were clean-cut, the messages of the sculpture were known and desired, the uses of the buildings were accepted as important. They were architectures in which *all*, the artists, sculptors, painters, gilders, stonemasons, and carpenters as well as architects, were expected to participate skillfully and lovingly; they were buildings that the state desired and appreciated; those who contributed to them were regarded not as wastrels but as estimable men. So in such moments of precarious balance the Parthenon and Chartres were achieved. They offer us standards for comparison.

7

FOR ARCHITECTURE, AS WE HAVE NOW SEEN, MUST MEET SO MANY CRIteria that there never has been a perfect building. To meet the demands of commodity, solidity, and aesthetic satisfaction, a building must not compromise in any area. Unfortunately, that is impossible, for the sev-

eral measures, as we have said, make contradictory demands and often
cancel each other. Perfection in formal design tends to be sacrificed to
expression or utility, structure impinges on utility and elegance defers to
expression in an endless round of concessions. The architect would prefer not to compromise, but he cannot avoid diminishing the pleasing,
the stable or the useful aspect of his buildings. Sometimes he will come
near perfection. But the Parthenon leaked; its spaces were ill adapted
to new uses; its form did not express the double chamber within; its
triglyphs looked like the ends of wooden beams that were not there;
its structure was inefficient; and it did not reflect Athens' immediate
need for the courage and will to win against Sparta. Early Christian
basilicas, though their affirmation of Christianity has seldom been surpassed, often were motley assemblages of columns borrowed from
classical buildings; their structure was weak, their spaces cramped. The
beautiful central-altar domed churches of the Renaissance were ill
adapted to the Catholic liturgy, which had to move along a processional
nave towards a climax at the altar. Even Chartres has moments of chaotic, though highly expressive, design where the Romanesque and
Gothic parts join; and the nave had no adequate climax until a baroque
statue was placed at the eastern terminus. All the Gothic cathedrals
sacrificed comfort, efficiency and stability to religious atmosphere. The
men who built them decided where the compromises would be made
and which measures would be foregone. But in the end the most important were given precedence; for the men of the thirteenth century the
elevation of the Host clearly outweighed the comfort of the worshiper;
in Protestant churches of the twentieth century, where pew location and
rent were related to status, this was possibly less clear.

The issues involved have deep implications. If all designers must compromise, then perhaps the greatest buildings are those that exhibit a
compromise made powerfully and decisively. Perhaps the Erechtheum
is less wonderful than the Parthenon because it still shows all the hesi-
tancy and indecision of a designer and a society that refused to subordinate all the diverse shrines within a well-unified design, even though
they had accomplished that subordination in the Parthenon. Perhaps
the realistic and economical display of spaces in Early Christian basilicas was the strongest possible decision in favor of internal function
rather than external unity. On history's larger scene, the decision to
strike for unified design rather than stylistic expression has been greatly
debated; few indecisive solutions stand the test of time. The greatest
designers sacrifice some utility to design and expression. That fact may
reward the designer with the laurel of history, though the client is bound
to be disturbed.

These buildings required wealth, power, certainty of purpose; they announced an agreement as to what was important for the society, the will to lavish treasure on the desired building; they coincided with fleeting moments of classical stability when traditions were clear and not scorned.

On the big scale of history it is evident that great styles have taken a long time to develop and this suggests the question whether we should expect too much from an America that has only a three-hundred-year history. Many things have accelerated now and the new ways may develop and die more rapidly, even too rapidly. But up to now the periods of gestation, fruition and decay have run into centuries. The Greek temple was on the way to development at least as early as 700 B.C., had its finest hour at around 400, and though it has never died away altogether ceased to be a vital form by the first or second century of the Christian era. It was an architecture of a millennium.

Early basilicas that paved the way for the Romanesque and thus the Gothic had taken a recognizable form by the reign of Constantine. They were well developed by the eleventh century; they reached their peak in the Gothic of the Île de France in the thirteenth century; like the Parthenon, they never died away but they stopped being a living force toward the end of the fifteenth century. Thus their span was also a millennium. The buildings that are genuinely Renaissance began with the fifteenth century and they have been moribund perhaps since the eighteenth, and surely after the Crystal Palace of 1851. This leaves us four or five hundred years for the Renaissance-baroque-Georgian stream. The Roman architectural reign was about as long.

One cannot extrapolate with confidence to guess how long it will take to evolve an architecture of the industrial revolution. It did not begin to be suggested until well after the industrial changes were under way. When did the modern movement begin? Was it as early as the first uses of iron by Frenchmen in the Galerie d'Orléans and similar structures, near the beginning of the nineteenth century? With the Crystal Palace of 1851? With the reconstruction of Chicago after the Great Fire of 1871? With the first writings and speculations of Le Corbusier, Mies van der Rohe or Gropius? In any event, a new attitude toward building has been held for not much over a century at most; and it has been widely acceptable, even inevitable, only since the Second World War. It is not yet ubiquitous; there are those who yearn for the fancied elegance of yesterday. All the battles are not won, any more than they were when Chartres was completed. But it is also clear that the significant battles have been won and that rear-guard actions will not matter in the end.

This does not mean at all that the new architecture is perfected, that it has been distilled into its classic forms. We cannot really say that we are in the center of the history of the new great style, much less that we are seeing it at its apogee. What is certain is that we are watching the development of the first potentially great architectural period in which America has had a chance to participate nationally.

Great building periods have always focused on the creation of one or two, and usually not more than two, important building types on which the people were prepared to lavish all their greatest architectural skills. This attention was possible because the belief was there. These were not the conditions in nineteenth-century America. The society was not wealthy enough, though it was becoming so. It was not powerful in the world sense, though it was getting ready to reach such power. It had no very clear purposes, it was vigorously discussing everything. It was not prone to waste money on the arts, it did not have a single dominating admiration for which it wanted to build the best buildings that could be built. It may not even have cared to build any "best" building. The evolution of its architecture had come at second hand and colonially at that. If the conditions of Chartres and the Parthenon were essential conditions for a great architecture, nineteenth-century America could not be expected to produce one. It would be hard even in the mid-twentieth.

The greatest architectures have arisen in support of religion (but not always the Christian religion). It is possible that this is not essential but that the important thing is that there should be a strong common belief, religious or not. There is nothing to insist that this belief should be mystical or even anti-intellectual. But the great models of history suggest that the greatest artistry has come in times with unifying concepts, even *a* unifying concept, about which most people, *including the artists*, agreed. This proposes questions for Americans. When were Americans near to such unity? Were they ever near to it? Are they nearer or farther now? Is it true, as Mencken insisted in a dark period of America, that artists are always in rebellion against their time? Or is this a late and unhappy state of the Western world, not experienced before Galileo, Machiavelli, Montaigne and Luther, ominously growing through the nineteenth century and into the twentieth? Is a former American unity proclaimed by the New England village green or the manor on the James? Was the confused, even bad American architecture of the nineteenth and early twentieth centuries simply a reflection of the turmoil of a people who had lost the values of a unitary, agrarian, Protestant society and were trying to come to terms with a pluralistic, technological-urban, heterogeneous, Catholic or rabbinical one? If there was a schism, was it the artists or was it the people who were the wiser?

Had any building types emerged that seemed so desirable to Americans that they would lavish upon them kindred sacrifices of extra money, extra labor, extra love, such as we think were brought to the Acropolis or to Mont St. Michel? If there were no such dominant types, was the pluralistic society nonetheless reaching towards an agreement on some common values to be expressed by many architects, ordinary and extraordinary, to be accepted, even admired, by many people, not only by a few self-indoctrinating critics and connoisseurs, to be offered and accepted as a record not only of what the time *might* have been like in twentieth-century America but also of what the times *were* like?

These were the continuing problems. If the American work was not often good work, it may be explained quite as much by the uncertain dialogue that was going on in America as by any lack of talent in the unfortunates who, in a given moment, were trying to make architecture. If the newer work has promise, its promise is partly related to the fact that Americans in general may be almost ready to decide what is worth while, admit the decision, and then lavish effort on it. Our study is, then, less one of great achievements than one of great debates.

As soon as the serenity of tidewater colonialism was disturbed by the thrust across the Alleghenies, the American architect's life began to be complicated by the perplexing questions that rose from these debates.

How was he to work with an enormous and varied terrain, and its multifarious materials and climate? Should he try to preserve the innate regional qualities or should he deliberately negate them? Should he seek personal uniqueness or a classic result which might be called a "carbon copy"? Should he let his work be controlled by nature, or should he as a "pilgrim of power" seek to control nature? What would his genesis be; how much should he let others affect him; how much should he accept from other countries, how much attempt to stand as an American? How could he manage to produce first-class architecture in a nation of the middle class? What would happen to his profession as bigness was laid upon it? What limitations would be put upon his work by the "rural" or "village" mind?

How much should he subscribe to the Emersonian dream of unique America? In the great debates, where was he to take his stand? Would he be for tradition or innovation, for the frontier or the cultivated area, for preservation or demolition, for evolutionary or revolutionary change, for classicism or originality, for big cities or for villages? Should he believe in and try to serve an egalitarian or an aristocratic taste? How much should he be willing to satisfy the docility of his society, how much should he affront it? Was any other building worth more of his love than a church, and if so what should it be, and why? What position would he take between the hand and the machine? How much should he condone frugality? Should he suppress or reveal any ecstasy he felt in this work? What was to be his stance with sculptors and painters? Should he woo them or repel them? Control them or be guided by them? Use them as collaborators or as tools? Or should he reject them altogether on the ground that architecture was now its own sculpture and painting, the architect a better sculptor than the sculptor, a better painter than the painter, an artist complete and self-sufficient?

These were the questions he had to meet and to answer. Sometimes he answered them one way, sometimes another. But all the time it was quite a slalom course to run. Not very many American architects got to the bottom with all the flags still flying.

I

1600-1860

I

1900-1850

THE GREAT AMERICAN ARCHITECTURAL QUESTIONS
have never quite been answered but the argument about each has
ebbed and flowed so that now one, now another, has seemed the
more important. It is simpler to examine each at the time when it has
been most actively discussed. But in choosing to do this we must not forget that none of the questions is ever entirely suppressed.

They have arisen from fundamental conflicts in the American personality. They involve the struggle between the desire to be gay, hedo-
nistic, expansive, even extravagant, and the restraints imposed by caution, frugality and the sense that in the worship of beauty there may be
sin; between the instinct to wipe out the past and the nostalgia to preserve it; between the notion that cultivated taste does deserve to be
heeded and the egalitarian idea that the people can judge as wisely in
the arts as they are presumed to be able to do in politics; between a love
for the machine and a fear of it; between the admiration for the expert
and the distrust of him; between the sense that man must conquer nature and alter it to his will and the reverence that argues rather that man
should accommodate himself to nature. From this too comes one of the
most durable of all the debates, that between country and city, yeoman
and urbanite, farmer and factory hand, West and East.

I

FIRST, BEFORE THERE WERE ANY QUESTIONS AT ALL, THERE WAS THE LAND.

Each of its details was nearly duplicated somewhere in the world. But
when you put all the American land together it seemed different. Abra-

ham Lincoln said it was a land suited for one people, but it took a large
mind to see that. Individuals loved the details.

The details began at the shores. There was the sheer bare geometry of
the rock cliffs at Castle Head, Mount Desert, where the waves dashed
against the rock and the brittle spray fell back into a dark cold sea.
There were the gentle estuaries dotted with piles of salt-water hay near
Newburyport. There were the tall waving pampas grasses of the Jersey
meadows, the ragged scarred palms on the tiny hill of a sandy beach in
Florida, the ominous boom of the Pacific as it rode under the kelp to
the steep sides of the Big Sur, or the rough and foggy coast of California
north of Fort Ross where lumber schooners tied precariously near while
redwood logs were lowered down to their decks. But the coasts were not
places where many people might live. They were often too bold or too
marshy or too sandy. We can remember our coastal architecture, its light-
houses, its salt-gray shingles beaten by the weather, but for America
most of the buildings were inland. Some American writers wrote of the
seacoast but it was the inland continent that entranced most of them.

Thomas Wolfe told of the New England autumn with its frost "sharp
and quick as driven nails," its blazing, bitter red maples, and other
leaves "yellow like a living light . . . falling about you like small pieces
of the sun."

Thoreau observed a whole world in the passage of freight trains on
the Fitchburg Railroad bearing Manila hemp, coconut husks, English
ginghams, hides from the Spanish pampas, but also lumber, lime, salt,
fish, and molasses, and sounding through snow and rime "the muffled
tone of their engine bell from out the fog bank of their chilled
breath . . ."

The winter of old England was clammier. In Minnesota or Montana
the winds blew more bitterly. Blizzards from the west piled the snow
higher around Buffalo, but New England would come first to mind
when you read in Henry Adams of "straight, gloomy streets, piled with
six feet of snow in the middle; frosts that made the snow sing under
wheels or runners."

Very little of the land was east of the Appalachians. As you crossed
them, you might, if you had never been farther west, agree with Jefferson that the "passage of the Potomac through the Blue Ridge is, perhaps, one of the most stupendous scenes in nature," admire the small
catch of blue horizon through the cleft, speak of the "terrible preci-
pices hanging in fragments over you." There were other water gaps like
the calm one of the Delaware below Stroudsburg, and beyond the Blue
Ridge were many rivers: the French Broad as it poured out of the
Smokies or the serpentine Tennessee as it meandered around Chatta-

nooga and the wind-and-water-scooped rocks of Lookout Mountain. In the end all the rivers of the western Appalachian slopes would take you to the Mississippi but before that there was the Ohio valley and before you came to the Great River there were the remote lands of its fertile eastern basin as Hamlin Garland came to know them in the late 1860s.

Here Green's Coulee, Wisconsin, offered timbered knolls and little steep ravines, obdurate oak stumps and ditch-demanding marshes dotted with lakes which make the West seem "a fairer field of conquest."

Before the West there was the Mississippi. It dominated a great deal of American thought. Like multifold American nature, the Mississippi was many rivers. It was the steep-banked sky-blue stream of Hennepin and Hiawatha and the flat black bayou of Evangeline. But for most Americans it was the broad and muddy river of Huckleberry Finn with its coves, knee-deep above sandy bottoms, its bullfrogs, its gray sunrises, its rafts and its snags, its log cabins, and its fresh morning breezes, "and everything smiling in the sun, and the song-birds just going it!"

After New England and Virginia and the Appalachians and Wisconsin and The River there was the prairie. The Garlands came there, to the meadows so wide that they stretched unfettered to the western rim, to the "grass tall as ripe wheat," to the remote, dim clumps of trees, to "the hawks lazily wheeling in the air," and to the land billowing "like a russet ocean."

West of the plains and before the mountains there were the Bad Lands. Frank Lloyd Wright saw the Bad Lands of the Dakotas as architecture — "a distant architecture, ethereal, touched, only touched with a sense of Egyptian, Mayan drift and silhouette. . . . Endless trabeations surmounted by or rising into pyramid (obelisk) and temple, ethereal in color and exquisitely chiseled in endless detail . . ."

Entry to the plains, crossing them, was to be a dominating and persistent part of American experience. The Spaniards had known it, too, oppressed as De Voto reminds us by the ball-shaped sky-surrounded land, the dusty willows and cottonwoods along the shallow watercourses, and the incessant grass which "bent as the wind trod it; the line of horsemen bent it too as they crossed; it rose again from wind and hoof and closed behind them and no sign of their passing had been left."

In the long run, whether through the Bad Lands or through the grasses, you came to the Rockies, laminated and sheer as they were in Montana, pointed and serrated as they were in Wyoming, massive and dry as they were in Colorado, sculptured into monuments as they dwindled south into Arizona and New Mexico. They were hard enough to pass but the low and tractable places could be found. Then you met the sand, the insistent barrier of all American transcontinental experi-

ence. The desert could not be avoided. It subsumed the world's experience of deserts. Walter Prescott Webb has called it the overriding influence that shaped the West, its one unifying force, permeating the
plains, climbing the mountains to strip them of their vegetation, drying
up the inland lakes, plunging "down the Pacific slope to argue with the
sea. . . . It is the great designer of the American West, painting the
landscape with color. . . . It shortened the grass on its borders before
destroying it in the interior. . . . The trees it could not destroy it shriv-
eled, and those it could not shrivel it petrified."

To the north the desert was sometimes kind. The good dirt might be
carried from Washington and Oregon on to the rolling dunes that
covered the great lava beds of Idaho and a handsome fertile wheat belt
like the Palouse could be born. Beyond the rolling hills that would some
day bear the great grain crops were the wet and wooded Cascades, the
gorge of the Columbia, where Indians precariously speared the salmon,
and the expansive conifered region of Puget Sound. But to the south
the desert was more insistent and after you had crossed it there was still
the Sierra, that fantastic mountain range that Clarence King knew and
loved so well, its eastern foreground of whitened plain, its sapphire
mirages, its frowning eastern wall, marked with the shoreline of an ancient sea. But when you saw it from the west the brown foothills were
gentle, now purple, now full of orange-colored flowers, the sky was beryl,
the summits sharp but unforbidding, the green-roofed pines separating
the foothills with their rusty mining-town ravines from the not quite
perpetual snows which at sundown "burned for a moment in the violet
sky, and at last went out."

Beyond there was only the complex Pacific, here craggy-beached,
there sandy, here bearing fog-laden forests of giant trees, there sun and
scattered live oaks, madrones and clumps of manzanita, but the end of
the line for America unless subtropical Hawaii and arctic Alaska were to
be counted.

This was the majestic framework. Within it the details might be collected as much as you liked. You could note the cliffs of the northern
Atlantic as they dwindled into a broader and broader sandspit from
Long Island to Florida where everything became sand. You could notice that the White Mountains had spines, the Alleghenies wrinkles,
and the Smokies majestic domes; that the valleys of the North were long,
those of the South tortuous and appropriately called "coves." Even the
gaps to the west would vary, the easy one along the Great Lakes, the
long ascent over the Cumberlands, the steeper and shorter rise across
the Blacks and the low, hot, red-earth and resinous way south of Atlanta
where the ranges gave out altogether. You could admire the exciting

differences of river systems, the rushes of the eastern streams, the rages of the St. Vrain or Thompson, tearing their way eastward through the red rocks of Colorado, the turbid fall-offs of the Missouri and Platte, the narrow lava-cut course of the Snake, the Humboldt dying in the sand, the varicolored Mississippi, whose sky-blue water from Minnesota was dyed brown under the bluffs off St. Louis, only to rest in black-patched backwaters in Louisiana. You could think of the lava flows of Idaho, the shiprocks of Arizona, the Blue Grass plain, the Ozark plateau, the channeled tablelands of eastern Oregon, the volcanic peaks from Rainier to Shasta. The land offered every splendor except those of the tropics and the Arctic, the whole range of nature's palette, varieties of sight and sound, of animal and bird, of wet and dry, of heat and cold, of light and dark, of eminence and depression, of fertility and sterility, all often in close and dramatic contrast.

It provided almost every kind of material for building: hard and soft woods, woods that were white or red or blue, woods that came curling clean off a plane and woods that splintered at a touch, close-grained oak, tractable pine, wild-grained fir, cherry, maple, cypress, redwood; and tropical woods were not far away. It offered many clays that would provide hard bricks and soft bricks, warm red ones, delicate pink ones, simple grays and dirty yellows. It supported icy granite and burning lime, sandstones and limestones that carved easily, a variety of marbles. It had dirt for adobe, and grass for thatch, and all the building metals, copper, zinc, lead, aluminum and the bounteous supplies of iron and coal and flux which made steel easy to come by. Whatever the climate demanded of the architecture, the land responded to with useful and handsome building materials. But like the climate and the terrain the range was fantastic. There was almost too much abundance, too much freedom. How could any such variety be served by a single architecture; how could men coming on such wonders be content not to wonder?

In almost any condition, except the American condition, this land would have dominated a variety of peoples, have preserved and intensified their differences, have supported an interesting range of diverse architecture, dress, food, speech, ways of life. It began that way in America too. But it could not last. After modern technology had obliterated the differences, unprotected as they were by national frontiers, and had made it really impossible that they should ever be sharpened again, some Americans came romantically to regret the regionalism that was gone and even to try hopelessly to revive it. But the wave of technology was as inexorable for men's buildings as it was for their clothes and their food and even their thoughts. By 1960 it had filled even the coves of the black mountains of Tennessee and Kentucky and justified

Jesse Stuart's plea, "If there are ballads left among us, they should be gathered now."

To be a continental nation, containing within one boundary most of the temperate elements of a continent, was reserved as a unique experience for the United States. The vastness, not yet fully sensed, had impressed St. John de Crèvecoeur, back in the eighteenth century, when he reported that no European foot had traveled half the continent and that it would take many ages to "see the shores of our great lakes replenished with inland nations," and it was not one of the great cultural achievements of the airplane that it made the vastness seem banal. But before the airplane and not much more than a hundred years after de Crèvecoeur, a Middle-western historian, Frederick Jackson Turner, was happy to announce, perhaps prematurely, that the vastness had been consumed.

In the century between de Crèvecoeur and Turner many Americans had a wide variety of love affairs with American nature. But the characteristic American romance with nature involved more conquest and pillage than love and care. De Tocqueville understood this well enough in 1831:

> . . . the Americans themselves . . . are insensible to the wonders of inanimate nature and they may be said not to perceive the mighty forests that surround them till they fall beneath the hatchet. Their eyes are fixed upon another sight: the American people views its own march across these wilds, draining swamps, turning the course of rivers, peopling solitudes, and subduing nature. . . .

Later on, the American romance of nature was composed of a strange mixture of admiration for ancestral self-reliance and a belief in change, of nostalgia for a past that was gone and a craving for the exotic that may never have been. But when the chips were down and the choice needed to be made between the virgin forest and the bulldozer, there would be no doubt which the American people would choose.

Against this choice the land was not impregnable. It did have endurance and resiliency, as a single example will illustrate. As Ray Whitbeck and Olive Thomas have noted, the upper peninsula of Michigan and the corresponding part of Wisconsin were first deeply forested and filled with rivers. Indians of the Stone Age dressed local flints into heads for arrows and spears, stripped bark from the birches for canoes, attired themselves in furs and skins from the abundant animals and fed on their flesh and on the river fish.

When wealthy European taste declared furs luxurious, the rivers bore the boats of French and English trappers who came to take as many furs as possible, to loot and exploit a resource.

There were other things to be looted. Soon the loggers came. The helpful rivers carried the log drives when they were in spring flood; winter snows supported sledges that carried the logs to the streams. The trees had been growing for a long time and the logs were big. But the logging camps among the pines and the sawmills along the banks did not multiply until the prairie began to be settled by people who were unable to cut any timber on their own land. Towns and railroads came to the peninsula but not the seeds of new trees; and in the end many of the logging camps were ghosts and the land desolate, while the streams had either been choked by detritus, or, stripped of cover, had flooded and eroded their courses.

By the third quarter of the nineteenth century another way of life was dominant. The day of wheat began in lower Wisconsin where conditions were favorable but it soon spread northward where they were not. The land was cheap and fertile, it opened eastwards via the Great Lakes. It attracted Germans and Scandinavians for whom it supplied more than one recollection of home. Wheat was a fine cereal, it was in world demand, it shipped well, it grew well on fertile virgin soil in a favorable climate and it could be forced, even high in the peninsula. But in the long run the ardors of Wisconsin farmlands seemed too heavy and the wheat farmers moved on to the "sunset regions" of the prairie.

Today Wisconsin produces more cheese than wheat, and the northern lake shore yields copper. There are vestiges of fur hunting, there are lumber mills which work the local woods into paper, furniture, wooden ware and wallboards; there are shrunken wheatfields, most of which have yielded to the drier, pest-free, cheaper lands of the plains. The soil and the climate and the waterways are not as they were. What might have been indigenous for Wisconsin yesterday is not indigenous today and will not be indigenous tomorrow. Now the cool nights help preserve milk, but of course electricity can do that also. Now the summer favors the growth of ensilage corn and hay for dairy cattle, but they can be trained to eat other things.

If you drive through the state, the farms will look solid and permanent but in laboratories at the University of Wisconsin there are no doubt biologists who are dreaming of days when men will prefer algae to cheese and agronomists who are figuring how to maximize the production of algae on the Wisconsin waters. The red men were nomads; the *voyageurs* and *coureurs de bois* were nomads; the loggers were nomads; the wheat-growers were nomads, and there is nothing to say that the Wisconsin cheese-men will some day not move on or out. Wisconsin recapitulates in a nutshell the history of American land and its ingenious occupants, the vigor, the ruthlessness, the restlessness, the perpetual hope, the nomadism, the desolations, and the elegancies that were possible on a resilient land.

The ultimate American uniformity did not come about solely through the leveling ministrations of the machine or the pollen of American nomadism. It was also prepared for by the shared mysticism that a man was a different man the moment he set foot on the new continent and that the continent had a mystic unity. You can find this belief in many famous passages from John Winthrop and de Crèvecoeur down to the present. But the early Europeans, like de Crèvecoeur, holding an eighteenth-century European view of nature, thought that the Americans, "incorporated into one of the finest systems of population which had ever appeared," would in the long run "become distinct by the power of the different climates they inhabit." They did not, could not, foresee that Americans would reverse previous human procedures. Instead of being affected very long by the power of the land and the climate, they would affect the land and the climate by their power. It would even seem more important to Americans to apply the power than to be careful not to apply it carelessly or adversely.

This spirit would boil up in little ways and big ways. It could produce an impression such as the St. Louis Exposition did on Henry Adams in 1904, when he saw

> . . . a third-rate town of half-a-million people without history, education, unity or art . . . doing what London, Paris, or New York would have shrunk from attempting. This new social conglomerate, with no tie but its steam-power and not much of that, threw away thirty or forty million dollars on a pageant as ephemeral as a stage flat.

It was something that Adams found possible to enjoy with "iniquitous rapture"; it gave hope to a "pilgrim of power," it foreshadowed that Americans would soon have all the power they wanted to throw away. But Adams also noted another American characteristic in St. Louis. It "industriously ignored" its only element of natural interest, the River.

The spirit of the frontier laid waste the hills of West Virginia, the cut-over areas of northern Michigan, the rivers of the California gold dredges; brought grime and flood to the confluence of the Allegheny and Monongahela and called it a Golden Triangle; shrouded the Sierra Madres in smog; ignored minor desolation in every city every day so that Mencken could justifiably talk of the American libido for the ugly; it was never patient enough to work out the destiny of one place before it pulled up stakes and moved on to another. But it also made Rockefeller Center and the Tennessee Valley Authority; it carried the waters of inner Colorado through the massive Front Range to bring bloom to the eastern slopes. You might love a more intimate nature and pray that grand nature would not be demeaned by man, you might deplore dese-crations, weep over the ruthless, thoughtless, even aimless despoliation of natural resources, but you would generally be loving, praying, deplor-ing and weeping in a small company. You might dream yourself back into the imagined richness and integrity of an eighteenth-century New England village or Virginia manor. You might seek desperately to pour water on the dead roots of a never flourishing regionalism, you might hate the machine and the city, you might insist on a diversity for Amer-ica which Americans did not want, but all your dreaming, seeking, hat-ing and insisting would be quite in vain. All your piety and your wit and your jeremiads would not cancel either the record or the promise. There was the land and its continental embrace, its enormous scale, its indirect and elusive unity, and there was the pioneer, always changing the scene he stopped briefly to change, always moving on until there was no-where else to move; but then going back to remake what had in the meanwhile become desolate. So the frontier returned from the West to Pittsburgh, Chicago, Detroit, New York and Boston to begin a new cycle. This circular frontier had no end.

There was the great basic fact that man had come to alter nature and not to be altered by it. You might love this or hate it, admire it or fear it, or you might just try to be indifferent to it, but you would not have much chance of understanding what was good and what was bad about American architecture if you tried to pretend that this relation of the American man to the American land was different than it was.

About this land there had to be some pivotal decisions. Not all the decisions were unanimous, conscious, wise or even democratic; but some were irrevocable.

The continental decisions came first. The management of the con-tinental nation was to be undivided and English, not French or Spanish or Dutch. This determined what our underlying architectural inheritance could be, what influences from Europe would in later years most stead-ily be brought to bear, and most importantly what the dominant lan-guage would be.

Had the French remained in the Mississippi Valley, the Spanish in the Southwest and in California, even if each had gained independence from Europe, the parochial limitations would have been very different. The tide of common practice might well have been delayed at the boundaries, even checked altogether. As it was, materials and ideas could flow freely across one almost limitless, duty-free, continental market.

There was the decision about independence from Great Britain. The most superficial examination of the architecture of New Zealand, Australia or Canada will show how different things might have been. As they were, America felt few British architectural shackles after 1820, though Ruskin captivated some minds for a brief period after 1860. Since British architecture was decaying, except for sports like the Crystal Palace, we were lucky not to go through a colonial watering down of what was a weak effort in the motherland. On the other hand the War of Independence had initiated a durable affection for France and for French culture which influenced American architecture at least up to the Second World War.

Next came the decision about slavery. Perhaps the faulty economics of the Cotton Kingdom had doomed the feudalism of slavery; but the Civil War sealed the doom abruptly. It seemed to decide that America should not be a pair of nations, one agrarian, one industrial; one feudal, one almost democratic; one educated and scientific, the other gentlemanly and vague; it guaranteed that the Greek Revival plantation house was not a way of life, even for a few Americans, in the society that now had to emerge; it destroyed almost the only group of patricians who might have provided a continuum of cultivated understanding of architecture, however conservative that sympathy might have been. In exchange it offered a further chance for technological development, unity of national purposes on most questions, development of a kind of uniformity as to what architecture would be considered satisfactory; it did not succeed, South or North, in releasing anything that might lie in the Negro which would suggest any new themes for American architecture. When the Civil War was nearly a century in the past, honest Americans would have to admit that they had merely sat on the curbs of the wells of Negro culture without trying to draw from the sources which seemed to have served Mexico and Brazil so well.

There were other racial decisions. First there was the rejection of the indigenous peoples that refused to let American Indians play any significant role in the future development of the country. De Tocqueville remarked that Americans had learned how to exterminate the Indians "tranquilly, legally, philanthropically, without shedding blood, and without violating a single great principle of morality in the eyes of the world." And so it was. Perhaps a cross-mix was impossible in America though it had been achieved elsewhere, even on the American continent. When Americans declined the experiment they lost a chance to add elements of symbolism, irrationality, and ritual which might have tempered our expansionistic, technological and materialistic drives, for good or ill. But it did not happen.

Then there were the immigrations. At the end of the Revolution in 1790, the population was three-fourths of British descent and largely Protestant. To this we now added five million Europeans who came during the forty years of continental expansion that coincided with the years of great European political turmoil. Most of these came from England or Germany still; but there were French and at least a third were Irish, Gaelic, Catholic, the first group to offer any problems of assimilation at all, to be a minority even if only for a time.

Then the rapid industrialization after the Civil War brought another kind of immigrant, uneducated, uncomplaining, to be enticed to labor by steamship companies for the fares they would pay, by plant managers because they provided the possible oversupply of labor in which hard bargains might be driven. They came from Russia and Italy, from Poland and Rumania, from Croatia and the Levant.

This was the flood that poured into what Israel Zangwill perhaps too optimistically called "the melting pot." The new people offered problems. Their urban huddles became enclaves and often the enclaves were ghettos and slums. Their groupings and their ignorance and their habits of political thought or indifference combined to make them natural supporters of machine politicians. As soon as economic forces fed social resentment, the immigrations were stopped. This was another critical decision.

The immigrations, even the small ones of "exotic" Koreans, Chinese and Japanese, had been indispensable for the arts which for a long time might not have survived at all without immigrants, permanent or temporary. For most "old" Americans and most of the later Irish, Scottish and German stock were not expected to join the ranks of painters, sculptors, architects, musicians, cooks, decorators, opera singers and actors, though they might venture at being poets. This remains true despite the brilliant examples of the Irish Sullivan and the Welsh Wright. For a long time American parents thought it tragedy when their children sought careers in art, and perhaps still do. But the later immigrants produced progeny who, American-born and half American-bred, had talents resting in both worlds. The puritan ethic might have held it unsound for a scion to be either painter or scientist. The European view was different. In the end it might even be fashionable for an American whose ancestors had arrived in 1620.

Thus the large immigrations brought different kinds of people for different purposes, offered particular contributions to the composite culture of America.

Then there were decisions about how American wealth should be distributed. These, too, were evolutionary. The general tendency was to level incomes, whether by higher wages or higher gradations of income and inheritance taxes, whether by farm-support programs or by the distribution of federal funds for education in the illiterate states, whether by support of disaster-ridden citizens in an emergency or, by social security and job insurance, the support of those who were ridden by disaster in fair times as well as foul. When we exaggerate we say that America has delivered the classless society promised by Marx but a classless society of the middle class rather than of the proletariat. Or again we say America has become one great middle class; and we are partly right. This has a great deal to do with what our architecture has been and what it is likely to be. It has meant, for example, an upgrading of the standard of the average dwelling. But an average standard, which might have produced some elegant uniformities as it has in other times and places, has been degraded by an absurd demand for an insecure individuality. The leveling of incomes offers the risk that a comfortable middle class may supply no patrons interested enough in architecture to aspire to the best. There is nothing yet in architectural history to suggest that great works of art are likely to be made or even approved by middle-class committees.

Moreover, the American suspicion of public spending has thus far been justified in American architecture. However Swedes and Danes and Finns may have succeeded in achieving fine design in nationally commissioned buildings, the American successes are uncommon. There is no basic principle, perhaps, which says that large government buildings are unlikely to be distinguished in America, but there is plenty of historical evidence to suggest that lack of distinction is probable.

Then there was the decision about farm and city which continued to provoke debate long after it had been taken. It was not a conscious decision but it was none the less real; the surge to the city was relentless, beyond the power of any critical Canutes to halt. In the rush to the cities Americans, never strong at long-range planning, overlooked, even lost, the real advantages of urban life. But the consequences of the decision to be urban if not urbane ran through all of American history after 1880.

Finally, there was the difficult, halfhearted decision that we should play a leading role in world affairs. For American architecture this meant many things. There was the infusion of new architectural ideas brought by foreign visitors or by Americans who had sojourned in many lands. The things Americans wanted, the things they would accept were influenced. The opportunity to build abroad had a similar result. The result might be superficial and appear in thoughtless imitations of the Katsura Palace or the Masjid-i-Shah at Isfahan as happened in the nineteenth century. But later on, in men like Edward Stone or Harry Weese or Minoru Yamasaki, the experience seemed to settle into the spirit and be distilled later in forms that were not imitative.

These were the questions that seemed reasonably on the way to settlement — the continental extent of the nation, its racial pluralism, its early English understructure, its rejection of exotic people whether they were Indian or Oriental or Negro, its partial acceptance of the almost equally exotic Jew, its unification, and its destiny as an industrial, technological, and urban rather than as an agrarian nation, its development into a vast middle class and its emergence as a world power, but the arguments did not always die down even after the decisions seemed irrevocable.

They were all debated before the backdrop of "the American dream." The dream existed long before James Truslow Adams named it about a quarter-century ago, "that dream of a better, richer, and happier life for all our citizens of every rank which is the greatest contribution we have as yet made to the thought and welfare of the world." Almost all Americans subscribe to the dream, no matter how they differ about what is better, what richer, what happier.

Despite its illusory nature, despite many disillusionments, the dream has been durable. It has three main ideas. First, there is the idea of progress, perfectibility, the new and better life. Second, there is the idea of a democracy forming a new kind of commonwealth. These alone could not define the American dream, for they have been imagined by other dreamers of dreams, for Edens, Utopias, Atlantises. The dream became American when the powerful conviction was added that it could come true and in a specific place and that the specific place was America. The idea that "this is the place" is the conviction of most Americans and of many foreigners, too. It runs through most American documents from Edward Johnson's seventeenth-century *Wonder-Working Providence* through Emerson and Whitman to the Four Freedoms. It is in the Declaration of Independence, Brook Farm, the TVA, and Frank Lloyd Wright's proposal for Broadacre City.

The dream sought reality in countless specific examples, some in architecture. There was for example the early American prison in Virginia, the first one conceived architecturally in America. For it Benjamin Henry Latrobe provided the inscription "The Legislature/ of the Commonwealth of Virginia,/ having abolished the ancient sanguinary criminal code/ The first stone of an Edifice/ The Monument of that Wisdom/ which should reform while it punishes the Criminal/ was laid on the 7th day of August/ in the year 1797/ . . ." When French experts criticized the plan, it was the American dream which answered that the prison was different because "it was planned to emphasize reform and hope."

Observers like Frederic I. Carpenter have suggested that the dream at its best thought of universal freedom, not of nationalism; of the advance of science, not of materialism; of the intelligent cooperation of educated individuals, not compulsory social reform; of self-realization through struggle, not simple individualistic successes in pragmatic terms. The recurrent ejaculations have been "freedom," "progress," "democracy." They were powerful words, sometimes mouthed uncritically, sometimes not quite believed, but always powerful.

In the present day, Americans have been less steadily sure that the dream was true; some may have doubted whether it was even admirable or desirable; more have been able to see its weaknesses, to distrust it. The attitude of most American artists can be studied against the texture of the dream, tragically for men like Melville, O'Neill, or Jeffers. Not many architects except Louis Sullivan, John W. Root and Frank Lloyd Wright stand as clean-cut examples of the power of the dream. For it would be absurd to assert that many American architects felt the challenges and disappointments of the dream as intently as the poets and the novelists; only poets among them like Wright and Sullivan would utter such thoughts. The many American architects who sought their sources in Europe, who sought to bring European culture to America, explicitly denied a new architecture and thus explicitly denied the dream; and not many architects would quote Jeffers, "it is time to begin to perish," and create buildings for people they believed to be standing on the peak of time. Critics may be Jeremiahs at heart; architects cannot be.

If architects and their work do not show the extremes of ecstasy and despair about the dream that we can find in the writers, if architecture has supplied but a limited and restrained criticism of life, then this is but another affirmation of the fact that architecture is only partly an art. If the reflection of the society it holds up is pale, it may be that the society itself was a little pale. This, of course, is what the writers were suggesting.

But there was a good deal of agreement about one aspect of the dream — the notion that "this is the place" — and there were sub-dreams about sub-places so that Texas or California or North Carolina, not the United States, was "the place." Out of this mystique of "the place" grew the myriad demands for the maintenance of a regional and a national architecture, if there were one, and the invention of such a distinctive expression if it did not exist.

2

AMERICA, LIKE EVERY OTHER COUNTRY, HAD ITS OWN PRIMITIVE, NAÏVE and indigenous original architecture. But this was the architecture of Indians — the bark houses of the Penobscots, the long houses of the Iroquois, the tipis of the Crows, the mounds of the Mandans, the pueblos of the Zuñi, the hogans of the Navajos, the log dwellings of Puget Sound. Some of these were even elegant, many contained seeds of promise; but we swept them all aside. Indian words and Indian foods passed into the American culture but nothing important from the Indian architecture, save a belated effort to imitate the form but not the function of the pueblos.

It was not unnatural that Americans should have ignored the indigenous American dwellings, for the evolution of buildings from comparable European primitive types had gone a long way before European settlers came to America. Their own experience and their memories provided them with more advanced solutions than those of the Indians.

For much the same reasons the more sophisticated arts of the pre-Columbian Indians of Mexico and Peru were rejected by the Spaniards who saw in them nothing worth adopting or even something idolatrous to be shatteringly repudiated. So Spanish-American buildings recapitulated the achievements of Spain on land which had much in common with the Spanish land, just as the English efforts were to be on land which, in New England, if not in Virginia, had much in common with English land. Much of the great prehistoric Indian work was not known; what was known was ignored. It was not until the twentieth century that Americans began to pay attention to it; that Mayan and Inca ornaments and decorations interested American artists; that a marriage of cubism and a pseudo-regionalism and a false nostalgia combined to reawaken interest in the pueblo as a form for new buildings, but purely as a form.

Of the European invaders only the English left a large, durable and extensive residue. The purposes of the French were not to establish permanent settlements; the *coureurs de bois* and the *voyageurs* were brilliant explorers and trappers and they opened up the great rivers; they brought an interesting vertical version of the log cabin up the Mississippi, perhaps a better version than the horizontal, but in the long run their influence was trivial; and the great contemporary and monumental styles of France were inappropriate for poor Frenchmen in America even while French colonization was vigorous.

It was a little different with the Spaniards. The church and the army

marched hand in hand, and though the main search was for gold there
was also the matter of converting souls. The churches of Mexico did
leave a mark. It was the mark of the Spanish Gothic and later of the
Renaissance and baroque. Such churches appeared briefly in the United
States, too, as in the eighteenth-century St. Xavier del Bac in Tucson.
Florida's St. Augustine contained the Spanish Governor's house and
cathedral. But they are not so important as the more primitive missions
of California built by Father Junipero Serra later, long after the con-
quistadores, not long before the conquest of California and Texas by the
United States. The missions have influenced California thought ever
since, sometimes far too directly. They are handsome in their honest
and human simplicity; and touching when they contain examples, as
at Ventura, of the Indian primitive rendering of ancient Biblical subjects. They were fine of their kind but came only at the end of a Spanish influence, and did not move into the main stream of the indigenous
California building which would endure. So they have not had the durable and insistent influence on America that the transplanted English
house did via Massachusetts, Virginia and South Carolina.

The California "adobe" did have such an influence, for it was a good
design for California living if California was to be a land of far-riding
rancheros. It offered enough combination of outdoors and indoors,
enough free ventilation with its through rooms and its double verandas
so that it was useful for much other Californian life, too, and it can be
called genuinely indigenous. It has been resilient, even in modern
hands. But there is at least a good chance that the "adobe" was not
Spanish at all. Its primary form may well have been brought to Monterey by Thomas Oliver Larkin, who had lived in South Carolina before
he came; after it was introduced it may have been adopted by wealthy
Mexicans like Vallejo, for men of this type did not hesitate on another
occasion to replace Spanish forms with those of the Gothic Revival. In
any event there were adobe villages from Mexico to Kansas in the end.
Whatever its source, the California indigenous was real and more independently contrived than the New England indigenous. But its influence was not widespread nor really durable. Easterners like Richard
Henry Dana, coming by Monterey in 1834, thought it pretty and exotic;
but fifteen years later it was dying away and Bayard Taylor came to
examine what seemed to be the last of the old Spanish way of life;
while the semblance of Mexico was all on the surface by 1890.

For the same reason it is not necessary to dwell on details brought
early from other parts of Europe, as in the Vieux Carré of New Orleans;
or even late in the nineteenth century and duplicated from memory by
Germans, Swedes, Danes, Norwegians in various parts of the agrarian

West; or on the earlier contributions of the Danes or the Dutch to localized regional architecture in the East. This implies no disrespect for the
Swedish introduction into Delaware of the log cabin, which would
spread across the Appalachians and have a powerful, if ephemeral, life
on the frontier, or the French use of timber-and-nogging walls in New
Orleans as early as 1716, or the stilted first floors and long porch designs
of the French for a tropical climate of the lower Mississippi, or the yel-
low-brick kilns of the Dutch that provided stepped gables for early Albany (1657), or the cloisters of the Baptists at Ephrata. Some of the
buildings are handsome and characteristic. All partake of the same fine
qualities as the English development in New England and Virginia and
Carolina; all endured the same later history and we can remember
them while considering only the primary sample, since in the long run
they remain less as influences than as memories.

All were based on the rectangular construction which dominated
Europe and hence the United States. If the walls were to be made of
stone or mud or brick, then the principal structural problem concerned
the roof only, and this was the problem for the Dutch brick house or the
California adobe. But in regions where mud was unavailable or unde-
sired and where brick was costly if desired, while wood was plentiful, it
was inevitable that wood would be the predominant material. Wood
offered more structural problems and also more structural freedom.
Many Europeans have forgotten their wooden beginnings and tend,
unless they come from the North, to scorn wooden buildings as inferior;
Englishmen have forgotten that England was a land of wood until
Samuel Pepys devoured the English forests to make England empress
of the seas. One of the few pleasures available to an American trying to
show a friend from abroad anything that he will admire is to see how the
attitude towards wooden architecture changes as the friend is toured
around New England. But the wooden architecture did not begin this
way. It was a matter of necessity; refinements came later.

As soon as the colonists emerged from their temporary burrows, such
as they dug at Concord, they began to build their version of the English medieval development from the Saxon cruck house. Wood was
plentiful as bricks were not and the colonists made the most of this and
of their memories.

The houses did not long resemble their medieval prototypes, perhaps
no longer than the first winter. The exposed Elizabethan struts, stuffed
with bricks or lath and plaster, simply let in too much air and the
American addition of heavy siding was urgent. Otherwise the houses
still had a distinctly medieval cast. But within fifty years after their
arrival the colonists had developed a style of house which had distinc-

tive American characteristics. The chimney was the dominant factor in this, and out of it in the long run came four basic plans, one with a great central hearth, one with a chimney at each end, one with two chimneys set in the center of each of two wings, and one with four chimneys, two at each end.

Such primitive constructions were refined rapidly. In other parts of the colonies a few other American innovations were being made, such as the gambrel roof which the Dutch seem to have invented here. But though we can still see a few of these ancient American houses, they are not really what we associate with New England. The buildings that come most readily to mind are of later date and the result at first of considerable native development, then modified by self-conscious efforts at refinement of details, first from memory, then with the aid of books, and finally by the efforts of professional architects. Between 1607 and 1800 dormer windows had appeared, thatched roofs had disappeared, and stick chimneys had been abandoned for brick. The roofs were flatter, the second-story overhang was disappearing. Iron railings had become readily available, houses could be built even as high as five stories; iron-backed fireplaces were known, and the Franklin stove had appeared as early as 1742 but was not exceptionally popular. Carpets were beginning to be used, but sanded floors were common and remained popular in Boston for a long time. After the early handmade crude pieces there was very little American furniture and until 1795, when Duncan Phyfe began his work, almost everything was imported.

Yet a glass works had been operating in Salem from 1638, printing in Cambridge from 1639, an iron works in Saugus from 1646. By 1778 a "defector" had brought us the English textile secrets, the first iron-rolling mill had been organized, and in 1793 Whitney invented the cotton gin. At this point America was ready to enter the industrial revolution as an aggressive participant. But her architecture, though it would be carried far and wide over the land, was not necessarily well fitted to serve every terrain and every climate that was now to be encountered. As the Romans had marched across Europe and deposited the atrium wherever they marched, so the English and their descendants now marched across America and most of the time deposited the New England house. As it became less and less suited to its surroundings, it also suffered depreciation.

We must not let small details within this one dominant tradition confuse us. You may associate white-painted wooden forms with New England; you may think of Virginia in terms of Jeffersonian bricks and two-story porches. Bucks County will recall stone barns to you and you will remember others from Wisconsin, Illinois and Kentucky. If you see a round stone silo with a conical roof resembling a tower of ancient Carcassonne, you will be right to associate it with Maryland and not South Dakota. You will associate adobe with Taos and not with Meriden, Connecticut; you will think of Oregon or Washington when you see a barn with vertical boards and battens; of the Piedmont of the South or even of the Great Smokies when you see a high, thin house carrying a breezeway between small wings, and a lean-to porch; you would be surprised to find it in Minnesota. In all of this there was and is a minor regionalism and a charm, but almost without exception it is the ringing of changes on a single theme.

The changes do matter and they do make us aware that we are in one place and not another or even that the building is a church or school and not a house. The rectangular plan may support one story or more and the proportions are made very different by the decision. The pitch of the roof matters; it matters whether it has dormers or not and whether these are large or small. A gambrel roof alters the form materially, and so does a roof that sweeps down on one side in a great curve or a pair of roofs standing out from the flanks. Poke the barn form up much higher, make it narrower, and you have the grain elevator, that beacon of the Middle West which replaces the New England church steeple as the sign you are nearing a town. A verandaless house is different from one with a veranda; if there is a veranda it matters how high it is, whether its roof is flat, or flows from the main roof or is separated from it, drooping from the front wall, so to speak, as it often does in rural Carolina and Georgia. Replace the central chimney by a cupola and there is a sensed difference although the form is much the same. Take the cupola from the middle of the barn to one end and you have the simplest form of church like the little country ones of the South, pathetically standing in their meager cornfields as at Manning, South Carolina. Put the door at an end under the gable, hoist a flag pole over it, put the chimney at the other end, append two outhouses and you have a country school of Ward County, North Dakota. Pitch the roof more steeply, enter the side through a door with an ogival top, perforate the end with two narrow and ogival windows, put a small circular window just under the ridge, poke a belfry through the roof to replace the chimney, treat the wall vertically with boards and battens, and you have the "Gothic" church of Lancaster, New Hampshire. Use the end for an entrance, cover the whole gable with a rectangular false front, and you have the beginning of a western Main Street. Farmhouse, barn, elevator, school, church, store, town house, town street, all come from this one bolt of indigenous cloth; and you will hardly confuse it with the dwellings of the Cameroons, of the Swiss Valais or the Norwegian fiords.

Good or bad, this is something that has already gone beyond the primitive, has in it something of the self-conscious, is relying in part upon the book to jog a failing memory or to supply what memory never had. As the carpenters, armed with their simple books of proportions and their own manual skills, began their embellishments of windows, edges, chimney tops, pediments, cornices, quoins, and corbeling, they followed well-established patterns almost as traditional as the original peasant style itself, patterns for details that were originally in stone, as the granite façades of Georgian London were reproduced in wooden house façades of 1716 Portsmouth, New Hampshire. The results were of high quality in New England. Was this because it originated there and was sensible there, or because craftsmen were better, or because New England was richer, or because New Englanders cared more, or because their memories were greener, less plagued by the daily grinds and desolation of the west-bound frontier? Something of all of these, no doubt, but was there something more, as Lewis Mumford insists, the result of the "common spirit, nourished by men who had divided the land fairly and who shared adversity and good fortune together"?

3

IN THE PERIOD BETWEEN 1800 AND 1860 THE CENTRAL PART OF THE North American continent was to be joined to the United States whose boundaries would then touch the Pacific. But at the turn of the century (save for New Orleans) everything that was really civilized in this land stood east of the Alleghenies. Nor was it anything to be ashamed of for this young and provincial land barely released from colonialism. It was a testimonial to people who built well.

Even today, a town like Shirley Center, Massachusetts, settled in 1750, makes a happy impression. Its triangular green stands at the intersection of three roads leading through rock-fenced fields bordered by deciduous woods. Its meetinghouse and town hall are white and large enough to dominate the town while proclaiming their communal functions. Nearby, along the roads, trim houses stand four-square beneath arching elms, facing the green or the roads, backed by sprays of cedars, maples and oaks. The common character of the village is asserted by double-pitched roofs, red-brick chimneys, white clapboards, modulated windows, dark trim. Other towns of that day, like Salem or Newburyport or New Bedford, perhaps more prosperous, perhaps more worldly, sometimes have a more elegant architecture; but the plans and scale of all speak of orderly societies whose enormously independent builders contrived to produce individual houses that did not contradict the whole. This common understanding can be observed again on the Connecticut River where Deerfield, Massachusetts, Orford, New Hampshire, and Putney, Vermont, reveal the common understanding of the early builders.

What they built looked well in many landscapes, served efficiently in many climates, could be built of many materials, permitted a good amount of adaptation. It was less elegant than romance depicts it; it cannot solve all the problems of today but it is one of our finest architectural heirlooms. What one sees today at Williamsburg or Cooperstown is glamorized historical fiction and may lead to the belief that a historical style, rather than scale and town planning of spaces and a way of life, was the source of what is admirable. But Shirley Center, where time stopped in 1860, is a genuine witness to the sure eye of builders who, while working sincerely in the style of their period, insisted on the good design of spaces. Thus they created comfortable, dignified houses and handsome public and religious edifices even in quite remote and small places.

When we think of a New England village, we think of it as white although white was not universal, for there were still reds and yellows and grays which, in isolation, played a part in the New England scene. Nor was white the only possible color for such a landscape, as a short tour of Norway will demonstrate. But it was a good choice, perhaps the best choice. It offers a brilliant and American example of how an anonymous architecture may arrive at a right solution through no apparent intellectual process but a considerable amount of emulative conformity, while efforts in the minds of mediocre innovators will fail.

This white has a severe test to meet. It must be at home as background for the stark skeletons of the winter-shorn branches, the small red berries of the winter bushes, the green and blue of the firs and balsams; it marries the snow and lets the purple shadows of the drifts flicker up its sides. When spring comes it offers the gentlest foil for the burgeoning yellow of the forsythia, the fragile leafage of the budding trees, so thin and lacelike, so pale and yellow a green, but also for the bold red buds of the maples; in summer it sits cool beneath the shadows of great elms and is at once noticed and unnoticed, reposed and quiet; in the autumn it again becomes part of the lively palette of the autumnal conflagration. No other color might perhaps manage it so well, but it must be kept white and not allowed to be dingy and this, too, is a New England symbol and a New England pride. So it offers the capstone to the perfection of the New England indigenous form and it sits with equal felicity throughout the seasons, a symbol of growth and stability but prepared for eccentricity at the same time.

It was not long before New Englanders demanded greater amenity and elegance than their early architecture afforded. Many Americans, especially in the South, had risen well past primitivism by 1800. Only a few surviving houses, like the Fairbanks House in Dedham, Massachusetts, or the John Ward House in Salem, recalled the privations and hardships of colonial life. Unsubstantial wooden structures like the many-gabled Old College at Harvard had long since rotted, burned or been demolished. Even Williamsburg's Capitol had nearly disappeared, and the so-called Wren Building at the College of William and Mary no longer satisfied eighteenth-century men like Thomas Jefferson who called it a "den of noise, of filth and of fetid air."

Urbane, cosmopolitan people readily felt at home in some of the American cities, many had a special and personal character: there were the rows and stoops of Baltimore and Philadelphia; the squares of Savannah; the gracious verandas of Charleston; the gold-domed State House on Beacon Hill rising above the Boston Common. Local flavor was Spanish and French in New Orleans, Quaker and German in Philadelphia, English in Boston, Dutch in New York whose step-gables had not yet been replaced by ubiquitous brownstones.

Dugouts, sod houses, tents and shacks were emblems of the frontier or of the destitute. On the frontier there were log forts like those at Marietta, Ohio, Harrodsburg, Kentucky, and Fox River, Wisconsin, but as the Indians were pushed westward by wars like the Black Hawk of 1831, more substantial dwellings appeared on the rivers and even in clearings at the very edge of the forest. The Swedish log cabin was never regarded in America as anything more than a makeshift on the way to better things and by 1840 it was well down in the social scale. It had advantageous political symbolism for a wilderness campaigner like William Henry Harrison but his own house in Vincennes, Indiana, though simple and lacking in elegance, was much more than a log cabin.

The westward expansion tended to reduce diversity and erase primitive enclaves. New England houses were provided in California and Oregon during the Gold Rush as New England pianos and window curtains were ferried around the Horn. Mormons, moving westward from New York, left a trail of buildings in Kirtland, Ohio; Nauvoo, Illinois; St. Joseph, Missouri; and finally in Salt Lake City. As more up-to-date ways of building came to the frontier, they were quickly adopted, usually more coarsely than in their Eastern prototypes.

There were islands of resistance to Eastern fashion. Usually these were associated with special religious groups of Amish, Rappites, Baptists or Shakers in New Harmony, Indiana; Ephrata, Harmony and Economy, Pennsylvania; New Lebanon, New York; and Shakertown, Kentucky. They built substantial and simple buildings of brick or stone or wood, in a peasant vernacular, almost always well proportioned, showing some but not much increase of refinement as they prospered, sometimes as at Ephrata clearly retaining their memories of the late-medieval architecture of their ancestral home. The Shakers in particular insisted that craftsmanship could capitalize on the nature of materials even when the building was modest.

Other religious groups, often partly socialistic as well, built similar communities at Red Bank, New Jersey; New Icaria, Iowa; Bethel, Missouri; and Aurora, Oregon. Their architecture was much the same, sturdy, dignified, unembellished, whether they called themselves the North American Phalanx, the Old Icarians, or the followers of Keil.

The Mormons went further, particularly in their towered and buttressed Temple at Salt Lake City (1853-1893) or the specially dormered "Lion House." So did the Oneida Community when it erected its mansarded Mansion House at Oneida, New York, in 1860-1871. But these architectures are interesting more as an expression of social objectives than because they have any excellence as art or because they have really demonstrated a revolutionary style comparable to the life they house. In the end all such efforts had little influence.

For most other centers were not interested in trying to resist the fashionable architecture of the East. On the contrary, they welcomed it. Radical differences remained between the North and the South, between New Orleans and New York, but these differences were less marked than the colonial ones had been.

A major factor in the diminishing regional differences was the national acceptance of a professional architecture, American Georgian. Derived from Palladio, the sixteenth-century Italian architect, this style had been modified in England by architects like Sir Christopher Wren and James Gibbs, whose work was known in America through books like William Salmon's *Palladio Londinensis, or the London Art of Building,* first published in 1734.

The cast of Georgian architecture is well exemplified by a famous eighteenth-century Virginia house, Westover, located twenty-five miles above Williamsburg on the James River, built for William Byrd II about 1730-1734. Educated in London, Byrd was a wealthy plantation owner who directed public affairs in the colony. One of our finest national monuments, his mansion is approached from the north side through wrought-iron gates that open beneath a scrolled overthrow. On either side, brick piers, bearing large birds, mark the beginning of handsomely wrought fences that stretch across the forecourt to the house. The entrance façade is symmetrical while the first floor is raised three feet above grade on an English basement. The central doorway is the fulcrum of the composition, reached by a pyramidal flight of stairs. The windows in the two main stories, spanned by low brick arches, form a regular rhythm clearly centered on the axis of the doorway. The roof rises steeply to a sharp ridge which is stopped by two pairs of end chimneys. A belt course and the main cornice, with rows of dentils and modillions, wrap the whole design. The south or garden façade is identical except for the doors, which were modeled after plates in Salmon's book and may have been imported from London with the wrought-iron entrance gates. The fore-hall is off center to gain light from one of the windows; beneath the stair landing it opens into a more commodious after-hall whence one may enter a music room, a drawing room, a dining hall or a library. Each has its own deep fireplace and is fully paneled to the height of cornice moldings.

Houses such as this, or Carter's Grove, or the ballroom wing of the Williamsburg Palace, the product of skillful imported master carpenters like Richard Bayliss and master designers like Richard Taliaferro, perfectly exhibit the character of Georgian architecture. They shame the better-known architecture of Monticello or Mount Vernon. Their fine compositions overrode all minor differences. An English house, designed by James Gibbs and published in his *Book of Architecture*, served perfectly well, for example, for the south front of Mount Airy in Richmond County, Virginia, built by John Tayloe in 1758-1762; differences in national origin, site and terrain might affect the level of craftsmanship or cause minor adjustments to windows and chimneys, but they did not seem important enough to require modification in the basic harmonies of Gibbs's design.

Washington's Mount Vernon, 1757-1787, has a Palladian plan that was transferred from northern Italy. Its walls, which look like blocks of stone masonry, are actually planks of long-leaf pine beveled and painted with a sand finish. The Palladian window of the banquet room, whose prototype was a plate in Batty Langley's *Treasury of Designs*, is decorated with Adam detail on the interior at a scale incompatible with the Georgian exterior. Furthermore, the exterior by no means expresses the interior. For example, to express the two-story banquet room, which had no bedrooms above it, would have required a blank wall on the upper story, but this would have thrown the whole design into embarrassing asymmetry! So two false windows were created, complete with sashes

and blinds, but with a blank wall immediately behind them. But no
false way was found to resolve one of the glaring inconsistencies of the
east or porticoed façade, where the rude staircase adjacent to the library
cuts diagonally across a window. Such aberrations illustrate the degrees
of artificiality that a prescription of rigid formalism can impose on architectural design. To achieve the classic result, many utilitarian, material, and structural aspects were sacrificed to formal composition. Such
sacrifices were to be challenged later by professional architects like Benjamin Henry Latrobe, who thought Mount Vernon a result of "indifferent taste."

Still the best Georgian managed to reconcile beautiful form with useful performance, and that excellence so endured that what was essentially an English style continued to fascinate Americans from 1700 until
1850 even while they were toying with other ways. The strength of the
Georgian lay in its unerring aim at beautiful form and repose. It permitted considerable variety, particularly as houses were adapted to
tropical or temperate climates to produce differences such as those between the Gibbes House in Charleston, South Carolina, and the Jere-
miah Lee House in Portsmouth, New Hampshire. But this variety did
not disturb the basic homogeneity of the form. Even public buildings
resembled houses so that Independence Hall in Philadelphia or the
Old Colony House at Newport have a domestic character.

It was possible for a gifted man to study Georgian precedents and
produce fine buildings. Thus Peter Harrison, of Newport, often called
the first American architect, achieved notable successes in his Touro
Synagogue and Redwood Library in Newport, his King's Chapel at
Boston and Christ Church at Cambridge; all are beautiful and dignified buildings, especially admirable inside, and all are within the common tradition he had studied in his books. The amateur, Jefferson, did
not stray far from the Englishman Robert Morris's books when he rebuilt Monticello. Where, as in Salem, such scholarship was combined
with the skill of a great woodcarver like Samuel McIntire, the general
beauty imparted by formal composition was enriched by mantelpieces
and paneling, as in the Gardner-White-Pingree House. It was a tradition
that set American architecture upon a good beginning; we should not
be making the mistake of trying to continue it in modern Lexington
or Shaker Heights; but what remains of it should be zealously preserved
and will always enhance our landscape and our life while it lasts.

But the serenity of the Georgian experience was threatened by the
Revolution and by the subsequent demand for a new expression of the
new land in every sphere of American life. One could sense this in the
first national architectural competition, held for the Capitol in Washing-

ton in 1792. Naturally, it drew a group of designs in the accepted Georgian idioms. Some were amateurish, like Philip Hart's badly scaled and ineptly phrased elevations; others like James Diamond's clutter of roof trusses, arches, pediments, domes and other discrete elements failed to provide the desired dignity. Several were surprisingly competent, notably McIntire's, a well-proportioned and monumental English palace. But Washington and Jefferson looked for something more classical than any of these. Such a spirit appeared in the domed and porticoed designs submitted by Samuel Dobie, Stephen Hallet and Dr. William Thornton. Thornton's design won the competition, and to it are due the general scale and features of the old Capitol, still visible in the rebuilt east façade. Hallet was asked to modify details and to supply a technical competence which Dr. Thornton lacked. Later, Latrobe executed much of the interior work and the dome over the Halls; in 1818 Charles Bulfinch was called from Boston by President Madison to redesign the portico and to achieve a better unity between the wings. Still later, in 1851-1867, Thomas Ustick Walter raised the great dome over the center and constructed two outlying wings whose heavier scale balanced the dome and the central block. This succession of designs was often the result of bitter political and aesthetic bickering. The atmosphere was normally one of great personal rivalry, machination, anger. Men were freely accused of incompetence, extravagance, even venality. Congress and the President were forever interfering. But the fact that so many designers, working in such an unhappy climate, could nonetheless achieve improvement, and maintain an essential architectural unity as they worked across the sixty years, indicates the basic unanimity of agreement about classic design. To compare the situation with the present, we have only to ponder the disruptive proposals made for the completion of the crossing of St. John the Divine, or the additions our contemporaries make to an old American bank or to Grosvenor Square in London. The history of the Capitol reveals also that local traditions were disappearing as the "national" art emerged. The Capitol set the mark for later government buildings like the Department of State and the old General Post Office in Washington, and most of our state capitols have since reflected it. Boston's State House of 1795 by Bulfinch, has been mocked in later designs for schools and even office buildings by architects who have mistakenly been more interested in form than in performance.

The decay of the Georgian and regional architecture was brought about by several forces; there were the designers themselves who began, self-consciously, to import English architecture through books, often incompetently, unimaginatively, merely degrading the native traditions; there was the decay incident to careless handling of details on a frontier indifferent to details since it was always preparing to move on; there was the decay implicit in attempting to put a form where it did not belong, in modification to make it more useful, destroying the old but not creating a good new one since the limitations of the residue were too cramping; there was the decay incident to the unification of a land, tending to level out ways of life. Decay by design could be best seen in the old places where the original memories were greenest, decay by neglect could be seen across the prairie, decay by modification could be seen in the more prosperous parts of the Middle West, and decay by unification was a national experience.

The designers took the low rectangular houses and made them square and high, attached classical pilasters and cupolas and captains' walks, cut wood to look like stone. Soon the men who had used the books fancied themselves competent enough to get along without them. So the style decayed; a glance might not show that the proportions had changed, but closer inspection revealed that ornaments had become an "illiterate reminiscence," that windows were bare openings; as Lewis Mumford observed, "Alas for a bookish architecture when the taste for reading disappears!"

There was more and more of this on the American scene and it was bad enough. But it was nothing when compared with the way the fine native and anonymous work petered out as it crossed the Appalachians and the way it disappeared altogether when it left the Ohio River and started west. Thus what in Kentucky and Ohio, on the very edge of the frontier, had been made with skill and beauty and even refinement, farther west became crude and transient; the versions of the now much changed and aged vernacular became unrecognizable without emerging into a clear local type. The early Oregon houses of New England type built under the guidance of the early settler, Dr. John McLoughlin, look interesting in Oregon but would seem inconsequential in any old New England town. The efforts of the men of the mining towns, whether in Colorado or along the Mother Lode of California, often move us and remind us of something we like from Mark Twain or Bret Harte but their architecture will not stand any real analysis. The charm of the Victorian relics of Aspen, Colorado, should not lead us to overestimate their absolute excellence. They are all betrayals of architectural illiteracy rather than of any desire to build something particularly suited to the place, the times and the conditions. The courthouses at Guthrie, Oklahoma, or Tombstone, Arizona, are but two among many mute witnesses to an effort at architecture by someone without any understanding of it. They are indigenous only in the sense that they look

like other things on the frontier and that they used a nearby and unusually ugly stone. Their like can be found all over Kansas and Nebraska
and they are only a small step better than the tin shacks that now adorn
the great national roads in these areas.

In the mining or logging towns or wherever men came to loot the
earth and then move on, the situation was even worse. We may ignore
for the moment the shacks of Pittsburgh or Altoona. But the general
disorder of the communities was but a reflection of the attitude of the
exploiter, whether he dug the earth for minerals or plowed the plains
for a cash crop. In either case he lived in perpetual debris, as Mumford
reported, and when it got too thick or when the soil or the forest or the
vein ran out he simply moved on. Anyone who becomes too enamored
of John Kouwenhoven's theory of the American "vernacular" based on
the superiority of American tools must remember that these communities too were products of the same Americans and the same tools.

But the greatest leveler was the development of a national instead of
a regional pattern of life. This was substantially a product of technology and especially the technology which made it possible for materials
to be sent anywhere, for all parts of the country to know overnight
what every other part of the country was doing, of inventions which
made the climatic necessities no longer binding on the builder.

The balloon frame was such a leveler. For the critic-historians John
Kouwenhoven and Sigfried Giedion it is a symbol of the properties of
the American "vernacular." Certainly this light wooden frame covered
by boards was an American invention. Certainly Chicago readily accepted this quick, economical and often insubstantial way to assemble
a house after Augustine Taylor of Hartford, Connecticut, arrived in
Chicago in 1833 and proceeded to build St. Mary's Church on such a
frame. First described in Gervase Wheeler's *Homes for the People*, of
1855, this structural system soon replaced the old heavy methods of
timber framing. Its speed of erection permitted whole towns to spring
up overnight looking much the same wherever they rose.

The professional architects were less enthusiastic about the invention
and were not necessarily blind in this attitude. Not imaginative enough
to see what could be done with it, they were all too reasonably depressed by what was being done. Thus Calvert Vaux called the new
buildings of 1857 "bare, bald white cubes." Distressed by these, his
strange remedy was to use the frame to build Moorish arcades and
Chinese balconies.

The suggestion does point out that the balloon frame did suffer from
its own versatility. Almost anything was possible. Instead of yielding a
new American native style, more American than the old colonial, it

produced instead, as Kouwenhoven admits, "the bare, unimaginative, depressing houses which stalked both sides of Main Street in Western manufacturing and mining towns, and . . . the pointlessly mendacious pseudo-classical and pseudo-Renaissance public buildings which were pompously erected in the proudest cities of the land."

In the largest sense of the word there never has been a handsome American vernacular save the old one bedded in the traditions of Europe; there has been a common and more recent American wooden house and it is anonymous enough; but it has no regional character; it has no distinction; it contributes nothing but anonymity to town after town. The leveling may have been inevitable; the specializations of the technological age may have guaranteed that there never again could be a spontanous regional architecture in America.

That the indigenous and the regional would decay was seen as early as 1819 by Latrobe when he entered in his diary of January 25 the note that the French flavor of New Orleans would be reduced to the standards of Baltimore and Philadelphia. "We shall introduce many grand & profitable improvements, but they will take the place of much elegance, ease, and some convenience."

A nation which has become one great middle class, which is nomadic, which has much the same education throughout, which is urban and not agrarian, a melting pot even if racially pluralistic, which handles most regional eccentricities by nationally standardized means, which admires change and makes it synonymous with progress: such a nation is unlikely to preserve an ancient and honored traditional indigenous architecture.

4

ALL THIS DID NOT HAPPEN OVERNIGHT. AS AMERICANS STOOD POISED IN 1800 for the great western expansion, they were still rural-minded, racially homogeneous, economically differentiated, regionally oriented, unprepared for the onslaught of technology. They lived in a clear architectural tradition of neat domestic buildings in which a city was only a larger village. The natural expectation was that these cultural traditions would simply spread westwards with the men who carried them. But the West itself, together with the rapid change in industrial technology, declined such a conclusion; first the results and in the end the aspirations as well.

In retrospect, the early Federalist days may seem more attractive than they actually were, but attractive or not they must now pass. Industrialism was beginning to stamp the new pattern. Its rise prompted Emerson to remark. ". . . a cleavage is occurring in the hitherto firm granite of the past and a new era is nearly arrived."

In the sixty years after 1800 Americans occupied the most productive parts of their continent from ocean to ocean and the western expansion on the land flowed from the industrial expansion of the East. Furs, farms, speculative land profits, and precious metals had drawn Americans westward in that order. By 1849 all these magnets still had power. At the time of Lincoln's inauguration, however, the total population mustered but a little over thirty millions; the center of it was only at Chillicothe, Ohio, though it had moved steadily westward along the thirty-ninth parallel from Baltimore, where it lay at the end of the Revolution. Now the industrial Middle West had joined the older New England and Middle Atlantic states in accounting for three fifths of the population and almost all of the industrial wealth; another three tenths were in the Southern states east of the great river; only a tenth of the Americans lived west of the Mississippi; only a handful had reached California. The coming years belonged to the Middle West, and nowhere was this more clear than in the Civil War itself, which was won by U. S. Grant in the valley of the Mississippi despite the brilliance of Jackson and Lee in the valley of Virginia.

The people of the United States, with the exception of the Negro slaves and a declining number of Indians, continued to be essentially a single race, and it was not until the reactionary troubles in Europe of the 1840s that Germans came to change the long-enduring pattern of an immigration ninety per cent of which had been from the United Kingdom. But the Germans, quantitatively significant, did not offer any problems of assimilation or any serious change in the cultural outlook.

America was moving toward urbanism, but slowly. If five thousand people were a city, then perhaps one fifth of Americans lived in cities in 1860. The area around New York held a million people but no other American city came near to it. There was but one other with more than half a million, only nine altogether to boast more than 100,000 while only one twelfth of the people lived in such great congregations. Three fifths of all of the workers were in agriculture, even before you counted the Southern slaves. We were still basically a rural people following the pattern that Thomas Jefferson had laid down a half century before.

Major technological changes were preparing in the wings but the actors on the stage were horses, whale oil, and illuminating gas, canals, and paddle wheels; even the locomotive now snorting its way across the Mississippi was a romantic adolescent.

Only a foresighted man might note that the independent yeoman of Jefferson would soon be replaced by the businessman farmer of the prairie. The transportation system had just begun to open the markets to Western agriculture; the new wide fields encouraged the use of horse-drawn machines that might not have been maneuvered over a rocky hillside or in a forest glade. Machines cost money and the farmer began to yield some self-sufficiency for more cash, to become an employer of semispecialized transient labor. By 1860 this was not an uncommon practice in Ohio, Indiana, Illinois, and Michigan; crop specialization had begun; more machines demanded larger acreage and required fewer hands; so the agrarian exodus was prepared if not in full swing.

In the city, urbanity was uncommon. City streets when they were lighted at all relied on gas which had increased in popularity from Murdock's inventions of 1798 and particularly after the demonstration of street lighting on Pall Mall in 1807. Domestic lighting came from gas or candles or the whale oil of Nantucket and New Bedford. Electricity was still largely a matter of scientific curiosity. In the century after Franklin caught the lightning with his kite, noteworthy and fundamental discoveries about currents, voltages, resistances, electromagnetism, and induction had been made by Galvani and Ampère, Volta, Ohm, Oersted, and Faraday, so that by 1830 the fundamentals for electric lighting and power had been prepared. But for the time they lay fallow and there was a still greater delay in applying the discoveries of the late '50s by Planté of the use of lead in a storage battery or by Plücker of the glow on the glass wall of a gas-filled tube near the cathode.

The only certain use of electricity was in the telegraph which expanded rapidly after 1844 when Samuel F. B. Morse tapped out his credit to God over the experimental line from Washington to Baltimore; still, stretching wires all the way across the empty West seemed unrewarding to those who initiated the pony express between St. Joseph, Missouri, and Sacramento, California, in 1860.

Electricity had thus no significant effect on architectural developments between 1800 and 1860. Neither did petroleum. In 1859 a well was dug near Titusville, Pennsylvania, but the few who saw riches at the bottom of the pipe thought in terms of kerosene and a way to light homes. To be sure, an Englishman named Samuel Brown had succeeded in exploding gas in an atmospheric engine as early as 1823 and had moved to some exploitation of the internal combustion principle for stationary engine purposes at Croydon. Thus the knowledge of internal combustion, the storage battery, and the fuel to be used were all ready but it would be a long time before architecture would become servant of the automobile.

For the time being the people of these sixty years moved rapidly to develop water and rail transportation. In the sixty years after Fitch, Fulton and Stevens carried out their faltering demonstrations, the trans-oceanic steamship became a clear success, reasonably safe, reasonably comfortable. Over much of the period, canal and river-boat systems were important modifiers of American development. The Erie Canal began to operate in 1825; it brought prosperity to the state and city of New York and produced backwaters in Massachusetts and Pennsylvania. The Ohio and Mississippi were alive with paddle wheels. Ideas and people moved with the steamer; and despite the picture of wide-hatted, long-cigarred, drooping-mustached gamblers in fancy vests, the arts traveled more smoothly on the river boats than they did on the prairie schooners. Architecture and building materials alike moved down the Ohio from the English East and up the Mississippi from the French New Orleans; they met at St. Louis. Even the architectural fashions were reflected in the river boats and from the river boats to the adjacent land.

But of all the advances in transportation, the growth of the railroads was most prophetic. It had taken more than forty years to get from Newcomen's pumps (1726) to Watt's condenser (1769) and almost as long again to Stephenson's locomotives. In 1830 the engine Tom Thumb raced against a horse for the Baltimore and Ohio Railroad — and lost, but it was almost the last defeat. In the next thirty years the rails entered Chicago and crossed the Mississippi. By 1830 there were 31,000 miles of railroad track, heavily concentrated however in the Northeast. As the rails pushed through the land they too carried ideas and materials to hammer at the palisades of regionalism; but for the moment transportation charges discouraged the architectural use of exogenous materials, and the main effect of the rails was to cut the cities in pieces, to create perpetual blight along their smoke-blackened rights of way, and to begin the demand for some less matter-of-fact approaches to the station whence a traveler would launch his exciting journey and at which he would alight at journey's end.

Public urban transportation systems were inadequate in 1860 but the larger cities had some horse-drawn cars which had been used in old towns like Boston for more than a quarter of a century. They were fast enough for existing urban needs. There were portents of how they could be faster in London's new underground railroad.

The power which made the locomotive possible had also been har-nessed to manufacturing. Indeed, the two things went together for without a strong manufacturing industry there would have been no need for the railroads. There had been a productive textile industry for a long time and by 1798 Eli Whitney had taught the virtue of interchangeable parts. Americans were ingenious in developing the machine tools which lie at the base of any serious industrial expansion. They had found ways to make other articles, such as wallpaper and furniture and clothing, in considerable supply by standardizing their designs and though these ways were tentative it was sensed that standardization is essential for large-scale manufacture, and that it is not *ipso facto* harmful.

The most exciting promise for architecture was no doubt the new metallic material, steel. The recent inventions of Bessemer in England and the possibly less well-known American, Kelly, were being adopted by 1860 in America for rolled rails, but the beams and the columns were yet to come, so the promise of steel for architecture could only be felt in a future time.

Thus the period was rather one of preparation for a technological-industrial nation than of its realization. It was an age of horses, gas, coal, steam, iron; not an age of automobiles, electricity, petroleum and steel. It was an age in which education was either remarkably theoretical and classical or overly practical. Technological education was in its infancy. West Point and Rensselaer Polytechnic Institute were the only senior institutions in which rudiments of a technological training might be sought; M.I.T. was founded only at the end of the period.

Nor had the development of industry yet led to significant changes in the lot of the workingman. Labor had attempted to organize as early as 1830 with the Mechanics' Unions of Philadelphia but strikes by these nascent craft organizations lost as often as they won. Organized labor was inconsequential and unorganized labor could not play a forceful role in architecture.

Still less influential on the American scene were the theories of Marx and Engels which were advanced in Europe after 1848.

What was more evident was the physical devastation of the countryside brought on by careless applications of the new technology. Where once painters had delighted in the apparition of gleaming and gay locomotives chugging across an English moor, now a poet like Wordsworth could see only the desecration of the land and the degradation of the cottager. Even the optimistic Dickens turned from the cheery prophecies of *Pickwick Papers* to the dismay of *Hard Times*, after the Chartist riots. No doubt the dinginess and despair of industrial England were greater than the dinginess and despair of industrial America, for England was at the moment moving at a faster pace. But the results were the same in America. The new industrial works *were* dirtier than a New England village; they *did* produce smoke and grime; the rails *did* chew up the hillsides to get through; and the conditions of labor *were* uncomfortable and unsafe. In this stage of its development, industrial America destroyed more beauty than it produced, uprooted better habits of life than the substitutes it proffered.

One might wonder then what were the beckoning lights of this will-o'-the-wisp of industrialization; for some no doubt the lure of large and fast profits; for some the excitement of inventing or the prestige of being an early patron of a new innovation; for some the allurements of the transcendental mystique of the American dream; and for others no doubt nothing but apprehension; for most perhaps only the sense of being carried along and presumably forward on a belt and the exhilaration that the belt was moving fast. Thus despite the enthusiasms of the innovators and the pioneers, the people were clearly ambivalent about what they were doing. Industrialism was exciting and promising but it was also dirty and vulgar; it needed counterpoint in a different world. For the moment anyway the gate between the two worlds could be shut and safely guarded and there was little doubt which was the more pleasant side of the gate. It is not surprising that the artists were the greatest victims of this ambivalence.

The depiction of American historical events which had fascinated painters like Benjamin West and John Trumbull no longer seemed to fascinate. Contemporary painters of other countries might lean upon their literature, including their national epics. But though the American past contained epical material, American painters had no epic literature. Thus many of the painters were preoccupied with classical subjects which had little relation to the lives or education of the Americans who were living in the industrial towns spread out near the factories. It was possible for them to understand and love the American landscape whence they had so recently moved and it did not trouble them that it was usually cast in the romantic haze of English landscape painting as it might be by Thomas Cole and others of the Hudson River School. Indeed, the bolder excursions of Inness on the Delaware were troubling. A closer documentation of the real America did wake interest when men as talented as Audubon, Catlin, and Bingham or Mount portrayed the details of the birds, Indians, or life on the rivers. But even the frontier ought not to look too raw and it was the romantic Bierstadt who knew what kind of West was wanted in the salon.

But the rollicking and gargantuan industrial infant did not often seem a suitable subject for any painter, just as novelists did not know how to come to grips with business and, saving Hawthorne, did not even seem to want to try. A painter like John Neagle might idealize a blacksmith as a representative of American technology, but the blacksmith was remarkably clean and really a symbol of the village rather than the industrial economy. Despite a few exceptions it was left to Currier and Ives to see the excitement of a steamboat, a railroad, or a steel mill. But Currier and Ives could not be called artists until a later day, just as the primitive Hicks and his *Peaceable Kingdom* were not much noticed until years after when interest in the French *douanier*, Henri Rousseau, reflected back on this atypical American artist.

The *cognoscenti* were few in number, aloof, and self-satisfied. They looked to Europe for their references in the arts, were happy that the "best" painters like William Morris Hunt should study with and be influenced by Millet or the classicist Gérôme and not by the more contemporary Delacroix and Courbet. They looked to Europe but overlooked industrial England as firmly as they overlooked industrial America. When murals were needed for the national Capitol they turned naturally to Italy and the subjects were not to be those of the frontier or the factory but rather abstractions in the form of classical allegories.

Beyond the *cognoscenti* nobody cared. The public might be interested in and buy the latest Currier and Ives but would not be offended if the *cognoscenti* rejected the prints as outside the boundaries of art. For the Americans of 1800-1860 did not care about painting. Benjamin West had learned this earlier; Samuel F. B. Morse epitomized it when he deserted painting for electricity. Whistler wasted no time in leaving America for good. The magazine *The Crayon*, devoted exclusively to the arts, was founded by the painter Stillman in 1855 and foundered six years later. It was not suprising that Americans painted less well than Europeans; seldom studied with *avant-garde* painters; invariably lagged behind the European movements by a quarter century or more. It was even less surprising that their subject matter avoided the forces which, outside the arts, were most moving America.

If this were true for our painters it was even more true of our sculptors, who went in for the literal interpretation of native subjects or of heroes from the American scene or for the rendering of a few imagined classical topics. It does not matter much whether you talk of Powers or Crawford or Rogers or Hosmer or even of Greenough, however the latter may have protested in his essays. Powers's *Greek Slave* which was so much admired from 1840 on had literally nothing to do with anything that ever had existed in America. Rogers groups were more indigenous and homely, like Neagle's blacksmith, and found their way, as Maxfield Parrish would later, to many an American parlor.

The trail of the American writers was more complex. Whatever the talents of the tragic Melville and the dark Poe, they did not grapple directly with the American industrial scene, whether or not they blamed it for the defeat of the American dream. Together with the more popular Hawthorne and Emerson they were the American giants to be measured against the contemporary Europeans, Carlyle, Thackeray, Dickens, Balzac, Stendhal and Hegel. Thus while Paris met *Les Fleurs du Mal* and *Madame Bovary*, Boston and New York savored the *Song of Hiawatha* or *The Autocrat of the Breakfast Table*. And even when they imported their reading, Americans who enjoyed Longfellow and Holmes were likely to cherish Sir Walter Scott and Edward Fitzgerald. The contest between Americans and Europeans was hardly more equal in letters than it was in the visual arts. Despite all of Emerson's fanfares the shackles of colonialism had by no means all been severed by 1860.

For architecture, American engineers and particularly their European stimulators had paved a road more brilliant and daring than was yet to be trod. The Howe and Pratt trusses were well known. Roebling's cables at the Niagara Bridge had demonstrated the potentialities of suspension. Labrouste, Horeau, and Baltard in France and Paxton in England had built or proposed highly imaginative iron structures at the Library of Ste. Geneviève, the Bibliothèque Nationale, Les Halles Centrales, and at the later Crystal Palace of 1851 in London. James Bogardus had demonstrated a five-story iron factory in New York; in 1853 Elisha Graves Otis showed that an elevator could be safe; steel was just around the corner while Aspidin's Portland cement was known from 1824. In a humbler sphere the balloon frame, as we have seen, had opened wide flexibility for wooden structures.

Thus from 1830 on, technological opportunities beckoned feverishly to the architects. By 1860 most of the potentially revolutionary materials and methods had at least made their debut. Bunning's iron-domed Coal Exchange in London could have been visited any time after 1849. If American architecture chose, on the whole, to look rather to the neo-Renaissance gentilities of Barry's Reform Club or the Red House built in 1859 on Bexley Heath by Philip Webb and William Morris, it was not exactly the fault of the engineers, although most of them had a taste in architecture which was even more conservative than that of the architects. And if the various American architectural efforts seem to have centered around matters of eclectic choice, the architects were not behaving differently than other Americans. The whole long debate about whether American buildings should be Georgian or Greek or Gothic or Egyptian was quite unrelated to the fact that Americans were moving westward, that railroads were building, that the big shift from an agricultural life to an industrial one had clearly begun to accelerate.

In 1800 the scale of the American production was small but by 1860 it was conspicuous. In 1800 there was more of peace and less of ugliness. In the early days a sophisticated European visitor might find the face of America less primitive than he had anticipated without conceding that it had attained the standards of Europe. Coming in 1860, he could have found distinguished individual buildings but none to surprise him; several dignified communities but none to impress him. He would have seen few signs of even a beginning of architectural independence. What was fine in American architecture derived from earlier European achievements, was colonial in the truest sense. The country was agrarian; its democracy was not egalitarian; its taste was sure; its life simple.

There were few specialists in those early days and they were good at more than one thing. A doctor, Thornton, won the architectural competition for the national Capitol; a painter, Peale, was a skillful inventor of mechanical devices; an architect, Latrobe, was a good engineer, wise enough to be commissioned by the American Philosophical Society to make the official response to an inquiry from Holland on the state of engines in America. A president, Madison, personally sought a new architect for the Capitol and had the sure taste to choose Bulfinch; another president, Jefferson, had ideas of his own about architecture and they were not entirely naïve or untutored. He was almost the last president of whom this could be said.

The American society still thought essentially in village patterns, even in the city; expected to solve all the problems of Federalism in the terms of Madison rather than those of Calhoun; found it reasonable that the finest buildings should be devoted to the offices of democracy and to the service of the church. And at the beginning Americans knew how to build such buildings.

During the sixty years before the Civil War they forgot how to build so well and so beautifully. They left the security of the Georgian rules but found no compensating security elsewhere. They experimented with rationalistic architecture as proposed by Latrobe. They left this promising theory before it was mature, to dabble with a variety of associational ideas about nature and about earlier buildings. From the experiments with association they gleaned a moment of dignified aesthetic success in the Classic Revival; and a more dubious sense of moral fulfillment in the first Gothic Revival. But associationalism also led to importations from Egypt, India, China, via Victorian England, in two orgies of eclectic fashion which left their cities without dignity or repose. At the end rationalism was recalled in a utilitarian cast-iron architecture which had some good qualities. Once the Georgian convention had been abandoned, though, the experiments swirled through time with no clean-cut beginning and end. Always the choices seemed to involve little concern with the vital questions of the needs of the new cities, of industry, of technology. Never afterwards would so much of the architectural debate be centered on style set apart from major social questions. But even the debate was in the temper of the times, measured, quiet, slow. The clamor would begin only with Reconstruction. In some ways it was a long, last look back at a serene past.

We shall never forget the charm of Charleston, South Carolina, even though we may never again achieve it. That it has lasted so long depends upon its failure to keep pace with the times after the Civil War. But admire its ancient glories as we may, we must not forget that the streets of Charleston below Broad Street represent the Indian summer of a way of life and owe their continued elegance to an escape from reality. But there was a time when Charleston was not an escape.

5

IN THE BEGINNING THE STEEPLED CHURCHES AND PORTICOED COURTHOUSES spoke of a settled, balanced life among agricultural and commercial people. But by the eve of the Civil War, steam engines snorted and drilling rigs whined; the ring of the steel rail sounded louder than the rumble of the cobblestone; tall-masted ships were more urgent than Gothic church spires; telegraph wires sagged across the colonnaded faces of Roman banks; cast-iron stores challenged the right of pedimented government buildings or crenellated churches to speak for America.

As the debate grew louder it brought dissensions and jealousies. Architects divided into camps, each championing a style. If you listened to them all you might come out like young George B. Post, who began to study architecture about 1860; to him it seemed as though there were only confusion. Medievalists saw no merit in classic art; devotees of the Renaissance thought modern Gothic beneath contempt; pre-Raphaelites believed in neither. Over all, Post noted that American painters and sculptors frankly stated that they believed there was no art in architecture.

Post's bewilderment was understandable. By 1860 there was little agreement about any of the big architectural questions. One thing, though, was obvious: no matter how beautiful they were, Georgian Annapolis, Federalist Salem and Greek Revival Marietta could not meet the challenges of the new industrial society; in Post's own lifetime the dignified agricultural villages and the commercial towns were erased unless, by accident, prosperity passed them by. Some new men supported regionalism as others had once favored a national architecture. Other new architects sought something more personal than the anonymous classical results. Some argued, as more talented men have done since, that nature should be the chief determinant of architecture; but others insisted that geometry and formal composition should not be abandoned. No one could escape the great argument between those who wanted to derive a national architecture from Europe and those who exhorted young artists to aim at all costs for something indigenous. One might want to cling to the faith that churches would remain the dominant symbols of American society; but he could not ignore Bogardus's successful prefabricated-iron emblems of business enterprise. Was America to remain a collection of picturesque, peaceful, rural villages, or to become a nation of large and elegant cities, or a nation of small planned industrial communities? Where was each American to stand on questions of taste — with the naïve Jacksonian hope for egalitarian art, with Jefferson's distrust in it, with the effort of Calvert Vaux to find a democratic way of controlling it? There was an easy way (and there always has been) to avoid such questions. Men like George Post took it. Like most architects, before and since, they drifted with the crowd, never doing anything distinguished, willingly adopting what was fashionable at the moment even though the changes were frequent and violent. Those who did debate the questions were naturally less content than Post to satisfy current fashion, more willing, even anxious, to affront it.

By 1840 a young aspirant to architecture might gain only a confused picture of America by walking, for example, the streets of New York. At Hudson Park there was a serene moment in the contemplation of John McComb's dignified St. John's Church of 1803-1807, but nearby the Infant School Society met in a ramshackle basement. Wall Street clearly revealed a society in transition; plain brick houses alternated with Greek temples, occupied by banks or the Merchants' Exchange, and here too were drab houses for insurance companies and newspapers. At the Fulton Street Market in 1821 one might walk along cobblestoned streets, past arcaded stalls, only to pick a way among barrels, casks, wheelbarrows, hucksters' wagons and horses toward the tower of an undistinguished church. From the ferry at Brooklyn Heights one could see Underhill's handsome Colonnade Buildings, while at the North River he would meet a jumbled assemblage of utilitarian brick buildings forming an iron foundry where locomotive parts were made. Or one might visit Henry Brevoort's Ionic-porticoed three-story brownstone at Fifth and Ninth, designed by Alexander Jackson Davis. All its interior spaces, from the library and parlor to the entrance with its curved stair, announced a New Yorker of taste and distinction; yet not far away at the headquarters of the Fourteenth Ward on Broadway in 1840 the presidential campaign of William Henry Harrison was conducted from a synthetic log cabin fitted chiefly with hard cider. It would be easy to wonder which was the true America, and perplexity might mount when one compared Rogers's Mercantile Exchange of 1836-1842 and its giant Ionic portico and large Pantheonic dome with Barnum's Museum on Broadway, its upper face covered with a giant billboard showing the picture of a menacing serpent. A note of the future was suggested in James Bogardus's cast-iron house; or by 1857 in the Haughwout Store at Broadway and Broome, where Elisha Graves Otis installed the first passenger elevator with automatic safety devices; but these were still incidents within a city that was undecided about its future form, as indeed it still is. The chaos of 1840 may not seem remarkable to an American who knows the contrasts of Manhattan in 1960 but it was more perceptible then, standing as it did against the background of a time when cities had managed more unity, dignity and repose.

Indeed, not all American cities had yet followed the example of New York. Philadelphia, more than most of the others, demonstrated that a commercial architecture might be dignified. From her eighteenth-century heritage she had retained an orderly plan, a small scale and attractive residential squares. Latrobe's Bank of Pennsylvania, 1799-1801, with its Ionic portico and rotunda banking room, had shown that art and commerce were not intrinsically enemies. William Strickland's Second Bank of the United States (later the Customs House) had a fine banking room framed by Ionic colonnades under a barrel-vaulted ceiling; its Doric porticoes were modeled after those of the Parthenon. With Thomas U. Walter's Philadelphia Saving Fund Society Building of 1839-1840, these established a classic precedent for banks. Anyone who knew the Burlington Arcade in London would have noticed similar corridors of interior shops in John Haviland's Arcade of 1827. More elaborate Greek Revival architecture could be found at the Merchants' Exchange designed by Strickland in 1832-1834; its Doric west front, its curved Corinthian façade at the east, and its finial from the Choragic Monument taught lessons in archeology, a gentlemanly study. There were innovative structures too like the cast-iron plated office building Cummings erected for the Penn Mutual Life Insurance Company of 1850-1851. A prescient visitor might have seen in William Johnston's ten-story Jayne Building, of 1849, a premonition of the skyscrapers that would rise soon enough. Altogether no one could deny that commerce was well served by art in Philadelphia.

How such scenes appeared depended upon the point of view. When Mrs. Trollope arrived in America in December 1827 it did not take her long to conclude that we were harbingers of a decaying European civilization. Many of the inferior details Mrs. Trollope saw justified such a conclusion. It could be said even of Philadelphia. But if one looked beyond the façades which might please Jefferson if Roman, and Henry Cleveland if Gothic, one could observe that most of the buildings were constructed upon utilitarian plans in the shape of L's, H's, or T's, all quite innocent of Greek or Roman or Gothic precedent. Even Robert Mills's buildings, clumsy as they often were in proportion or detail, were bold compositions of serviceable, sometimes heavy, geometric elements; they lent conviction to his advice, "Go not to the old world for your examples . . . it is our destiny to lead, not to be led." By 1860 American clipper ships, machinery, and even a few buildings like the Astor House in New York and the Tremont House in Boston, hotels by Isaiah Rogers, encouraged a young architect, James E. Cabot, to believe Emerson's self-reliant rationalism and naturalism; to deny the copying of the Greek or the Gothic; to assert that beauty, convenience, grandeur, and "quaint expression" were as possible in the American as in any nation. If the American artist would only recognize that "All good architecture must be the gradual growth of its country and its age," then we might obtain houses whose "beauty must grow as naturally from their use as the flower from its stem."

The evidence for such a hope was not often clear. Charles Dickens did declare his amazement at the sumptuous galleries, colonnades, piazzas, and passageways when he visited Boston's Tremont House in 1842; yet he hastened to add that Boston was special, that America was not often so refined.

Thus he was not nearly so pleasant about the national capital, which all Europeans and many Americans agreed was a mess, despite its pretensions. Though it later became America's best tribute to monumental urban design, Washington was nearly ruined by abuse in the period before the Civil War. The term "magnificent distances" was used in scorn. Abigail Adams who was used to only modest luxury in Quincy complained about the mud of Washington; she was forced to use the incompleted East Room of the White House as a drying room for her laundry, there was no running water, and only temporary stairs afforded access to the upper story. Conditons were not much better at the time of Lincoln's first inaugural. Even after the Executive Mansion was burned by the British in 1814 (and its blackened sandstone walls were painted white), successive Congresses begrudged any funds spent upon improving its furnishings and setting; they permitted public and private architecture to destroy the brilliance of the city plan that the French engineer, Major Pierre Charles L'Enfant, had laid down for Washington beginning in 1791. This plan proposed a grand development of the area on the land lying at the confluence of the Potomac and Anacostia Rivers. The best sites were to be reserved for principal buildings, of which the most important, the Capitol, would stand on Jenkins Hill, a plateau some eighty feet above the rivers: it was "a pedestal waiting for a monument," said L'Enfant. On a line westward from the Capitol he laid out a grand avenue, four hundred feet wide, where foreign ministers might have spacious houses and gardens. A mile and a half northwest along the Mall, a second axis would strike north and south, leading from the White House to the Washington Monument's knoll and southward to the marshy estuary of Tiber Creek, which L'Enfant proposed to canalize. Such principal sites were to be coordinated upon a gridiron of streets running east-west and north-south. Broad diagonal avenues or "lines of direct communication" would connect principal points. Where two or more diagonals intersected there would be squares or circles, carefully adjusted to afford "reciprocity of sight" from one civic space to another. The squares and principal sites would provide opportunities for fountains, statues, a national church, residences and small churches, colleges, academies and buildings for various societies. Leading from one large square, near the White House, L'Enfant proposed to have an avenue lined with shops and an arched covering over the pavement. But his intention — to "unite the useful with the commodious and agreeable" — almost went unrealized at all and was never realized in full. The scale of his avenues acted as a challenge to later architects to erect overblown classic buildings. His formal scheme was not protected from those who tried to turn the Mall into a romantic garden and built the Smithsonian Institution, an ugly red-sandstone building, a medieval castle with towers and turrets, designed by James Renwick. Washington developed westward rather than eastward as the planner had proposed; the site of the Washington Monument was shifted southeast so that the axes were thrown off; Tiber Creek was allowed to become a menace to health. Beginning in 1835, the tracks of the Baltimore and Ohio Railroad were laid to the capital, and the Pennsylvania Railroad built a terminal on the Mall itself. Areas but a block away from the great avenues, even near the Capitol, became squalid slums. L'Enfant languished in poverty and obscurity until his death in 1825, and his plan was progressively misinterpreted, disfigured and neglected until a commission appointed by Senator

ROBERT D. HARVEY STUDIO

Shirley Center, Massachusetts

WAYNE ANDR

Charles City Co., Virginia, "Westover," ca. 1730

Salem, Massachusetts, Gardiner-White-Pingree house, 1810,
Samuel McIntire, arch.

WAYNE ANDREWS

RALPH THOMPSON, U. OF VA. NEWS OFFICE

Charlottesville, Virginia, University of Virginia, 1817-1826,
Thomas Jefferson, arch.

NATIONAL BUILDINGS RECORD, LONDON

Shrewsbury, England, St. Chad's Church, 1791, George Steuart, arch.

Philadelphia, Girard College, 1833-1847, Thomas U. Walter, arch.

WAYNE ANDRE

LONGLEY STUDIO

Cincinnati, Ohio, Plum Street Jewish Temple, 1866, J. Wilson, arch.

WALTER FLEISCHER, HARVARD NEWS OFF

Cambridge, Massachusetts, First Parish Church (Unitarian), 1833,
Isaiah Rogers, arch., seen from Harvard Yard

BROWN BROTHERS

New York, St. Patrick's Cathedral, interior, 1858-1879,
James Renwick, Jr., arch.

WAYNE ANDREWS

New York, Haughwout Store, 1857, J. P. Gaynor, arch.

New York, Old Grand Central Depot, 1869-1871, Isaac C. Buckhout and
J. B. Snook, archs.

NEW YORK CENTRAL RAILR

James McMillan of Michigan revived it in 1901. Unfortunately, no similar enlightened interest has resurrected the comparably urbane plans made for Detroit and Indianapolis, which fell victim to the disregard that destroyed the eighteenth-century American city plans and left the cities that had them in not much better shape than the cities with none.

Even the most confident architect must have entertained the lurking suspicion that America might never achieve a great architectural tradition of its own. Primarily the arts had still to struggle against three old things: utilitarian standards, commercial expediency and puritanical simplicity. James Jackson Jarves thought that the spirit that sustains trade could do nothing except debase art. Evidence for such a belief was bountiful. Even the railroad stations, which should have intimated America's future architecture, were uniformly bad. There were heavy Romanesque buildings like Thomas Tefft's station in Providence or the one in Salem, Massachusetts. Dull, utilitarian buildings like Baltimore's Clare Street Station were only occasionally offset by the sight of a whimsical pavilion like Austin's New Haven station of 1848. The adventure of traveling was often announced by bizarre entrances, like the Egyptian portico of New Bedford's Old Pearl Street Depot. Such absurdities in the name of the arts were enough to damage even the true arts and to do it even in the eyes of those who were not unsympathetic. Besides, there were many Americans, not all yokels, who were unsympathetic to, even suspicious of, the arts as a matter of principle.

6

THE FIRST MAJOR ATTEMPT TO GRASP THE SCEPTER AND BRING SOME higher degree of order to American architecture was made by rationalist architects, who now sought the throne that Georgian formalists had held. Beginning in France and England, some architects now began to question classic unity. They argued that form should be a rational expression of spaces that were arranged strictly for use. Critics and architects alike heaped scorn on Palladian excesses that permitted false windows and façades which masked interior functions as at Mount Vernon. Architecture, the rationalists asserted, must be adapted to use, to climate, to structure, not to abstract principles of unified form. Adaptation became the basis for a new international architecture. The Italian Lodoli expressed an extreme view: "In architecture only that shall show that has a definite function, and which derives from the strictest necessity."

England developed philosophers like Francis Hutcheson who applied this doctrine to aesthetics in 1725. Their works circulated in America in the early nineteenth century and were popular with American architects. So was the writing of the Scottish philosopher, Archibald Alison, whose essays on taste written in 1790 were republished in Hartford, Connecticut, in 1821: ". . . all machines or instruments," he wrote, "are called beautiful by the artists, which are well adapted to the end of their arts."

Such avowed espousals of mechanism are too easily misread by modernists, who are inclined to interpret them as premonitions of the machine aesthetic to be announced fully almost a century later, in 1925. But Lodoli, Hutcheson and Alison had no such intentions even when they said that forms should be adapted to use. The forms they had in mind were classic elements; the point was that they should be composed on non-classical rules and without regard to the classical principles of unity.

Rationalism led to a new architecture, distinctly different from the preceding Georgian and its Renaissance precursor. The movement began in Europe, moved later to America. It appeared in England in Sir John Soane's Bank of England and enjoyed popularity in France where Nicholas Ledoux built the Barrière de la Villette in 1785-1789. The work of Valadier and Piranesi announced it in Italy; it was the hallmark of the German designers, Persius, Gilly and even Schinkel despite his romantic deviations. By the early nineteenth century when it came to America, the style had even invaded Russia so that the New Admiralty at St. Petersburg by Zakharov of 1806-1815 and the Belfry at Gruzino, near Novgorod, by Stasov, about 1815, resemble the most advanced work in America and England.

St. Chad's at Shrewsbury, England, designed by George Steuart (1791), exhibits the major characteristics of rational architecture. It has four parts: an entrance hall preceded by a portico, a two-storied tower, a staircase leading to galleries, and a large church hall. Each part is distinct; the cylinders are opposed to each other; from the exterior they exhibit an array of self-centered, independent rooms of different shapes. Unlike baroque effusive architecture, St. Chad's is reserved, and baroque unity disappears as parts are placed in strong isolation so that they rebel against any blending and harmony; they are juxtaposed without easy rhythms, regular cadence or suave intersecting curves. This composition of pure geometric shapes — with classic features — is a presage of an aesthetic that gains dynamism by ignoring unity, and gains useful disposition of interior spaces by refusing to be ruled by classical balance, hierarchy or axial arrangement.

The Frenchmen Joseph Jacques Ramée, L'Enfant, Joseph F. Mangin and Maximilian Godefroy were principally responsible for bringing rationalism to America. Ramée's design for Union College at Schenectady was characteristic. So was Godefroy's First Unitarian Church in Baltimore of 1817-1818. The most notable thing about the church is its geometry; it is a single cube capped by a hemispherical dome, with a deep entrance designated by a triangular pediment that is carried upon arches supported by columns. The massive, simple geometry, the monumental scale, and the bold juxtaposition of strong shapes are all quite different from such Georgian buildings as the neighboring Otterbein Church of 1784. Subsequently, architects who were born in America took up the style. It was the characteristic motif of Robert Mills, whose Sansom Street Baptist Church in Philadelphia was in that manner. Isaiah Rogers scored notable successes with it in his hotels, and Alexander Parris in Boston designed the Quincy Markets as a series of strong volumes extruded as simple masses, distinct from each other, kept separate without blending and without subordination to any dominant part. Towards the end of his career, even Charles Bulfinch began to break out of the Georgian and towards rationalism with his University Hall at Harvard and the Church of Christ at Lancaster, Massachusetts.

But the most important American designer in the new style was the English-born Benjamin Henry Latrobe, whose architectural and other knowledge merited the respect of Jefferson. Latrobe recognized that architects must seek more than harmony of form. He was almost unique in early nineteenth-century America for achieving an integration of "firmness, commodity and delight" within forms that were expressive as well. His deprecations of Mount Vernon must be understood in terms of that synthesis. It led him to deplore the misdeeds of carpenter-builders like those who submitted plans for the national Capitol; it also led him to disagree with gentleman-architects like Jefferson who too frequently fell victim to copying classic forms.

Latrobe's contribution appears in many buildings of which three examples will suffice. In Center Square, Philadelphia, in 1799, he built an engine house for the pumps that raised water from the Schuylkill River. The building had a parallelepiped base that supported a tall cylinder terminated by a low dome. Its basic conformation was similar to Ledoux's Barrière at Paris. Like the French building, its proportions, emphatically unclassical, were tall at the top and low at the base. No blending ameliorated the abrupt junctions of the strong geometrical parts. The building announced the architect's intention to utilize classical elements, like columns, within pure geometric forms, to keep the buildings simple in silhouette and allow use to be the major determinant in the composition. "I would never put a cupola on any spherical dome. It is not the *ornament*, it is the *use* I want," he once wrote.

The Merchants' Exchange and Custom House at Baltimore, begun in 1816 and opened in 1820, was a collaborative work of Latrobe and Godefroy. An original drawing of the Gay Street façade shows a dignified entrance composed of three arches within a pavilion that stands forward in front of two well-proportioned wings; they enclose an interior court that is capped by an octagonal drum and dome. Again the composition is boldly geometrical; light and air are easily obtained; the stone construction is solid; the whole building has a workmanlike appearance that shows the kind of serviceable and attractive buildings America might have had if such designers had been given more commissions. It was eminently well fitted for the stock exchange and bank it housed. These were nineteenth-century institutions; no ancient formalism, whether Greek, Roman or Renaissance, would produce buildings suitable for their use. "Our religion," Latrobe wrote, "requires churches wholly different from the [Greek and Roman] temples, our Government, our legislative assemblies, and our courts of justice, buildings of entirely different principles from their basilicas; and our amusements could not possibly be performed in their theaters or amphitheaters." He insisted that architectural form proceed from the character of the institution it was intended to house, rather than from books about design. This led him in 1807 to try to invent new minor architectural elements as well, such as the American maize capital for the new vestibule of the Old Senate or the tobacco-plant capital for the Senate Rotunda.

His Roman Catholic Cathedral in Baltimore, begun in 1808 and dedicated in 1821, is a fine example of a new building for an old institution. It was a succession of surely designed spaces, beginning with a portico and vault, proceeding to a small dome and culminating at a major dome over the crossing. All these spaces were rational volumetric interpretations of a liturgical plan, and they determined the enclosing masses. No one can mistake the plan, clearly visible in the elevation, and no one can misinterpret the structural system that encloses those spaces. But Latrobe did not let the desire for a simple, distinct form lead him to subordinate the masses beneath the dome or shorten the nave. He began with a freedom of planning and expression unknown to Georgian formalism and produced this remarkable concatenation of unblended elementary spaces and masses. There are classical details to be sure and they were made more classical by the porch added in the 1870s but they are combined non-classically in a composition that is sustained only by the balancing of pure, elementary geometry.

No matter how much he respected Latrobe's rational exposition of useful forms, and though he frequently consulted Latrobe about his plans for the University of Virginia, Thomas Jefferson was never able to bring himself fully to relinquish formalism.

His initial proposal for the University was a direct attack on the problem, seeking a practical correction of the defects he had criticized in the dormitory at William and Mary, but the solution lacked architectural character. Following some suggestions made by Latrobe, Jefferson revised the plan so that it provided for an academic community centered on a dominant rotunda, the library, which stood upon an eminence, whence lawns descended in a series of terraces. Two rows of parallel buildings stood on each side of the lawn. The innermost row contained pavilions for classrooms or faculty residences. These were connected by covered passageways that gave access also to low buildings where some of the students lived. Beyond the first row, or lawn, there were gardens enclosed by serpentine walls; these were closed by the second row of buildings, called "ranges," providing more dormitories. The excellent site plan achieved a community of buildings each of which served a definite purpose; it permitted variety within an overall integration; it protected the community against the spread of fire or disease; it isolated noise. Thus far it obeyed good rational principles. But Jefferson could not follow rationalism to the end. Instead, he ransacked Palladio's books to find temple façades for his pavilions; he studied drawings of the Pantheon, made them more classical by altering the proportions of the porch, and transformed the whole thing into a library which was essentially the Pantheon at half size.

Thus Jefferson represented the two sides of the architectural situation in America at the turn of the century; the eminently practical builder who insisted upon precise cost estimates and good performance; the amateur gentleman-architect who demanded correctness of form, who was willing to copy earlier buildings no matter how incompatible or disjunctive the resulting combinations might be. It did not disturb him at all to hang a practical balcony from the center of the columns in an otherwise classical façade.

The dichotomy amazed some of Jefferson's friends. Latrobe, for example, disliked the reliance upon precedent which appeared again in the house at Monticello. Here the principal façade was a restudy of a design made by the English architect, Robert Adam. But this overt formalism was incompatible with Jefferson's other interests so the classical sophistication was at once denied by the lobby of Monticello. George Ticknor, an urbane student of cosmopolitan life, did not like the contrast when he met, in the entrance hall, many kinds of ingenious mechanical clocks, weathervanes, buffalo heads, Indian maps on leather, in short the paraphernalia of Jefferson's private *Wunderkammer*.

We do not find such extravaganzas surprising in the nineteenth-century home of Theodore Roosevelt at Oyster Bay but they are less easily associated with Jefferson. Yet Jefferson prized both the enclosure and the museum. The native element, Lewis Mumford recently noted, appeared raw and unassimilated but the classical past was the real intruder: ". . . it was contemporary America whose spirit cried to be represented in other forms than those of extinct mammoths."

Yet, if Mumford were correct, that spirit should have been best manifested in Jefferson and it should have found form with Latrobe and Godefroy, Rogers and Parris, Ramée and Mills. The fact is that the real spirit of America, all romance aside, was, as Mrs. Trollope insisted, oriented toward Europe, and it was satisfied by Jefferson's copies of European architecture rather than by Latrobe's insistence that nothing could be "beautiful which appears useless or unmeaning."

Latrobe's attempt at developing an American architecture with classical elements composed in a useful, rational exposition of spaces was rapidly submerged after 1825. Romanticism and formalism of the kind Jefferson displayed at Monticello and the University of Virginia swamped rationalism.

7

RATHER THAN WORK OUT NEW BUILDINGS WITHIN A SINGLE RENAISSANCE tradition, as the Georgian builders had, the new generation followed the lead of the amateur. They took their architectural ideas from many sources, plunging into eclecticism for the first if not the last time. The whole encyclopedic history of architecture became a possible mine for American buildings. In 1829 the *American Quarterly Review* devoted forty pages of its March issue to Egyptian architecture. The *American Monthly Magazine* for April, 1835, contained an editorial, "Architectural Designs," which was a savage attack upon Town and Davis's design for the New York Customs House, an "utterly monstrous and barbarous" sin, combining a dome with the temple form of a Greek Parthenon or Thesion (Hephaistaion). The demand was for copying, and for correctness. The editorial praised Haviland's Egyptian prison at New York, the morbid "Tombs." In 1844, Arthur Gilman reviewed Edward Shaw's *Rural Architecture*. He expressed keen dislike for both Greek and Gothic forms in America, but admired the simpler colonial churches and Georgian houses. He advised architects to seize upon Renaissance styles and develop them further. His own approach was fully eclectic: his Arlington Street Unitarian Church in Boston, he said, was based on the English Renaissance of Gibbs on the exterior, while its interior was inspired by the Santa Annunziata at Genoa. Americans now built villas modeled after Tuscan country houses and Chinese temples; from Asia, Indian sources were invoked, too, as at Armsmere and at P. T. Barnum's Iranistan near Bridgeport, Connecticut. Barnum said he hoped to repeat in America the success scored by King George's Brighton Pavilion but in the end Iranistan was not a copy. Instead, it was an American country house with a square central block and balanced wings but it was all bedecked with bulbous domes and exotic minarets. Easily seen from the New Haven railroad trains, it was an early example of American architectural advertising from 1848 when it was built to 1857 when it burned down. All this was, it must be said, not merely an American extravaganza. Again the Europeans were leading the way and with more *brio*. Now the lead was notably English again and the pipers to this architectural masque played even more boldly and of course much earlier in the motherland.

Much of eclectic architecture depended for its impact upon what has been called associationalism. Here the chief merit of a building was thought to lie not in its power to present a clear and distinct sensory impression, nor in its power to display the useful and structural organization of volumes of space, but rather in its power to evoke secondary reactions generally associated with the form. Those reactions might be subjective, personal, local or national; they might be purely literary. Such a view was derived from the philosopher and precursor of logical positivism, Hume: "Beauty is no quality in things themselves: It exists merely in the mind which contemplates them. . . ." Many of the Scottish philosophers of the eighteenth century expanded Hume's associationalism. They admitted the value of all kinds of non-Palladian and non-classical architectures, which were admired because they stimulated moods. What was admired was not necessarily beautiful; it was sublime, as Burke called it; it was expressive. Jesuit missionaries to China and Japan brought back an irregular and asymmetrical way of gardening, called Sharawadgi; Horace Walpole began his initial remodeling of the country house at Twickenham, a "Gothick" castle he called "Strawberry Hill." In France, too, the rustic and primitive, the asymmetrical and non-classical, appealed to the followers of Jean Jacques Rousseau. Marie Antoinette's Petit Hameau at Versailles was a rustic hamlet entirely devoid of the artificial formalism of seventeenth-century Versailles. Landscapes painted by Claude Lorraine, Gaspard Dughet and Salvator Rosa emphasized the wild and unruled. Often a ruined ancient temple stood as a mark of nature's victory over formalism.

Claude's paintings were admired by Richard Payne Knight, the philosopher whose *Analytical Enquiry into the Principles of Taste,* of 1805, fought Georgian conventions: "Houses should be irregular where all the accompaniments are irregular. . . . The best style for irregular and picturesque houses . . . is that mixed style, which characterizes the buildings of Claude and the Poussins." His house, Downton Castle, was irregular and eclectic; it is properly imagined set in a wild, irregular terrain, where trees have torn and shredded shapes, where dead branches are scarred, even burnt, look menacing by moonlight, as in some of the romantic scenes of Fuseli, Blake, or Schinkel; waterfalls and precipitous crags, rude bridges and ruins announced nature as wild and uncontrollable, the destroyer of man's artifacts, unencompassable by formal geometry or reason.

In 1761 William Chambers adorned Kew Gardens with a full-sized Chinese pagoda, and Hindu, Turkish and other exotic motives were imported from the "mysterious East" or the "barbarian Goths." William Wrighte's book of 1790 dealing with "Grotesque Architecture, or Rural Amusement" and offering plans for "Huts, Retreats, Summer and Winter Hermitages, Terminaries, Chinese, Gothic, and Natural Grottos, Cascades, Baths, Mosques, Moresque Pavilions, Grotesque and Rustic Seats" came to America in 1835 after the conventional time lag. Americans could not be immune to such heady mixtures in the days of their high romanticism; they are scarcely immune yet. But again their native sobriety and restraint made their picturesque work less extreme and therefore less effective than the work in Europe. Whatever might happen in American literature, American architectural romanticism was nearer to the spirit of Cooper or Irving than to that of Poe.

8

ASSOCIATIONALISM SPAWNED MANY PROGENY. IT BRED SPHINXES AND ZIG-gurats and produced an Egyptian hospital in Richmond, Virginia; it put Chinese temples in rural New York and artificially ruined castles in a St. Louis park. It might lead to a careless or a careful Gothic revival. But it could also lead back to a tender reconsideration of Greece and Rome. One of our finest architectural residues, the products of the Classic Revival, must thus be numbered among the offspring of associationalism.

It was perfectly possible, then, indeed easy, to be romantic about this most regular of architectures, especially if one looked upon it as the product of democratic societies, entertaining incomplete notions about the Periclean orations or the character of the early Roman Republic whose stalwart farmer citizens might seem to resemble the citizens of the new American Republic. It was many years later that other Americans, not much more sure-footed about their history, insisted on construing the classic symbols as those of imperialism. For the day they were taken as the symbols of democracy and heartily welcomed on that ground. Again European archeological knowledge supplied the preliminary fodder. Wood and Dawkins published their book about Palmyra's ruins in 1755; their study of Baalbek followed in 1757. Leroy, a French archeologist, described the ruins of Greece in 1758. His work was followed by a more detailed and systematic investigation, Stuart and Revett's *Antiquities of Athens*, a four-volume study, published consecutively between 1762 and 1816. The Palace of Diocletian at Spalato was described by Robert Adam in 1764. Meanwhile Winckelmann in Germany had presented the political, social and intellectual conditions that underlay the "noble simplicity and tranquil greatness" of Greek art in his *History of Ancient Art*. Excavations were begun at Herculaneum and Pompeii in 1735 and 1755, and buildings, furniture and household utensils were gradually recovered from layers of ash and lava; Herculaneum's treasures were published by Cochin in 1765. In 1774 Clérisseau published his *Antiquités de la France*; the first volume, *Les Monuments de Nîmes*, included the famous Maison Carrée, which Jefferson, in collaboration with Clérisseau, imitated in the Richmond Capitol a decade later. Even there, American fashion followed a practice of scientific reconstruction initiated in 1760 when Chambers erected in Kew Gardens a Temple of the Sun derived from Baalbek.

Scientific archeology provided a means for exact imitation of classic architecture. Architects constantly railed against such subservience to precedent and warned of the shortcomings of formalism. "Wherever the Grecian style can be copied without impropriety, I love to be a . . . slavish . . . copyist," Latrobe wrote in his most patronizing way, but hastened to add that classical styles are inapplicable to modern uses and climates. At the Franklin Institute in 1840 Thomas U. Walter, the architect of the dome on the Capitol at Washington, lectured: "The popular idea that to design a building in Grecian taste is nothing more than to copy a Grecian building, is altogether erroneous. . . . If architects would oftener aim to *think* as the Greeks thought, than to *do* as the Greeks did, our columnar architecture would possess a higher degree of originality, and its character and expression would gradually become conformed to the local circumstances of the country, and the republican spirit of its institutions."

But clients and amateurs demanded correctness rather than adaptation, much as Jefferson had. In September, 1835, Philip Hone noted the ability of architecture to recall the grandeur and beauty of far away and long ago. In February, 1838, he recorded in his diary: "How strange it is that in all the inventions of modern times architecture alone seems to admit of no improvement — every departure from the classical models of antiquity in this science is a departure from grace and beauty." Such a feeling among patrons of art stifled art; as Talbot Hamlin, the historian of the Greek Revival, noted, "at last, under the heavy blanket of correctness, it was smothered to death."

Thinking of that sort brought the fiasco at Girard College in Philadelphia — a story that might well give pause to more than one present-day well-intentioned university trustee. Stephen Girard, the merchant-financier, had specified in his will the exact dimensions of the building he intended to have for instructing the orphans at the college he founded. He offered a premium for the best plan submitted in a closed architectural competition. The contest was won by Walter. Although his plan pleased the building committee, it did not please Nicholas Biddle, president of the National Bank, traveler in Greece, admirer of Byron, and amateur, who immediately wedged his way into membership on the building committee. He weaned Walter from the original plan and persuaded him to "take advantage of this rare opportunity of immortalizing himself by a perfect, chaste specimen of Grecian architecture." The trustees and councils hesitated, thinking a Greek temple out of character with Girard's request for a simple building; but Biddle rallied them to lay the foundation stone on July 4, 1833, and the Corinthian temple with elliptical groin-vaulted classrooms was warped to fit the dimensions specified in Girard's will. When, in 1847, the main building at Girard was completed, the taste of the day was again affirmed by a client, a literary man, not an architect. Joseph Chandler spoke of it as "the whited sepulchre of ancient art [that] shall . . . become the temple of moral life."

No style since the Georgian captured American hearts more fully than the classical, especially the Greek Revival. When they were permitted to do so, professional architects used Greek architectural elements, but applied them to modern practical plans. Scale and workmanship were often exquisite; the best results may vie with the best Georgian as America's finest effort to date. A Greek Revival town is a fine and handsome assembly of stately colonnades and well-turned building masses. One can catch glimpses of this civic beauty at Nantucket, where the whaling captains built Greek Revival houses, churches, banks and libraries in 1840-1860. The style moved westward to grace Saratoga Springs and Ovid in New York, Dayton, Ravenna and Newark in

Ohio, Detroit and Chicago; it moved south to Frankfort, Kentucky, to Tuscaloosa, Alabama, and Athens, Georgia. The buildings in those towns were not reproductions of whole Greek or Roman buildings; at most their porticoes or cornices were copies; but largely they should be regarded first in terms of their plans and sections, where the results were practical and graceful, and then in terms of their details whose refinement was frequently original as in Mills's Customs House at New Bedford or the church at Wickford, Rhode Island.

The vitality of Greek Revival design stemmed from a sure sense of architecture as a combination of use, construction and beauty, first of all in spaces. This can be clearly seen in the old Capitol at Frankfort, Kentucky, by Gideon Shryock. It has an excellent plan, in which an axial arrangement admits visitors past a portico to a one-story hall and then to a central, double circular stair of marble, built as a curved arch, which rises gracefully beneath the overarching dome. The spaces for the court of appeals, library, offices and committees are clustered on the first floor around the stair hall. Ingenious planning enabled the architect to gather the House of Representatives and Senate Chamber at the front and rear of the second floor. Minor entrances and stairs, toilets and coat rooms, windows and doors are all placed perfectly to give excellent circulation and control. A section through the building shows a sure grasp of the space under the rotunda; the circular stair spirals gracefully upward through the space, which is pinched inward at the summit and funneled into a side-lighted cupola. According to Shryock, the inspiration for this old Kentucky Capitol was the temple of Athena Polias at Priene in Ionia; but he referred only to the portico; the arrangement of the whole building is as original, practical, and modern as it is beautiful; no Greek temple ever had a rotunda or staircase like those of the Capitol; none had a dome and lantern. Shryock thought as the Greeks thought, but he did not do as the Greeks did.

It is exciting and pleasurable to follow the course of the Greek Revival as it moved across the land until one meets the pathos of it as it dried up in the plains. Besides Shryock, there were other fine practitioners like another of Latrobe's apprentices, William Strickland, the Philadelphia architect who designed the State Capitol at Nashville as well as St. Mary's Church there. Belmont, near Nashville, reveals once again the sureness of geometry which Strickland shared with other Greek Revival architects. Others like Francis Costigan showed more caprice but still dealt skillfully and with charm in buildings such as the Lanier House (1844) at Madison, Indiana, or the many-domed Institute for the Blind at Louisville (1851).

Boston was to see the Greek Revival in heavy buildings like Young's

Doric colonnade around his cruciform and domed Customs House.
New York had a more graceful composition in Isaiah Rogers's Merchants' Exchange (later Customs House). Here a tall Ionic colonnade
robustly screened an interior containing a handsome rotunda in the
Corinthian order. Virginia's Berry Hill was a plantation equal to any
of the Georgian ones, and North Carolina's State Capitol at Raleigh
(1833-1840), despite its awkward massing and heavy base, had some
interesting moments in the fine detail of the Corinthian order in the
rotunda.

Other houses like the Roper House in Charleston and Belo in Winston-Salem revealed to what a degree Southern taste in architectural
matters would be missed after the Civil War. This impression is borne
out as one moves into Prince Street in Athens, Georgia, or into Tuscaloosa, Alabama, where the house for the President at the University reveals an architectural taste that Northern cities neglected to their detriment during the '80s and '90s. No hotel in the North could boast
greater elegance, magnificence or lavish formality than the rotunda of
the St. Louis Hotel at New Orleans, designed by Jacques Bussière de
Pouilly and built in 1836-1840. Urbane and monumental, its polychromed interiors were superb, reaching their climax in the columned
rotunda and dome at the center. In the lower Mississippi Valley, the
Greek Revival reached an apogee of refinement, with attenuated columns like those in Stanton Hall at Natchez and the Governor's Mansion at Jackson, Mississippi, and with original detail like the faceted
blocks in the frieze of Shryock's State Capitol at Little Rock, Arkansas.
The Greek Revival was especially popular for schools, like the one built
at Norwalk, Ohio, in 1848, where Ionic columns, as graceful as any in
the East, punctuate the façade. At Columbus, Ohio, the State Capitol
exhibited the strong geometric forms of the style, and even farmhouses
in remote Michigan, Gordon Hall at Dexter, for example, had a practical plan graced with a Doric portico. As it moved westward, the style
declined; but federal buildings carried it nationally and even the gross
scale of the United States Mint in San Francisco shows that the Greek
Revival was a national style that was seldom used so poorly as to prevent
its buildings from remaining superior to most in any city.

9

DURING THE 1840S AND '50S THE GREEK REVIVAL, ESPECIALLY IN THE
copied forms amateurs and clients often insisted on, was attacked by
many critics. The most effective were associationalists who denied the

democratic association to argue instead that Greek forms spoke of a pagan civilization incompatible with a modern Christian nation whose true architecture should be the Gothic. When Alexander Jackson Davis completed his Gothic hall for New York University, the critic Henry Cleveland, writing in the *North American Review* of 1836, declared his pleasure upon learning that Gore Hall Library at Harvard would also be Gothic, restudied from King's College Chapel at Cambridge, England. Cleveland admired Gothic. He criticized Egyptian and Greek architecture because their religions were pagan, not Christian, disgusting, absurd, superstitious. Gothic, he said, besides being Christian, allowed close adaptation of form to use. But expression was more important than use: "There is a style of architecture which belongs peculiarly to Christianity . . . whose very ornaments remind one of the joys of life beyond the grave; whose lofty vaults and arches are crowded with the forms of prophets and martyrs and beatified spirits, and seem to resound with the choral hymns of angels and archangels . . . the architecture of Christianity, the sublime, the glorious Gothic."

Cleveland's sentimental yearning reflected a growing amateur taste for Gothic architecture, which had already gripped England. There the Oxford Movement, begun in 1833, and the Camden Society, founded in 1839, had initiated greater liturgical ceremony within the Church of England and influenced architects to follow medieval precedent. The eighteenth-century "Gothick" of Walpole's Strawberry Hill had already been undermined by archeological investigations into true Gothic buildings which Rickman, Britton and Pugin published in 1805-1821. One notable architectural success in the perpendicular style, Barry's and Pugin's Houses of Parliament, encouraged a taste for better modern Gothic buildings. The older "Gothick" succumbed. The zealous high priest of the new Revival in England was Augustus Welby Pugin, whose *True Principles of Christian Architecture* confounded aesthetics and ethics in the assertion that Gothic was a Christian architecture, and Gothic buildings would influence people in Christian ways and beliefs. Gothic churches inspire moral behavior, he thought, and medieval towns were better than those of the nineteenth century. The idea came to America in essays like Cleveland's and in one small American book of naïve drawings, Bishop John Henry Hopkins's *Essay on Gothic Architecture*, published in 1836.

The early Gothic Revival, which entranced Americans in 1830-1860, was a considerable advance beyond the picayune details of earlier essays by Latrobe and Godefroy in that style. But it often simulated effects by any available means, rather than building in accordance with Gothic as a whole structural system. The climax of many designs was a lath-and-plaster vault carved to imitate stone, as in Richard Bond's Gore Hall at Harvard. Stuccoed walls were routed to suggest stone joints, and falsery was coupled with overwrought crenellations to create picture-book castles. Such faults were not corrected until Ruskin's freer interpretation of the Gothic Revival insisted upon honest construction. When this was coupled with the serious scholarship of Viollet-le-Duc, original compositions employing Gothic structural principles began to appear after 1860. Meanwhile, the typical church was a somewhat boxlike affair, Gothic only in having buttresses, vaults and pointed windows; notably deficient in the sculpture and stained glass that were essential features of true Gothic architecture. Only rarely an Anglo-Catholic church such as Notman's St. Mark's in Philadelphia of 1848 displayed the colorful, picturesque masses that would characterize the later Ruskinian churches.

The most interesting and famous architect of the early American Gothic Revival was Richard Upjohn, the architect of Trinity Church in New York. Typical of the literary quality of this architect was the strong morality that dominated his response when asked to design a church for Unitarians in Boston. According to an account in the *Boston Christian Register* for Saturday, November 28, 1846, "Upjohn replied, that after having anxiously and prayerfully considered the matter, he had come to the conclusion that he could not conscientiously furnish a plan for a Unitarian Church, he being an Episcopalian."

The best feature of Upjohn's architecture was the freedom of planning he achieved by using many separate Gothic units, dispersed siting and picturesque silhouettes, but his Gothic was still mainly pictorial. Oaklands, the R. H. Gardiner House at Gardiner, Maine, of 1835-1836, has an L-shaped plan and an extended symmetrical wing from which a semi-hexagon is extruded; each room is shaped well so that the spaces are firmly modeled and flow through the plan. Churches allowed Upjohn no comparable freedom nor did he have the imagination to demand it. Trinity at New York, 1839-1846, is an English country parish church. Except for a soaring spire, it is boxlike, decorated with planar sculptural ornament, and lacks the depth and plasticity of true Gothic. Its plaster vaults and ribs mark a heavy geometry that depresses a space which refuses to be shaped by the wide nave and boxed-in side aisles; the nave arcade bifurcates the interior, a fault that Gothic architects had corrected by using the triforium gallery. Upjohn was more successful in simpler, rural churches like St. Mary's at Burlington, New Jersey, of 1846-1854. There, stone walls and buttresses retain a brittle character which gives "punch" to the sharp spire on the tower, and wooden rafters and hammer-beam vaults are sufficiently heavy to indicate that they truly support the roof over a space that is well proportioned and well sustained by the Gothic arch at the crossing. In fact, the more rustic and modest they were, the more successful were Upjohn's designs. His board-and-batten churches, like St. Thomas's at Hamilton, New York, of 1847, have vigorous forms that are well scaled by the shadows of the battens, while the truss that supports the roof is a complex foil to the austere simplicity of the white walls on the interior. Upjohn's best work carried Gothic Revival into an original phase. It was not nearly so fine as the classic moments of the Greek Revival, but it deserved at least part of the eulogy of Thomas U. Walter, who praised the "purer and more artistic forms of medieval art" that Ujohn developed.

I O

BEGINNING WITH BUILDINGS LIKE HUGH REINAGLE'S MASONIC HALL IN Broadway, started in 1826, the American landscape had long supported a weird collection of foreign visitors. But now the floodgates of eclecticism opened wide. There were picturesque Gothic rural villas like Upjohn's Edward King House at Newport of 1845. Stranger still was Wilson's Moorish temple on Plum Street in Cincinnati, complete with minarets, serving ironically as a Jewish temple, and a prime illustration of the fact that there was no Jewish-American architectural tradition (and there still is none). A church at Sag Harbor, Long Island, erected in 1844, was Egyptian, designed by Minard Lafever whose crude archeological notions led him to suppose it recalled the Temple of Solomon. Alexander Jackson Davis's Pauper Lunatic Asylum on Blackwell's Island, New York, presaged more Italianate developments, like Notman's "Prospect" at Princeton and later villas by Davis, including the Litchfield House in Prospect Park of 1853-1854. At Washington, the National Soldiers' Home of 1851 was a foretaste of Ruskinian Gothic. It was a time of the Roman and Tuscan villa, the Lombard church, the Roman of Pliny and Palmyra, Vitruvian, Norman, American farm or country house, suburban Greek, Regency Moorish and the Byzantine cottage. If we rely solely upon the names they assigned their work, we shall miss seeing that architects accomplished more than novelty of effect. They also apportioned spaces rationally and freed planning and silhouettes from the limitations of strict Greek and Gothic forms. One could notice this in the creative though eclectic work of architects like Detlef Lienau, whose commercial buildings like the Noel and Saurel Warehouses in New York, of 1864-1865, stem from the eclectic architectural tradition that developed strongly in the '40s; underlying his use of picturesque forms like the mansard roof on the Schermerhorn House of 1859 was the strong insistence upon adaptation to use which eclecticism sometimes fostered when it was not mere façadism.

It did not seem to occur to many designers that the new plans and performances might yield their own new appearance. We need raise no eyebrows at this. It was natural for the men of a society which liked to adorn its steam engines and machines with fluted Ionic columns in iron, carefully placed where they would not interfere with the practical workings. It was a sincere, if inept, search for something good-looking, no less sincere than the flight to streamlining three quarters of a century later. There were some voices speaking the other way. In *Hints on Public Architecture*, an account of the eclectic Smithsonian Institution at Washington, Robert D. Owen advanced the view that "in planning any edifice, public or private, we ought to begin *from within*; that we should just suffer the specific wants and conveniences demanded . . . and then adjust . . . its architecture . . . to the individual form." But at the same time he praised the elevations of Renwick's Smithsonian building, which were Lombard Romanesque, for reflecting the plan and he did not doubt that they were well adapted to America or to Washington in 1849.

Use and expression — the watchwords of eclecticism — were the mainstays of the diet Andrew Jackson Downing fed his readers. *Cottage Residences*, which he published in 1842, offered a strange paean to rusticity in a nation which was headed for industrialization and which had already produced such urbane cities as Philadelphia and Charleston. His most ambitious publication, *The Architecture of Country Houses*, published in 1850, showed a genuine, almost overwrought, attention to natural landscape. He insisted that houses be adapted to the rocks and ground, the trees and plants, where they stood. A house should look "domestic" and fit its environment. Expression was for him merely a matter of style. He showed Italian villas, Swiss houses, Gothic rustic cottages and English rural houses, championing the fallacious notion that each style was suited to a particular landscape, and he wanted "harmoniously [to] combine rural architecture and rural scenery."

Even the meanest mechanic knew better. In 1838 some of the mechanics in Michigan were setting themselves up as architects and engineers. They were incensed at Alexander Jackson Davis's proposal for a Gothic hall for the University of Michigan. One of them wrote to ask why the Lieutenant Governor had not given the citizens of his state a chance before calling in a New Yorker. "I suppose," wrote one man, "it was because the Mechanics of Michigan do not assume that dignified name called *Architect!* or any of those *lofty* titles as Esq'rs &c." He found nothing "attractive about this Gothic elevation, without it is

those towers of Babel between 200 and 300 feet high, and the two negroes in the attitude of skating in front of the plan." "Pray, why does
Michigan want to imitate the fooleries and splendid extravagances of
Europe? The whole of the funds appropriated will be expended before
there will be conveniences for a single Professor. Why are those four
mammoth windows necessary, and the large chapel which will require a
fortune to provide fuel to keep it comfortably warm in winter?"

In *Rural Architecture*, of 1852, Lewis F. Allen urged farmers to be as
simple as they were alleged to be and "leave all this vanity to town-folk,
who have nothing better — or who, at least, think they have — to amuse
themselves." In *Village and Farm Cottages*, published in 1856, the authors, Cleaveland and Backus, gained the confidence of suspicious farmers by remarking about the Greek Revival that they hoped "this folly
has had its day." They proposed a way to develop varied, useful plans
into picturesque, rural compositions. Again there was the American
dream, announced in Messianic terms, that a proletarian art would bring
good housing for everyone. At its wildest, this could lead to the proposals of Orson S. Fowler, a phrenologist, who wrote *A Home for All, or
the Gravel Wall and Octagon Mode of Building*. In this he prescribed
the spiritually medicinal properties to be found in concrete octagonal
houses such as those by Goodrich which he had seen near Janesville,
Wisconsin.

The musings of medicine men and mechanics were anathema to professional arbiters of taste; yet they, too, paid lip tribute to use and morality. Downing shot darts at the "coarse and brutal" frontier: "So long as
men are forced to dwell in log huts and follow the hunter's life, we must
not be surprised at lynch law and the use of the bowie knife. But, when
smiling lawns and tasteful cottages begin to embellish a country, we
know that order and culture are established." Here, again, was the curious belief about good architecture: that it improved moral conduct!
Americans guiltily demanded and demand some justification for beauty
to be found beyond beauty itself; they naïvely confounded and con-
found aesthetics and ethics — to the disservice of architecture and ethics
as well. Not quite convinced of the alliance, Downing stepped into a
second and still seductive trap; joining aesthetics with economics, he
intended to prove that the superior, beautiful and harmonious forms
"may be had at the same cost and with the same labor as a clumsy
dwelling, and its uncouth and ill designed accessories."

He argued too for expression of purpose, that is, that banks should
look like banks, churches like churches, and not all be confused together behind common, impassive, impersonal, Greek porticoes or
Georgian façades. But the appropriateness was not to be unlimited. The

building must still be rustic and "natural" in a strictly romantic sense. Here was an exultant affirmation of the countryside over the city; of the alleged farm purity over urban decadence. Downing's village mind recoiled at the urban houses that expressed "sensuality instead of hospitality"; setting the stage for the later censures of John Bascom, he thought that "gaudy and garish apartments . . . will express pride and vanity" since "a house which is beautiful . . . deadens or destroys its beauty by overlaying its fair features with a corrupt or vicious expression." Small wonder that the *Broadway Journal* poked fun at Downing's books.

But journalists could not stem the tide of picturesque eclecticism. Artists like Thomas Cole depicted "sublime" landscapes such as *The Architect's Dream* where piles rise high in a kind of classic Xanadu. But he was more at home when commissioned to paint some landscapes in 1826 by Robert Gilmor, Jr., of Baltimore. Gilmor insisted that they be the kind of setting Downing and Davis envisaged for their houses: "Water should be introduced in one, and would be well in both, one being *falling water*, and the other *still lake*, reflecting the play of light on a slight motion of part of it, which may also be effected by introducing deer or cattle drinking or a canoe with Indians paddling on it. The boat race in Mr. Cooper's last novel would be a happy introduction. . . . It would give animation and interest to the whole; — I should also like to have in the other some *known* subject from Cooper's novels to enliven the landscape." Thus the literary quality of the visual arts was affirmed.

Indeed, Cooper had greatly fortified the canons of the picturesque tradition. His views on architecture were set forth in *The Pioneers*, *Home as Found* and *Afloat and Ashore*; he sided with the Goths. In *The Pioneers* he ridiculed the Jones-Doolittle attempt at turning the Templeton manor into a Greek Revival temple; in *Home as Found* the Effingham family went up the Hudson expressing scorn for the "vulgar pretension" of the Greek Revival country seats and public buildings they saw; John Effingham thought it a sickness: " . . One such temple well placed in a wood, might be a pleasant object enough; but to see a river lined with them, with children trundling hoops before their doors, beef carried into their kitchens, and smoke issuing, moreover, from those unclassical objects, chimneys, it is too much even for a high taste." It was no surprise to Cooper's contemporaries at Cooperstown when the novelist got Samuel F. B. Morse to remodel his father's house from the Greek Revival to a Gothic dwelling; though the hoop-rolling children were no more compatible. His voice was markedly different from that of Mark Twain whose *Life on the Mississippi* spat tobacco juice at the Gothic pretensions of the State House of Louisiana.

All of this was a long way from the rationalism of Latrobe and the best Greek Revival architects. None of the leading intellectuals of the '40s and '50s was duped by picturesque eclecticism. They shared the farmer's suspicion of the Europeanized architect and distrusted the aristocratic arbiters of taste. The opinion of leading writers like Greenough and Emerson was far removed from that of Downing, while scientists seem to have received favorably the aesthetic ideas of the physicist Joseph Henry, of the Smithsonian Institution, whose speech at the meeting of the American Association for the Advancement of Science in 1854 was a strong avowal of utilitarian building — a point of view we shall meet later in other scientists like John Shaw Billings, Thomas Huxley and Charles William Eliot.

Henry insisted that it was bad taste to make a candlestick in the likeness of a statue of Apollo, or to use a fine painting for a fire board. Buildings should be planned from the inside. They should have a character expressive of their age. The Greek temple was intended for external worship and "an old Greek would laugh to see us construct a Grecian temple for a treasury building or a meeting house. . . . architecture should be looked upon more as a *useful* than a *fine* art."

It seemed to many that machines and clipper ships showed how strict adherence to utility might produce a beautiful architecture. James Russell Lowell, Samuel A. Eliot and Clarence Cook praised the new American ships about 1850, and Emerson, writing in *The Dial*, in 1840-1841, described how a tyrannical nature forces men's designs to be subordinated to her wishes: "It is the law of the fluids that prescribes the shape of the boat — keel, rudder, and bows, — and, in the finer fluid above, the form and tackle of the sails." As early as 1836, John Willis Griffiths, who designed the first extreme clipper ship, began lecturing about new mechanistic bases for ship design. His lectures given at New York in 1841 were later expanded into his *Treatise on Marine and Naval Architecture*, first published in 1849; his *Rainbow* and *Sea Witch*, launched in 1846, were revolutionary: "We have spread our banner to the breeze bearing our motto of *fitness for the purpose*, and *proportion to effect the same*." That was Griffiths's definition of beauty as well as his guarantee of performance.

Behind the image of the ship lay the notion that nature herself demanded functional form. Nature was regarded as the selector of the form best adapted to perform well in a given environment. The idea was proposed as a law to describe evolution when Darwin published his *Origin of Species* in 1859. The idea was particularly attractive to men of the Darwinian days when descriptive biology was at its height and when men like Robert Louis Stevenson could write intelligible essays on the physical properties of a grain of dust. Nature, always a favorite of poets, could now be scrutinized at least in a pseudo-scientific way. It is not an accident that *The Chambered Nautilus* should appear at the same time that architects, engineers and critics were once more proclaiming that nature offered models of excellent adaptation. Marc Isambard Brunel constructed the Great Shield that enabled him to tunnel beneath the River Thames by taking as his model the structural shell that enclosed the wood-gnawing mollusc, *Teredo natalis.* The structure Joseph Paxton invented for the Crystal Palace of 1851 developed from observation he made of a water lily, the *Victoria regia,* and a year earlier he had described the beautiful engineering in the underside of that Amazonian plant: "Nature was the engineer. Nature has provided the leaf with longitudinal and transverse girders and supports that I, borrowing from it, have adopted in this building." From similar examples of engineering based upon organic forms, Emerson developed a principle about nature's resources for engineers: "Smeaton built Eddystone lighthouse on the model of an oak tree, as being the form in nature best designed to resist a constant assailing force. Dollond formed his achromatic telescope on the model of the human eye. Duhamel built a bridge, by letting in a piece of stronger timber for the middle of the under surface, getting his hint from the structure of the shinbone."

Of all the men who rode these currents at their full, Horatio Greenough was the most convincing as a writer if not as a sculptor. He sensed the urge of America to become a new and great civilization; he was saddened by our youthful misadventures, by our failure to learn deep lessons from Europe, by our insistence on founding institutions on hope rather than experience. It is tempting to interpret Greenough as a seer, well ahead of his time, a precursor of the architecture that Le Corbusier, Wright and Mies van der Rohe developed in the twentieth century. His criticism has been read that way. But, lest we think of him wrongly, we must recall his sculpture. His "Washington," now in the Smithsonian, sits on a classical throne, nude to the waist, a Zeus, in a toga, capped by Gilbert Stuart's face of the sage of Mount Vernon. It is as remote from cubism or machined forms or adaptation to America as it could be. His portrait of Lafayette had a realism that caused Cooper to insist that he recognized it immediately as an American work; but it too was classical. In his treatise, Greenough was no more seeking a mechanistic architecture than such a sculpture. He sought adaptation within a classical tradition. He thought no architecture complete unless it were ornamented; he opposed reconstructions of Greek temples but

not the kind of rationally planned classical work that Latrobe and Isaiah
Rogers had designed. In fact, he championed a future development of
the rational architecture that had been the most vital work in Europe
during the 1830s when he was living in Italy. "Instead of forcing the
functions of every sort of building into one general form, adopting an
outward shape for the sake of the eye or of association, without reference to the inner distribution, let us begin from the heart as a nucleus
and work outwards."

Exactly that kind of adaptation, so firmly advocated by Latrobe, had
been missed, even disclaimed, by Greek Revivalists and amateurs like
Nicholas Biddle and Thomas Jefferson. Girard College, Greenough
wrote scornfully to his architect brother Henry, was like "seeing the
Pitt diamond upon an Indian squaw."

Some indication of an architecture Greenough might have approved
is the work of this brother; buildings like the Orthodox Church in
Cambridge and the Museum of Comparative Zoology at Harvard were
pragmatic and utilitarian; severely plain masses revealed the shape and
apportionment of useful spaces. Apparently Greenough thought well of
the German architectural work of the early nineteenth century, especially that of Schinkel who, admiring the utilitarian factories at Manchester, England, had designed buildings like the Bauakademie in
Berlin, and St. Nicholas's in Potsdam, in the rational tradition of eighteenth-century classicism. In 1838 Greenough wrote a letter to Charles
Sumner, who was then in Berlin, asking him to relay impressions of
Schinkel's work, "as regards distribution & adaptation, *organization* in
short."

Use and expression, the two standards of eighteenth-century criticism,
are also the chief themes of Greenough's writings. There were, he said,
two distinct kinds of building: what he called the monumental and
the organic. The *organic* is "formed to meet the wants of their occupants."; the *monumental* is "addressed to the sympathies, the faith, or
the taste of a people." They had separate rules. The organic had its
own laws: ". . . the laws of structure and apportionment, depending
on definite wants, obey a demonstrable rule. They may be called machines, each individual of which must be formed with reference to the
abstract type of its species." But different laws guided the monumental:
they occupied "the positions and assume the forms best calculated to
render their parent feeling." Greenough offered a concise summary of
the architectural philosophy of "organic adaptation" in a letter he wrote
to Emerson which was later published in *The Dial*: "Here is my theory
of structure: A scientific arrangement of spaces and forms to functions

and to site: an emphasis on features proportioned to their graduated importance in function; color and ornament to be decided and arranged and varied by strictly organic laws. . . ."

Such a theory caused Greenough to turn associational ideas back on themselves. Medieval architecture seemed un-American. Roman governmental buildings seemed undemocratic. He accepted the theory of associations which picturesque critics like Downing alleged to be the content of historical architecture, but he claimed that Downing's associations were particularly bad. The Romanesque Smithsonian Institution was a specter. It spoke to him of "medieval confusion, stamped itself on the halls of Congress, as ink on paper! Dark on that whiteness — complication on that simplicity! It scared me. . . . It seemed to threaten."

His was the voice of a man recalling the aims of Latrobe, but Americans of 1840 paid no more attention to Greenough than Jefferson had to Latrobe in 1820.

The American client and his architect were not often mindful of the nationalism that Greenough thought should divorce us from Europe; nor were they willing to espouse Greenough's belief in a vernacular art, or an architecture similar to "the trotting wagon and the yacht America." They might agree that "If a flat sail goes nearest the wind, a bellying sail, though picturesque, must be given up," but they saw no point in transferring this metaphor to architecture. Least of all did they agree with him that if we could "carry into our civil architecture the responsibilities that weigh upon our ship-building, we should ere long have edifices as superior to the Parthenon, for the purposes we require, as the Constitution or the Pennsylvania is to the galley of the Argonauts."

All of this met favor with Greenough's friend Emerson, who subscribed to Coleridge's idea of how the artist should shape form: "The organic form . . . is innate; it shapes, as it develops itself from within." The process of designing a building should then be natural, not literary; spontaneous; aimed at giving good performance first. Consult nature; once consulted, nature revealed an authority that allowed small scope for choice. According to Emerson, ". . . . nature tyrannizes over our works. . . . Nothing droll, nothing whimsical will endure. . . . Man seems to have no option about his tools. but merely the necessity to learn from Nature what will fit best, as if he were fitting a screw or a door . . . his works become . . . hers and he is no longer free." He attacked the revivalists, both Greek and Gothic, and insisted in his essay on self-reliance that architecture should be expressive of American aspirations. That idea was promoted by his circle of friends, including the architect Samuel Gray Ward, whose "Notes on Art and

Architecture," published in *The Dial* of 1843, advocated organic adaptation and an architecture in which a cornice — "a wreath of thistles and
burdocks curiously carved or cast" — might express the American landscape.

Indeed, Americans at mid-century revealed a growing sense of "natural" landscape. Downing thought buildings should form a harmonious
part of their settings, and Olmsted and Vaux, who created Central Park
in New York City, valued romantic landscapes within urban settings.

This was a nature the urban, classic and conventionalized man would
soon lose. It remained real for Thoreau, or so he said. Even Calvert
Vaux, at work on Central Park, sensed "an innate homage to the natural in contradistinction to the artificial . . . with all its town-bred incongruities and frequently absurd shortcomings. An actual love for nature, however crude it may be, speaks clearly of a possible love for art."
There was also a purity and a simplicity in nature which led Thoreau to
question, even if self-consciously, whether civilization had improved
man's condition. "I would rather sit on a pumpkin and have it all to
myself, than to be crowded on a velvet cushion."

Neither Thoreau's primitivism nor Greenough's organic adaptation
was to be the way of architecture. The city was to invade Thoreau's
wilderness; European taste vanquished Greenough's pleas. When Thoreau speculated that a man might be well content with a shelter that
was a mere box where railroad men kept their tools, he effectively drew
a curtain between himself and all but the most romantic Americans,
and he did not even often live that way himself.

I I

THE FUTURE OF AMERICA, FOR BETTER, FOR WORSE, LAY ALONG THE CA-
nals and waterfalls of the New England rivers, not in the quiet
shallows of Walden Pond. It lay in Fall River and Woonsocket and
Pawtucket where Samuel Slater had established the first cotton mill
back in 1793. It lay in Manchester, Nashua, Lawrence and Lowell —
industrial communities, neither agricultural nor commercial. At first the
scale of those factories was easily accommodated within buildings that
preserved much of Renaissance design, such as the mill at Lowell, Massachusetts, founded about 1827. They were neat, attractive buildings,
standing in open countrysides; races brought water and dropped it over
giant wheels. Nearby, as at Harris, Rhode Island, stood trim, white cottages for workers; their communities were villages in the traditional
sense with well-appointed churches, schools and stores. By 1850 the

older means of wooden architecture no longer provided the strength or size or safety demanded by the more powerful means of production introduced when steam engines, heavy machinery, and more elaborate belt systems became the armature within the buildings. Wood beams carried on cast-iron columns were tried in many large brick factories like those at Lawrence, Massachusetts. They lost the scale and grace of the early mills. Crowding and massiveness became characteristic of the later development of Lowell. Workers' houses deteriorated in quality. It was obvious that architects and engineers had not yet developed adequate architecture or city planning for the burgeoning industrial society, nor had critics like Greenough and Emerson encouraged mill owners to find an adequate substitute for the Renaissance tradition, once the magnitude of the industrial city overstepped the Renaissance scale.

The possibilities of a new pattern for the environment of industrial society made initial appearances in the '50s. Some architects seized upon relatively new materials like cast iron and sheet glass to develop new structural forms. Sometimes those materials supported traditional forms, as when Walter produced his brilliant design of wrought and cast iron for the dome of the Capitol at Washington. The Penn Mutual Life Insurance Company Building in Philadelphia of 1850-1851 indicated one possible way of using cast iron in sheets, as a sheathing for the exterior, but that was usually only a means of simulating stone in iron, much as John Haviland used it in his early bank at Pottsville, Pennsylvania. The greater potentialities of iron as structure began to be realized about 1850. James Bogardus's Harper Building in New York, done in collaboration with the architect John B. Corlies, employed iron to form a cage of columns, discontinuous at each story, which supported beams made of wrought-iron tension members and cast-iron compression supports. Foundries, like Badger's Iron Works, began to turn out prefabricated parts that were assembled to form columns and capitals made of iron. Most of these still simulated classic and Gothic forms. But increasingly a form more suited to iron appeared in buildings like the *Baltimore Sun*'s iron building, R. G. Hatfield's design of 1851, and in the interior of Baltimore's Peabody Institute Library. Many of the cast-iron buildings achieved a dignity that had not been seen in city streets since the 1820s. Frequently that dignity was due to the modular design of cast-iron prefabrication and to classical principles of composition, as they appeared in New York's Broadway Manufacturing Supply Company of 1857 by J. P. Gaynor and the Haughwout store of 1857 on Broadway at Broome. Neither of these had the spatial excitement that Paxton achieved in London's Crystal Palace, nor the soaring adventure of Bunning's rotunda and his iron skeleton dome on London's Coal Exchange. Americans treated new materials as replacements for wood and stone, rather than extending them to their limits, whether they were iron, steel, or concrete. Even when Walter followed the precedent of the remarkable cast-iron dome of the Cathedral of St. Isaac's at St. Petersburg, Russia (erected 1840-1842), he was too cautious to press that experiment to a new stage; Jefferson's mechanical interest had never led him to provide in America something he admired in France, the iron-framed dome of the Halle-au-Blé at Paris of 1811. When in 1853-1854 a competition was held for the Crystal Palace to be erected at New York's international exhibition, the most progressive design was bypassed. Bogardus with Hoppin and Leopold Eidlitz proposed to build a roof that would be suspended by wrought-iron chains from a central tower; but their radical design lost out to a pedestrian and pale reflection of Paxton's building, prepared by G. J. B. Carstensen. Americans valued iron for the ease with which it could be erected and because it was an economical way of gaining the effect of stone in structure and ornament. But they were a little ashamed of it, too! By 1859, some of its possibilities were visible, notably to the architect Henry Van Brunt who read an important paper to the American Institute of Architects, later published in *The Crayon*. He approved the repetition he saw in cast-iron buildings; far from being a deficiency, that repetition expressed industrial production, mechanical assembly, and standard design: "As regards truth of material," Van Brunt said, "monotony in iron is as noble as variety in stone." Traditional design must give way to new kinds of composition, in which superimposition, intercolumniation and proportion must be reanalyzed and given forms different from stone construction. Such ideas opened a new field for design — one that the picturesque tradition had not contemplated.

In the years just before the Civil War and right after it, the cast-iron façade waxed fat in America. Foundries in San Francisco made parts for buildings in Portland, Oregon, and so it was throughout the land. Thus a national façade developed rather rapidly. The details of the castings were often atrocious, and sometimes the proportions of the columniation too. But on the whole the fabrication imposed a kind of order and regularity which was not lacking in vigor and architectural interest. It could be found from east to west, from north to south. It embellished the river fronts of Cincinnati, Louisville, and St. Louis, and the streets of many cities. It even invaded old cities like Charleston, where it came to the landward side of Broad Street. Charlestonians still try to forget that it is there, and wrongly. It does not have the great quality of the residences south of Broad but it is not without dignity and it was an effort to say that new things could happen in Charleston as well as old. If we wish to conjure up one picture of an American city street as representative of the style of America just before the Battle of Bull Run, we might be hard put to it to think of anything more characteristic than the façades of iron.

Unfortunately, no comparable progress was made in city planning for industrial communities. Villages and towns rapidly became choked by new growth. No controls, either legal or more broadly cultural, prevented a village like Centerdale, Rhode Island, where the Allendale Woolen Mill was built in 1822, from becoming clogged with buildings. A town like Waltham, Massachusetts, rapidly deteriorated when the Boston Manufacturing Company of 1813 was followed by other factories that crowded upon the land. Some efforts were made at ideal communities. Utopians tried to establish new agrarian-industrial communities like New Harmony, Indiana, or the town, Hygeia, which J. B. Papworth proposed to construct in Kentucky; but when Robert Owen attempted to interest Congress in planning for industrial communities, it turned a deaf ear to the Scotsman in spite of his years of experience with industrialism in Scotland; agricultural and commercial attitudes could not imagine the nascent industrial world. Nothing comparable to Saltaire, England, established near Bradford, in 1850, was erected in the United States. In answer to the question whether industrialism could produce a new and better environment, or whether we should once again follow historical styles, some would turn hopefully toward a revival of pre-Revolutionary and Georgian architecture, others might listen to Ruskin, who recoiled from the Crystal Palace and the mills of Manchester to praise the guilds of Venice. Few dared to hope for more.

Over all the major question was how to achieve a serviceable and attractive form for an industrial civilization. Few could doubt now that the commercial agricultural community was a thing of the past, and the Civil War would seal its doom. It was obvious that Georgian and classical and medieval architectures were not the right forms for industry. But whether they could still be warped to serve was the question that perplexed many young architects, including George Post, as we have seen. There was little to suggest that the vernacular or the democratic might guide industry into a cultural form that was meaningful. Yet, if one were a democrat, that assumption was part of the American dream. Thus Greenough had an unlimited naïve, Jacksonian faith in the common man: "It is the great multitude that has decided the rank of the statesmen, the poets, and the artists of the world. It is the great multitude for whom all really great things are done, and said, and suffered.

The great multitude desires the best of everything, and in the long run
is the best judge of it."

Such an egalitarian basis for the American dream seemed false to
many cultivated and serious-minded men who had seen the collapse
of Georgian taste and saw now only the ugly side of the industrial *sequitur*. The common man seemed neither to want nor to get the best.
Ruskin saw no way out beyond general education of all working people. Charles Eliot Norton set out to establish some model dwellings
for them, particularly immigrants, but his motive was fear: "The lower
classes here, as in the old world, are the *dangerous classes*. . . ." Such
fears were not well received in a period that savored phrases such as
faith in the common man and political equality. On the other hand, belief in the phrases undercut the professional arbiter of taste who might
set himself above the vernacular and mechanics' habits of building.

It was at this juncture, and in these days of bewildering and divisive
contention, that architects climaxed nearly thirty years of ineffective
efforts at being recognized as professionals by founding the American
Institute of Architects in 1857. For two years before this some architects
had belonged to the American Society of Civil Engineers but it is not
surprising that this arrangement did not satisfy the need for a new
society. Richard Upjohn was a prime mover in the founding and was
the first president, a post he held until 1876. The membership included
most of the actors, yet living, whose roles we have rehearsed, including
Walter and some like Richard Morris Hunt whose arrival on the scene
would not be much noticed for a while. The aim of the founders was to
establish a concerted effort at improving architecture by exchanging
ideas, establishing ethical codes and fees, and publicizing the way their
functions differed from those of the ordinary builder. But the way of the
professional architect remained almost as difficult as it had been in
1820 when Latrobe had complained bitterly about it.

Calvert Vaux sensed the difficulty of the professional architect in a
democracy where cultural integrity had been destroyed by a violent
social change; in 1857 he wrote in *Villas and Cottages*:

> Continuous ease and leisure readily welcome art, while con-
> stant action and industry require time to become acquainted
> with its merits. . . . The industrious classes . . . decide the
> national standard of architectural taste. . . . How is this uni-
> versal taste to be improved? . . . To secure any thing perma-
> nently satisfactory . . . , professors . . . , workmen . . . ,
> and an appreciative, able public are necessary. . . . The press
> is the improving power that is to be mainly looked to. Cheap

popular works on architecture . . . , popular lectures, popular engravings . . . are the . . . means . . . to influence the
public.

It seemed a strangely weak conclusion to a period that had started so
well; yet it was inevitable that America should turn to popular education, to England and to Ruskin once she was frustrated from developing an architecture for industry comparable to the Georgian. After
1860 Ruskin bewitched America more than the hardheaded Latrobe
had done. In the contest between the rationalism of Latrobe and the
medievalism of Upjohn, the medievalist had emerged the prophet.

Thus a period which had started simply, even elegantly, ended in
confusion. The confusion would become worse before any clarity might
appear again but at least people were beginning to understand what the
question was. For architecture it could be stated simply, although that
did not usually happen. America was becoming an industrial society
and not very many wanted to stop it, while no one knew how. She
might continue to pretend that this was not happening by the witness
of her architecture or she might admit that she was what she was and
try to display it proudly. It would take her nearly three quarters of a
century before she could bring herself to the latter alternative.

II

1860-1885

II

1860-1885

ONE IMPORTANT ITEM OF THE AMERICAN DEBATE, recurrent at least until the Second World War, concerned the dependency of the New World upon the Old. It asked how much Americans should borrow from their motherlands, whether American culture should develop as an evolution from the past or whether the American land and the American democracy would inevitably evoke a new culture, as complete a break with the aesthetic past as the American republic seemed a break with the political past. Actively discussed even before the Revolution, it had encouraged Emerson to some of his most hortatory language. But though heavily debated in theory it never became much of an issue in the practice of American architecture until after the Civil War. In the peaceful and pleasant days of the Georgian and the Greek Revival buildings, their modest American modifications seemed enough.

But when expanding and turbulent industrialization spread over the land in the wake of the Union victory, the devastation it brought was more apparent than the improvement. This led some sensitive Americans to yearn both for the handsome past which was being stamped out and for a European approach to the fine arts. Men like Richard Morris Hunt who led such movements gained their understanding of what was happening in Europe mainly from capital cities like Paris and London which felt the impact of industrialization for the most part on the exchanges, or in the villages of Provence which felt it not at all; they ignored Manchester and Sheffield and Lille, which were the centers of the industrial movement and which were, if anything, more dismal than their American counterparts. The argument for or against European influence was to continue with greater vigor in the next quarter century, culminating perhaps in 1893, but it was vigorous enough even in the seventies.

Those who coveted the European way were by no means characteristic of the groundswell of America. They might seem important in the salons of New York, but were only the butt for merriment on the frontier; they were repudiated by Twain and Whitman; and in the long run of history they were swimming upstream. The adverse current that would sweep them under was the current of advancing technology and industry. The buildings of religion and of government, the houses of the opulent, were to retain some prestige but the dominant cultural premise, usually unspoken, often not even realized, was that the new world of technology and industry would have its own importance, would cry for its own symbols.

If less turbulent times can be epitomized by one or two buildings, the contentious themes of the post-Civil War period require nearly a dozen. Shirley Center was now a memory, its place in the sun preempted by such industrial metropolises as Cleveland, where crass expediency downtown was coupled with an ideology about cultural institutions which romantically decked them in Gothic and classic costumes. Concurrently there were vigorous, uncouth striplings, the bald working machines of commerce, like the John Shillito Company store in Cincinnati, and useful expedient buildings for the new sciences, like the Johns Hopkins Hospital at Baltimore. There were emblems of the new technology and wealth, skyscrapers like the Western Union Telegraph Building at New York or the Gothic mansion erected for William K. Vanderbilt by Richard Morris Hunt, affirming the wealth, denying the technology. At the opposite end from the pragmatic, there were the Victorian Gothic buildings of cultural institutions — the National Academy of Design at New York and Memorial Hall at Harvard. There were also signs of a titanic energy, nascent and undecided, perhaps best felt in the rustic, Romanesque buildings Henry Hobson Richardson designed at North Easton, Massachusetts, and the jail he did for Pittsburgh.

Reflective people were disturbed by the schizoid culture they saw. America seemed to have her abundant energy, even her distinctive gait, but no integrated personality. The factories belied the pretensions of the churches; the government buildings bore no mark of the laboratories or even of the political climate. In 1864, James Jackson Jarves raised a telling question in *The Art-Idea*. What would be thought of us, he asked, if as had happened to the Egyptians, Ninevites, Etruscans, Aztecs, and Central American races, some cataclysm of nations destroyed everything except our buildings; ". . . what would they directly express of us? Absolutely nothing! . . . the one intense, barren fact which stares us fixedly in the face is, that, were we annihilated tomorrow, nothing could be learned of us, as a distinctive race, from our architecture."

The brighter side of our coin might show only if, as Jarves predicted, future scholars fell upon "the mechanical features of our civilization . . . our ocean-clippers, river-steamers, and industrial machines . . . They bespeak an enterprise, invention and development of the practical arts that proclaim the Americans to be a remarkable people." But at the end of the period, the evidences of American personality, especially the city, continued to disturb artists.

I

Perhaps the most difficult tension of all was between the city and the vanishing country. It, too, would be stretched tightest in the next quarter-century but the pull was already beginning. In America, up to the Civil War, the city was not much more than an overgrown village. Its congestion was not much greater, its pace not much faster. The country was not remotely different. But now the industrial peripheries and even the industrial centers made the city into a different thing. The countryman could no longer feel at ease in the city street or the city man in a rural hedgerow.

Thus for America there was finally a reality to the dispute between city and country which has been argued elsewhere through history from Aesop and La Fontaine to the most contemporary Parisian *boîte*. All through this history the city slicker and the country bumpkin had their own self-consoling images of the stupidity of the other. But there was this difference between the conditions in America and those in Europe: there were no true peasants and no genuine rural tradition in America. If the barriers between town and country could then be more readily leveled, it also meant that the distinctive virtues of town and country were always blurred, until the factory made them clear.

Most Americans would agree with young Henry Adams that "Town was winter confinement, school, rule, discipline. . . . Town was restraint, law, unity. Country, only seven miles away, was liberty, diversity, outlawry, the endless delight of mere sense impressions given by nature for nothing."

The country suggests freedom to most men and the virtues of the country were imputed also to the countryman. Rousseau proclaimed it but Adam Smith confirmed it on what seemed hard economic terms. The farmer was supposed for practical reasons to be naturally frugal, disinterested in profit; he was more intelligent and resourceful than the factory worker. The farmer was more universal, it was thought, because he had not been required to, nor was he able to, specialize his task as much as the factory worker. He made a better soldier because he was healthier and more resourceful. And the country tended also to preserve his morality, if only by keeping an eye on it.

In America, Irving painted the picture of the aesthetic peasant in *The Sketch Book*, a life full of wonderful observances and rituals and ceremonies; in England Wordsworth mourned the industrial desecration of the countryside and the degradation of the peasant thereby; but neither was picturing a peasantry he had ever known; instead, they were harking back to the conjectural peasantry of Elizabethan England.

The invasion of the country by the factory was longer in coming to America and protests like those of Wordsworth naturally were not heard so soon in the New World. The appeal of the country or the woods, with or without peasants, was couched in different terms, notably those of Thoreau who went to the woods "to live deliberately, to front only the essential facts of life."

As time went on, the farmer became less dominant in American thinking. There were many places where his life deteriorated and this bothered countrymen like Whittier.

> Our yeoman should be equal to his home
> Set in the fair, green valleys, purple-walled,
> A man to match his mountains, not to creep
> Dwarfed and debased below them.

The pictures the poets made were becoming harder to see; the single haycart creaking down the hill, with the driver asleep on top, the drowsy smell of heliotrope, white clover, and mignonette, the locust stabbing the sharp silence of noon, could be matched by curtainless windows, shiftless rags, rubbish piled up the chimney's back, rampant honeysuckle and burdock.

But the agrarian myth was more durable in America where there were no peasants and where agriculture was less central than in older countries such as France where there were peasants and where agriculture provided the heart of the economy. What America wanted, of course, was to have it both ways. So the agrarian myth was a happy one which has only recently been deflated by scholars like Richard Hofstadter, who coined the phrase for what he was to deflate.

Even city-oriented men like Franklin and Hamilton joined in praise of the yeoman farmer. Franklin thought farming the most honest national way to wealth since growth from seed was a miraculous demonstration from God that he approved the farmer's "innocent life and

virtuous industry." The Jeffersonian belief in the small farmer and in
the national need for agriculture lay behind the first moves for Western
expansion and the assertion in his first inaugural address, that our
chosen country had "room enough for our descendants to the hun-
dredth and thousandth generation." A century later Franklin Delano
Roosevelt was still an agrarian at heart.

Food production was not long the only reason for westward expansion. The first mining push was concerned only with the precious metals
which could be minted into currency. The more complex and widespread mining of other metals had to wait for the technological revolution. But the speculative nature of prospecting and the restless life it
engendered were matched by the life of the speculator in land. Thus the
image of the sturdy and virtuous yeoman wandered farther and farther
from the truth. Many of the pioneers were, in effect, not farmers at all
but land speculators, men of Mark Twain's *Gilded Age*, constantly seeking the end of the rainbow, like Squire Hawkins of Obedstown in East
Tennessee. Such men did not always move on because they thought the
land might be more fertile farther west, although many clung to that
illusion even when the green grass of Iowa gave way to the brown grass
of Kansas and both in turn to the sandy desert. But the need to move
on, the dream of the oasis over the hill, the craving for speculative profit, became all mixed up.

Indeed, de Tocqueville noted as early as 1831 that the agricultural
society of America was not really attached to the land but rather to
land values, that even the farmhouse was built on speculation. A century and a quarter later Hofstadter differentiated American rural life
from European by saying that it was not only that the Americans of the
prairies and the plains produced for a market and with no emotional
attachment to the soil but also that they were "so speculative, so mobile,
so mechanized, so 'progressive,' so thoroughly imbued with the commercial spirit." But the myths about the farmer, the country, and the
pioneer persisted nonetheless.

America had no Zola to tell the truth about life on the farm and
among the peasants. As the city gained on the country, as the city
represented machines, immigrants, bewilderment and expense, it looked
even to unemotional people as though there were some menace in the
metropolis. People of the country came to view the city as a godless and
parasitical growth upon the country. The banks to whom the farmer
owed money were there; the immigrant and the foreigner were there;
the urban slum was more apparent than the rural slum; urban immorality was gayer and more constructive but also more visible than what
went on behind the barn and in the hayloft. It was perhaps inevitable

that Bryan would come along to portray farmers not as part of a system but as pastoral victims of a flagrant conspiracy. The farmer felt a bitter discrepancy between the verbal deference he was paid and his economic position.

This boiled later into the struggle associated with the Progressive and Populist movements. The antagonisms had a considerable effect upon the immediate architectural sequels. But in the end, the country and the city were to become alike, the urbanite and the farmer almost undistinguishable.

The myth of the village was at least as durable as the agrarian myth. Again it conjured up a group of self-reliant, tolerant, charitable and understanding citizens, communicating with each other, loving each other, working at a "human" scale, acting, in other words, as village-lovers think all human beings should act. The Georgian village had perhaps some of these characteristics. But that villages can also be narrow, circumscribing, censorious, bitter, was well known to many who had been brought up in them and who could dispel the fogs of sentimental memory. They knew all this well enough before Sinclair Lewis peeled a layer of skin off Gopher Prairie. If the city created anonymity, the village insisted upon surveillance. Yet this myth too died hard and at the Corning, New York, conference in 1951 there were many city men weeping for the villages to which they had no intention of returning.

The promise of the metropolis was that its size might permit it to cater fully to a maximized diversity of interest, both intellectual and aesthetic. For this it exacted the price of impersonality and the unnecessary tax of noise and dirt. Not every one minded the impersonality. For within the metropolis there could be communities of common interest, and the main virtue preached for the village was community interest.

The evolution of American architecture had to take place for the most part in the growing city. But for most American cities industrialization succeeded in retaining the less desirable village characteristics while destroying the village virtues. Thus few American cities were really metropolises. They grew too fast without enjoying the centuries of evolution which had characterized the great centers of Europe and Asia. New York was no real exception. It never became truly urbane. Los Angeles was obviously a city of farmers and milkmaids. In Atlanta the Governor of Georgia was supposed to keep a supply of red mud to smear on his boots when he walked the streets at campaign time; Boston and Philadelphia owed most of their charm to the dignity of their early village remains; and there was no greater rural scene than Broadway at night, enjoying much the same kind of events that used to line the carnival streets of a small town, right down to the frequent chances to see Little Egypt.

At first the architectural problem was affected by the clear antagonisms between the rural people and the city people; one of the problems of the architects, almost all country-born, was to avoid being overwhelmed by the fancied superiorities of the urban European culture and thereby led into a denial of the machine. In good part this happened to Richard Morris Hunt from Brattleboro and, later, to Ralph Adams Cram from Hampton Beach, Charles Follen McKim from Chester County, and Bertram Grosvenor Goodhue from Pomfret. Village-bred architects were trying to deal with country-bred patrons, with rural taste, conservative taste, frugal taste; and it was the agrarian or village mind quite as much as the Puritan inheritance which imposed restraint on the splendor and elegance of American buildings.

Peasants have traditionally made handsome objects and provided the beginnings of art but they have not needed very sophisticated art. American countrymen were more, and unhappily less, than peasants. The anonymous peasant art and craft was replaced for them by the produce of the machine; they lost the aesthetic instincts of the peasant but retained his narrow prejudices. So the agrarian and the village mind became, in the end, the enemy of art and architecture in an America where there were few urbane minds to offer opposition. American architecture, produced by village-bred architects for village-bred clients, has had to breast the adverse stream of rural intuition. It is only in the last quarter-century that most of the leading architects of America have been brought up in cities, while the ultimate arbiters of their work particularly in Congress are still victims of the village background.

But the rural mind caused an even greater difficulty. Americans were not really ready to have great cities. Instinctively they followed the gospel of the country and the village and lived by the country and the village myths. Thus they preferred to travel long distances to suburbs to avoid the responsibility and the privilege of making and paying for great cities. The early suburbs had perhaps some autonomy and some sense of differentiated communal life, but the modern collections of anonymous buildings betray city and country alike — too scattered to provide any of the advantages of the city, too anonymous to provide any of the community spirit of the village. Distilling a process which began in the '80s, Americans, following their rural noses, succeeded in averaging down both the city and the village.

Thus in an extraordinary way the more urbanized America became, the greater the victories the country seemed to win. We tend to think of this as a recent paradox but it became manifest soon after 1860.

2

THE QUARTER-CENTURY BEGAN WITH THE GREAT WAR BETWEEN THE states, a war which had to end with victory for the industrially more powerful North. The North had four times the population of the South, more than twice the number of miles of railroad lines, and almost all the serious manufacturing facilities. The victory was bound to rest with the greater producers and depended at least as much upon their productive skill as upon the bravery of the Union armies, the skill of the Union generals, the statesmanship of Abraham Lincoln, or the righteousness of the cause. Slavery was abolished in name and the South condemned to a period of disintegration before it could start again on a new tack.

After the war the national population soared from 31 million to 55 million. Its center marched farther westward along the 39th Parallel from Chillicothe, Ohio, to a point just inside the eastern Indiana border. The industrial eastern quarter of the nation held a slightly smaller per cent of all the people but still had half and remained the vital heart of the nation. The relative position of the South dropped abruptly, and it virtually ceased to produce great architecture, while the Northern Shermans had destroyed many of its earlier achievements. The agrarian West, including the states of Iowa, Minnesota, Nebraska, Kansas, Missouri, and the Dakotas, was a large gainer and by 1885 had doubled the 7 per cent it held in 1860, marking the high point of immigration into the rich farmlands. The Southwest, whose petroleum reserves were still not much coveted or even imagined, was beginning a slow gain; the Pacific states showed a large proportional gain but were negligible on any absolute basis. The center of the stage, which had been on the Massachusetts-Virginia axis in colonial days and located around New York and Philadelphia for the first half of the century, was now between New York and Chicago or at the farthest St. Louis. The Mississippi River valley was about to become the aorta of the nation. San Francisco and Los Angeles may have been romantic, Portland and Seattle tempting, but their contribution to the national economy or the national culture was not yet serious.

There was still the frontier, small in size, dramatic in the eyes of all, a place where a single second-rate villain or a minor cavalry officer could be blown up to extravagant proportions by the tall tale, romantic for its associations, meaningless for its architecture.

You can wander down the deserted streets of Nevada City or Grass

Valley or Volcano in California, or the later Cripple Creek or Lead-
ville in Colorado, and find buildings or sites (hanging-trees) to cause a
sigh of remembrance. The buildings are sometimes quaint, even bizarre,
and there is always a Chinaman's shack and a simple Assay Office. It is
not hard to feel nostalgia among these backdrops for *High Noon*. But
they have less than nothing to do with American architectural history.
The people of the boom towns built cheaply and clumsily. When they
aimed higher they usually became fantastic. An occasional building like
the old hotel in Georgetown, Colorado, peers through its modern re-
visions to suggest a shadow of dignity; the simple brick of the much
restored Columbia, California, suggests that a rare town may have had
repose. At their best the magnates of the mining frontier imported what
they could afford and recaptured the best recollection they could of
what their surroundings might have been like had they lived in the
East.

While population was growing on the frontier, in the East the movement to the city accelerated. Two fifths of the people now lived in
"cities." New York remained the only city of a million but by 1880 there
were four cities of more than half a million; the expansion of smaller
cities was even more amazing. The nine cities of 100,000 or more of
1860 had become twenty by 1880. It was these larger cities that would
determine the urban patterns. In 1860 one twelfth of all the Americans lived in cities of 100,000 or more, in 1880 one eighth, and in 1900
nearly one fifth. There was a corresponding decrease in the proportion
of farmers but America had not yet become an industrial or a city-domi-
nated society. Almost half of the working population was still on the
farm.

At the beginning of the Civil War the population of the country was
predominantly Anglo-Saxon with a substantial Gaelic minority. Immigration dropped to a trickle during the conflict but along with all the
other expansions of the times built up to a considerable peak as soon as
hostilities ended, with a crest of 800,000 in the year 1882. The immigrants were now a serious element in the *total increase* of population,
accounting throughout the quarter-century for about a third of this
increment. Yet the consequences were not spectacular. Even in the
peak years most of the newcomers were from the British Isles and the
north of Europe, primarily from Germany and Scandinavia, brought to
America in great numbers by the advertising efforts of railroads and land
companies and their agents on the continent of Europe, by the promo-
tion of steamship companies, by the bureaus of immigration set up
in some of the Western states, particularly Wisconsin, Minnesota,
Nebraska and the Dakotas. The German-Scandinavian immigrants

expected to stay on their farms, enlarge them, make them more prosperous, surround themselves with married sons and daughters on adjacent land. They built their barns firmly and for a long time; they were not very interested in the speculative profit to be taken from the land nor in the restless search for richer land the other side of the next range. They provided some stable rural enclaves quite different from those of the frontier and these can be found in many parts of the Midwest, even in Texas. Though Minneapolis had some Swedish or Norwegian characteristics, and Milwaukee or Chicago a mild German flavor, the differences were superficial and did not, save for a brief time, have an important effect on the architecture of the cities.

It was, however, a period of one other significant immigration, entering from China, induced to come by jobs on the railroads and in the mining camps. Though not enormous in numbers and though forbidden after 1887, this immigration provided the first new group that was difficult to assimilate into American life. Poor at first, playing menial roles as servants, mine and railroad workers, cooks, laundrymen, the Chinese were frugal and grew rich. Drawn from coolie, not sophisticated, stock, removed from the traditions of great Chinese art or religion, they developed islands in most of the large cities. In the great seaports where their trading skills could be exercised, they created "Chinatowns" which held both mystery and beauty and even imagined danger to romantic Americans. But such Oriental images as they erected came late in the day and were debased. The benign influence of the East on American taste could be experienced only much later, after Americans had gone to China and Japan and encountered the real thing. In the long run the culture immigrants brought was more modified than the culture to which they came. They all became Americans.

Despite the earlier notable contributions of imported architects like Latrobe, L'Enfant, and Upjohn, despite the work of imported contemporaries like Vaux, Americans were learning more by visiting Europe than from European visitors. It is not so clear that the American architects visiting abroad were looking at the right things or working on the right problems. Not only did they stay away from Manchester and Lille but they were even selective in Paris and London. Before Richard Morris Hunt came to Europe, Cubitt had provided a forceful expression of the train shed of King's Cross Station in London and Duquesney, the provocative Gare de l'Est at Paris, but they interested Hunt less than Lefuel's classic addition to the Louvre.

3

STILL LESS WAS HE OR ANY OTHER INFLUENTIAL AMERICAN ARCHITECT prepared to understand or care about what was happening on the frontiers of science. These frontiers were alive with the magnetic field theory of Maxwell, the electromagnetism of Hertz, the vacuum tubes of Crookes, the hybrids of Mendel, the phase rule of Gibbs, the light-velocity measurements of Michelson, the psychological experiments of Wundt, the tubercle bacillus of Koch and the work of Burbank on the cross-breeding of plants. All these were laying the foundations for extensive immunology, for some of the theory and more of the experimental practice of modern physics, modern psychology and some of modern genetics. They were to move the center of scientific interest first from Paris to England and then to Germany but they seem to have made no impression on nineteenth-century architects or their architecture.

What did make an impression was the theory of Darwin announced just before 1860. Orthodox theologians and scientists locked horns. On the face of it architects were not lively debaters of these issues, at least until the later generation of Louis Henri Sullivan. But like other successful entrepreneurs they were no doubt happy to credit their successes to a strained interpretation of the meaning of the comforting phrase "survival of the fittest" and to expect that architecture too might evolve, even be subject to the processes of "natural selection" so that nothing that was not fitting could survive.

It was a time for many new learned societies and professional organizations, for great expansions in geographic and geologic exploration and of great expansion as well in the university and college systems. The emphasis now lay on increased education for women and still more dramatically on the growth of technological instruction.

Commerce, mining, industry, agriculture — all demanded men trained in science, engineering, and the practical arts. The traditional liberal arts colleges, none too interested in utilitarian education anyway, dealing by habit with theology and teaching, grudgingly with medicine and the law, were doing almost nothing about preparing men for demanding industrial careers. West Point and Rensselaer Polytechnic Institute were inadequate to the national demand. With the founding of the Massachusetts Institute of Technology in 1861, William Barton Rogers, its first President, saw the realization of a hope he had entertained for many years, a prophecy made by his brother Henry a decade earlier, "an important revolution. . . . The old institutions with their vast funds, educating youth at enormous expense, yet fitting them for nothing truly useful or calculated to advance the age, must soon meet the rivalry of institutions which will embody modern ideas."

M.I.T. was only the vanguard. Many followed, and soon: Lehigh, Hampton Institute, Stevens Institute, Virginia Polytechnic, Case Institute, Georgia Institute of Technology. In 1862 Congress passed the Morrill Act for Agricultural Colleges which applied to engineering colleges as well. Not only did this foster the engineering taught at older state universities in Michigan, Minnesota, Iowa and North Carolina, but it stimulated the founding of twenty new state universities including those of California, Illinois, and Ohio. The Sheffield School was established at Yale in 1861 and the first American Ph.D. granted at Yale in the same year. Purdue followed in 1869, Johns Hopkins in 1876 and Leland Stanford, Jr. University in 1885. From the outset Hopkins and Stanford were interested in science. In 1869 Harvard made the revolutionary choice of a layman and a chemist, Charles William Eliot, as its President. That there was a technological wind blowing through American education there could be no doubt. Whether architects would feel it was more questionable.

The question was real despite the fact that the first American architectural schools were located in schools of engineering. Prior to 1860 the only way to qualify for practice in America had been by the English pupilage method, although some design had been taught as part of the science of building. The first independent course in architecture was established at the Massachusetts Institute of Technology in 1866 and schools soon followed in departments of engineering at Cornell (1871) and Illinois (1870). The University of Michigan had had a vacant chair in architecture since the '30s but had never filled it. Columbia established a school in 1881 but the first one to be seated in a deliberately fine arts environment was that at Harvard in 1890.

Most of the architects in America at this time were under the influence of English romanticism, but the engineering faculties, in so far as they taught design at all, leaned on the classics as interpreted by Vignola. Conflict was bound to ensue. Architectural students fled abroad when they could and began their misguided worship of the École des Beaux-Arts in Paris which few of them really ever understood. Had they but known it, American engineers had a fleeting chance to develop in nascent architects an understanding of the relation of technology to architecture. Instead, they themselves ignored the relationship, took refuge from it in aping the classics. Thus the architects were alienated both from engineering and from the growing activity of their times. The alienation left a stubborn residue in the mutual distrust between architects and engineers. It meant that the architects would never really understand their quarter-century, would try to deny what they did understand, and would usually join the anti-scientific and anti-rational forces of the day. The things they built would betray this all too clearly as would the experiments they failed to make. Most of all perhaps the attitude would be betrayed by the contempt in which architects and clients held the most important building types of their generation. Indeed, manufacturing seemed so vulgar as to be beneath the attention of most architects.

The new and coming building types were the industrial and commercial centers and the exchanges for communication and transportation. Technological improvements in the telegraph and expansion of lines caused the demise of the short-lived pony express by 1861, when the wires reached San Francisco. Peter Cooper and Cyrus Field made the Atlantic cable secure in 1866 and by 1885 there were connections with France and Brazil as well. But despite mounting mergers and years of prosperity for Western Union, the telegraph remained for most Americans an instrument of emergency. The wire services began to carry stock exchange reports and news of crisis but they were not material conditioners of architecture.

A more seminal influence in communications was in preparation when Alexander Graham Bell sent his historic message to Mr. Watson on March 10, 1876. The new device caught on rapidly enough after it was demonstrated at the Philadelphia Centennial of the same year. The first exchange was built at New Haven two years later, to serve twenty-one subscribers. By 1884 long-distance telephone connections had been established between New York and Boston. One year after the demonstration there were 1300 commercial telephones. By 1880 there were nearly 50,000 but this was still a little less than one phone per 1000 population, and the telephone was thus still far from being a standard part of American life. But its potential influence on building was enormous. It was one of the devices which collaborated to make life in a big building or a high building possible. It opened many opportunities for planning a city, including imaginative decentralization. But in the beginning, like most innovations, it was treated as a novelty. Jordan Marsh of Boston was quick to install it. It would speed internal communication and it was regarded as good business for a store to be able to say, as witness of its modernity, that it had telephones. For the moment the main effect on the urban landscape was a proliferation of unsightly poles, joined later by those for electricity and still standing gauntly on most rural roads and village and city streets, though we have learned not to notice them.

Just as the intimations of the telephone would be felt only in later buildings, so it was for the automobile whose faint shadows were cast by Otto's four-stroke internal combustion engine of 1876 and Daimler's motorcycle of 1885.

But the bicycle was in full swing; the "safety bicycle" with its two equally sized wheels, and the Dunlop pneumatic tire, created such demand that forty-three manufacturers exhibited bicycles at the World's Columbian Exposition of 1893 and there were perhaps a million bicycles on the American roads. Commentators noted that young people who could not afford carriages and were thus condemned to stoop-sitting could now explore the countryside. We may speculate that if the bicycle had persisted as a feature of urban life, the demands upon American urban architecture might have been quite different, as Amsterdam or Stockholm or even Mackinac Island will suggest. But it was not to be, and no serious provision was ever made in America for the bicycle as a primary means of local transportation.

All the known devices naturally enjoyed improvements, some spectacular, such as the use of turbogenerators in steamships following the invention of Parsons in 1884. The railroads made notable innovations such as the Westinghouse air brake of 1868, the Pullman car of 1864, the tank car of 1865, the refrigerator car of 1875. There were steady improvements in the power and efficiency of locomotives, in the details of car construction, in traffic controls. But the most exciting developments were to be noticed in the lengthening miles of track that now were tying the nation together.

Now Americans left the rivers for the rails. For the railroads it was the time of enormous consolidations; of transcontinental expansions assisted by federal land grants; the time of Leland Stanford and Collis Huntington; of Cornelius Vanderbilt and Jay Cooke and Henry Villard. In 1869, amid a country-wide celebration, the Central Pacific and Union Pacific were joined at Promontory Point in Utah and the first transcontinental link was forged. In the same year Vanderbilt consolidated the lines from New York to Buffalo. The first through car came from the Pacific Coast to New York City the following year. In 1873 Vanderbilt leased the Lake Shore and Michigan Southern and thus completed his line from New York to Chicago just a year and a half after the big Chicago fire. By 1879 he had moved the railroads into the region of finance capitalism when Morgan and Company sold some of his New York Central stock on the London market.

Now what was bad for the railroads was bad for the country. Over-investment in the Northern Pacific by Cooke, which caused his down-fall in 1873, brought on a subsequent September panic in Wall Street. But financial reverses or not, the rails stretched on and by 1883 there were three transcontinental lines, one north and one south of the pioneer venture. In the same year four standard time zones for the nation were suggested and gained by the railroads.

The major effect of the railroads on architecture was naturally to be a transporter of goods, people, and ideas which broke down regional differences. But there was a railroad architecture as well, and it was not good. The rights of way destroyed the unity of most towns, introduced an area of blight, often established a right and wrong side of the tracks. Union Pacific yellow adorned the Western landscape. Refrigerator cars which could carry fresh meat for long distances permitted large meat-packing establishments, cars brought stock over distances cattle could not have been driven and thus stockyard towns were born. Pullman cars fostered some ideas of interior elegance that might better have gone unfostered. And the railroads made rich men who like Huntington and Stanford gave away large fortunes in the founding of great libraries and universities. The railroad men, pirates or not, were among the giant builders of America and many of them were substantial patrons of architecture.

But they were not the only giants. There was Andrew Carnegie, en-tering the steel industry during the time when the American production would multiply ninefold by 1885 from the 190,000 long tons of 1867. After his experiences as bobbin boy in a cotton factory, as a telegraph clerk and operator, as superintendent of the Western Division of the Pennsylvania Railroad, all preparation for his success in only the most general terms, the Scottish immigrant's subsequent moves were but an exaggerated example of what was going on all over America, what was happening to a number of people. After the Civil War he foresaw the demand for iron and steel and started the Keystone Bridge Works, built the Edgar Thomson steel rail mill, bought out the Homestead steel works, and by 1888 controlled a great plant, tributary coalfields and iron mines, a line of lake steamers to carry the ore, and almost five hundred miles of railroad. At the same time Bethlehem Steel had been founded in Pennsylvania (1873) and in 1882 F. W. Taylor, gang boss for the Midvale Steel Company, had introduced scientific manage-ment. By 1901 this large beginning had blossomed in the enormous United States Steel Corporation with a capitalization of almost one and a half billion dollars. Carnegie was clearly one of the leaders of his society.

Another of the great consolidations of the day was going on in oil. Here the operations of John D. Rockefeller and his colleagues had resulted by 1870 in the Standard Oil Company, incorporated in Cleveland. By 1879 this company was producing 95 per cent of the refined oil of the United States. The Standard Oil Trust was organized in 1882.

There were comparable if smaller beginnings headed in the same direction in Minneapolis where the Washburns and the Pillsburys were building flour empires, beginning by adopting in 1874 the Hungarian system of grinding wheat between chilled iron rollers; in Chicago the Union Stockyards opened on Christmas Day, 1865, and the Armour meat-packing establishments were formed thirteen years later; there, too, Montgomery-Ward was rising as the first large mail order house, starting with a single-sheet catalogue in 1872. Appropriately, Horatio Alger published his first book, *Ragged Dick*, in 1867 and advanced the obvious thesis, "There's always room at the top."

By modern standards this great growth did not demand much in the way of physical energy. The 3100 trillion BTU's produced in 1885 were but a tenth of the amount available to Americans in 1955. Of the 3100 trillion of 1885 more than 2800 were produced by the burning of coal. So little energy came at that moment from electricity that it was not even recorded.

So the country was alive with innovation and change, with building and rebuilding, with consolidation and speculation. Enormous fortunes were made and sometimes lost. It was a country of soot and grime, of ugly cuts in the landscape made by the thrusting rails, but it was a busy country, and an exciting country, in which the opportunities for some at least were unlimited.

Observing these new institutions, exulting in the patent successes of the new technology, progressives could not help but look forward to an era of material prosperity and progress. President Daniel Coit Gilman of Johns Hopkins prophesied, "The improvements that result from the employment of steam and iron . . . are so varied that those communities will henceforth be most prosperous and happy where intelligence is allied to Industry and where appropriate education is most widely diffused."

As the period advanced, though, there seemed less reason to be so optimistic about the diffusion of education or the alliance with industry. The laboring force did not seem more prosperous or happier and the towns were certainly getting uglier. Even among those who cared almost nothing about the lot of the working class there were those who did not like what they saw. But men like Charles Eliot

Norton of Harvard or President Noah Porter of Yale, however much they detested and inveighed against the aesthetic and moral temper of the times, could not reverse the ugly utilitarianism of a society made prosperous by mining and industry and made profligate by rapacious victories won by forming exclusive combinations of mutually beneficial monopolies. At best they could offer, at Harvard or Yale, a genteel education, oriented towards European, especially upper-class English, values, capable of producing a Henry Adams who was able to master the ideals and the ways of the agrarian and commercial society that was disappearing but unprepared to understand, much less master, the symbol of his age, the dynamo. Destined to glorify the Federalist period as America's Golden Age, such a product was bound to see his hopes betrayed by the degradation of the democratic dogma. Unfortunately for American architecture, too many architects had the same instinctive revulsion from coal and iron.

The changes of scale were enormous and might have tested any mind to understand. In 1860 nine tenths of the clothes were made at home; twenty-five years later homemade clothing was unimportant. In the 1880s men could still remember when a farm worth $1500 was a sign of prosperity and when a fortune of $50,000 would earn the title of "magnate." But when Carnegie sold his holdings to United States Steel in 1901 his daily income was estimated at $40,000. At the end of the Civil War there were but a handful of millionaires; by 1892 there were more than four thousand.

4

MEANWHILE CHANGES IN URBAN TRANSPORTATION WERE BEGINNING TO make larger cities possible and to change the requirements for an urban building. The first urban mass transportation system had originated in Paris in 1819, while horse-drawn omnibuses had been introduced into New York in 1831. When flanged-wheeled cars riding on rails, pulled still by horses, were adopted in New York in 1832 an important and inflexible conditioner of the city plan had been introduced. By 1890 American cities would employ 105,000 horses and mules to pull 28,000 cars along 6600 miles of track. Despite the importance of cable cars on the hills of San Francisco in 1873 and trials of their remarkable techniques in Washington, New York, Seattle, and a few other cities, notably Chicago, they never accounted for more than one tenth of the urban systems. Electricity for urban transport was introduced by Siemens in Germany in 1881 and caught on rapidly, first in Richmond,

Virginia, but the period was clearly one dominated by the horsecar.

Although the London Underground had been in existence for some time and experiments were conducted in New York in 1867 with a cable-driven elevated railroad on Ninth Avenue, off-street transport had a setback when the cables failed and steam locomotives had to be used as an unsatisfactory substitute. Subways did not come to America for another generation.

The development of fixed lines of urban mass transportation froze the city plans, congested the city centers, determined the kinds of building that would go in the centers. The horse-drawn streetcar made it possible to conceive of a great department store located at the convergence of the various lines. There was a big development of horse-drawn buses in Paris in the early 1850s and in 1852 Boucicaut founded the first department store, the Bon Marché. Lord and Taylor and Jordan Marsh had begun business in America well before this innovation but had confined their business to traditional retail lines, mostly dry goods. But now wider horizons could be viewed, wider markets served; Stewart in New York, Wanamaker in Philadelphia and Marshall Field in Chicago were the first to expand into department stores. Others followed. They created a demand for an entirely new type of building.

But the rails had other effects. The Loop beckoned to any activity that much of the population might patronize. Theaters, museums, central libraries sought to be near the focus of urban travel. Companies that needed many office employees could draw and hold them better if the office building were in the center. The cross-country railroad brought the visitor to the center and his hotel ought also to be nearby.

The urban rails represented a big investment and they were not easily moved. Cars on a street meant a noisy street. So the character of streets was defined, almost irrevocably. People tried to get their houses near a car line but not on it. Small neighborhood shops profited by being on the line. Streets like North Halsted in Chicago or Sixth Avenue in New York were colored by the passing trolley or El and their complexion was not easily changed later even after the rails and the pillars were taken away.

Had there been a pneumatic tire, had there been a smooth pavement that horses would not slip on, had there been a better omnibus so that rails were not needed for comfort, the system might not have been so rigid. The coils of the city might not have been so inexorably laid. For the want of a tire, perhaps a city was lost. It was not inevitable, despite the rail, that the city pattern should have become as desolate as it did; the absence of a rail does not guarantee serenity to a city, as modern

Los Angeles attests. But certainly the urban rails did not make the city problem easier. In this decision about shape through *laissez faire* the other technical services below the surface of the street were also staking out rigid boundaries. The result was seldom attractive and a century later cities were spending colossal sums to free themselves from their self-imposed chains while new and free cities were spending as much on divisive superhighways to impose new ones.

Americans brought up in villages had a hard time deciding how to live in a city. The *American Architect and Building News* of 1876 reported that living in flats was spreading. It had long prevailed in Edinburgh but had been resisted in England. It was of course much more common on the Continent. Paris led the way. "It seems . . . to be the best contrivance of modern times, for the secure and comfortable housing of a large number of people of different conditions, in the narrow spaces of the city." But a year later the same journal noted that New Yorkers were spending an hour each way in transit between home and work. It remarked that the Americans (and the English) in contrast to the French had tended to separate commercial and residential quarters and suggested that we too build dwellings above stores. All this offered American architects an opportunity to provide more urbane cities, had the clients desired them. But Americans generally did not want them. They approved rather the morality of Van Osdel, Potter Palmer's architect, who refused to build "French" apartments, fearing they would destroy family life. Some apartments were built near towns but most Americans clung, as they still do, to the notion of "owning" a single-family and detached "home" — even when the "owning" consisted of so small an equity that it could be wiped out by a small business reverse and the detachment consisted of nothing more than a six-foot strip of grass between neighbors' bedroom windows. Insistence upon the detached dwelling made the cities larger in area, stretched out the lines of public transport to the point where they were too thin. Serving only small communities, they could not operate efficiently and as soon as other means of transportation offered them competition they were in trouble. Some of the ills of the American city of the twentieth century stem from the determination of nineteenth-century Americans not to live like Europeans; some, but not all, for twentieth-century European cities have their problems too.

The urban transportation had a great deal to do with the kinds of building that might be required downtown but not much with what they would be like. Other innovations, seemingly far from architecture, played roles in this. Sholes invented his typewriter in 1868 and

Remington Fire Arms Company purchased it for $12,000 in 1873. Exhibited at the Philadelphia Centennial in 1876, it caught on quickly. Edison invented the mimeograph in 1876. This with the typewriter, the telephone, the electric light bulb had much to say about what urban buildings would become. But since the same innovations were available in European cities which did not make skyscrapers, evidently there was another competitive and symbolic ingredient belonging exclusively to the American scene at the moment.

But the commercial prestige attached to height could not be realized until passenger elevators were available. The idea of elevators was an old one. They had long been employed for hoisting goods to the tops of warehouses, often by horse power. A familiar sight from Clark Street in Chicago had been that of a horse's head thrust out of the window of the top story of such a warehouse. By the middle of the '50s steam-powered grain elevators were common in America and were replacing rope whenever new installations were made. When the future Edward VII visited Chicago in 1860 he was most fascinated by Sturgis and Buckingham's Elevator B, a block from his hotel. A year later Anthony Trollope saw it too and thought it interesting enough to describe in his book, *North America*.

Such elevators were for freight and were sold almost exclusively to warehouses and factories. The change came after Elisha Graves Otis demonstrated his safe passenger elevator at the New York Crystal Palace Exhibition of 1853. It was not long before elevators became as important a part of modern hotel advertising as bathrooms later were to be. When the Tremont House was refitted to be the largest hotel in Chicago, in 1867, its proprietor, John B. Drake, advertised that it had all the modern improvements and illustrated this specifically by only one example, "including a passenger elevator." A year later the Sherman Hotel made the same point. Hydraulic elevators remained dominant for many years and the faster electric elevator was left for the future.

Although the ability to generate electricity by steam had been shown at the Philadelphia Centennial, the Corliss engine which had far less long-range significance stole the show. In 1879 the first experimental central electric power station was tried by the California Electric Light Company in San Francisco; in 1881 alternating current was demonstrated by Gaulard and Gibbs in Paris. In 1882 the Holborn Viaduct electric power station was built in London and the Edison central power station on Pearl Street in New York. But both were direct-current stations and New York's provided current to only eighty-five buildings. Tesla's alternating-current motor did not come until 1888 and there were few central power stations even by then. City streets were generally lighted by gas. In 1862 Davey equipped the lighthouse at Dungeness with an arc light and in 1879 Brush arc lighting systems were installed on the streets of Cleveland and San Francisco. A year later Brush conducted a public demonstration of the system at Wabash, Indiana, and in 1881 one mile of Broadway was so equipped. Electric street lighting was on the way but it came slowly; one often saw a gas lamplighter walking the streets of Chicago as late as 1910.

Domestic lighting by electricity was also on the way. In 1879 Edison got his patent for an economical incandescent bulb and the next year he brought New Yorkers to Menlo Park, New Jersey, on a special train to view his demonstration of three hundred lamps. In the same year the new S.S. *Columbia* advertised that she had a five-candle-power lamp in each stateroom. By 1882 Edison plants had been installed in 150 factories and residences. Perhaps some of the householders used them only just long enough to adjust the wicks of their kerosene lamps. No doubt many of the venturesome factory and store owners were adding electric lamps more to show progressiveness than to have better light. There were not many electric light bulbs in 1885 when Welsbach brought out his new gas mantle which postponed the decline of gas lighting for many years. In 1881 there were not many more than 5000 electric lamps in use, only one tenth the number of telephones; the number doubled in a year and increased dramatically in the next four years so that 200,000 lamps were in use in 1886. But the numbers were still small, the use sketchy until 1890. Indeed, Sullivan's use of electric bulbs to light the Chicago Auditorium at the end of the decade was thought a daring novelty.

Innovations in building techniques were more quickly adopted. By 1867 cast-iron columns had reached their peak in the Paris show. In 1871 Jules Saulnier built the first building of true iron skeleton in the modern sense, at Noisiel-sur-Marne near Paris. It was widely published. But the problem of building intelligently with iron and later with steel was not solved overnight or by a single inventor, whether the claim be made for Leroy S. Buffington of Minneapolis or William Le Baron Jenney of Chicago.

The city of Chicago did offer a specially fertile field for the innovations of the moment. Having burned down in 1871, it needed a great deal of building in a hurry. During that fire hundreds of tons of pig iron in the McCormick reaper yards had melted and flowed in rivulets and this made the builders realize that iron buildings were not necessarily fireproof. The same fire had shown that a "fireproof building" like the Grannis Block, made of heavy mill construction, could burn down and this had caused a shock. Whether Major William Le Baron

Jenney was forced to the steel framing of the upper part of the Home
Insurance Building in 1883 by a bricklayers' strike, or whether, as
Henry Ericsson suggests, Jenney got the idea from the accident of
laying a heavy book on Mrs. Jenney's wire birdcage, we may leave to
the romancers. In any event the steel frame and the notion of using
stone or brick, not to support loads, but to form curtain walls and to
fireproof the metal, were born at this time. The story of their adoption
is the most rehearsed of any in American architecture.

In a short time the engineering, if not the architectural, possibilities
of the frame were realized throughout America. The chance to use them
often was augmented by the development in 1878 of the Thomas
alkali process for making steel since this open-hearth method proved
more effective than the Bessemer furnace.

As the frames came along, the cast-iron fronts had to go. From
Bogardus on, they had permitted great speed of construction but
they were not so fire-resistant as people had hoped. Cast iron had
brought a certain dignity and even elegance to an age in which ele-
gence and dignity were rare. The skyscraper as it evolved from Jenney's
preliminary use would not always acquire an equal dignity.

Reinforced concrete, one of the great building materials of modern
times, was not yet available. Natural cements were still the most useful
and continued to be common until the end of the century. They were
less dependable than artificial Portland cements were to become and
they were not available in large quantities. The manufacture of artificial
Portland cement began in the United States at Lehigh, Pennsylvania,
in 1875 but a decade later the material was still not an important ingredient in building construction. Indeed, it could not be until a great
deal of experiment had been conducted. Concrete is strong in compression and weak in tension. The Romans had used their pozzolanic cements only in compression systems of arches and domes and these forms
were not always suitable for building needs of the nineteenth century.
Using concrete in blocks simply offered an alternative masonry material
no more plastic than a brick. Perhaps it was the French gardener,
Monier, who in 1868 first thought of using wire mesh to strengthen the
concrete of some water basins he was casting. In any event, the idea was
born at about that time and it could not be worked out for serious building construction in a hurry.

A writer in the *American Architect and Building News* for 1878 noted
a book by Thaddeus Hyatt accounting for some new experiments with
Portland cement concrete and iron, and said, "If a floor could really
be composed" using iron to take the tensile strength only, "a monolith
of indestructible concrete enclosing iron ties, in which the strains and

resistance could be calculated with as much certainty as in a floor of brick arches between iron beams, but requiring only one-third the iron, we might consider that the perfect fire-proof floor had been attained."

Thus the society of 1860-1885 was one in which railroads were the dominant transportation, gas the dominant lighting, the telegraph the dominant means of fast communication, wall-bearing buildings and cast-iron fronts the dominant ways of building important buildings, the horsecar the dominant means of urban travel. Iron was more common than steel, natural cement more common than artificial. But in this time electric lights, telephones, electric streetcars, elevators, steel frames, fire-proofing, and reinforced concrete were all suggested. In terms of the changes of daily life they implied, the innovations of 1860-1885 were explosive.

5

AS AGRARIAN INFLUENCE DIMINISHED AND MORE WEALTH WAS ASSOCIATED with business, industry took on an added responsibility for the national welfare. You heard less scorn of merchants, bankers, and manufacturers. Once men had seemed blessed of God when they succeeded, for God would not bless the unrighteous with success. But as Calvinism became less convincing, a successful man found it harder to believe that his successes had been ordained by God. A misconstruction of Darwin might be substituted. If "survival of the fittest" could be construed broadly, then the man who went to the top was but a justification of the laws of nature while the poor man in general was obviously unfit, a man for whom "a litany might be sung" but who was not much to be regretted. "The growth of a large business," John D. Rockefeller, Jr., told a Sunday School class later, "is merely the survival of the fittest."

It is not surprising that Herbert Spencer was given an ovational banquet at Delmonico's when he came to America in 1882. Even the barons with the larger consciences admired him. In 1868 Andrew Carnegie thought that the amassing of wealth was the worst sort of idolatry. He thought that if he continued to lavish most of his thought on the making of the most money in the shortest time, he would be degraded beyond hope of permanent recovery. But after he had misinterpreted Herbert Spencer's misinterpretation of Darwin he proclaimed that he had "got rid of theology and the supernatural" and "found the truth of evolution. 'All is well since all grows better' became my motto, my true source of comfort." The new millionaires continued variations on the theme well into the oncoming century.

The fortune-makers were of many types. There were sharp bargainers of character like Andrew Carnegie, who thought that higher wages and contented employees paid good dividends, who valued his Lord Rectorship of St. Andrews above a favorable listing at the hands of Ward McAllister's social twenty-five, who was prouder of his friendship with Gladstone and Matthew Arnold than of his relation to George Pullman and J. P. Morgan, much as he admired these business leaders. In the middle ground were the rough, tough, public-scorning Vanderbilts, pouring thousands of dollars of "absolute water" into the New York Central, but taking risks, building the railroad, and building America. There were socially registered speculators like Jay Gould, capable of selling fraudulent stock in the Erie Railroad and a consort of Jim Fisk, the one-time circus hand, hotel waiter, peddler, dry-goods salesman, stock-broker, and consistent briber of legislatures and judges. There were bosses like Tweed, for whom Gould was a prominent and generous bondsman. The most serious enterprises could play fast and loose with economic morals. The owners of the Union Pacific could engineer the Crédit Mobilier to give shares to more than one Congressman and resign under fire although the House merely censured its own culprits. Besides the Crédit Mobilier there was the Whiskey Ring of revenuers and distillers which made millions by frauds on internal revenue taxes in St. Louis. There were the Star Route frauds which involved Senator Dorsey of Arkansas and employees of the Post Office Department. Sometimes the waves of scandal washed the feet of U. S. Grant, the President himself. But hardly anyone except Boss Tweed was ever convicted and it was the temper of the times to feel rather sympathetic with the charming and wealthy scoundrels and to wish them the light sentences they usually got. The charming and wealthy scoundrels were, alas, often the best patrons of art and architecture and the quality of their patronage was not proportioned by their morality or lack of it.

But in the '60s there were already those like John Bascom who worried about the possible corruption of the millionaires, reiterated Downing's moral concern, asked whether a house with forty rooms could provide a family with a "pure" life. In his *Aesthetics, or Science of Beauty*, published in 1862, he railed against extravagance and luxury with a puritanism unexcelled even in the seventeenth century: "Extravagant dimensions and elaborate ornament bespeak an expenditure utterly uncalled for by the end to be reached . . . it speaks of an eager, selfish gluttony of enjoyments . . . A baronial mansion implies superior rights, deep-seated hereditary inequalities . . . The dwelling which shows the lavish prodigality of fortune toward a favorite teaches the immorality of chance government and of irresponsible expenditure." Here was a note indicating that further excesses would arouse voices of reform, a preview of positions to be taken in later days by social critics like Thorstein Veblen. A report of the Senate Committee on Education and Labor as early as 1885 spoke of legislation to put a ceiling on the amount a millionaire might spend for a house.

Despite the long hours of work, the terrible working conditions, and the poor wages in most of the new industries, labor organizations were only beginning to be effective. Until Samuel Gompers organized the Federation of Organized Trades and Labor Unions of the United States and Canada at Pittsburgh in 1881, most of the efforts of the various labor groups were politically oriented and consistently abortive. Strikes did begin, grew more violent and occasionally successful. Conflict reached a momentary peak in 1886 when 610,000 workers were out with a monetary loss of 35 million dollars, which was enormous for the times. But in all this labor gained little. Gompers had done away with the Utopian political proposals of earlier groups, had introduced pragmatic policies of a gradualist sort, declining to define any ultimate ends but working on the problems of the here and now. Yet even he was not very successful. The Gompers Federation began to lose strength soon after it was founded and in 1884, when the eight-hour day became its issue, the membership was cool.

Moreover, the theories of Marx and Engels proved of small interest to most American laborers and the first international organizations of the European socialists were no more exciting to them. Forty years after the *Communist Manifesto*, twenty years after *Das Kapital*, the gospel was still not powerful in America. Still less influential were the recommendations of the British Fabians, seeking to reconstruct society in accordance with moral possibilities. This lack of interest in communism or socialism went hand in hand with an apathy, even among labor leaders, towards efforts at public or any other form of communal housing. Lewis Mumford was not exaggerating a great deal when he wrote, ". . . at no period in American history has the working class in America been more desperately enslaved."

In contrast, a few wealthy men in New York engaged in increasingly extravagant and snobbish actions. The Saratoga race track was opened by John C. Morrissey. The foppish Ward McAllister organized the Patriarchs, a group of twenty-five socially impeccable gentlemen who were prepared to censor the guest lists for social gatherings in Manhattan and who played this trivial role for years. Lawn tennis was introduced but not on public courts. James Gordon Bennett, Jr., brought polo to his friends. William K. Vanderbilt held his extraordinary fancy dress ball in March, 1883.

The architects' social choice was clear enough. They were more interested in building mansions for Vanderbilt than railroad stations for him. They preferred a McAllister to a Gompers every time. With a few striking exceptions architects have not been great friends of the poor or even very interested in the common man or in the waves of reform that have swept the land. They have not often manned the barricades of causes.

Indeed, all through the period the *American Architect and Building News* was clucking nervously about the labor situation. In 1877 and 1878 it was particularly apprehensive. It gave accounts of trade unionism in London and expressed fear for its spread. It thought that labor revolts indicated a "gradual consolidation of the men into a united class with class-feelings, class-prejudices, class-aims and class-politics." Such a class, it believed, might become completely stratified and might be used as a tool of the politically ambitious or the unscrupulous. It did not ask whether McAllister's twenty-five were stratified; did not consider that there was danger in the cohesive unity and power of Vanderbilt's associates. Instead it asserted that society existed by the poise of a great many nicely balanced forces. Perhaps unions did not at once menace this balance but complete unity of the workers' classes acting according to their leaders' recklessness or to mob thinking could. "It is not much, perhaps, that architects can do, but it becomes them since they continually have to do with workmen, to keep some watch on them, to understand as well as they can their aims and feelings, and to be awake to what good influences it may be in their own power to favor."

Although the time is generally regarded as high, wide and handsome, the fact is that many important reform movements got their quiet start in this boisterous era. The labor movement was about to become serious. It was also a time when many legislative controls had their inception. The first tenement law was passed in New York City; the Civil Service Commission was established; state boards of health were organized in some of the leading Eastern states; Illinois, Wisconsin, and Iowa created railroad and warehouse commissions with power to fix minimum rates and to prohibit discrimination, and this right to regulate was held by the Supreme Court to exist in the states. Women's suffrage amendments were introduced and defeated but in 1879 women at least could practice before the United States Supreme Court. Societies for the prevention of cruelty to animals and later to children, for barring obscene literature from the mails, for national prohibition, for divorce reform had their start. Anthony Comstock was well known; Brigham Young was arrested on polygamy charges; Moody conducted his spectacular evangelistic revivals. The first pure-food laws were enacted in

New York, New Jersey, Michigan, and Illinois. An intimation of another future set of controlling actions was given in the publication in the *Atlantic Monthly* of Henry Demarest Lloyd's attacks on the Standard Oil Company in 1881, called "The Story of a Great Monopoly." With political and social reform there were new bursts of charity such as gifts to hospitals and universities. Characteristically the Salvation Army and the Red Cross were founded in this time. In 1890 Andrew Carnegie endowed his first American public library at Allegheny and this was an event of great importance to the ultimate culture of America if not to American architecture.

6

THE CULTURE OF THE MOMENT, EFFERVESCENT AS IT WAS, NEEDED TO BE understood by the American artists if understanding was possible. The painters were characteristic. Vedder, Homer, Eakins, William Morris Hunt, Inness, Whistler were not necessarily inferior in absolute skill to their European contemporaries, Manet, Monet, Renoir, the young Cézanne, Van Gogh and Seurat. The differences went deeper. The Europeans were more imaginative and daring experimenters. Millet's approaches were abandoned by Monet, who discovered that a town or a city could also supply a landscape, and only Pissarro remained faithful to the pastorale. But a more important step was the one from *pleinairism* to impressionism. Light became pure color but the conventions of perspective or correct proportions were not destroyed. Even in the work of Whistler and Inness there was nothing so bold as this. Experimental and advanced as they seemed to most Americans or to Ruskin, they were nonetheless following in the steps of old Courbet, whose technique more than his revolutionary activities was what interested Whistler.

It must not, of course, be imagined that European society as a whole or European critics generally took kindly to the new experiments, either. No society after the Renaissance has taken kindly to the new experiment in art until long after it has been successful, or at least so the artists like to think. Both Manet and Monet were attacked. There had to be a *Salon des Refusés*. But this is not the point. The European painters were at the cutting edge of experiment in painting, the Americans were living in the past and when they came nearer to the present there is no suggestion that they were anything but derivative.

Neither group could be said to be avid as documentarians of their own day. It could be argued that Winslow Homer's pictures of prisoners during the Civil War or of the parasoled ladies standing on the cliffs at

Long Branch, New Jersey, were just as observant of a society as Degas'
pictures of ballet dancers or of the orchestra at the opera, or the cotton
office in New Orleans, or other French painters' pictures of each other
in boats or on picnics. Eakins's careful painting of *The Gross Clinic*
might be called an effort to understand and portray one element of the
advancing technology of the day. But it can hardly be placed on the
same footing with the general discovery by the Europeans of the city as
a proper landscape and more particularly with the announcement by
Monet that the train shed and the locomotives and the smoke and
steam of the Gare St. Lazare were suitable subjects for an important
painter in the age of coal. Little protest would be found in either group
outside of Daumier unless one wanted to call Van Gogh's *Potato Eaters*
of 1885 a form of protest. On the contrary, when American painters did
come near to industry they made it look more than presentable. An-
shutz's painting of *Steelworkers' Noontime*, for example, offers a bland
description of a contented group of men amiably flexing their bare
biceps in the sunshine. Finally, though there were counterparts in Europe to Vedder's fantastic *Lair of the Sea Serpent* or to the romantic
classical allegory *The Flight into Night* prepared by William Morris
Hunt for the State Capitol in Albany in 1875, the Europeans held them
in less esteem. They might even have suggested that Hunt's Albany mural with its rearing horses and gods and goddesses perched atop cumu-
lus clouds was an absurd statement for the halls of the capitol of New
York State at the end of the nineteenth century, however good its
brushwork, however ideal its composition.

The American painters, indeed, had little affection for the whole
American scene and seemed to love only those parts of it which were
reminders of a past that was quite clearly slipping away, or romantic
fragments of a West which occupied the place of science fiction in our
day, or enclaves in the halls of Vanderbilt where the throbbing pulse of
America outside could not be heard. Thus though this was precisely the
time when most of the famous art museums of America were established, they were evidently designed for the art of history and not the
art of the day. If prophecy were to be sought in the American arts, it
was better to examine the photographs of Muybridge or Matthew Brady
than the wistful children of Mary Cassatt or the haunted nightmares
of Albert Ryder. To the artists the world was evidently a troublesome
one, full of manufactured goods in which the machine had replaced
the hand. Did this foretell the destruction of the "beautiful"? Were
machine-produced and machine-ornamented articles implicitly ugly?

In 1876 the Centennial at Philadelphia made the question more explicit. The Corliss engine was a prominent exhibit and its calibrated,

sheer lines were much admired; but nearby there were exhibits of manufactured bric-à-brac suggesting only that machine tools might be a
bountiful source of meretricious ornament.

But even if the industrial designers of 1885 had been more skillful
than they were, even if they had not tried to clothe sewing machines in
classic capitals, still there would have been a gap between them and the
architects and painters just as there is today. If the serious artists failed
to understand or to want to be a part of their new society, others
would.

With the exception of Twain and Whitman, American literature
stood largely on the same grounds, remote from the incipient technology, inferior to European letters. To cite parallel productions of the
same years is not exactly fair but not without meaning: *Crime and Pun-
ishment* versus *Snow-Bound*, *Anna Karenina* and *L'Assommoir* versus
The American; *Also Sprach Zarathustra* versus *The Story of a Country
Town*; *Ghosts* versus *The Celebrated Jumping Frog of Calaveras County*
and *Uncle Remus*. Europe was older, more aware of the changes that
the industrial revolution was bringing, but the physical and economic
conditions in a French mine were not much worse than those in America; yet it was the Frenchman, Zola, who wrote *Germinal* and there was
no serious American counterpart in this generation. The fact was that
American novelists and poets, except the radicals, had hardly known
how to come to grips with the businessman after Hawthorne had tried
and failed — and they may not know yet. Surely they knew that in business lay part of the American strength, even part of the dream. But they
could not bring themselves to try to understand it and left it to muck-
rakers while they cultivated American regionalism. Mark Twain, one
of the greatest, demonstrated clearly enough the new democracy's contempt for authority but like others he was more complete when adorn-
ing a past than in welcoming a new age. *Huckleberry Finn*, the regional
classic, may be eternal. *The Gilded Age* which dealt with larger social
forces is ephemeral. On any terms, as Edward Chase Kirkland has said,
"Business affairs and activities were dirty, dusty and personal and occupied a low priority in any absolute scheme of values. Ideas on religion
and politics might be literary material; conceptions about making a living were not such stuff as books and articles were made of."

In one sense some American writers tried to come to terms at least
with a new audience. Twain asserted that he never attempted "in even
one single instance . . . to help cultivate the cultivated classes." Even
William Dean Howells, who did not scorn the cultured, thought that
the more important audiences were among the masses. At the head of
the list of those who preached the notion of art for all, especially for the

common man, was Walt Whitman, whose affection for the crowd never abated. He at least could see in a glass works a paean to the colors of the glowing molten mass of silica, could hear a melody in the "see-saw music of the steam machinery," could sense architecture in the "vast, rude, halls, with immense play of shifting shade, and slow-moving currents of smoke and steam, and shafts of light," as he wrote in *November Boughs.* He was not offended by the stench of steel and did not try to look the other way. Indeed he spoke of "effects that would have fill'd Michel Angelo with rapture." No American musician at this time had found a comparable stimulus to his music; no significant painter had yet seen the beauty in technology and industry and their potentials for humanity. The question for architecture was whether it too might have a Whitman. No influential architect was prepared for the role; nor did society clamor that any one should essay the part.

In retrospect not available to the architect of the time, it seems clear enough what the architectural problems of the age were. First, there had to be an understanding of the new technology and a skill in taking advantage of it, a way of making the most of elevators, glass, steel, fireproofing, new foundation schemes, typewriters, telephones, and electric lights. Second, there was the problem of accepting the new building types as significant and therefore of developing them ardently and excellently, types such as office buildings, railroad stations, large banks, department stores. Beyond this was the clearly impending need of being more foresighted than this and thinking about new forms for cities, housing and schools. Last, and possibly most difficult of all, there was the question of developing an aesthetic expression commensurate with the importance of the new technology and the new culture, which required in the first place an understanding of the times and in the second an enthusiasm for them. One would not do without the other.

In a general way architects did understand that all these problems existed, except perhaps the problem of the city. With greater or less success they made some effort to solve each of them. But surveying the scene of industrial might and millionaires' fortunes, they most often envisioned themselves in the role of cultural impresarios, experts in matters of taste, cultivated in all matters of European fashion, ready to provide the stage where the merchant prince might strut. They allied themselves not with the new institutions, not with the scientist and engineer, but with his critic; not with Daniel Coit Gilman and Thomas Huxley but with Noah Porter and James McCosh and Charles Eliot Norton, who attempted to polish the raw edges of industrial society with European grace and sentiment. The architects, no less than the clients, sought to ignore the ultimate sources of wealth, in industry, with the consequent conflict between a technology underlying prosperity and an art that ignored or denied the technology. They were themselves divided as was the society. They did not know whether they coveted an advance or a retreat; they were not sure they could preserve all the serenities of the old while enjoying all the practical advantages of the new.

Their indecision seemed to make them no more receptive to warnings from the more heavily industrialized countries of Europe. Nor were they willing to forego reviving the old, castoff architectural scenery of Romanesque France and Gothic England. No one in America, especially those who were intent on importing European styles, seems seriously to have believed the Frenchman Viollet-le-Duc who prophesied an architecture of metal and glass, nor did they act upon the suggestion of Sir Joseph Paxton, whose Crystal Palace alerted the English historian, James Fergusson, to note that "at a time when men were puzzling themselves over domes to rival the Pantheon, or halls to surpass those of the Baths of Caracalla," it was wonderful to see the magnificent conservatory made in iron and glass; it was, Fergusson said, "the most fairy-like production of Architectural Art that had yet been produced."

The fact was obvious: the first exhibition of the industrial world, held in 1851, had been inaugurated together with a new architecture. Other Englishmen also greeted the new style enthusiastically. An anonymous writer of a book bearing the significant title *Examples of the Architecture of the Victorian Age*, which appeared in 1862, praised new railroad stations, especially that at Munich, and the Crystal Palace: "We consider that iron and glass in conjunction have succeeded in giving a distinct and marked character to the future practice of architecture." Two years earlier, the rather eccentric architect and writer, Thomas Harris, published a book, *Victorian Architecture*, which joyfully embraced the argument that a new society requires a new architecture. "This is an age of new creations," Harris exclaimed, "steam power and electric communication [are] entirely new revolutionizing influences. So must it be in Architecture . . . We must no longer grope about amongst the usages of former ages, but . . . chisel out for ourselves new expressions, being content with simple, and, it may be, rude achievements at the outset."

But these calls to boldness in a new age no more alerted Americans than they inspired Englishmen. Each remained content to fritter away his opportunity by improvising on Gothic and Renaissance themes. Thus a curious paradox underlay the architecture: the age that proclaimed their art of building to be concerned with beauty *and* social improvement refused to treat the centers of mining and manufacture as architectural problems, even though they were the ultimate sources of prosperity and ultimately might even become, through neglect, sources of powerful social protest. The paradox, it is true, alarmed several people. It alarmed Ruskin; it provoked William Morris to start reforms in design and education; and it encouraged Charles Eliot Norton to inaugurate housing reforms, to write about the need for better architecture and to take active part on building committees. But the suggestion they made for solving the paradox was to roll back history, bring about a moral reform, and build once again a handicraft architecture. That answer was all too acceptable to trustees of institutions and even to business managers.

7

IN EARLIER DAYS, AS WE HAVE SEEN, FACTORY TOWNS BUILT AT LOWELL or Pawtucket had been communities; they were small, complete villages. Community functions were given proper spaces and special locations. Now this planning sense was lost and with it architectural scale. In the coal towns, the oil towns, the mining villages there were only shacks, wooden stores, saloons, warehouses and the necessary or abandoned rigs and pitheads. Foundries whose sequence of operations gave some incentive to plan presented a better order. This was true, for example, of iron and steel units such as Carnegie's Lucy Furnace of 1872 in Pittsburgh. But these had no architectural character either and an industrialist would have thought any one crazy who suggested they should. Most small manufacturing was done in old warehouses and mill buildings made of wood and brick.

The advances made in industrial architecture at this time were more technological than social or aesthetic. Following the series of factory reform laws enacted during the '60s and '70s, mills were forced to meet minimum state requirements for health and safety. Still, good design of a producing unit was not yet identified with advertising and prestige; nor were the social, economic, and political pressures to provide amenities for workers exerting any great force.

Industrial architecture consisted, then, simply of those buildings needed for the storage of raw materials and the manufacture, storage and distribution of finished products all on a very simple basis. The mill engineer's chief objective was to put together an inexpensive, stable, fire-resistant building which would withstand the motions of heavy, vibrating machinery, to protect this from the dangers of fire or boiler explosion, and to keep the whole arrangement compact so that materials could be moved without long hauls and so that power could be transmitted by pulleys and belts with minimal loss. He met these objectives by using "slow-burning" or "mill" construction whose brick walls enclosed a frame of thick wooden columns, carrying heavy wood beams and plank floors. Later the wooden columns were replaced by cast iron.

Occasional attempts to give architectural character to such mills ought not to mislead us into thinking that they were common. Just as Paul Nelson in the twentieth century drew theoretical hospitals, so young architects like Hapgood and Whiting drew factories in the nineteenth; these were speculative if not completely theoretical designs for ideal mill buildings. More rarely a successful architect, such as Thomas Tefft, whose early brick factory at Cannelton, Indiana, evoked praise during the '80s, attempted to create industrial architecture. But these exceptional forecasts should not confuse us about the general situation. Neither the client nor the architect regarded factory architecture as a subject fit for a first-class and fashionable artist. The view was held by Charles Follen McKim and Richard Morris Hunt and even by Henry Hobson Richardson despite the fact that he did design railroad stations and warehouses and proclaim that he craved to design a Mississippi River steamboat. Factory owners did not ask great architects to work on their problems; great architects might not have deigned to try. Instead the owners who tried any dressing up at all were content to borrow architectural or decorative trappings, to apply mansard roofs and corbel moldings, or to trick out a factory in the fashionable French baroque of the Louvre pavilion as they did at the New Harmony Mills in Cohoes, New York.

Some recent writers have praised the early industrial architecture, and have pointed out aspects that were, indeed, admirable. Some farms, silos, elevators, roundhouses and other specimens of "anonymous architecture" contain such elements. The old grain elevator or mill does stand out before the sky of a flat prairie. Often such buildings have an elemental geometry such as the rhythmically repeated cylinders of a large grain storage unit, built solely for the purpose of storage, stripped of everything that does not contribute to the construction or the work to be done. They photograph even more marvelously against a thunder-filled sky or with the long shadows of dawn or dusk. They are, seen thus, modern enough to please a Le Corbusier or a Giedion or even less sophisticated men who trouble to look at them. But when examined as a whole they reward the scrutiny less frequently. This is even more certain about the seductions of pictorial details; the camera can abstract from an undistinguished whole a rich pattern of bricks or a suggestive rhythm of windows; but collections of such pictures are often false to

the whole of the building, to the relation of machines and human beings in the spaces that lie behind the photographic fragments. Thus to
worship the current fetish of anonymous architecture resolutely is to be
led into a kind of romanticism about past builders and clients that does
not tell the truth about the actual aspirations of their period. The plain
fact is that almost no industrialist then regarded the seats of production
as aesthetically significant or even thought much about their other cultural significances; nor did his architect when he had one.

This becomes clearer when we observe the site planning of the new
factories that rose after the Civil War. When compared with the earlier
ones they seem, in the ensemble, to have disregarded the architectural
possibilities. We may recall that the early factories such as the ones at
Lowell were set in large spaces, laid out on axes, and that such schemes
persisted as late as 1850. But thirteen years later Lowell was crowded.
Transportation had not been developed to bring workers to an out-of-
town factory. So the old buildings were kept for economic reasons
while the needed new ones were simply crowded onto the same sites.
Bleak canyons, spaces choked of air and light, deprived of vista, were
inevitable.

The steady degradation of housing for the employees was equally
characteristic. The older paternalism had prompted industrialists to attract workers, especially farm women, with offers of comfortable houses
in a community containing churches, schools, libraries, recreation halls,
even lyceums. Now the utopianism of the early mill village was replaced
by real-estate exploitation; the industrialist went by on the other side;
the laborer found only row housing of inferior quality, the tenement,
the slum. In the big cities the exterior alleviations for the slum were
harder to come by and pressure for reform of the physical conditions
of the dwellings was steadier. But even then improvements such as those
made in the railroad and dumbbell apartments of New York were
minimal. They left a fine vision of misery for the cameras of Jacob Riis
and other reformers of the next generation.

George Pullman, who was an unusual industrialist, tried to do something much better when he built a whole town at Pullman, Illinois,
but he was near to unique. Even then, as we shall see, the temper of
the times was such that his experiment failed in a short while. The
significant generalization about American architecture of 1860-1885 is
that the most needed building types of the period, that is, the factory
and its supporting housing, were excluded from architecture altogether.

If industrial architecture and housing lay outside the responsibilities
of the architect this was no longer so for centers of commerce, distribution, management and professional services. The architect soon was

Cambridge, Massachusetts, Memorial Hall,
1866-1878, William Ware and
Henry Van Brunt, archs.

HARVARD NEWS OFFICE

.TER FLEISCHER, HARVARD NEWS OFFICE

Cambridge, Massachusetts,
Memorial Hall, interior

P. B. WIGHT, "NATIONAL ACADEMY OF DESI

New York, National Academy of Design, 1865, Peter Bonnett Wight, arch.

Hartford, Connecticut, Trinity College, 1876, William Burges, arch.

TRINITY COLLEGE, "CATALOGUE,"

"AMERICAN ARCHITECT AND BUILDING NEWS," 1877

Cincinnati, Ohio, John Shillito Company, 1877, J. McLaughlin, arch.

Baltimore, Maryland, Johns Hopkins Hospital, Isolation Ward Pavilion, ca. 1888, John Shaw Billings, engineer

JOHNS HOPKINS HOSPITAL

MIKE ROBER

Eureka, California, Carson House, 1886, Samuel and Joseph Newson, archs.

BROWN BROTHERS

New York, W. K. Vanderbilt House, 1881, R. M. Hunt, arch.

Washington, D. C., State, War and Navy Building (Executive Offices),
1871-1875, Alfred B. Mullett, arch.

ABBIE ROWE, COURTESY NATIONAL PARK SERVICE

BRIAN SHAWCROFT

Boston, Trinity Church (John Hancock Building in
background), 1872-1877, Henry Hobson Richardson, arch.

Boston, Trinity Church, interior (chancel remodeled by
Maginnis and Walsh, 1938)

ANDRÉ SNOW

WALTER FLEISCHER, HARVARD NEWS OFFICE

Cambridge, Massachusetts, Harvard University,
Austin Hall, 1883, Henry Hobson Richardson, arch.

Cambridge, Massachusetts, Harvard University,
Austin Hall, detail

WALTER FLEISCHER, HARVARD NEWS OFFICE

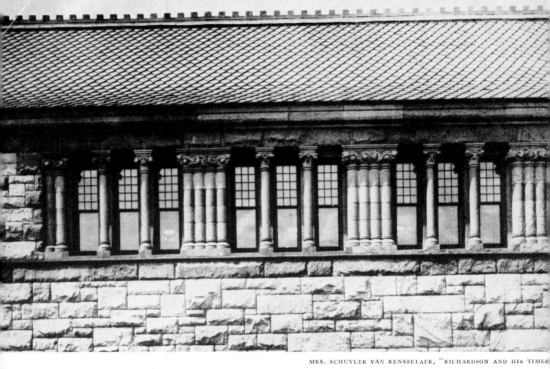

MRS. SCHUYLER VAN RENSSELAER, "RICHARDSON AND HIS TIMES

North Easton, Massachusetts, Library, 1881, Henry Hobson Richardson, arch.

Chicago, Illinois, Marshall Field Wholesale Warehouse, 1885-1887,
Henry Hobson Richardson, arch.

CHICAGO ARCHITECTURAL PHOTOGRAPHING CO.

identified in the public mind as a creator of symbols of commercial prestige, of lures for catching patrons. He was supposed to make banks seem substantial and reliable, stores enticing, offices imposing. Following English practice, the banks emulated Barry's Travellers Club and Reform Club in London. They were modestly monumental buildings designed to resemble small Italian Renaissance palaces such as the one Leopold Eidlitz created in his American Exchange Building of 1857-1859 in New York. Alternatively and following a turn in England towards the medieval, they appeared in Gothic dress, popularized by Russell Sturgis at Albany and Frank Furness at Philadelphia (Provident Trust Company, 1879).

This commercial demand for architectural advertising rapidly destroyed the older type of coherent shopping district. There, as in the Washington Stores in New York (1845), identical small units had provided a homogeneous pattern with uniform bays, floor lines, windows, all under one roof. Stores were distinguishable by modest displays and emblems or by discreetly lettered names. Now even the small retail store departed from this pattern. Thus Bruce Price tried to attract attention to a small store in Wilkes-Barre by protruding a large show window from a deep recess and surmounting it with richly ornamental brick details. Stores demanded show windows surrounded by ornamental frames. Even architects whose instinct was literally archeological were tempted to become adventuresome, to capitalize upon the long spans and thin mullions obtainable with iron to invent vigorous modern ornament. The Noel and Saurel Building (Crosby Street, New York, 1864-1865) by Detlef Lienau shows how far even an historically oriented architect was willing to go to achieve a good display area and distinctive decoration.

Although commerce encouraged architects to cherish such new ideas, few moved much farther than Lienau. One could satisfy most commercial clients and their buying publics by forcing the new institutions into older architectural plans and fashioning new materials to resemble older ones. The shopping area developing in New York between City Hall and Twenty-third Street was made up of fashionable retail shops and large department stores. The goods were set out on counters with the prices clearly marked. The whole atmosphere of such establishments called for a different relation between buyer and salesman than the whispered confidences prevailing in the small shops of a nineteenth-century Savile Row. Buildings to serve this sort of enterprise needed large display windows on the ground floor combined with inviting, almost grasping, entrances. They demanded large well-lighted floors for displaying goods in separated areas. They needed storage

space. Over all they needed to create the atmosphere of a fashionable
bazaar, incessantly exciting the window shopper to buy. In 1876, comparable requirements for the new Bon Marché in Paris led Eiffel and
Boileau to design a superb store. Its large glass surfaces forming the
show windows were protected by a glass canopy carried across the whole
front. A prominent pavilion was set at the corner. The interior was divided and perforated by iron columns and bridges to offer a series of
courts. It was lighted through skylight canopies billowing above the
floor spaces and mezzanines. American architects were not so imaginative or straightforward in designing their commercial buildings. They
took from English precedent the idea that a store should resemble a
palace outside and a group of private chambers inside, ignoring the
better English and even Russian practice of arcades which had also
been used in America earlier. Thus, New York's Haughwout Store of
1857, previously mentioned, foretold the future development of the
American department store. While J. P. Gaynor, the designer of this
building, availed himself of two technological advances, the elevator
and ready-made cast-iron columns, lintels and capitals, the plan and the
envelope were each conceived in terms inherited from masonry buildings. The result was naturally not much different from the masonry
building Griffith Thomas had erected for Lord and Taylor's on the
corner of Grand Street and Broadway in 1859. This, the *New York
Times* noted, was "more like an Italian palace than a place for the sale
of broadcloth."

Thus, for the moment, the elevator, the building materials and the
functional requirements of the department store were not permitted to
condition architectural design. The iron front was not adopted for its
own properties, but for its commercial value; as William John Fryer
wrote in 1869 it could be repainted periodically, thereby overcoming
the disadvantages of brownstone which flaked and eroded or of marble
which stained and became discolored. ". . . place two merchants respectively in a stone front and an iron front store, side by side," he
challenged, "and he in the clean, bright, attractive front will do the
most business, and can afford to pay the highest rent." He might have
added that those who came in to see an elevator or an electric light
bulb or a telephone might remain to buy something.

Advertisements for iron fronts produced by Daniel Badger's Iron
Works about 1865 emphasized that they could reproduce any historical
architectural form, obtain a sharper outline, achieve more elaborate ornamentation, and do all this at less cost than stone. A product of the
requirement that each store have a distinctive façade, an iconography
that would advertise itself and attract customers, such versatility further

stimulated the demand. The palace-type store, such as the enormous
A. T. Stewart store (later Wanamaker's) in New York, designed by
John Kellum in 1859-1863, with its dignified rhythmic repetition of
standard elements, was bound in these circumstances to go out of
fashion. The Grover and Baker Sewing Machine Company was no more
ready to use cast iron in a structurally direct way in buildings than in its
sewing machine legs. The company erected a store at 495 Broadway
with a front suggesting an entrance to a large Gothic cathedral. In 1875
Richard Morris Hunt designed a Moorish cast-iron façade for another
store. To be sure, the more pretentious and vulgar of these façades
brought contempt from some, and considerably simpler, less cumbersome designs occasionally seemed to indicate a chastening taste. But
later buildings, such as the Mercantile Exchange of 1882 by Herman J.
Schwarzmann, suggest that idiosyncratic and lavish ornament continued
to serve the demands of advertising better than good design.

The office building, too, was clothed in an architectural dress intended to make its form an advertisement and its offices attractive to
renters. Architecture was now a financial investment, no longer a tribute
to the Virgin of Chartres or Bourges. The growing complexity of modern commerce, not yet much aided by the telephone, required quick
physical connections between stock markets, banks, railroad offices,
factories and warehouses, and even with a sales force. Physical propin-
quity was the only immediately satisfactory solution. This demanded
concentrated administrative centers to house large office staffs. Since
the areas adjacent to leading banks, stores, restaurants and hotels were
already densely crowded, the land use was now intensified to the burst-
ing point. This swelled land prices, made it seem important to maximize
the use of each square foot, to support on it as much rentable office
space as possible. The buildings also advertised the company that owned
them. Both forces suggested that buildings be larger and, if possible,
higher, though not so high as other ambitions would push them later.

Early insurance offices, for example, were small, usually simple, even
when they looked a little like the houses of Italian merchant princes
of the Renaissance. But in New York the Mutual Life Insurance
Company outgrew such modest accommodations in the thirty-six years
between its founding in 1843 and the day in 1879 when it was acclaimed as the largest corporation in the world with more than ninety
thousand policies and gross assets of ninety million dollars. Specifically
designed to house the Mutual and two tenants, John Kellum prepared
a new building in 1865. It was still a palazzo but much larger. Tenancy
turned out to be so attractive that Henry Baldwin Hyde, Vice President
of the Equitable Life Insurance Company, persuaded his colleagues to

erect a new building in New York which would include six floors of rentable office space. Forceful, energetic, alert to money-making possibilities, Hyde saw that the limitation upon financial income from leases on properly located properties was not imposed so much by building construction as by the difficulty of making the top floors conveniently accessible. By using an elevator, which had proved successful in stores and hotels, he hoped to attract renters even on the top story in the roof which was 130 feet above the street. It now seems strange that this idea was timidly accepted as a speculation. Designed by Gilman, Kendall and Post and erected at 120 Broadway in 1870, the new building proved so popular that the architect, George Post, who had agreed to rent a suite of offices there as token of his faith in the idea, sold his lease six months later at a profit of $6000. The building helped establish a type for future insurance buildings so that a distinctive insurance style spread across the United States.

Having broken through the traditional restrictions upon height, office buildings started the flight skyward. In 1865 New York was a city of four- and five-story buildings. By 1875 several office buildings had attained nine or ten stories. The change was accomplished without any alteration in building structure. The elevator alone had enabled investors to stretch wall-bearing construction to give as much rentable space as possible. Nor was there any change in street dimensions or in aesthetic conception, even when the new masses strained traditional architectural vocabularies. Ornate Renaissance detail, domes, tympana and giant orders gave a confused and ridiculous appearance to a 110-foot building like that of the Domestic Sewing Machine Company. They dwarfed its scale, much as the *New York Evening Post's* domestically dimensioned windows diminished its true size.

The quest for rentable space drove buildings still higher, long before there were any new technological or aesthetic solutions for the skyscraper. In 1873-1875 George Post built the Western Union Telegraph Building and Richard Morris Hunt the *New York Tribune* building. They rose to vie in height with the dome of St. Peter's at Rome by reaching 260 and 230 feet, respectively. Yet both were of wall-bearing construction. Each was a large block which sprouted into a tall tower. Each appeared as a sequence of floors, separated by band courses and cornices, grouped by giant pilasters, capped by a tall roof. Neither design had any sense of unity. Neither had a scale which represented the building. Neither intimated the relationships that existed between the interior spaces or the nature of the vertical or horizontal circulation. These matters were unimportant to the client so long as renters did not mind. The space was expected to have commercial and not aesthetic value and the tenant would have subscribed to the same view had he ever thought about it at all.

Other cities besides New York accepted the commercial, advertising and prestige values of the skyscraper. The more conservative Philadelphia and Boston experimented. Chicago, in particular soon developed the financial and urban conditions which gave rise to concentrated office buildings. Having begun as a city of wood, cast-iron and brick buildings, largely razed by the fire of 1871, Chicago now began the erection of large commercial structures. In 1872 Henry Hobson Richardson designed the American Merchants Union Express Company Building, as a large block of masonry bearing-walls, with interior columns of cast iron and an exterior Gothic treatment. But before taller buildings could be erected on its mud flats, Chicago needed a lighter form of construction. Each floor must weigh less if there were to be more floors. The foundation would have to ride on the mud. The great fire was a vivid memory and fireproofing would have to be achieved. The city sky was already dark with the promise of abundant industrial smoke and so there must be as many large windows as possible. Finally, the speed of construction must be increased.

Such technological problems had to be solved before the aesthetic problem could even be considered. They were solved, brilliantly, and mostly in the Middle West by George Johnson and his hollow-tile fireproofing in the Kendall Building of 1872, by Burnham and Root with their raft foundations under the Montauk Building of 1882. Builders learned to use salt in brick mortar so it could be set in freezing weather; they adopted canvas enclosures and electric lights so that they could work when it was cold, rainy, snowy or dark. But the buildings were still earthbound as long as the outside walls must be of masonry.

Each floor added its weight to be supported. Each increment of weight required a thicker wall. So the higher the building, the thicker its outside wall must be at the ground. As it got thicker, it had also to have smaller or fewer windows. Thus the commercially desirable window and floor space was smallest precisely where it was most valuable, that is, on the accessible ground floor. Indeed, there might be a critical height which could not be exceeded because at that point the lowest floor would have become all masonry, or at least as densely peopled with columns as the Great Hall at Karnak. So the metal-cage theories revealed in Leroy S. Buffington's patents and the practices of Major William Le Baron Jenney were the great liberators. The break-through seems to have been realized when Jenney erected the Home Insurance Company Building in Chicago in 1883-1885. Once skeletal or hung-masonry construction had been invented and proved, the main technological barrier to higher buildings had been removed. The technical questions, if not those of aesthetics, remaining for later generations were distinctly minor, at least until the buildings rose so tall that the question of wind-bracing became difficult; or demanded so much climatic control that the problem of where to put the air-conditioning units became a dominant one. In the meantime the problems centered on what materials to use on the armature, how to relate the spandrels and the windows in the curtain walls.

It was characteristic of this generation that it would find ingenious, if unrefined, solutions to its technological problems but pay little attention to the aesthetic ones. Essentially, the aesthetic problem was twofold; whatever its structure, the tall building should have a unified composition in which a single theme dominated and ordered windows, piers, and spandrels; and second, the elevations should express the organization of space, structure, circulation and use within the building. Neither of these was solved by Post or Hunt in New York; they were designing their tall buildings on the formula of a multi-layered tower. Stripped of all its Gothic and Renaissance ornament, the Montauk Building in Chicago by Burnham and Root was, on the contrary, something radically bold. The vertical piers somewhat dominated segmentally arched window openings which were slightly recessed. But the small windows were not phrased so as to form a composition equal to the scale of the whole.

The aesthetic problem intrigued the young architect, Louis Henri Sullivan, who had come to Chicago from his Boston birth and early upbringing, from brief stays for the study of architecture at the Massachusetts Institute of Technology and L'École des Beaux-Arts in Paris. Each he had quickly rejected although he had more good things to say for the Paris than for the Boston school. He had worked for a time for Frank Furness in Philadelphia and owed his skill as a delineator and perhaps some of his affection for detail to this experience. A rebellious, inconsistent, poetic, iconoclastic and utterly romantic Irishman, he found his spiritual home in Chicago even in the very days when he was calling it a pigsty. Imaginative as he already was, and great as he later became, Sullivan did not find a solution to the problem of the skyscraper in the short time he practiced before 1885; and it is even stretching things to pretend that in his experiments of this time he was working in a straight line to the great solutions which he ultimately provided a few years later in St. Louis and Buffalo. In the Borden Block of 1879-1880 he made the horizontals dominate. His Rothschild Store of 1881 reversed the premises with assertive verticals. But each was covered with a profusion of heavy and crude ornament which concealed the simple organization he was trying to achieve.

Nor was the engineer any more effective. Major Jenney covered the technological progressiveness of the Home Insurance Building with a jumble of rustication, ineffective arcades, giant pilasters, all breaking up the mass. The aesthetic problem of the tall building was simply not solved in the days of its youth.

8

MEANWHILE THE TALL BUILDING EMPHASIZED AND INTENSIFIED THE shortcomings in the total urban form. In the absence of zoning controls, factories and warehouses were built at points where discontinuities in transportation by water, rail, or street conveyance suggested a way of capitalizing upon the transfer of goods and people from one means of conveyance to another. Warehouses were piled on wharves; foundries and factories filled the ocean or river flats, alternating with dump heaps. Tenements were stuck anywhere. Retail stores crept out along the street-car lines and invaded squares which formerly had been residential or reserved for civic buildings. Dense concentration of tall buildings choked space and movement in the commercial centers. Factories extended out along the railroad, slicing through the city. The city became increasingly a daytime place of work, a residence mainly for poor families, and a place for entertainment. As it became less desirable as a living place, the suburban areas developed as dormitory communities. Throughout this process, the various social, economic and cultural institutions were not assigned the kinds of space or the locations which would have allowed them to operate effectively.

The growth of Cleveland during this time offers an example of the chief stages and the chief faults in city expansion under industrialization. With the completion of the Erie Canal in 1825, western trade funneled through the Lakes to New York; Chicago, Cleveland and Detroit now found ready outlets for their products. Cleveland had an advantageous location. She drew iron ore from the North, over the Lakes, coal from the South, over the rails. So she grew in eighteen years from the small commercial city of 25,000 in 1852 to an industrial center of almost 93,000 in 1870. Railroads, industry, and large-scale immigration stretched the city boundaries eastwards and westwards along the lake. The commercial warehouses and stores on the Cuyahoga River front disappeared as the river flats were cut by canals to carry heavy ore-laden freighters, crisscrossed by railroads, sidings, freight yards, roundhouses, repair barns, foundries, fabrication plants and their retinue of materials dumps and slag heaps. Dozens of competing railroads, encouraged by grants of land and subsidies from state and town, carved rights of way, disrupting the natural terrain, tearing through residential and commercial areas, crossing traffic arteries. One, the Cleveland and Erie, was laid out on a level stretch along the shore of Lake Erie, pre-empting the shore line and drawing to itself a wall of industrial plants that prevented subsequent use of the area for the excellent residential and recreational purposes for which it was uniquely qualified. Still another railroad pushed past Clinton Park, a protected residential area on a fine site near the lake, forcing the owners to abandon it. As rivers were widened and canals dug inland, wedges of blackening desolation and confused congestion were driven upstream by railroads and factories; rivers were fouled by sewage and industrial waste, land made barren and corrupt by slag heaps and dumps, air polluted by smoke and stench. Even the public square which had been Cleveland's civic center was not inviolate; mercantile firms and retail businesses transformed it from a village green to a commercial center, further decreasing the capacity of the central core to serve as the cultural and civic climax of the city.

While obviously ruining Cleveland for generations to come, it was also clear that prosperity had created material advances and economic development. But the society never solved the basic issue, namely, how to make private wealth serve common wealth, how to ensure that private enterprise would not undermine public interest. Here the private interests enlisted the support of their newspapers to threaten voters with personal loss of income and property should controls be placed upon their "free" enterprises. A proposal for an ordinance aimed at controlling the smoke problem met determined opposition in 1860 from a prominent newspaper, the *Cleveland Leader*: "This action should be spiked at once. If coal oil can't be refined in the city, no other factory should be allowed to produce in the city." By indicting a railroad iron mill company as a nuisance, a grand jury raised the ire of the *Leader*: "The idea of striking a blow at industry and prosperity . . . is an act that should and will be reprobated by the whole community." Reform had no appeal. An ordinance of 1857 against polluting the Cuyahoga River with refuse was followed in 1861 by a motion to repeal. "This petition," the *Leader* said, "should be granted. To refuse to do it, is to pursue the same policy toward manufactures that has diverted trade and business to other more favorable points, and has greatly retarded the legitimate growth of our city. Our prosperity hereafter will be measured by our manufactures . . . Pittsburgh is not a pleasant city, but under its dense smoke, and its begrimed atmosphere, it has a sub-stratum of manufactures that will enable it to bid fair defiance to all ordinary panics and dull seasons. . . . Cleveland, on the other hand, indicts her rolling mills because they smoke, and prohibits coal refineries because they smell badly, and gets laughed at by all her sister cities." If there were a progressive architect, what was he to do when this was the set of his society?

Bradford, Pennsylvania, offers a possibly extreme suggestion of temporary expediency and shortsighted exploitation, accompanying the drill, pump, and move-on mining industry. Oil was discovered at Bradford in 1860, only a year after the first discovery at Titusville. Thus Bradford began its existence as a town only a generation or so after eastern rural towns like Shirley Center or Woodstock had revealed the orderly settled plan of late New England. Bradford lay on an ingratiating terrain. But the purposes of the men who came to Bradford were different from the purposes of those who had come to Shirley. They had no intention of staying. So Bradford grew up as a boom town. A photograph of 1880 shows its horror. The scene is full of eroded hills, denuded of trees, a creek glutted with refuse, covered by oil slick; temporary wooden shacks, pitched at random, hang crazily on the slopes. A few steeples offer a feeble counterpoint to the desolate stores and saloons; they clearly are subordinate to the bristling oil derricks, perhaps appropriately since these were the reason for the town. Indeed, the derricks may be the least repulsive feature of the entire aggregation when viewed from a distance and in a favorable light. The town shows no evident symbols of education or of government. It displays none of the order that would indicate a population intent upon cultivating land, and caring for it by returning part of the usufruct to insure productivity for future generations. We know now that one can extract oil under precisely the conditions of Bradford without desolating the oil area, and without requiring the extractors to lead a desolate life; but even with our knowledge we do not do much about it save occasionally in Latin America. In 1860-1865 Americans did not know how, did not care, did nothing.

Indeed, whether or not Bradford was horrible may have depended upon your point of view. The neat Andrew Carnegie visited the comparable Oil Creek in 1862 and was not repelled. He was impressed with the ingenuity and adaptability shown by the men in managing places to sleep and eat, and, above all, with the good humor of those working there. "It was a vast picnic." The future was built into what he saw but he did not notice that. What he did notice was that Oil Creek was producing wealth. It might some day be large and rich if not dignified or commodious, but if not, it would not matter much; at least there had been the picnic. Carnegie did not, of course, have to linger on and see the refuse from the picnic. He could repair instead to Skibo. There was no Skibo for the families of Bradford, Pennsylvania.

But Carnegie saw more than most men of his station. He came home to Pittsburgh in 1860 and found it disagreeable. "Any accurate description of Pittsburgh at that time would be set down as a piece of the grossest exaggeration. The smoke permeated and penetrated everything. If you placed your hand on the balustrade of the stair it came away black; if you washed face and hands they were as dirty as ever in an hour. The soot gathered in the hair and irritated the skin, and for a time after our return from the mountain atmosphere of Altoona, life was more or less miserable." The Carnegies escaped to suburban Homewood as soon as possible.

There is nothing particularly reprehensible in this. Andrew Carnegie or anyone like him was less responsible for Bradford and Pittsburgh than the people who swarmed there with their high hopes and their vulgar ambitions. No distribution of Carnegie's wealth, no appropriation of the profits of his companies to all the laboring force could have at that moment raised the standard of living substantially; and such a distribution would have prevented the capital formation that was essential if Gargantua were to grow up. The magnates were not villains or criminals or even insensitive men. They were nearer to heroes than to knaves. It is possible to state their position without indulging in any value judgments at all. The fact is that the frontier town was of interest to them only as a resource and they could admire it only if it were energetic and productive. As for its future, they were unconcerned; but if asked they would have been optimistic and would have said, somewhat in the terms of John Adams, that once wealth had been achieved it might be wisely spent to produce the amenity that was now missing. Those few important but unrepresentative attempts at reform in the cities held little interest for the typical business magnate or industrialist. Indeed, if he perceived the implications of such regulations he would have to oppose them because as a follower of Herbert Spencer he would have to believe that they were bound to fail, acting as they did contrary to the processes of natural selection. The fittest would get out of the slum; the less fit would stay there as natural science seemed to be saying was inevitable.

Yet above the congestion and pollution of their cores American cities began to present soaring skylines. None of these was studied as a whole, from an aesthetic, social or any other point of view. They were the result of chance and of competition for rentals or prestige waged under the most lenient conditions of *laissez faire* and with almost no concern for anything other than economic gain. Yet they were not always ugly. From the Brooklyn Bridge, from Hoboken, and especially from the Lower Harbor, the tip of Manhattan Island began to take on its handsome, aspiring shape, so reminiscent of Mont St. Michel in form, so different in meaning, clearer then than in today's smog-laden air, though much less dramatic since none of the greatest pinnacles were to be achieved for another quarter-century. But whatever the promise from afar, as soon as one went ashore into the deepening canyons, the appearances were less amiable. People no doubt soon learned not to see the impedimenta of poles, wires and arrogant street signs which still clutter the American urban landscape from New York to San Francisco and which we also have learned not to see. Worse than this disorder, which might have made some plea of necessity, were the long rows of high tenements, wooden lodgings, the alleys of stores and lofts for sweatshops. The elevated railroads added trestles, ramps, stairs and stations plus an endless rumble to many streets; any street they contaminated was unlikely ever really to recover. Vast areas of the cities with the shining front towers were slums where immigrants managed to cling to a little of their traditional culture but which, all too often, were, like New York's Tenth Ward, foci of infection threatening the whole city with disease and crime.

Such areas would get much worse before they got better. They were to become most serious in the following quarter-century but even in this growing age their threat began to be revealed. As is so often the case in the throes of economic growth, the slums far outweighed any feeble efforts at reform as represented, for example, by new tenement laws or by model tenements such as those of Calvert Vaux. Occasionally there were new, foresighted park systems such as R. U. Copeland's pioneering "city plan" in Boston or Frederick Law Olmsted's magnificently conceived Central Park in New York. But even these, ample as they were for the moment, did not have a scale which could do much to alleviate the despair of the writhing ghettos.

Since other reforms were the harbingers of greater efforts in years to come, they are noteworthy even when meager. A few private industrialists such as the men of the Ames family established local philanthropies in towns like North Easton, Massachusetts, attempting to improve their factory town by hiring a man like Richardson to design town hall, post office, library and railroad station. But even North Easton, a monument to one of our greatest architects, did not achieve the over-all plan or the communal character of an earlier village like Shirley Center, the harmonious product of several generations. North Easton was less complete, put together too suddenly, and did not have the advantage of the cooperative effort of the townsfolk as well as the benefice of the patron. Perhaps the town did not have enough history. There is nothing to show that either the patrons or their large-scaled architect thought in terms beyond those of the individual buildings.

Of all the new towns of this quarter-century, perhaps Pullman, Illinois, previously mentioned, can best be compared with Shirley Center. But it, too, although designed as a whole and by an architect, S. S. Beman of Chicago, fell far short of the earlier village and very likely for the same reason as North Easton. But even with their shortcomings, villages like North Easton or Pullman were more typical of the thinking of the men of several generations later than of their own times. Ordinarily the villages of this time were low in quality. Many of the company towns had but a brief existence as such. It was difficult for the management to evict striker-tenants for non-payment of rent; in days of violence it might even have been impossible. Yet, if not evicted, the tenants were, in effect, being subsidized by the employer in their strike against him. Considerations of this sort, rather than that of avoiding paternalism, caused most manufacturers in the long run to turn against the idea of providing housing for their workers and generally to maintain this position to the present day. All too often this reasonable business decision led them also to ignore other responsibilities to the manufacturing community.

In addition to the experiments with company villages there were a few civic movements for reform. Early tenement laws had failed to correct the slum conditions that were described in articles such as the series called "Our Homeless Poor" which appeared in *Frank Leslie's Illustrated Newspaper* for 1872. Occasionally a society in Boston or New York would produce an isolated example of something better such as the White model tenements in Brooklyn. The legislation passed in New York in 1879 was stronger than the earlier laws, called for better construction, assumed higher standards of living in the tenements. But the writing of laws guarantees little; the enforcement of the regulations was often, perhaps usually, slack. Moreover even those tenements which faithfully adhered to all the requirements of the new laws did not reach the standards at which the reformers were aiming. Thus it was that a new model tenement built at First Avenue north of Seventy-first Street by Calvert Vaux in 1880 was publicized by pamphlets with engravings and descriptions and exhortations to others to go and do likewise.

But many people thought it impossible, under a *laissez-faire* system which few wished to change, to achieve enough reform housing to begin to cope with the need. Most people were quite indifferent to the whole question. Others thought that major alleviations might be provided as they seemed to have been in some European cities, if only there were enough grass and open space and playgrounds so that the people of the tenements might find their life confining only during their hours of work and sleep and that all this confinement could be atoned for by a Sunday in the Park. But the quarter-century seldom succeeded in providing even such alleviations. The trend was the other way. Philadelphia continued to fill in her grid plan as it had been laid down in the seventeenth century by William Penn, not even reserving the squares he had then proposed. Detroit and Indianapolis followed the example of Washington and neglected the radiating avenues and circles proposed by their early planners. Even when cities and states created land artificially, the use of these lands seldom was well controlled.

Boston did better than most. Here a large portion of the Back Bay marshes was filled in by the Commonwealth of Massachusetts and the city, working with several private corporations. A semi-cultural center was put on the filled land, developed as Copley Square, which is still something of an ornament to the city; Commonwealth Avenue stretching out towards the higher ground became a broad, green, arbored boulevard with generous pedestrian walks down the middle, ending in what would become the distinguished Public Garden which led in turn to the Boston Common in the heart of the retail district, a group of features which together with the Charles River Basin combined to provide the main ingredient in Boston's pleasant flavor and one which has been remarkably resistant to later desecration. But otherwise the plan was an unimaginative grid which forced commercial developments to be made along traffic arteries, prevented all but one row of houses from having a view of the river, laid major streets east and west so that their sidewalks could catch the full blast of the prevailing winds while the houses fronting them would receive a minimum of sunshine, if they received any at all.

Meanwhile the foresight of Olmsted and the designing skill of Vaux had succeeded in persuading New York City to protect the large area of Central Park from being divided into the gridiron proposed by the Commissioners of 1801. Instead, the area was laid out into rustic woods, gardens and ponds, crisscrossed by a network of paths for pedestrians and roads for vehicles, with pedestrian bridges where the paths crossed the roads. Most of the Park begun in 1859 was completed by 1876. Some cities followed the New York example as best they could or to the extent they willed; but few willed enough to overcome the difficulties in acquiring substantial land holdings at their cores and so Central

Park remains the largest single public area of open space in the center of any American city. As transportation has changed, peripheral elements of the park system may have become more interesting to some urban dwellers, but the flight from the city might have been less vigorous if all the cities had preserved spaces like that of Central Park. But Central Park was not enough. Manhattan needed many Washington Squares and Gramercy Parks; it made little effort to find new ones; it did not preserve all the ones it first had.

It is possible to live a healthy, perhaps even a happy life in the woods or in a village in Iowa, under physical conditions which would be intolerable in a metropolis. Consequently the rural slum has never been so frightening as its big brother in the city. The frontier was one big rural slum, saved only by the fact that the open spaces were not far away, by the general optimism, even gaiety of the life, by the openhanded attitudes of men and women who had little to lose today but expected to gain a great deal tomorrow. The newer towns of America were therefore no better at bottom than the decaying old cities, but they were saved from the most dire consequences by their surroundings and no doubt by the fact that they were smaller.

It did not matter whether such towns were in the cattle kingdom or in Golconda. The cattle towns were established around a courthouse and a settlement of stores and became places like Abilene and Dodge City. Some, like Lockhart, Texas, or Globe, Arizona, might not only escape the worst faults of the industrial city but even make some modest claims to amenity. In any event they created no waste in the form of mine tailings or industrial slag. Their prosperity was seasonal. After the cattlemen had ridden through, drinking and yelling, and leaving fewer new graves than is generally believed, the town settled down again. But such towns never achieved the real quality, the real serenity of Shirley Center. The nature of their infancy was such that they show no signs of attaining it even in maturity.

A place like Miles City, Montana, not so romantic as a gold-rush town, takes on a certain glamour when it is reported by contemporaries of the '80s like Brown and Felton. But the biggest glamour is picaresque, associated with gun fights, or gala balls, or strange conduct at the opening of a hotel or opera house. The architecture was as romantically synthetic as the pleasure. All the commercial buildings had false fronts. Brick was the front of prestige and naturally the first brick was plastered onto the First National Bank. The heart may easily go out to those who toiled to bring the bricks all the way from St. Louis at a cost of about seventy-five cents a brick laid in the wall. But no yearning will make this anonymous architecture good architecture. The hope and the aspiration were not matched by the performance. A town like Miles City burned frequently, and gradually most of the wooden buildings were replaced by two-story brick affairs. But every sequential photograph shows that Miles City was an architectural mess, as it still is. So is almost every other town which was once on the frontier and which boasts a residual Main Street, every town from Keokuk, Iowa, to Placerville, California. The development of a university in a town as at Iowa City can work minor ameliorations; an unusual number of trees and minor buildings by Louis Sullivan and Walter Burley Griffin may add a little interest to Grinnell; Frank Lloyd Wright sometimes made small islands like the one he created in a miniature gorge at Mason City; there were occasional, but only occasional, better things in Denver or Salt Lake City or Kansas City; Lincoln, Nebraska, has gained spires by Bertram Goodhue and Henry Magonigle. But the average Western town from the Mississippi to the Sierra cannot be spoken of in the same breath with Concord, Massachusetts, or Pendleton, South Carolina, or Marietta, Ohio. This has not been a question of money, geography, climate, water or flora. The industrial age and the frontier attitude simply made too few provisions for urbanity.

9

EVEN IN THE OLDER CITIES WHERE THERE WAS NOW A RICH SOCIETY, IT WAS of form and display, curiously indifferent to the bold adventuring that had provided its financial position. One could see the difference in its architecture. A. T. Stewart was an adventuresome man when he created his large and prosperous, if architecturally recessive, department store. He was more cautious when he approached the problem of a family mansion. For this he did not demand of the same architect any degree of originality or fitness comparable with that he had expected in the store. Thus Kellum provided Stewart with a large mansarded palace on the corner of Fifth Avenue and Thirty-fourth Street. It was lavish, comfortable, a flagrant display of wealth, and clearly an emulation of European traditions of imperial, not even domestic, architecture. Similar mansard palaces, often grosser and more lavish, followed the march of prosperity across the country, appearing in Cyrus H. McCormick's house at 675 Rush Street, Chicago, in 1875-1879, in Independence, Missouri, in the Vaile Mansion of 1877-1882, and in the Carson House in Eureka, California, in 1880-1886. Perhaps the Carson House is the most ludicrous of all unless one regards it as fit material for Charles Addams's cartoons, for it stands there in the California landscape, piling dome on tower, thrusting dormers through mansard roofs, mounting story on story in castellated hyperbole, adding insult to insult until its swagger betrays a man of wealth who wistfully hoped to acquire prestige through foreign forms, no matter how grossly mishandled, while ignoring the wealth of resource that California could have yielded.

The grandest of all these mansions was the one executed with great skill by Richard Morris Hunt for William K. Vanderbilt. Built at 660 Fifth Avenue, on the corner of Fifty-second Street, it alerted a whole city of modest brownstones to recognize how French sixteenth-century architecture might advertise wealth and social position and be the stage for the social maneuvers of the choice Four Hundred selected by Ward McAllister's committee of twenty-five. William Stewart's palatial mansion in white marble showed well enough how a client might encourage a modest architect like Kellum to become a scene designer, and the family of patriarch William H. Vanderbilt lived lavishly enough, occupying brownstones on the block between Fifty-first and Fifty-second Streets on the west side of Fifth Avenue. But these houses were architecturally careless, having been designed by the Herter Brothers, contractors, who created no dominant features, no development of masses or lines, vertical or horizontal, no interpretation of the openings. These failures were avoided somewhat by George B. Post when he erected a limestone and red brick mansion on the northwest corner of Fifth Avenue and Fifty-seventh Street for one of Vanderbilt's sons, but none was a brilliant success until Richard Morris Hunt turned a millionaire's house from a bourgeois mansion into a palace.

Having begun his training in Switzerland and spent the nine years between 1845 and 1854 studying at the École des Beaux-Arts in Paris, Hunt was without any rival; he was the best-trained architect on the American scene in the immediate post-Civil War period. Under his *patron*, Hector Lefuel, he had served as inspector in charge of work upon a new pavilion at the Louvre, and he was conversant with that charming architecture, combining Gothic and Renaissance forms, which flourished during the fifteenth and sixteenth centuries in France. An increasing affection for it prompted him to abandon the heaviness and spottiness of his earlier buildings, such as the Yale Divinity School and the Rossiter House. The late French Gothic of the Palais de Justice at Rouen, of the Hôtel de Cluny at Paris, and Francis I's château at Blois showed him how to compose masses upon a varied asymmetrical plan, capping each with tall, steep roofs, keeping the base of the building massive but lightening the effect with carved ornament to produce a rich skyline. Hunt carried off a successful design in this style for the

Vanderbilt House so brilliantly that later architects, notably McKim, derived special satisfaction in looking at it over and over again. Whether one studied the gray limestone walls or the hood moldings around the windows or the carved figures, one saw the result of refined attention to design. Hunt lavished such care that we can safely doubt the story that one of the sculptors surreptitiously modeled the face of the architect on the statue of a mason at work. For Hunt here scrutinized every detail, bringing all his art and knowledge of French ways to the service of his client and escaping the traps of ostentation and vulgarity that pervaded the millionaires' row on Fifth Avenue. Nonetheless Louis Sullivan would later poke fun at the contrast between the silk-hatted Vanderbilt and the feather-hatted architecture of his house. The fun was justified, not by the bad quality of Hunt's design but by its false premises. For Hunt's job was a first-class development of a theme which had no relation to the real meaning either of the society or of the owner. The evasion was at least as much the fault of the client as of the architect. It was inevitable that this first-class achievement could have no important place in serious architectural history.

There were other houses besides those for the millionaires. A retinue of lesser dwellings elbowed each other for room near the elite. There were new row houses, usually more elegant than those designed in earlier periods. In the hands of an architect like Lienau, they could be designed so as to constitute a fine street façade, as in the houses of 1869 for Mrs. Colford Jones at Fifty-fifth and Fifty-sixth Streets and Fifth Avenue. The apartment house, too, was introduced at this period, though it could not have great popularity in an age when servants were liberally supplied by open immigration practices. But Hunt designed the Stuyvesant apartment house complete with a *concierge* living on the ground floor, and J. C. Cady designed the Aurelia, which provided ample apartments for those who wanted to experiment with a way of living well known in Europe. Alongside the houses and apartment houses were gymnasiums and libraries and clubs. Not many of the new clubs seem to have been avidly devoted to intellectual pursuits as the Athenaeums and Institutes of the preceding period had been. The Union Leagues were inaugurated with a political purpose, and the Northern Leagues catered to rich members with impressive, even splendid, clubhouses. Perhaps the best of these was the Union League built at Philadelphia in 1864-1865, a bit of the French Louvre transported to Broad Street. Art associations were popular, and they built headquarters possessing architectural distinction, such as the Boston Art Club designed by W. R. Emerson. Many of these buildings deserve to be given large places in local histories of architecture but they were not representative; they were merely intimations of building types that would become important in the future.

I O

OTHER BUILDING TYPES ALSO ENRICHED THE URBAN SCENE. THE HOTEL, for example, introduced during the earlier period, loomed much larger on the cityscape. The Grand Central in New York offered visiting businessmen and tourists a great lobby, small shops, dining rooms, elevators, and suites of rooms fitted with modern conveniences. It could not accommodate conventions of Shriners and businessmen and professional societies, for conventions did not yet seek hotels, but it was the stage for parties and debuts, and the decoration of its grand rooms therefore rivaled in show if not in quality the lavish mansions of the rich.

Besides the office buildings and the mansions and the hotels, the American city occasionally suggested the future. By 1865 Europeans had built a number of magnificent railroad termini. There were the earlier Parisian stations like the Gare de l'Est (1847-1852) and the Gare Montparnasse (1850-1852) in which the brilliant engineering of the train shed was boldly emphasized on the façade. But Chicago's Grand Central Terminal of 1855-1856 and the New York, Harlem and New Haven Terminal of 1857 were little more than ugly tunnels in or through nondescript edifices. The Columbus, Ohio, Union Depot of 1862 was almost exactly a barn, the Boston and Maine Depot in Salem a kind of castellated tunnel. They were in striking contrast to more opulent examples in Europe, such as the St. Pancras Station of 1863-1876 and the second Paddington Station of 1852-1854, both in London, and the earlier magnificence of Hardwick's Grand Hall for London's Euston Station (1846-1849).

Arriving at such European stations or departing from them was exciting; they were truly the gateways to the city. One entered an office building or perhaps a hotel, arrived at a large lobby filled with activity; then boarded the train in a separate building, the train shed, a single vast structure spanning the tracks. Great vaults above the tracks were filled with glass supported on iron arches, creating a space filled with steam and smoke and muffled sounds. These train sheds caught the spirit of adventure and comfort then associated with railroad travel, as Monet was to show in his studies of the Gare St. Lazare. America lagged in building such train sheds and it would not be until the '70s and later that American railroads followed the insurance companies and banks by building an architecture expressive of themselves.

A certain quaintness had been achieved occasionally at way stations such as Henry Austin's amazingly exuberant Union Station for New Haven (1848-1849) or Thomas Tefft's more restrained Lombard tower and Romanesque cloister for Providence (1848). But for the most part the early railroad tycoons, the Vanderbilts, Huntingtons, Stanfords, Villards and Cassatts, displayed the wealth and power of their railroads by the visible evidence of the president's house and not by the railroad station, which often, as at Baltimore's Calvert Station of 1855 and the Camden Station of 1856, had a form that might have suited a warehouse rather than a railroad terminus.

There were a few other fabulous way stations like the gay Union Station at Worcester, Massachusetts, by Ware and Van Brunt (1875-1877), with its high machicolated clock tower a little like a tower of Florence, a little like a tower of Rothenburg on the Tauber, but not anything like Worcester, Massachusetts.

The tower was to be a popular accretion to railroad stations and would be used by Eidlitz at the Polk Street Station in Chicago (1883-1885) and by many others right down to the twentieth century, but it could not conceal the fact that the train shed, the waiting rooms and other important elements of train use were casually studied or ignored.

The single glowing exception was the Grand Central Depot at New York, built in 1869-1871. The important elements of a railroad station, the train shed and waiting room, were not handled equally well. Nor did the designers, Buckhout and Snook, follow the excellent European practice of making the exciting canopy of the train shed a principal element of the façade. Nevertheless, if one could push oneself blindfolded past the entrance façade, escaping the menacing riot of quoins and arches, pilasters, pediments and mansard roofs, the train shed spoke in earnest of the three railroads, the New York and Harlem, the New York, New Haven and Hartford, and the New York Central and Hudson, pusillanimously announced by small signs affixed to the three pavilions on Forty-second Street. Perhaps few people ever seriously considered the architectural character of the train shed; we can be certain that even fewer saw the rear entrance to it, which had the stately rhythms of a ferry slip or pier head, directly expressing its purpose, the work obviously of an engineer who, left alone, accomplished something greater than the Forty-second Street entrance. But if one ignores the shell surrounding the great vaulted space, the train shed at the old Grand Central was magnificent. It was spanned by trussed arches that formed spider-web patterns against the clear glass of the ribbon lighting at the top and sides of the vault. It would have been better had later designers followed this lead, instead of encasing the railroad within Gothic filigree architecture as was done at the Park Square Station in Boston, the Baltimore and Potomac at Washington, or the somewhat more robust design made for the Union at Worcester, Massachusetts.

The railroads seldom demanded great architecture; they frequently ruined many potentially fine sections of cities, as they did at Cleveland; but they also supplied a means for escaping the city. Commuting was by no means so prevalent then as now, but it was sufficiently common by 1885 so that English visitors were amazed to find how many people followed the railroad lines to places which had been countryside only five years previously. Suburban villas were starting up like mushrooms, according to an English observer, and the value of property everywhere, but especially along the various lines of railroads, was increasing at an incredible rate. Small fortunes were made by owners of land in Yonkers and other places along the Hudson River, and the Main Line of the Pennsylvania Railroad, running west out of Philadelphia, soon brought clusters of villages and estates within twenty-five minutes of downtown offices. Meeting the train was more ceremonial then than now, in the twilight of the train, as we may learn from Edward Lampson Henry's painting, *The 9:45 A.M. Accommodation, Stratford, Connecticut,* of 1867. Migration to suburbia was actively encouraged by railroads, which purchased rights of way, laid out towns, developed residential communities and advertised their advantages. The Marietta Railroad published a brochure at Cincinnati in 1874 inviting businessmen to buy large, comfortable houses set in parklike communities with all the allurements of schools, churches and restricted admission.

Outlying communities, tied to the city by railroads, excluded industry and most commerce. An existing street or turnpike, such as the Lancaster Pike in Philadelphia, might support intermittent sequences of clustered stores, taverns and inns. But the residential area serviced by these and by the railroad was a "greenbelt," a romantic park, with winding drives leading to large houses set in wooded land. Many of the villas built there resembled large Elizabethan manor houses. Such a house was built on the Main Line in 1869 by Alexander J. Cassatt, of the Pennsylvania Railroad. But more noteworthy were later houses created by a number of highly able American designers. The new country residences were remarkably free from historical ornament; their plans took advantage of irregular sites and orientation, and met the prevailing demand for many large specialized rooms with different moods. Frequently, entrance vestibules, drawing rooms, dining rooms and libraries were interlocked spaces; areas were defined but not enclosed, and sequences of walls, windows and columns produced some of the vistas characteristic of modern open planning. The Stoughton House in

Cambridge, Massachusetts, of 1882-1883, is an especially vivid example of this new sort of house. Here on a corner lot Richardson developed the house on an L-shaped plan, filling the angle in the garden with a curved bay containing the staircase. Rooms opening off the main hall are variously shaped, and their strong volumes are enclosed by exterior walls covered with shingles.

Other houses, similar in style, were built by Hastings, Price, McKim, Stevens and Emerson, all of whom owed much to Richardson. They left many fine suburban and country houses. Their plans and shapes came to be highly regarded by architects during the twentieth century, especially by men like Frank Lloyd Wright who saw similar houses in the region around Chicago. There was no real counterpart to these houses in Europe. They were peculiarly well suited to American materials, climate, workmanship, terrain, and to American domestic life during the '70s and '80s. They seemed in that period to epitomize what so many had felt about the American landscape. No civilization would want to rest its architectural case only on its domestic buildings, especially if they were built of a material as ephemeral as wood, but the Stoughton House and its progeny captured the heart of a society whose major interests lay within the family and the private house, not in the cathedral or market place or in the cafés along an urban boulevard. The American tourist might participate as much as any foreigner in the night life of Paris or Berlin, but in his own land the *"boulevardier"* came home after work to a dwelling eminently private and lordly. Even a Western engineer like Jenney wanted nothing else. His essay, "A Reform in Suburban Dwellings," written in 1883, paraphrased the main objectives of Eastern architects, championing rural settings, the rustic use of native materials, especially stone and wood, picturesque compositions, rooms adapted to use and site.

Through the open lands beyond the suburbs, railroads carried a small clique of rich Americans to country places, not yet so remote as Florida but to Long Island and to Saratoga Springs and even to Bar Harbor. At Saratoga the grandiose United States Hotel of 1875 was an enormous Mississippi River steamboat planted on turf, with a veranda in place of promenade decks and serving much the same function. There one could take the waters, follow the races, and gaze at the Vanderbilts. Saratoga Springs lost out in the end to Newport, Rhode Island, which had long welcomed a small colony of visitors but now became the summer capital of American society.

Gradually the face of Newport was transformed by the new elite. The eighteenth-century houses and libraries and churches had been set around the cove and on the hill nearby. About 1835 and farther to the

south, Edward King had built a fine Gothic villa designed by Upjohn.
Even the summer houses of the '50s were small and rustic, while the
small mansards of the '60s hardly intimidated old-time all-year-
round residents. But now these were dwarfed by new extravagant mansions, euphemistically labeled "cottages" by the Newporters. Richardson, whose recognized talents now rivaled and would soon surpass
Hunt's, created a large manor house for Watts Sherman in 1874-1876,
of stone, red brick, and half-timber; it sturdily carried great sweeping
roofs punctuated by tall chimneys and dormers. It had the most domestic character of any of the large country estates at Newport, but these
merits were not appreciated by people like the Fearings, who built their
lavish cottage in the form of a French château in 1871-1872. Succeeding
"cottages" like the Château au Mer by Hunt of 1877, Robert Goelet's
house of 1883, and others by the rising young firm of McKim, Mead and
White went full tilt towards the Renaissance palace, providing their
owners with colossal halls less fitting to their lives than to those of the
Italian princes who had invented them.

Shadows of this taste stole westward, where the meridian of fashion
was at least a decade behind the East. The "Gothick" Moss Cottage at
Oakland, California, of 1864-1865 would not have seemed unfamiliar in
upstate New York during the '50s when Downing was promoting the
same idea. The few Western buildings with serious pretensions toward
architecture tended to be crude, overly concerned with detail, badly proportioned, even impractical. Western taste was epitomized by the
steamboats *Thompson Dean* (1871), *Grand Republic* (1876), and
J. M. White III (1878), which churned the Mississippi sporting 260-foot
dining saloons with gleaming white filigreed wood, plush red carpets,
and extravagant chandeliers.

Peter Bonnett Wight, who had pro-Eastern and Ruskinian ideas, reported of the Western states in 1880 that only their commercial buildings had quality. What the architects of the West called Renaissance
had little in common with the historical Renaissance of Italy and
France; the style commonly called Gothic had only a vague resemblance
to the original. Chicago was still behind New York, but many years
ahead of San Francisco.

In that romantic coastal city the transformation of Nob Hill had begun. Its abrupt raw heights were the setting where Mark Hopkins,
Charles Crocker, and Leland Stanford chose to erect their grandiose
palaces of brick and wood, often relying upon sheer mass for magnificence, with towers, battlements, and fortified walls. Crocker's house cost
$1,250,000 and had a 76-foot observation tower up which the corpulent
host hauled his guests to point out the harbor. One contemporary ob-

server of Nob Hill thought the builders had carried " 'a bit of ancient Carcassonne to the shores of the Pacific'; another labeled Crocker's home 'a delirium of the wood carver' and asserted the common feature of the whole architectural array was an expense which could not be taken away from it." This the Nob Hill Franciscans — not then absorbed with the necessity for an "indigenous Bay architecture" — might have gleefully admitted.

But if San Francisco was not yet self-conscious, the Middle West was beginning to be. In a few places one could, indeed, find intimations of an approach to architecture that would be independent of historical eclecticism, suggesting a basis for today's design. The flavor of the West was evident if one compared the cast-iron Gantt Building in St. Louis of the '70s with the ornate classical arcades of iron buildings in New York. The St. Louis waterfront buildings displayed their iron for what it was, a cast metal, crisp and sharp, made in sections, handsomest when laid out as lintels and posts with no emulation of classical or Gothic forms. Even the Easterner Peter Bonnett Wight, who did not like it, saw that this commercial architecture was Western, identified by straight lintels, flush with the walls, continuous band courses and sills, cornices intended only to protect the walls, not to cast a great shadow, minimizing an ornament that was confined to the surface of the walls. A little-known building, for the John Shillito Company at Cincinnati, erected in 1876, showed these features brought to a scale and organization that anticipated the solution of skyscraper design worked out in the late '80s. Pier and spandrels were separated, as in some English warehouses and stores of the period; the theme was one of dominant verticals standing in front of recessed horizontal planes.

But such buildings appealed no more to other Eastern architects than they did to Wight. To them it was a "vernacular" or mechanic's style, perhaps acceptable for industrial buildings, even for some kinds of commercial buildings, but hardly architecture at all. Certainly it could not be satisfactory as the "national" style campaigned for so fervently by architects in the new American Institute of Architects and by architectural magazines such as the *American Architect and Building News,* based on the conviction that theirs was clearly a new age demanding a new style in architecture, that it must express this new national unit, America. This had been and would be a recurrent refrain sung to different tunes. The current theme was that the new age ought not be frighteningly new. America might be a new phase of European history, but not a complete departure from Western heritage. Their interpretation of the relation resulted in the magnificent historical inconsequence that the new architectural style should be a continuation of the last phase of Gothic, having at most an admixture of Renaissance elements, all mixed up with the idea that great architecture can effect moral and social improvement, and that it was the architect's duty to improve his society.

I I

No ONE IN THE ENGLISH-SPEAKING WORLD SPLIT THESE VARIOUS CURRENTS of architectural sentiment more fully than John Ruskin. *Seven Lamps of Architecture*, 1849, and *Stones of Venice*, 1851, were widely read and more editions of them were published in America than in England. American architects followed Ruskinian doctrine even more literally than Deane and Woodward had in designing the Oxford Museum.

During the '40s Ruskin had seen in England the horrifying spectacle of industrialization that would appear later in American cities. He despised its disintegrating effect on urban life, its mechanized products, its degraded workmen. Believing that lasting reform could come only through education, he organized museums of art and science, taught at Oxford, established lecture programs for factory workers and artisans, emphasizing always the influence of good art on morality. His interests were wide-ranging, sometimes progressive as in his support of housing reforms and his critical appreciation of the painter Turner; sometimes scientific, though his affection for geology tempered his dislike of any science that enjoyed anatomical dissection; but his disposition was mainly historical and religious, even mystic, and this led him to an unqualified admiration for the medieval guilds. He drew well and wrote with passion. When he looked at a sunrise, one of Ruskin's friends remarked, he doubted there could ever be a sunset. He was the leading spokesman for the dubious idea that art and architecture must contain moral expression, insisting that good architecture makes men good. His lectures about art, as well as his books, were Messianic sermons, pontifically pronounced, melodiously phrased, and they spellbound his audiences and his readers into believing that Gothic architecture, alone, was appropriate for use in a Christian society and that its revival was necessary to correct modern paganism and to temper the onslaught of industry.

Such sermons were well received in America, particularly by those who despaired of factories, cities like Cleveland, or the Vanderbilt mansions. They ignored the rational architecture proposed by Latrobe and Greenough, preferred the conversion to medieval piety offered by this English high priest. By 1875 a few people discredited Ruskin but most of the disenchantment had to wait for later generations. Few in the

'60s had the discrimination necessary to discern Ruskin's art, to separate his knowledge from it, or to measure his genius.

Nor were many Americans aware how fitful that genius was. Groups in New York, Boston and Philadelphia set out to emulate his example. Their love affairs with Victorian Gothic are commemorated on many college campuses today. Some of the buildings like Memorial Hall at Harvard and the Chancellor Green Library at Princeton have long since ceased to serve their original purposes and modern students perhaps too readily wish them ill. But their colorful ornament and rich silhouettes endear them to others, especially if the later architecture seems excessively bald and inexorably ruled by straight lines. No one will doubt that the American acceptance of Ruskin diverted her leaders from industrial horrors to the ultimate loss or at least postponement of great opportunities.

Ruskin's inaccurate observations and *non sequiturs* were well suited to beguile Victorian sentiments and open Victorian pocketbooks. It was not surprising that a group of young architects and critics living in New York in 1863 should have founded an astonishingly naïve society, The Association for the Advancement of Truth in Art. Dedicated to promoting Ruskinian principles, the Society's magazine, *The New Path*, attacked the Renaissance style, whose morality they judged corrupt as Ruskin had also: "It is base, unnatural, unfruitful, unenjoyable and impious." The Society could find no American architecture worthy of praise before the National Academy of Design was constructed at New York between 1862 and 1865. Polychromed and carved enough to make spectators giddy, the building was designed by Peter Bonnett Wight. It was the Society's greatest triumph, a colorful palace more or less in Venetian Gothic, a bit of whimsey livening the commercial scene with tracery and brick patterns polychromed in reds, ochers and yellows. Ruskin had set an example at the Oxford Museum when he brought plants to the brothers O'Shea which they copied into the capitals. Now Wight followed this and brought indigenous foliage to the stone carvers to be studied as models. For he subscribed to Ruskin's belief in the moral efficacy of having workmen who were craftsmen and creative artists; he wanted "to give workmen opportunity to think."

Having moralized the stones of New York, the Ruskinian muse perched on the shoulder of Charles Eliot Norton at Cambridge, where this distinguished Harvard professor of fine arts successfully inspired many an undergraduate to believe that "we have, as a nation, painfully displayed our disregard of the ennobling influences of fine architecture upon national character." Like his close friend Ruskin, Norton believed that morality and aesthetics were inseparable. This belief led Norton to attempt to enhance the beauty and presumably the morality of the Harvard environment by taking an active part in overseeing the character of Memorial Hall, built in 1865-1878.

Norton wanted Memorial Hall to be Gothic. His hopes were high when Ware and Van Brunt's Gothic design won the competition, and he even solicited Ruskin to express interest in the building. The architects designed a cathedral form, the nave becoming the dining hall, the apse a theater, and the transepts a Memorial surmounted by a tall ornate tower. When completed, it was a picturesque and solemn monument to the Civil War dead, an imposing mass of red brick with colorful designs in the shingled roofs and topped by a cast-iron coxcomb — dreadfully effective when washed by moonlight. But it was a tragedy of errors in design all the way from a scale that violated the collegiate theme established in the Yard to the carving and brick patterns and cast-iron filigree and stained glass and moralizing inscriptions that seem to modern students so maudlin and contrived, though they perhaps did not seem so to contemporaries. Norton himself was disappointed in the result. It was his misfortune, as it was for many Americans versed in the best European traditions, not to find any modern architecture that met his standards for beauty and morality; he was to have his hopes for something better revived during the age of reform but as late as 1904, still dissatisfied, he continued to seek in aesthetics an ethical ideal, "fine architecture as an influence in the education of youth."

Norton's disenchantment with Ruskinian medievalism did not prevent a whole American generation from erecting Victorian Gothic buildings for their cultural institutions. In the Gothic, American trustees found a "civilized" style; they would not often use it for factories or machines nor would they attempt by and large to surround their workers with the kind of environment the Society for the Advancement of Truth in Art tried to promote. When acting not as practical businessmen but as preservers of culture they took on the *alter ego* of trustee personality and insisted upon having "important" institutions housed in buildings redolent of history, perfumed with the spices of France and Italy and Araby, if not of Cathay. In this they followed English example. The fitful aberrations of modern Gothic appearing at the Natural History Museum at South Kensington and London's New Law Courts and the University of Glasgow reappeared in the old Art Museum at Boston and the Springer Music Hall at Cincinnati. It was a style with many merits: it permitted highly utilitarian, informal planning. It offered large open areas between buttresses where good lighting could be obtained. Frequently it provided a drab town with its only Xanadu, its one spot of fantasy, exoticism, color or romance. While it seems to us today to have had no contact with or relation to the burgeoning industries that paid for it, we must recall that this Victorian Gothic floridity was balm to a soul divided and that it was a feverish attempt to compensate for the ugliness produced by machinery run solely for economic advantage.

Indeed, the Memorial Hall of Harvard and the Chancellor Green of Princeton as well as many less exuberant Old Mains on American campuses, fail as they may in absolute architectural terms, deserve preservation as part of American university history and even applause as graceful reminders of our enchanting interlude with Ruskin.

Victorian Gothic was not the only competitor to become the American "national" style. Dr. E. A. Freeman, an Englishman who visited Albany in 1883, was convinced after seeing Richardson's Capitol that the true style for America, the one that "really flourished best on American soil," was the style of Pisa and Lucca, that is, Italian Romanesque. The *American Architect and Building News* in 1885 was convinced that the Théâtre Lyrique and the Chatelet in Paris proclaimed the style of the century which would be that of Louis Philippe and Napoleon III. Out in Chicago John Wellborn Root was expressing a liking for Flemish Gothic but he understood history too well to mock it as the Victorian Gothicists unwittingly did. What Root said about the classic could as well have been heeded by the nineteenth-century Gothicists, "this very perfection, which was only attainable when life was simple and the world was young, . . . makes it forever impossible that Greek detail should be successfully 'adapted' to modern buildings." The Middle Ages too had been young.

At first glance it might have been expected that ecclesiastical buildings would express differences in ritual or creed. A Roman Catholic cathedral might reasonably have been high Gothic; a Congregational church might have resembled an early New England meetinghouse; a synagogue might have had a Near Eastern expression. Occasionally this was so, especially when the churches were built for people with memories. So in New York and Cleveland and Seattle basilicas arose for the Russian Orthodox church, provided with onion-shaped domes that would have been quite at home in Moscow or Kiev. At New York James Renwick provided Catholics with the Gothic St. Patrick's. Sometimes memory slipped as when Leopold Eidlitz supplied a Jewish synagogue in New York with minarets more familiar to a muezzin than to a rabbi. But denominational differences soon could not be distinguished in an architecture which, for the moment, was drowned by Gothic.

It was during this period in Boston that Unitarians built their Gothic

First Church, by Ware and Van Brunt, the Congregationalists their Gothic New Old South Church, by Cummings and Sears, the Episcopalians their Gothic Church of the Advent by Sturgis and Brigham. The distinctions among these remained more in plan than in elevation or detail, but even planning differences tended to disappear as social aspects of church activity became increasingly prominent and the shrine was correspondingly reduced.

Identification of Victorian Gothic architecture with the liberal arts was common. The collegiate tradition was so firmly rooted in English institutions that the President of Trinity College journeyed to England in 1875 to find an architect capable of designing a massive medieval pile in the tradition of ancient Oxford and Cambridge, to be built in Hartford, Connecticut, a place the architect did not know and would never see. He found William Burges who conjured up a whole Gothic monastic collegiate community for this unfamiliar place and land. Princeton, Harvard, Yale, the Union Theological Seminary, Columbia and Knox College all emulated the quadrangles of Oxford, and it was a durable idea as the University of Chicago proved from 1892 to the 1940s. The values inherent here were exactly what was needed and would become effective in the age of reform, but the whole dream was totally unrelated to the potential for a new aesthetic residing in science and industry. One could sense the dichotomy at Cornell, where one side of the campus displayed rude, calloused academic and dormitory buildings and utilitarian machine shops, all erected by the businessman Ezra Cornell, while on the other side were Victorian Gothic "sermons in stone," as President Andrew Dickson White called them.

With all of this the scientists and those awake to the potentials of the new civilization were quite out of sympathy. While the businessman misguidedly fulfilled his trusteeship by following the lead of Hunt or Van Brunt or Burges or Potter or Sturgis, the scientist was willing to build Johns Hopkins in Baltimore or M.I.T. on Boylston Street (with nothing but the most utilitarian expression or perhaps at most a single classic porch) in which money was spent upon good apparatus rather than on art. That simple building could also be art occurred to no one. The dichotomy between utility and art had to be asserted every day.

Official architecture for government buildings was less uniform, but equally impervious to utility or vernacularism. The official style varied with the man who was acting as Supervising Architect of the Treasury. Throughout the '60s and '70s, a classical Beaux-Arts manner ordained the billowing domes and myriad colonnades of the buildings designed by Assistant Supervising Architect Alfred B. Mullett. Aggrandized versions of the Louvre pavilions appeared in the post offices of New York and Philadelphia and Portland, Oregon, and in the State, War and Navy Building in Washington, and were emulated in the City Halls of Boston and Philadelphia. When the State, War and Navy Building was completed it was described by deB. Randolph Keim as "the finest edifice of the kind in the world." Its "Roman, Doric, originally treated" was much admired. Now known as the Executive Office Building, it is no longer listed even in the *World Almanac* as one of the buildings to see in Washington.

The official buildings veered to Victorian Gothic when Supervising Architect William Appleton Potter covered the Middle South with courthouses and post offices in the Ruskinian vein. The impending controversy over what our official national architecture ought to be became of more public concern after the State Capitol at Albany was taken from Thomas Fuller's office and given to Richardson and Leopold Eidlitz. Then Richardson built a grandiloquent Senate chamber and entrance in the Romanesque style, whose appropriateness evoked the praise of the Englishman, Freeman, already cited.

All of this dabbling in archeological styles in an attempt to find something appropriate for an emergent American culture was enforced by a literary, musical and philosophical heritage quite unrelated to, indeed regarded as an amelioration to, rather than an expression of the industrial civilization. The schism in the culture was revealed by the Centennial Exhibition at Philadelphia in 1876. There were many wonderful things there. Japan sent a sectionalized house and workmen to erect it; Germany sent a fascinating exhibit of Froebelian educational methods. Both of these would profoundly affect later American culture and American architecture, and not only through Frank Lloyd Wright, whose mother learned from the Froebel exhibit a system of three-dimensional block training which Wright claimed gave him his start. But architectural progressivism hardly was the dominant theme of the Fair. American steam locomotives amazed a Russian engineer by their functionalism. Many a visitor caught the sense of power appearing in the Corliss engine. But these were housed in buildings that suggested no architectural recognition of mechanism. Turning his back upon the Crystal Palace, the architect Schwarzmann tricked out Horticultural Hall in Moorish fantasies. The buildings failed to catch the vigor and scale of America's future, failed to stretch iron and glass to a point of audacity where a speculative nation could dare ensnare great volumes of billowing space, to charge them with the urgency and stress and precision obvious in the Corliss engine.

Surveying the architectural scene in 1876, then, one saw the same confusion of tongues that one saw in the society. Victorian Gothic threatened to become a national style, but other languages abounded. There was the Romanesque, chaotic and eclectic, of the still immature Richardson to rival the classical idiom. There was even at this late date some pure Greek Revival building in Philadelphia as at the Ridgway Library. Architects shared and abetted this confusion. Asked to enter a competition for completing the Washington Monument, most of them submitted fantastic proposals for completing it in Gothic, Romanesque, or mansard styles.

Worse yet were proposals submitted for a "national" style. Such a proposal appeared from the hands of John Moser in 1884 when he suggested a building for the American Institute of Architects, to be built at New York. In his description of the building, Moser advised an explicit eclecticism: from bottom to top it was to go from Egyptian to Victorian Gothic, "an embodiment of the history of our art . . . where every epoch in architectural history shall be represented by details from the best examples now obtainable, following each other in regular and orderly sequence." By 1887 Moser hoped that America might develop her own new style, "Aim to unite the quiet serenity shown in the Greek with the heaven-aspiring tendency of the Gothic. Aim to have the proportions as agreeable and the whole as harmonious as the Greek. As agreeable as the French. As vigorous as the English. As refined as the Florentine. As systematic as the German . . . and the time may come when foreigners will copy as eagerly from us as we now do from them." At no time was the chauvinistic American professional architect so far from the truth about his art and his mission.

This was no indication of the prophetic design nascent in the earlier John Shillito Building; it was rather a synopsis of the architects' library of plates, not so well composed nor so consistent as *The Architect's Dream* of 1840, painted by Thomas Cole for the neo-classic architect Ithiel Town, where the essentially Roman cityscape was overshadowed by the Great Pyramid of Cheops. Erastus Salisbury Field's *Historic Monument of the American Republic*, of 1876, was a similar compendium of ten skyscraper towers covered with archeological remains. "Progress" had been backward.

I 2

THIS SORT OF ARCHEOLOGICAL ARCHITECTURE WAS ATTACKED BY SEVERAL kinds of critic, all of whom sensed in the American scene a destiny different from that of the "tastemakers." Clarence Cook, a convert from a youthful confirmation in Ruskin's parish, excoriated the taste-maker architect and his merchant-prince client: "The Museum of Fine Arts [Boston] and the Memorial Hall in Cambridge . . . are examples of what comes of buildings getting into the hands of the literary, critical men, art-students with their heads crammed full of remembered bits of Old World architecture, and their portfolios stuffed with photographs of more and more bits. . . . Where architects abound, the art of building always deteriorates."

Like many an apostate, Cook was enormously aggressive in his new cause. By 1882 and in the *North American Review* he had turned even on Renwick's Gothic Cathedral of St. Patrick at New York. He asserted that Renwick's design, like Trinity Church in Boston, was nothing but "borrowing, borrowing everywhere; an original motive almost impossible to find." Nor did he think the Vanderbilt houses were any better. "Where is the profit in being a millionaire," he asked, "if all one's money cannot command better design than this?" He thought the trouble lay in the ascendancy the professional architect enjoyed over the vernacular building: "and in architecture . . . the field has fallen into the possession of a set of clever, accomplished, but over-cultivated young men who have come back from French and English studios, offices, and pedestrian trips, with a plenty of 'material' in their sketch books." It seemed to Cook as to many other thoughtful people that American architecture had run steadily downhill from Westover to Memorial Hall.

Cook's attack upon the architectural profession, though bitterly rebutted in the architectural press, simply drove home the wedge of functionalism which was being fashioned by nineteenth-century industrial engineers and scientists. For them, adaptation to use was a simple principle that guaranteed performance, of course, but that might frequently result in beauty as well. To prove it there was always the Corliss engine. Daniel Coit Gilman, President of Johns Hopkins, made the conventional, unimaginative, almost irresponsive, pragmatic answer, testifying that machinery "brings to every cottage of our day comforts and adornments which in the days of Queen Bess . . . were not known outside of the palace." But Gilman also saw machinery as a source of beauty as well as comfort. It was apparent to him in the Brooklyn Bridge, in ships like the *Aurania*, in complex machine tools such as Rowland's dividing engine which "has beauty of its own; not that of the human form nor that of a running brook, but the beauty of perfect adaptation to purpose," much as some contemporary scientists assert that a beautiful formula is a poem. Quite obviously a man like Gilman would not want medieval buildings for his university at Baltimore, but rather serviceable, economical structures. Gilman coupled a dislike for the modern medievalism he saw at the University of Glasgow or in the plan for Trinity College with a disdain for professional architects whom he considered both ignorant and incompetent in technical matters. He wrote gleefully about architects' failures to provide drains from roofs and courts, of bad orientations, of long staircases, of doors too narrow to pass machines and laboratory equipment, of the absence of lifts or ventilating hoods. He wanted buildings at Hopkins which would have good machinery for heating and ventilation, be well supplied with gas, water and light, with ways of removing noxious dust or gas from the laboratories, all arranged, without architectural assistance, by a "professor who looks after these things in advance — instead of an architect who forgets them altogether."

Bad as the architects doubtless were, the professors were worse. What Gilman got was an array of remodeled houses, carriage sheds, bald laboratories erected to suit the taste of professors of physics, chemistry, biology and philology. Developed in the middle of Baltimore, the University grew without guidence from a master plan. The utilitarian aspect of Hopkins attracted only local attention, however, until the notoriously contentious Thomas Huxley journeyed to Baltimore in 1876 to participate in opening the new University. His speech made headlines and raised the hackles of the architectural profession. He was not disappointed by the utilitarian appearance of Hopkins. On the contrary, he said, "It has been my fate to see great educational funds fossilise into mere bricks and mortar, in the petrifying springs of architecture, with nothing left to work the institution they were intended to support . . . whenever you do build, get an honest bricklayer, and make him build . . . just such rooms as you really want, leaving ample space for expansion." Huxley envisioned the future Hopkins as having serviceable laboratories and museums of science, "then, if you have a few hundred thousand dollars you don't know what to do with, send for an architect and tell him to put up a façade. If American is similar to British experience, any other course will probably lead you into having some stately structures, good for your architect's fame, but not in the least what you want."

Huxley's attack upon the architectural profession, which many a reader may still relish, upset architects almost as much as his theories about evolution had angered religious fundamentalists. They were pressing by concerted action against American apathy towards the arts and American reliance upon the "honest bricklayers" in matters of building. Their task was not made easier when a well-known scientist espoused amateurism. Huxley's opinion moreover denied the claims of European-oriented architects such as Hunt and Eidlitz that America would have no worthy culture until she was refaced in the image of Bourges or the Baths of Caracalla.

But it was on exactly this score that Europeans and Americans sensitive to what was best for America disagreed with the professional architects. Huxley did not want us to repeat the errors made at Oxford. Physicians who saw monumental hospitals designed more like palaces than as places for the sick and wounded cautioned us not to build architecturally. Architects seldom accepted the advice. Hunt's Episcopal Hospital at Philadelphia as well as his Presbyterian Hospital in New York, built in 1872, were multi-story structures with dark interiors, monumental stairways, all in medieval dress, more attractive to donors and trustees than to nurses, physicians and patients. What the physician wanted was a hospital built as a series of independent ward-pavilions supplied with good lighting and ventilation, easy to supervise, easily cleaned, easily separable for the isolation of diseases. A ward-pavilion at the Johns Hopkins Hospital was the ideal. It was designed by a physician, John Shaw Billings, who was asked by the benefactor, Johns Hopkins, to make a modern institution built upon a plan fit to obtain "ventilation and heating and light and sunshine, as curative agents." He adopted the idea of one-story detached pavilion wards which had been advocated by experts like Florence Nightingale, based upon observations made during the Crimean War. Set upon north-south axes so that the sun gained access to both sides during the day, each pavilion, standing apart from the others, would have ventilation and sunlight. Walls were double, enclosing a hollow space that insulated the ward. Further attention to utility appeared in abundant provisions for heating and ventilation, consolidation of plumbing, elimination of all moldings and ornament to facilitate cleaning, and a plan which enabled a single nurse easily to supervise a large number of patients. These arrangements made the ward as efficient a machine as a hospital management could then conjecture.

Physicians had long hoped to be able to operate such a machine. One doctor blamed architects and trustees for the backward state of hospital design, and nearly all physicians echoed Huxley's lament about the useless expenditures made by architects; thus Dr. Francis Henry Brown wrote in 1879: "Architects are tempted with permanent materials in their hands to devote too large an expenditure to display and effect, making the buildings expensive in indirect proportion to the use for which they are intended."

But perhaps the most serious of the charges physicians made against the architect was that he strove for permanence and monumentality. Experience during the Civil War with temporary wooden barracks convinced Surgeon-General Woodworth that "The old, magnificent hospitals, built as monuments for all time, will be abandoned for the simple pavilion of indefinite existence." Dr. Billings agreed: ". . . no hospital should be constructed with a view to its being used more than fifteen years."

Nonetheless Billings was forced by the donor's will to make a city monument out of the façade of his Johns Hopkins Hospital. This task was entrusted to Cabot and Chandler who produced an unbelievably bad composition, and the investment conditions required that the pavilions be permanent instead of the ephemeral ones Billings thought wiser. But despite these fundamental difficulties he persisted in the primacy of utility and achieved a building that performed well while lacking any architectural merit. It was a bald brick working machine sprouting ventilators, windows, and chimneys in ugly disarray.

The medical success of such a building caused scientists to suspect the assumptions underlying professional architecture. Charles William Eliot, President of Harvard, once a chemist, struck at the heart of associationalism when he observed that art and morality were two separate things. He was suspicious of anything involving mysticism or ritual, identified medieval architecture with Catholicism which he thought idolatrous — regarded cathedrals as bad things because they were unsuited for rational worship. The seat of all virtue for Eliot lay in the intellect. The emotional and the intuitive he discounted as vague and deceptive. His democratic taste countenanced no high priests of the arts. He was repelled by Ruskin's remark, "It is not to the public that the judgment is intrusted. It is by the chosen few, by our nobility, and men of taste and talent, that the decision is made." He too suspected professional architects, and preferred the "honest bricklayer" to any tastemaker. Architects might insist, with Leopold Eidlitz, that "An architect who consents . . . to permit a layman to decide upon the merit of his work, to gauge it, correct it, accept it or refuse it — has already given up his position as a professional man." This was a professional posture, a sentiment that would be respected by many an architect right down to such different men as Frank Lloyd Wright and Ralph Walker, but it was not a sentiment many other Americans would accept. On the whole, they would agree rather with Greenough's apostrophe to the common man, previously cited, "The great multitude desires the best of everything, and in the long run is the best judge of it."

Such desires and judgments as "an honest bricklayer" might entertain would, it was thought, inevitably align architecture with progress — that *leitmotif* of the modern age. Buildings should be for useful purposes; they should be extendable, temporary, flexible, expendable. According to the scientist G. Stanley Hall, "partitions should be rather temporary, for in science the changes in methods of research so often necessitate changes of partitions." Nor was flexibility the only concession to be made to progress. Buildings should be expendable. Having planned the chemistry laboratory at M.I.T. and having seen the difficulties of remodeling various monumental buildings at Harvard, Eliot expressed a common American thought which had been voiced long before in *The House of the Seven Gables*, "our way of building for the present generation only is the best way. . . . It is not well that a house should last a century — it becomes unsuited to the improved habits of succeeding generations. The same is true of public buildings."

Utility, then, conditioned the plan and bleak appearance of the University Museum at Harvard begun in 1858. The museum is largely a monument to one great scientist, Louis Agassiz, the biologist, who intended it to be a center for object-directed education about flora and fauna and the laws governing their growth, though not their evolution which he was not to accept. The museum's factory-type structure, consisting of cast-iron columns embedded in brick, carrying brick vaults, enclosed many isolated and fireproof rooms, two stories high, with balconies around their perimeters. Such rooms enabled Agassiz to display a series of biological ideas, assembling within one exhibition all the animals and plants, mammoth to microscopic, stuffed specimens or fossils, that might be needed to show a new typology. Here was a museum building, lacking any artistic merit, which enabled scientists to provide public education in the "vast connections between animals, both fossils and modern."

The uniqueness of the Museum, generally unobserved by professional and European-minded American architectural writers and architects, was not lost upon the Europeans themselves. One of the great naturalists of the day, Alfred Russel Wallace, gave Agassiz full credit for a great advance in educational building, for having produced the best example of a functional and economical museum.

The sacrifice of architecture to science pleased Wallace especially, for he had come to dislike Victorian Gothic monuments such as the Museum of Natural History at South Kensington because they taught nothing about biology. A dozen visits to the Museum at London would not distill the lesson so clearly told at Harvard — "the lesson that each continent has its peculiar forms of life, and that the greatest similarity in geographical position and climate may be accompanied by a complete diversity in the animal inhabitants."

It was ironic that such compliments to a product of American culture should come at the very moment when the American merchant and his tastemaker architect were attempting to reproduce in America an overlay of European art culture, when we were seeking to borrow exactly what the most creative and forward-looking Europeans were trying to discard.

But the functional view had its myopia too. "Honest bricklayers" did not abound nor did they build beautifully. For this there was plenty of evidence from Cambridge, Massachusetts, to Guthrie, Oklahoma. There was some right on the side of Charles Eliot Norton who cried that Agassiz's museum was no more than a massive and drab pile of utilitarian rooms, failing to convey any impression of the intellectual spirit pervading the research inside. "Its bare, shadowless walls, unadorned by carven columns or memorial statues, will stand incapable of affording support for those associations which endear every human work of worth."

1 3

A MAJOR RECONCILIATION, AN INTELLIGENT AND SENSITIVE INTELLECTUAL and intuitive synthesis between the demands of science and the needs of art, between pragmatism and idealism, between the real and the imaginative, the material and the human, was manifestly needed in architecture.

Among the architects who were the leaders of the period there were surely few who could even essay such a synthesis — a synthesis which compromised neither commodity nor delight. The power was not in Jenney, despite his functional ingenuity, for he had no skill in composition and no understanding of symbolism. It was not in the symbolists like Van Brunt, whose worship of architectural "morality" left them indifferent to the building needs. It was not in eccentrics like Furness; nor in followers of stereotypes like Mullett and Potter. It was not in the arrogant would-be tastemakers led by Hunt who denied their day altogether.

In the next period men like Sullivan and Root would come nearer to the goal though they too would fail to reach it. But that utility could be accommodated to design might not have seemed to them a thing to be believed had it not been for the incomplete examples offered by the greatest American architect of his day, one of the few great American architects of all time, Henry Hobson Richardson.

He entered an America ready for an architectural catalyst. There was, on the one hand, the boisterous roar of a nation exerting colossal energies, taking great strides, ripping ore from the earth, mastering coal and steam and iron and electricity, intent upon exploiting, content with the makeshift and the utilitarian, ready to flee to a new frontier whenever the social consequences of the past became too appalling at home. There were on the other hand the picayune and often effeminate pratings of a people who might gloss over their own rudeness but who did not yet know that their own aesthetic and intellectual resources were good enough, who sought to emulate the surface flourishes of European manners and customs. Men like Henry James and Whistler might flee to Europe; men like Henry Adams might worry ineffectually about the dynamo while writing inaccurately about the Virgin of Chartres and Japan. What was needed was something lusty and American. For architecture, the first useful image was provided by Richardson. That his image resolved the dilemma of his culture, at least in architecture, was sensed by many of his contemporaries.

A poll conducted by the *American Architect and Building News* in 1885, when Richardson was forty-eight, showed well enough that architects favored large, imposing buildings, regardless of the style of their interiors. Voting for the ten best buildings in the United States, seventy-five architects selected a total of 175 different buildings. None of those selected dated from before 1790; only two were of the period prior to the Civil War. These were the United States Capitol, placed second, gaining 55 per cent of the 75 votes, and Upjohn's Trinity Church, New York, fourth with 45 per cent. Choice number six was the wildly eclectic State Capitol at Hartford, a creation of Upjohn's dotage. Such a choice seems almost to have been an aberration in the overwhelming voice of the jury, for five of the top ten buildings were the work of Richardson. Hunt's Vanderbilt House, it is true, was a favorite, gaining 49 per cent of the vote for third place. But Hunt had definitely lost to Richardson whose Trinity Church in Boston stood easily in first place with 84 per cent of the votes; and this was followed in various positions by his Albany City Hall, Sever Hall at Harvard, the State Capitol at Albany, and the Town Hall at North Easton, each a unified, strong building. This was amazing acclaim for a man who was still young. It goes far to prove that he was indeed a hero, but a hero respected in his lifetime, not a hero in revolt against a time that did not understand him. It is well to underline this event, for architectural historians, abetted by romantic architects, themselves, as well as by modernists who had to fight for a while to gain acceptance, have tended to think of heroes of architecture as having always to work in the face of unbelievable opposition.

America was ready for Richardson. Out of the musings of Hunt and Eidlitz little good would have come had not Richardson shown a way of speaking the new scale of industrial life and of considering its architecture as a whole, rather than as an assemblage of quotations from European sketchbooks.

The Johns Hopkins Hospital with its utilitarian wards masked by a gilded front would not do. Neither would Memorial Hall's infatuation with Ruskinian moral symbolism. The two great streams of development slowly found a single current. It was no longer possible for an engineer like Jenney to be satisfied merely with technical innovation, as he had been in the Home Insurance Building. Now he must seek aesethetic refinement of total form as well. It was no longer possible for a man like Hunt to pretend that the new, huge, commercial buildings would achieve dignity and visual prestige with awkward silhouettes festooned with pages from history. The buildings and their builders had to acknowledge technology, and to be concerned with total form at the new enlarged scale.

Ironically, the building that did this was not technologically progressive at all. This was Richardson's wholesale warehouse for Marshall Field, built in Chicago in 1885-1887, now unhappily destroyed. Here Chicago saw great architecture for the first time, and the impression struck home. Looked at critically, the building revealed neither the obvious reminiscences of medievalism nor the spurious yearnings of the skyscraper, but simply an ideal commercial edifice. It was one great, single, plastic mass, with all the grandeur of a simple form which springs boldly from the ground, which is precisely defined at all points, which is terminated by a fine and decisive cornice. Throughout, each mass and space meant what it said. Everything was clearly organized, emphatically stated, whether one followed the superb rhythms of the arches or studied the heavily textured walls. Standing before it, Major Jenney must have felt that he had covered his frames with banal and confused clichés. We know that Sullivan learned from it how to express what was really central in architectural composition, and that this pulled him out of the morass of minor themes and decorative touches in which he was floundering. Here in the sight of this building, Sullivan found what others would find later, a way of form so that the technical need not be ugly and the aesthetic need be neither borrowed nor flimsy. Richardson gave to young architects a goal of quality, an index of scale, a sense of stateliness possible in architecture for an industrial civilization.

Thus 1885, just before Richardson's death, was a point of climax. The dichotomy between symbolism and utility had produced a clientele which might demand a new sort of architecture. After Richardson such an architecture was possible and it became evident very soon.

Richardson, himself, seems to have sensed the fact that the American architectural scene needed a living hero. He came from a rich and cultivated plantation family in New Orleans, and might have been a Henry Howard, designing elegant houses for the landed gentry. He was popular at Harvard, where he won membership in the Porcellian. Thus he might have rivaled Hunt as aesthetic docent to Northern Society. He studied at the École des Beaux-Arts and might have transplanted the architecture of the Second Empire to America. But he did none of these things.

The Civil War cut him off from his family funds; his friends in the North dissuaded him from returning South after the war. He was to become the architect for many wealthy people, including industrialists like the men of the Ames family. He thought money was best used on architecture to which posterity might point with pride. He preferred the company of the Adamses and the Olmsteds and of artists like La Farge and Saint-Gaudens to the *nouveaux riches* of the Newport châteaux. He refused to transplant a French architecture to America, saying that "it would not cost me a bit of trouble to build French buildings that should reach from here to Philadelphia, but that is not what I want to do."

If you will know Richardson, you must look at some of his sketches. They are rough vignettes, capturing bold masses and spaces, circumscribing the major masses of a composition, firmly rooting it to the earth, juxtaposing masses against each other in dynamic balance. No one else on the American scene could plan with his authority. Nor had anyone else yet grasped the majesty of the elementary forms he drew in a composition for a lighthouse or an icehouse beside a small pond with its sheds and long chute leading down to the water. Contrasted to the work of Downing or Upjohn, Richardson's sketches seem to have dropped all that smacks of interior decoration, effeminate scale, two-dimensional picturesqueness. Contrasted to those of Jefferson, whose scholarly habit ruled rigorously straight lines on blocked paper and showed the façades of different temples, annotated with statistics of materials and costs, Richardson's sketches reveal an architect who seeks the organizational whole of spaces and masses first, plunges into the composition emotionally, and preserves all the fire of first impression. Elementary and machine-serving forms appealed to him; they were the new America, and he realized that no amount of paper and T-square geometry could capture the spirit he saw in them. He worked with builders and masons and artists, altering his design on the site until it lay "in stone, beyond recovery." Nothing could be more different from Jefferson's rational way of working than Richardson's creed. "The architect acts on his building, but his building reacts on him — helps to build itself. His work is plastic work, and, like the sculptor's, cannot be finished in a drawing. It cannot be fully judged except in concrete shape and color, amid actual lights and shadows and its own particular surroundings; and if when it is begun it fails to look as it should, it is not only the architect's privilege but his duty to alter it in any way he can."

Working in this way, Richardson did not soon or easily arrive at the answer that would provide a working image for the oncoming age of reform. Few great architects should be remembered for their first works; he was no exception. His first commissions, obtained after discouraging delays, were hardly above the common taste. Sharing the prevailing belief in "appropriateness," he used Gothic for churches at Springfield and West Medford during the '60s, Renaissance for business buildings such as the Western Railroad offices and the Agawam National Bank at Springfield at the end of that decade. None of these is distinguished by control over great masses of simple composition. There were even lapses in coloration and scale and proportion, such as produced the pitiful tower of the Worcester High School of 1869-1871.

The 1870s saw Richardson gain control. The tower of the Brattle Square Church (1870-1872) gave some intimation of the masses and the interior a hint of the large expansive spaces he would later develop.

Trinity Church at Boston, which he won in a competition over Hunt, brought him to the manner which would become identified with his name. Although the exterior was still a combination of many fragmented parts, the interior presented a strongly unified space arranged for the preaching of Phillips Brooks. Among other things it was the first American church to have a whole interior decorated by any single painter of ability, John La Farge. What Richardson learned at Trinity about handling a total mass and volume appeared fully in the Cheney Building at Hartford in 1875-1876, with its massive and stately arches framing smaller parts. This office building is progressive in the highest degree. On the other hand, the house built for Cheney at South Manchester, while its inside has a free plan like that of the house of Watts Sherman at Newport, is still just a Richardsonian version of the kind of house Richard Norman Shaw was making for neo-Elizabethans in England. Richardson had not yet found his domestic style of the Stoughton House at Cambridge, and his clients seemed to be content with houses far less bold than their office buildings. Perhaps the things that best reveal his capacity in this period are the magnificent staircase and Senate Chamber at Albany.

By 1878-1879 he had achieved something more than a new imported style. He had learned how to plan great and complex series of spaces and to surround them with elementary masses vigorously proportioned, varied in shape, balanced on the land, and energetically counterbalanced by each other. We can see this in the Town Hall at North Easton, which sits on the crest of a hill, rising mountainlike from ledges of granite. The great circuitous approach stair undulates with the land. The Library below sits on the side of the hill. Its arched entry forms a point of balance between the long handsome stack wing with its irregularly rhythmed windows and the tall tower on the lower side. The railroad station at North Easton again displays simple, big forms. The Ames gate house may be the prize. Here huge glacial boulders project two feet or more from the surface, but never escape their imprisonment in the battered walls that shape a rough geometry. All this is executed in autumnal browns and reds and earthy colors. A giant conceived of those stones, not a man inspired by Godey's *Lady's Book*. Van Brunt was right when he said it was "a specimen of boisterous Titanic gamboling."

In the '80s and particularly in his last four culminating years, after his trip to southern France and northern Italy and Spain, all of Richardson's work tended in the direction of simplicity of forms, compactness of mass, monumentality of scale. But this was not a copied inspiration from a new foreign source, merely a recognition of some fundamental principles with which he found himself in accord. The designs were always conceived as a whole; the rhythms were always all-inclusive whether the building was a library in Quincy or a bridge over Boston's Fenway. The materials became more natural, the planning more "open." The series of railroad stations and small public libraries of the '80s all led him to segregate functions, to envelop them with basic geometric shapes, and to weld these into an over-all design. Sever Hall, at Harvard, begun in 1878, reveals his ability to handle brick beautifully, to gain a monumental envelope, even if in this case he followed the lead of other great architects by compromising the spaces, circulation and lighting within the building. It shows also how he could strike his own theme while yet making his building compatible with others, even with such ancient buildings as Bulfinch's august University Hall which lies opposite to the west.

Contrasted with these, his buildings in Pittsburgh and Chicago were simpler still. Seldom has any architect handled a difficult problem better than Richardson did when he designed the Allegheny Courthouse and Jail at Pittsburgh of 1885-1887. One can imagine Hunt attacking this problem with a quotation from European town halls. Richardson did no such thing. Even the Bridge of Sighs became in his hands a massive arch springing between the buildings. Giant stones in walls and arched openings fairly scream the custodial finality of the jail. No doubt Richardson here thought himself working with all his power; he believed it would be his greatest achievement, and said, "Let me but have time to finish Pittsburgh . . . and I should be content without another day."

All this work of Richardson's came to fruition in the Marshall Field warehouse. Here was his *chef d'oeuvre* and his swan song. It suggested to his successors how they might begin to make the details of a fine city of industrial buildings. It did not propose the larger truth that a great city must be more than a collection of fine individual buildings. There is nothing to suggest that this idea ever occurred to Richardson, much less to any other architect of this period. That revelation was saved for the age of reform and for Daniel Burnham of Chicago.

Yet Richardson, dying before he was fifty, had done enough. He was a hero. Henry Adams said Richardson was the only really big man he had ever known. He loved the remark of a German admirer, "*Mein Gott*, how he looks like his own buildings." He would have loved the epitaph by Phillips Brooks in the *Harvard Monthly* for October, 1886: "The man and the work are absolutely one. The man is in the work and the work is in the man." This is a good thing for architects (and others) to remember. It helped the succeeding generation, including McKim and Sullivan and Wright, to aspire to the best, to be themselves.

I 4

STILL IT WAS NOT ENOUGH FOR THE POST-CIVIL WAR GENERATION TO HAVE one great architect, nor is it ever sufficient even when he is as creative as a Richardson or a Wright. Richardson's greatness, like Wright's, lay in a personal achievement that could not easily be wrenched from the personality that made it. His was a personal triumph over the society in which he lived, but his art could not become a universal expression like the genuine Gothic, nor attain the universality of the Georgian. His personal stature majestically commanded a following among young architects who carried the Romanesque throughout his empire, but as their weaker versions of Richardsonian royalty revealed John L. Faxon, Robert H. Robertson, or Frank M. Howe in disguise, the style languished and its passing carried away the most important lessons of design Richardson had taught. A later generation thought of Richardson as the purveyor of still another foreign style, the Romanesque. In the *Atlantic Monthly* of 1886, Van Brunt hoped for something gentler, more cultivated and urbane, with less of "savage and brutal strength." It seemed to him that Richardson's experiments were "often open to the charge of an affectation of barbarism and heaviness inconsistent with our civilization."

Thus the next generation begun in 1885 had still the pressing problem of developing a beautiful and amenable architecture and a plan for industrial cities. Neither the idealism of European-minded architects like Hunt and critics like Norton nor the pragmatism of Huxley and Gilman had found a way of improving the slums that mocked the American dream. The opening of the West had not carried with it an architecture commensurate with the landscape; the South no longer could offer examples of an aristocratic architecture; and as agriculture declined in importance, the city, with its swollen immigrations, became entangled in a paradox in which cultural institutions were preoccupied with European achievements and architectural dress, while the industry and commerce that supported those institutions addressed themselves to the utilitarian and expedient. The vernacular might sometimes reflect the great movements in science, as it did in the Johns Hopkins Hospital and the Museum of Comparative Zoology at Harvard; but the cultivated architect preferred to ignore science while he erected a National Academy of Design or a Memorial Hall. By their sheer bulk alone, a Mutual Life Insurance Building or Western Union Telegraph Building indicated the power of national business concerns, but their architecture preferred to hide rather than exalt the telegraph, telephone, rails, steamships, typewriters, elevators, electric lighting, iron and steel, and oil that were the great technology of the time. Richardson showed an artistic way past the Home Insurance Building, by his jails and warehouses, but even he did not seize upon the technological resources available to him. Lesser architects, like those who designed the Cathedral of St. John the Divine or the proposed building for the American Institute of Architects, could not be expected to do so. The resources were great, but there was little to suggest in 1885 that architects might ever learn how to use them.

III

1885-1913

III

1885-1913

T HOUGH THEY PROBABLY NEVER CONSIDERED IT, Hunt and Richardson had but one dominant ideological question to answer: Do you welcome the science and the technology of industrial America or do you prefer to pretend they are not there? The next quarter-century added others, as change in the characteristics and the aspirations of the American people accelerated. Lilienthal's gliders developed to Sikorsky's four-engine aircraft; Daimler's erratic internal combustion engine matured, was abetted by Kettering's self-starter, and one million automobiles thronged American roads; a paper patent on a motion picture device grew to a full-length feature, *Ben Hur*, as popular in its day as the new version of 1959 was later.

Architecture moved from Jenney's modest Home Insurance Building to the soaring white spire of the Woolworth Building; the novels of Stevenson and Hardy gave place to those of Proust and D. H. Lawrence; serene Parisians carrying their umbrellas over the sward of the *Grande Jatte* of Seurat were succeeded by the violence of Chagall's drinking soldier or the emptiness of Chirico's lonely spaces. Saint-Gaudens's statue of Lincoln became less moving to new generations than Lehmbruck's *Standing Youth*. In 1886 New Yorkers marveled at the new Statue of Liberty just installed on Bedloe's Island; in 1913 they met the works of Duchamp, Matisse and Picasso at the first Armory Show. The quarter-century lifted its curtain to the brassy *Death and Transfiguration* of Richard Strauss and brought it down with the primitive woodwinds and the excitement of Stravinsky's incessant drums, celebrating *The Rite of Spring*. The buccaneers of American industry gave way to the barons. Plutocracy and monopoly and organized labor waxed and sometimes were restrained. The federal giant began to intervene in many matters. It was a time of bitter polemic, and of transient reform.

It witnessed the largest immigrations the United States had ever known, accompanied for the first time with great variety among the ethnic groups that furnished the immigrants. It saw the "passing of the frontier," the emergence of Chicago as a national center. It experienced a culmination of the antagonisms that farmers felt toward city men, the West toward Wall Street and the East. It saw America begin seriously to interfere in the outside world, to shake the Big Stick, to send her fleet and her Presidents traveling, to challenge the seapower of England, to assert a national belligerence built on a faith in manifest destiny, which, despite disclaimers, often seemed imperialistic.

Thus a philosophical architect found himself puzzled by a number of questions beyond the still urgent one of the relation of technology to art. Federal government was rising. Did this demand or deserve a new or a refurbished architectural symbol? Large business corporations were beginning to do business on a national scale. Ought one to try to produce fine railroad termini, factories, power houses, a corporate architecture? There was interest in social settlements and in alleviating the lot of the poor. Did this call for attention to parks, playgrounds, hospitals, collective housing, a social architecture? Reform was in the air. Could there be such a thing as a reform architecture? Should there be, would there be a bimetallic architecture, a Populist architecture, a Granger architecture, a labor architecture, a Western architecture? Clearly enough America was yearning for world influence. Would her architecture turn imperial, too? Many people thought too many buildings were designed for the taste and use only of the rich and powerful and that this was undemocratic. Beyond that there was a mystique. Men like Sullivan and Wright cried for "democratic" architecture. Was there, could there be any such thing?

What architecture was democratic, what was not? Louis Sullivan and Frank Lloyd Wright, for example, were ambiguous about it. On the one hand, they said that the individual in a democracy should have what he wanted. On the other, they berated the "imperialistic" planning of McKim and Burnham. But the American public, from William Jennings Bryan to J. P. Morgan, liked such "imperialistic" buildings very much. What, then, was the more democratic, to let them have what they wanted or to provide what a few architectural leaders of the opposition thought they knew to be better? The American dream persisted; but it was too vague to be expressed in some democratic symbol as unequivocal as a Thomist cathedral.

I

NONE OF THE AMERICAN ARGUMENTS EVER SEEMS QUITE TO BE SETTLED. From 1885 to 1913 Americans continued to debate how much influence to yield to the future, how much to the past; whether to prize innovation or tradition the more; whether the country or the city offered the finer way of life; whether common men or an elite should be the arbiters of the arts; what were the respective roles of God and science, of the hand and the machine. Today we have lost most of our fear of subservience to any motherland; the city has, at least on the surface, prevailed over the country. But discussions of emancipation, and of the city, came to their fever point in the twenty-five years that bracketed the beginning of the twentieth century.

They were debated by Americans whose general characteristics have been described for over a century by many observers and with remarkable agreement. Americans, most of them say, have prized individualism, pragmatism, work as a value in itself, change in itself, education for useful work; they have usually been generous, optimistic, deferential to women, given to overstatement, anxious to make sweeping generalizations, prone to moralizing; their definite acquisitiveness is not really cupidity; they reveal strange combinations of lawlessness and respect for law, humility and exaggerated humor and bombast; the arts have always seemed less important to them than a high physical standard of living. They have been remarkably prone to solve problems by moving away from them, to despoil a land and then to move on rather than to try to preserve it. Thus they have been and are paradoxical (but no more so than the Athenians), idealistic and materialistic in the same breath, practical about details, flighty about generalizations, suspicious of forward plans, but impatient for a quick resolution of every difficulty.

As the nineteenth century drew to a close the discussion of the past and the future was carried on in a new key. In the beginning it had been mostly a denial of Europe, a solicitude about preserving the special and vaguely defined American treasure against the corruption of the Old World. It was often manifested by demands for a national art, a national literature, even the unifying and different national language proposed by Noah Webster. It had reached its peak in the ringing words of Emerson's 1837 Phi Beta Kappa oration, *The American Scholar*. This was far more than a mere declaration of literary independence. It applied to all employments of the mind and even more; Europe was the paterfamilias, now rejected.

Whitman carried rejection further and added egalitarianism. He enjoined the muse to "migrate from Greece and Ionia" not only because America was to be self-reliant but because she was the absolute antithesis of Europe. She was to be a place where the average man, with the most common qualities, could be divine.

But now the true issue was no longer that of America versus Europe, if it ever had been. Instead, it was the more general one of change against tradition, expressing the urgent necessity, felt by many Americans, to lift the heavy bolt of the past which barred the door to the future. In the beginning the barrier was epitomized by the Europe from which our cultural as well as our economic and political independence must be wrested. In accepting this epitome, it was convenient to forget how many innovations were, in fact, coming from the "tradition-fettered" and "tired" Old World. Later on the same mistake was made in the opinion Western America held of the Eastern seaboard.

But even among the wise extremists of either side there was an American ambivalence, one which Santayana noted when he said that America was really a country with two mentalities: "one a survival of the beliefs and standards of the fathers, the other an expression of the instincts, practises and discoveries of the younger generation."

2

REJECTION OF EUROPE AND OF THE PAST WAS BUT A FACE OF THE CONtest between the transcendental sword of self-reliance and the historical shield of the genteel tradition. Each had its romance. The men of the tradition loved a Europe that may never have been. The transcendentalists imagined a frontier that never was.

The self-reliance of transcendentalism demanded a democratic tolerance of the self-reliance of others, perhaps even an enthusiasm for it. It might content itself with gradual change, but, sprung as it was from Puritan pietism, it must identify change with progress. For the transcendental romance, the frontier was the cutting edge. Viewed another way the frontier was then and now an escape from failure; but to the transcendental mind, failure was synonymous with the past, and the past was always in the East, European or American as it might be. What was there was doomed to passivity. The pioneer obviously had to be self-reliant; the self-reliance involved in coping alone or almost alone with elemental forces was more evident than the self-reliance that might be required to cope with the complex problems of the settled community. Now towards the end of the century as the obvious frontier was disappearing, it was around the frontier that the controversy swirled.

On this vanishing frontier the rage against the East was hot and deep. Tragedy on the plains might be deferred for another three decades and in the end self-reliance might not be enough. But already life on the land was becoming marginal whether the cattle empire remained or the nesters fenced it in. There was still some Indian land but the war whoops were practically stilled after Geronimo, the Apache, was captured in 1886 and the Sioux put down in 1890. What was left on the reservations was not very good land but nonetheless it was distributed bountifully to the thronging whites. The "boomers" did not always move as fast as those of 1889 who built the tent towns of Guthrie and Oklahoma City between noon and sundown of an April day, but they moved fast enough. After 100,000 of them had poured into the Cherokee Strip in 1893 there were no more great reserves of land worth stealing, annexing, bartering, or "buying."

On July 12 of the same year, Frederick Jackson Turner, the Wisconsin historian, delivered his classic address, *The Significance of the Frontier in American History*, and it was appropriate that it should have been delivered in Chicago. In Turner's view America was not an inheritance from Europe, but the product of action and reaction with Europe. He took the big position that appealed to a farm belt which still thought of itself as part of the frontier. "The existence of an area of free land, its continuous recession, and the advance of American settlement westward, explain American development." The region of sparse settlement to the west, "the frontier," was "the meeting point between savagery and civilization." In that lay its strength. As the frontier went west, it moved farther away from the influence of Europe and this meant a steady growth of independence along strictly American and, therefore, better lines. When the frontier closed there would be a real risk of decay. Such a theory naturally distrusted the industrialized and urbanized civilization of the East.

Nevertheless, the government in the East was beginning to think about the problems of the farmer, over and above the measures taken in response to his political power which, then as now, exceeded the realities of his numbers or importance. Of long-range significance were the federal surveys of the arid regions of the West and the New Lands Reclamation Act of 1902 which authorized the government to build great irrigation projects served by such structures as Wyoming's Shoshone Dam or the Roosevelt Dam on the Salt River of Arizona. The great conservation movement was on, supported by President Cleveland and especially by President Theodore Roosevelt, in whose administration almost 150 million acres were set apart for the public domain, establishing reserves of minerals and forests, conserving watersheds, providing the prospect of bounteous national parks.

But even the most direct benefits of such programs did not appear to farmers a sufficient recompense for the drain on their slender cash which seemed always to be flowing to the city and to the East. The interests of farmers in Oregon and Nebraska, of silver owners in Nevada or Colorado, united in a suspicion of financiers, of cities, of the East. Some motives were economic, some psychological. But they pooled their often contradictory resentments and ambitions; they voiced political discontents which were really economic discontents. In the end they coalesced into the Populist party, joining farm needs with the different purposes of the advocates of free silver, abandoning convictions in search of a victory which was not to be won, at least directly. In the end most of the serious part of the Populist program became a part of the American system. But it was later and at other hands.

The high-water mark for Populism was reached in 1896 when William Jennings Bryan came nearest to victory. But for a long time after that he was still indefatigable and a durable symbol with his bald head, his fringes of side hair, his rumpled linen suit, his incessant palm-leaf fan, spellbinding the Westerners at fair-grounds and under Chautauqua tents, standing against wealth, against the East, against bankers, against the gold standard, against alcohol, against the theory of evolution, against science, against culture.

What could a movement like this do for or to architecture? Had farmers' organizations been stronger, wealthier, wider of purpose, more durable, architecture might have emerged to serve their needs but a Grange building is not Populist architecture and is seldom architecture at all. The frontier was an abandonment of architecture by the nature of its mobility. It never settled long enough in one place to develop the log cabin or the sod house into architecture. The Populist movement had the same characteristics. It too was not firm enough to have any architectural symbols; and its taste would have approved the present Corn Palace at Mitchell, South Dakota.

But there was an ideological residue of importance for American architecture. For Sullivan and Wright and other architects the frontier theory provided the genesis for an insistence on "regional architecture" and the belief that American architecture could be born only in the West. Each expressed the same conviction although quite differently.

Sullivan was the vaguer. He fancied himself a poet and wrote a great deal of flamboyantly bad poetry. A professed nature lover, his words seldom revealed any close observation say of the blade of flax bent by

the wind or the ruffled underfeathers of a blackbird's wing. His ornament, unlike that of medieval Bourges or Chartres, was not often
drawn from the neighborhood, the immediate prairie sources. His detailed observations when there were any came mainly not from Illinois
where he worked but from Biloxi where he occasionally played. But
usually his Byronic terms were broad and general. He wrote of "surging
forests," "vasty plains," "angry waves," "forest monarchs," "the lily's
aromatic luxury," and spoke most often of "flotsam and jetsam." In
architecture he almost never dealt in clichés; in poetry he seldom wrote
anything else. Thus it was with his views of democracy. They centered
not on the political process but on the one thing he felt essential, the
full development of every individual as an individual. In this there was
an implicit assumption, borrowed perhaps from John Dewey, that every
person has a will and a capacity toward individuality. But Sullivan's
interpretation of individualism was as confusing as his interpretation of
feudalism. Feudalism meant, roughly, the men who had power and
money in his day, mostly, though not all, in the East. Individualism
meant the farmer standing alone in his fields facing the rain. Of the
Western European mind he said, "It is at home in turmoil, and loves
urgency, and stress and chance. It loves to build up, and tear down, and
build up again; it loves change, novelty, progress. It loves to destroy."
Of world peoples he asserted, "Their ancient polychromatic thought is
turning white," implying the degradation of individuality.

Sullivan thought that both New York and Chicago were fatally bad.
The belief that few great men are born in the city, that the individualist
will always be associated with the noble countryman, the perpetuation
of the agrarian myth of the stalwart yeoman, the notion that the Western city always had a better chance of regeneration than the Eastern —
all these are Populist. But this does not make Sullivan's architecture
Populist. The Prudential Building for Buffalo could have been for
St. Louis; the Wainwright Building of St. Louis could have been in New
York. Thus the words and the architecture were almost unrelated. It is
the architecture that matters.

Frank Lloyd Wright was in most ways the greater man and the
greater intellect. His writing, too, often betrayed the influence of Populist thought, soaked in Carlyle and Thoreau. The doctrine of individuality colored all his pronouncements though he did not often stretch
this doctrine to include the right of other individuals to do the awful
things they did. In his definitions of democracy, Wright like Sullivan
often sounded transcendental. Wright's picture of Sullivan and himself
suggests the lonely revolt they led against any classic school of design, even a contemporary one. It was an extreme statement of the

transcendental notions of the self-reliant pioneer, appropriate to the "frontier" climate of Chicago.

But despite the brillance of men like Wright and Sullivan and despite the underlying national affection for transcendentalism, men of the genteel tradition were in the saddle during the whole quarter-century. The polemical debates were almost always won by the transcendentalists but when it came to getting important commissions or leading their professional societies it was the traditionalists who came out on top. And if, much later, the victory seemed to have gone the other way, the durable question was how permanent it might be in a democracy which, as de Tocqueville described it, was one where "each new generation is a new people." In his view American conventions of literature and by implication of the other arts must be ephemeral because "If it should happen that the men of some one period were agreed upon any such rules, that would prove nothing for the following period."

3

BUT, EVEN IF AMERICAN TASTE WERE TO BE AS VOLATILE AS DE TOCQUEville thought it must be, the nationalist debate went on. The arguments were pitched at two different levels; there were those that can be regarded as simple chauvinism, a kind of extrapolation of Stephen Decatur with the footnote that my country is not likely to be wrong and is certainly capable of the best. This merged with the sense that there *is* something different about America and that it is not only essential but inevitable that this difference will ultimately find its different aesthetic expression.

At its lowest level the chauvinistic view simply manifested itself in uncritical statements about American buildings. In 1887, for example, the *American Architect and Building News* asserted that Henry G. Marquand's new house in New York was going to be the most beautiful in the world. Such hyperboles run through American criticism but were usually balanced by equally strong statements to the effect that American work was the worst in the world.

Even thoughtful and temperate Americans like John Wellborn Root, one of the most sensitive leaders of the architectural development of Chicago in the '90s, were not immune to such thinking. He believed with others that Richardson's buildings were much better than the most pretentious contemporary buildings of Europe, voicing the mysticism of the American dream in architectural terms: "In the American works we find strength and fitness and a certain spontaneity and freshness, as of stately music or a song in green woods."

In the conscious search for an American art form, as well as in the assertions that we have one and that it is superb, there is no doubt the underlying anxiety of a young people to be praised for doing well. About this the American people have had a normal youthful ambivalence. On the one hand we have paid European emissaries well to come and tell us how badly we are doing and how much better things are back home. Resenting such criticism, we have nevertheless demanded it.

Some of the thrust for aesthetic independence no doubt came from the conviction that history demonstrates that there is no sure way save the way of independence on all fronts, including the aesthetic. A young nation may feel it necessary to cultivate a national outlook if only to slip the bonds of colonialism. But it is a paradox of the nationalist movement in American architecture that at the time when we were most shaky in our independence, most likely to be overwhelmed and restored to a colonial role, we followed a colonial tradition of architecture with great success and that we became generally self-conscious about our national style only after the threat to independence or a renewed colonialism had really vanished.

Against the nationalist view there were those Americans, often the most cultivated, who thought American productions in general were uncouth. This too was a natural attitude; a sound corrective to chauvinism; when it extended to accepting only things from abroad it was absurd, but this was often the extreme position of the Americans who supported the genteel tradition in America during the last half of the nineteenth century. So much of the argument for a national style roared out of Chicago instead of New York that the debate appears in part to have been between Fifth Avenue and Newport on the one hand and Halsted Street and the Loop on the other, the "cultured and leisured" versus "the uncouth and untutored," the East against the West, a regional argument conducted in national terms.

John Wellborn Root thought we might have a national style because American students, "reinforced by what is now conceded to be a great national spirit," had the advantage of having no ignoble history; this might more than compensate for the lack of a great national art history. "They are, therefore, free; free in a deep and significant sense." To this the genteel would of course have countered that it was necessary for Americans to turn to European pasts precisely because they had no history of their own.

But quite aside from the question of freedom from history there was the persistent feeling that Utopia was just around the corner and that the corner would be located in America. This notion has engaged European theorists and practitioners alike from William Penn, Bishop Berkeley, Coleridge and Southey to D. H. Lawrence, Katherine Mansfield and John Middleton Murry. Lawrence for example proposed locating a new state in Florida in 1915 because of the "living sky" he thought was above America. It meant to all of them an escape from the corruptions of the Old World, so that Wyndham Lewis could call America "the antechamber of a world state."

Freedom from Europe, from the East, from history, Utopian necessity, separation from other nations, progressive government, all these spoke in the '80s and '90s to Chicago architects like Root, Sullivan, Wright and George W. Maher for a particular American style.

All this too was confused with the argument about democracy which is still going on. Americans have cherished the undemonstrated theorem that a democratic society is essential for the highest development of art or science despite historical evidence which is less decisive. Many autocracies have, as a matter of fact, done very well by culture. But the view that the arts need democracy remains an essential part of the American conviction and can always be stated as a hope that the whole thesis will be proved tomorrow. Louis Sullivan asserted it over and over again. He made his great affirmation in *Kindergarten Chats*. "Arrange your architecture for Democracy" because "a certain function, democracy, is seeking a certain form of expression, democratic architecture." Yet what "democratic architecture" was he could hardly define. Nor have others done much better. There have been those who have insisted that democracy must have its own symbolic interpretations and men, like Jefferson, who have found these symbols in the classic adaptations of the Enlightenment. Others have said that Roman monumentality had no place whatsoever in a democracy. Could democracy have symbols; could they be invented or must they simply grow; was there any such thing as a democratic architecture? Is Sullivan's original bank at Owatonna as democratic as the classic White House? Or more so? What was undemocratic about the contemporary Japanese temple built by Hunt as a teahouse overlooking the ocean on the Belmont estate at Newport? All were being produced in the democracy; why were some democratic, others not? As a final test case, was the Egyptian obelisk, taken from a totalitarian scene, planted on an artificial knoll near the Potomac, a proper memorial to the first President of the United States; was it democratic just because it was in democratic Washington? Was the White House democratic simply because its fences seemed frail? Despite the confusion, it was easy enough for architects who do not enjoy long stays in the realm of rigorous argument to fall back on the main theme; there is such a thing as democracy; there can be such a thing as a democratic architecture; America is a democracy; there are differences in democracies, and America's, though not the only one, is a different democracy. Therefore it should have a different democratic architecture. This will be American architecture.

There were about as many thinkers who believed that we could not produce a unique American architecture even if we tried, or should not if we could. They rested their arguments on the idea that a national architecture would destroy a desirable individuality inherent in the region, that the scale of the country made a national expression impossible, that by seeking a national norm we would be shackling individual independence, that nothing of this sort could ever be achieved deliberately; that the time was not ripe, America not ready for it, or that the whole notion was contrary to the trend of modern history.

Before such arguments could be joined, one had to meet those who were dubious about the whole spread-eagle thesis on the ground that the American people were crude, likely to stay crude for a long time, and that the best that could be done would be to borrow as much refinement as possible to soften our crudities. This was, for example the position of Stanford White, a popular architect at the end of the nineteenth century. But White, though a good artist, was a lightweight thinker, and serious men rested their opposition to architectural nationalism on more defensible grounds.

4

REGIONALISM, DEEPLY LOVED, STOOD IN ANTITHESIS TO NATIONALISM, JUST as doctrines of states' rights struggled with federalism. Men of a self-loving region could argue that a nationalism which represented all regions would inevitably destroy the loved special qualities of each.

To those regionalists who thought national architecture undesirable, there were added those who thought it impossible. Frederick G. Corser, a Minnesotan, writing in 1885, took an equally strong stance against both importers and nationalists. The best periods of art, he said, had always been those when art was indigenous. Better buildings were made, even if they were crude, when they were "done in response to the living needs of a people." He insisted that if you would "adapt your buildings to the nature of things instead of trying to get up national styles or import the fashion of King this and Queen that . . . your work would stand some chance of outliving you." The climate of Versailles, he liked to remind his readers, was not the climate of Minneapolis; and St. Paul boasted no Marie Antoinette or Henry Tudor.

Beyond those who thought that a national style would either be impossible or would shackle regionalism, there were those who opposed it as a shackling of independence in general. This was really Wright's position although he was identified by the *Architectural Record* of 1908 as an exponent of the New Nationalism. In fact Wright denied Americanism in favor of a much broader kind of individuality which should be consistent with the personalities of clients, artists, terrains and climates. "A man who has individuality (and what man lacks it?) has a right to its expression in his own environment." Adherence to such a doctrine not only means that there could not be a national style, but that even an international style could not properly develop. "I do not believe we will ever again have the uniformity of type which has characterized the so-called great 'styles.' Conditions have changed; our ideal is democracy, the highest possible expression of the individual as a unit not inconsistent with a harmonious whole." But was this idea in itself so American that the expressions which would arise from it would in themselves define an American architecture of maximized diversity? To call such architecture American was probably to avoid the issue; and surely it was the antithesis of what the ardent nationalists were looking for.

Finally even among those who thought we might some day achieve a national style there were some who were convinced it could not be force-fed or brought into being by *force majeure*. This was essentially the position of Barr Ferree, who wrote in 1891, at the height of the debate, that any attempt deliberately to design an American style must fail, that styles cannot "be designed or drawn to order on a sheet of paper."

Even among those who wanted a national style there was no agreement as to what it should be. The national eclectics wanted to repeat the works of the Georgian past. The traditionalists wanted Americans to work out their own version of Roman architecture which would somehow have a new national flavor. The innovators insisted that eclecticism of all sorts be abandoned, historical models discarded entirely, even those from the American past.

Thus the architects were, as usual, arguing about too many things at the same time; did we need a national style at all; how could we get it; must it be eclectic; should the eclecticism be national or world-wide? Where should eclecticism stop and innovation begin? These were questions that could be answered categorically only by the opinionated.

The more thoughtful were, perhaps, in the camp of Root when he said, "broad influences of climate, of national habits, and institutions will in time create the type, and this is the only style worth considering."

But the sober Root tried nonetheless to state the American traits that might be expected to appear in an American architecture. He did his best in his main address at the Illinois symposium of 1887. It was about as well as anyone has ever done. He thought American architecture would be catholic:

> The American people . . . tend to the adoption of any new thing, provided it merely seem better than the old, which often leads to a too sudden abandonment of older modes cutting off slow and yet promising developments and inflicting the newer fashion with certain harshness and crudity. . . .
>
> It will be grave. . . . Though Americans are really grave, the gravity . . . has a humorous complement, strongly marked, which will give to the architecture of the future, a certain "lightness" . . . grace of detail . . . or . . . occasional touches of fancy, or even whimsicalness. . . .
>
> Our architecture will probably remain practical. This means not only that structures of purely decorative character will be few in number, but that each important detail of a building must have some immediate, easily recognized and practical use.

Then he summed up by describing our architecture as catholic, grave with modifying grace, utilitarian. Perhaps as afterthought, he suggested it might also show some trend toward splendor.

5

SUCH SELF-CONSCIOUS INTROSPECTION INTO AMERICAN PERSONALITY TO discover what the American dream meant for architecture came in a period of drastic changes in population, cities, science, technology, business organization and labor patterns.

Many more people now lived on the American land. The population of 1913 was double the fifty million of 1880. Its westward drift persisted, still along the 39th Parallel, its center reaching Bloomington, Indiana. The Pacific Coast and Mountain states grew at two or three times the national rate but still claimed a mere fifteenth of the population. The farmlands of the Middle West were about full. The industrial states around the Great Lakes continued to expand vigorously but the industrial northeast quarter of the country still held more than half the population and vastly more than half of the wealth, monetary, productive, or intellectual.

The long swing from country to city was now more apparent. Agricultural valuations had accounted for a third of the national wealth in 1880 but by 1912 they were only a fourth. Half of those gainfully employed had worked in agriculture in 1880 but by 1910 they were down to a third. A little over a quarter of the people had lived in "urban territory" in 1880; by 1910 it was nearly a half. In 1880 only one city could claim a million people, by 1910 there were three. The twenty cities of more than 100,000 became fifty. Chicago's population doubled in the single decade 1880-1890; the Twin Cities trebled; Detroit, Milwaukee, and Cleveland grew by 60 to 70 per cent. And a great many of the new urbanites were alien.

After 1882 immigration increased precipitously. In the twenty-four years between 1891 and 1914 sixteen and one-half million new Americans entered, so that by 1910 one seventh of the whole population was foreign-born. The newcomers, moreover, were concentrated in the big places. By 1900 they represented a quarter of all the people in cities over 100,000 and up to one half of those in the largest cities.

The great older cities of the industrial Northeast felt the new immigration most forcefully. The native stocks of Boston, Philadelphia, New York were outnumbered by the unassimilated foreign-born and their immediate children. The Italian population of New York exceeded that of Naples, the German population that of Hamburg, the Irish population was twice that of Dublin. Rudyard Kipling, who had little affection for "lesser" races, described the government of New York City as a "despotism of the alien, by the alien, for the alien."

The ethnic composition of the immigrants was important. Up to 1880 they had almost all been British, Irish, German, Scandinavian or French. Though not all had been literate, they often belonged to the middle and professional or farming classes and were not generally drawn from or destined to become an urban proletariat.

But the composition changed almost as the Statue of Liberty was being set up. By 1900 practically all the newcomers were Italian, Greek, Hungarian, Polish, Czech or Baltic. Many were Jews trying to escape the ghettos of Russia and Poland. During the decade 1905-1914 this new type of population accounted for more than half the total American increase. Brought in mainly to supply a plentiful source of cheap, unskilled and uncomplaining labor, the new people settled in the big cities, huddled together in their distress, were both bewildered and submissive. The men who brought them help, who managed their quick naturalization, who got them jobs, who watched out for their social welfare, who defended them in court, were inevitably the agents of the local political boss. While the advocates of good government sniffed and drew their coats away from the stench and the sordid dwellings, the bosses won friendship and support. From this the whole chain of graft in municipal services, of collusion between the policeman and the purveyor of vice, was easily forged. Lord Bryce thought American municipal government the worst failure of democracy in the United States. Andrew D. White asserted in 1890 that American city governments were the worst in the world.

But that was not all. For the cities were not the result only of this torrent of immigration. There had also been a substantial migration of native Americans from the farms. These were small-town people, usually Protestant, usually accustomed to familiar neighbors and to a simple and superficially virtuous life. They were depressed by the anonymity of the city, confused by its crowding and its noise, astonished and repelled by the blatant exhibition of extremes of wealth and poverty, angered by vice and crime and corruption, ill-concealed, often jubilantly paraded. All of this they blamed on the alien and "idolatrous" newcomers. With Josiah Strong they proclaimed that "The first city was built by the first murderer, and crime and vice and wretchedness have festered in it ever since." With Hamlin Garland they entertained lurid dreams of the dangers attendant upon a callow youth who might venture to walk across downtown Chicago even at midday. But it was the new immigrants who were most resented. By 1910 they accounted for two thirds of all the workers in twenty-one major branches of American industry. Unwelcomed by the more skilled native workers, they were even kept out of unions. Demagogic violence, such as mobbed eleven Italians in New Orleans in 1891, was joined to spiteful racist writing. Mary E. Lease proposed massive movements of races so that Northern whites would run everything and be waited on by Orientals and blacks whose proper spheres were servile. The Populist hero, Ignatius Donnelly, asserted that America was "united by a ligament to a corpse — Europe!" By 1914 Professor Edward A. Ross had produced a tract to show that the new immigrants were destroying America. They had forced down the living standards of all labor "toward their 'pigsty mode of life,' just as they brought social standards down to 'their brawls and their animal pleasures.' They were unhygienic and alcoholic, they raised the rates of illiteracy and insanity, they fostered crime and bad morals . . . they threatened the position of women with their coarse peasant philosophy of sex and debased the educational system with parochial schools; they spurred the monstrous overgrowth of cities . . . they threatened to overwhelm 'American blood' and bastardize American civilization."

Despite all the clamor, presidential vetoes by Cleveland and Taft prevented Congress from placing any significant limitations on the immigrants from southern and eastern Europe in this quarter-century. For them the inscription on the Statue of Liberty was still true, at least as far as the Open Door. But the Chinese and the Japanese felt the hand of exclusion in this time and even segregation efforts, such as those in California which prohibited aliens from owning land. The greater segregation was retained for the Negro; a white President might dine a Negro at the White House, appoint a Negro to office, but the Jim Crow laws grew while the Supreme Court affirmed them. Simple intimidation, tar-and-feathering, rape and lynching were all so common in the Negro experience that they were hardly reported. The National Association for the Advancement of Colored People was organized in 1909 but was ineffective for a long time. In the moment the only recourse an enterprising Negro had was to run away to the North and this is what Negroes did in increasing numbers, adding to the distress of the cities.

The smooth face of American buildings seemed unwrinkled by these intolerances but what was going on had its effect on American architecture nevertheless. The migration made the American metropolis what it was to become. For a time it produced large congregations of people of wide enough variation in needs and possibilities so that the city called for large and important buildings for government, education, commerce, religion, recreation. Supplying audiences big enough to support activities that would have languished in the villages, it demanded concert halls, opera houses, theaters, coliseums, libraries, museums, railroad stations, cathedrals. The ingredients for urbanity were there and in the moment the desire as well. But at the same time the growth of the city was too rapid, too thoughtless, too indigestible. The city lost what traditions it had, dissipated its early order, became a jungle. The immigrants contributed to the jungle; though they brought new tastes for music and painting, and the promise of new artists to come, urban indigestion was the most obvious immediate consequence of their arrival.

6

WHILE ORDINARY IMMIGRANTS AND OLDER AMERICANS WERE MILLING about, seeking to accommodate themselves to each other, scientists, principally in Europe, were preparing a connection of conclusions which would be earth-shaking. The effects of their penetrations cannot yet be fully assessed. But the merest schoolboy knows that they have yielded unparalleled weapons of destruction, unparalleled sources of potential peaceful energy, unimagined opportunities to alter what would once have been thought to be immutable substance or immutable theology. There was Hertz and his observation of ordinary ultraviolet light when it ionized air; Roentgen to show that X-rays would penetrate materials. In the sixteen years after 1895 a galaxy of investigators from Becquerel and the Curies to J. J. Thomson and Lord Rutherford had achieved so much that physicists were beginning to have a definite picture of the atom.

Then there was Planck's quantum theory of 1901 which said that energy could not be transmitted continuously but only in definite hunks or "quanta." Hard as it was to reconcile with Newtonian mechanics, the idea could not be dismissed after 1912 when Poincaré proved it was the only hypothesis that explained the way spectral energy was observed to be disturbed. At the very end of this period Bohr successfully applied the quantum theory to electron orbits. The third revolutionary development was Einstein's theory of relativity, announced in 1905.

These were difficult ideas, not well comprehended in the beginning even by many members of the scientific community. They could not so easily be explained to the public as the theory of evolution, for example, had been. No social Einsteinism or social quantum theory came to replace social Darwinism.

Outside the domain of natural science there were other influential theories and observations. This was the time when Freud published his three great studies of hysteria, dreams and sexual theory, soon followed by Jung's investigations of the unconscious. All these came quickly to America, as the ideas of Darwin had before. In September 1909 Freud lectured at Clark University in Worcester, Massachusetts.

The effect of Freud and Jung on later twentieth-century thought, education, literature, painting, medicine was enormous and direct and more quickly felt than the derivations from the work of Rutherford and Bohr. But in this moment there was no obvious effect on the thinking of American architects. Though men's minds were marching close to the gates of Heaven or the jaws of Hell in this quarter-century, there was nothing on the American architectural scene to indicate such a fearsome crisis.

If a time is producing brilliant science, must it be concluded that it will also produce brilliant art? Even if all the efforts of men are not equally well displayed in any given era, would not the *Zeitgeist* at least expect that the participants might interact with each other? By the end of the nineteenth century the different voices were becoming unintelligible, even antagonistic to each other, and interaction was becoming more difficult and less likely; perhaps even less desired.

7

WHETHER THE INTELLECTUALS OR THE ARTISTS OR THE PUBLIC HAD ANY basis for an accord with the scientists' science, everyone could see and most would applaud the accompanying technological revolution, based as always on preceding accomplishments of science. The break-throughs were, on their own terms, as astounding as those of science.

First there was the automobile. Again the basic inventions were European, Daimler's internal combustion engine, Dunlop's pneumatic tires, Benz's gearbox and his reliable combustion engine, all conceived between 1886 and 1895. These innovations did not put the gasoline engine beyond challenge as a means of self-propulsion. Steamers and electrics appeared too. But the noisy, stuttering, explosive, wideranging gasoline buggy prevailed. On Patriots' Day, 1892, Charles E. Duryea finished his "buggyaut" at Springfield, Massachusetts, the first American automobile. Almost exactly a year later Henry Ford wheeled his contraption out of the barn for its initial road test. At the turn of the century there were 8000 automobiles in the United States, about one for every ten thousand persons, but they still had less than 150 miles of hard-surfaced roads to travel on. On August 1, 1903, the first transcontinental automobile trip was successfully completed in New York City. It had begun ten weeks earlier in San Francisco.

Formed in 1903, it took the Ford Motor Company five years to get its classic four-cylinder Model T on the market. Assembly-line technique was adopted in the Ford factory in 1913 and in a new modern building by Albert Kahn. From the first sputtering hand-cranked engine to self-starters and assembly lines had taken only twenty-eight years; the 8000 registered cars of 1900 became two and a half million by 1915.

The airplane was not far behind. It was less than two decades from Lilienthal through Langley to the full-scale if short success of the Wrights at Kitty Hawk in 1903. These were quickly followed by longer, higher, faster, more hazardous flights by such other pioneers as Bleriot and Glenn Curtis. Only eight years after an automobile had crossed the continent, Galbraith P. Rogers flew a plane from New York to Pasadena. The actual flying time was 82 hours but the elapsed time demanded by repairs and weather was only three weeks less than the auto crossing had required.

Despite the excitement and the portent of these events the important immediate change in transportation came from applying electric power to street, elevated and underground railway systems. At the beginning of the period there were some twenty electric street railways in the United States. Five years later there were a hundred. The first elevated railroad came to Chicago in 1892, a rudimentary subway to Boston, first, and to New York by 1904. In 1905 London's Underground was electrified. Now cities quickly achieved rapid and relatively comfortable local transportation and the horse began to lose ground although he continued to serve breweries and policemen for years to come. With the new transportation it was possible to live farther from work. More people could be collected in a single place at about the same time. Thus the public transportation of New York was one of the things essential to permit a Woolworth Building. But it did not demand one.

Overland the main long-distance travel still belonged overwhelmingly to the railroads, as minor improvements continued to be made and as transcontinental lines grew to seven. Now the goods of the nation could be carried almost anywhere. Passengers in sleepers and dining cars found physical comforts not all of them could enjoy at home. All this new comfort and success evoked an interest in impressive railroad stations; it seemed fitting that a new Grand Central Terminal should arise in New York City and it did not seem absurd to stretch a red carpet under those who boarded the Twentieth Century Limited. So the quarter-century saw the flowering of the American railway empire and of an imperial railway architecture to fit it.

The revolution in communications technology was quite as spectacular if not yet so influential. By 1901 Marconi's experiments had matured so that from a point in Newfoundland he could hear signals from England. Eight years later, radio saved passengers when the *Republic* sank off Nantucket. Thereafter Congress required it on all steamers leaving American ports and carrying American passengers. But national radio and television were still far away.

It was the quarter-century, too, when the movies were born. Edison's kinetoscope patent of 1887 was followed by the first public showing of a movie the following year when the Lumière Brothers projected film in a basement of the Grand Café in Paris with a different machine. *The Great Train Robbery* became the first commercially successful movie in America in 1903. Early movies often came to the country in tents, the "Black Tops," that toured Kansas in 1910. In the city they were usually shown in vaudeville houses and but rarely in a special if modest establishment like "Parisiana, the King of the Cinemas," built in Paris in 1911. Few thought that the movie might ever be an art form. The important thing was that by 1910 ten million Americans were sharing common theatrical and other visual experiences as they had never been able to before.

The telephone was getting more reliable and cheaper every year, although in 1900 a private phone in New York still cost 240 hard dollars a year. In 1880 there had been but one telephone for every thousand people; in 1910 there was one for every dozen. Transcontinental calls were possible after San Francisco was connected to New York in 1913 but they were not common and not yet reliable. Meanwhile, together with the telegraph and the transportation systems, the telephone helped in enlarging cities, pushing buildings higher, decentralizing life.

Along with this there were expansions of all kinds of energy, the development which most contributed to the expanded material well-being of Americans. While the population was doubling, the energy consumption was increasing more than fivefold. Though petroleum was increasing rapidly as a source of energy almost 90 per cent of the nation's power came from coal even in 1910 and most of this was soft coal. Thus the factories were still limited in location to places where coal was easily found or delivered and the urban air grew grimier. The freedom and the cleanliness that would come later with electricity was still mostly a prophecy. By 1912, much as hydroelectric installations may have impressed men like Senator Norris, they provided a negligible amount of the power. Whether the electricity was generated by steam turbines, as was possible after the innovations of Laval in 1889, or by water, as became promising after Westinghouse built the first American hydroelectric plant at Willamette Falls in Oregon in 1891, it was alternating current that was the important innovation since it permitted long-distance transmission without undue loss of energy. Westinghouse built his first plant for alternating current in New York in 1886 and by 1895 had built a large hydroelectric generator at Niagara Falls capable of sending electricity twenty miles.

Electrical energy would finally permit the city to explode into the country. For the moment it was important in other ways; for transportation, horizontal and vertical, in small amounts for communication and potentially for its illumination. The small domestic use of electricity was limited to the light bulb. Rapid progress in the design of the lamps followed the happy demonstration at the White City in Chicago in 1893. Production increased thirty times between 1891 and 1919 and each American citizen had twenty-two times as many lamps on the latter date while these yielded 230 times as many lumens of light. Expansion in later days would be still more spectacular but the electric light had arrived.

Architects had a potentially new design force in electricity. For the city as a whole it meant that it could be a twenty-four-hour place. For buildings it meant that the forms need not be seen only as white in the day and black in the night against a dimly lighted sky. It meant that the night forms could be revealed by floodlights, or reversed from the daylight form by lighting visible interiors. It meant that buildings no longer had to catch every minute of daylight from the ever dingier industrial skies, that the effort to get larger and larger windows could abate; indeed that there could be a complete retreat from the window if this was desired, as soon as better ventilation could be found, and this too was implicit in electricity. The large bay window was no longer essential even in Chicago. Within the building electricity called for the inauguration of a new kind of lighting fixtures and asked the question, still not well answered by architects or decorators, whether the electric light should inspire its own forms. A few men like Adler and Sullivan tried, as in the Chicago auditorium, to come to grips with the new lighting, and McKim made a different try in Boston's Symphony Hall, but for most architects of the day the electric light was simply a convenience and not a stimulus. Not many architectural oversights have been greater.

These were the influential or potentially influential technological achievements of the generation on the large scale. In building technology itself Hall developed his process for extracting aluminum from ore but aluminum buildings did not spring up for fifty years. The United States Bureau of Standards was established in 1901 and served the building industry well in routine matters if not very imaginatively and if not always courageously. The first successful electric elevator was installed in 1889, the escalator in 1900. But the most important of these developments for the building art was the enormous increase in the production and use of steel.

In 1885 the country made three million long tons of rolled iron and steel, but probably half of it was iron. By 1894 the Carnegie-Phipps Company of Pittsburgh had circularized a trade catalogue of standardized steel sections for use in the building industry, and in 1910 there were 21 million tons of rolled shapes, practically all of steel.

What this meant for architecture was that there was plenty of steel to let the buildings thrust skywards. At the same time there was a more modest improvement in concrete technology though not so dramatic as the introduction of the open-hearth process. A Montgomery-Ward warehouse of reinforced concrete was built in 1908 in Chicago; one concrete skyscraper of modest size appeared in the Ingalls Building in Cincinnati, a building of no distinction save for its innovation; but the

imaginative uses of this resourceful plastic material were to be deferred
to a later day, although Europe had begun to reveal its potential. The
steel, the subway, the elevator, the telephone, the typewriter, the adding machine, the electric light, all stood ready to conspire to give to
men's vaulting ambitions a vehicle for trying to scratch the skies.

To scratch the skies required the collaboration of engineers and the
desire of businessmen. Whether the architect could cope successfully
with either seemed for a time in doubt. Of the two marriages, that
with the engineer was the more precarious. When the Forth Bridge
was revealed in 1890, William Morris called it the "supremest specimen
of all ugliness." Sir Benjamin Baker, the designer of the Forth Bridge,
replied to William Morris in a lecture he gave at the Edinburgh Literary
Society on November 27, 1890: "beauty relates to function." This was
the essence of the debate. The architect looked on the engineer as a
servant, a kind of Caliban to do the behests of the architectural Ariel;
the engineer thought the architect an effete fool. Montgomery Schuyler,
the leading American critic of the day, saw the dichotomy: "The
architect resents the engineer as a barbarian; the engineer makes light
of the architect as a dilettante. It is difficult to deny that each is largely
in the right. The artistic insensibility of the modern engineer is not
more fatal to architectural progress than the artistic irrelevancy of the
modern architect. In general, engineering is at least progressive, while
architecture is at most stationary."

8

WITH THE BUSINESSMAN, THE ARCHITECT COULD FIND MORE IN COMMON.
Thorstein Veblen was not speaking for architects when he castigated
the aesthetic standards of the rich of 1899. The funds they spent on endowed buildings showed, according to him, the "pervasive guidance
of the canons of conspicuous waste and predatory exploit." Some critics
at a later date, entranced by Marx, have insisted that these difficulties
were intrinsic to capitalism. Industrialists, on this theory, would support
engineering and technology in building because industrial production
demanded better performance. But their ideology would be heavily conservative so they would demand, as James Fitch says, "imperial symbols
for their new imperialism," As a diagnosis of the dilemma of architecture in the '90s the comment was valid; as an analysis of "capitalist
architecture" it was wide of the mark, as the USSR's architecture of
1950 would show.

The trend of business was certainly toward empire. The quarter-century was the scene of titanic struggles between businessmen trying successfully to build influential monopolies and reformers trying to curb them. In this contest the power of the federal government to interfere in business affairs, adversely as well as favorably, was demonstrated, tested, and eventually, if grudgingly, accepted. But despite antitrust legislation like the Sherman Act of 1890, a few families became very, very rich, a few men sat in seats of enormous power, and corporations could not be kept small. Every time a judge cut off a business head with a court decree, a larger hydra appeared. It was the day of trusts in whiskey, sugar, cordage and lead. A succession of skillful corporate moves was inevitable once New Jersey and Delaware had opened the way to bigness with their new laws of incorporation. The consolidation of the railroads by Morgan and Kuhn-Loeb were paralleled by the action of the Standard Oil Company of New Jersey in absorbing the whole oil trust. Veblen published his bitter attack, *The Theory of the Leisure Class*; President McKinley in his third annual message requested that "Combinations of capital organized into trusts . . . should early claim the attention of Congress"; but the combinations persisted.

By 1900 large corporations produced two thirds of all our manufactured goods. In 1904 John Moody in *The Truth about the Trusts* listed 318 corporations of great size. A company like that of Morgan easily controlled the interlocking managements of diverse operating companies. So did the Rockefellers, who influenced not only oil but the National City Bank and the Union and Southern Pacific Railroads. The larger the growth, the louder the protest.

Theodore Roosevelt recommended regulation in presidential messages; in 1905 *McClure's* tried the trusts before the bar of public opinion, using such prosecutors as Lincoln Steffens, Ida M. Tarbell, and Ray Stannard Baker. *Everybody's* followed suit with articles on "The Beef Trust" by Charles E. Russell and "Frenzied Finance" by Thomas W. Lawson. Now the tide began to turn toward the reformers. You could sense it in Charles Evans Hughes's successful prosecution of scandals in the life insurance companies of New York; in Employer's Liability Acts, Pure Food and Drug Acts, Meat Inspection Acts, the prohibition of corporate contributions to election campaigns. You could see it in extension of Interstate Commerce Commission's jurisdiction to telephone, telegraph, cable, and wireless companies. All this agreed with some of the ideas of nationalization advocated by the progressives. One of them, Herbert Croly, a liberal editor of *The Architectural Record*, wrote *The Promise of American Life*, which T. R. said had brought him back from the jungles of Africa determined to strengthen the national government in order to attain constructive social and economic ends. Not long after, Roosevelt made his declaration for the New Nationalism at Ossawatomie, Kansas: "I stand for the square deal — property shall be the servant and not the master of the Commonwealth." In such a climate it was not surprising that Woodrow Wilson as the reform governor of New Jersey quickly obtained election reform, utilities regulations, employer's liability and a corrupt-practices act; that in March of 1911 the Supreme Court upheld the corporation tax and in May addressed dissolution orders to the Standard Oil Company of New Jersey and to the American Tobacco Company. In 1912 the House appointed the Pujo Commission to investigate money powers in the United States. The Supreme Court dissolved the merger of the Union and Southern Pacific Railroads. Woodrow Wilson was elected President and told the Commercial Club of Chicago that "The business of the United States [must be] set absolutely free of every feature of monopoly." But the bigness did not die so easily. In 1913 the Pujo Committee brought in its report which said that the people who were attached to the Morgan interests held 341 directorships in 112 corporations, banks, trust companies, transportation systems, insurance companies, manufacturing and trading companies and public utilities with total resources or capitalization of 22 billions. Louis D. Brandeis estimated that this was "more than three times the assessed value of all the property, real and personal, in all New England. . . . It is more than twice the assessed value of all the property in the thirteen Southern states. It is more than the assessed value of all the property in the twenty-two states, north and south, lying west of the Mississippi River."

In the end the will of the country insisted that the big interests of the Morgans and the Rockefellers should not go unchecked. Part of the forging of this will was no doubt due to the writing of the Tarbells, the Steffens, the Lloyds, the Veblens, even the Donnellys and the Bryans. Such writing was demagogic more often than not; usually unbalanced, unrestrained, not always factual. It has left an unfair residual picture of the barons. They had much to be blamed for, but they ought not to go unpraised.

To management they brought new efficiency and not all of it was fiscal; they built better plants; they introduced the methods of Frederick W. Taylor with corresponding large increases in productivity per hour of a man's work; they improved materials as Rockefeller did when he employed chemists to salvage the evil-smelling oil of Ohio. They consolidated railroads and utilities, and the consolidated units usually gave better services than the unconsolidated. They made notable contributions to education and to culture with massive, usually unimpeded gifts. It is inconceivable that anything like the same funds and the same freedoms could have been found from any other sources in those days, and to imagine the importance of the barons we need only to recall the memorials, foundations, hospitals, institutes and universities that bear their names and the great collections of paintings and sculpture and books that distinguish our museums and libraries. In these men there was a certain statesmanship, a certain magnanimity, not often to be found in the writing or the legacies of their detractors.

Yet the detractors were right on the main issue, which was how much raw power could be left in the hands of private individuals. Unfortunately their attacks were not often pitched at this level. We know little, for example, about Ida Tarbell's own taste. But we do know how she attacked that of John D. Rockefeller. Of him she said that his houses showed him to have "no pleasure in noble architecture, to appreciate nothing of the beauty of fine lines and decorations." But in such a discussion an overly rich man could not win. If he built a fine house of its kind, as Morgan and Henry Frick did, then he was subjected to the opposite attack of being over-luxurious, perhaps even immoral. Certainly Rockefeller's taste was quite irrelevant to Tarbell's main hunt. Neither good nor bad taste would justify the operations of the Standard Oil if they were wrong; and if they were right, then Rockefeller's personal taste was a matter of no concern. But the reformers caught on wherever they could. Henry Demarest Lloyd spoke of the power kings as one-generation men, "Without restraints of culture, experience, the pride, or even the inherited caution of class or rank." Joseph Medill Patterson's *A Little Brother of the Rich*, published in 1908, described a Watteau-like fete given for the Anti-Vivisectionist Society of Boston. A Brahmin dilettante read Chaucer with a Middle English accent. His soft and white hands, Patterson commented, were kept so by child labor in the mills of South Carolina. Cartoons in *Life* showed the idle rich treading elegant marble floors upheld by starving men and women.

There were stupid rich men like Harry Lehr, who dined his friends' dogs, or those who rode horses into ballrooms and lighted cigars on hundred-dollar bills. The real men of power, the Morgans, the Rockefellers, the Carnegies, danced on few marble floors, recited little Middle English. But they were callous enough and after the writers were through with them, after the reforms had been made, the imperial men never looked so glamorous again.

But they were imperial men. Social Darwinism was slow in dying. It was still persuasive, for example, to E. L. Godkin. In *Forum* for 1894 he wrote an article called "The Duty of Educated Men in a Democracy": "The great law which nature seems to have prescribed for the government of the world . . . is that the more intelligent and thought-ful of the race shall inherit the earth and have the best time, and that all others shall find life on the whole dull and unprofitable." This was the spirit which moved the powerful Charles Elliott Perkins to write Edward Atkinson in 1881, "I think it would answer an extremely useful purpose if as able a pen as yours would show what I suppose to be the fact, that the Standard Oil Company is simply a product of natural laws and laws which it is not safe to touch."

Men like this might have had a certain respect for the bold defiance of young Frank Lloyd Wright but they would prefer the classical archi-tecture of Stanford White. They were conservative about art and they desired, consciously or unconsciously, an imperial architecture. They wanted it for their offices, their railroad stations, their houses, their libraries, their museums, their universities. And they had a way of get-ting what they wanted.

9

IT WAS A TIME WHEN MOST OF THE AMERICAN PUBLIC LOOKED WITH AP-proval and even with pride upon the forays of the flag into far waters. Perhaps it began with the exploits of imperial businessmen like the Keiths in Costa Rica who built a railroad and then developed a banana business to support it; or the Guggenheims who sought copper and silver estates in Mexico and South America, or the sugar planters of Cuba and Hawaii and the oil drillers of Venezuela. You could see our navy grow after the affair with Spain until by 1911 it was being sent to danger spots in the popular practice of naval diplomacy. You could see our concern about Japan magnified after the acquisition of the Philippines which T. R. called our Achilles' heel, and so it was a time for the building of bases in the Pacific and for annexations of Samoa, Hawaii, Guam, Puerto Rico, the Panama Canal Zone. As a nation come late to imperialism, we were acquiring lands in ways we would have berated in others. Where we did not acquire lands we often sent the Marines, as we "helped" Venezuela, Cuba, Nicaragua, Costa Rica, Honduras, San Domingo and Mexico, impartially upholding administrations of tyrants and democrats. We engineered a flagrant *coup d'etat* in Colombia to promote the secession of Panama and took only seventy-six minutes to recognize the new *de facto* government.

We often seemed belligerent, expecially when the Monroe Doctrine might be invoked. When Secretary Olney "invited" Great Britain to arbitrate her boundary dispute with Venezuela he reminded the world that the United States was practically sovereign on the American continents, and did not hesitate to cite our raw power. Senator Beveridge envisioned a world covered with the American merchant marine, "Great colonies, governing themselves, flying our flag and trading with us, will grow about our posts of trade." Senator Champ Clark debated for the Canadian reciprocity agreement because he hoped "to see the day when the American flag will float over every square foot of British-North American possessions clear to the North Pole."

There was another and more amiable side. A procession of Secretaries of State consistently assured the Central and South Americans that we coveted no territory south of the Rio Grande. It was Americans who promoted the Pan-American Conferences, the Pan-American Union, the Pan-American Exposition, the American Court of Justice. It was a citizen of the United States, Carnegie, who built the Peace Palace at The Hague, and paid for the Pan-American Union Building at Washington, who established the Carnegie Endowment for International Peace. It was another American, Ginn, who founded and endowed the World Peace Foundation. The divided personality represented two views of America's new position in the world, which no longer could rest on a policy of isolation. Americans *were* affected by the agricultural, industrial, and commercial successes and failures in other lands; Americans *were* genuinely sympathetic to the human plight of Armenians and Chinese.

Whether benign or sinister, the new world view in the United States made it inevitable that the doors of America were opened to an influx of ideas from the East and from Europe. There was, for example, the acceleration of the strange, long-drawn-out, love-hate affair between America and Japan. Japan held some fascination for America that other Asian countries did not. In the beginning the architectural results might seem superficial, as in the effect the Japanese exhibition of the Chicago Fair of 1893 had upon Frank Lloyd Wright, or the influence of Japanese houses on the lesser Pacific Coast architects Bernard Maybeck and the brothers Greene. But the course of this stream ran deep, surviving wars and treacheries, and it would appear far more influentially in American architecture of the mid-twentieth century.

For the long pull the big thing was that American architecture began to identify itself with international architecture and not with colonial architecture; that it was anxious to excel, to have something that could be put before all the world and announced with pride as American. We found it in the skyscraper. But for the moment there was a more direct connection with our imperialistic spirit as well. For the individual who commissioned it, the skyscraper, trying to go higher than any competitor, was the demonstration of a personal imperialism, even if it were that of a ten-cent-store owner. In a more conventional sense what Wright excoriated as the imperial spirit was demonstrated by the almost universal adoption of Roman architecture and Roman site-planning in government work after 1893, by the extrapolation of this to other "important" buildings of all kinds, and by the use of similar expressions in buildings placed even in exotic Manila.

I O

NATIONALISM, IMMIGRATION, URBANISM, INNOVATION, INDUSTRIALIZAtion and imperialism were the main themes of the quarter-century. They were not the only themes of the American dialogue of the time, indeed not even the loudest themes. Those arguments were about the tariff, the frontier, the currency, and the lot of labor. Tariffs and currencies do of course affect how wealthy a nation is and which groups have the disposition of the wealth — and to both of these architecture is sensitive. They may influence the importation of building materials. But for this analysis it is not helpful to remember more about the tariffs. Similarly, the debate about bimetallism which was vigorous in this time is of negligible interest here.

Even the violent emergence of the labor movement had a less direct influence upon American building than it might have in another day. In the first decades, and right up to the panic of 1893, the purchasing capacity of labor improved slowly. Relentless manufacturing competition and increased productivity per man-hour drove the men hard and forced a speed-up without adequate compensatory safeguards; accidents increased without economic compensation. Labor won few of the great strikes of 1886 and at the outset had the bad luck to be linked with the Haymarket bomb incident which destroyed the Knights of Labor. But the needs of labor were such that new organizations were inevitable. First was the American Federation of Labor of 1886 and four years later the United Mine Workers. With extraordinary foresight, such groups discarded political organization and legislative reform programs in favor of collective bargaining on practical issues such as the closed shop, increased wages, shorter hours, and improved working conditions. They started auspiciously by negotiating a successful contract or two. But after 1892 the years were bloody and disastrous.

The guerrilla warfares of the silver mines at Coeur d'Alene, Idaho, the Pinkerton operations at the Homestead steel strike, the stabbing of Manager Henry Frick, the effort to boycott Pullman Palace cars and the subsequent indictment and imprisonment of Eugene V. Debs, the unsuccessful later boycott effort of the Danbury hatters leading in turn to the jailing of Samuel Gompers, all these reminiscences remain fresh in the American mind.

As prosperity returned, there were fewer and less violent strikes and they were more often successful. In 1897, for example, the soft-coal miners won an eight-hour day, semimonthly pay, abolition of company stores and biennial conferences after a twelve-week strike. But the attitude of management of 1902 was well stated by George F. Baer, President of the Philadelphia and Reading Coal and Iron Company, spokesman for the anthracite mine owners, "The rights and interest of the laboring man will be protected and cared for — not by the labor agitators, but by the Christian men to whom God in His infinite wisdom has given the control of the property interests of this country."

But the national temper was not disposed to leave the lot of labor to the good will of any manager even if he were the benevolent Andrew Carnegie, the paternal George Pullman or the God-fearing George Baer. The trickles of legislative control of management grew in number and in force, mostly in measures governing health, liability, hours of work and minimum wages. Such measures, though subject to many judicial reversals, began to be passed from Massachusetts to Oregon, often being more advanced in less industrialized states. Moreover the importance of the labor force was recognized in another way when, early in Wilson's administration, separate Departments of Commerce and Labor were established. But the period ended as it had begun — with violence. A coal miners' strike of the United Mine Workers in southern Colorado produced unusual conflicts and in the end the federal government had again to intervene. Out of all this turmoil no labor architecture had arisen, but better amenities for plant labor had become inevitable.

There were other architectural effects. The most important was on the building industry itself. Almost all the important craft unions of this industry were established in this time. Bricklayers had been nationally organized in 1865. But between 1881 and 1900 almost every other craft was organized, beginning with the carpenters and followed by plumbers, painters, stonecutters, electricians, tile-layers, wood and metal lathers. Elevator workers, marble workers and hod carriers and building laborers joined in the first three years after 1900.

The whole sentimental idea of a happy group of building craftsmen, perpetually singing at their work, is one of the legends of architectural reminiscence. The Egyptian and Greek and Roman slaves probably did little singing although an occasional classic sculptor may have. The insistence of the medieval guilds on standards of performance may be overrated. There were fewer "honest bricklayers" in Huxley's day than he imagined. But it is safe to say that there were some in earlier times. The drawings were less complete; more skill and ingenuity were required of the laborer and the buildings were often of a size where his personal contact with the architect could be maintained. All this led to a better human relation and, it is not unreasonable to think, a higher quality of work.

Whatever the views of the medieval guilds may have been, the laborers who organized in America were usually concerned more with maintaining their wage scale than they were with improving their standards of workmanship in building. Not that they were more ignoble than any other labor force, or any other management force for that matter. But they met with a particular difficulty not very much of their making though certainly supported by them. This was that the building "industry" was fragmented from top to bottom. It did not have the advantage of bigness. No Vanderbilt or Carnegie ever thought to give it his attention. Even if every building worker had remained exactly as competent as his father, the plain fact is that the makers of materials, the contrivers of methods for assembling buildings, and the architects themselves were not interested in producing spectacular technological advances in the economy of building based, as it was, entirely on handicraft methods. While on the farm the amount of produce per man-hour of work went up steadily and in the factory the rise was dramatic, there was essentially no change in the productivity per man-hour in building on the site. The slight improvement was trivial in terms of the improvement elsewhere. Under a perfect system of exchange this might have reduced the wages of the building laborer so that the building did not cost more relative to other goods. But the unions were able to prevent this. By keeping their wages constant or raising them slowly while producing no more, they were out of economic balance with the rest of the work force. They were able easily to effect these wage arrangements because any single building-trade union could stop the whole building operation. The owner of the building could not afford a long strike once the building was under way for he then had too much capital earning nothing while tied up in an incomplete building. Thus every year the cost of a unit of building increased with respect to the cost of any other article subject to machine operations. This was not inevitable, but it came about through the feeble organization of the building industry. Few building workers and few architects would have wanted it otherwise.

Among all these groups, leading contractors seem to have felt the most elation. Their diaries and articles sing many a paean to the symphony of the whistles, the jack-hammers, the dynamite, the caissons, the steel drills eating granite rock, the rivet guns clinching the white-hot steel, the turning concrete mixers, the cable hoists and compressed-air lines. They exult in the pressure of work against the clock. But even this was a kind of romance akin to Kipling's personalization of a ship on her maiden voyage. It did not bring the productivity of the building industry in line with the productivity of the factory.

At some point in this losing battle of relative costs it was inevitable that Americans would have to be content with less space in their buildings and perhaps even with less architectural amenity. To the competition of relative costs there was added the competition of the increased cost of the new services desired in every building. This led to an unpleasant choice. Given such a choice it was inevitable that an American society should have agreed to demand less and less of its architecture. If a cubic foot of enclosed space costs twice as much as it needs to, there may not be much left for fountains or sculpture or paintings or even grass or trees — or even for enough space, especially if you want automobiles, air conditioning, television and cosmetics more.

This was perhaps the main effect of the labor movement on American architecture. It could not be blamed on labor alone. The architects' ignorance of and lack of interest in technology was quite as retarding. But, ironically, it helped to make the housing of labor almost impossible. When society began to be aware of the folly of bad working and housing conditions and to wonder how to ameliorate them, almost nothing was possible through an improvement in productive efficiency — and the ameliorating measures had to come through preventive law and assisting subsidy.

I I

SUCH A SITUATION LED A FEW ARCHITECTS TO FEEL COMMON BONDS WITH urban reformers but these bonds could not be stretched very far. More architects looked at urban reform in poetic terms than as a pragmatic challenge to organize. Wright was calling attention to the degradation of the city in stentorian tones. In his 1901 address at Hull House in Chicago, he said, "Chicago in its ugliness today becomes as true an expression of the *life* lived here as is any center on earth where men come together closely to live it out or fight it out. . . . We must walk blindfolded through the streets of this, or any great modern American city, to fail to see that all this magnificent resource of machine-power and superior material has brought to us, so far, is degradation." But as Wright looked further he betrayed his admiration for the potential when he revised *The Art and Craft of the Machine*. Now he advised the listener to go at nightfall to the top of one of the downtown steel giants and "you may see how in the image of material man, at once his glory and his menace, is this thing we call a City." Then he provided a prophetic and poetic picture of the skeleton, the musculature, the blood vessels and the nervous system of this glory and menace. Although he did not like what he saw, he was not then, anyway, in despair about the end. Nor did he provide any useful practical suggestions.

Moreover, though it was an age of enormous reform in many cities; though names emerged which are still familiar — "Golden Rule" Jones, Brand Whitlock, H. S. Pingree, Tom Loftin Johnson, and on the national level Theodore Roosevelt, La Follette, Folk, Johnson, Wilson, Norris and Lindsay — still few of these reformers or their reforms had much direct effect on the slums or on architecture.

Often the reform movements stemmed not from a desire to improve the living conditions of the poor or the morals of politics but just as a way of conquering vice. Thus the reformers made strange bedfellows like Steffens, Jacob Riis and the Reverend Charles Parkhurst in New York. To be sure, a model tenement was built here or there but on the whole the reformers did more to clean up the police departments than they did to clean up the slums. Only an occasional mayor like McClellan of New York had any interest in the arts of the city. Reform Presidents had no better, if no worse, taste than those who ran on less humane platforms. Senators elected by popular vote were not more or less wise or concerned about architecture than those who had been selected by venal legislatures dominated by the silver lobby. The effect of the reform movement on the slums or on urban architecture, if there was any, was indirect. It rested on a changing concept of taxes after the Sixteenth Amendment went into operation in 1913. By then everyone had forgotten that twenty years earlier Joseph C. Choate had called a 2 per cent income tax "communistic" and "socialistic" and that the Supreme Court had wasted no time in voiding this modest provision of the Wilson-Gorman Tariff Act. This changing concept would tend to level incomes, reduce the number of poor, increase the middle class; it might bring large enough sums to government so that serious efforts could be made both for slum clearance and for rehousing. The taste of the country in these matters was surely changing. Rugged individualism was less popular even on the vanished frontier. Thus for the few who saw other expedients failing, it seemed that something at least might be accomplished by regulatory acts, preventing the worst abuses of sanitation and safety. In these crusades a few but not many architects might occasionally be enlisted.

I 2

OTHERS WHO HAD NO DESIRE TO APPLY LEGAL MEASURES OR TAX-SUP-ported subsidies reasoned that the slums might disappear if the building industry could only manage to obtain the same increase in productivity per hour of labor that had been common in the manufacturing industries. This was an entirely reasonable economic analysis. In time it led a series of men of fine intentions to break their hearts and sometimes their pocketbooks trying to invent and establish new ways of manufacturing a building.

The Hodgson Company had been making prefabricated wooden houses successfully since 1892 but these were combustible detached buildings and could not contribute to the supply of urban dwelling. About 1907 Thomas Edison experimented with a form for pouring a whole house of monolithic concrete but despite his reputation, work, and many patents, nothing came of it. The most noteworthy effort of the day was by Grosvenor Atterbury, an architect, who from 1907 on experimented with large pre-cast panels, first with his own funds and later with support from the Russell Sage Foundation. He applied this construction to the houses he designed for Olmsted at Forest Hills Gardens, New York, and used it with moderate success for some time, but the system produced no imitators and no successors.

All of this effort at innovation came to naught. Nobody seemed to know how to invent prefabrication. Nobody seemed to want to exploit it if it were invented. Some interest groups were categorically opposed to it; among these, architects usually stood in the front row, arguing that its standardization would impose limitations on their freedom of design. Mediocre architects were particularly sure of this. Social reformers who were looking for subsidized housing or a socialized state had no interest in higher productivity — and little faith that it could be achieved. Moreover the efforts were not convincing. The prefabrication movement was so weak that it was readily killed by massive indifference. The dimensions of the failure became more apparent in the next decades of severe housing shortages.

There were still other ways to alleviate the lot of people in slums. Octavia Hill had experimented successfully in London with purchasing, restoring and then personally managing three verminous and decaying houses in Marylebone, using John Ruskin's capital. Now Octavia Hill

Associations were founded in America, a noteworthy one in Philadelphia in 1896. Even if the economic principle was sound, which is open to doubt, there were just not enough Octavia Hills to go around. The effect was like that of a drop of rain on an endless sand.

Then there were the social settlements designed to bridge the gap between the life slum dwellers were now living and the lives they might live later, to bring them together in some kind of decent community exchange that their home surroundings could not foster. The first one in England was Toynbee Hall in London in 1884. The first one in America was the Neighborhood Guild established on New York's East Side in 1886. This was quickly followed by Hull House in Chicago (1889), Andover House in Boston (1891), and others in New York. Staffed by admirable and sensitive men and women like Robert A. Woods or Jane Addams, the settlement house movement was unquestionably a force for good at the level of the individual or of the individual family.

Finally there were efforts to reclaim the city altogether and the beginning of theories about garden cities we owe to this period, though not to the United States. The important person was Ebenezer Howard. There had been places called "garden cities" before, but these were merely real estate developments. Howard produced his thesis, *Tomorrow; A Peaceful Path to Real Reform*, at London in 1898. In it he described a garden city set in a large area of protectable farmland; a complete town would be surrounded by a wide belt of rural country; the town would be essentially self-sufficient and certainly able to provide housing, farming and industrial employment for all its residents; its extent would be limited; it would not be allowed to encroach on the green belt; it should contain about 30,000 persons, small enough to be human, big enough to match most of the magnetism of the large city. Groups of such towns could support activities which demanded larger populations. Any rise in land values would be shared by the community which had itself created them. By such devices, Howard suggested, rural depopulation could be arrested; the constant growth of the metropolis into something too big to be managed would stop. Such a garden city must never be confused with a suburb. The autonomy, the profit-sharing and the fact that it was a cross-section of the society all differentiated it both from the company town and the one-class dormitory suburb.

The publication was followed by the Garden Cities Association in 1899 and the first garden city, Letchworth, in 1903. (The second city, Welwyn, was not built until after the first war, in 1920, and the first one in America was later still.) Despite the attractiveness of the notion and the success of the individual towns, despite the strong support the movement has had from a number of eloquent voices, it affected little urban development.

Howard was followed at the end of the period by Patrick Geddes, a Scottish-Australian physiologist, zoologist, botanist, sociologist and zealot who started the regional survey movement in Edinburgh and a study of the "organic" relationship between city, country and industrial area, a sort of urban ecology on which he wrote voluminously for thirty years. In 1913 he produced *Cities in Evolution,* a book carrying his persistent slogan about the city as a trinity of place, work and folk, as the rural village had in fact once been. He is more important in the American scene for the impression he made on Lewis Mumford, who subsequently made a comparable impression on many Americans, than for anything he himself wrote. In all of this as in everything else about housing and slum clearance, the period 1885-1913 simply set the stage for a future performance.

1 3

INDEED, MUCH OF THE VIOLENCE OF THE DEBATE ABOUT REFORM APPEARS more in words than in deeds. American writers were now concerned with American problems as they had not been in the earlier day. There was much less escape writing, much less effort to be sentimentally regional. A few writers looked back with nostalgia. Some of these, like Willa Cather or Edith Wharton, resembling the architects in this, were among the best craftsmen. But the vast majority were concerned with but one thing, the decay of the American dream. A subtle thinker like Herman Melville wrote *Billy Budd* (it was not published until 1924). The least subtle and most flamboyant, Ignatius Donnelly, orator of the Populist movement, wrote the imflammatory *Caesar's Column,* in which workers and capitalists alike were overcome by the demons of Caesar Lomellini, heading a sadistic and proletarian Brotherhood of Destruction. But with the possible exception of Melville, the writers were at bottom optimists. They believed that reform was possible if things as they were could but be exposed to the American view. So the center of American writing was the documentary exposé. It might be as violent and insincere as Jack London's *The Iron Heel* (1908), which described the march of the People of the Abyss. Here were Carlyle's monsters of the Faubourg St. Antoine and Zola's women of Montsou marching again, but as in most American radical novels marching to slaughter under the Iron Heel of indicted capitalism. Others painted

the picture sordidly but with less flaming brushes in the manner of
Norris or Upton Sinclair; they dealt with the problem more personally
in the way of Dreiser; they produced quasi-fiction in the muck-raking
essays of Tarbell or Steffens; they yearned for Wisconsin with Hamlin
Garland; or leaned on piety with Edward Sheldon; they couched their
criticism in pseudo-philosophical terms with Veblen; or tried a serious assessment of the times like Croly; advocated the solution of the
strenuous life with Roosevelt, or the technocratic city with Utopian
Bellamy, whose *Looking Backward* started abortive Nationalist Clubs
off on an attempt to rear a middle-class version of state socialism; they
sought with Henry Adams to explain the dynamo by contemplating
the Virgin or with John Dewey to turn pragmatism to social ends.
But all the time the writing that focused on the industrial and cultural
life of America was really cast in optimistic terms. Not a doom-sayer
believed in doom.

Henry James, perhaps the greatest American writer of the time, was
an exception to this general attitude, as perhaps Lafcadio Hearn was
when he emigrated to Japan. But James was made of sterner stuff.
When he returned to America in 1904 he found it much changed. He
did not pretend to like the change but he did sense the grandeur in this
world of the office building, "huge constructed and compressed communities, throbbing . . . with a single passion." He could understand
how the skyscraper had earned a right to soar above the church. Though
he rejected this outcome for himself, he did not deny that it might do
for others in the future. So even with James we must conclude that the
writers of America continued to believe that the new age was still possible even though it had not yet arrived.

This belief, fostered by the pragmatic philosophy of liberalism, was
more evident among the architects of the Mississippi valley than in the
work of reform novelists or painters. Men like Wright and Sullivan,
Root and Elmslie, shared many tenets of Dewey's instrumentalism,
Croly's progressivism, and Veblen's economic theories and especially
their appeal to the ultimate authority of experience.

14

FOR SUCH MEN THE PAINTERS OF THE TIME HAD LESS TO SAY, FOR FEW
painters of Europe or America concerned themselves directly with
social protest in paint, although they joined freely enough in verbal
manifestoes. But the architects could not go unaffected by the experimental and provocative experiments the painters were making with

space and light. It is sometimes easy to forget today how violent the painting revolution was in Europe in this period.

Beginning with Van Gogh and Seurat, it continued with Cézanne, Gauguin, Ensor, Bonnard, Munch, Matisse, Rouault, Braque, Gris, Utrillo and Dufy. It saw the cubist and classic Picasso and the Picasso of the Harlequins; it included the experiments of Fauvism, cubism, futurism. There were new organizations, new manifestoes, the *Salon d'Automne*, the *Deutscher Künstlerbund*, *die Brücke*, and the first *Blaue Reiter* Exhibition of 1912 revealing the work of Arp, Delaunay, Kandinsky and Klee.

All these men of change did not find a common answer to the problem of expressing ideas on the flat surface of a canvas. Painters and architects of Europe were able, nonetheless, working on different problems but contemporaneously, to be satisfied by similar kinds of organization and space. For example there are many points of resemblance between a painting like Seurat's *Le Dimanche sur la Grande Jatte* and the interior of the Dufayel Store at Paris. Some are superficial, like the similarity of bustled, bosomy, curving form, bespeaking the ephemeral ways of the haberdasher and couturier. But more significant ones lie in the composition of light and form and space. Both architects and painters silhouetted form against light, flattened it, revealed volumes only by half-light; both edged the forms with penumbras of shimmering, form-breaking light; both isolated their forms and made them stand free, in deep voids; both emphasized the structural elements that made up the forms; and both adopted one type of composition as meaningful.

Americans could see the new painting even if they did not make it. This was due principally to the efforts of Alfred Stieglitz and his Photo-Secession Group, who opened the 291 *Gallery* at 291 Fifth Avenue in 1906. Through it Picasso and other important European painters paraded their works; 291 was not slow either to reveal the work of promising young American painters. Marin's first one-man show was held there in 1910 and the work of Max Weber and Marsden Hartley appeared there in the same year.

These young Americans were not yet much admired by their compatriots. The average citizen hardly knew of and certainly would not have accepted even the work of the Eight, — Henri, Luks, Glackens, Sloan, Shinn, Prendergast, Lawson and Davies. Davies painted idyllic subjects; Prendergast and Lawson were impressionists; the rest painted realistically but chose subjects that were not popular with the accepted American painters of their day. The new men painted New York, its East River, its birds, its children, its ferryboats, its skyline, its cafés, its boxing clubs.

But American architects still esteemed the Sargents, the Abbeys, and the La Farges. They were not ready for the Sloans. They were even less pleased with the work from Europe. In 1913, when the Armory of the 69th Regiment offered its great exhibition of 1,100 works by painters ranging from Ingres and Delacroix to Duchamp, Matisse and Picasso, it was well attended. But *Nude Descending a Staircase* was the most discussed picture, whether for its manner or its "risqué" title is hard to say. Theodore Roosevelt attended and then wrote about it in *The Outlook*. He was emphatic about the right of "progressive painters" to paint progressively and to have their work examined, but he had many personal reservations. "Probably we err in treating most of these pictures seriously. It is likely that many of them represent in the painters astute appreciation of the power to make folly lucrative which the late P. T. Barnum showed with his faked mermaid." In some ways he found the American work most interesting. Then he approved the absence of the commonplace and felt that perhaps any reform movement risked the penalty of being liable to extravagance. "It is vitally necessary to move forward and to shake off the dead hand, often the fossilized dead hands of the reactionaries; and yet we have to face the fact that there is apt to be a lunatic fringe among the votaries of any forward movement. In this recent art exhibition the lunatic fringe was fully in evidence, especially in the rooms devoted to the Cubists and the Futurists, or Near-Impressionists . . . *it is just as easy to be conventional about the fantastic as about the commonplace.*" (Italics added.)

On this score Roosevelt, even with his reservations, was far to the left of the American public. The show was coldly received by art viewers in Boston and Chicago and by most American architects. The few experimental American architects of the day did not do well by revolutionary artists. Sullivan commissioned or permitted bovine banalities by an itinerant painter, for his lunettes in the Chicago auditorium and the Owatonna bank; Wright had little taste for any other art than architecture, despite the Japanese screens at Taliesin and the sculpture of the Midway Gardens. More conventional architects like McKim, who did want painters, invariably selected Sargent or Abbey; if they went abroad for their painter they chose the pale and aged Puvis de Chavannes rather than even Derain or Utrillo, not to mention Picasso, Braque or Léger.

15

NOR WERE AMERICAN ARCHITECTS OF THE RIGHT OR LEFT PLEASED OR IN-fluenced by the advanced architectural work of Europe. This was so even when the manner was related to that of the earlier Richardson as in Berlage's Stock Exchange in Amsterdam of 1898-1903; or could be seen as an imaginative extension of the principles of Jenney as in Victor Horta's splendid glass and iron Maison du Peuple in Brussels in 1897.

By 1900 the lively and varied Art Nouveau movement was a major current in the cities of western Europe. Its representatives worked in highly different styles though most of the work was decorative and floral as in Horta's interiors or biomorphically sculptural as it was when Gaudi began mixing it with symbolism borrowed from world religions for the Sagrada Familia in Barcelona. Exponents of the style offered some major structural innovations, especially the fascinating Gaudi, who seemed to try to escape the tyranny of the classical past; but the group in the mainstream tended to emphasize the structural possibilities of iron and stone, while treating them plastically as in Hector Guimard's Humbert de Romans Building in Paris. Guimard, the architect of many Art Nouveau stations for the Paris Métro, became a spokesman for the movement, publishing a book, *Le Castel Béranger*, with delicately colored plates; it espoused a triadic philosophy of logic, harmony and sentiment. The movement produced a more angular version in Scotland through the work of Mackintosh and Mackmurdo, and this in turn influenced the Finn, Eliel Saarinen, and through him such later American architects as Goodhue and Magonigle. More directly, some Americans if not many American buildings took notice of the modern French school itself. The *Architectural Record* in 1902 reviewed Guimard's book, published photographs of his work, and an account of the important exhibit of Art Nouveau held at Turin in 1902. The more plastic aspect of the movement greatly influenced the American designer, Louis Comfort Tiffany, whose glass curtain for the National Theater in Mexico and whose studio in New York City owed their curious exoticism to the new art in France. The more rectilinear design of the Scottish group appeared in the buildings of Frederick Scheibler, who worked in Pittsburgh about 1900. His Heidelberg Apartments and Highland Towers Apartments (1911) there are important examples of the modernism springing up in the Middle West soon after the turn of the century. Surely the greatest expositor of Art Nouveau design in America was Louis Sullivan, whose decorative ornament, almost Celtic

in its interweaving of form, seems to have developed independently of
the Art Nouveau in Europe, though perhaps from the same sources as
the iron ornament of the Bon Marché and the Eiffel Tower. But the
movement never became widespread in America. It had a long development in France, becoming more cubistic at the time of the 1925 exhibition at Paris, and it was this late decorative version of the Art
Nouveau that appeared in America much later in the Barclay-Vesey
lobby by Ralph Walker and in many other buildings of the 1920s.

Alongside the fantasies of the Art Nouveau interiors, there were
revivalists and realists and modern classicists, all defying any attempt
to subsume the ferment of ideas under a single designation. In
Liverpool, Giles Scott was beginning his Modern Gothic Liverpool
Cathedral, and Voysey was simplifying the picturesque house of Morris
and his followers. In Sweden, Ragnar Östberg attempted to develop
a modern folk architecture by his arts-and-crafts interpretation of the
Town Hall at Stockholm. A vigorous group of men in Austria proposed
simple geometrical forms and angular decoration, visible in Otto Wagner's railroad station at Vienna and his chapel at a sanitorium near Vienna. A further insistence upon cubical form, composed asymmetrically
and decorated rectilinearly, appeared at Darmstadt in Ölbrich's Habich
House of 1906 and also at Brussels in the Stoclet House of 1905.
French architects tended to remain under the wing of the classicism
associated with the École des Beaux-Arts, but Anatole de Baudot found
in the Church a loyal client for his pioneering reinforced concrete
frame and his Art Nouveau space and decorative forms, while Auguste
Perret broke headlong towards modern architecture in his Theatre
des Champs-Elysées of 1911-1914, his apartment on the Rue Franklin
and the garage in the Rue Ponthieu.

If there was any one center for the diverse currents of modernism, it
surely lay in Berlin and in the office of Peter Behrens, where the important modern architects Le Corbusier, Mies van der Rohe and
Walter Gropius were taking their apprenticeship. Behrens's house at the
Darmstadt Exposition of 1901 revealed his assimilation of the tendencies towards simplification and unification that gripped all architects at
the turn of the century; it seemed a thing of planes, precise but thin.
That impression was changed entirely by the buildings coming from
Behrens's office after the works of Frank Lloyd Wright were made
known in Germany. The Berlin AEG Turbine Factory of 1910, for example, is a building of tremendous power, developed upon masses
struck firmly, exposing the nature of brick and glass, and unified by the
dominating form of the building. Behrens's pupil, Walter Gropius, revealed his knowledge of the industrial architecture being produced in

Chicago in 1914 when he designed the Werkbund Exposition building at Cologne, a model factory which in one jump took the German architects far beyond anything produced for industry in America with the exception of Wright's Larkin Building. His Fagus shoe-last factory at Alfeld-an-Leine was a thoroughgoing modern presentation of the steel and glass architecture being developed for factories in New York and other American cities. It was characteristic that these German architects picked up what was being developed in America in a slipshod and non-architectural way — by all save Wright — and made it monumental and architectural. Later, they were amazed at the time of the Chicago Tribune competition (1922) to find that their architectural postulation of American building tastes was inaccurate, that America had scorned its factory architecture in favor of skyscrapers festooned with classical and Gothic ornament.

Equally characteristic was the fact that America ignored one of the best lessons to be learned from Europe, the lesson to be gained from the modern city planning of Beaux-Arts men like Perret and Tony Garnier. In 1901-1904 Garnier created one of the most far-reaching plans for a modern city ever conceived by any architect. He called it *La Cité Industrielle* and to it Le Corbusier's later proposals are but rich and copious footnotes. Garnier proposed a vast city, with transportation centers, separated residential quarters, circulation patterns adapted to vehicular traffic, industrial centers and business quarters, all given areas compatible with their requirements and buildings functional in form but possessing good scale and silhouette. Unfortunately this city pattern was not published until 1917, and American city planners paid little attention to it, preferring the grandiose monumental planning of the kind Haussmann had made in Paris.

Suggestive as this all was of the ferment in European architecture, the fact remains that even the most imaginative and sensitive innovators were confused when they attempted to relate their efforts to the largest movements of the times. Thus in 1894 Otto Wagner made a sonorous statement of the kind European architects (and some Americans) like to make: "Our starting point for artistic creation is to be found only in modern life." But anyone could say that and many would. The question was what the words "modern life" meant. Was it the life of Lorentz and the electrons; was it the Freudian world; was it the life of the space the cubists were uncovering, or the life of the screaming people of Munch, or the Polynesian life of the people of Gauguin; was it a Gare St. Lazare or a haystack of Monet? Was it the life of Marx? Or was it just an immediate life which would use the devices technology offered? The Karlsplatz station of the Vienna subway and the Savings

Bank, both by Wagner, with their metal and glass canopies and reminiscences of classicism must have been what Wagner meant, by buildings whose starting point was in modern life, but they were still far from coping with the promise of modern science.

If European architects were lagging their own scientists and technologists by several decades, what was to be expected from the architects of America where a lag behind adventuresome Europe had always been acceptable? Although they may have discussed art with painters and sculptors, the American architects were not accustomed to the cross-cultural, cross-disciplinary discussions of the European intellectuals and artists. They knew nothing of science, almost nothing of literature, and the history they paraded was more often than not half-studied and ill-remembered. They were interested in the political and social climate. The "gay" discussions between St. Gaudens, McKim and Hunt seldom turned on the gloomy philosophical questions their friend Henry Adams was asking of the atom, or on such social puzzles as the slum. It was more pleasurable for them and more characteristic that they bandied jests about the vulgarity of Chicago, pretended to chase bulls around the amphitheater of Arles, exchanged reminiscences of the boulevards.

The clearest American architectural genius of this or any other day, Frank Lloyd Wright, had little time for such vaporings. But he too seems to have made no effort to comprehend the theories of science or to look for messages in the work of contemporary painters. He was as sensitive to primitive art as Picasso or Braque. Some of the great themes of Mayan architecture leaped from the pages of Catherwood's drawings or the books of other archaeologists and found their new statements in his Wisconsin warehouse or, later, in the patterns of the textile blocks of his California houses. He was among the first Americans to sense the organic unity of Japanese houses, to glean from the Japanese exhibit at the Columbian Exposition a message of how space could be defined by hovering planes; in this experience he was not led astray by trivia into the idea of copying or modifying the bracket details or the wooden screens as the brothers Greene did in California. He developed his own cubist ornament for the Midway Gardens and here came as close as he ever did to being influenced by the European movement. But Wright was never a great admirer of painting anyway and asserted that he was no admirer of the architectural work of others. How much he really examined, only he could know. In the end he seemed always to find his own nature without the aid of others' eyes. If his work could influence science or art he might regard it as well and good; if not, they might go their separate ways.

Thus practically all American architects of the day preferred to stand aloof from the social, aesthetic and intellectual ferments. The most prosperous and worldly of them were still of the middle class, employees of a financial upper class. The more revolutionary like Sullivan and Wright were not so far to the left as the Populists. The indifference of the architects posed problems for architecture which to measure its times needed to pay attention to the factory, to provide symbols for big business, to make imperial houses, museums and libraries, to provide churches for an enormous range of liturgies and social attitudes, to produce schools and universities that would take account of the new pragmatism; architecture which needed also to use steel and electricity well, to begin to work on the problem of the slum, to prepare at least for the later and almost predictable onslaught of the automobile. The architecture did not manage all of these problems equally well; it was at its best with the ephemeral imperial problem; at its worst with the technology and the slum. The result was often cacophony.

1 6

IN RETROSPECT IT IS EASY TO SEE WHICH BUILDINGS WERE MOST PRESCIENT. But it is not extraordinary that the most famous architects and critics, the most influential clients, the best educated public of the day did not see them in that light. They acclaimed Boston's Public Library, New York's Pennsylvania Station, West Point's Chapel, Vanderbilt's Biltmore at Asheville, and Washington's Pan-American Union, works of imperial quality, executed by admitted and successful leaders of the architectural profession, McKim, Cram, Hunt, and Cret. The idea that many were repelled by the display at the World's Columbian Exposition of 1893 is far-fetched. The frontiersman liked it just as well as the effete Easterner — perhaps better, for he had never seen Rome.

Later historians would praise Sullivan's Wainwright Building in St. Louis, Maybeck's Christian Science Church in Berkeley, Greene and Greene's Gamble House in Pasadena, or Wright's prairie houses, Unity Church in Oak Park and the Larkin Building in Buffalo; all of these were foresighted leaders to the future, the work of able designers well out of their cocoons, but they were not what most men of the day admired.

Although imperialism was making the louder noise and although imperial architecture was making the louder show, the most important motif of the period seems now to have been the drive towards increased industrial productivity. When a comparable drive was occurring in Western religion the great Romanesque churches were born. One might, then, have expected some fine factories and warehouses to reflect the new and great importance of industry. But industry was not yet ready for symbolism. Most industrial buildings remained purposefully utilitarian and incidentally ugly. They grew larger; they cast deeper and longer shadows over the streets they walled; they took more and more green space from the city. But they were given little aesthetic and not much more social consideration. Those still extant reveal the attitudes of the businessmen who built them with small sense of civic obligation.

There was a social program that might have been well expressed still in terms of the engineer's structural aesthetic. Industrialists were having to act a new role. Bankers or lawyers might remain in New York playing baron, but manufacturers were not so remote from what was happening in the labor force. Squeezed between government and labor, they felt impelled to reinstate some form of paternalism or "fraternalism" as some now preferred to call it. They came to regard good working conditions as synonymous with good business. The treasurer of the Reeves Engine Company in Trenton, New Jersey, said his company provided the best conditions possible to help it get men who were able to do more and better work. The Weston Electrical Instrument Company of Newark, New Jersey, noted "how frequently the health of employees, and the requirements of business, are best served by identical conditions." Such statements were typical.

But such a social program focused on health, morals, education and efficiency did not necessarily lead to a fine architecture. Industrialists could provide better washrooms and rest rooms and libraries and gymnasiums without designing beyond utility. They could build more substantial and comfortable housing, such as that of the Colorado Fuel and Iron Company, without creating architecture at all. They could add equipment for ventilation without making shops and lofts less ugly. Design could improve only when the pragmatism of health and education took account also of the pragmatism of aesthetics.

But paternalism did effect some aesthetic improvement. You could see it in a village like Whitinsville, Massachusetts, where the Whitins' houses stood opposite the machine factory, surrounded by comfortable houses for the workers. Such arrangements were not unique. They were to be found at the Fairbanks Scale plant in St. Johnsbury, Vermont; at the Kilbourne and Jacobs Manufacturing Company in Columbus, Ohio; at Proctor and Gamble in Cincinnati; at South Manchester, Connecticut, where the Cheneys who owned the silk mills of the town also built their residences. Many of the new industries came to be

located in rural settings or in landscaped parks. There had been
European examples of this in the '80s when famous English candy
manufacturers had moved out of Birmingham and York into the adjacent country. In 1889 Lever Brothers removed their soap works from
Warrington to Mersey and established a model village there.

In the United States, we recall, most factories like those of the Merri-
mack Manufacturing Company at Lowell had expanded on crowded expensive land and had built densely and to great heights. Others, such
as the Waltham Watch works, near Boston, were more fortunate. One
English visitor, Budgett Meakin, praised "the handsome buildings . . .
surrounded by well-kept lawns, overlooking on the one side the
river, and on the other a park-like village, inhabited by the employees."
The Crane Paper Mills near Pittsfield, Massachusetts; the Bullock
Manufacturing Company seven miles outside of Cincinnati; and a
number of others sat in rural parks, sometimes not even fettered by
fences. Some urban factories like those of the Acme White Lead Works
at Detroit, the Cleveland Varnish Company, or the National Cash
Register Company at Dayton were provided with landscaping and gardens; the Natural Food Company's plant at Niagara Falls was set in a
ten-acre park overlooking the Falls.

Even where there were no gardens there were interior improvements.
Many emulated the Weston Company in providing libraries, kitchens,
dining rooms, gymnasiums, natatoria, bicycle depots, hospitals and
rest areas. Many, like the McCormick Harvester, introduced safety
appliances, used vermilion paint on dangerous machinery, took pre-
cautions against fire, introduced advanced sanitary or ventilating equipment. Almost all the new factories had extensive areas of glass to obtain better light; the Natural Food Company's "Conservatory" boasted
30,000 panes. Some electrical shops were now lighted through sawtooth
roofs, whose glass faces were oriented to the north to keep out direct
sun.

Of course this entire social program could be and usually was
realized without architectural intervention. As it became more complicated, however, it cried for the work of imaginative minds, trained
planners. But even as late as 1909, the *Architectural Record* could
still remark: "The American manufacturing plant is a commercial
type of structure which the architect has so far played an insignificant
part in developing." The editor appealed to industrialists to hire
architects, suggesting that a well-planned factory would not only lead
to operational economies but that an attractive factory would bring
prestige and good workmen.

This argument, most appealing perhaps to those whose business depended most directly on good public relations, seemed confirmed by the successes of such organizations as the Natural Food Company or the National Biscuit Company. One or two buildings of the time used steel columns, recessed spandrels and large windows, but the examples provided by such factories as those of Stein and Company in Chicago or the Fisher Marble Company Warehouse in the Bronx were not much imitated. A notable plant was owned by the National Cash Register Company at Dayton, Ohio, where buildings were set on well-landscaped sites and arranged to enclose generous courts. The buildings themselves were orderly. Their four stories used bricks in narrow, continuous piers, setting a clear cadence for recessed arched spandrels above wide windows. The owner's concern for moral education was revealed by mottoes prominently lettered on the walls, proclaiming for example that "Labour is a Girdle of Manliness." The owners were justly proud of such buildings. They encouraged visitors who, around 1905, were inspecting the plant each day in groups of fifty to five hundred, enjoying a conducted tour, complete with tea served in the adjoining clubhouse.

One could sense the breath of this new attitude even in cities like Cleveland, whose early industrial history had been so deplorable. There, Robert D. Kohn, always social-minded and progressive, was employed by H. Black and Company, manufacturers of women's wear, in 1909. He provided a picturesque group of basic manufacturing elements set in an open field. The long low skyline was livened by sawtooth roofs. The water tower was a strong vertical accent sculpturally emphatic from a distance, presenting rich patterns of brick and terra cotta. In an article in the *Architectural Record* of 1909 Kohn openly avowed his intention to create attractive as well as useful factory architecture.

Factories and warehouses of some distinction thus began to replace some of the shabby wooden structures and disorderly piles of brick which had so often been acceptable earlier. "Realistic design" became almost a national movement. In Chicago Richardson's Marshall Field Wholesale Warehouse gave the lead to many praiseworthy expressions by Hill and Woltersdorf, Argyle Robinson, or Nimmons and Fellows. Outstanding among these was the Walker Warehouse by Adler and Sullivan. Here Sullivan came as close as he ever did to mimicking Richardson, using a massive arch to frame the lesser parts of the design and developing the whole building as a single unit. Other Midwestern cities found their tradition in the cast-iron buildings of St. Louis or the John Shillito Building at Cincinnati. Minneapolis, too, was a center of realistic design, at least in part. There the Metropolitan Building of 1888-1890 by E. T. Mix belied its romantic exterior with a splendid twelve-story interior well. The gay railings, the exposed elevator shafts, showed how charming, even adventurous, realism might be.

Factories equaling those of the Middle West began to appear in Boston and Philadelphia and Baltimore. New York buildings such as the Hanan and deVinne Press Buildings by Babb, Cook and Willard were sufficiently numerous and impressive to stir critical comment in the leading architectural magazines. One would scarcely have expected Russell Sturgis or any of his Ruskinian friends to admire unornamented, utilitarian buildings. Yet they were recovering from their first love affair with the Gothic. Matured under the tutelage of Viollet-le-Duc, they had found a manly hero in Richardson and were now ready, within limits, to accept a hardheaded philosophy of realism in design. Russell Sturgis led the way. His eye was never so sure, his judgment so dependable, as Montgomery Schuyler's. But like Schuyler, he admired the steel web of the Brooklyn Bridge, preferring it to the stone towers with their Gothic vestiges. Now he went further and championed the new industrial architecture. In 1904 he wrote an account of the buildings designed by Babb, Cook and Willard and some others including the Judge Building by McKim, Mead and White: ". . . one sees in the treatment of these recent and very plain — very utilitarian — structures, a wholesome architectural influence." Sturgis could not bring himself to go the whole way in asserting the falsity of the prevailing monumental architecture, but he readily admitted that there was something in the proposal that "designers should be restrained to square masses and sharp corners and plain windows for twenty years to come — with sculpture denied them and all the bad architectural forms *tabu*."

At Chicago in 1910, Peter Bonnett Wight published his essay about warehouse architecture, called "Utilitarian Architecture in Chicago." Like Sturgis, Wight was an ex-Ruskinian, with several recognized Gothic successes to his credit, including Yale's School of the Fine Arts and the National Academy of Design at New York. But in Chicago he abandoned his medieval ways and embraced realistic architecture. The conversion was greeted as an encouraging sign by young architects like Richard E. Schmidt whose warehouse for Grommes and Ulrich excited Wight's praise. The warehouse interested Sturgis too, who once suggested that it showed how professional architects should treat the problem of library design. There had never been, he thought, a better device for giving light to a building which needed all the light there was. He suggested applying the maxim to the fronts of the Carnegie libraries.

It would be wrong to conclude from Wight's and Sturgis's criticism that a new architectural age had arrived in America. Indeed, the fight had hardly begun. A number of able designers, it is true, eagerly embraced industrial problems, happily designed buildings using new materials and structures, successfully developed a new philosophy of total design. They were not entirely neglected by critics and they found some business and industrial clients, motivated, at least in part, by a desire to create something beautiful. But the critics were still hesitant in their praise, the commissions still relatively few.

The important fact is that no one yet seriously proposed that the new way should be applied outside of industry to buildings intended for monumental sites or for major civic or cultural purposes. By 1913 America had achieved many admirable industrial examples of the type prophesied by the scientists and theorists of the '70s and '80s. But while Huxley's point of view was acceptable to many industrialists and to a few architects and critics, if it were limited to factories and warehouses, the same men usually insisted that eclectic design, Gothic or classic, be used for churches and courthouses at the upper levels of the cultural hierarchy. Thus criticism and theory worked to a dual standard.

The dual standard had strange consequences. A supreme example was Albert Kahn, an immigrant who came to America from Germany with his rabbi father at the age of eleven and settled in Detroit. His first factory, made of reinforced concrete and steel sash, was commissioned by the Packard Motor Company in 1903. He inaugurated the all-under-one-roof type of factory and followed this with the even more revolutionary all-on-one-floor design. In such work he was brilliantly innovative and architecturally sure-footed. He designed rigorously and imaginatively planned factories for the Ford Motor Company such as the Highland Avenue Factory in Detroit where the first mass-produced Model T rolled down the wooden ramp in 1913. Buildings such as this commanded great respect in Europe, encouraging men like Gropius and Neutra to develop a consistent theory of modern architectural design. Kahn's achievements in this field were in the end genuinely colossal. But he could not universalize them. Suffering the ambivalence of his colleagues he hardly thought of his best works as architecture at all. He confined realistic design to the lower echelons of the building hierarchy. Thus when he was later asked to design an administrative building for Ford, or the Detroit Public Library, or large office buildings in Detroit for Fisher and General Motors, he and his clients rejected the factory experience and ventured into eclectic dress and ornament. Thus the buildings he wanted most to be fine were least fine.

Only a hierarchical attitude, combined with a literary symbolism which imputed certain built-in excellences to various historic styles, can explain such vagaries. By the turn of the century Americans might have learned that a single well-considered approach to design could produce beautiful buildings for any purpose. But for the next fifty years many American towns and practically all American colleges and universities persisted in the curious belief that a building with Georgian detail on it, for example, would be attractive no matter how poorly planned, how ill adapted to its non-Georgian use, how disruptive to its environment, how ill scaled.

One must not leap too quickly to a conclusion about which of the Janus heads was the more reliable expression of its day. We think we know which head was looking forward. But a great many Americans of the day were more than happy about the noble Boston Public Library and many fewer cared for or were even aware of the Wainwright Building. Those who made the Boston Public Library and its kind were sincere and upright men, doing competent and sometimes brilliant jobs, given their premises. Our cities would be meaner today without their work. It is as silly to call these men stupid or even "dishonest," as some contemporaries have, as it is to wish to return to their theories as a few contemporaries urge. It is time now to be firm about not reviving the theories; it is time also to recognize that some of their proposers were designers of real stature. They, too, thought that architecture should not be Janus-headed. They favored a single style, the one used for buildings at the top of the hierarchy, wished to rebuild the national face in the likeness of classical Rome. In time their point of view became the prevailing one. It dominated the imperial days between 1900 and 1913; it rode over the messages from Europe, the messages from the American factories. So most American cities ended with buildings that paraded the classical façades and the classical ornaments, whatever their purpose.

17

No CITY DISPLAYED THE CONFUSION BETTER THAN NEW YORK. ITS NUMEROUS factories, shanties, warehouses and docks, all utilitarian, lay at the foot of its towering symbols of the commercial spirit, usually tricked out in classical dress. During the '90s the race to the skies began to grip America. Advertisements showed dramatic bird's-eye views of tall buildings seen from above, looking down into the deep canyons, while boasting for the topmost offices that there was "nothing between us and the sun." Height offered business distinction. Tall buildings began to appear in all the other large cities east of the Mississippi, concentrating in the business section, creating for the moment for each city a more or

less distinctive profile depending on the shape of the land. In Chicago
the expanse of lake front made the buildings into a wall; on Manhattan
the point of the island piled them into a pyramid. The skyline, a word
coined about 1897, intrigued New Yorkers. The skyline of Manhattan,
changing enormously even in the three years between 1894 and 1897,
impressed itself as a symbol. It was a theme that photographers recorded, artists depicted, poets sometimes praised.

In 1897 Fred Panning of *Harper's Weekly* recorded Manhattan's
jagged silhouette as it was seen from north to south. There was the tall
Home Life Building, a more or less standard tower; next was the Pulitzer (or World) Building, raising its dome into the skies; then the two
tallest buildings in the world, the Park Row and the St. Paul. The
steeple of Trinity Church, long the most prominent feature of the
New York skyline, now stood dwarfed between the Bank of Commerce
and the giant block of the Surety Building. The vista terminated at
Number One Broadway, where the Washington Building was partly obscured by the new and gigantic Bowling Green Building. It was an impressive silhouette but like the Bolshoi Ballet of later date its power lay
in the aggregative mass and not in the fine details. Montgomery
Schuyler remarked, "It is not an architectural vision."

The sheer immensity and audacity of the new commercial skyline
drowned both an appreciation of the tremendous city planning problems it imposed and the enormous architectural possibilities that lay
in the component skyscrapers. However the masses might glow from
the river, the new form was not so glamorous at the level of the ordinary pedestrian. A walk down Wall Street or Broad Street or Nassau
Street by 1905 was a passage through sunless gorges. But the gorges
seemed exciting still to illustrators like the one of 1911 who drew a view
for *Judge* looking upward from an open street intersection to a sky
framed on all sides by the distant roofs of huge buildings that pointed
still higher toward weird aircraft. King's *Dream of New York* of 1908
envisioned a future Broadway lined with buildings all of which would
be higher than the 612-foot building Ernest Flagg had designed for
Singer. At their upper stories, some 500 feet above the ground, the
buildings were to be connected by bridges while their roofs were hangars and mooring stations for huge balloons which carried signs indicating that they were departing for the Panama Canal, Europe, Japan
and the North Pole. But all this excitement did not lead architects in
New York to discuss the real and mounting urban problem.

Nor did they usually approach the individual skyscraper as a new
problem, requiring first a utilitarian analysis of its structure and function
and then an aesthetic expression of them. The Pulitzer Building, for

CHICAGO ARCHITECTURAL PHOTOGRAPHING CO.

Chicago, Illinois, World's Columbian Exposition, 1893

Dayton, Ohio, National Cash
Register Company, ca. 1885

NATIONAL CASH REGISTER

Chicago, Reliance Building, 1890-
1895, Daniel Hudson Burnham and
John Wellborn Root, archs.

CHICAGO ARCHITECTURAL PHOTOGRAPHING CO.

Proposal for A.I.A. Building at
New York, 1884,
John Moser, arch.

BRIAN SHAWCROFT

Berkeley, California, First Church of Christ Scientist, interior, 1912,
Bernard Maybeck, arch.

WAYNE ANDREWS

U. S. ARMY PHOTOGRAPH

West Point, New York, U. S. Military Academy, Cadet Chapel, 1908,
Ralph Adams Cram and Bertram Grosvenor Goodhue, archs.

Guthrie, Oklahoma, City Hall, 1902, J. Feucart, arch.

BRYAN STU

BRIAN SHAWCROFT

Boston, Massachusetts, Public Library, 1888, McKim, Mead and White, archs.

Asheville, North Carolina, "Biltmore" (Vanderbilt Estate), 1896,
R. M. Hunt, arch.

WAYNE ANDREWS

Buffalo, New York,
Guaranty Building, 1895,
Louis H. Sullivan, arch.

CHICAGO ARCHITECTURAL PHOTOGRAPHING CO.

Owatonna, Minnesota, National Farmers' Bank, 1908,
Louis H. Sullivan, arch.

WAYNE ANDRE

CHICAGO ARCHITECTURAL PHOTOGRAPHING CO.

Chicago, Illinois, Schlesinger and Mayer Building, now Carson, Pirie, Scott & Co., 1899-1904, Louis H. Sullivan, arch.

Chicago, Illinois, Rookery Building, interior, 1886, Daniel Hudson Burnham and John Wellborn Root, archs.; Staircase, 1906, Frank Lloyd Wright, arch.

CHICAGO HISTORICAL SOCIETY

CHICAGO ARCHITECTURAL PHOTOGRAPHING CO.

Riverside, Illinois, Avery Coonley residence, 1908, Frank Lloyd Wright, arch.

CHICAGO ARCHITECTURAL PHOTOGRAPHING CO.

Riverside, Illinois, Avery Coonley residence,
living room, Frank Lloyd Wright, arch.

Pasadena, California, D. B. Gamble residence, 1909,
Charles Sumner Greene and Henry Mather Greene, archs.

WAYNE ANDREWS

example, rose through many layers of classic ornament to a summit crowned by a Renaissance dome, as ludicrously ill proportioned as the hat of a clown. The Park Row Building, erected in 1897-1898 to be the tallest building in the world, rose majestically from a throne of classic bombast to end near the clouds in silly rabbit's-ear turrets. The cornices of its tall neighbor, the St. Paul Building, turned the corners and stopped, providing a mere starched front to give surface respectability to a dirty brick rear. Bradford Gilbert's Tower Building at 50 Broadway built in 1888-1889, did nothing to reveal that it was the first steel skeleton erected in New York. Its ill-organized tower emerged from a rusticated stone base, fronting a mediocre loft.

The newer cities of the Midwest offered a better opportunity. The problems of skyscraper design called for a group of well-trained designers who had had experience with the utilitarian architecture required by industry and who were not saturated in classicism. New York architects had been insulated from the commercial significance of the skyscraper by their background, their professional education and the nature of their work. But after the fire, Chicago attracted a number of young Eastern architects, like Sullivan and Root, who were to become great designers. In Chicago they found competent natives like Jenney, Holabird and Roche who were already struggling to find an aesthetic for the tall building. They found too the pragmatism which called for adaptation to use. It inspired them to seek a way of beginning with the program for a building, developing the forms it required, modifying them in accordance with the materials and the structures, and making the result beautiful.

Curiously enough this almost unconscious search for a modern architecture derived inspiration from the theoretical, prophetic writings of the French archeologist Viollet-le-Duc. His studies of medieval structural systems had not inspired the generation of the '60s who followed Ruskin's lead in admiring Gothic architecture for its ornamental and moral qualities. But Viollet-le-Duc insisted that structural organization lay at the base of any great architecture, including any future one. His own generation saw only the Frenchman's detailed and factual examination of medieval structure; for them it lacked the poetic fire of Ruskin's crusading prose. The new buildings Viollet-le-Duc designed, such as the Gothic chapel near St. Denis, showed no inventiveness or warmth comparable to the best buildings inspired by Ruskin. Neither did they reveal his bold prophecies of a future architecture built with an iron structure. His audience at the École des Beaux-Arts, including Richardson, failing to recognize the implications of Viollet-le-Duc's thinking, rioted when he was appointed by Napoleon III to

teach at that center of modern classicism. They did not see the basis for
a new architecture in his drawing of a vast space supported by iron
members. Richardson, like most of his contemporaries, brushed aside
the challenge offered in the second volume of the *Lectures*. "A practical
architect might . . . conceive the idea of erecting a vast edifice whose
frame should be entirely of iron . . . and . . . preserving . . . [that
frame] by means of casing of stone."

Nevertheless these ideas had been widely broadcast during the '80s.
Henry Van Brunt had translated Viollet-le-Duc's *Entretiens sur l'Architecture* for an edition called the *Discourses* and published in Boston in
1875; later, in 1877-1881, it appeared in England with the title,
Lectures. In 1880 Buffington, the Minneapolis architect sometimes
credited with inventing the "cage," read the passage referring to an iron
architecture. He began to investigate the possibility of developing such
a structural skeleton for skyscrapers, and in 1888, but after Major
Jenny's Home Insurance Building had been completed in Chicago,
received a patent for a skeleton with laminated steel columns.

1 8

FAR MORE IMPORTANT THAN BUFFINGTON'S LITERAL AND EXPLICIT READ-
ing of the sentence was Viollet-le-Duc's over-all message to Americans.
He insisted upon "truth" in architecture, and by truth he meant adaptation to use and to structure: "There are in architecture . . . two indispensable modes in which truth must be adhered to. We must be true in
respect of the program, and true in respect of the constructive processes
. . . fulfill exactly, scrupulously, the conditions imposed . . . employ
the materials according to their qualities and properties." The program
of the "realistic" architects which we have already mentioned called for
truth to structure, materials and program. They aimed at "rational
building," a term lifted from George Martin Huss's translation in 1895
of Viollet-le Duc's article "Construction."

The group in Chicago might, of course, have applied the idea of
rationalism to continue medieval forms as Charles Eliot Norton construed it in Cambridge, or as Major Jenney did in churches, and Root
in his occasional use of Richardson's adaptations of Romanesque. But
in Chicago there was another set of ideas. These we may link together
under the general term "organicism." The young designers in Chicago
came to believe that each building should be regarded as an organism,
subject to laws analogous to those of biological growth. Reading the
Origin of Species and Spencer's *Principles of Sociology* Louis Sullivan

thought he found a guiding principle for design: the form of a building should be adapted to its function and its environment. The architect would act in the role of nature to choose that which was best adapted. In his *Autobiography of an Idea*, Sullivan said of himself: "In Darwin he found much food. The theory of evolution seemed stupendous." What they learned from evolutionary theory was reinforced by their knowledge of a German theorist and architect, Gottfried Semper, whose writing was translated by Root and frequently quoted by Adler. In 1860, Semper had written: "Every technical product [should be] a resultant of use and material. Style is the conformity of an art object with the circumstance of its origin and the conditions and circumstances of its development." In following Semper, the Chicago architects put themselves in the mainstream of eighteenth- and early nineteenth-century thinking about adaptation. They forged a link relating themselves to Latrobe and Greenough and Emerson. They avidly read Whitman, whose *Democratic Vistas* envisioned a whole civilization unique to America. In him they felt an ally, hostile to the survival or revival of historical forms, demanding a new, modern form, expressive of American ambitions. They became conscious of living in a modern time, one that was unique in history. They followed Hegel and Taine in believing that the history of art was itself an organism, reflecting the changing natural and historical conditions that created it. Since the times had changed, it must be that a new idea was required, one related to the qualities of the new times. The Chicagoans, sensing their departure from the past, their difference from the East, determined to emphasize and preserve it, founded the Western Association of Architects. Their publications, *The Western Architect* and *The Inland Architect and Builder*, spoke of a West trying to assert its modernity. They remained in accord, however, with Populist notions and with the Sullivan-Wright theory of the identity of democracy with individuality. Each building in such a view was unique. This was at odds with biological classification where individual differences do not conceal the classic forms of the phyla and the genera and with the principles of biological growth which encourage uniqueness only through modest deviations from the norm. But when it becomes convenient to drop a scientific analogue, artists will jettison it with alacrity.

Wright was the great expositor of these ideas. He began very early. In his *Architectural Record* piece of 1908 he spoke of a new attitude towards building. Businessmen were more likely than the "cultured" to be men of "unspoiled instincts and untainted ideals," capable of judging for themselves, of encouraging the new work. An artist's limitations were his best friends. The machine should not be denied. There was "no more important work before the architect now than to use this normal tool of civilization to the best advantage instead of prostituting it as he has hitherto done in reproducing with murderous ubiquity forms born of other times and other conditions and which it can only serve to destroy."

He said, too, what he meant by "organic" inspiration. It was indispensable for an architect and it could be best developed in the school of nature. "A knowledge of the relations of form and function lies at the root of his practice; where else can he find the pertinent object lessons nature so readily furnishes? Where can he study the differentiations of form that go to determine character as he can study them in the trees? Where can that sense of inevitableness characteristic of a work of art be quickened as it may be by intercourse with nature in this sense?"

But neither the theories of organism nor those of rational design would have created a great architecture had there not been some enormously talented designers in Chicago. They saw that mere adaptation of form to use, materials, structure, environment, would not prevent an ugly result. Great building required more — that the form be adapted to emotional and aesthetic as well as utilitarian needs. Since these were not always consonant with maximum physical utility, each designer was faced with the necessity of resolving a personal conflict between use and beauty. Many, like Jenney, Holabird, Roche, took the rigid course, deciding in favor of the expression of use and materials. Greater men, like Root and Sullivan, took the way of all great designers, starting from pure theory, but modifying the conclusions to their greater ends. In this they were following the basic principles of the Beaux-Arts. This statement seems paradoxical simply because long years of opposition have blinded our eyes to what the Beaux-Arts once was. But since it does seem paradoxical, it must be defended.

The only authorized account of the modern teaching offered at the École is contained in Guadet's *Elements and Theory of Architecture*, published in 1902. In a chapter called "General Principles," he summarized the theory taught by him and by other teachers like Pascal, Daumet and Laloux. These were principles of *design*, not *style*. They were matters of unity, balance, proportion, rhythm and scale — not of classic or Gothic plans. Americans, such as Daniel Burnham, who did not attend the École, and some who did, like McKim, tried to legislate a style, an historical one, the classic. That led the Beaux-Arts architecture they perpetrated here to be held in disrepute. But the Parisian Beaux-Arts men had long since attempted to evolve a modern style, and they were not concerned with recreating classical buildings, nor indeed with imposing the classical style upon modern institutions.

Guadet himself had designed a Romanesque monastery for the Alps, Viollet-le-Duc was a Gothicist, and the École produced modernists like Tony Garnier, Auguste Perret and Anatole de Baudot at the turn of the century. Many of the Beaux-Arts students might turn out arid and stiff buildings, like the Museum at Grenoble, which obeyed all the superficial formulas, but they seldom produced an ugly building comparable to the *Record* Building in Philadelphia. Few European Beaux-Arts men were pedantic. They would have been the first to recognize McKim's sources and first to criticize his Tiffany Building and Pulitzer residence and the general waiting room of the Pennsylvania Station for being based with almost sycophantic correctness upon the Grimani Palace, the Cornaro Palace and the Baths of Caracalla, respectively. Copying was not the goal of the Beaux-Arts, however much it was the students' device for passing examinations. The École taught general principles of composition, and it is as unwise to judge the École by its worst practitioners as it is to judge Christianity by all its professors.

No school, not even one favoring a modern style, can defend itself against what every student who passes its courses may later turn out to be. The École des Beaux-Arts was vigorous and strong through a century of changing styles and changing problems and has suffered too much at the hands of its German and Swiss critics. It drew students from all over the world. Its education was so impressive, unfortunately, that American architects set out to duplicate it when they established the Society of Beaux-Arts Architects in 1894. This weak effort, too far removed from the fountainhead in Paris, should not cause us to view the Beaux-Arts in its light. Richardson and Sullivan, as well as Hunt, studied at the Parisian Beaux-Arts. Richardson finished the course, and though Sullivan gave up, he never spoke of it with real disrespect. This is forgotten by critics who identify the Beaux-Arts with what it became in the hands of McKim, the aging Hunt, the lesser Bacon and Pope or the even less talented men who later founded the Beaux-Arts Institute of Design in America in 1916, at a time when the École had lost its vitality, and who would continue to man its misunderstood barricades to the death. But to make such an identification is to forget that the older system in Paris had stood for the designs of Labrouste and Laloux and that Sullivan was the greatest American in the real Beaux-Arts tradition.

This was recognized easily enough by the French architects who visited Chicago at the time of the 1893 Exposition. They admired Richardson's work. They disapproved of Hunt's. They agreed that Sullivan, alone, had fully understood the principles of the École which would be listed nine years later by Guadet. These include six principles of design. They involve the rationalism of Viollet-le-Duc and also his realism: (1) You must be faithful to your program and see what is the character to be kept in the building; (2) the ground, location or climate can modify the expression of a program; (3) all architectural compositions must be constructible; every inconstructible scheme is absurd; (4) truth is the first requirement of architecture; every architectural untruth is inexcusable; (5) effective strength is not sufficient — it must also be apparent; (6) designs proceed by necessary sacrifices; a design must be good first of all, but it must also be beautiful. "You must compose then with a view both to the utility and the beauty of the building. And, as an element of beauty, you will try to obtain character by variety." That could stand as the credo for Sullivan.

1 9

THE VARIOUS COMPONENTS OF THE NEW THEORY DEVELOPING IN CHICAGO during the '80s began to appear visibly in a series of brilliant designs for office buildings erected during the period after 1890. Each building had utilitarian features; many contained technical innovations; each had a powerful structural basis and expressed it; all were modern and well adapted to their use and site; each showed the hallmark of a designer who understood matters of unity, scale and refinement achieved through ornament. In greater or less degrees, all had beauty. Gone was the bleak utilitarianism of the Montauk Building of 1882. The structural innovations introduced by the Home Insurance Building were no longer obscured by confused patterns of exterior form. Nor did the designers repeat the unsatisfactory superficial ornamentation of Sullivan's early attempt in the Rothschild Store to find an expression adequate to the modern office building. They had encountered the Marshall Field Wholesale Warehouse, and as Sullivan wrote in *Kindergarten Chats* had seen "stone and mortar, here, spring into life."

The Rookery (1885), at 209 South La Salle Street, was Burnham and Root's first successful office building. Its granite piers and columns support the brick piers and arches of the upper stories within strong horizontal divisions framed by arches, the unifying arcade that Richardson used. But the design is still heavy and granitic and the exterior does not indicate how interesting the interior is. Here one finds a court whose cast-iron columns and wrought-iron spandrel beams display an open skeleton, with airy but vigorous curving iron stairways and the decorations added by Wright in 1906. The interior court was awaiting recognition from a designer who would develop an entire building accordingly.

This transposition of theme was made by Holabird and Roche in their Tacoma Building of 1886-1889. Now they sought lightness throughout the building. The metal columns wore only a minimal covering, while the spaces between them were filled with large areas of glass — a systematic expression of the processes of obtaining light, useful interior space and firm construction.

The Monadnock Building by Burnham and Root of 1889-1891, although of old-fashioned construction, was another triumph of unified design, the last great monument of the wall-bearing age. It is a tremendous unadorned slab, two bays wide and sixteen stories high, built with masonry bearing-walls and an interior iron frame. The narrow slab provides outside exposure for every office but this utility is combined with severe simplicity and fine proportions in a powerful composition of horizontal and vertical lines worked out with a magnificent sweep from the batter of the base to the curve of the cornice. If the Marshall Field Warehouse was the first, the Monadnock was the second great lesson in unified design. Strangely that lesson came, as in the first case, within traditional walls. Yet perhaps it was not strange — all it meant was that the best designers had not yet come to grips with the metal frame while the greatest innovators were not often, unhappily, the best designers. This has happened before and could happen again.

Even the untalented Major Jenney was led by the new insights to create a bold and vigorous design for the Second Leiter Building (now Sears, Roebuck) in 1889-1890. It is a huge rectangular prism, and its gray granite facing over the columns and spandrels fully reflects the interior skeleton in a large and unified pattern. The interior presents sweeping open areas divided into broad avenues by rows of tall, slender columns which created a dramatic impression of open and airy space, much diminished today even on the upper floors, by the plethoric placards of Sears, Roebuck.

Louis Sullivan took a less literal direction but achieved greater artistic expressions. The tall narrow piers of his Schiller Building of 1891-1892 extend to the sixteenth story where they bend into an arcade. This arcade does not express the shape of the underlying structure but is used to close the composition at the top. Form follows function here but the function is aesthetic, more than structural. He made the same flight from literal engineering in his Wainwright Building at St. Louis, one of the great triumphs of his career. Built in 1890-1891, the building rises from a U-shaped plan in a classical arrangement of masses and voids. The base has a large module at ground story and mezzanine; a smaller module through the shaft; an impressive roof and cornice terminates it at the skyline. The shaft makes no distinction between mullion and pier; only every other vertical element contains a load-carrying steel column; but the failure to express the "honest" structural fact is not aesthetically "dishonest," not a failure of architectural morality. Instead, it follows a higher honesty and a higher morality than that of disclosing the skeleton; it gives the vertical lift and scale that express height and unify the composition. It is an almost perfect outcome of the theoretical and artistic and engineering work in Chicago around 1890.

While each of these buildings had merit, no single style was evolving. Instead each was a highly individual, "democratic" variation of a common theme. This troubled some visitors to Chicago, such as C. H. Blackall, who praised the Rookery Building, but went on to say "that there has been, as yet, no real style developed. Each building is a law unto itself, and no architect seems to feel called upon to follow even his own precedent, either in the choice of design or the character of the detail. There seems to be, throughout, a restless striving after originality; a seeking for striking effects, which . . . is not always good, and generally serves to belittle the character of the architecture." The Chicago work in 1890 included several individually brilliant office buildings, but no convincing demonstration of a national or even regional architecture, and even the brilliance could be negated. Chicago was far from beautiful, and its appearance was not improved by dull exercises like Jenney's Fair Building of 1891, split absurdly in the middle by an obtrusive horizontal element. Moreover the new theory could spawn monsters like the Fagin Building at St. Louis. Built in 1888, this was not widely recognized until 1893 when the *Architectural Record* gave it the ultimate accolade of being the most discreditable piece of architecture in the United States. Then the writer labeled it with the most damning phrase an Easterner could muster; he said it had all the vices and crudities and vulgarities called "Western."

This was indeed the attitude which pervaded the East at the time of Chicago's World's Fair of 1893. Sullivan himself often spoke disparagingly of Chicago's culture as fit only for hogs and butchers. Once he said that Chicago had been a mudhole fifty years ago and was one still. McKim's scorn was more superficial and not born of love. When his agent was trying to buy a piece of sculpture for the World's Fair, consisting of a bull, a ram and a boar, he was able to get only the boar and tried to persuade McKim to accept the compromise. McKim refused but added that it would be appropriate enough for Chicago. When the Frenchman Bourget went into ecstasies over some of the Chicago buildings, it was not because he liked them but because he thought they expressed the American character as he understood it.

Thus, on the eve of the World's Columbian Exposition of 1893, as the New York firms were assembling to advise on its planning, they were not disposed to take Chicago seriously. They accepted Burnham and Root, and Adler and Sullivan, and both firms were in on the ground floor of the planning. Indeed it was they who had summoned the Easterners to help. And the world would have thought them right. The West seemed to most to have produced but little. Of 129 buildings compiled as notable by the *American Architect and Building News* in 1891, most built after the Civil War, only ten were from Chicago, only fourteen from the vast area west of it. Of the ten from Chicago only the Pullman Building, the Auditorium and the Rookery suggested that the compiler realized that a new style was developing there.

2 O

GIVEN SUCH AN OPINION OF THE WEST AND ITS ARCHITECTURE, THE classicism of the Columbian Exposition was almost a foregone conclusion. Eastern architects went to Chicago with the firm intention of providing the Middle West with a dazzling spectacle of the best; of showing how a national style in the grand classical manner might be modified for modern use even on the prairie. The goal was much like that of a missionary to a "savage" land. The missionaries, like others who seek to convert from without, failed to note that the natives had something of their own to say.

It was an attitude which was unfair to Sullivan and equally to Root. It was the latter who had said that we could not live like Greeks or build like them because we were no longer simple enough. He had his own idea of what the Fair might be and it was not the idea of the New Yorkers. His adulating sister, Harriet Monroe, insists that his colorful proposal did not tolerate "imitations in staff [white plaster] of marble palaces." He wanted the Fair to express its temporary character; the buildings should be lighter, gayer, more decorative than the solid structures along the streets. But this was not to be.

On the first day of the first conference of the World's Fair Board Root caught pneumonia; he died before the conference was over. Harriet Monroe insists, "If he had lived, there would have been another battle of Chicago against the East, new methods against old, our own beauty against the past." Perhaps so, perhaps not. Anyway, in Root's absence, his partner Burnham offered no opposition to Hunt, St. Gaudens, and McKim; without Root at his elbow, Sullivan made no headway.

So the Easterners succeeded in putting on their display. Henry Adams blamed the Middle West for regarding art as a stage decoration. He sat down on the steps beneath Hunt's dome at the Fair and pondered, "if . . . the new American world could take this sharp and conscious twist towards ideals, one's personal friends would come in, at last, as winners in the great American chariot-race for fame. If the people of the Northwest actually knew what was good when they saw it, they would someday talk about Hunt and Richardson, La Farge and St. Gaudens, Burnham and McKim, and Stanford White when their politicians and millionaires were otherwise forgotten. The artists and architects who had done the work offered little encouragement to hope it . . . to them the Northwest refused to look artistic. They talked as though they worked only for themselves; as though art, to the Western people, was a stage decoration; a diamond shirt-stud; a paper collar." Adams could not see that it was his Eastern friends who were creating his "shirt-studs."

The fact is, though, that the Western work was not much better. Cobb's Fisheries Building may be assumed to have been the nearest to what Root had in mind, and certainly was the most representative of what Chicago architects had been doing, but it was of no distinction. Sullivan's Transportation Building attracted the most attention. But it too was a shirt stud. As a picture it was marvelous. A great Romanesque arch held five voussoirs, each brilliantly decorated with Sullivan's most exotic ornament. The whole arch-portal was then framed by a large projecting horizontal member at about the level of the springing of the portal arches. This motif had been suggested on a smaller scale at the Auditorium and would be used again later by Sullivan in appealing ways on some of his Iowa and Minnesota banks, especially at Owatonna. The building had originality and freshness to the extent that it was in opposition to the prevailing classic detail of the Fair. But Sullivan had created no Galerie des Machines, no Crystal Palace, not even a true exemplar of the work of the Chicago school. It is quite unjustified to say with James Fitch that it was "the only structure which disdained the dull and hackneyed idiom of the last Classical Revival." At that particular moment the Richardsonian idiom was if anything more hackneyed than the classic. The building made no statement about the arched iron structure of the shed behind it, no statement about transportation; it made no important prediction for future railroad stations either, although the door details turned up the very next year in the Union Station at St. Louis. Its charm lay in its difference; its quality lay in Sullivan's decorative genius which, great as it was, is not his main claim to fame. It was appropriate enough for the Fair, in the terms of Root, but had American buildings of the next fifty years followed its lead, the Transportation Building might well have been as great a barrier to the future as the conquering classic turned out to be.

Yet Sullivan's later words of criticism seem to have convinced more people than the art in his buildings was able to do. Thus we find interpretations like the one advanced by John Kouwenhoven, ". . . the work of men like McKim . . . had less relation to the vital contemporary forces of American life, and to its future, than even the crudest, least ingratiating examples of small-town dwellings or the most materialistically functional office buildings." That this is distorted history for its day, however sound as prophecy, seems established by the numerous commissions given to McKim by men who were heavily involved in the then vital contemporary forces; and if the wide acceptance of the new classical manner is any sign, almost everyone of the times must have been ignorant of them and of the place of architecture in them. For there can be no doubt that the new classical manner was exactly what the society wanted.

Somewhat later Paul Cret pointed out that "Nobody imposed French architecture on the United States. It was of their own free will that hundreds of Americans went to Paris and that thousands more took their inspiration from the ideas they brought back. Were all these men fools? What were they looking for in France? . . . It was composition and design." Only hindsight could lead Sullivan to assert, and Wright to quote, and those who accept an unusual version of history to believe, that the Fair dealt American architecture a blow from which it would not recover for fifty years. It was fifty years before the new ideas came to fruit; but to blame their lag on a single summer's show and not on the national disposition is to put too much faith in a minor event.

Certainly the view could not have been entertained in the year 1892, while the Fair was being planned. The Chicago architects, like Atwood from Burnham's office and Sullivan himself, went right along with the group from New York led by Hunt and McKim. Moreover the greatest buildings of the Chicago style were built *after* the Exposition. Burnham's Reliance Building, one of the finest examples of the steel cage enclosed in terra cotta, was only a small four-story building in 1890, not completed until building was resumed in 1894. The Marquette Building and Beman's Studebaker with its all-glass façade topped inconsistently with Gothic fretwork, all lay in the future. The Fisher Building, the marvelously simple Gage Building of Sullivan, and the McClurg Building came at the end of the century. The great Schlesinger-Mayer Store, later occupied by Carson, Pirie and Scott, was not built by Sullivan until 1899. Thus the World's Fair did not nip the Chicago School while it was still in the bud. It had barely shown what might be done by 1893; it continued to develop long after the Fair was closed. The Fair did offer American clients a choice, and most of them, as we now think unwisely, chose the classic revival. But the Chicago school had its chance to show competing work off the Fair grounds and American clients were prepared for a while to support the Chicago school for industrial, commercial and residential architecture. But the old law of hierarchy of building types still operated to insist that cultural buildings should be in the grand tradition of classical design. The Fair merely stated the accepted law and possibly revealed and emphasized it to more people. In the end the classic mania overtook the "non-cultural" buildings too but this was after Sullivan had dissipated his energies, after his break with Adler had deprived him of strength, after the death of Root had weakened the aesthetic powers of Burnham's firm, after Purcell and Elmslie had aged and only Frank Lloyd Wright was left, and he in eclipse.

2 1

BUT THERE WAS A MOMENT WHEN SULLIVAN SHOWED THE WORLD HOW A tall skyscraper ought to be built when his Prudential Building at Buffalo, completed in 1894-1895, repeated the success of the Wainwright Building. It expressed Guadet's principles perfectly, as Sullivan's own explanation reveals. This appeared in an article he wrote for *Lippincott's Magazine* for March, 1896, "The Tall Office Building Artistically Considered." The essay began by describing the practical conditions to be met; he found five: first, a story below ground containing the equipment for power, heating and light; second, a ground floor with an entrance common to all spaces in the building, devoted to stores, banks or other establishments requiring large area, ample space, ample light and great freedom of access and display; third, a second story accessible by stairs, broken into large subdivisions with liberal spacing of structure and liberal expanse of glass; fourth, above this, an indefinite number of stories of offices built layer upon layer, all alike. Fifth and finally, at the top, a space that is the attic: "In this the circulatory system completes itself and makes its grand turn, ascending and descending. The space is filled with tanks, pipes, valves, sheaves, and mechanical etcetera that supplement and complement the force-originating plant hidden belowground in the cellar."

Having distinguished the five major subdivisions, Sullivan next described the module for the whole design. It was the standard office room which determined the structural unit and the size of the window openings. The openings in the base needed to be the largest, those in the attic were unimportant. "Hence it follows inevitably, and in the simplest possible way, that if we follow our natural instincts without thought of books, rules, precedents, or any such educational impedimenta to a spontaneous and 'sensible' result we will . . . design the exterior of our tall office building." This statement is characteristic of Sullivan's acceptance of the belief that "every problem . . . contains and suggests its own solution," a firm avowal in architecture of the principles of instrumentalism in teaching which John Dewey was developing in Chicago to challenge academic methods of relying on the old process of memorizing facts and rules.

Consider now how Sullivan proposed to organize the chief and possibly conflicting requirements of good performance, structural stability and beauty. Beginning with the first story, he would create a main entrance that attracted the eye; the remainder would be treated "in a more or less liberal, expansive, sumptuous way — a way based exactly on the practical necessities, but expressed with a sentiment of largeness and freedom." The second story would be similar, and above this, through the indefinite number of office tiers, he took his cue from the individual cell, which required a window with its separating pier, its sill and lintel, all looking alike because they were all alike. The whole would terminate at the attic, "which, having no division into office cells, and no special requirement for lighting, gives us the power to show by means of its broad expanse of wall, and its dominating weight and character, that which is the fact — namely, that the series of office tiers has come definitely to an end." So much for the strictly functional aspects of the office building and their expression in the design.

But thus far, Sullivan's results were merely partial and tentative; his form had followed function, but only physical function: ". . . we must seek a fuller justification, a finer sanction. . . . We must now heed the imperative voice of emotion." What is the chief feature of an office building? "And at once we answer, it is lofty. This loftiness is to the artist-nature its thrilling aspect. It is the very open organ-tone in its appeal. It must be in turn the dominant chord in his expression of it, the true excitant of his imagination. It must be tall, every inch of it tall . . . It must be every inch a proud and soaring thing, rising in sheer exultation that from bottom to top it is a unit without a single dissenting line." Now Sullivan prepared his reader to accept the idea, that form must not only be adapted to function, but that it must *express* that function: "All things in nature have a shape . . . that tells us what they are . . . Unfailingly in nature these shapes express the inner life . . . of the animal, tree, bird, fish, that they present to us. . . . Over all the coursing sun, *form ever follows function*, and this is the law. Where function does not change, form does not change. . . . It is the pervading law of all things organic and inorganic." It was that general principle of organic expression, not mechanical functionalism, which led Sullivan "readily, clearly and conclusively" to give the lower stories a character suited to commerce, the tiers of typical offices another, and the attic still another. Each form revealed a different function; but where, as in the offices, function did not change, neither did form. He arrived at a three-part division "naturally, spontaneously, unwittingly . . . not from any theory, symbol, or fancied logic."

Yet Sullivan's interpretation was open to misunderstanding. Years later his word "function" would receive only a mechanistic interpretation, denying that form should be modified for expressive and aesthetic, rather than utilitarian, reasons. Equally misinformed were those who ignored the origins of expression in function. For example, Sullivan's desire to express the verticality of the tall building led him to introduce extra vertical, decorative, non-structural elements between the structural piers; but from the exterior no distinction was visible. Expressive form here took precedence over structural function, with no nonsense about "honesty." Furthermore, the terra-cotta protection was not self-supporting. Therefore the casing was treated with delicate ornament. Here form alone scored a triumph unbounded by any efficiency or economy. The ornament was a great personal accomplishment, but it opened the way to lesser designers to develop form that was unrelated to structure and function, obeying the rules of form alone.

The achievement of Sullivan both in the Prudential Building and in theory was widely recognized and immediately acclaimed. In the beginning his influence was usually salutary. Many of the tall buildings erected between 1897 and 1913 expressed the theme of tall vertical lines, and most were divided into base, shaft and cornice. The functional mode of design he championed gained signal triumphs in the field of industrial architecture. Able designers, like Ernest Wilby working with Albert Kahn, achieved a characteristic expression for American industrial buildings, such as the Brown-Lipe-Chapin factory at Syracuse of 1908. Frank Lloyd Wright, Sullivan's most able draughtsman and probably the designer of some of Sullivan's best ornaments, developed an idiom of space and form that soon created houses and industrial architecture more original than any the world had known in many years.

Even the eclectics gave at least lip service to functionalism and attempted to respect structure. New Yorkers studied their new skyscrapers to achieve more unity than the World and the older Tribune Building

had offered. Tortured picturesqueness such as that of the Wolfe Build-
ing in 1895 was quickly outmoded. The Prudential and the Condict
(Bayard) Buildings of Sullivan, erected in 1897, showed Buffalo and
New York what might be done with the vertical theme.

But most designers could not resist thinking first of form and in the
end that stopped the clock. It was not long before New Yorkers reverted
to the classical envelopes. The St. Paul Building, erected by George B.
Post in 1898, obeyed Sullivan's formula of tripartite division and vertical expression, but all the dividing elements and details were derived
from the classics. The Metropolitan Life, erected in 1899, became a pile
of Renaissance palaces one atop the other. The Flatiron Building, done
by the Chicago firm of Daniel Burnham Company, was a classic column widened and imposed on a triangular site. Playing with the forms
independently of the structures, some designers soon exacted excessive
freedom from the structural and functional expressions. This characterized the highly eclectic New York Times Building by C. L. W. Eidlitz
and the pitiful tower added to the Metropolitan Life Building by Napoleon Le Brun who started the long shaft with vertical elements and then
could not end it without stuttering through successive strata of balconies, cornices, roofs, more cornices, pavilions and spires. Other designers, recognizing that such extravagances vitiated their effects, attempted
to simplify classic expression and bring it into accord with the structural
facts of the tall building. Carrère and Hastings essayed such a skyscraper
in 1903 when they built the Blair Building, called Beaux-Arts by contemporaries. In 1905 *The Record* urged New Yorkers to emulate the
modernized, simplified, almost classic expression Burnham had supplied
to such buildings as the Railway Exchange in Chicago, an expression
which Holabird and Roche then broadcast in buildings throughout the
West. The critic wondered whether the Railway Exchange was "not
much closer to a thoroughly sound starting point for the design of a skyscraper than the more pretentious methods of our school-men."

A distortion of Sullivan's idea that a tall building needed a primarily
vertical expression then led eclectic designers to abandon horizontal
Renaissance models for the Gothic. Vertical piers became buttresses,
ending in Gothic forms at the summit. The major achievement of
this kind was Cass Gilbert's Woolworth Tower, certainly a landmark of
the day in 1913 when it was completed. This 792-foot "Cathedral of
Commerce" was the highest building in the world for almost twenty
years. Gleaming white, it proclaimed its steel frame. Wide piers around
the columns and thin mullions between accentuated the verticality by
subdividing the wide spandrels. A tall tower rose from the main mass to
carry the long piers to the summit where they ended as buttresses, carved

into Gothic forms and giving the top a rich silhouette. The envelope of the building had been studied with regard to the setback of form at the top, and the tower, therefore, unlike the Tower Building by Bradford Gilbert and most other skyscrapers, was a finished form on all sides, not a façade masking a brick-walled loft. The scale of the Gothic ornament at the top was impressive enough. It provided labyrinthine spatial sequences. But the intended effect was to create a distinctive commercial building, one whose height readily proclaimed its position in the city. It was a frank avowal of the fact that mere functionalism was inadequate to express the role of business; it showed how the expressive function demanded of a cathedral of commerce might lead an architect to appropriate the Butter Tower at Rouen. Montgomery Schuyler went overboard about it. He praised the plasticity of terra cotta, the successful scale, the sharp outlines, the detail. The gargoyle he thought was the equal of true Gothic. He said that the loss of space caused by the recessions of the upper stories of the tower, to give a more artistic lightening of the mass, commemorated the client's sense of civic obligation.

The Woolworth Building was a major concession to the idea that there should be an historical style, but that the form of a building should also express its structure. Other buildings went straightaway towards formalism, ignoring structure. By 1910 leaders of the formalists like Charles Platt and Charles McKim had relegated the structure to second place and judged it unworthy to appear in the final result. Their tall New York apartments on the east side of Central Park were simply huge masonry Renaissance forms hiding steel. Thus by 1913 the issue of expressing the steel frame and remaining true to structural and functional fact had become dead; "art" had gone in pursuit of varied composition in mass, despite the examples of Sullivan.

The result could not have been otherwise, given the critical reception accorded the pioneers. Even the most progressive critics were intrigued only by the new forms and intellectually stimulated by the new theory; they did not think the results beautiful. Thus the critic writing about the Railway Exchange Building at Chicago in the *Record* of 1905 approved the theory underlying it, but found it "monstrously ugly, a tremendous affair of window sashes." He argued, "It would be a queer eye that would claim beauty for the result. No! the design is not beautiful — it is merely interesting because it is rational."

It seemed still more difficult to accept the early work of Frank Lloyd Wright, capped by his splendid Larkin Building at Buffalo. Some critics, it is true, joined advanced Europeans like Behrens and Gropius in praising Wright's office building. The *Architectural Review* (U.S.), which seldom failed to support Beaux-Arts principles, was nevertheless ecstatic in 1907: ". . . about as fine a piece of original and effective composition as one could expect to find. This sort of thing is absolutely in the line of creative architecture." But most of the country preferred industrial architecture like that erected at Morley, Colorado, in 1909-1910, for the Colorado Supply Company, a building in Santa Fe Colonial style. Not even Russell Sturgis could bring himself to admire the Larkin Building for more than intellectual reasons: ". . . this monument . . . [is] an extremely ugly building. It is, in fact, a monster of awkwardness . . . It is only capable of interesting that student who is quite aware that the architects of the modern world . . . have failed to make anything of . . . following the ancient styles."

Yet the Larkin Building was one of the greatest achievements of the Chicago school. It was planned around an interior court, skylighted from above and surrounded by balconies leading to the offices. The well, itself, had an exultant vitality, relying on the rhythmic statements made by the repeated forms of the several floors. The general idea had appeared earlier in stores such as Eiffel's Bon Marché in Paris. Now it had become a popular and excellent device, used in the Rookery, the Union Trust at Pittsburgh, the Metropolitan Life at Minneapolis, the Brown Palace Hotel at Denver, the Bradbury Building at Los Angeles, all of which had deep central wells similar to that of Bunning's Coal Exchange at London. But of these the Larkin Building was easily foremost. Elevators, plainly seen, brought the clerks to the balconies. Four corner towers, ninety feet high, contained the staircases. Many technical features showed great imagination. All furniture was designed by the architect, and much of it was built in. The building was hermetically sealed against the dirty industrial environment. All plumbing was concentrated in stacks. The quarters were light, wholesome and well ventilated. The outside walls were made smooth and hard to defeat the smoke and dirt of the locality. There was a restaurant on the fifth floor for employees opening in turn to a recreation area on the main roof.

But the major accomplishment was to have expressed a magnificent interior space. The massiveness and strength of the exterior forms, their monumental scale, prevented contemporaries from giving this building universal acclaim. They could appreciate the rationale of the building, but it all seemed too harsh: ". . . the square corner, the right angle, the straight edge, the sharp arris, the firm vertical and horizontal lines, unbroken, unmodified, uncompromising in their geometrical precision . . . [these] incongruous parts, leading to . . . a hopeless result." The critic failed to recognize, in a building he knew was important, anything beautiful or prescient. Later, in 1950, the people of Buffalo hardly knew they were tearing down an historic monument. Wright's own claim was modest enough, "The work may have the same claim to consideration as a 'work of art' as an ocean liner, a locomotive or a battleship."

2 2

BUT FOR ALL THE PROGRESS IN DESIGN OF THE SKYSCRAPER, THE FACT WAS that it still stood low in the hierarchy of architectural interest. Critics and architects were far more ready to accept a new style that was a matter of superficial detail than they were to accept excellent design based upon structural and functional realities. That was why it was so easy for McKim to rally an influential group of art collectors to support his idea for establishing a new academy of architecture. He felt that the role of this country for some time should be to catch up rather than prematurely to attempt originality, and he did not sympathize with those who would close the book and in their impatience start a national art. As Rome went to Greece, and later France, Spain and England went to Rome, so must we become students and study, bring back and adapt to American conditions the splendors of Rome He believed that great modern architecture demanded the example of great past architecture, and that young architects needed contact with originals, much as painters needed to study excellent examples. "No other city offers . . . an atmosphere so replete with the best precedents."

Such arguments persuaded J. P. Morgan and Henry Frick of New York and H. B. Walters of Baltimore, art collectors all, to help McKim establish the American Academy at Rome, organized in 1894. In this McKim carried the sentiments of most of the profession, except for Gothicists like Ralph Adams Cram. But most architects would have agreed with Burnham, who once offered to send Wright to Paris, and they would have agreed with McKim's letter of advice to Burnham about the kind of candidates to be sent to the new Academy; namely, to stick to classic and ignore any "Yahoo or Hottentot creations." What McKim failed to see was that the Yahoos and Hottentots would exist, Academy or not, and their vigor would breed a style capable of giving form to modern institutions.

In establishing the Academy at Rome, McKim was not making taste, but following it. His scheme was consonant with the national sentiment. Consider, for example, how business reacted to the Schlesinger and Mayer department store in Chicago. Here Sullivan had designed one of the most audacious, far-seeing buildings in America's history. It had no technical innovations; the interior was still of the loft-building type with large floor areas divided by the skeleton. All the innovations were artistic. Along the sidewalks, one saw the relentless precision of piers faced with terra cotta, richly embellished with the elaborate floral ornament characteristic of the architect. Here the show windows drew the pedestrian toward the great corner entrance where the rhythm was climaxed by a protruding rotunda with beautifully molded, bronze-framed bull's-eye windows. Above this base, the building made a strong statement with continuous horizontal spandrels running their long courses over recessed piers. The geometry was perfect in proportion, exact and definite, and the thin metal frames of the windows stated a subordinated theme. This large grid was terminated at the top by a wide-spreading cornice, wrapped around the whole design to bring the eye back to the strong vertical mullions and piers at the corner. No designer in America had more successfully turned a corner on a busy street intersection. It was all a direct consequence of the need for advertisement, for circulation, for light, and yet the whole was animated by great originality in detail and great discipline in the over-all composition.

In spite of this triumph, Sullivan was not asked by other Chicago businessmen to attempt anything so wonderful. Instead they tended to support the dreary and monotonous work of Burnham's firm, now bereft of Root. One would hardly suspect that a Burnham building like the Wanamaker Department Store, erected in Philadelphia in 1911, had come out of the Chicago tradition at all. Its innovation and values were all technical. It used a steel skeleton, but it hid it in masonry. To be sure, it had sixty-eight elevators, plentiful electric lighting, isolable sections of fireproof escape areas. Tanks on its roof held in reserve more than 80,000 gallons of water to supply automatic fire sprinklers; in all technical ways it was advanced, yet the architecture was dull, an embarrassing exemplar of what the commercial spirit was willing to purchase. This gargantuan Renaissance palace standing on stilts, monotonous, impersonal, inconsistent with its structure and use, had an exterior envelope which fulfilled all the superficial rules of classical composition, and the underlying principles of structural integrity, but missed the expression of character, conformity to program, and adaptation to cultural environment which all good architecture, including good Beaux-Arts architecture, has followed. The entrance was a give-away to the mentality of the designer; classic columns stood before a façade of steel and glass. The grand court on the interior took the same idea Wright had used in the Larkin Building but turned it into a pusillanimous mockery of a Roman basilica. Burnham willingly created one hall complete with palmetto patterns in the light shades hanging from the ceiling. It was called the Egyptian Hall, and its function was to sell pianos! And this was the usual end. Despite the noteworthy suggestions of Sullivan's Wainwright, Prudential and Schlesinger Buildings, despite the brilliance of Wright's Larkin Building, the image for most commercial buildings was eclectic. It was even more so for banks and bourses. The Knickerbocker Trust Company in New York City followed prevailing fashion by hiring McKim, Mead and White to design a Roman building, complete with an order of giant columns, and this example was followed by most banks in large cities.

Meanwhile Sullivan, when he was given the chance, created a few superb small bank buildings in Iowa and Minnesota, notably the one at Owatonna. There he provided a simple cube, beautifully proportioned, clad in magnificent brick, ornamented with terra cotta and bronze. This Owatonna bank was the most memorable one of its day; it affected the later architecture of the whole town square and made this small farming center a place of international pilgrimage. Unfortunately it was not the national symbol of a bank, even one in the country, and the classic columns that fronted its neighbors in Minnesota were but weak reflections of the grandeur established by much larger clients, men like the members of the New York Stock Exchange who commissioned George B. Post about 1905 to set up a Roman temple, fronted by a Corinthian colonnade, among the skyscrapers of lower Manhattan.

If commercial buildings were to be so garbed it was not surprising that public buildings should look like banks. A competition held in 1908 for the New York Post Office found no entries appropriate to an age of steam and steel, more or less efficient governmental services, a new culture based on science and technology, the huge transportation and circulation problems imposed by the vast area of the metropolis. The winning design by McKim, Mead and White might, *mutatis mutandis*, have stood in the Forum centuries before. McKim's Municipal Building of 1908-1910 turned the whole Forum up on its side to create a classic-bedecked skyscraper, while the Customs House at New York, done by Cass Gilbert in 1902-1907, was only less ridiculous than the tall shaft built later for the Customs House at Boston, topped by a mausoleum emitting smoke and suggesting that the whole building was nothing but a vast chimney stack, rising from a Roman temple. The citizens of Nashville voted to erect a plaster copy of the Parthenon in 1897; state legislators in Rhode Island and Minnesota and Missouri supported architects who crowned their Capitols with domes resembling that of the national capitol. Usually this work was composed effectively, the design was skillfully scaled, the grand escaliers were imposing, and the sculpture and murals were executed by artists who had the skills if not the talents of masters. But they remained reminiscent of another civilization and unfitting for the habits of the legislators who walked into them from the prairie. Measured against the Larkin Building they were foreign visitors, or Americans speaking with an affected accent, wearing costumes borrowed from a stranger.

Such designs unfortunately were carried even to distant lands to become the badge for American imperialism in Cuba and the Philippines. When Burnham went to Manila to design a civic center, he took with him the style of the World's Fair and laid out great areas among the bamboos, much as the English had done in India.

Once in a great while the government abandoned a strictly classic requirement and encouraged a talented architect to create something more original and appropriate. A noteworthy example of this is the Pan-American Building built in Washington in 1907-1910 and designed by Paul Philippe Cret, the Beaux-Arts architect who came from France to the United States in 1903 at the age of twenty-seven. Professor of design at the University of Pennsylvania from 1903 to 1937, Cret became the most respected French Beaux-Arts man in any American school. His building revealed how a good Beaux-Arts designer handled problems of siting, planning and expression. The Pan-American Union required offices, a library, and a suite of reception rooms, all with some elegance, all to be in a building on an important site, facing the Ellipse on one side and Constitution Avenue on another. Cret reinforced the grandeur of the site by the stately scale of the entrance, in which the central arches were framed by lofty pylons. Through the arches, one caught an intimation of a handsome skylighted courtyard beyond the entrance vestibule. The patio was perhaps the most impressive feature; it was surrounded by an arcade and open galleries. The pavement was of handmade tile with black figures displayed on a field of red. The rough white stucco arches supported a frieze bearing the coats of arms of the twenty-one republics. At the center was an Aztec fountain. Plants grown in the tropics — bananas, palms, coffee, rubber, papaya — as well as the noisy and bizarre macaws in the foliage, combined with the fountain and sculpture to make an interesting blend of classical architecture with the art of Central and South America. Sculpture designed by Gertrude Vanderbilt Whitney, Gutzon Borglum and Isidore Kouti harmonized well with the architecture. Besides the sculptors, it is noteworthy that Cret himself paid special tribute to Andrew Carnegie who gave most of the money for the building, to President Theodore Roosevelt who symbolized his international role by laying the cornerstone in 1908, and to Elihu Root, Secretary of State, whose knowledge of architectural problems Cret respected.

2 3

THE BIG TOWN HOUSE BUILT FOR THE RICH WAS ONLY A SMALLER VERSION
of the palaces of commerce and government. The individuality characteristic of mansions like the William K. Vanderbilt house, by Hunt, disappeared in favor of formal, uniformly anonymous houses, usually in
Renaissance or Roman styles. The New York houses for Henry Villard
set the theme in 1885. Characteristic of the best academic work, these
houses by Wells, of McKim's firm, were well designed. Their elevation
had a planar restraint like that of the Cancelleria Palace at Rome. But
they gave, also, an impression of restrained monumentality, much superior to the chaotic and picturesque skylines of earlier houses. They
boldly combined several houses into one large palazzo, surrounding a
court left open to the street.

Similar houses quickly became fashionable and were freely provided
by competent men like Ernest Flagg, Charles Platt, or Carrère and
Hastings. They were planned for a luxurious way of life, unsurpassed
in the countries from which their style had been imported. During the
'70s and '80s when the Carnegies and Rockefellers were building their
empires, their residential requirements in Pittsburgh and Cleveland may
have been modest. But at the turn of the century everyone had to have
a Renaissance palace, with detail taken from Italy, France or England,
and Carnegie had one built for himself on Ninety-first Street in 1905.
Some of the rich people hired architects much as they might hire
secretaries, keeping them on a permanent basis, charging them personally with all the family architectural work. This was the way for example of the Wideners with Horace Trumbauer. Such houses were unrelated to American workmen and to any other American resource
save money. They were bound to disappear as the economy and the
culture matured. But meanwhile this lavish clientele brought in not
only foreign styles but foreign architects who provided examples of
the full Beaux-Arts version of an elegant town house such as the Clark
Mansion in New York, erected in 1901, by Paul Chedanne.

The clients were often as princely as a Florentine patron, not prone
to cut corners or to make merely a plaster show as some of the motor
magnates were willing to do later. When McKim was designing the
Morgan Library, he is said to have tested his client by seeking to use
joints as tightly sealed as the stones in the splendid wall of the
Erechtheum. "I would like to follow their example, but it would cost a
small fortune and no one would see where the additional money went."

"How much extra?" Morgan asked. "Fifty thousand dollars," was Mc-
Kim's reply. "Go ahead," Morgan said. Such respect as Morgan
showed for McKim's talent and knowledge and such devotion as he
showed for excellence and permanence were emulated by other clients
in the houses they built in the East and, wherever sufficient money was
available, in the West. By any absolute standard they are superior to the
earlier Victorian fantasies of the Californians, Crocker or Carson. They
were an expression of an influential element of American life of the moment. The resentment leveled against them by Veblen or Tarbell was
not that of an absolute standard of designing taste but hinged on the
question, rather, whether any man should have such money to "waste";
whether men of such imperial power and ambition could be tolerated in
a democracy. If they could, the architecture of their houses was neither
inappropriate nor bad, and when Frick called in Hastings to design a
house that would hold a collection of paintings so well that it might become (as it was intended from the beginning to be) a museum for the
nation, the millionaire himself was stewarding his wealth for a common
interest in the tradition of Carnegie.

In such an atmosphere, it is not surprising that the old brownstones
began to give way to large palace-like apartment buildings, uniformly
classic in design, such as 925 Park Avenue by Delano and Aldrich or
Charles Platt's design for 131 East 66th Street, the Mills House Number One by Ernest Flagg, or the Apthorp Apartments by Clinton and
Russell, erected in 1908, which were said to be the largest in the world.
To these classic versions of opulent domesticity architects like McKim
added buildings like that for the University Club at New York, of
1900, whose impeccable façade adroitly masks the interior halls with no
obvious relation between the two.

2 4

THE SAME CONCERN WITH ARCHITECTURE AS PURELY FORMAL DESIGN
spilled over more appropriately on "great" hotels like the Waldorf-
Astoria, begun in 1893, or the "greatest" of them all, the eighteen-story
St. Regis Hotel of 1904, then the tallest and costliest hotel in New York.

Hospitals also followed the trend, with much less justification, becoming well-equipped, lavishly appointed buildings wrapped in formal
envelopes. Some, such as the Johns Hopkins Hospital, were still able to
command sufficient space to be spread out into pavilions. This was also
the early fortune of the Peter Bent Brigham at Boston, designed by
Codman and Despradelle. But more often they were consolidated on

many floors, as in St. Luke's Hospital in New York of 1896, by Ernest
Flagg, and the Bellevue Hospital of 1908 by McKim, Mead and White.
The plan of the Mt. Sinai Hospital of 1905, published by *The Record*
of that year as the ideal modern hospital, revealed that advancing technology in the better control over disease had reduced the amount of site
planning and architectural planning needed to make the hospital perform well. Consequently, the architects could become much more
formalistic.

Indeed, the hospital of 1885-1913 demonstrates how the advancing
technology now made it possible for architecture to turn away from rational planning. In earlier times if a building had clearly defined functional needs they could be met only by courting nature. Good and
therapeutic light could be brought to the building only from the sun;
good ventilation could come only from the prevailing breezes; coolness
could be supplied only by shade, by the suspiration of trees or by the
surround of non-heat-absorbing surfaces like grass. People had to move
about on foot and at the speed of foot travel. They could talk to each
other only by meeting face to face or by writing messages in longhand
for someone else to carry on foot. This meant that a successful building had to take account of nature in the fullest sense even in its functional planning; and such an account had to have an effect on the basic
composition of areas and masses. Now all these limitations were swept
away almost in a stroke. Elevators, telephones, electricity, heating and
ventilating machinery, insulating and acoustic materials, could be combined to make almost any scheme work. Thus for a while technology
seemed to free the architect from the excellent and unforgiving discipline of natural forces; he no longer had to make the design conform
to stringent physical necessity but could manage the necessity within
a preconceived and purely visual pattern.

2 5

IN THIS A GOOD DEAL OF BETRAYAL AND SELF-DECEPTION WAS POSSIBLE,
and an architect who turned his back on natural forces was not likely to
face unpleasant social realities any more squarely. He was aware of the
mansions, hotels, and clubs along Fifth Avenue that provided a fitting
background for the funeral cortege of General Grant in 1885, and the
more lavish if less military procession that moved along Fifth Avenue in
1895 behind the hearse of Ward McAllister. The kind of life Caroline
Schermerhorn Astor saw from her windows in the mansion at Fifth

Avenue and Sixty-fifth Street revealed no sense of what reporters like the Danish Jacob Riis were discovering in the Bowery's Tenth Ward where people were packed 522 to the acre by 1890. They photographed life in those quarters, using the photographs in lectures such as the ones Riis gave throughout New York. His book, *The Other Half: How It Lives and Dies in New York*, published by Scribner in 1890, shocked a city of minor Astors into recognizing the degraded condition of the slum people: "In a room not thirteen feet either way slept twelve men and women, two or three in bunks set in a sort of alcove, the rest on the floor. A kerosene lamp burned dimly in the fearful atmosphere, probably to guide other and later arrivals to their 'beds,' for it was only just past midnight."

Few architects seem to have been much interested in such problems. There were, to be sure, no government or private agencies for housing reform or urban renewal, to call upon architects to solve the kinds of problem that the social reformers were uncovering. The magazines addressed particularly to architects, even the *Architectural Record* under the editorship of the liberal Herbert Croly, displayed little concern about the slums. Attention was directed to elegant hotels and apartment houses, to lavish private estates, and big churches. Students in architectural schools would more often be asked to design a fountain or an orangery or an Explorers' Club than a low-cost housing scheme. The student could readily find an article about the bricks of Siena, the fountains at Tivoli, or the gardens at Versailles. No architectural magazine seems to have reviewed the spate of literature appearing about reform questions.

This revealed the enormous gulf between architecture and a large segment of American society. Concerned with questions of form alone, the architects had lost a social message. They were at their best as interpreters and fashion designers for a small clique of rich Americans oriented towards Europe. Even the radicals like Sullivan and Wright were not radical about the pressing social problem of the slum. Architecture had been in such dangerous waters before, and it would be again.

For architecture gains widest respect when it is allied with important social causes, emotional tones and intellectual ideas. The art of form is at best a narrow section of architecture's spectrum, and those who dally only with this drive architecture further and further from public reality whether they work with classic or "modern" forms. The professional architects of the generation 1885 to 1913 failed to read the lesson of recent history. They ignored the kinds of challenge Greenough and Huxley and Cook had given to professional architects. They created for their profession the reputation of being a luxury, something less than engineering or medicine or law, a reputation it still sometimes has if not enjoys.

The great and powerful architects of the generation seldom lent support to the many institutions being formed for welfare work. Leading architects did not enjoy commissions for frugal institutions such as the Y.M.C.A. or the Y.W.C.A., though these did build enough buildings so that the journals of 1910 carried special articles about them, and even evoked a distinctive if not distinguished architecture. Charities such as the Henry Street Settlement House in New York or Hull House in Chicago required architects to design new quarters. They hired such firms as Pond and Pond or Henry Ives Cobb to design respectable, modest, non-imperial but still eclectic Colonial or Renaissance buildings. But the architectural leaders of the conservative tradition, the Hunts and McKims, never showed up in these places. Wright went to Hull House in 1904 to deliver his forward-looking lecture about using the machine in future architecture, but this said little for the architecture of the poor of his or another generation. Wright could at least do this much, but McKim's designer-partner, Stanford White, complete with red mustache and cape, preferred to make a grand and late entrance to the opera. He was not noticeably in the headlines of the reform movement when Tammany was temporarily ousted from New York City in 1894 and Mayor William L. Strong's reform administration started cleaning the rubbish-piled streets of New York. He was not listed as present at the opening of the Henry Street Settlement in 1893 but was very conspicuous at the fashionable ceremony dedicating a temporary wooden and plaster triumphal arch erected on lower Broadway for a trivial pageant.

Some architects but again not the famous ones became active in the reform movements involving recreation. There were a few public recreational buildings such as the free baths for New York's East Side, designed by Aiken and Brunner in 1905. But such buildings were less typical than parks and gardens. Conspicuous features in many of the parks were boathouses, bandstands and refectories. Popular amusement parks like Coney Island were still more characteristic. Here the architecture tended towards the fantastic though not towards fantasy. Electric light was used profusely for advertising and to turn the night into day. Although the early American amusement parks were less vulgar than those that came later they never achieved the serenity and gaiety of Copenhagen's Tivoli or Stockholm's Skansen.

A zoo was another prominent feature of the city parks intended to enliven the lot of the poor while enlightening all youth. Buildings like those of Franklin Park, Philadelphia, or Central Park, New York, offered architects an opportunity to develop a major circulation pattern connecting a variety of uniquely shaped buildings. Each might have been appropriate to the specific type of animals housed, and a considerable degree of fantasy would have been permissible, even desirable. But in this period of the formal envelope, few buildings at any zoo had the gay variety which the London Zoo achieved later or the naturalistic environment for the animals found in recent moated zoos. In 1905 the American Beaux-Arts society set a competition for an elephant house in a city park and the results were quite indistinguishable from the designs for a library or a school.

26

THE PARKS AND PLAYGROUNDS OFFERED MODEST AMELIORATIONS AT BEST. Anything more fundamental seemed to require drastic steps, perhaps even moving people bodily to new centers planned upon better lines. We have already noted how Ebenezer Howard proposed the garden city movement in England. Europe had seen many earlier model villages built for and by individual companies, stretched over the fifty years after 1846 when Bessbrook had been built for linen mills near Newry, Ireland, including famous ones at Saltaire; Essen; Bourneville, England; Noisiel-sur-Marne; Port Sunlight; Creswell; and in 1905 Earswick, England, designed by the planners Barry Parker and Raymond Unwin. In the United States, too, employers had offered improved living conditions in an effort to get better and more faithful workmen. Leclaire, near St. Louis, and Berwick, Pennsylvania, had single-family houses set in parklike surroundings. Other attractive industrial villages were located at Vandergrift, Pennsylvania, for the American Sheet Steel Company; at Wilmerding, Pennsylvania, for the Westinghouse Air Brake Company; at Sparrows Point near Baltimore for the Maryland Steel Company.

But these were not conceived on the broad lines of Howard's garden cities. They were one-industry, one-company towns, and therefore not in any sense autonomous; they had no planned relation to other towns; they had no planned limit of growth; they had no protective green belt and bore no particular relation to agriculture; the residents were tenants; the profits from increasing land values fell to the company. Few of them were anything more than business investments by the companies; most of them were only superficially self-governing, and there was almost always some paternalism such as the stipulation that liquor could not be sold on the village property.

There were other and stranger towns, founded by crusaders like Dr. John Alexander Dowie, who established Zion City, Illinois, in 1901. Such men imposed harder conditions. Dowie permitted inhabitants to hold land until the year 3000 under a lease which restricted them in many ways: "No saloons, no harlots' dens, no tobacco shops, no theatres, no gambling halls, no opium joints, no drug stores, no secret lodges, no pig markets, no surgeons' offices, no labor unions, no oyster traffic."

There were also several attempts at founding fine parklike residential suburbs near large cities such as Baltimore, Chicago and Philadelphia. The most famous among these were two built on Long Island, Forest Hills and the so-called Garden City, though neither was a garden city in the sense of Ebenezer Howard. A. T. Stewart who started Garden City frankly intended it for the well-to-do. It had large houses surrounding a cathedral, schools and a public park, and it was well serviced by a railroad. The kinds of control and the kinds of industry that would give any organic character to towns of this kind never matured, and they remained dormitory suburbs serving only the small portion of metropolitan populations who needed service least.

Probably the best-planned was Forest Hills Gardens, Long Island, the work of Olmsted and Atterbury in 1911. Supported by the Russell Sage Foundation, Forest Hills aimed at a lower-income group than it reached. Aside from its curving streets and ample tree-shaded lawns and its concealed prefabrication, Forest Hills, however pleasant, was a romantic reincarnation of Tudor housing; one stepped off the Long Island Railroad into a charming synthetic village square of an England that never was, even in a Rackham drawing. In the distance one could hear not cowbells but the thud of tennis balls on the courts of the West Side Tennis Club. Just across the Long Island tracks the residential appearance was grim.

No doubt this sort of planning might have dug deeper into the social structure had legislation supported zoning and other planning needs, or had the experience with company housing in industrial towns proved more satisfactory. The country was not ready for a more public intervention, much less public subsidy; moreover, the American worker was not ready either. Like other Americans, he hoped to own his own house, even on a scanty margin of equity and even if it were inferior to the one his employer might have supplied. He was suspicious of paternalism; he mistrusted the company store to which historically he had been almost always in debt. On the industrialists' side there was the sad example of Pullman, Illinois, where President George Pullman had employed architect Solon Spencer Beman to design a model industrial town.

Many had looked to the Beman-Pullman scheme with great interest and hope; and by 1892 it was generally agreed that Pullman had a salutary effect on the workers living there, "a training school for the development of thrifty and thoroughgoing American workmen and mechanics." Attractive as Pullman was, it was not all cakes and ale for its residents, who found that the amenities of wide streets and lawns, the red brick row houses or the small private gardens did not fully atone for the loss of private rights. The company owned the theater and decided what would be shown, it owned the schools and decided what would be taught, it owned the public library and decided what books would be shelved, it owned the church and perhaps decided what would be preached. The employees could not buy property, could not acquire real political rights, could not even express opinions in print. Moreover, on the periphery and outside the boundaries of company control there was a wasteland supplying any of the lower human wants that the company denied. At any rate, in 1895 the Supreme Court of Illinois handed down an opinion that the company must dispose of all its land, homes and buildings not strictly employed in the manufacturing authorized. It is difficult at this stage to tell whether the initial mover behind the action was a group of real estate operators who wanted to gain control over the dwelling properties or whether the company itself wanted to get rid of properties which, beneficial in times of labor happiness, were a source of expense during strikes. Without the company, the town quickly ran down. After the dissolution the population waned from the 14,000 of 1895 to 10,000 in 1905, and by then only 6000 were still company employees. The appearance and tone of the village deteriorated as the streets and lawns and buildings got less and less care. In the long run the ten miles which separated it from the metropolis were built over, and Pullman was engulfed by Chicago.

2 7

THE IMPERIAL ASPECT OF THIS AGE DOMINATED THE REFORM ASPECT AND so it is not surprising that the "City Beautiful" movement was far more influential than philanthropy in the decisions that were made about planning. It was this movement with its bias towards classical architecture that gave to a few American cities a little of the spaciousness that French designers had achieved in the Place de la Concorde and the Champs Élysées at Paris and of course in Washington, D. C.

The movement owes nearly everything to the men who planned the series of great fairs, especially the Columbian Exposition of 1893. Despite modern criticism, it was a dream city of a summer; its axes, wide malls, lagoons, classical façades set on monumental sites, its spaciousness and cleanliness — all these were to last longer as ideas than the brief summer the plaster stayed white and uncracked. Other, later exhibitions were less glorious, but they carried the same message throughout the country; the Trans-Mississippi and International Exposition of Omaha in 1898; the Tennessee Centennial Exposition of the same year; the Pan-American Exposition at Buffalo in 1901. The Louisiana Purchase Exposition of 1904 in St. Louis was set in a large wooded park; its major buildings, all classical, were laid out on a long axis with plenty of space between them; one of the buildings, the Palace of Arts, designed by Cass Gilbert, stands today and serves St. Louis as a monumental if not very efficient gallery for the fine arts. Even the Alaska-Yukon Pacific Exposition at Seattle in 1909 had a formal plan and was classic except for the California building in Mission style. These fairs gave visitors a taste for architecture in the monumental tradition and a liking for one kind of urban planning.

Certainly the malls of the fairs were seemly compared with the disorderly streets of American industrial cities. An observant architect, Claude Bragdon, blamed *laissez-faire* individualism for the eclectic and licentious nature of our urban growth. "One of our streets made up of buildings of diverse styles and shapes and sizes — like a jaw with some teeth whole, some broken, some rotten, and some gone — is a symbol of our unkept individualism, now happily becoming curbed and chastened." It was not easy to cut into the living tissue of cities, particularly where tremendous real estate values existed on any downtown piece of property. The absence of any restrictions upon the use of land had inflated values to a level that seemed to justify only the tall office building. But various communities began enacting legislation, zoning for specific uses, requiring, for example, that all buildings in areas like Boston's Back Bay remain lower than a hundred feet, and there were attempts at maintaining architectural homogeneity in towns and historic parts of cities.

But the main renovations within cities stemmed more directly from the Columbian Exhibition itself, especially from the Court of Honor which fixed in the minds of Americans a higher ideal of aggregated architecture than they had previously had. Washington itself offered the best basis for improvement. Its grand plan, it may be recalled, designed by L'Enfant at the end of the eighteenth century, had never been completed. Indeed many of his planned spaces had been filled by miserably unmonumental buildings during the nineteenth century. The Union Railroad Station had ruined the Mall near the Capitol. Finally, about

1900, protests by many writers and some Congressmen began to bear fruit. Strongly supported by Theodore Roosevelt and Elihu Root, the Washington Park Commission was created to investigate improvement of the city and federal properties. Characteristically, Daniel Burnham was hired to extend and improve the L'Enfant plan. He opened the Mall and placed major buildings on the axes. The president of the Pennsylvania Railroad was persuaded to agree to remove the existing station and Burnham designed a new and monumentally impressive building, the present Union Station, below Capitol Hill. The total result of Burnham's work was to restore Washington to a plan that gave it spaciousness and its buildings a chance for dignity. In many ways it became the most beautiful city in the United States, particularly if you remained within the confines of the major axes and the parks along the Potomac and the creeks leading to it, and if you did not approach it with a disposition to be nauseated by its classicism or its "imperialism." But it was less rewarding if you strayed from the avenues of the northwest quarter. The peripheral areas were still slums and some of these lay in the shadow of the Capitol.

Inspired by this partial success, other American cities tried to carve consolidated space out of the old privately owned urban cores. When they succeeded they erected civic buildings on some sort of mall or square. It was an action of civic reform quite contrary to the attitude that had allowed Cleveland's commercial and industrial growth to destroy her early village green. But it had its own absurdities. When Burnham's firm was called on to design a civic center in the downtown of Cleveland, land was cleared at enormous expense and the city began to build major governmental buildings, all classical, on an open court. But this center lay outside what became the foci of the main activities of the city so its character is not only often missed by visitors but, even for the citizens themselves, it tends to be an empty, lifeless memorial to the City Beautiful idea. Burnham developed similar civic centers as the dominant foci of other large formal plans, for San Francisco, for Manila and in the end for Chicago, itself. The powers of persuasion of this able and energetic man are best summarized by the paragraph his assistant, Willis Polk, the architect, compiled from various passages in his speeches and writings, including the famous lines, "Make no little plans; they have no magic to stir men's blood."

The civic planners addressed a public distressed by the chaos and ugliness of their fast-expanding and uncontrolled cities. Accustomed to legislative curbs on *laissez faire* in business, it conceded the right to enforce conformity on urban development. The planners were so sure of the public support that the Group Plan Commission of Cleveland felt no arguments were needed in 1902 to prove that their new civic center required an architecture "derived from . . . the classic architecture of Rome; . . . one material should be used throughout and . . . a uniform scale . . . should be maintained. . . . The cornice line . . . should be uniform in height." Even buildings to serve radically different functions "should be of the same design and as uniform as possible."

It hardly needs to be said that these ideas were effective, but they were not enough. When they were good they owed their visual success to the organization of the spaces between the buildings and not to the adopted style. When they were bad they demonstrated that city planning will never be more than a monument to the passing whim of an aesthetic unless the plans are developed on sound social, technological and economic as well as physical and spatial lines.

The strengths and shortcomings of the City Beautiful movement are visible today in the civic center at San Francisco. The plan for that impressive complex was made in 1912 by John Galen Howard, Frederick Meyer and John Reid, Jr. They envisioned a long-range development, completed between 1919 and 1933, in which a large open square would be faced on the north by the auditorium, on the south by the State building, while the City Hall, dominating the west, would be the pivot for a large mall stretching eastward for 1800 feet, past the opera and library to terminate at Market Street. The group of buildings was to be balanced and classic, a foil to the earthy ugliness of the "Slot." But, admitting its obvious formal merits, the scheme failed to meet many basic functional requirements; it was hard to expand; it offered badly shaped sites for future buildings; it brought noisy traffic past the buildings and into the square; its classic dignity was soon marred by seas of glistening and unforeseen automobiles. Today it needs to be extended and revised to cope with traffic problems and new needs. San Francisco would make a sad mistake if its new plan were merely to follow the fashion of another aesthetic whim, however contemporary.

28

A CITY BEAUTIFUL DEMANDED MONUMENTAL BUILDINGS TO STAND AS ITS gateways. Of these the railroad station became the most important. The railroad was at its zenith, prosperous, luxurious; it demanded an architecture of size and prestige. Some of the early stations, to be sure, were still large, dark affairs, great train sheds with skyscraper overlays or machicolated towers such as Frank Furness's Broad Street Station in

Philadelphia of 1893 or the old Union Depot in Detroit designed by Isaac Taylor in 1889. Throughout the West picturesque stations had been built by a number of architects, notably Henry Van Brunt. Romance still lingers in the Romanesque clock tower of Milwaukee's Northwestern Station by Charles S. Frost (1899), or, at its highest and fanciest, in the long, complicated, quaint façade that T. C. Link and E. D. Cameron provided for the great train shed of the St. Louis Union Station in 1891-1894. Even its individually interesting tower bore no relation to the other masses or to the elegant Grand Hall whose colossal barrel vault sat at right angles to the vault of the train shed.

But these medieval reminiscences had all been built before the turn of the century and most of them antedated the Columbian Exposition. After that, stations took on a more monumental and a more Roman appearance. By 1914 the *Architectural Record* recognized that railroad architecture had become the second most important symbol of the imperial era, next to the skyscraper.

Washington's Union Station of 1904 by Daniel Burnham is representative of the new classic gateway to the city. The plan is simple; an enormous Roman waiting room, modeled after the Imperial baths and penetrated by arched portals, stands parallel to a functional arched concourse which leads passengers to canopied platforms beside the tracks. The façade facing the Capitol presents three arched doors of great scale, designed like a triumphal arch with surmounting statues, and corresponding to the whole length of the vault of the great hall. This central portion is flanked by two long and lower wings in the best manner of the Beaux-Arts classic. Inside, the ceiling of the hall is broken everywhere by impressive coffers. The spaciousness of the hall is not seriously diminished by the absurd statues which loll on the cornice.

Only a little later McKim, Mead and White provided the epitome of an Imperial railroad station when they built the Pennsylvania Station in New York in 1906-1910. Entering from Seventh Avenue through a long, street-level, Roman arcade, past shops and restaurants, the traveler walks towards a grand staircase. Pausing at the top, he looks down into a great hall containing ticket counters and an information booth. This hall, taken straight from the Imperial Roman Bath of Caracalla, does not suggest that the voyager may later detrain at Metuchen, New Jersey, or Altoona, Pennsylvania; its décor derives from the nineteenth-century reconstructions of what might have been in Rome. The scale is colossal, compatible with the throngs who pass through to destinations made clear by the symmetrical plan laid out along the main axis. Passing the hall, the traveler arrives at a wide central corridor, between waiting rooms. Eventually he emerges into a second great space, presented now in terms of modern engineering and not in those of Rome, thought by many people to be more exciting than the great hall. This is the concourse, still one giant level above the train platforms. But however clear the engineering may be aloft, it is in the subterranean chambers that the circulation breaks down amid a confusion of stands and markets and separately beckoning gates.

Architecturally the concourse space has the majesty of its steel arches and trusses and their glass plus the great stairs descending at each end. It has been less corrupted by time than the barrel vaults of the main hall which now also suffers from the ultra-modern canopy the railroad has thrust into the waiting room to its architectural degradation and the confusion of its circulation. But even when both rooms were pure there was no fusion between the unimpaired design of the concourse and the concealed engineering of the great hall. Pennsylvania Station is not, strictly speaking, great architecture; but its surface effect captured the literary heart of Thomas Wolfe and made Wayne Andrews speak wistfully of an Age of Elegance, now past. Even Claude Bragdon, himself the architect of a splendid space at the station in Rochester, New York, felt the dichotomy between the architect and engineer in Penn Station but had to admire a building that "raised its proud head amid the pushcart architecture of that portion of New York."

A drawing of this area made about 1910 shows the station in relation to the Post Office, also by McKim, and to the hotels nearby. It reveals the degree of harmony in the architecture, and shows how the architects expected the two buildings, one belonging to the federal government and the other to a private railroad, to constitute a monumental unit that would one day provide a transportation and communications focus in a large City Beautiful. It was a tremendous idea and the architects promoted it so well that they were allowed to develop substantial sections of cities more readily than many of our contemporaries have yet had the chance to do. Both the architects and their clients were Titans.

One can still see the titanic quality, refined and thereby subdued, in the Grand Central Terminal of 1903-1913, the work of Reed and Stem in collaboration with Warren and Wetmore. This building was erected athwart the axis of Park Avenue, which in turn covered the tracks entering from the north. Traffic past the building climbs upward on ramps straddling the Terminal, descends through a building on the other side to flow northward on the Avenue. The concourse, surrounded by a city of shops and theaters, galleries and hotels and restaurants, is one of the best-proportioned spaces in the United States, able to survive, or almost to survive, monumental Kodachromes and inappropriate three-dimensional advertisements as well as the display automobiles that revolve on its floor. It offers a background fitting for drama and was suitable thereby as a place for the Bishop of the Diocese of New York to launch a campaign before hushed thousands to collect donations for building the Cathedral of St. John the Divine. It is still a space in which Christmas singing sounds well, and it has a little, though not enough, in common with an important public square, or the Galleria at Milan.

Neither Pennsylvania Station nor Grand Central reached the full dignity of a monumental gateway, for they were not fronted by appropriately scaled plazas. Few stations in America save Washington ever gained one. Generally they simply sat on the side of a remote street. The station in St. Louis does have a small boulevarded park containing an important fountain by Carl Milles and the later station at Cincinnati is approached by a long avenue, but neither is typical.

Other main components of the image of the City Beautiful were the opera house, the library, the museum, all, save with the most modest bows to purpose, cast in the same mold. Theaters, big or little, were sometimes more ornate or occasionally more restrained as was McKim's Symphony Hall in Boston. Sometimes small legitimate theaters like the Century built in New York in 1906 by Carrère and Hastings might blow a great fanfare of swollen Beaux-Arts décor; sometimes outside New York they might be Romanesque or Gothic. But despite these sports, the Renaissance and classical image was firmly established as the norm.

29

SUCH ARCHITECTS WERE CAPABLE OF A FINE SOBRIETY IF NOT OF MUCH functionalism. To modern users, their designs for libraries of American cities seem to have been completely incompetent. There is no doubt that the imperial function overcame the function of purveying reading material. Formerly the libraries had been small buildings, storing books in alcoves extending around a central reading room. When collections became larger and the reading public more numerous, such plans were quite inadequate. The American architects had some good models from earlier European building, notably the Bibliothèque Ste. Geneviève at Paris of 1843, the Bibliothèque Nationale at Paris of 1854 and less fortunately the Bristish Museum at London, built in 1857. Each frankly segregated a large and often handsome reading room from an enormous utilitarian area where books were stored. But none was really appropriate for American purposes since they were designed for the comfort

and peace of the sophisticated scholar and not for the omnivorous reading and browsing habits of a half-literate general public which could
hardly be trained to use a card catalogue.

Though librarians like W. F. Poole favored bookrooms with shelves
rather than unsightly, badly lighted and frequently dirty stack-storages,
the European system was adopted, and perhaps with justification, for
the Library of Congress at Washington when the firm of Smithmeyer,
Pelz and Casey prepared a Greek-cross plan for a reading room and
placed a stack beneath it, like that in the British Museum; the building
erected in 1888-1897 was in full classic panoply with strong touches of
the Grand Opera House at Paris.

Among the earlier examples, the Bibliothèque Nationale by Labrouste
had solved the problem of furnishing a unified envelope around a large
reading room and a utilitarian storage room. It was his solution that
McKim modified to solve the difficult problem of the Public Library in
Boston's Copley Square which was to be so located as to confront
Richardson's Romanesque Trinity Church.

Viewed only as an architectural composition, McKim's design was
masterful. It picked up the theme of the arches in Richardson's church
but made it no other stylistic concession. The center of the new building, strongly emphasized by three arches, enclosing fine iron gates, was
out of line with the center of the church across the triangle, thereby
creating a discontinuity that forced attention on the intervening space.
To either side of the Library entrance small rectangular windows admitted light to the stack, and above these the visitor reached the main
floor by a grand staircase which rose through the center of the building.
This handsome stair was embellished with pleasant, pale murals by
Puvis de Chavannes. The great hall on the second floor which formed
the reading room was modestly lighted by large, beautifully proportioned windows in an arcade that ran across the whole façade. Arches
and columns framed a court on the interior of the building, and this
was surrounded by rooms decorated with sculpture and murals, to display exhibits of books and drawings, but also less efficiently to house
the public catalogue and the circulation desk. The handsome composition, the elegant choice of elegant materials, the dignity of the court
arcade have seldom been surpassed in American architecture. The
equally beautiful façade dignifies a civic square near a major residential
area.

While Boston's Public Library could hardly be outdone within the
premises of Renaissance design, its excellence as a form did not prevent
readers from discouragement and librarians from outright criticism. By
1890 the latter had formed a vigorous society with annual meetings

where they discussed library administration and the proper planning of library buildings. In 1891, C. C. Soule, writing for the *Library Journal*, stated that the architect was the librarian's natural enemy. After this there were many statements about the utilitarian standards librarians demanded from their buildings. The Boston Public Library achieved few of these; that a library should be planned for economic and efficient administration; for economy of the reader's time; that convenience of arrangement should not be sacrificed to architectural effect; that only what was needed for reading, storage and administration should be built, leaving land and space for future enlargement; that the library should have ample natural light; that the decoration should be simple; that the reading rooms should be in a separate building or pavilion to gain better light and to free the storage area for easier extension. It sounded like Huxley and the Johns Hopkins hospital all over again. But it was characteristic of the Imperial period that such pleas should be ignored both by the architects and by those who paid for the buildings, or that they countered, with some justification, by looking at librarians as enemies of the arts. So the Public Library at Washington, built in 1905, was a mammoth affair in the new classic vein, self-indulgent of decoration, haughtily ignorant of utility. This might have been permissible for the small private library McKim built for Morgan in 1906, but monumentality purchased at the price of utility did not seem a wise choice in the Carnegie public libraries, for example.

But from Bangor to San Francisco classic monumentality overrode all other considerations. In any American city the passer-by could identify the library when he saw it, unless he took it for the museum. For museum buildings were also designed more as civic monuments than as places to show pictures and sculpture. This was the program for the new buildings of the Boston Museum of Fine Arts, the Art Institute of Chicago, Buffalo's Albright Art Gallery, the Museum at Cleveland. A wing added to the earlier Romanesque museum at Cincinnati was in the same classic vein. By 1900 even the Gothic Revival Metropolitan in New York had been given a classic face on Fifth Avenue. Few designers asked practical questions as to how heavy works of art were to be moved about; how paintings were to be hung, lighted, best seen or best arranged; they recalled old palaces like the Louvre, later converted to museums, and believed that such palaces were adequate emblems of the European art Americans collected.

3 0

INDEED, FEW PUBLIC BUILDING TYPES ESCAPED THE CITY BEAUTIFUL IDEA. The most notable exceptions were the public schools. A few succumbed and were built as single masses, covered with Renaissance or classic detail. But even then they did not often achieve the monumentality that characterized railroad stations, museums or libraries. Nor were they placed so strategically. Some, like the series designed in Boston by E. M. Wheelwright, were even functional. The same could be said of Public School Number 17 at Rochester, New York, the work of Walker and Briggs. But it may be significant that the names of the most prominent architects of the day do not often appear as designers of school buildings. The best schools were done by men like William Butts Ittner of St. Louis or Dwight Perkins of Chicago, whose names are known mostly only to historians of school architecture. Myron Hunt built a few schools at Pasadena and Los Angeles and William Templeton Johnston erected one at San Diego — all with interior courts surrounded by one-story buildings; well lighted, acoustically treated, sensitive to the scale of children and to the emotional aspects of education, they offered a slight foretaste of the future, but, unhappily, were not widely emulated.

3 1

CHURCHES, TOO, GENERALLY REMAINED OUTSIDE THE CLASSIC IMAGE. BUT, in 1904, Trumbauer used Palladio's classical Redentore at Venice as his model for the Chapel of St. Catharine at Spring Lake, New Jersey. In 1908, Howells and Stokes installed the First Congregational Church of Danbury, Connecticut, in a Federalist exterior. The Peddie Memorial Church at Newark, in 1890, was Romanesque but with classic details. On the whole the Protestant sects and new church organizations like the Christian Scientists seemed to prefer classic or Renaissance forms, especially in New England, but it could not be said that any particular architectural expression was widely identified with the aspirations of any faith. So the First Church of Christ Scientist at Boston acquired a classic dome between 1893 and 1906 while another at 96th Street and Central Park West in New York was a Renaissance temple. The early Christian basilican design was adopted by McKim for the Madison Square Presbyterian Church in 1906 and by Maginnis and

Walsh for the Roman Catholic Church of St. John at Cambridge, in 1905.

Nonetheless the dominant image was Gothic, for which there was a strong prejudice in those churches whose service was vigorously liturgical. Henry Vaughan's chapel at St. Paul's School, Concord, New Hampshire, was a popular type of chapel borrowed from England, including the feature of having pews face each other across an aisle leading to the altar, as was common in English school chapels and choirs of English cathedrals. Even the usually Roman firm of McKim, Mead and White demonstrated their versatility and their tractability (and some would say their lack of conviction) by designing Gothic churches such as St. Peter's at Morristown, New Jersey.

Among the exponents of Gothic churches, the high priest was surely Ralph Adams Cram, another kind of Imperial man. A High Church Anglican, he believed that the heart of religious worship lay in the service at the altar, in the Mass, in the other liturgical elements, not in the sermon. He wished to surround the essential mysteries with all that the art of liturgy, music and iconography could add to their reality, saying, "It is the dogma of the transubstantiation, the cultus of our Lady and the doctrine of the Communion of Saints that made Mediaeval Christianity what it was and gave to . . . Mediaeval art its supreme beauty and its everlasting appeal." Cram's love of ceremony, his conversion to Anglicanism, his contention that "Luther killed art," show that Christian worship appealed to him on aesthetic grounds. Protestants might build in the Georgian mode, indeed he believed they should, and even designed Georgian meeting houses for Unitarians, such as the Second Church in Boston. But any service in which the Communion served as a major demonstration of theological beliefs should be held in a Gothic building. This latter-day Ruskinism attracted many clients; when Cram's literary force and scholarly understanding of true Gothic were accompanied by the skills of the highly talented designer, Bertram Grosvenor Goodhue, the architectural results were often impressive.

Cram's mission in life was to preach a new Gothic Revival, an archeological one, and to build it reverently and completely, not only as regards materials, plans and structures (though he often suppressed the side aisles, the clerestories and the triforia) but so far as possible to include the iconography as well. He led a few architects toward a "creative" scholarship of the Gothic form by articles such as "Good and Bad Gothic" in the *Architectural Review* (U.S.) of 1899. Meanwhile his partner Goodhue created some masterful churches; St. Thomas's in New York City was perhaps the zenith of this third and latest stage of the Gothic Revival. Its screen and sculptural reliefs rival the stained glass and the structure and space in their harmony of rich effect, quality of execution, and appropriateness to a beautiful ceremonial. Aesthetic environments of this sort fitted in well with the tendency among many church congregations, even among the Protestant, to become increasingly liturgical as their parishioners became more affluent and socially more self-conscious. They were aided in this by the followers of Cram and by the skill of his collaborators of whom none was more skilled than Charles Connick, the designer of stained-glass windows. So, liturgical or not, Gothic architecture now triumphed over acoustics and Protestant reserve, and now many a dissenter's sermon died away in the groined vaults before it reached the ears of the congregation.

The new Gothic Revival swung church architecture from the position in which Richardson had left it with Boston's Trinity Church. The large cathedral of St. John the Divine, in New York, had been begun in Romanesque when Heins and La Farge won the competition in 1892, over Cram's 1889 submission in Gothic. But in the end Cram prevailed. After the arches over the crossing had been erected in Romanesque, the commission was awarded to Cram who warped the whole thing into a Gothic cathedral. A similar building was started for the national Episcopal Cathedral, St. Peter and St. Paul. Even the Swedenborgians built a Gothic church at Pitcairn's model village for artists in Bryn Athyn, Pennsylvania. Some architects carried the romance so far as to build entirely by hand, using wooden pegs instead of wire nails, employing artists in residence to work out the iconographical program desired by those who were trying to play the role of modern Abbot Sugers. In 1892, one of these, George W. Shinn, wrote in "The American Cathedral" to praise deliberately slow building, "It would be well for us if more of our . . . buildings were built by degrees and paid for as the work went on . . . on and on, until a stately edifice rises where, under our present way of hurrying, we get a finished but very cheap and flimsy thing." He was thinking more of excellence than of keeping the church budget balanced; and he forgot how rapidly the great parts of the French cathedrals were actually built in the thirteenth century. Indeed in the end it took longer to finish some of the large American cathedrals than it had to achieve their thirteenth-century models. It hardly seems possible that such a piece as Shinn's could have been written in 1892, after the Home Insurance Building and the Reliance Building had already been built in Chicago, and buildings that had formerly taken two years or more were now being assembled in four or five months.

Whatever their style, the churches, like the great classic secular buildings of the period, were designed by men who insisted upon excellent detail, workmanlike construction, and colorful decoration executed by skillful artists. A good example of the high level of performance is Christopher Grant La Farge's St. Matthew's Roman Catholic Church in Washington, begun in 1893. Its cruciform plan carries a large dome over the crossing, recalling the form of north Italian churches. The exterior is a firm mass, imposing and simple, notably courageous for its colorful red brick and stone walls surmounted by the green copper-ribbed dome outlined against the sky. The massive effect of the exterior contrasts well with the interior, where, in the dim light admitted by translucent windows, the piers and arcades supporting an ornate vaulted ceiling carry the eye past bright mosaics to the space under the dome and its octagonal drum; beyond the delicate alabaster rail in the chancel, one sees a gleaming white altar, made more outstanding by its contrast with the delicate arabesques and bronze at the portals. Stanford White's Madison Square Presbyterian Church in New York City (destroyed in 1919) offered excellence of a different kind, and was perhaps the best central-type Renaissance church in America. For Gothic, one would go far to find anything more winning than St. Thomas's. Perhaps at no period in America's history were artists more skillful in working with architects, nor were many periods able to boast of greater sincerity in church design. Churches of this quality shame much though not all modern work and only fall into their true perspective and lose some of their romance after one has visited a few European originals from the twelfth and thirteenth centuries.

Against the prevailing medievalism oriented towards handicraft and a worship occurring in the chancel at the high altar, there was a strong opposing force within church organizations and architecture, the growing emphasis on social and educational activities. Ever since the Akron plan had been developed for Sunday School use, churches in the Middle West, especially Protestant ones, had tended to be large auditoria, almost lecture halls, with small rooms arranged on balconies that could be opened to admit a larger audience to the main hall. P. B. Wight had noted in 1880: "The average Western church . . . is a combination of a lecture-hall, a school, and a club-house. It is a congregational home for social as well as didactic purposes." It is "always well heated and ventilated . . . thoroughly comfortable, and even luxurious." The popular minister, Frank Gunsalus, made no difficulty of preaching in Sullivan's Chicago Auditorium. Though not one of his best buildings, churches like the one Sullivan designed for Cedar Rapids reveal the inclinations of the Midwest in this matter of planning. The social organization of the church had become as important as the religious purpose; it was a central bureau for charities, diffusion of knowledge, social assembly. One architect who was in favor of designing buildings for such institutions struck a blow at medievalism; it was not, he said, an invective against embellishment but just that too much money is "spent on buttresses that resist no thrust." This took no account, if any should have been taken, of symbolic thrust. But he went further. Apart from objections to sham he insisted that "these forms . . . were originally born of conditions and necessities that have . . . ceased to exist. The governing requirements . . . today are much the same . . . as a lecture room or concert hall . . . seating capacity, ventilation, heating . . . light, and acoustic properties." It was this point of view, a reflection of Huxley again, that brought about some of the early modern churches that appeared in the West, such as Maybeck's Christian Science Church at Berkeley, California.

In retrospect Maybeck's famous building shows some interesting personal features but was not really so great a departure from prevailing ideas as Wright's distinguished Universalist Church, the Unity Temple at Oak Park, Illinois, which was both less romantic and much more noteworthy as a work of art. Built in 1906 this remains one of Wright's greatest works. Long interested in poured concrete, he now had a chance to use it in a moderately important public building. Characteristically he livened its dead surfaces by letting the stones of the aggregate be exposed. The building was a functional dumbbell with the shrine to the left and the social activities to the right. The exterior was quite formal, clearly monolithic, dominated by a projecting roof slab which demanded a large scale in the other parts. Abstract capitals were placed at the top of the piers which framed the clerestory set in panels above a high unfenestrated wall. This was a motif he had used before, for example in his project for the Yahara Boat Club at Madison, Wisconsin, of 1902, and would use again in the Coonley House, the Roberts House, the City National Bank at Mason City, Iowa, but never with greater skill and power and appropriateness.

The inside of the church is more complicated but the remarkable interpenetration of the spaces is apparent at once, as balconies and floors at many levels cross and intersect but never without purpose. The electric fixtures and the wires that connected them were made part of the design. The building was quite as revolutionary and quite as important as the Larkin Building. It is difficult to realize that such a temple, of reinforced concrete, entirely modern in form and decoration, appropriate for a service based on the sermon and for a considerable number of activities outside the fane, could have been constructed in an age when Cram and Shinn were getting the leading commissions.

Towards the end of his life Wright sometimes called the Unity Temple his masterpiece and this may well be so.

32

UNIVERSITIES HAD AS MUCH TROUBLE AS CHURCHES IN DETERMINING WHAT their image should be and they were becoming self-conscious about it. A few had ancient buildings of dignity such as Nassau Hall at Princeton; some could show, joined to these, distinguished recent work such as Richardson had bestowed on Harvard; more boasted nothing of distinction but their alumni were developing a strange unreasoning affection for their Victorian "Old Mains"; a few like the Gothic University of Chicago were having the bad luck to spring architecturally full-panoplied from the purse of a contemporary Maecenas. None in this moment cared to listen to the messages of contemporary science or technology — or to heed the rational proposals that had been advanced only a few years before at Johns Hopkins. Protestant colleges appeared in the dress of Catholic monasteries, institutes of technology were equipped with Gothic or classic dress; a Texan campus offered a shotgun marriage between Venice and Valladolid.

Major new institutions did appoint architects to develop large and comprehensive master plans. The most impressive of these plans no doubt was the winning design for the University of California at Berkeley, submitted to the Hearst Competition of 1898-1899 by Henri Jean Emile Bénard.

The winner was a Frenchman directly out of the Beaux-Arts and so was his large and expansive site plan. It planted a long and strong axis running straight down the slopes towards the Bay, from an observatory set high on Berkeley Hill. It was a freer plan than the Roman arrangement of the Chicago World's Fair — the minor axes varied in their spacing, and there was room for informal woods and gardens up on the hill and along the lower flanks. Bernard Maybeck, also a student from the Beaux-Arts, had made it possible for the University to have a plan. Having designed a mining memorial to Phoebe Apperson Hearst's husband, he was asked by President Kellogg where to put the building on the then largely empty terrain of Berkeley. Competent to design the building, he did not feel competent to settle such a question and proposed an international competition. Mrs. Hearst approved.

Maybeck felt that Oxford had the ideal campus with its "absolute stillness and the atmosphere charged with historical association," but the historical associations could not be discovered or invented at Berkeley and the silence would inevitably be broken by the thousands of students who rushed for trains at the end of day. All Maybeck asked from the general plan was that it should place the buildings and arrange the communications. Its aim was "to simplify and not to embellish. . . . *Fifty years from now the plan of the University will have become modified and softened*; it will be transformed many times, because so easily done."

It did not take fifty years. Bénard came, took the prize money and then declined to be supervising architect. A German critic-architect writing for the *San Francisco Bulletin* predicted this, in saying that Bénard's plan was un-American, pretentious and imposing, did not express any deep thought. Bénard, this critic thought, would feel out of place. Whether disturbed by the criticism or simply through lack of interest Bénard did make what seemed to many Californians the incredible choice of Paris over Berkeley.

There was perhaps a moment when attention might have been paid to the *Bulletin*'s plea, "This should be a new University, typically, racially American — not a Chicago World's Fair." But soon the mantle fell to John Galen Howard, also a product of the Beaux-Arts, who moved from New York after 1901 to build the first buildings of the new campus, to be supervising architect, first head of the Department of Architecture, to plant the prevailing Renaissance firmly in California, and to modify the Bénard plan until by 1913 it could hardly be identified with the original except that both had the strong and clear axes of the best Beaux-Arts plates.

California critics, proud of their campus, have been kinder in their estimates of Howard than they have of his opposite and often more talented numbers in the East. The fact remains he was cut from the same cloth. Berkeley has a good campus but by no means one of the finest in the land. The multiplicity of buildings now has destroyed any sense of the master plan for the pedestrian if not for the map-reader. The predominant impression is one of buildings which are too white for the California sun, laid out and designed in the American classic manner and of only modest excellence.

But the campus is saved from the desolate Imperialism of comparable Columbia by a number of things, if not by its main buildings. The Berkeley hills still seem more pastoral than Morningside Heights, even though the smog and the population are both thickening from Richmond; the eucalyptus trees are big enough to provide a merciful contrast to the architecture; the Howard classic buildings are less congested, less monumental, less Roman, less demanding and pretentious than those of McKim at Columbia; and here and there minor buildings remain that have been built in the warm, vigorous, human mood of what people have liked to overstress as the California style. Buildings like Maybeck's Faculty Club, the Music Building, and the long set of low sheds stepping down the hill, that have served the School of Architecture so well, provide the grace notes of the campus at Berkeley and most of its grace. Without them it would be ordinary and dull.

Still, treated as at California, the grand plan yielded some order without becoming formidable; at Columbia the new court of honor by McKim forced library, engineering buildings, and students alike into an unnatural life. Even Harvard had a moment of flirtation with the image of the big classical campus of which the new Widener Library was to head an axial mall stretching to the Charles River. In the end, and mostly because land for the mall was so costly, Harvard escaped these toils, turned the Widener around, presented its small rear entrance to Massachusetts Avenue and pushed its colossal façade with giant columns and enormous and fatiguing steps into the small quadrangle at the north, where it dwarfed its more distinguished neighbors.

During this time many universities held competitions for master site plans, and these provided campuses temporarily more integrated but no more pleasant than the older ones. Carnegie Institute of Technology and the University of Pittsburgh were laid out by Palmer and Hornbostel on large classical lines although the later University buildings became Gothic. Ernest Flagg produced a plan of modern Beaux-Arts classical design for the Naval Academy at Annapolis, whose chapel is similar to that at the Sorbonne. There were also Gothic master plans. Beginning about 1893, Henry Ives Cobb developed Rockefeller's University of Chicago on such lines. But even where the grand plan did not prevail, universities sought order by freezing their architecture at a point in time, usually an ancient time.

Cope and Stewardson confirmed the fashion for this about 1886 when they designed picturesquely composed Gothic buildings for Bryn Mawr College and followed these by similar work at Pennsylvania, Princeton and Washington University at St. Louis. When the plans of establishments such as these are contrasted to vigorously classical campuses like that proposed by Cass Gilbert for the University of Minnesota, one notes greater flexibility of arrangement, more dramatic use of landscaping and land contour, much more human scale and better use of quadrangles and courts; but both stem from the idea that the environment for higher education must be beautiful and ancient and that there must be a controlling master plan in order to get good results. By 1905 even Johns Hopkins University, which had earlier carried the torch for urban *laissez faire* utilitarianism, held a competition for a new campus to be built outside Baltimore. The campus was ultimately developed there, and it was a highly integrated community of buildings carefully studied as to site, all clothed in Georgian Revival. Thorstein Veblen, followed by Upton Sinclair, inveighed against such dismissals of progressive skyscraper architecture.

The power of strong-minded architects and their academic clients often left an impress that could not soon be effaced. Nowhere was this more evident than in the Graduate College at Princeton.

Princeton acquired the first plant totally devoted to graduate students when her Graduate College, designed by Cram, was erected in 1913. It is a picturesque Gothic mass, perched on the crown of a small hill, dominated by its Cleveland Tower, looking out over a lush golf course and a tree-lined stream, beloved by ducks and geese. The impression is therefore reasonably bucolic. The buildings offer a residential complex providing suites of rooms which originally were elegantly appointed for a comfortable private life. It has a large commons room with bad acoustics, an unnecessary library, a refectory and breakfast rooms all arranged on the perimeter of two seclusive quadrangles. The sculptural and architectural form of these buildings well exemplified Cram's belief that "art . . . as a system of spiritual and psychological influence is perhaps the greatest teaching agency." Today his aversion to modern resources seems peculiar until we learn that it stemmed from his belief that "The liberal arts of age-long human culture have nothing to do with the current seventy-year-old technological civilization (except as a corrective which has thus far failed to work) and consequently the . . . artistic expression of the latter phenomenon can have no part in the manifestation of the older and eternal entity." Hence at the Graduate College this "humanist" used the precedents of English collegiate work of the fifteenth century, especially of the type employed by William of Wykeham at New College, Oxford. Cram wanted an architecture "consistent with . . . that sense of historic and cultural continuity that I am persuaded is fundamental in all educational and ecclesiastical work." Even the bracketing of school and church is significant. He rejected the classicism of the Renaissance and Academic periods in order to return to "our own racial style that was developed while we were yet consistent Christians."

Cram's Presbyterian clients sought exactly that. Long before the architect entered the scene, Andrew Fleming West, Dean of Princeton's Graduate School, had visualized the future college he wanted: "old associations . . . the peace of rural life. Quadrangles enclosing sunny lawns, towers and gateways opening into quiet retreats, ivy-grown walls . . . vistas through avenues of arching elms . . . the exquisite collegiate Gothic . . . of Oxford and Cambridge. Nothing so fully accords in spirit with our desires for Princeton." In such an environment he thought "liberal studies at least find their greatest charm" and the word "charm" reveals the tone of a literary man's architectural standard. We may doubt West's wisdom in so blatantly and arbitrarily trying to return the modern student to his medieval heritage; to many young men of a generation only forty years removed from West, the stained-glass windows in the refectory, portraying the "Light of the World illuminating the Seven Liberal Arts of Christian Learning," seem totally out of place with the science, logic or architecture he is studying, while the idea of donning a gown to enter the refectory for dinner seems an artificial absurdity. Yet it cannot be denied that some have found solace in the superficial cloisters.

33

AS THE GOTHIC AND CLASSIC FORMS GREW TO BECOME NATIONAL EMblems of cultural institutions and as technology tended to destroy regional differences, self-conscious retarding movements developed, aimed at regaining an expression of local and regional character. Ever since the Philadelphia Centennial of 1876 there had been an interest in reviving Georgian architecture. This received further impetus when McKim and White studied the excellent houses that still stood in places like Newburyport, and began to design handsome contemporary houses on Georgian and "Colonial" lines. The fashion for domestic Georgian was so pronounced by the turn of the century that it threatened to become a national style for domestic architecture and for some institutions as well. In 1904, when Wright was designing the Larkin Building, Joy Wheeler Dow published an influential book, *The American Renaissance*, to document the resurgence of good Georgian design throughout the country but especially in New England. Such a formal return to eighteenth-century architecture, if not to eighteenth-century manners or habits, encouraged other sections of the country to resurrect or, if necessary, to invent their own regional heritages. An especially attractive recreation, made out of whole cloth, was the one that occurred around Philadelphia; side by side with the revival of Pennsylvania Dutch houses, architects built handsome estates that imitated the farm houses and small country houses of rural France and England. The Southwest sought an architecture recalling the missions and churches of Spanish origin, most of which had disappeared or been greatly abused. Now they were copied in residential and ecclesiastical work. Few were really impressive architecturally but they were consistently well designed, well executed and thoroughly charming in the spaces and arrangements for comfortable living. There was less fake about them than in those of the later regional revival of the '20s.

Architecture built in the countryside and at resorts tended in some instances to show regional characteristics, but more often reflected the monumental character of town houses. In either case, the prevailing fashion was for greater unity in design. The picturesqueness of an early Georgian Revival house, like the H. A. C. Taylor House at Newport by McKim, Mead and White, was replaced by classic unity such as that of the Low House, built at Bristol, Rhode Island, in 1887, one of the finest of the shingle houses. The Renaissance palace dominated many countrysides and resorts. Perhaps none was more lavish than the Breakers at Newport, designed by Richard Morris Hunt for Cornelius Vanderbilt in 1893, unless it was the colossal François I château, Biltmore, built for George Vanderbilt, at Asheville, North Carolina, in 1895, also the work of Hunt. There were many others: the Marble House at Newport of 1891 for William K. Vanderbilt, by Hunt, and the estate of E. T. Stotesbury, a Versailles raised outside of Philadelphia by the French architect, Gréber. For clients like these, Hunt became an authority on taste and made each palace rival the last by its lavish size, European appurtenances, gardens, fountains and monumental gateways, all built independent of region or location. Another of the most popular architects in this manner was Charles A. Platt, who designed the residence of William G. Mather in Cleveland and many other estates in Connecticut, Long Island, Detroit and Cincinnati. At Lake Forest, Illinois, in 1912, he completed the house of Harold F. McCormick; it was a Renaissance villa seeking to rival the Villa d'Este in its gardens, and it was published in the *Architectural Record* in 1912 in an article titled "The Renaissance Villa of Italy Developed into a Complete Residential Type for Use in America."

Able voices spoke against this kind of adaptation. The strongest voices were surely those of the giants of the Middle West. But the men of the Pacific Coast were quietly active, too, and much later, when California grew more self-conscious, Maybeck, Howard, the brothers Greene, Mullgardt, Polk and Julia Morgan were given an abnormal amount of publicity. These Californians did not leave an enormous legacy in the quantity or magnificence of their buildings but it was an enduring legacy. They did not create a style. They sensed or analyzed what an informal way of life, growing out of ranch life, would demand of a house. They loved native materials. The climate permitted them, indeed invited them, to minimize the distinction between indoors and outdoors and they worked at this problem though less boldly than others would do later. They noticed that almost every site in the San Francisco region and many around Pasadena had brilliant views and so they were early to use large panels of glass to frame these outlooks. They arranged a relatively free flow of interior space. They loved the aggressive vegetation and their external woodwork embraced the vines and the gums. It is these things more than the romantic and pictorial quality of their roofs, the carving of their screens or rafter ends, the mysterious darkness of their redwood interiors, the occasional flashes of Japanese detail, that make them of some importance. They offered the best contemporary regionalism of the country, and the finest and most genuine form California regionalism has achieved.

But the architects were not so distinguished as they have been made out to be by local patriots. None was consistent. None avoided the Imperial image in other contexts as Maybeck's Packard showrooms and Anthony House sadly reveal. Willis Polk was so ambivalent that he could create some charming houses of the best California type on Vallejo Street, the brilliantly anticipatory glass wall of the Hallidie Building, and yet for more important commissions welter in the classic manner. The architecture was not an architecture of masterpieces and it did not last very long. It was overwhelmed soon after 1913 by the Expositions at San Francisco and San Diego.

Meritorious as several of the dwellings were, admirable as was the influence of the patriarchal Maybeck, we cannot insist unless we are being sentimental that these buildings should be bracketed with the most seminal buildings of history, not even with those of American history. Maybeck's houses and churches on the Bay, Greene and Greene's houses in Pasadena, are not in any sense Villa Capras or even as influential as the Savoye House of Le Corbusier. For their time they were however unusually good, not as absurd as a new Villa Capra would have been, and the times were far from ready for a Le Corbusier. If any domestic masterpieces were being created they were being made back on the prairie where a still more direct regional assault was made by Purcell, Elmslie, Griffin, Schmidt and Maher who were working on the Midwestern problem with about the same intensity, integrity and imagination as Maybeck and the Greenes in the West. But Chicago also had a genius in Wright.

It states the obvious to repeat that Wright was the most talented and able of all the regionalists, superior actually to regionalism as a doctrine, resisting the formalism of the monumental or regional favorites of the East, resisting absurd history, resisting the formal training that might have been his in Paris for the asking. He made no attempt, as a foolish man might have, to produce an elegant revival of the log cabin or the soddy, though in less obvious terms this is exactly what was happening in New Mexico, Florida and New Jersey and would happen later in California. Instead he went straight to the point and to the conditions of the prairie. His Willitts House at Highland Park, Illinois (1902), was the first of his masterpieces after he broke away from the office of Louis Sullivan. It stretched wide on broad lawns, its long horizontal roofs hovered over large units of space, clearly exhibited, simple in form, tied together by the strong planes of the roof. It was, Wright insisted, an architecture appropriate to the prairie, a new style for a new region uninterested in the medievalism of Cram, hoping to disavow the imperialistic pretensions of McKim. Wright's ability as a designer was recognized internationally by 1905 and stimulated the modern movement beginning in Germany, Holland and France; but as early as 1900, and consistently thereafter, architectural magazines in America acclaimed him as the greatest architect on the scene. *The Architectural Review*'s (U.S.) study of his work published in 1900 was followed regularly by essays published particularly in the *Architectural Record* from 1905 to 1913, but in other places, too. The fact that he was so often extolled by the architectural writers and publishers goes far to destroy the myth of the neglected hero which has built up around his career; it also proves the ineffectiveness of the tastemaker-writer or professional journal; for Wright did not gain a public following, either private, corporate or governmental, comparable to those gained by McKim and Hunt and Cram.

It is not at all clear, and the problem is worth studying, whether Wright alienated potentially big buyers by his arrogance more than he frightened them by his work. This certainly affected his relations with other architects. But clearly one of the reasons for his recognition and for his neglect was the tremendous modernity and strength of his designs. The Unity Temple announced a straightforward, even harsh cubism. The exciting spaces and planes were totally uncontaminated by classic traditions or details. But at the same time Wright prepared his forms in harmony with his idea of a progressive social program even though he did not intervene in other and more far-reaching efforts at reform. His strong view of nature was conceived in terms of Carlyle but even more in the organic vitalistic terms he attributed to Darwin. He insisted in words and deeds that the form be related to the immediate environment. The Coonley House of 1908-1910 at Riverside, Illinois, is a good example of the planning and elevations he worked out to express his beliefs that a house should use contemporary forms, should encourage domesticity, should serve as a shelter for cultivated activities and should accord with the personal needs of the owner. This complex served also as a school run by the Coonleys. The educational advisers were John Dewey and his sister, and the building was Wright's expression of Dewey's principles of progressive education. Both house and school were of domestic scale, intended to encourage creative activity, to permit no separation between the atmosphere surrounding education and that in the child's home. Gardens were to be important instruments of education, and the main one, lying in front of the house, had a stage where the children acted Greek plays in Greek attire, and he saw no inconsistency in retaining the Greek play while discarding Greek architecture, as indeed there was none. Other great Wright houses of this time such as the Martin House in Buffalo (1904), the Westcott House in Springfield, Ohio (1907), the Roberts House in River Forest, Illinois (1908), the Baker House in Wilmette, Illinois (1909), and the Robie House on Woodlawn Avenue, Chicago (1909), as well as the first Taliesin at Spring Green, Wisconsin (1911), told the same messages; they are now so firm a part of American understanding that they need no further description, although unhappily not many of them are still to be seen, and fewer still in good repair.

34

BUT THE BIG CLIENTS AND THE MAJOR CITIES OF THE MIDDLE WEST AND the Far West were really no more ready than the East to accept the implications of what was being done by Maybeck, Kahn, Sullivan or Wright. One after another each city abandoned any regional distinction it might have had, to become immersed, sometimes drowned, in the monumental City Beautiful idea of the Columbian Exposition. Technology had helped to break through regional differences, carrying the factory and the railroad and their architectures into the West, into places which had fomerly had only houses and churches all in some historical style. But more effective even than technology was the steamroller effect of the classical ideology.

When the image of the City Beautiful was at its very best, when McKim or Cret presided over its execution at the top of their bent, we cannot truthfully insist that the results were inelegant or that they did not provide an amenity for the cities that owned them. Insofar as an architecture can express the transient feelings of a people, they were eloquent testimonials to the Imperialism of the day. But the Imperial view was fortunately short-lived in America and the Imperial architecture had no justification or chance of a long career. This is the pathetic oversight in the recent efforts of men like Henry Hope Reed, Jr., to talk America back into an architecture it never needed very much.

Later on American architects would move towards a goal which was in part the goal of Sullivan and Wright. But before that could happen there had to be another interval. In this interim, belonging to an age of complacency, Sullivan would die in poverty and Wright would go into temporary eclipse. New men would walk the stage in place of Hunt, McKim, Cram and Cret. They would be less imperial, more experimental. But they would also be less certain. They would be men like Goodhue carrying on to his flowering and new men like Harvey Corbett and Raymond Hood and Ralph Walker. Meanwhile another drama would be acted in Europe, partly but only partly reared on the revelations of Wright. The gestation had to take place in Europe and not in America. But when it was finished the great time would begin. Still it was a quarter-century or more away. And in 1913 if you asked people in the know, men of certain taste, to tell you who had done the most for current American architecture, they would probably say that Sullivan had made some imaginative proposals and designed beautiful details, that Wright had built some interesting houses in the Middle West, that Cram's Gothic churches were excellent, that Cass Gilbert had mastered the skyscraper and Paul Cret the problem of a government building, but that if you were looking for giants you had better first go to New York and seek out the elegant taste and the highly developed talent of Charles Follen McKim and his partner Stanford White; they might go further and tell you that the heart of the whole enterprise lay in Chicago in the resourceful and indomitable planner, the real Titan, the emperor of architecture, "Uncle Dan" Burnham. Because in 1913 it was not apparent to any of the "right people" that the long-outstanding account with the past had been so emphatically overpaid. For the moment it was almost as though Richardson and Sullivan had never lived or written or built; as though the Unity Temple and the Larkin Building did not exist.

IV

1913-1933

VI

1913-1933

THE TWENTY YEARS AFTER THE VICTORY OF THE progressive movement, the Armory Show, and the completion of the Woolworth Building were years of confusion and retreat. Reform at home, idealism abroad, lost their luster. Repression of dissent, begun in war, became commonplace, manifesting itself in the experiment of prohibition, the heresy trial of Scopes in Tennessee, or the symbolic trial and ultimate execution of Sacco and Vanzetti in Massachusetts. The notoriously corrupt Ku Klux Klan now staged its largest and finest public parades.

Technology advanced, little inhibited by the general smug, aloof, prosperous complacency of the American people or the anger and despair of American novelists and poets. The latter observed the American scene with no great pleasure, but the focus of their attention was on the general disillusion, and the great industrial targets were no longer of interest. Babbitt replaced the Titan.

This was the trend in business, too. Henry Ford had less real power than Vanderbilt or Morgan. The power was passing to different and more anonymous hands. By 1930 the two hundred largest non-banking corporations controlled nearly a quarter of all the national wealth. Nickel and aluminum were virtual monopolies. Four companies accounted for one half of the copper industry; another four mined half the anthracite; two made half the steel. Three corporate groups controlled half the electric power; two thirds of all the automobiles were made by two companies; three quarters of the cigarettes came from three manufacturers; one company produced half the agricultural machinery. By 1932 six hundred corporations owned two thirds of American industry. Their directorates interlocked and added up to about six thousand individuals of whom two thirds may have been inactive. Thus perhaps two thousand men virtually controlled American private economic life.

The two thousand were captains of industry, not buccaneers, not malefactors of great wealth. Wealthy they might be, but they were not personalities as Peter Cooper, Commodore Vanderbilt and J. P. Morgan had been. They suffered more governmental if not more public surveillance. Most of them were obscure and preferred it that way.

This central group of American industrial power was not hereditary, dictatorial or feudal. In the years from 1920 to 1930 it showed great skill in applying scientific management to production. It learned how to make all sorts of goods in mammoth quantities and at midget prices. But it did not learn so well how to distribute the produce, or the wealth which would make it possible for the produce to be sold. The top was glamorous, the base in sand, and in the black autumn of 1929 it all came crashing down.

Thus Americans of the period began with reform; they knew a high moment of idealistic elation in the crusade to make the world safe for democracy. But quickly they retreated from their contacts with the world, consoled themselves with the lesser fruits of technology, abandoned themselves to an uneasy prosperity which troubled their young people, and saw this vanish almost overnight. Though Harding had sounded a popular note in 1920, the same words were hollow in 1932: "America's present need is not heroics but healing; not nostrums but normalcy; not revolution but restoration."

By 1932 America needed a hero and was ready even for nostrums. Often called a traitor to his class, Franklin Roosevelt saved it; regarded as an enemy of private industry, he probably prevented a larger experiment in socialism.

Posterity might find many a fault in him but it could not honorably divest him of the laurel of a hero. His buoyancy brought confidence to Americans with none; they believed him as they had not believed Hoover; they took his advice not to fear fear. Thus the period ended on an heroic note as it had promised to begin; but between beginning and end there were not many heroes.

There were not many in politics and there were not many in American architecture. By 1925, Sullivan was dead after years of partly deserved neglect, Wright in momentary eclipse. The influence of McKim and Cram was on the wane. The architectural giants were gone or were yet to come. In the same time the most seminal builders of the twentieth century were making crucial architectural statements in Europe, artists like Le Corbusier, architects like Mies van de Rohe and Gropius and Aalto, engineers like Freyssinnet and Maillart. But their works scarcely rippled the bland eclecticism of our leading schools or of our leading offices. They were jeered at by critics like Mencken whose basic toryism was concealed by his espousal of "advanced" literary causes; and they were rejected by "humanist" literary critics like Babbitt and More.

Eliel Saarinen, a master in his day but already one generation behind the thought of the times, was the most revolutionary architect who could be welcomed in America. Ragnar Östberg's Town Hall in Stockholm, a brilliant combination of reminiscences, was thought to be the thing for revolution-minded young Americans to see. What the country wanted for architecture was what it wanted in economics and in politics: normalcy, not nostrums; restoration, not revolution; healing, not heroics. There were numerous architectural Hardings and Coolidges ready to supply what was wanted. Thus except for a few sports like Rockefeller Center and some tentative seeds which would mature at mid-century, the architectural development in America between 1913 and 1933 is epitomized by the Woolworth Building which began it and the Empire State Building which ended it. The latter was taller and bigger but in no way better; its major achievement was the demonstration of managerial skills involved in coordinating so many tasks into such a large and effortless, if in no other way beautiful, productivity. Big management had moved into architecture as it had into business and like business management it was often anonymous. That it could produce big buildings it demonstrated; whether it could produce fine buildings remained to be shown; whether the new organization implied the death of the artist-architect in an America which had never known many was a question yet to be weighed. But neither the artist nor the businessman could see beyond the bigness of the single building; the bigness of the city escaped him.

It was a twenty years of missed opportunities. The ocean barrier was parted by World War I and more than a million young Americans marched through but most marched back and the inspirations to be found in what others do were deferred for another and larger exodus a quarter-century later. The automobile and the highway were beginning to be vital forces in American life, rural and urban, but we allowed the roads to grow at random, producing street patterns that were obsolete before they came into use. It was a time when great imagination was lavished on the processes of making everything but buildings. Abundant surpluses of income might have provided splendid housing and recreational facilities for all, but in the end the paper profits were gone and a third of the nation was still badly fed, badly clothed, badly housed. The means of transportation made all kinds of materials available anywhere in the United States; technological controls of environment were so advanced that the limitations imposed in earlier days by local climates were no longer serious conditioners of design; motion pictures and radio rapidly obliterated pockets of local ignorance as to how others were living. It was a time, then, which should logically have witnessed the triumph of technology over the indigenous.

Instead, two expositions on the West Coast did to these rapidly emerging regions what the Chicago World's Fair had done to the Middle West twenty years earlier. The Far West became as culturally self-assertive as the Middle West had formerly been. The pseudo-regionalism that sprang up notably around San Diego and Santa Barbara permeated not only California but the Southwest and the Midwest and the Northeast. It played hand in hand with eclecticism to create an environment in which serious contemporary architecture, public or domestic, could only mark time.

For American architecture, then, the '20s were timorous, not turbulent; elephantine, not elegant; prosperous, not perceptive. American architectural genius had burned for a moment in Sullivan and Richardson; it was kept alive in Wright; after these years of complacency, stimulated by a small wave of great immigrants, it grew on the power of American technology and the expanding American need. But for all this the '20s were not, save in the technological sense, even a preparation, unless a time of reaction and lassitude, of smugness and mediocrity, is needed by a national culture as a kind of sleep in preparation for a vigorous effort on the morrow.

I

LARGE HISTORICAL MOVEMENTS FLOW LIKE GLACIERS AND NEITHER LITTLE Coolidges nor large Roosevelts will change them much. So it was for the westward course of the American people. Between 1910 and 1930 the whole population increased by one third to 123 million. The agrarian Middle West, the Middle Atlantic, the Great Lakes and the Mountain states grew at about the national rate; the Deep South and New England well below it; while the Pacific region began its fantastic climb. For the first time the absolute weight of the Far West was felt as the nation and Charles Evans Hughes learned when the late returns from California changed an apparent Wilson defeat into victory.

For the moment and perhaps for a long time to come another distribution was more important. Here, too, there was an inevitable and perhaps an even more irresistible tide, the steady, even accelerating flow to the city. Where 45 per cent of Americans had lived in urban places in 1910, more than half were there by 1920, and in 1930 56 per cent. Of the total increase of 31 millions, 27 millions were registered in cities.

The larger cities grew the most. The three cities of over a million people became five; where they had housed an eleventh of the national population in 1910 now they accommodated an eighth. There were nearly a hundred cities of more than 100,000 where there had been fifty, and they held three tenths of all the people in America. It was evidently but a question of time when more than half of the people would live in such great aggregations.

Nor were all the big cities any longer in the older part of the country. The metropolis had become a national phenomenon to be noted in California, Florida, and Minnesota as well as in the more congested Northeast. The time was near at hand when almost every state in the Union would have a big if not an urbane city.

An almost continuous urban pattern was in the making along the Atlantic Seaboard from Boston to Philadelphia, perhaps even to Washington, D.C.; another one was forming south of the Great Lakes from Toledo to Milwaukee; the intimations of Los Angeles, San Diego and their strip were there to be seen, though it was not yet clear that there could be another one along both sides of the bay of civilized San Francisco, from Richmond or Sausalito to San José. The Woolworth Building in elegant and relative isolation might have worked well, even brilliantly; when its like was proliferated in hundreds they did not work so well.

The concrete highway, it seems now, might have pricked more imaginations. It was invented as an almost inevitable response to the multiplying internal combustion motors which, emerging from mud and gravel, frayed the macadam, then rutted the asphalt. Cities that had become ever more dingy and congested became too dingy and too congested. The concrete road and the automobile multiplied the avenues of escape as the suburban train and the interurban trolley had been unable to do. More and more people found easy exits from the dingy city into the sunshine and open air of the suburb; and the freedom of movement of the automobile made it possible for suburbs to grow up almost anywhere, without roots, without convictions, without permanence. This hegira was only a prophecy between 1913 and 1933, another nascent example of the easy American way of solving problems which was to leave them behind; its terrible toll would not be felt until the middle of the century. But already suburbanites, caring no longer to be urban (if they ever had), left the city as a home, withdrew their tax support, depleted its finances; withdrawing their political influence as well, they left its management to the venal. Yearning for space, few found as much space as they had dreamed. Hoping for an autonomous and democratic village life, they found the autonomy expensive and the democracy elusive. Accepting the ever longer and more fatiguing trek to and from the city, they ended by finding no stirring amenity at all, in city or in country. By mid-century it would appear to some sociologists that suburbia had so trained its dwellers that they did not want stirring amenities.

There was a fine irony in this. For the most distinctive American accomplishment in this time was the conquest of vertical space through brilliant engineering. Yet this was wedded to an abysmal management of horizontal space. More and more Americans found themselves working in the day amid the brilliant verticality, and earthbound at day's beginning and end in a snarl of horizontal traffic. And as the motor commuting increased, the quality of the road to the city deteriorated. A commuter on the Staten Island Ferry might at least see the miracle of lower Manhattan at every dawn and dusk; but more and more of the millions of commuters to America's centers of culture moved through visual deserts, tunnels and canyons to arrive finally at the office that was their urban home. For many other millions who might call themselves, for example, New Yorkers, it meant that they never made the one- or two-hour journey to Manhattan at all. And if they never made the journey they might as well have been living in any other enormous Brooklyn or Bronx, for the urban advantages of the metropolis were not being used; thus cities became anonymous for most of their residents, whatever false fronts they might present to the tourist; and even for the tourist they began to look more and more alike for each coveted the same symbol of prestige, the skyscraper; it was as much wanted on the broadest acres of Texas as on the tightest ground plots of lower Manhattan Island.

This was the time when the disease that was beginning to gnaw at the American city might have been detected, and even cured. In the '50s it would take surgery with no clear prognosis that it would work. But no one looked at growth or lack of urbanity as a problem. Indeed most cities no doubt coveted New York's size; and Los Angeles certainly looked forward to the day when it might call itself the largest city in the world, even if it had to set its boundaries fifty miles from the center, even if it never actually were to become a city, but only a collection of a lot of people.

The time had long passed when the practical and the aesthetic problems of the city could be solved by mere growth or by individual buildings, no matter how carefully zoned, no matter how elegant, no matter how colossal. Today the self-satisfied '20s offer an object lesson — for they show how clearly the urbanization and suburbanization of America, combined with our vertical skill and our horizontal incompetence, our tendency to solve a problem by leaving it, our zealous maintenance of the wrong kinds of local autonomy have unfavorably conditioned not only American architecture but also American life and to a considerable degree negated the potentials for a better life that lay in the new technology.

2

THE POPULATION WAS CHANGING IN OTHER WAYS. THE MAMMOTH IMMI-grations came to an end. Soon after the First World War ended, the flood had begun again and 800,000 came in 1921. But now when increasing union power frowned on additional supplies of competitive unskilled labor, mounting restrictions were placed on immigration so that 1931 was the first year in our history when the number of American emigrants exceeded the number of immigrants. The ghettos were beginning to change, growing less Italian, Polish, Jewish, more Negroid.

Now only one fifth of the employed, the farmers were getting older as well as fewer; they were older than the national average, for their young people went off to the city and usually never came back. Farm technology was becoming almost too competent as it produced crops that outran the world's capacity to pay for if not to use. Ability to pay was the only measure in the days of Coolidge so there was an oversupply of American food. Farmers who had fought trusts in an earlier day now began to establish their own. Unable any longer to dominate American political action by sheer numbers, they learned how to exercise the disciplined power of a bloc.

Although reforms and prosperity had placed the farmer in a fair, even a preferred position, the country still was obsessed by the upsetting ideological concept of the "corrupt" and "immoral" urban mores, the dragons in the fiery wood. So farmers and villagers formed ranks for their last defeat in the '20s. But farmer support for the gallus-snapping fringe began to die away, however long it might linger in the red clays of the Southern cotton states; this came about less from the wise-cracking about boobs by the boorish Mencken than from the impact of technology. Radio turned Chautauqua weeks into losing enterprises; the men at the microphones were country boys trying to be more urbane than the urbanites. Even if Elbert Hubbard had not gone down on the *Lusitania,* the days of *The Little Journeys* and of the imitation-Morris craft of the Roycrofters of East Aurora would have lost their savor. Mail-order catalogues became increasingly sophisticated and bred sophistication on the farm which in the sequel would own Aalto stools; so did improved roads, automobiles and trucks, rural electrification, telephones, radio, and perhaps most of all the motion pictures. The farmer met the same entertainment as men in the suburban middle class. The corn belt furnished more movie stars than Broadway. So the distinctions between the rural and the other middle-class cultures of America grew indecisive. Well before he collapsed at Dayton, Tennessee, William Jennings Bryan must have drunk the gall of knowing that he was no longer the idol of the prairie; and indeed this sense may have helped to drive him into narrower and narrower positions, commanding fewer and fewer supporters, doomed to more and ignominious defeats.

The immediate outstanding development in the relations between the farmer and his nation was but one of several portents of a future time when the American public would generally accept the view, with an obbligato of ineffective grumbling, that the federal government would become a steadily bigger factor in the life of every American individual. From the grain corporations required in the First World War through the fumbling efforts of McNary and Haugen to hold up farm prices; the droughts and the grasshoppers; the erosion of the plow-broken plains; to the situation of 1932 when almost every farmer was a debtor, the hourglass marked only fifteen years, now almost lost in memory. In this the concept of the farmer as independent yeoman inevitably vanished. He could no longer honestly imagine himself as really free to drive his plow through any piece of grass, to sink his ax in any tree, to pen up any stream. Unable to survive in a "free" market, he could no longer reasonably declaim against the labor union or the corporate trust, for he had built his own kind of union and his own kind of trust. He could no longer consistently argue against big government, for he was asking big government to help him.

Thus the path was cleared for soil conservation, irrigation, flood control, rural electrification and other projects which would generally bring new technologies to farm operations, make farms more prosperous and American food production more secure. But this could not happen unless many of the farms were much larger than had previously been necessary; so corporate farming got its start.

Out of such crises and such organizations several things happened to rural architecture. Always and everywhere prudent farmers who were even modestly prosperous had maintained farmsteads that had much visual, even architectural, delight and sometimes even a trace of elegance. The village commodity which had been so common in the eighteenth century had long ago deteriorated into the drab mediocrity of places like Abilene, Kansas. Now the farms were to change too and lose their character; more comfortable, better equipped with labor-saving devices, bombarded with news on the radio and style by the movies, the farm establishment soon acquired the aesthetic values of the suburb.

The little red schoolhouse was no longer going to be little or red. It would no longer try to teach all grades in a single shed with a pendant pair of privies. Country children would become used to being driven miles each day in public buses to reach large school buildings and these buildings might often not be Georgian. Indeed you might soon have quite as good a chance of finding Mies van der Rohe on the prairie as in the metropolis. As the city man tried to pretend he was living in the country, so the countryman began to act like a city man.

3

JUST AS THE ENVIRONMENT OF THE FARMER WAS SHIFTING, SO WAS THE environment of the laborer. Within the plant his physical task was becoming much more specialized and in most physical ways easier. For the man who had individual skill and pride in it, the new methods of mass production raised serious questions; some of an economic and some of a psychological nature. Would his skill be displaced by that of the machine? If so, how was he to live? If there was a task for him in the new fragmentation of work, would it reduce his role to that of a robot, however essential, and thus remove from him the incentives that rest in pride over a task well done? The new processes were demanding larger factories, more remote management. Could he know the boss any more as he had known him in a simpler village factory economy? Whether this knowledge had bred love or hate, and it had bred both, was less important than that the lack of contact on both sides might breed the subtly poisonous hostility of indifference. If management were to be more remote, might not his own union representatives also be so? If big unions were needed to cope with big management, might the laborer as an individual lose any sense of identification with his own agents? Was the unemployment of a specialized worker a more frightening specter than unemployment of an individualistic jack-of-all-trades?

On the whole, the larger philosophical problems, the broader economic and political issues, did not enter labor thought. For the most part it concentrated on getting a greater share of the new productivity and on asserting its right to organize for joint action in pursuit of this share. When real economic disaster hit the country the labor movement lost its teeth for a while; the labor power simply merged with that of the other beaten groups, who identified themselves with the "forgotten men" and so voted in the election of 1932.

Between 1919 and 1929, only ten years, due largely to scientific management and new machinery and the redesign of products to make them
easier to make, the productivity of the average American worker increased by 43 per cent as compared with a 30 per cent increase in the
whole quarter-century between 1890 and 1914, probably the greatest
American accomplishment in this age of complacency. But workers'
take-home pay necessarily increased by only half as much and what
they had did not make workers into effective consumers of the goods
pouring out from the new factories.

In 1929, at the height of the "prosperity," the Brookings Institution
reported that 42.4 per cent of American families had annual incomes of
less than $1500. At the same time a mere 0.1 per cent of the families each
had incomes of more than $100,000.

All this was ignored by businessmen and intellectuals, too, as they
happily consulted the euphoric stock market figures every night while
talking about car loadings and other market indicators. Democrats and
Republicans alike were sure to agree with Hoover's acceptance speech:
"We in America today are nearer the final triumph over poverty than
ever before in the history of any land." Even Al Smith was not of a
different view although he campaigned for better housing, better factory
laws, care of the insane and better provisions for child welfare. In this
climate labor gains were slight; Henry Ford made his own wage scales
and seemed a renegade to many employers when he paid unnecessarily
high rates, introduced short hours and added a profit-sharing plan. The
war control measures were not quickly relaxed when it was over.
A. Mitchell Palmer enjoined important strikes; the Wilson program of
the New Freedom was not intended to make drastic changes in the
conditions of labor.

So far as architecture was concerned the slow progress of the labor
movement in this time was of little direct consequence. Labor unions in
the building trades did not make important contributions to the productivity of the building industry and were seldom if ever interested in
building aesthetics. Labor leaders on the broader front did not lead
their groups in support of better urban or regional plans, or even of parks,
playgrounds and certainly not of urban beauty. An individual laborer
with enough money to spend to build a house at all invariably had conventional tastes and simply tried to make it as much like a middle-class
suburban house as possible. Workers rarely built cooperatively as they
were frequently doing in Europe; even when they did one cannot point
to their projects as important American architecture. Unions did not yet
have large enough coffers to build office buildings, nor large enough
staffs to fill them; such symbols of the growth of a union would have

In the next three years the American economy ground to a halt. The national income was cut in half; the national wealth shrank by a third; stocks sold at a tenth of their 1929 prices; farm prices stood at 40 per cent, exports at one third, industrial production at one half; nine million savings accounts were wiped out; municipal employees could not draw their pay for months; in cities like Chicago one out of two workers was unemployed. The national birth rate was 17 per cent below that of 1921. The bread lines and the apple salesmen were real. The businessman never looked as infallible again. After the New Deal the merchant princes built no more private palaces.

Franklin Delano Roosevelt proclaimed the "forgotten man" in April 1932. In July he flew from Albany to Chicago to accept the Democratic nomination. "I pledge you, I pledge myself, to a new deal for the American people." In November he polled three popular votes to Hoover's two, gained eight out of nine electors, carried all of the important industrial states except Pennsylvania and Connecticut. The mandate was clear.

Although the hero of this drama had himself a vigorous interest in architecture, he also had extraordinarily bad taste. Nonetheless the inauguration of Roosevelt marked the end of a bad period of American architecture and the beginning of a new and better one.

5

MEANWHILE ANOTHER SET OF IMPORTANT FORCES WAS WORKING ABROAD. For the first time since America had been a colony, our foreign relations were a vital factor in determining what and why we would build and how we would build it.

In the Western Hemisphere some of the more blatant big-brotherliness was disappearing. American troops were still dispatched freely, but the justifications were more often challenged at home. Black Jack Pershing's Mexican expedition seemed comic opera but was not, for a real revolution was going on there, sometimes peacefully, sometimes violently, and its impact was brought to Americans through painting and literature as well as pocketbooks. The real successes of the revolution came after 1933 and the permanency of the success was clear by 1950. In 1913-1933 the revolution was going on, and after 1917 it progressed without American troops although there were many other American attempts to intervene or intercede.

But even if the Marines left Mexico alone, it is true that throughout these twenty years there were few months when American troops were

been neither appropriate nor welcome. The only good architecture for labor was the architecture of the factory and that was supplied by management.

4

WHILE LABOR WAS FARING MEAGERLY IN THE COMPLACENT YEARS, AT least in everything except the fullness of the dinner pail, government actions and public opinion were operating in favor of business. Woodrow Wilson held that private monopoly was "indefensible and intolerable" but regarded the Clayton Act as enough protection. Beyond the Clayton Act the Wilson administration was content with setting up a Federal Reserve System and a Federal Trade Commission, and with sequestering some naval oil reserves to keep them out of private hands.

Moreover, the governmental mobilizations of industry during the First World War which even put the government into manufacturing for a moment were abandoned with alacrity after Versailles and scant attention was paid to halfhearted proposals by Glenn E. Plumb that employees should share the ownership and operation of the railroads; or to the suggestion by the United Mine Workers that the coal mines be nationalized.

A more troublesome residue for the businessman as individual or corporate executive was the philosophy if not the actual size of the new tax structure. The principle of a discriminatory tax on annual incomes of over a few thousand dollars had, it will be recalled, been established in an earlier period when Joseph Choate had protested that it was a "drift towards socialism." But the objections had not been extensive because they were objections of principle and nobody had been hurt in a practical way.

If the tax adventure had not revealed any philosophy, Republican or Democratic, that would call for a serious revision in the distribution of net income among Americans, it had during the war years established the precedent of graded taxes related to "capacity to pay." The cuckoo was in the nest. It was not clear at what point graded income taxes would destroy "individual initiative."

Tax measures could be and were used to provide a half-accepted principle of "from each according to his ability, to each according to his need." For architecture it meant that a greater number of important decisions about what to build, where to build, how to build, including many aesthetic decisions, would be made not by private clients whose individual imaginations might be piqued but by public committees who seldom had imagination at all. Public committees would be subject to all the inertias of the bureaucracy of public servants plus the individual and usually ignorant prejudices of the individual legislators who sat on the Congressional committees. It would take time before progressive architects could find a way through competitions, for which the juries were often rigged, through new advisory committees, occasionally to push back the wall of federal indifference or hostility to good contemporary architecture. Meanwhile the attitudes of the Supervising Architect of the Treasury limited by the censorious village minds of the Congress were likely to prevail in government architecture.

Increased status for businessmen, decreased status for ministers, professors, editors, doctors, and even lawyers left the architects in some doubt as to where they stood. The architects were not exactly artists, not exactly professional men, not exactly intellectuals. As time went on intellectuals, almost to a man, deserted the standpat side while the professionals, like the doctors, seemed to become more and more conservative. This was noticeably true of the engineers and the architects, who could work best in a society which conserved things. Both might always want innovation, engineers more than architects. But both needed clients with funds. These funds had either to be in private hands or in governmental hands; they would not constructively be in revolutionary hands. On the whole the architects and engineers alike had found the bureaucracy of big business far more flexible than the bureaucracy of big government and as believers in conservative change it was not unnatural for them to stay on the side whence such change was most likely to be supported. Some engineers found the doctrines of technocracy appealing as they premiated the technologist but to the architects these were less convincing, though not because architects were wiser, but because they did not look upon themselves as technologists.

The artist in America might feel no such changing status. His position had always been ambiguous. Art was an afterthought for most Americans and the artist of second-rate importance. In a war for survival the poetic stock was expendable as the scientific was not.

It is not at all clear who wanted to be an architect in this situation or why. It does seem clear that few architects of the day came from or joined the angry classes. Few were seeking an economic or social upgrading through successful practice of their profession. Few were burning to rebuild America in some great new image. Architecture was too often regarded as a genteel profession, suitable for the man who had attended an Ivy League college, made the Grand Tour of Europe, caught the lively spirit of the École des Beaux-Arts, knew his wines and brandies and old châteaux, married a suitably wealthy and cultivated

wife and could stage grandiose settings for wealthier men whom knew at social clubs.

It was not a profession which would appeal to many intelligent ambitious Jews, for example. If they burned with talent to create could find higher, purer, less circumscribed opportunities in scie music or one of the fine arts; if they burned with the desire to serve could be more certainly useful in medicine or law; if they burned get rich they could make more money in almost any activity chosen random. And for even more reasons the profession was effectiv closed to Negroes.

It is not surprising that few architects of those days were to be fou among the agitators, or in the vanguard of the liberal parades.

Not all architects were smug. A small group of men like Robert Ko Clarence Stein, Henry Wright, and Arthur Holden were beginning press for a different concept of housing and urbanism and men of t stamp stood with the liberals of other professions. But the He Wrights and the Clarence Steins in this time of prosperity and self-sa faction were not conspicuous leaders of the whole profession howe many accolades they may have since received. With the New Deal th came for a moment into their own but only for a moment. Even fr the New Deal, the neutrals got most of the commissions.

The satisfied architects were undoubtedly more typical of the Ame can consensus than the few professors or ministers or lawyers or nov ists or poets who were not so sure that everything was lovely. For t architects, the American dream seemed in no jeopardy. Nor did it f the American people. Moreover, the people had no doubt where th prestige lay. It belonged to business and not to the arts. There was question of any sort, including that of architectural excellence, on whi the opinion of the successful Andrew Mellon would not be taken mo seriously than the opinion of the "unsuccessful" Frank Lloyd Wrigh

After the early years of the Wilson administration, criticism of bu nessmen abated. Business leadership was accepted not only in practic matters of economics, politics, and welfare, but in matters of aesthetic philosophy, or morals as well. People liked Harding's 1920 statemen "What we want in America is less government in business and mor business in government." They applauded Coolidge's philosophy tha "the business of America is business." They agreed with Andrew Mello that initiative could be associated only with acquisitive opportunity.

Soon enough, the years of business in government were measured an found wanting, while the years of government in business were to com mence. Hoover accepted the nomination of 1928 with his assertio about the American abolition of poverty.

not standing guard somewhere else in the Americas, in Haiti, Santo Domingo, Nicaragua. The Marines did not always limit themselves to short visits. In 1925 they ended an occupation of Nicaragua which had begun in 1912 but they were back by 1926 and the last of them did not come out until January 2, 1933.

Still we were becoming gentler. There were more Pan-American conferences; our Presidents went on good will tours; we finally paid some reparations to Colombia for the Panama steal.

Of course United States power continued to be felt in Central and South America and it was not always in a velvet glove. But the way of wielding was becoming, at least, more subtle. The influence was economic, not military, cultural more than crassly political. Many more young Latin Americans came to the United States for higher education. Many more Americans went to South and Central America for business or pleasure. Here they found different and interesting cultures. The interest might be wakened by the romantic residues of the European Renaissance culture of Castile, but soon it turned to the indigenous pre-Columbian work of Mayans and Aztecs or to the attitudes of the contemporary Indians. The Americans began to admire the revolutionary paintings of Siqueiros, Orozco and Rivera and so invited these powerful muralists to paint inappropriate social messages in such places as the Dartmouth College Library. As time went on we found that the new wealth and the new freedoms were uncovering unexpected new talents. Imaginative native architects and sculptors and painters sprang up in Mexico City, Cuba, Venezuela, Brazil, as wealth released opportunity. The artists were more exuberant than the artists of the United States; the public was more interested and more tolerant; for a time the achievements could even embarrass those Americans who made comparisons with their own more cautious efforts. Thus in the years which were coming the new Western Hemisphere was one in which nations would contribute to each other's culture. In the long run the greater influence on American architecture might come no longer from Europe but from the mixed and awakening people of Mexico and Brazil; thus in a roundabout way the Indian and the Negro would have their say.

The second great international change was America's entry into the First World War, and even more its sequels. After it was over we might try to disentangle ourselves but we were never to succeed and thus the whole course of our destiny was changed. In many ways the American participation in the first war was fragmentary, romantic, quite uncomprehending of the real dimensions and the real complications of the conflict, as our diplomatic actions during the Russian Revolution remind us. From it we achieved a sense that we could have military power if we wanted it; we learned that we could apply controls to our national life without demoralization, at least in crisis, that we could sustain a national draft of manpower, that government controls could sometimes even promote efficiency. We learned but forgot rapidly enough that no nation was really independent, that a complex modern world might be one of continuous crisis.

But we did not learn as much as we might have. To most of the dough-boys, Winchester meant the mud of the base camp at Winnal Down and not the Cathedral, the Round Table or the School. To an American Legionary the symbol of France was a boxcar for forty-and-eight, the culture of France was to be found on the Butte Montmartre, the women of France were the mademoiselles from Armentières. For the architects the coin was a little different though perhaps as spurious. They had a predisposition to like France. Many had studied there; many understood the French cuisine; a few were honest oenophiles. They knew where some of the fine buildings were and managed to see them when on leave. Thus the architects of the AEF did bring something back, a pleas-urable nosegay of nostalgia, delightful for the individual, harmless enough for him, damaging to his architecture. For though France offered a wide variety of the finest architectural experiences created over a thou-sand years, and a few competent contemporary ones, it was the old ones that were visited. These were in themselves seldom eclectic but they could be imitated and adopted eclectically, overromanticized by sketches and etchings and water colors. The pleasurable encounter with France simply enticed the young American soldier-architect to put on his beret and to try to bring old France to young America.

But these were perhaps trivial failures. The bitter pill was the retreat from greatness. When Woodrow Wilson's hopes died, so did those of many other liberals and it does not matter how much it was his fault and how much Lodge's and how much the sheer inconsequence of the American people. For if the people had had what they wanted in the Wilson of 1912 and what a scant majority wanted still in 1916, the Hard-ing they got in 1920 was what a considerably larger majority thought they wanted then. Though the American Federation of Labor sup-ported the League of Nations, its members repudiated it. The Daughters of the American Revolution and the American Legion had never had any truck with such nonsense. In the long run few others did either.

We made proposals for the rehabilitation of German finances but did little to rehabilitate the German people. We lowered the Italian interest rate almost to zero but did not help the Italians to stay the hand of Mussolini. We were shocked when other nations broke their promises or when Japan walked out of the League of Nations after the

Lytton Committee report, yet we never joined the League ourselves. When Japan attacked Shanghai we buzzed with protest and then fell silent, for we were invariably quick with verbal moralizing but quick to make it clear also that we were still too proud to fight.

We thoroughly miscalculated the Russian Revolution, and ad-libbed through the critical days, as George Kennan has reported. Finally, after doing either too little or too much, we got out. We were the first to recognize the Kerensky government of Russia which was admittedly *de facto*. But we declined with equal celerity to admit that the Bolshevist *coup d'état* of November had taken place and tried to pretend officially that Lenin and Trotsky did not exist while maintaining representatives not in Moscow but in nearby Vologda.

In all this inconsequence we watched the rise of Tojo and Mussolini and, most of all of Hitler. After 1931 there was no turning back. The decision as to the time and place of war had passed to the dictators. Americans stood enwreathed by a garland of pious platitudes and clucked gently. At least the Italian trains were running on time.

6

WITHOUT DOUBT IT WAS A TIME OF BAD TASTE AND CORRUPTION BUT mostly it was a time of complacent lassitude, in which a local and temporary material prosperity seemed to be the be-all and end-all of American life. If any one man were to epitomize the complacency and the stupidity of the attitude it was President Calvin Coolidge. If anyone were to play the wasp it was Henry L. Mencken. His acid observations on the American scene help us to recall it better than Coolidge's platitudes.

Mencken was a Southern Tory who detested almost everything and particularly liberals, uplifters, professors and New Englanders. He did not like successful businessmen at the Babbitt level though as they got bigger he became less critical. He hated also the Bible Belt, the Rotary Club, the American Legion and the YMCA. It is to be doubted if he really had any significant respect for any part of American culture — or Anglo-Saxon culture for that matter.

America needed, he said, and did not have a civilized aristocracy and that was partly because of the catastrophe of Appomattox. For him Freud was a quack, Lodge the prince of cynics, Theodore Roosevelt the emperor of mountebanks, Anglo-Saxons incompetent and cowardly, the least capable of civilization. Preachers and bishops were ignoramuses; professors were fools. Democracy was a self-limiting disease.

Public schools were a drag on the community. Wilson's style was balder-
dash and buncombe; Coolidge a man of sad necrotic humor; Franklin
Roosevelt a man whose only asset was his name. Perhaps all Coolidge
could ever really think of was his electric horse but it was better to have
a nincompoop doing nothing in the White House than the world-sav-
ers who preceded and followed him.

Anyone who lashes out at so many targets will hit some that any
given reader rejoices to see hit. Thus Mencken may be everybody's man
— or nobody's. For the '20s and especially for the younger generation,
including the architects, he, along with Huneker, was very much the
man and they liked to read him even when he was telling the truth about
themselves. He was wrong about Le Corbusier and wrong about the
genius being always at war with society, both of which they liked to
hear. He was right about something they may not have liked to hear: "In
the arts as in the concerns of every day, the American seeks escape from
the insoluble by pretending that it is solved. A comfortable phrase is
what he craves beyond all things." That was too often the architectural
condition as well.

7

AMONG THE INTELLECTUAL ACTIVITIES OF MEN, MODERN SCIENCE SEEMS
best able to divorce itself from some of the general political, social and
moral milieux of its day or at least this was so before science needed such
large public funds to do its work and before scientists felt any particular
need to be acclaimed or loved. Thus despite the general languor of the
times the science of 1913-1933 made great strides. The bigger ideas had
been laid down in the previous period by Einstein, Planck, Rutherford
and Bohr; but a much more elaborate structure was now erected on
these foundations. In physics the great task was to summarize the properties of matter in terms of electric charges and radiation. It was the
time when protons, neutrons and spinning electrons joined the company of familiar words and by its end Enrico Fermi had shown that
nearly every element in the periodic table would undergo a nuclear
transformation when bombarded by neutrons. The threshold had been
laid down for the use of nuclear energy on a big scale.

Meanwhile the quantum theory of Planck was coming to maturity.
After Bohr had put together many of the relations there was a serious
exploration of different but not alternative aspects of the theory such as
the transformation ideas of Dirac and Jordan, the matrix theories of
Bohr and Heisenberg, the wave mechanics of Broglie and Schrödinger.

This led to the doctrine of kinetic indeterminism and in simple terms it could be stated as Heisenberg's uncertainty principle of 1927 that there was a limit to the precision with which nature could be observed, or more concretely that one could not determine simultaneously the position and the velocity of a particle as accurately as one wished; that the more precise one got about one of these the less precise he would have to be content to be about the other.

Remembering the misinterpretations of Darwinian and other scientific concepts through false analogies to social situations, physicists like Percy Bridgman were alarmed at what laymen might make of the postulates of Heisenberg. In 1929 he wrote, "The immediate effect will be to let loose a veritable spree of licentious and debauched thinking. . . . One group will find in the failure of the physical law of cause and effect the solution of the age-old problem of the freedom of the will, and on the other hand, the atheist will find the justification of his contention that chance rules the universe."

One should not expect to find direct applications of the work of the scientists in the contemporary Empire State Building but one could not expect even an indirect effect if the architects were formally ignorant of everything that was going on in physics, as undoubtedly they were. For a moment the implications of the atomic work for architecture were only philosophical, if they were anything; a little later and briefly they would pose concrete questions of location for survival; and still later they might ask architecture what to do for a world in which energy might be essentially free. But at the time they had none of these effects. The architects were then, as now, formally ignorant of science and not anxious to change the situation. Thus even the serious efforts of Sigfried Giedion could not build believable connections between Duchamp's *Nude Descending a Staircase* or Gropius's Werkbund Building at Cologne and the recondite space-time of Einstein. Exactly what architects might have done with the knowledge had they possessed it may be hard to define but that still leaves unanswered the question whether architecture can express its times well while the architects are deaf to some of its most important manifestations. To the physical sciences they seemed quite indifferent though it was from the physical sciences that a new and formidable philosophy was emerging.

If new work in vitamins, hormones and insulin prolonged life, stimulated gerontology and changed the age distribution of the American people, the architects could perhaps defer their interest until this distribution called for new buildings, even new building types. If theories of adsorption, concepts of unit operations in the chemical industry, many developments in synthetic chemicals prophesied whole new lines of materials they could perhaps wait until the materials were on the market. But psychology was moving into the architectural backyard. Architects might not enjoy the labor of trying to make a direct connection with the new psychology, behavioristic or Gestalt, or to encounter Jung's efforts to explain the psychology of art. They might find it easier to take at second hand through critics like Read and Burke, novelists like Mann and Joyce, painters like Miró, Klee, Tanguy, Masson, Ernst, Picasso, Dali, and Man Ray. The few psychological statements that architects might essay were in the end rationalizations of what they had done intuitively and subjectively to produce work that was satisfying for them. They could seldom adduce experimental evidence to support their views, for example, as to what was the right light or the right number of convalescents in a single hospital room, or the effect of color upon the patient, though they might now begin to "talk psychology."

There were a few architects like American-born Paul Nelson, living in France, who pressed the idea of doing what they called architectural "research," applying it notably to the study of hospital design. But such men seldom got their buildings built at all, and even when the details seemed interesting or useful the buildings often offered less delight than the intuitive ones. This was not of course a demonstrable denial of the virtue of knowledge in design but it seemed to architects to absolve them from any necessity for paying attention to the dusty and often boring methods and findings of "research." In terms of true scientific laboratory techniques and attitudes, the research of those contemporary architects and foundations who worked on architectural problems seems to have been remarkably primitive, even subjective, and never at best much more than empirical. Thus to praise it with the title "research" is to magnify it beyond its deserts. And it made almost no dent on the world of the architects in which very few even were interested in watching the researchers, much less in emulating them.

8

TECHNOLOGY ALSO MOVED FORWARD IN THE COMPLACENT YEARS AND INdeed contributed to the complacency. For Americans found it easy to confuse technological change with "progress." On many counts the material standard of living became higher although not necessarily on all counts. A high material standard of transportation was attained, including speed, comfort, flexibility and general availability. But the landscape through which the Americans traveled did not become finer and the speed at which they traveled did not improve its visibility; the stand-ardization of communities might even make the purpose of the travel more dubious. But given such choices Americans have never wavered. They selected the speed over the amenity and called it a better way of life. They accepted the slag heap and the smog as a reasonable price for fast travel and electric appliances in the house.

Now the railroads which had provided the backbone of American transportation for freight and passengers alike began to pass their ma-turity. There would continue to be innovations in railroading right down to 1950 but the once piratical and adventurous railroad manage-ments had become conservative and unimaginative, unable to vie with the competition of the air and the highway.

By 1915 railroad construction had begun to slow down almost every-where in the world and perhaps forever; except for a brief spurt during the Second World War the marks of railroad supremacy reached their peaks and fell back during this quarter-century. All the red carpets and extra-fare trains, all the stewardesses and the too few other practices borrowed from the airlines simply postponed the demise. The passenger railroads were heading towards senescence and no hormones would post-pone the process much. But no one foresaw this at the moment and so the spate of imperial railroad stations continued until almost every city had one. Indeed a few of the interesting ones were built in this time.

Innovations and improvements in the airplane, on the other hand, came along at a headlong pace. Biplanes, triplanes and quadruplanes gave way to the single wing. The engines became more powerful and reliable, permitting faster and longer flights until the oceans could be crossed. The technological advances in these years were notable but they had all to be tested by men and women working in a time when there was still a good deal of mystery as to why airplanes stayed up at all. The airplane needed engineers but it also needed heroes and it found them in the Doolittles, Turners, Alcocks, Posts, Lindberghs, and in women like Amy Mollison and Amelia Earhart. They launched parachutes from 26,000 feet by 1921; they flew the Atlantic both ways and by 1933 had gone 5650 miles non-stop. They stepped up the speeds. The fifty-nine days it had taken C. P. Rodgers to fly from New York to Pasadena in 1911 were cut down to twenty-two hours in 1922 when Doolittle made the trip from Jacksonville to San Diego, and in 1933 Turner halved that time in a flight from Los Angeles to New York. They got around the world and by commercial services — John Henry Mears in forty days in 1913, Edward Evans and Denton Wells in twenty-eight days in 1929. They drew away from the competition of the dirigibles. But after all the heroism and all the excitement of the pioneering innovations had become common fare, there remained the drab problem of building a transportation system. And for some time Americans were less daring about this than they were about the flying itself.

Thus Americans concentrated for a long time on carrying air mail while Europeans quickly developed the passenger service. By 1919 you could fly commercially between London and Paris, between Moscow and Petrograd and a number of other important European centers. Meanwhile we worked on the mail, which went transcontinental in September 1920 when a service was opened between New York and San Francisco, but it was not until 1924 that a successful night flight was made over the relatively safe terrain between Chicago and Cheyenne.

The airplane posed many problems to architecture as it grew. The most primitive questions were simple, such as those of the appropriate location and design of air terminals. The beginnings were not imaginative as again we showed that we could solve the difficult problems of dynamics with more verve and imagination than the simpler static ones of architecture. Again we showed we could manage vertical travel better than horizontal. It was not time to wonder what the airplane said about the aesthetics of the city; not time even to guess that the freedom of movement between old civilizations and today might affect them both profoundly. Indeed architects were more likely to discuss the risk that planes might bump into the Empire State Tower or how to use the Tower as a dirigible mooring mast; or the even more fascinating if less consequential question of how to adapt the Petit Trianon or the Imperial Roman Baths to airports since they had manifestly served so well for railroad stations. Hangars and other utilitarian aircraft barns might be seen to have an admissible beauty but it was a beauty that belonged to the engineer and one that seemed to most architects not to have any transferable suggestions for their less utilitarian needs. So the effect of the airplane was postponed to the future.

What was squarely in the present was the automobile, although the magnitude of the urban disaster it was preparing was but vaguely foreshadowed. The mass production started by Ford in 1913 required the concept of a public need of which the public was not yet aware. Fourteen years later Henry and Edsel Ford drove their fifteen-millionth car out of the plant and most of the fifteen million had been the sturdy, uncompromising Model-T. But at the end of that year Ford showed the new Model A and this reluctantly adopted change broke the ice for the continuous and trivial changes of the present.

The 181,000 cars that were made in 1910 became almost four million by 1930. Truck production increased from 6000 to 571,000. The 458,000 registered passenger cars became 23 million and now there was one car on the road for every five Americans. There were still only 40,000 buses but trucks on the road had increased from 10,000 to 3.5 million. The miles driven in America multiplied by ten.

Enormous credit belongs to the early manufacturing pioneers, whether inventors like Ford and Kettering or engineers like Sloan. But it must not be forgotten that the great improvements in rubber, alloys, fuels, made in laboratories that did not belong to the motor magnates, were of major importance in permitting the automobile to grow. The automobile manufacturers did bring big mass production and distribution to the American people; they also developed enormous integrative concepts whereby they set out to own their own mines, steel plants, ships. But automobiles were not articles of household use. They needed roads to run on and the early roads were mere remnants of ancient carriage tracks. In old areas and in many new ones they were quite unsuited even to modest speeds. They abounded in sharp curves as they twisted around ancient property lines, steep grades as they assaulted hills head on, short lines of sight that had been perfectly safe for horsedrivers. They were narrow, they were replete with blind intersections, their surfaces were uniformly bad.

Indeed, the first problem for the national roadbuilders, aside from providing a system on which even the markings would be consistent and there would be a certainty that one route did lead into the next, was to make surfaces that could be traveled on at all. For a long time after cars began the gentle trickle from the cities it was a real question whether the open road could ever keep up with the national demand. By 1914 it was clear that the prevalent macadam was failing under the increased traffic. Nor could the brick roads of Ohio endure, or the cobblestones of Chicago's North Side. The decade between 1914 and 1924 saw the 2300 miles of concrete increase to 31,000 and by that time concrete roads were being laid at the rate of 6000 miles a year, exceeding everything except the still most common gravel. By 1933 the national road system had been completed as to routes and was thoroughly obsolete, since it consisted almost entirely of two-lane highways connecting main settlements but passing through every congested center and debouching into clotted city squares. The first rotary grade intersection was provided in 1920 and the first cloverleaf in 1930, both in New Jersey. The first few miles of an American superhighway with a grass strip between lanes came in the same year. The Holland Tunnel became the first to carry automobiles beneath the river in 1927 when it opened a new road from Jersey to Manhattan. But the builders had no concept of the dimensions of the oncoming flood and no realization yet that the critical point might be at the tunnel mouth or the bridgehead. So the new river crossings simply dumped the traffic onto conventional city streets quite unprepared to take away the flow.

All this certainly posed immediate problems and a potential crisis for architecture but the architects seem not to have done much about it. The trailer, invented in 1929 by Glenn Curtiss, was displayed in the Hudson showrooms without causing a tremor in architectural circles. The motel crept in quietly, first as a mediocre economy for a few travelers or as a source of small change for a farmer. As the automobile destroyed urbanity and civilization within the city, muddied the difference between city and suburb and country, spawned a massive, uniform, banal and horribly ugly highway culture, the architects did not complain. Twenty years too late they began to see the damage to the land, cry outrage among themselves, ultimately join more seriously with others in an effort to cut out a cancer that had cried for an earlier diagnosis.

It may be idle to bang this drum. There is no reason to suppose that city politicians and businessmen would have believed the architectural alarm had it been sounded. But the architects were not active even on lesser and more obvious problems. They might, if asked, design an inadequate storage garage but their interest stopped at the building line and they were quite willing to let the incoming and outgoing cars pile up at an unchanged street. For their other buildings they made no pretense at providing off-street parking; for theaters, opera houses and other buildings which many people would approach and leave almost simultaneously they provided no off-street roadways, no entries more sophisticated and comfortable than the ancient marquees. In all of this there was an irresponsibility that was something less than charming.

9

MEANWHILE ELECTRONICS, TOO, WAS PREPARING TO LAY ITS HANDS ON the American culture. Telephone service became automatic, almost foolproof, and common. The 8.2 telephones per 100 Americans of 1910 was doubled by 1930. By 1923 there was transatlantic service to London. After radio-telephone service was set up between New York and London at the beginning of 1927 and at midyear between San Francisco and Manila, the world had been almost girdled with a fast communications network.

The use of radio signals for commercial broadcasting was on the verge of developing. The first known American program had been beamed from an experimental station at Brant Rock, Massachusetts, on Christmas Eve of 1906 by Professor R. A. Fessenden. In 1910, Lee de Forest had installed a 500-watt transmitter at the Metropolitan Opera House and broadcast a program in which Enrico Caruso took part. After the war evolution was rapid; KDKA began the modern era in Pittsburgh in November 1920 by providing returns from the Harding-Cox election. By 1922, 564 stations had been licensed to operate. By the end of 1933 an enormous fraction of the twelve million homes then housing thirteen million sets were tuned in for the first of Roosevelt's fireside chats.

Significantly, radio began in strong hands and never really left them. National networks dominated the scene by 1927. The effect of the national and simultaneous distribution of the same music, the same comedy, the same sporting events, the same political speeches, the same news and the same comments about the news, the same advertisements, changed the music, the comedy, the speeches, the interpretations and in many ways standardized them. Depending upon how it was used, national radio might have been able to cultivate or destroy regionalism, elevate or debase national taste.

But meanwhile the engineers were preparing an even more ominous development of electronics. As early as 1884, Nipkow had demonstrated a way to the future television when he used a circular, spirally perforated scanning disc behind which he placed a phototube pickup. Practical use had to be deferred until de Forest invented his thermionic amplifier in 1907. By the early '20s theoretical cathode-ray devices which had long been known were shown to be operative as pickup tubes. On April 7, 1927, Walter S. Gifford, President of the American Telephone and Telegraph Company, conducted a public display of television, showing on New York sets a picture of Secretary Hoover sitting in his Washington office. For the period 1910-1933 whether this cultural infant would turn out to be Michael or Lucifer could not be perceived.

Another mass medium was very perceptible. By 1930, it is estimated, 100 million Americans were going to the movies weekly. The old vaudeville theaters with their makeshift arrangements no longer would do. The Strand Theater in New York opened in April 1914 with 3300 seats, a 30-piece orchestra, elegant popcorn-vending machines, glamourously caparisoned ushers who drilled every day and carried magic light wands to speed their work. *The Spoilers* of Rex Beach, the picture with the first long fist fight, set a record by playing to 40,000 people in a single week. Gone was the nickelodeon. *The Birth of a Nation*, the first long combination of spectacle and drama, played in theaters which often charged two dollars a ticket. New types of showmen, like Roxy of the radio, had movie theaters built in their honor. The New York Roxy had 6250 seats, a cooling plant, fancy service and stylized courtesies, stage shows based on a permanent *corps de ballet* that moved with the precise impressiveness if not the meaning of the great ballets. All this picture was framed in velvet and introduced with fanfare. The film was approached with something of the awe that befitted a cathedral of the cinema. Given any kind of picture, people would stand in line for hours, would buy so many tickets that the place could gross nearly $150,000 a week.

In this as in almost every other art of the time, even in the art of designing a forthright motor car to succeed the forthright Model T, Americans were showing themselves more adept at massive manufacture and distribution than at imaginative and varied production of more exciting things for a more critical clientele. Despite the fact that American moviemakers had far greater financial and technical resources at their disposal or perhaps because of it, the list of outstanding American pictures of the day will not stand comparison with the list from Europe. In Europe the makers of movies walked hand in hand with the painters and the writers of higher capacities, sometimes were themselves the painters or the writers. A few Americans were able to see such European productions as Wiene's *Cabinet of Dr. Caligari* or Murnau's *Last Laugh* or Léger's *Ballet Mécanique* but this could be done only in out-of-the-way corners of large cities and not at the Roxy in New York or at the Balaban and Katz palatial and perfumed Chicago Theater in the Loop.

For American architecture the movies posed no direct new problems. The cloak and suit makers who became first New York's and later Hollywood's cinematic tycoons had taste only for extravagance and a nose for the kind of delusion the public would take to. Movie theaters, or houses for magnates and stars, all called for the same program, something a little too big, a little too noisy, a little too bizarre, a kind of building that stopped just short of being a stage set, that was as artificial as the loving and surprised greetings with which the actors accosted each other in public. Nothing contemporary was needed. The new technical requirements were primitive. Almost any style would do that would lend itself to grotesque overornamentation, whether it was the preferred Italian or Spanish Baroque or Moorish, Gothic, Egyptian or Chinese.

At a deeper level the movies, along with the radio, did contain the power to expose large portions of the American people to some common standards of dress, clothing, manners, speech, even architecture. The movies had the advantage that many of these tastes can best be cultivated by vision. In the event they proposed no crusade, contaminated only in a mediocre way, elevated not at all. In the main all they really offered was another version of the steady threat to American individuality or American regionalism that was implied in the mass production of automobiles, of clothing, of soup, of housing, or of ideas. The mass media had the power to create a higher public taste or a lower one, or merely to pander to whatever taste they thought the public had; this is the role most of them chose, most of the time.

The radio and the movies were but two of the most immediately successful operators in the new mass culture. Another important one was born by the actions of two Yale graduates, when *Time* magazine began to influence American opinion in 1923. *Time* was a product of the technology which made its short deadlines possible, but *Time* owed its success to efficient, sometimes ruthless management, and to an idea. Affecting no editorial policy, every piece of news reporting was an editorial or a criticism. Moreover the editorials and the criticisms were anonymous. The criticism seemed to be criticism by committee and therefore to have more authenticity than the writings of an identified individual. *Time* was favorable to change and to much contemporary arts and letters. It struck useful blows (and so did its offshoot *Life*) for the public observation of and even favor for new things in the visual arts. In these respects it was more responsible and more creative than the movies or the radio. In the decades to come new journals of this type influenced general public opinion and taste in architecture and the arts as no earlier journal had ever succeeded in doing. Often it seemed that they were more interested in discovering new talent than in perpetuating old. The role of kingmaker can be too heady.

I O

THE ADVANCES IN THE OLDER TECHNOLOGIES WERE STEADY THOUGH TO the public they may have seemed less spectacular now that the novelty was gone. But the increase in use of electricity, for example, *was* spectacular. If the index of population increase for the period be taken at 100, the index of increase in kilowatt hours of electricity stood at 350, of residential consumers at 435, of kilowatt hours consumed in residences at 917, electric-lamp production at 398, while the index for lumen hours was 2930. Thus the lamps were larger, brighter, and more durable, and the number of lumens supplied per capita increased by nearly thirty-fold. This great invasion of night, Howard Mumford Jones suggests, had the profoundest effect upon the time sense, the space sense and the color sense of Americans. It also more effectively divorced them from a firsthand acquaintance with natural phenomena. They came to make less sharp distinctions between night and day, at least in the cities where most of them lived. They lost some of their seasonal sense. Most of all, perhaps, they lost any contact with primal sources, did not know or care whence their water, their light, their clothing or their food really came.

There were numerous minor changes in the building technologies. Steel structures were simplified but generally only along lines already well established and by way of larger or more elegant designs rather than by new ones. The Bear Mountain Bridge of 1632 feet in 1924 was stretched in 1931 to be the George Washington Bridge of 3500 feet. The Woolworth Building shot upward so that the Chrysler Building at 1046 feet and the Empire State Building at 1250 feet were 62 feet and 266 feet higher than the Eiffel Tower. When other ways for using steel were suggested in America they were likely to be fanciful like the suspended roof of the Transportation Building at Chicago's Century of Progress or R. Buckminster Fuller's demonstrations of tension in his Dymaxion House. Throughout the period, Mies van der Rohe's project for a glass tower, put forward in 1921, was left strictly alone except in the avant-garde magazines.

The dramatic uses of concrete were also reserved for a later time. In Europe parabolic arches were used for balloon hangars; Freyssinnet produced amazingly thin reinforced slabs of concrete bent into vaults for some locomotive sheds at Bagneux, France in 1929 but they seemed suitable only for things like locomotive sheds. The Swiss Maillart designed thrilling bridge arches out of concrete but even in tolerant Europe you had to search them out mostly in the remote cantons. In America there was nothing to suggest that architects found them fine, if they had found them at all. The problem of restoring Colonial Williamsburg or of carving a South Dakota mountain into the portrait busts of several former presidents was of more concern to the actual discussions of 1927. The War Memorial Opera House in San Francisco was dedicated late in 1932 by a performance of *Tosca*; it asked nothing new of engineering or of art and was itself an architecture consonant with Puccini.

There were of course many little contributions to efficiency: bulldozers, polishing machines, jets, cranes, scaffoldings, elevators, chutes, paint sprayers, cement guns, caissons, salamanders, and other ways to help winter building, and unless these had been used intelligently and to the hilt a monumental structure like the Empire State would have been quite impossible. There were improvements in the quality and consistency of cement, aggregate and the resultant concrete; there were the efforts of John Earley to make new and handsome concrete textures by brushing the cement surfaces away from selected colored aggregates. There were Frank Lloyd Wright's experiments in textile block construction which was the principal thing that interested European delegates who in any event were not interested in any other American architect. Glassmakers were learning to draw larger and purer sheets, to make them more consistently, to temper the glass against shock, to make it resistant to heat, translucent to some ultra violet, to tint it. They were developing industrially what was historically one of the oldest forms of glass, the thread. From this came new textiles and insulating blankets. Other insulating materials were being invented too, heat absorbents, sound absorbents, ways to reduce the reverberation in a chamber, to keep the sound from reaching another room. A science of auditorium acoustics was being born in the work of pioneers like Sabine and Watson; and of the proper physiological environment for the human body, especially the thermal environment, in the work of C. E. A. Winslow, sponsored by the John B. Pierce Foundation. Air-conditioning and ventilating systems were being invented or refined and thus engineers and scientists were creating a situation in which a sharper definition might be made as to what human beings needed from a given room and more satisfactory ways of providing for that need. These artificial environmental controls would become almost a standard element in the architect's kit bag later although the actual performance of air conditioning, of insulation, and even of acoustic design might remain tricky and not quite predictable for a long time. They would relieve the architect of any regional limitation but at the same time they would encumber him with the demand for a great deal of space for the ducts and other things that the environmental services demanded. But in 1933 all this was merely a promise as were resin-bonded plywoods and porcelain-enameled iron sheets. Buckminster Fuller's Dymaxion House called for a number of materials which, hypothetically possible, have not even yet been brought to the market place.

Behind all these detailed changes, mostly improvements, there was the feeling that architects must somehow come seriously to grips with the new techniques of mass production which were obviously changing the economy of so many things other than building. Michael A. Mikkelsen summed it up in 1929, saying that the outstanding problems of architectural practice were how to adjust design to the conditions created by mass production and how to adjust the practice of architecture to the conditions which tended to segregate architects into groups of specialists — on hospitals, schools, banks, and so on.

Both problems commanded attention in the field of housing. There was a general feeling that there must be an enormous market for a good and inexpensive detached house, that good dwellings might be more important to the national welfare than good automobiles, that good houses obviously cost too much, that it should be possible to design them for mass production and that not enough was being done about it. Some large companies like Johns-Manville and the United States Steel Corporation carried on desultory, modestly financed, almost entirely empirical investigations. The American Radiator Company maintained its captive John B. Pierce Foundation which was ineffective in its construction research. Sears Roebuck relied mostly upon attractive financing and found itself in the curious position of being a national manufacturer and distributor which had no real control over the quality of the houses it sold, since so much depended on the local arrangements. Many individual inventors including several architects tried out their dreams for a mass-produced house, almost universally with no success.

Lawrence Kocher and Albert Frey proposed an *Aluminaire* House supported on six duralumin columns standing inside the walls, thus offering a hung construction such as would be common in big buildings later. They put up a full-scale model in Grand Central Palace for the New York Architectural League Exhibition of April 1931 and later reërected it as a permanent summer house for architect Wallace Harrison at Syosset, and that was about that. Robert W. McLaughlin, Jr., another architect, designed the Motohome, based on a frame and asbestos-cement panels plus a lot of equipment. Assisted substantially by Gerard Swope and other important industrialists, he organized a corporation, American Houses, Inc., which stayed in business for years and sold a good many houses filled with gear including a month's supply of canned food but never became a real industrial giant although for several years it showed substantial profits. American Rolling Mill tried to find ways to use more strip steel in housing by designing what was essentially an all-metal chassis. Grosvenor Atterbury continued his experiments with concrete and finally invented a nailing concrete which he formed into blocks. The American Car and Foundry Company became interested in this by 1919 but by 1921 work at the demonstration plant stopped. At that point the inventor concluded that a proper method had been found, that one method of production applicable to successful commercial use had been developed, but then drew the other highly important and disappointing conclusion "that no commercial concern could be expected to solve these problems scientifically, economically, and rapidly with the sole object of creating a new basic industry devoted to the production of minimum-cost housing; that such work could be done satisfactorily only by some non-profit agency."

Such a confession was a retreat from the whole notion of successful pre-fabrication and the history of American private enterprise as it had been conceived up to then. Only the minor successes of American Houses and National Homes have suggested that Atterbury was wrong and no large company seems ever to have gone at the problem whole-heartedly.

Steelmakers all too often simply sought, by prefabrication, to put more steel into a house, even where it served no useful or economic function; other designs relied on precut wooden frames and panels; or concrete precast into all sorts of interlocking shapes or poured on the job in all sorts of standardized forms. Among all the experimenters, none was more devoted or more prolific of a variety of ideas than Albert Farwell Bemis of Boston and none spent more personal time and fortune on the experiments.

But in the end all of them really came to naught. Although some of the companies remain, although a few may have made small profits, the fact is that their history bore no resemblance to that of the motor industry; even today the factory-built house accounts for but a minuscule part of all the housing production in the country.

World-famous inventors like Thomas A. Edison and Simon Lake tried and failed. Elaborate schemes of financing, imitating those which had been used by Electric Bond and Share, were brought in and did not succeed. Howard T. Fisher in his proposals for General Houses had a scheme for integrating existing producers like the Pullman Company into a cooperative productive and distributional effort. If you believed the right issue of *Fortune* you would have thought that this show was really on the road.

The high point of the movement was no doubt reached when each of many producers and inventors actually erected single demonstration houses at Chicago's Century of Progress Exposition in 1933. The houses attracted few sales and many of the producers could not have made sales if asked to; the main effect in the long run was to acclimatize many Americans to some trivial changes in interior design and decoration and one or two other features, of which the parade was unfortunately led by the corner window. When the New Deal entered upon its housing program and sought to put every American resource to work, none of the great exhibitors at Chicago was really ready to make a major contribution. After that the romance of prefabrication never seemed quite so attractive again. The questions that were unanswered in 1933 could still be posed in 1960.

More quietly, mass production was moving in on the details of architecture. Individual parts — windows, radiators, ducts, panes of glass —

were becoming standardized in shape and sizes. For a full realization of
the potential benefits, architects needed to discipline themselves in a
way to which they were unused and of which most of them were suspicious. Standardized parts did not necessitate standardized buildings
as Bemis was constantly asserting about his modular proposals. The
German architect Walter Gropius praised the standardized part on both
ideological and aesthetic grounds. But large buildings used so much
of everything that they could really establish their own plant standards
and make their own module independent of any national norm. Little
buildings were usually in the hands of little men and such men feared
the "menace to design" of any standardization. Thus the profession
was unable and unwilling to take any concerted action although it did
set up committees. Buildings were partly standardized and partly not.
A few of the benefits of mass production were reflected almost acciden-
tally while many potentials went quite unrealized. Buildings were moving to an over-all standardization while preserving costly independence,
even anarchy of dimensions. So the editor of a leading American architectural journal could still truthfully write in a private communication
in 1956, "Having just gone through a hospital, a high school, and a
housing project under construction, I cannot testify to any influence
from objective technological improvements, such as the use of the
module, prefabrication, or whatever. Tile is still cut and fitted around
door frames, flooring is still laid by craftsmen on hands and knees."

This was surely one of the great recent failures of American technology and industry. Probably everybody was to blame; not enough imaginative men found themselves drawn to the technological problem
as they were to the problems of flight; no entrepreneur of enough
stability and power was interested enough, resourceful enough and determined enough. The organization of labor, of the politics of business
supervision, of the whole process of making a building was almost certainly in opposition. And what of the architects? Not solely culpable,
can they escape blame on the ground that it was somebody else's business?

On balance it seems we must say that the architects of 1913-1933 in
America failed their times. They were able to use modern industry
efficiently to make the Empire State Building but could not harness
themselves or the building industry to housing, or even to mass production in general. Buildings, therefore, suffered some of the limitations
of the new production without reaching to grasp its potential benefits.
The craft disappeared but the machine was not put to work. In all this
the architects were naïve when they were even interested. They were
incredibly innocent as inventors. They played with specialization but

hastened to disclaim it in the same breath. In these matters they were, to be sure, acting with less ignorance than they were in acting about science; with less indifference than they were in acting about the automobile and the movie and the electric light or about the social problems of the millions of ill-housed. But even in matters very close to their own business they seem to have been both surprisingly ignorant and surprisingly indifferent, following if you like the example in another sphere of President Coolidge. The charge cannot be defended simply by saying that architecture is not an intellectual business. The successful American architects, with a few exceptions were simply not full of the spirit of experiment that moved many of the painters, the spirit of compassion or angry repudiation that was common among the novelists and poets, the spirit of dedication to search that marked the scientists.

I I

IN SUCH A CLIMATE IT IS NOT SURPRISING THAT THEY IGNORED OR DEPRE-cated the important buildings and writings that were appearing in Europe, such as Mies van der Rohe's Glass Tower Project of 1921, Gropius's Bauhaus at Dessau of 1925, Oud's Café de Unié at Amsterdam of 1925, Aalto's Library at Viipuri of 1927, Le Corbusier's Savoye House at Poissy of 1929, the Siemensstadt Housing, the Tugendhat House, the Sundahl Cooperative, the Swiss housing at Neubühl, Le Corbusier's model for La Ville Radieuse. American architects might read Sullivan's *Autobiography of an Idea* now that he was dead but they gave shorter shrift to Le Corbusier's essays or to Paul Nelson's project for a City Hospital at Lille. The Chicago Century of Progress revealed its half-baked, halfhearted ideas in the same year that the Nazis were dissolving the Bauhaus. Fuller's Dymaxion House, Wright's Southern California houses, were also ignored. Current and choice were the Nebraska State Capitol, the Palmolive Building in Chicago, the new Bosworth complex for M.I.T., and the overcited Empire State. A civilization may provide its architectural symbols without intending to. The admired American buildings were appropriate to an age of complacency. The successful American architects of this day were complacent too.

This was not true of all the American artists. It was not true, for example, of the composers, who were entering upon a very experimental age. The period began with two great Europeans, Stravinsky, leader of the neoclassicists, and Schönberg, leader of the atonalists. Each wrote a fundamental statement just about when the period began. Such composers were trying, as the European architects were trying, to find out how they could break up the long-standing relations between the various traditional elements and recombine them in greater freedom. Alongside Europeans like Stravinsky and Schönberg, Prokofieff, Bartók, Webern and Berg, Milhaud and Honegger and Hindemith, Americans such as Piston, Sessions, Thomson, and Copland were working. It becomes clear in an instant that the work in American music was far more experimental than in architecture.

Also, the best writers, European and American, could not be accused of complacency about their times and their world although their standards of criticism and the things they chose to criticize were different. In France, for example, there was a towering group of novelists and poets headed by Proust, Valéry, Mauriac, Gide, Claudel, and lesser figures like Colette, Apollinaire or Cocteau. Among all of them there was a great uneasiness about the world. It was not a question limited to life in France or even life in the twentieth century, but rather a questioning of the human condition itself. Each in his own way, Joyce, D. H. Lawrence, Aldous Huxley, Mann and Hesse, were asking comparable questions. They were not all questions by outsiders. They did not have a monolithic point of view except on one point — that the individual in Western society was having a bad time and needed to take a new look.

American writers were thinking about the same things but in a delayed way, at a more parochial level, with more attention to the details of American life, more materialistically, less symbolically, with less style and, although angry, really with less pessimism as well. Most of the American writers, indeed, continued to use methods that no longer seemed appropriate to Europe which welcomed only Dos Passos, Hemingway and Faulkner as important.

After the first war, even before it, the typical radical and socialist literature was dying away. Of course there were remaining areas of protest. But Americans seemed to be generally prosperous, dressing up to go on what Scott Fitzgerald called "the gaudiest spree in history." There was too much success.

It was not really different a decade later when the success was not so evident. Some American writers were frightened and angered by the Sacco-Vanzetti execution, and Dos Passos stormed, "All right, we are two nations," but he was no revolutionary. Calling the novelist an "architect of history" he retained independence, refused to be an "artist in uniform," as Max Eastman called the Soviet writers.

The dedicated Communists were not good writers. They were trying to find glory in the American worker, a glory which he hastily disclaimed. In 1921 in *The Liberator* Michael Gold had defined "proletarian literature" that would be produced by men who would not be like the artists of the past, artists who had held themselves aloof from the people, even felt contempt for them, and as a result had become sterile. "The new artists of the people, on the other hand, will learn what Life is from their solidarity with the eternal, yea-saying masses." The social revolution was a religion of the new artists, Gold declaimed, and the American people would now be ready to "put forth those huge-hewn poets, those striding out-door philosophers and horny-handed creators of whom he [Whitman] prophesied." They would now be ready to follow "the massive labors of the earth-born proletarian culture." But the great roughhewn poets and the horny-handed creators did not stride forth from the nonexistent proletarian faubourgs.

This does not mean that the intellectuals and the writers of America were content. Indeed they shared an excitement to which the architects were immune. In 1913 they had been happy about the future. They thought a new America was on the march. John Butler Yeats announced, "The fiddles are tuning as it were all over America." Ezra Pound, acting as first foreign editor of Harriet Monroe's magazine *Poetry*, proclaimed an American Risorgimento that would make "the Italian Renaissance look like a tempest in a teapot."

The optimism faded away with the war, with the repudiation of the League of Nations, with the peccadilloes of Harding, the indifference of Coolidge and the ultra-conservatism of Hoover. The intellectuals found themselves again forced into revolt but the taste for proletarianism had dulled too and other ways had to be found.

The novelists continued to berate America in a quasi-naturalistic manner but now the butts of attack were not the great cities and the great tycoons but the little towns of Winesburg, Ohio, or Gopher Prairie, Minnesota; the targets were middle-class men and women like Carol Kennicott or George Babbitt just as they would later be the gray-flanneled men of Madison Avenue and suburbia. Unlike the contemporary writing of France the revolt was not, as Kazin notes, concerned with great questions but with "the sights and sounds of common life." In opposition to them stood the Baltimorean sage with the blunderbuss leveling shafts at all middle-class morality, and his disciples Nathan, Hergesheimer, and Cabell. Each in his way tried (and failed) to outdo the Mencken pronunciamento, "If I am convinced of anything it is that Doing Good is in bad taste."

The poets felt more of the world pain. Beneath their loving scenes Frost and Robinson etched the tragic aspects and the complexities of

American existence clearly enough. T. S. Eliot was the "laureate of nostalgia, of dwindling hope." *The Waste Land* of 1922 expressed the feeling of many Americans towards their times by examining many failures and disintegrations in an arid world that had once been green.

However they resolved their personal philosophies, the poets were moved by greater and more profound discontents than the novelists. In this they joined hands with their leading French colleagues. They were personally ill at ease with and socially suspicious of science, the new applications of technology, the ugly cities, the anonymous crowds, the incessant din, the cheap ways of making money, the cheaper ways of spending it, the worship of commercial success, however attained; the billboards affronted them and so did the radio, the movies, Clara Bow, the Charleston, Teapot Dome, Coolidge's Indian headdress; in short they rejected everything, big and little, that the middle generation of the middle class seemed at least to be content with.

Who were the architectural counterparts in America of Eliot, Faulkner, Dos Passos, Fitzgerald and Hemingway? The answer is none, really. Nearest were the less famous people who clustered around the housing movement: Arthur Holden with his early studies of the economics of mid-Manhattan; Clarence Stein with his planned communities, often done with the help of Henry Wright; Frederick Ackerman and Robert Kohn; all oriented in the general direction of Sir Raymond Unwin. But these men were not then regarded as very important architects and none of them was really ever an artist. The only great architectural artist, Frank Lloyd Wright, could hardly have been less interested in the social problem.

But artistic or not, the leadership of Stein and his associates did become important for the country when the New Deal offered them a chance to work at the vital center.

Before this happened most of the architectural attitudes had to be expressed by critics or by architects turned critics. It was the words and not the buildings that had to do the speaking. This is always unfortunate for architecture is not, finally, a matter of words. But in such a time it was inevitable that the leaders should be writer-architects like Clarence Stein or Henry Wright, historical critics and social philosophers like Lewis Mumford, then at the height of his powers and influence though not of his acclaim which came later, or sociologists like the young and ardent Catherine Bauer. Few of them were then identified nearly so closely with architectural reform as with political and economic housing reform and they worked more for social change than for a change in architecture — which is perhaps just as well. But Mumford wrote penetrating and important criticism of individual buildings while also preaching persuasively the theories of his idol Patrick Geddes improving and fortifying them as he did so. When the right moment came the work for which Stein and Henry Wright were responsible, and which Mumford and Bauer publicized, had a benign if brief effect upon the American scene, regrettably partial, regrettably ephemeral.

I 2

AMERICAN SCULPTURE AND PAINTING OF THE MOMENT STOOD SOMEWHERE between the architecture and the literature but was less experimental than the painting and sculpture abroad.

In Europe a certain tranquillity hovered over the arts for a few years after 1915. Cubism had worked itself out. The new movements had not clearly emerged. Painters played with mannequins that were modestly Freudian, tentatively symbolic; Picabia tried to construct machine ballets and to personalize the machine as in *La Parade Amoureuse*. Léger tried to stress the importance of the machine but more and more abstractly. Amadée Ozenfant and Jeanneret issued their purist manifesto, *Après le Cubisme*, in 1918. This said in effect that cubism had become purely decorative and that it had adopted elements of impressionism from which it ought to be purged. This effort to "reconquer the plane surface" was an essential element in the new architectural thinking. So were the architectonic studies of the constructivist Malewitsch. But the most concrete architectural stimuli came from the movement of the neo-plasticists called *De Stijl*, founded in 1917 by Theo van Doesburg. It included Mondriaan, Oud and van Eesteren. Best remembered through the early constructions of van Doesburg and the late flat, linear and usually rectangular abstractions of Mondriaan, it obviously, almost too obviously, suggested the inner space and even the façades of buildings that were to come; but it also repeated messages that had been stated in Frank Lloyd Wright's Unity Temple more than a decade before. The abiding principle insisted that "the universal is simple and through that abundant." The application forced concentration on the purity of planes and color.

The disciples of this movement were direct and forthright and reveal that even fellow soldiers in a movement can have differences. Today we recall the Bauhaus as one of the most influential forces in the modern movement up to the time when Hitler destroyed it. Certainly its subsequent influence on American architectural education was more than substantial. But van Doesburg went to the Bauhaus in 1921 and announced that it was romantic, that it permitted and even encouraged a

contradiction between theory and practice, between the functional theories of its architects and expressionistic abstractions of some of its artists
like Klee and Kandinsky. In other words, it did not have an adequate
theory, it was too permissive.

And indeed the Bauhaus both at Weimar and after 1925 at Dessau
did have its internal inconsistencies and this is a great tribute to Gropius,
who might have been more doctrinaire. Men like Albers and Moholy-
Nagy cannot really be said to be working in the same direction save on
the raw ground of discarding tradition, and perhaps liking each other
personally, as fellow battlers against conservatism.

But now painting would move away from architecture. After 1925,
Léger tried to let color define his objects. This provided a new concept
of mural space but more importantly suggested that interior space might
be less rigid, emulating the "elastic rectangle." This was the beginning
of the end though hardly noticed in America where architects did not
look to painters for suggestions.

One of the great European movements included the many efforts
to exploit the Freudian undertones of surrealism proclaimed by André
Breton in the surrealist manifesto of 1924. Arp worked sometimes with
the surrealistic and sometimes with the abstract, relying equally on
chance and intention, producing in either case ameba-like forms. Miró
combined spermatozoa, breasts, wombs and a humorous outlook on life
which may have meant much or nothing; Klee painted sophisticated
fantasies like *Um den Fisch* which were pitiless if often mystical satires.

Meanwhile Rouault made his highly personalized, stained-glass-like
studies suggesting pathos, and human injustice; Picasso dramatically
shifted from the gently classic *Woman in White*, of 1923, to the violent
Seated Woman of 1927. Braque continued to develop his great and
quiet still lifes. Germans like Schlemmer clung to the expressiveness of
human form however modified; Kandinsky splashed out complete abstractions by 1923; Schwitters made collages of great delicacy and Beck-
man and George Grosz made bitter and completely indelicate observations about human ugliness, physical and spiritual. All this effort was
manifestly very rich, very experimental, very skillful — and sincere; but
it was also very personal and therefore bewildering. How could it all be
called modern painting and have the term mean anything? How could
the work of the architects be so neatly subsumed in a catchy title, the
International Style? But the bewilderment was not limited to the enemies of the experimenters who might have been expected to pretend
bewilderment. It arose because if you believed there were some truth
about the world, and if all the painters were really trying to express
truth, then if some of them were right others were clearly wrong unless

the world was, after all, chaos. In freeing painting from tradition of manner it had also been freed from any common tradition of subject; and the messages of the world of the painters were too many and too contradictory. All they could agree upon was the inviolability of the personal expression. And this very determination to defend the personal expression at all hazard was a sharper indictment of man's twentieth-century condition than anything that the writers had prepared, since it seemed to be a thoroughgoing denunciation of the idea that there was any profit in or even chance for commonalty. If it was the last mad dance before chaos the painting nonetheless provided an exciting ballet.

In sculpture there were semi-realists who made semi-comprehensible human figures, often very sensitive to the tragedy of human beauty as the thin Lehmbruck and the fat Maillol and the polishing Zorach. There were Picasso's efforts at cubistic sculpture and Modigliani's stone heads drawn from primitive African sources. There were the concretions of Arp and his three-dimensional amebas. There were Brancusi's elegantly smooth abstractions of flying surfaces and eggs, Moore's manifold experiments with perforated forms quite architectural and the still more architectonic space-constructions of Gabo, who will perhaps be even more appreciated in the future. A great many much more than competent artists were flinging off a shower of suggestions but the few who tried to work and rework the suggestions to a conclusion were both outpaced by those who moved from innovation to innovation and seemed in the end not to have dug much deeper nor found much more perfection than was implicit in the first experiment. The final judgment on Picasso and the rest may be that they tossed off an enormous number of magnificent half-developed ideas for several arts that might have been.

By 1929 Americans had had a chance to see a great deal of this work at the exhibition with which the Museum of Modern Art opened its doors. But its effects had to come later, for in American painting the stir was much less vigorous and so far as the American architects with commissions were concerned there was no contact whatsoever between them and an even pallid follower of Arp or Picasso either as commissioners of work or as seekers after ideas. Whenever a building with a mural was to be put up, it would invariably be a neo-classic building and the mural demanded was not in the vein of the modern current of Europe.

Occasionally there were summonses for other murals but these were almost always disastrous. Orozco, Rivera, Curry, Benton were commissioned at Dartmouth, Rockefeller Center, Kansas State Capitol or the University of Indiana. The last two made trivial works in uncongenial architectural surroundings and the messages of the first two were too strong for the stomachs of the clients, although Dartmouth at least manfully maintained the painting once it had been revealed. But for the most part, and even in these cases, the architect-clients had no intention of using painters or sculptors at the center of the creative process, even in a collaboration such as that of Goodhue and Lee Lawrie.

Nor were the American painters ready for it, if it had been offered. First they needed to get away from the personal decorative impressionism of Prendergast as revealed in his *Arcadia* of 1917. Marin, Demuth, Sheeler, Max Weber, Stella, and Stuart Davis took some ideas from the Armory Show of 1913 but the new Museum of Modern Art Show left them cold. They were concentrating on purity of light, on good space construction, seeking grand effects still. In different ways they portrayed the complacency of their day or teased it gently. But at bottom the works were romantic American sentimentalities, less obvious than Benton's languorous Mississippi bathing beauty cast in the role of Susannah attracting the eyes of the rural elders, Curry's Moses-like John Brown braving the lightning and the tornadoes, Sheeler's photographic glorification of River Rouge plants, Grant Wood smoothing down the Iowa hills or making fun of the grim-jawed couple of *American Gothic* or the tea-drinking hard-bitten *Daughters of Revolution*. Hopper painted lonely houses by the side of desolate railroad tracks, or picturesque but slightly macabre recollections of late Victorian buildings. Reginald Marsh suggested another aspect of the slums as his *High Yaller* girl flounced down the streets. But none of these was really a serious criticism of America, an important suggestion for reform, or a large experiment with new means of expression, a new adventure in space.

Yet if American architects did not read the kicks to their complacency in the writing of their own land or suggestions for new ways in the work of local painters, they might have found plenty of both abroad. Unfortunately the local journals were not at this moment leading taste. Thus *The American Architect* was more likely to carry an article by Edward Pearce Casey to denounce the awkward appearance of parabolic arches, or one by Lorado Taft on recent tendencies in sculpture which would ignore everyone after Rodin. The readers of this journal might find favorable comments about Letchworth or the Rogers model dwellings on West Forty-fourth Street but they were given much more information on the dimensions of the Temple Antoninus and Faustina or the Arch of Constantine. They would also be told a great deal about the properties of such "interesting woods" as Demerara mahogany, the bullet wood of British Guiana, or Himalayan deodar.

By 1933 the tone of the magazines had shifted and contemporary European work was often published.

There was much to publish. As early as 1911, Gropius had used glass as a screen for iron-framed walls and joined the glass cleanly at the corners in his Fagus Works. In 1914, Behrens, Hoffman, and Van der Velde had shown precedents for the '50s at the Deutsche Werkbund Exhibition in Cologne. Here too Bruno Taut had exhibited a glass house and Gropius his design for an office building. This *"Fabrik"* had an abundance of glass, covered terraces, projecting horizontally planar roofs and at the ends pavilions reminiscent of Wright. By 1921 Mies van der Rohe had published his sketch for a glass tower. Gropius built the Bauhaus at Dessau in 1926. Again there were the glass curtains, the balcony slabs jutting into space. If the reinforced concrete skeleton was heavy it was because of German law. But the glass curtain was ubiquitous, meeting the horizontal white ribbons of opaque wall only at top and bottom and then only as a matter of closure. Here as at Fagus the columns were set inside. Here were many of Wright's principles, the regrouped planes, the many levels of reference, the glass curtains lacking only the solid anchorage to the ground which Wright never forgot.

And there was the work of Le Corbusier starting with that simple and revolutionary drawing of 1915 that showed nothing but four concrete posts, three horizontal concrete slabs and a connecting concrete stair. His major principles had already been demonstrated as Sigfried Giedion so clearly shows — the pillar, the functional independence of skeleton and wall, the free plan, the free façade, and the roof garden — all mightily obvious in this drawing but not obvious to men before. His Villa Savoye at Poissy of 1928-1930 demonstrated these in very pure form. Here the isolated lot had afforded him the freedom to build above the swell of the valley of the Seine. Where Wright would have hugged the rocks, Le Corbusier threw his platform skyward on triumphant *pilotis*. There was his design for the Competition for the League of Nations Palace of 1927, so near to winning but for the surprising defection of juror Victor Horta. Here acoustical and traffic problems had found masterful technical solutions, but, and more important, these limitations of the practical had been used to enhance the design. One could see also his Geneva apartment house of 1932, the Maison de Verre, a late extension of Jenney's Leiter Building and Sullivan's Carson, Pirie and Scott, especially as to the properties of the skeleton now boldly used for residential instead of commercial purposes. There were the powerful *pilotis* of the Swiss Pavilion at University City of Paris in 1931-1933. On the city planning side the skyscrapers-cum-greenspace of the proposal for Buenos Aires were ready for study.

In Switzerland many of Maillart's bridges were long completed, including the dramatic leap from cliff to cliff of the Salginatobel and the refined thin slabs of the marvelous Schwandback bridge. Karl Moser, too, had completed his magnificent, bald, concrete-ribbed church of St. Antonius in Basel. The CIAM had been organized at La Sarraz in 1928. In Barcelona after 1929 there was Mies van der Rohe's German Pavilion whose walls were thin planes of light materials easily rearranged for different spatial effects.

And there was much more. These architects might also have told Americans that architecture was a social as well as an aesthetic problem; they might have reported the change of status that Gropius foresaw when the architect would cease to be wholly subservient to client and contractor.

But when they did see the new European ideas, the leaders of American architecture sniffed. They read with approval Mencken's attack of 1931: "If I were building a house tomorrow it would certainly not follow the lines of a dynamo or a steam shovel." Of Le Corbusier's suburb he said that if it were to be built in America it would appropriately be laughed at. "When men really begin to build churches like the Bush Terminal there will be no religion any more, but only Rotary. And when they begin to live in houses as coldly structural as step-ladders they will cease to be men, and become mere rats in cages. . . . To say that the florid chicken-coops of Le Corbusier and company are closer to nature [than the 18th century] is as absurd as to say that tar-paper shacks behind the railroad tracks are closer to nature."

Comparable pronouncements were being made from the lecture platforms of nearly every American architectural school. At one a thoroughly mediocre critic-architect compared works of Le Corbusier with a Pacific-class locomotive much to the favor of the latter and then announced that neither was, of course, architecture. But more often the European work was not mentioned at all. Fortunately not all the students were hypnotized. Many had seen or would see Europe with their own eyes. They did not all follow their predecessors to the fountains of Rome. Some went to Viipuri, some to Stockholm, some to Zurich, some to Helsinki. When they came back they listened with less interest to the comments of reactionary critics or even to the words of men who, like Raymond Hood and Ralph Walker, had tried, if with only partial success, to find their own version of change. As the New Deal dressed itself to ring down the curtain on the age of complacency, American architecture too was getting ready to wake from its thirty-year sleep which had dreamed of the importance of business in America but had not created an architecture for American life.

PAN AMERICAN UNION

Washington, D. C., Pan American Union, 1910,
Paul P. Cret and Albert Kelsey, archs.

Washington, D. C., Pan American Union, interior, 1910,
Paul P. Cret and Albert Kelsey, archs.

PAN AMERICAN UNION

Worcester, Massachusetts, Worcester
Pressed Steel Company, 1930,
Joseph Leland and Niels Larsen, archs.

PAUL J. WEBB

San Francisco, California,
Hallidie Building, 1918,
Willis Jefferson Polk, arch.

MOULIN STUDIOS, S. F.

WASHINGTON CONVENTION AND VISITORS BUREAU

Washington, D. C., Lincoln Memorial, 1922, Henry Bacon, arch.

GOTTSCHO-SCHLEISN

New York, St. Thomas' Episcopal Church, 1913,
Bertram Grosvenor Goodhue, arch.

CHICAGO ARCHITECTURAL PHOTOGRAPHING CO.

Spring Green, Wisconsin, Taliesin East I, 1911, Frank Lloyd Wright, arch.

EDHOLM AND BLOMGREN

Lincoln, Nebraska, Plymouth
Congregational Church, 1931,
Henry Van Buren Magonigle,
with Robert McLaughlin, archs.

Lincoln, Nebraska, State Capitol, buttresses,
1922, Bertram Grosvenor Goodhue, arch.,
Lee Lawrie, sculptor

EDHOLM AND BLOMGREN

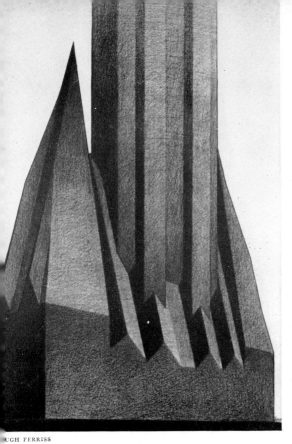

UGH FERRISS

Study for Maximum Mass permitted
by 1916 Zoning Law,
by Hugh Ferriss, 1922

New York, McGraw Hill Building,
1931, Raymond Hood, arch.

MUSEUM OF MODERN ART

CHICAGO ARCHITECTURAL PHOTOGRAPHING CO.

Chicago, Chicago Tribune Building, 1923-1925, Raymond M. Hood and
John Mead Howells, archs.

I 3

INDUSTRIAL BUILDINGS NOW RE-EMPHASIZED THE BELIEF THAT BETTER architecture might promote better business at least up to a point. Some factory designs consciously tried to nurture the team spirit which the Hawthorne Experiment and the work of the industrial sociologist, Elton Mayo, suggested might help to raise output. In 1918 George C. Nimmons, a prominent industrial architect from Chicago, argued that the heads of industry should use improved architecture to keep labor happy. He cited Eastman Kodak, National Cash Register, United Shoe Machinery, Armour, the Shredded Wheat Company, and did not leave out Sears, Roebuck and Company for whom he and his designer-partner, Will Fellows, had designed a plant that year. In this plant the plan had been influenced quite as much by the welfare program as by the production flow diagram.

An even earlier example was the "campus" built for the National Electric Lamp Association at Cleveland in 1914. Abandoning inefficient buildings in downtown Cleveland, this company decided to locate its new plant twelve miles east of the city center on forty acres of wooded, hilly land, readily accessible by trolley or automobile. There the architects, Wallis and Goodwillie, laid out what was called "a university of industry." It contained two quadrangles formed by two- and four-storied buildings devoted to administration and research for the plants scattered all over the country. The architecture was in true imitation of the university, an inappropriate late Georgian, sufficiently pleasing to prompt Montgomery Schuyler to write that it added to the character of the institution but was yet business-like in its convenience, concluding from this scene of cooperative industry that " 'big business' may be not only a very big, but a very beneficent thing." The *Architectural Record* of 1914 thought that Nela Park represented a new era that "Business men are beginning to recognize the financial value of good architecture."

The efficiency studies of Taylor and the traffic diagrams and flow sheets that were the trademark of the industrial engineer made an even more convincing case. In 1914 George M. Price published his influential book, *The Modern Factory*. It suggested standards for lighting, acoustics and ventilation, proposed standard layouts for various production schemes. But such studies tended to glorify the engineer. Matters of aesthetic form were either ignored or discussed only as products of functionalism. Following such theory the Austin Company and other

engineering firms such as Stone and Webster built efficient factories
whose functional approach occasionally yielded handsome forms like
that of the Conowingo Dam and Hydro-Electric Plant on the Susque-
hanna River of 1926-1928.

This dominance of the engineer was not overlooked by industrial
architects, who lost no time in exhorting their fellows to wake up. In
the *Architectural Review* (U.S.) for October 1915, Frank E. Wallis
asked, "Is architecture a live art or only a pedantic profession?" He reviewed a list of important industrial buildings in Berlin, Strasbourg,
Bremen, and Dresden; their merits persuaded him that American architects were backward: "If we had . . . made our architecture publicly
accepted as a live art, the dickie fronts, the raw and unsightly brick
back-sides and the tank sky-lines of New York would never have been
perpetrated." Wallis contrasted pairs of buildings to show that the engineers' solutions had been inferior to the architects'. He praised the
Storehouse for the Hoyt Company at Chicago by Nimmons and Fellows and the Continental Motor Car Factory at Detroit by Albert Kahn
and Ernest Wilby. "To-day America is a great manufacturing nation
. . . The use of Fine Arts in the market-place, in the slaughter-houses,
and in the shoe factories, where steel beams are rolled and where vege-
tables are canned, is necessary and financially important."

The field of industrial architecture now enlisted a number of able
men who continued to be led by Albert Kahn. They created buildings
like Frank D. Chase's Wilder Tanning Company at Waukegan, Illinois,
a simple and open expression of reinforced concrete construction. Kahn
produced a handsome and expressive modification of this structural
system by recessing the spandrels and carrying the piers upwards to support low arches in the Burroughs Adding Machine Building. These
American builders seldom used concrete plastically, seldom realized the
continuous curves that the contemporary Maillart was molding. There
was some development of the rigid bent frame in automobile factories
and reinforced concrete mushroom columns were sometimes used to
support continuous concrete floor slabs as in the Metropolitan Printing
Plant of 1922 at Long Island City. But Americans felt more at home
with linear structures based on grid frames whether the frames were of
wood, steel or concrete. The modules of such frames yielded rhythms
that they liked, such as those of Kahn's Woolen Mills at Mishawaka,
Indiana; and they liked the effect of clothing the frames in brick to provide a foil of color and texture against the mullioned glass, as in the
Lakeside Press Building (later R. R. Donnelley and Sons) in Chicago.

The American industrial architect was at his best when he worked
with steel, gaining relief by the forms of the columns and girders as

Alfred S. Alschuler did in Chicago's A. Stein and Company Building. One of the best examples was a building of about 1930 designed by Joseph Leland for the Pressed Steel Company at Worcester, Massachusetts. It was a prism of steel and glass, strong and clean, bent to form courtyards. The laminated steel columns were enriched only by their flanges and the exposed rivets; the girders carrying the second floor were marked by spandrels containing a floral pattern in iron. Large panels of glass set into the structural frame revealed the floor levels, staircases, and radiators with a directness quite as modern as the Bauhaus of 1926.

But "top" architects seldom undertook industrial architecture and were still less often successful. One exception was achieved by Cass Gilbert, the architect of the Woolworth Building, when he designed the United States Army Supply Base at Brooklyn. He later belied the promise of Brooklyn in his sterile, if stately, United States Supreme Court Building at Washington and the highly conventional Minnesota State Capitol at St. Paul. But the Supply Base showed how sensitive this man could be when he was working without historical presuppositions. The buildings were great gray masses, all one color, all one tone, yet the concrete was modulated by sun and shade, and the simple outlines and surfaces were broken by salients of fire towers, elevator shafts and utilitarian openings. The texture was simple, lacking, as Gilbert once wrote, any "trickets and gewgaws and patterns and . . . fictitious corbels. . . . The logic forbids such intrusions." He was justifiably proud of this work but could not imagine a comparable approach to the architectural problem of the Supreme Court which seemed to him still to cry for Roman symbols of justice.

No architect served industry better in its architectural drive for respectability than Albert Kahn. He was now at the height of his powers, world-famous, commissioned for work in many parts of the world including an enormous task in the Soviet Union. His various small plants like the one for the Ford Motor Company at St. Paul were exemplary arrangements of elements needed for production or display. The main plant at River Rouge, Michigan, begun in 1917, masterfully assembled complex production facilities, bringing together ore boats, and railroads and blast furnaces, rolling mills, dies and assembly lines, the whole grouped so effectively that it enticed photographers like Margaret Bourke-White and painters like Charles Sheeler to record the dramatic vistas of cranes, drive wheels, walls and chimneys. Kahn carried some of this directness and vigor into the administration buildings and research laboratories at Dearborn, Michigan, although the tendency for display here overcame his engineering skill, and he fell victim to the prevailing commercial habit of clothing the industrial firm in classic dress as soon as it was to meet the public. And the minute he tried what he felt to be "more important buildings," he remained a victim of the notion of hierarchy expressed through style and his skill fell away.

Now some concerns began attempts to develop their individually identifying corporate iconography. The Richfield Oil Company built a series of gasoline stations basically similar in form and color, each flanked by a tall steel pylon, as a kind of line of beacons guiding men across the deserts of the West. Sears, Roebuck, using its own architects, Nimmons and Fellows, strove for telling and identifiable silhouettes to characterize their buildings throughout the land. So did Montgomery-Ward. Such iconographic architecture was a new application in advertising terms of the notion of appropriateness which had so long affected church and college architecture. Later it played a part in gaining acceptance for the cubistic architecture of the late '20s and early '30s, when it was adopted by such national companies as those of the Bell Telephone System. Thus throughout the land corporate architecture was tending to transcend regional considerations.

Now the tall office building mounted to its zenith. It seemed to offer the most exciting problem on the American architect's drafting board, the telling sign of a society whose business was business. Solutions changed over the twenty-year period, moving all the way from McKim's classicism to the modernism of Raymond Hood's McGraw-Hill Building and Rockefeller Center. All designers felt excitement in the skyline of New York, all were able to reconcile their aesthetic sentiments with business. Some went much further. Thus Harvey Wiley Corbett explained the causes for the "beautiful ensemble which New York presents. First, the urge for greater beauty in surroundings, and, secondly, the greater mass efficiency arising from the concentration of business." You will not find in their writing any doubts about the efficiency or the necessity for the concentrations. You will find no deeper philosophy underlying design than that our constructions would demonstrate Americans to have been "a people of wonderful engineering knowledge and commercial enterprise." Even the ablest of these designers, Raymond Hood, moved from one traditionalist style to another and so on to traditional modern without formulating a personal philosophy of design that could be compared with Sullivan's or Wright's. In 1927 he admitted he was as much in the air about style as everything else and that if he had been interested in Chinese pagodas at the time he was designing the Chicago Tribune Tower or the American Radiator Building they might perfectly well have come out as horizontal compositions.

One does not have to search far to see that big business offered architects a compelling objective. The skyscraper architects proclaimed their clients' prestige through height, through peculiarities of form, through color, by dramatic night illumination. The publicity features of the new skyscrapers were designed to attract attention whether they were the gilded crest atop the jet black American Radiator Building or the Daily News Lobby filled with geographical and meteorological exhibitions. Searchlights hidden in the setbacks of the tall towers dramatized the buildings at night, maintaining the drama of the evening in April 1913 when President Wilson threw a switch in the White House to turn on 80,000 lamps in the gleaming new Woolworth Tower in New York.

"A style is developed," as Hood said, "by copying and repetition, both destructive to creation and maximum usefulness, which is essential to building." It also depends upon slow refinement through experience. The demands for advertising originality deterred the architects from working out a consistent "classic" form for the skyscraper. As long as each building was supposed to have a unique shape, as long as its usefulness was identified with display and prestige, pure talent was often seduced from clarity to novelty. Corbett was realistic about it in 1924: "Advertising, exploitation, publicity, by whatever name you call it . . . it is the animating agency behind the commercial age . . . in the United States . . . architects have evolved a type of building — the city sky-scraper — so daring, so virile that . . . It proclaims to all the triumph of industrial efficiency." Commerce had come to be placed above art with almost the same reverence as that with which the builder of Chartres might have placed God above his own aesthetic impulses, if they were in conflict.

Persuaded that their main objective was a search for distinctive form, the skyscraper architects moved rapidly to contrive emphatic silhouettes, struggled to be original, abandoned each form before they had perfected it. Technical advances only gave the designer more freedom. Improved skeletal construction, artificial ventilation, lighting techniques, all lessened any need for realistic expression. By 1913 Sullivan's structural realism was almost forgotten; when he died in 1924 Fiske Kimball had to recall for readers of the Architectural Record the contribution "the old master" had made. Only an occasional work like Severance and Van Alen's Bainbridge Building of 1924 remained true to the structural frame. A much more common treatment provided a column arranged with base, plinth, and capital. McKim's Municipal Building set the fashion for classic appliqué; Le Brun's Metropolitan Building of 1913 had shown how to stack a ladder of Renaissance loggias. Charles Platt tried to obtain a massive and unified business block by inflating the Renaissance Strozzi Palace to create the "princely" Hanna and Leader News Buildings at Cleveland in 1922. Benjamin Morris's

Cunard Building of 1921 was another classic column; while in 1924 for New York's American Telephone and Telegraph Building, Welles Bosworth piled eight tiers of Ionic upon a Doric hypostyle hall complete with a frieze of triglyphs and metopes carried on thirty-foot Doric columns!

The classic formula for the skyscraper was ridiculous when sequences of twenty or more plain stories were capped by cornices, temples or domes. Nevertheless its only serious rival was also archeological, emphasizing the verticality of the tall buildings and capping the towers with Gothic buttresses and Gothic ornament. The Woolworth Tower had set this fashion; it was succeeded in 1917 by the equally interesting and simpler Bush Terminal Tower Building, in midtown Manhattan, designed by Harvey Wiley Corbett. This tower gained impressiveness through its isolated position and its vertical expression of the frame. Piers were distinguished from mullions, while the general character of the detail was late Gothic. Since the tower could not be protected from future buildings that might be raised alongside it, the side elevations did not contain the shadow-producing voids and ornamental relief of the front and back. Instead the ornamental work was simulated in brick most of which was buff with white used for highlights and black for shadows. The device revealed the growing concern that the tower should be seen as a whole and from all sides, not merely as a facing for a loft building. It rose steadily without breaks until the top receded in several slight setbacks, suggesting a small chapel, the plinth being modified first to a large octagon and then to a small one terminated by copper finials. The setback was used here merely as a means for achieving a positive termination and perhaps for effective night lighting.

A different envelope appeared in a striking but isolated building at San Francisco, the Hallidie Building of 1918. There Willis Polk produced a fine if uncharacteristic façade, extending the theme of Beman's Studebaker Building in Chicago and with more restraint and skill. The frame of the building carried cantilever floors so there were no columns at the exterior wall; this permitted him to hang an entire glass façade divided into well-scaled panels against which he played brilliantly detailed balconies and fire escapes. A few other glass-walled buildings, such as the more capricious Boley Building built in Kansas City in 1909 by Louis Curtis, had explored this motif of a transparent glass wall enclosing an entire structure, but it had never been done before with such finish. The interesting lead was largely ignored by American architects of the period, however, as were the contemporary examples in Europe, and the message of the Hallidie Building was not really heeded until the middle of the twentieth century when a large photograph of it adorned the halls of Harvard's Graduate School of Design and appeared also in many other schools, now wrapped in the mantle of prophecy.

Whatever possibilities lay in transparency and a revealed frame were overwhelmed by the much-heralded Chicago Tribune Competition of 1922. The newspaper ballyhooed the competition with headlines, feature stories and large illustrations. Every Sunday supplement carried photographs of famous historical buildings and asked what the new building would look like. Drawings came from all over the world and they remain interesting on many counts, including the light they throw on what foreigners thought skyscrapers and Americans were like. A few of the submissions did not take the competition seriously. Some submitted lampoons such as one of an elongated Doric column, or another a skyscraper grown into the form of an Indian wearing a full ceremonial war bonnet. And of the 281 drawings which reached the final jury the majority were still unintentionally ridiculous by any architectural standard. The Italians and the British seem entirely to have missed the point. Their elaborately festooned drawings were filled with heavy classic and baroque detail; one even took the *Tribune* publicity seriously and multiplied the Doge's Palace indefinitely. The entry submitted by Gropius and Meyer from Germany was a stiff and logical expression of the tall frame. It showed much of what Gropius had done earlier at Fagus and would do later at Dessau. The basic skeleton was clear, the fenestration orderly, using the "Chicago" window as a kind of vertically-disposed reminiscence of Carson, Pirie and Scott. The occasional projecting slabs seemed less orderly, the project was quite clearly unfinished and even insensitive. But even if it had been in the best vein of the matured master, it could hardly have prevailed in McCormick's Chicago of 1922. The resemblance to Chicago of the '90s would have been repudiated, if noticed, since anything less romantic, less Gothic, than Eliel Saarinen's tower could not be entertained by the prevailing taste.

Of all the collective foreign entries, those from Holland offered most promise; one entered by Bijvoet and Duiker from Zandvoort was a highly advanced composition of long thin planes cantilevered the whole length of ladder-like bays. American architects did not present anything as good. Sullivan and Wright did not enter; their absence was only faintly compensated for by the entry submitted by Walter Burley Griffin, a former pupil of Wright. In the first two stages of the competition the chauvinistic jury awarded all three top prizes to Americans, and the newspaper proudly boasted that the judgment acknowledged the undisputed superiority of American design. Meanwhile an entry from Finland, the work of Eliel Saarinen, belatedly cleared customs and was rushed into the final stage of the competition. In the last vote, that entry stood beside the design of Hood and Howells, and the jury awarded the Americans the first and the Finn the second prize.

The winning design was built in Chicago by 1925; until diminished by the proximity of other buildings it was the ephemerally impressive landmark of the *Tribune,* though totally retrogressive as a work of architecture. Wright and Sullivan and Root and Jenney might as well have never lived and worked in Chicago. Despite its vertical emphasis, despite its search for light offices, the whole thing was a fraudulent stage set. The unnecessary Gothic tracery ended in colossal and meaningless flying buttresses. The door was the portal to a cathedral. Hood was as pleased as the owners; in 1929 he wrote to praise his buttresses, and the architectural effect of the whole, and insisted that the whole structure "soared magnificently into space."

Others were far less sure about the forty-foot decorative buttresses. They criticized the Gothicism as totally alien to American soil and having less than nothing to do with the structure it covered, much less the activities of the newspaper it housed. They preferred the second-prize Finnish design by Eliel Saarinen, whose tower played freely with the steel skeleton beneath the piers and spandrels; the whole envelope rose with discreet setbacks, each terminated by the jagged silhouette of pier tops, bracketing the sculpture carved above the spandrels, an elaboration of a manner he had learned from the Scottish architect Mackintosh and developed on the railroad station at Helsinki. Perceptive American critics openly suggested that the jury had erred in not awarding the first prize to Saarinen; H. Harold Kent was prophetic when he wrote, "We are confident that the second prize design will have such an effect upon our designers . . . that through its influence will be born a really distinctive, a truly American Architecture." The most fervid admirer was Louis Sullivan who wanted to reverse the verdict of the jury: "The Finnish master-edifice is not a lonely cry in the wilderness, it is a voice, resonant and rich, ringing amidst the wealth and joy of life . . . Confronted by the limpid eye of analysis, the first prize trembles and falls, self-confessed, crumbling to the ground. Visibly it is not architecture . . . Its formula is literary . . . It could be but as a foundling at the doorstep of the Finn." Architectural students in the schools of the day generally agreed. Saarinen's losing design drew so much attention to his talent that he was soon brought to Detroit to build the Cranbrook School, to direct it and to live out his life as an American architect who added much to the texture of the American scene, through his own buildings, through his son, Eero, and through the young men trained at his school.

The prize winner in the Chicago competition at least set one standard; the classic formula for skyscraper design would be discarded. Leon Solon, writing in 1924, recorded its passing, "We are about to bid a glad farewell to the standard formula for the skyscraper design, with its Graeco-Roman or Byzantine feet, its geometrically punctured torso, and its Renaissance topgear." But the replacement was a spate of minor Woolworths and Tribunes as the tall building took its motif from the perpendicular pier; Cross and Cross designed a Gothic tower fifty stories high for 570 Lexington Avenue, New York, in 1930; Day and Klauder appropriated the commercial form for the Cathedral of Learning at the University of Pittsburgh in 1924-1925.

Meanwhile leading architects, having abandoned the classic formula as well as the earlier Chicago functionalism, set out on a search for cubistic masses handled simply. It led them to the tower of setback blocks, the "ziggurats" that Wright scorned. The form was the result of a marriage of aesthetic style and legal restrictions, of cubism and zoning. Painters like the early Georgia O'Keeffe and John Marin and Charles Sheeler began to represent the towers of Manhattan as large soaring masses, boldly simple in silhouette, a vision Hugh Ferriss often published in Sunday supplements. Somewhat later these imagined multi-blocks appeared in actual buildings.

But the form was also a response to legal restrictions. Before 1916 John M. Carrère had drawn a scheme in which New York buildings would be held within the limits of a plane passed from the opposite sidewalk at an angle of twenty degrees from the vertical. The New York law of 1916 zoned skyscrapers to maximum envelopes that were supposed to let light down into the streets. By 1922, a series of studies had revealed that it would be possible to have rentable well-lighted offices on the top floors only by reducing the width of the building at the upper levels where banks of elevators had been dropped off and the central core correspondingly diminished. This relationship between the elevator system and the setback tower, existing even in free-standing buildings, reinforced the aesthetic origins of such designs as that of the Heckscher Building created by Warren and Wetmore on upper Fifth Avenue in 1921. Setbacks frankly acknowledged the prevailing opinion that offices more than thirty feet deep were unrentable; the offices clung to the perimeter of the elevator core.

This new tower form was proposed in a number of graphic studies. Of these the most influential were published by Corbett in *Pencil Points* of 1923. He visualized a tall tower, of indefinite verticality, with tall pyramids clustered about its base. This preliminary diagram was uneconomic since the pyramids dropped some floor area at each story. More advanced diagrams grouped the fall-offs in packages, leaving a central tower that rose inside lower, cliff-like blocks. Corbett himself failed to recognize the aesthetic power of his block diagrams but decorated the envelope with rectangular and circular temples of Greek and Roman origin.

Corbett's study might have attracted less attention had it not included a drawing by Hugh Ferriss. This showed a city of cliff-like towers. Cut off sharply at each setback, the buildings were cubical shapes, with grids of windows placed flush with the piers and spandrels. Ferriss's towering black mass made the skyscraper better and it made the skyscraper city seem not only plausible but exciting. The drawing became the touchstone for a new vision of the commercial skyscraper.

For a while the idea remained only a sketch while architects decorated the setback forms with colorful detail. A good example of the tendency was Hood's American Radiator Building of 1924-1925, a soft black mass with windows blended into the walls, beveled corners and vertical piers crowned by golden decoration. It was described as "one huge cinder, incandescent at the terminals." A retrogression from the simplicity of form predicted in Ferriss's sketch, it was the natural consequence of an advertiser's insistence that the skyscraper be readily identified by the florid character of its summit. Seen from Bryant Park in New York, Hood's example is still effective but the same doctrine led unerringly to monstrosities in less competent hands, the cluttered Paramount Building in New York with its capping glass sphere, the ribbed crest of Sloan and Robertson's Chanin Building.

The commercial spirit led architects to crown their setback towers with distinctive forms often inspired by the ornament and furnishings which had been shown at the Paris Exposition of 1925. Some were curvilinear simplifications of the Art Nouveau work of Horta and Guimard, made suave by machined precision, as in the stainless steel spire on the 1030-foot Chrysler Building at New York designed by Van Alen. The RCA Building by Cross and Cross was a surrealist stage set of cubistic forms intertwined with tracery, pyramids and lightning-shaped spires. A more rectilinear version of Art Nouveau appeared in the zigzags, chevrons, and cubistic forms of the Union Guardian Building at Detroit. One of the best of such efforts was the Barclay-Vesey or Telephone Building at 140 West Street in New York, completed in 1926, for which Ralph Walker received a Gold Medal from the Architectural League of New York and praise from Lewis Mumford. The massing was harmonious with the detail: the blocks, tied together by vertical lines, were broken into setbacks beginning at the eighteenth floor where the office building ceased to house telephone equipment. The weaving in and out of setback masses within the monolithic texture of buff brick and limestone was carried into the ornament, lighting fixtures and furnishings in the lobby. The decoration was no less superficially applied to the structure than the older Gothic and classic details had been, but it bore the imprint of a non-archeological search for an ornament compatible with the tall building's cubistic form. Whether or not a merely American lag behind Europe which was momentarily abandoning Art Nouveau, this was a distinct achievement in a time when the iconoclastic European modernists were turning "ornament" into a word of reproach and parading the misconception that great styles can be achieved without any scale-giving features.

By 1926 everyone in America agreed that the tall building should have a setback silhouette, but there was little further agreement. Some architects continued to insist that the towers carry the mausoleum of Halicarnassus as they did on the Los Angeles City Hall, or a Roman temple such as sat on top of the National City Bank at New York. Some labored for regional interpretations of ornament like the curiously contrived San Francisco Telephone Building of 1926 where Miller, Pflueger and Cantin ended the tiers of spandrels with ornaments based on campaniform flowers and made the entrance an effulgence of Chinese bracketing systems, moldings and screens. Still others carried forward the suggestions of anthropomorphically terminated pilasters that Saarinen had made in the Chicago *Tribune* competition. One of the best of these was Holabird and Root's building at 333 North Michigan Avenue, whose tower, set on a thick slab, had vertical piers capped by figures at the edges and terminals of the setbacks, and this idea, culminating in Goodhue's Nebraska State Capitol, was particularly popular in the West.

It is paradoxical that the search for archeological ornament led in the end to an elimination of all ornament. About 1925 Alfred C. Bossom, an English engineer who was working in the United States, advocated the pyramidal form for New York's skyscrapers, as others had before him. He called the 230-foot pyramid at Tikal, Guatemala, "the original American Skyscraper," and he proposed a 35-story modern building with a similar form and decoration. The idea was reinforced by current Mayan archeology and it intrigued many. Robert Stacy-Judd, writing in the *Architect and Engineer* in 1933, saw in it the long-awaited "All-American Architecture with Ancient Maya Motifs as a background."

Mayan forms had long impressed other American architects, notably Wright whose warehouse at Richland Center, Wisconsin, and handsome textile-block houses in Pasadena looked as though they owed something to Mayan inspiration. But the new grasp on Mayan was directed to the details and not to the forms as Bossom had suggested. The Sears Roebuck Store at Los Angeles of 1926 and the Telephone Office at Houston, Texas, carried Mayan ornament. An important building of the "Mayan Revival" was the one at 450 Sutter Street, San Francisco, built in 1929-1930 by Timothy L. Pflueger. It was a massive shaft twenty-five stories tall, with rounded corners and vertical piers. It loomed above the business district. It had modern notes, a thousand-car garage, broad windows flush with the walls to give a decidedly horizontal effect; but the ornament at the entrance and on the tower, convincing as it is, was Mayan and Aztec.

Designers soon looked beyond the decorative side of Central American architecture into its massive contours. The interest in cubistic forms led them to revalue the Pueblo architecture of the Southwest. Even modernists described Pueblo buildings as America's first examples of cubism; the comparison impressed the Austrian modernist Richard J. Neutra and in his book *Amerika*, published at Vienna in 1930, he displayed photographs of Pueblo architecture placed adjacent to modern skyscrapers, factories, and industrial products. Thus an interest in eclecticism and archeology joined momentarily with a modern taste for cubism.

About 1927 the office building became a cliff-like block of cubistic forms, massive, almost monolithic, the windows alone giving relief to wall surfaces. Even the windows were played down, the piers were broad vertical bands, and solid stone covered much of the space which the Tacoma and other early skyscrapers had given to glass. There were no belt courses; all divisions were accomplished by major setbacks and projections; decorative elaboration was left to movie houses and cheap theaters. The new fashion appeared in Chicago's Palmolive Building and the Daily News Building of 1928, both the work of Holabird and Root, and New York saw a cubistic form at 120 Wall Street, the work of Ely Jacques Kahn, who wrote, "The beauty of a plain surface, relieved in whatever way the artist may desire, is the ideal." The mood prevailed even among traditionalists like Coolidge, Shepley, Bulfinch and Abbott when they designed the cliff-like New York Hospital. Ralph Walker's Irving Trust at 1 Wall Street was a clear reflection of the new fashion. The same spirit moved the facile Raymond Hood and, as always, Hood created one of the best examples of the new mode, the Daily News Building in New York City. There a great mass was reduced to what then seemed an ultimate simplicity. A bold silhouette of setbacks and piers, shaped as tall thin slabs, emphasized the verticality. But at night it was noticed that the lighted offices revealed horizontal stripes.

Beginning about 1931 the horizontal dimension became dominant, a clear reversal of Sullivan's verticality, partly derived from European design. Functionally it was equally defensible. It appeared in New York at the hands of men like Joseph Urban, whose New School for Social Research had a façade made entirely of horizontal spandrels alternating with continuous strip windows, a device Wright had used earlier but which had then been ignored. The façade emphasized the structural function of the beams, played down the columns. Furthermore the façade was no longer a solid mass. The broad horizontal windows divided the building into long continuous planes of transparency and reflection alternating with planes that were opaque. The new spatial and formal effects led Hood to his handsome McGraw-Hill Building of 1932. The sheer unornamented prismatic tower was enriched by the transparency and reflectiveness of the glass walls and by olive-green bands which alternated with bands of dark blue in the glazed terra-cotta surfaces. Only a step beyond this building lay the possibility of an entire curtain wall of glass carried upon floors cantilevered outward from the columns as had been suggested by the façade of Polk's Hallidie Building of 1918 (illustrated in the *Architectural Record* of 1931) or by Mies's charcoal sketch for a glass tower of 1921. About 1930 Hugh Ferriss, too, imagined a skyscraper tower in which glass alone enclosed a series of horizontal planes, the floors. The essential structural and aesthetic principles imagined by all these pioneers, Polk, Wright, Ferriss, Mies, finally found realization in the bank and office building of the Philadelphia Saving Fund Society of 1931. Here the American George Howe joined the Swiss William Lescaze to create a fine tier of continuous spandrels and continuous windows all cantilevered from the columns which he set well in from the wall, as Gropius had done in the Bauhaus of 1926.

We have seen that early skyscrapers were massive blocks. Sometimes they carried tall towers, and in the end they were succeeded by skyscrapers built wholly as towers like the unfortunate Minneapolis lighthouse called the Foshay Building. Now the new characteristic form became the slab, a term applied to the buildings erected at Rockefeller Center beginning about 1930. The slab form had appeared briefly in the early history of the skyscraper, notably in the Monadnock Building and in Wright's unexecuted design for the San Francisco Press Building. The form did not become at all popular until the late '20s, although Albert Kahn's group of classical office buildings for

General Motors Corporation at Detroit suggested it. It remained isolated in works of the late '20s such as the Lincoln Building near Grand Central in New York and the Chicago Daily News Building of 1928. It remained for the architects of Rockefeller Center, notably Harrison, Hood and Fouilhoux, to modernize the slab, to make it thinner in relation to its height, to simplify it and to treat it with characteristic but underemphasized setbacks. The Center's buildings, taken individually, were retrogressive as contrasted to the McGraw-Hill Building; but their form contained a new aesthetic property, the horizontal direction emphasized by the axis of the slab, which became the important element in the grouping of tall buildings around open plazas.

The great slabs of Rockefeller Center paved the way to an important future, offered a new approach to urban planning, seemed to end all the flirtations of the skyscraper with classic, Gothic, Mayan, with elaborate theories of horizontal or vertical structure, with pyramids and setbacks. They opened a gate and it may not be surprising that they caused some dismay although they were not that revolutionary. The New York papers printed angry letters and *Pencil Points* for May 1931 published an article, "The Functionalist Design for Radio City Has Aroused Public Indignation." After Rockefeller Center, American tall buildings would never be the same again. There was a fair chance they would be better.

1 4

MEANWHILE THE NATIONAL IMAGE OF A BANK WAS THAT OF YORK AND Sawyer's classic Federal Reserve at New York in 1927, despite efforts at a late Beaux-Arts simplicity in such examples as Paul Cret's Federal Reserve Bank in Washington. But neither was suited to the skyscraper city and in the end the large banks joined the skyscraper's march towards modernism.

The urban scene was filled with other large structures. New hotels rose in districts filled with offices, stores, and transportation terminals, hotels like the Commodore at Grand Central Terminal or the 1931 Waldorf-Astoria. Despite their creature comforts, none was distinguished; few were in good taste; most were as eclectically stuffy as the Waldorf; and some, unfortunately, were monstrously ornate, like the Traymore at Atlantic City of 1918, with its assorted domes, buttresses, vaults, and towers, producing a riot comparable only to Russia's modern University of Moscow. The Los Angeles Biltmore was characteristic, with its four-story lobby beneath a gambrel roof vaulted and coffered in gold; a huge and ornate balcony stood upon a pair of curved stairs that led to a baroque entrance portico; the building realized the slogans of hotel designers: "Fine motor cars stop at fine entrances," and "Social functions need impressive settings." It was a design exactly like those that were currently winning the best prizes in American architectural schools.

Economics and social change, including the move toward a servant-less society, stopped the building of many large town houses and the new ones engaged the attention only of lesser architects. Old town houses like Vincent Astor's, obsolete, standing on land wanted by commerce, were doomed to demolition. Herbert Croly noted this in 1925: "New York society has changed much since the days of the old Mrs. Astor. It is no longer necessary for its queens and duchesses to build houses in which four hundred guests can be sumptuously entertained. . . . The only new buildings now being constructed on upper Fifth Avenue are apartment houses."

By 1929 the fourteen largest cities showed that three apartments were built for every one- or two-family house, although the figures were deceptive, since so many of those who worked in the city lived in suburbs where multi-family houses were rare, even forbidden. Apartment houses, built principally along main arteries or at the borders of open areas like Central Park in New York City, were reduced to a formula: a stone base with quoined corners, an arched entrance, a brick façade, string courses and banks of double-hung windows. The Vincent Astor Apartments at 530 East Eighty-sixth Street, by Charles Platt, were typical of the severe block-like form, which occasionally was decorated lavishly as in Cross and Cross's apartment at 960 Fifth Avenue.

John Taylor Boyd actively promoted the garden apartment about 1920, while Clarence Stein and Henry Wright made extensive studies of it in the early '30s. There was some experimentation with low apartment buildings grouped around courts, but the tower type enjoyed greater favor because it reserved more land for tennis courts, playgrounds, landscaped areas, gardens and promenades. Alden Park in Philadelphia epitomized the planning although its buildings were traditional. America's best sample of European apartment modernism was New York's Beaux-Arts Apartments designed by Murchison, Hood, Godley, and Fouilhoux. These modern, glass-filled buildings contained suites of studios and bedrooms arranged on long corridors. The ground floors provided cafeterias and other common or public spaces. The modernity of the buildings was here coupled with retrograde site planning, for they filled the site as tightly as earlier buildings had. Thus they showed that modernism could be as much a cliché of style as any other if it were dissociated from its planning principles.

While the apartment houses and tall commercial structures supported larger urban populations, transportation facilities abetted decentralization. The fringes of all major cities burst the previous boundaries. Roads and bridges were extensively overhauled or created, facilitating automobile transportation, breeding larger bridges like Philadelphia's over the Delaware or New York's George Washington of 1931. Commuting railroads added cars and buildings including important commuters' stations such as Philadelphia's at 30th Street and substantial parts of Chicago's Union Station of 1925 or Cincinnati's of 1933. These usually reflected the classical glory of the railroads' heydays though like those in Chicago and Cleveland by Burnham's successors they were sterile ghostly versions of the greater days. Only the functional plan and dramatic arched form of Cincinnati's Union Station of 1933 by Fellheimer and Wagner suggested that railways might still claim the right to provide the gateway to the city.

Now transportation demanded new buildings. The rough strips and rude hangars which marked the terminus of a hedge-hopping airplane were about all that had appeared before 1929 although by then you could find 49 airports and landing fields on the map of the Los Angeles region alone. By 1929 competitive designs for airports were appearing in the magazines and exploratory building-type studies were published in 1930. But the development was embryonic and the problems were not yet really understood, as the details of air transportation service were also in a state of rapid evolution.

The automobile now began to call for its buildings too and not only garages and bus terminals. During the '20s and '30s Ford and Packard dealers enlisted architects to design impressive showrooms such as Maybeck's grandiose Pompeiian affairs for Packard at Los Angeles and San Francisco. Gasoline companies began building service stations in cities and along highways. These stations started the ill-formed ribbon developments along rural roads and they were quickly followed by tourist camps, wayside refreshment stands, drive-in movies and modest stores. At the end of the period in 1933 architectural magazines had published drawings for suburban shopping centers, and the model town Radburn was being advertised as the town for the motor age.

Even as early as 1924-1925 the problem of urban transportation and congestion was looming large. It had not been solved by the City Beautiful, except in isolated grand boulevards which connected public monuments and squares. Better theoretical schemes had been proposed in Europe from Garnier's *Une Cité Industrielle* of 1901 to the exhibitions at Stuttgart where Le Corbusier, Oud, Gropius and Mies showed apartment houses. Under these proposals high buildings covered only a small portion of available land, large open areas were preserved. Of all the architects who worked on such proposals, Le Corbusier was the most imaginative. In 1920 he proposed an ideal project of tower apartments sixty stories tall, rising to a height of 700 feet, separated by 250 to 300 yards of landscaped parks. A drawing of 1923 showed the towers placed among gardens and playing fields, shielded from main arteries which were freed for rapid traffic. As early as 1915 he had proposed to raise all buildings one story above the ground which would be free for vehicular traffic while pedestrians moved on bridges at a higher level. In 1922 he advanced a plan for a whole park-like city of these tall free-standing business and apartment towers, and he contrasted the city of New York to the city model he proposed. Much of his thinking was broadcast in an important book, *Vers une Architecture,* originally published at Paris in 1923, followed by a translation published in England in 1927. The basic ideas proposed by Le Corbusier gained wide acceptance in Europe, and they began to appear in America soon afterward.

In 1923, following the Chicago *Tribune* Competition, Eliel Saarinen made his design for the Chicago lake front embodying some of the new principles of planning; this plan was followed by the Detroit River Project of 1924. His Memorial Plaza set tall buildings in open areas from which traffic was excluded by subways, underground garages, multi-level streets, and walkways. The chief plaza avoided the geometric alignment characteristic of Le Corbusier's city plans, and symmetrically placed buildings afforded dynamic vistas. Those features Saarinen had learned from Camillo Sitte's important *Der Städtebau nach seinen Kunstlerischen Grundsatzen* of 1889, and from Hegemann and Peets's *The American Vitruvius: An Architects' Handbook of Civic Art,* published at New York in 1922. Both books described the rich conformations of famous squares developed in Europe over long periods of time, and the authors favored an aesthetically pleasing city, filled with controlled variety, not one standard, not chaos.

Leading designers now began to study the skyscraper as it might be built under ideal conditions. In 1924, Corbett, always an advocate of building tall buildings in dense surroundings, turned out a serious study of traffic flow in relation to skyscrapers. In the *Architectural Forum* of 1927, he proposed that different kinds of transportation be separated on different levels, the rail traffic underground or carried in the air, vehicles on streets, and pedestrians on an elevated level. In this he built upon some of the ideas proposed by Saarinen in his work for Detroit, and he saw in Saarinen's plan "a very modernized Venice, a city of arcades, piazzas and bridges, with canals for streets, only the canals will not be filled with water but with freely flowing motor traffic, the sun glittering on the black tops of the cars and the buildings reflected in this waving flood of rapidly rolling vehicles."

The new scheme for cities appeared in Hugh Ferriss's *The Metropolis of Tomorrow*, published at New York in 1929. The book opened with a dramatic description of the early morning fog lifting from the skyscrapers of New York. A second section of the book offered suggestions about set-back envelopes and overhead traffic ways. The third and final section displayed an imaginary metropolis of free-standing towers: a government center, an art center, a business center, with large intervals between them. In the Science Zone of this metropolis there would be: "Buildings like crystals. Walls of translucent glass. Sheer glass blocks sheathing a steel grill. No Gothic branch: no Acanthus leaf: no recollection of the plant world. A mineral kingdom. Gleaming stalagmites. Forms as cold as ice. Mathematics. Night in the Science Zone."

The free-standing tower intrigued several designers. Harvey Corbett, writing in the *Saturday Evening Post* of 1926, explained that his Bush Terminal of 1917 was intended to be "a thing complete in itself, with fine, clean, uprising lines, a building that could be looked at from every angle." In the Radiator Building Hood had achieved a tower fronting a large space, Bryant Park, so as to be visible from almost all sides. The Daily News Building, he hoped, might become the first in a future city of free-standing towers. The idea was given rudimentary form in Hood and Walker's unexecuted proposal for Terminal Park, Chicago, of 1930. It received attention in Edwyn Rorke's Alden Park Apartments at Germantown, Pennsylvania, before 1930. Here six tall towers stood free in a rolling landscaped park. The scheme had defects: the rural setting was perhaps too informal; the architectural dress was Elizabethan; but it was a positive statement of a cluster of tall towers grouped in open spaces and it prepared the way for the greater creation of Rockefeller Center.

But even such a singular success as Rockefeller Center did not stimulate enough practical action in the cities. The plans may not have been well enough known by the electorate and in the centers of decision; perhaps the problems the plans were intended to solve were not yet excruciatingly painful or harmful to the prosperity of business and cities; they would have to become more than unbearable before any individual private interest would be prepared to make any sacrifice in the common good and the common good required sacrifice from all; perhaps the solutions did not really seem more attractive to the users than what they found elsewhere in the city. Until the designs were better understood and the pressures more wearing there could be no legal or economic instruments for guiding cities towards a better form. In their absence the commercial components of cities simply became larger and more centralized, while the arteries leading to them were further congested by *laissez faire*. Despite the disaster that we now know was being prepared it is idle to scold our predecessors. Any different arrangement would have required enormous changes in commercial and commuter habits. Workers *might* be brought to live at their places of business but Continental urban mores had never caught on in America; business might change its attitudes towards land ownership and use; both might in time accept more governmental assistance and control. But most American architects of the day realistically avoided socialist answers.

The problem remained then one of improving transportation and finding new sites for large apartment buildings. Consequently in 1924 Hood proposed that skyscraper apartments be built upon bridges surrounding Manhattan, an idea recorded in a sketch by Hugh Ferriss which appeared in *Metropolis of Tomorrow*. In 1929 Hood turned up again with an even more radical remedy, a 45-story building covering three city blocks and containing stores, theaters, offices, clubs, hotels, restaurants, and in the floors above the 35th, apartments for workers. He hoped that many such buildings might unite whole industries, housing "a city under a single roof," as he said in *Nation's Business*. But the American businessman preferred his daily jaunt to the city and his wife certainly preferred the country or seemed to. The automobile bridged the distance and the architects, more concerned with aesthetics than with social implications, did not press their ideas to the point of trying to get them executed. True, Lewis Mumford had begun about 1927 to ask whether the skyscraper was tolerable and to suggest that legislation was required to make it respond to social needs, but the architects Hood and Corbett did not seem disposed to share such liberal social beliefs, while Mumford's writing was more effective as criticism than as suggesting workable remedies. Moreover, most of the discussion centered on the urban residential problems of families of high income.

Nevertheless the period saw a few noteworthy advances in low-cost housing and community planning, including Goodyear Heights at Akron, Ohio, a garden city built by a private company. The war promoted industrial housing, and Lawrence Veiller, an authority on housing legislation, prepared the framework for governmental standards. The principal achievement was to set some low-cost houses in healthy surroundings. George B. Post and Sons planned Eclipse Park at Beloit, Wisconsin, while Sawyer Park at Williamsport, Pennsylvania, and a colony at Erwin, Tennessee, were also the work of architects. One of the best was Indian Hill, an industrial village at Worcester, Massachusetts, designed by Grosvenor Atterbury.

Development slackened after the war but now American architectural magazines began to publish German and Scandinavian work, notably the Danish housing schemes by Kay Fisker. The American designers Kocher and Ziegler proposed sunlight towers, and Duhrie, Okie and Ziegler developed a neighborhood of ingeniously planned quadruple houses at Chestnut Hill, Philadelphia. At Sunnyside Gardens, Long Island, in 1929 Clarence Stein and Henry Wright provided *cul-de-sac* groups of houses running through from street to street but facing toward the restricted part of the community. Their work culminated in Radburn, New Jersey, a town laid out by the City Housing Corporation, where *cul-de-sac* streets were separated from pedestrian ways on which the houses faced. Here Stein and Wright went far in the direction of providing a new social pattern for their town but the architect of the houses, Frederick Lee Ackerman, designed traditional buildings. At that point the social objectives of the planners had not yet been associated with modern architectural form.

It was a strange dichotomy. Architects like Hood and Howe who brought something of the modern European style into American work ignored the social ideas that had been associated with the style in Europe, did not change their social orientation when they changed their architectural costume. Indeed they probably enjoyed the superficial aspects of the new forms while deploring the social and economic penumbra that European theorists like Le Corbusier and Gropius cast around the new architecture. There were too many overtones of collectivism in the writings of men like Bruno Taut, for example, and those ideas, however necessary to the new European city planning, must have been anathema to most American architects of the day. Thus Taut's book, *Modern Architecture*, published at London in 1929, could not fail to raise hackles on those architects who glorified *laissez faire* prosperity even if its obvious Marxism was less distressing to men of 1929 than it was to men of 1959. Taut was an avid proponent of functional architecture. "Everything that functions well," he said, "*looks* well." From aesthetics he moved to morality: "If everything is founded on sound efficiency . . . its utility will form its own aesthetic law . . . The architect who achieves this task becomes a creator of an ethical and social character . . . Thus architecture becomes the creator of new social observances." Unlike Hood, Taut strained to ally the new aesthetic with a social mission.

His social interests took him to Russia during the '20s and he admired the new spirit of collectivism, feeling that the Russians were gaining the advantages of Americanism without "the absurd appendages of American culture." He applauded the communal organization he saw in city planning in Holland: . . . "the miracle actually did come to pass, i.e., the creation of a collective architecture, in which it was no longer the individual house that was of special importance but the whole long row of houses in a series of streets." He thought comprehensive unity was possible, under such collectivism, even when the buildings were made by different architects.

Such social theories, held by many other influential European architects of the day, implied a responsibility to society and to the architectural profession and perhaps a view of the economic order to which American designers did not often subscribe. It was not merely that Corbett or Hood used their facile pens in praise of commercial advertising. It was a more profound question of philosophy. Underlying the eclecticism, for example, of Ely Jacques Kahn and most others was the belief that style was no more than a superficial coating, intended to please without any relation to social objectives, and that modern designs could be adopted quite as readily as Greek or medieval or Renaissance. Such formalism was confirmed by Geoffrey Scott's *Architecture of Humanism* of 1914 which asserted that the aim of architecture has nothing whatever to do with expression of structure, use, function or morality. Its aim was solely to create pleasing forms and it was valuable only because the forms were pleasing. Scott totally disavowed the idea that social objectives were fundamental to style. His perfect formulation of art-for-art's-sake in design appealed enormously to most of the leading American designers of the day.

Indeed men who liked to build great suburban houses and skyscrapers were unlikely to heed any socialist attacks on individualism. Harrie T. Lindeberg, the famous maker of suburban villas, would have thought Taut was silly to say: "The small individual house, built in accordance with the wishes of an individual man or woman is . . . indicative of . . . the delirium of individualism . . . Only by its collection in a co-operative sense can it avoid the dreary schematism of international trash." Goodhue could hardly quicken upon learning from Taut that "Neither the Church, nor Autocracy, nor Feudalism can be regarded as style-forming factors . . . Neither cathedrals nor castles lead the building profession to-day. The fact that such edifices are still being

built cannot disprove the fact that they have relinquished leadership."
Nor could Corbett, Hood, Gilbert, or Wright accept the equalitarian
dogma of Taut: "Leadership has been transferred to other hands. To
the hands of those who erect buildings, produce building materials,
manufacturing them from raw materials, extracting them from pit or
mine, and working them up in factories; to the hands of those responsible for installation and transport, to those who can, in short, produce
everything that everybody needs." At this particular point in their history the thoughts of Gropius and Le Corbusier were not different although Taut went farthest and wrote the most. Reading him and seeing
the housing in Europe, industrialists and their architects could hardly escape the conclusion that modernists might be harboring treasonable
thoughts and thinking of other revolutions than an architectural revolution; so modernism came into some bad odor. Wright labeled the "International Style," "socialistic." Others used even more damaging ad-
jectives.

Similar social theories became more pointed after the depression.
Meanwhile city planning remained formal without regard to centraliza-
tion, traffic congestion, or legal, economic and social bases for better
city plans. In 1929 American cities had 377 skyscrapers more than
twenty stories high. Of that number 188 were in New York City and
fifteen of them were over 500 feet tall. Yet until Rockefeller Center
was built no city had provided an example of how a skyscraper might be
made to define handsome sequences of urban space, nor was there any
significant development of new patterns for pedestrian traffic or shopping centers.

I 5

THE NEW FAIRS HAD NOTHING NEW TO CONTRIBUTE EITHER. THE PANAMA-
Pacific Exposition at San Francisco in 1915 clearly elaborated the City
Beautiful plan with its long axis leading to the Court of the Universe,
terminated by the Art Palace and Machinery Palace, both classical; bordered by domed buildings and confusedly eclectic offerings like Mullgardt's Tower in the Court of Abundance. Maybeck's Fine Arts Palace
was fatuous Piranesi in full color, and, like the fair, offered nothing
to the knowledge of urban forms. San Diego was if anything even less
instructive. It attempted to embody the romance of a high Spanish
civilization that had never been, "to build such a city as would have
fulfilled the visions of Fray Junipero Serra as he toiled and dreamed
while he planted missions from San Diego to Monterey." Such a theory

ignored the historical fact of Serra's modesty but it appealed to Cram and Ferguson as they stated it in the California State Building's torrid Spanish baroque entrance and towers. Bertram Grosvenor Goodhue, the supervisory architect for the Exposition, outdid even the exuberant Balvanera Chapel in Mexico City in his Commerce and Industries Building, and he covered the grounds with polychrome domes which he took with him to most of the permanent architecture he built thereafter. Most of these buildings have been preserved and they contribute today the attractive fairy tale of Balboa Park, sitting above San Diego, but the buildings taught architects nothing valuable, nor did the grounds make any suggestions as to how a city might solve its modern problems.

Thus the City Beautiful movement persisted even though it had become a formal abstraction quite unrelated to the political and social problems of the cities to which it was applied. San Francisco and Philadelphia and Cleveland continued to work on their civic and cultural centers. Their monumental schemes inspired Denver to a reawakened interest in the improvement scheme Charles Mulford Robinson, the City Beautiful exponent, had made about 1904. Modified by Frederick Law Olmsted, Jr. in 1917, some of the scheme was achieved but it was inadequate, not really central, and was far from including the types of industrial, cultural, residential and commercial buildings that Denver actually needed and willingly supported.

So it was for Cleveland, which summoned tremendous energy during the '20s to complete its civic center which was already obsolete. This in turn encouraged leading institutions far from the downtown center to create their own cultural focus in University Circle at Wade Park. Hopes were high for developing the first natural American cultural grouping but rivalries among the institutions and failures to relate the new scheme to a comprehensive economic and social plan for the whole neighborhood and city led only to chaos. By 1938 the circle was a seriously blighted area.

Realistic city planning barely appeared in this time. Planners needed first to know more about society and its operation. The knowledge was long in coming. In 1929 Pitirim Sorokin's *Principles of Rural-Urban Sociology* still described a clear-cut distinction between city and country that was nullified by the intrusions of city into suburb. Adna F. Weber's classic *The Growth of Cities in the Nineteenth Century*, published in 1899, had looked towards rapid transit and the rise of suburbs as the amelioration of city evils resulting from overcrowding. The process was actually going on in the period 1913-1933, but the transportation system and the suburb somehow never managed to lessen overcrowding in the cities themselves. It was obvious that the planners were working with an unrealistic social unit. About 1920, two new units were defined on the basis of economics, geography and sociology. One was the comprehensive unit, the region, which grew out of studies by geographers, introduced into sociology by Warren H. Wilson about 1920. One real experiment in operative regionalism, the TVA, was established by Congress in 1933. The second unit was the neighborhood, which Clarence A. Perry made the basis for city planning in a study published in 1929. The neighborhood was not an aesthetic, purely formal unit, as it had been with the City Beautiful planners. It was a cohesive pattern determined by business habits, topography, physical barriers, street plans, transportation systems, locations of schools, churches, community organizations, social clubs and political districts. The determinants frequently existed within well-defined physical boundaries, as was shown by a study of neighborhoods in Chicago of 1929, which reached the conclusion that "In the planning of a neighborhood unit . . . boundaries . . . physical limits enable the public to see a local community as . . . a distinct entity."

The new determinants provided planners with sociological, economic and legal tools for guiding the growth of cities. Many designers still ignored them for the purely formal schemes of Ferriss or Hood or Corbett. But Lawrence Veiller and the National Housing Association attempted to place sociological foundations under their work. Robert Moses in New York City organized powerful administrative and legal means for public works projects and for preparing vast recreation areas like Jones Beach. Men like Mumford insisted that *laissez faire* skyscraper development, suburb and City Beautiful movements would not alone produce healthy and happy urban environments. The most effective new planner was probably Henry Wright, whose work on Sunnyside and Radburn with Clarence Stein has already been discussed. They followed this with the still distinguished Chatham Village at Pittsburgh. But these were not the areas where many architects had any interest, nor did many of the leaders find it interesting to provide architecture for social settlement houses or YMCAs.

16

THE SUBURBAN HOUSE COMMANDED MORE ATTENTION. UPPER-CLASS SUBurbs, on winding tree-shaded drives leading outward from nuclei of stores and churches, schools and municipal buildings, contained few if any industries or businesses; each was essentially an expensive dormitory. It protected its appearance with legislation aimed at preserving conformity in building height, land use, architectural style, and racial use. The Georgian house set on a broad lawn became the characteristic image of residential America and the lawn was as important as the building. It was in this period 1913-1933 that many of the famous and fancy American upper-middle-class suburbs were developed: Shaker Heights, Lake Forest, the Main Line, Glen Head, Chestnut Hill, Tuxedo, Grosse Pointe.

The emblematic building of the upper-class suburb became the Country Club to which the *Architectural Forum* devoted whole issues in 1925 and 1930. The architecture often resembled that of a stately country house of the ante-bellum South, like Guy Lowell's Piping Rock Country Club at Locust Valley, Long Island. Such buildings were seldom imaginative or significant architecturally, and while Albert Kahn might design the Detroit Golf Club and Robert Kohn the Sunningdale at Scarsdale, the country club set seldom had any desire to employ an artist like Wright.

The prevailing pattern for the country estate remained French classical. The house of Miss Laura Robinson at Greenwich, Connecticut, of 1913 was the Petit Trianon wrapped around modern fixtures. The H. C. Frick estate at Pride's Crossing of 1915 was the tribute of Carrère and Hastings to the genius of François Mansart. Horace Trumbauer worked in the style of the Louvre and Versailles when he did Whitemarsh Hall at Chestnut Hill, Philadelphia, in 1915 and the Rice Estate at Newport in 1920. Even Senator Clark of Idaho wanted Versailles balustrades, formal paneled rooms, and gold-fauceted marble tubs for the house Reginald Johnson built for him in Santa Barbara in 1932, the last of the great mansions. Departures went towards the picturesque where Gothic was favored. Goodhue used it for the Glen Cove estate of J. E. Aldred and it appeared in many other houses such as Rynwood designed by Roger Bullard in 1929 for S. A. Salvage of Glen Head, New York. Sometimes less clear-cut styles than the Gothic or classic appeared in English half-timbered manors like the residence of Clarence Lewis at Sterlington, New York, built by John Russell Pope in 1931. But attempts at forming a new picturesqueness outside the Gothic tradition more often led to abortive monstrosities such as the one Van Tine designed for Henry Ford at Dearborn in 1914, a clumsy and bizarre jumble of log-cabin construction, rustic stone chimneys, Louis Seize balustrades, Jacobean, rococo or Renaissance rooms *a choix*.

Some architects like Frank Forster were specialists in a particular style such as the Tudor but most could satisfy the varied whims of all possible clients. Delano and Aldrich for example summoned a variety of styles to please their clients, H. Payne Whitney, Willard Straight and Otto Kahn. Of all the chameleon designers Harrie T. Lindeberg was the most popular and versatile. At Lake Minnetonka, Minnesota, he provided an Elizabethan house for John S. Pillsbury; Duncan Harris's house at South Norwalk, Connecticut, was rustic rural; H. L. Batterman at Locust Valley, Long Island, wanted Roman Doric, while a slate-roofed Tudor housed Eugene du Pont at Greenville, Delaware; the dwelling for Nelson Doubleday at Oyster Bay, Long Island, was red-tiled Spanish Colonial, and Clyde Carr had a half-timbered dovecote at Lake Forest, Illinois. No two designs were alike, and though he tended to favor picturesque thatched-shingled roofs, Lindeberg was accurately praised for his "freedom from formula." He even put many of these together in the new Houston suburb of River Oaks.

For smaller houses domestic regionalism was durable, even self-consciously defiant against the universalizing technology, mass production, communication, and advertising. By 1927 A. Lawrence Kocher, editor of the *Architectural Record*, thought he had discerned three principal regional styles, the adobe house of the Southwest, the California ranch house and the Pennsylvania farmhouse. There were actually many more: for example, the Mediterranean Renaissance which was locally popular in Florida. There Addison Mizner built the J. S. Phipps house at Palm Beach in 1922, a lesser version of the greatest Florida villa, Vizcaya, the estate of James Deering, which had been designed by J. Burall Hoffman and Paul Chalfin in 1916. Vizcaya was a Spanish-Italian Renaissance-baroque ensemble of terraces, fountains, parterres and perspectives, combined into a fortress overlooking the Bay of Biscayne, and drawn from the Rezzonico Villa at Bassano. Boat landings, Venetian mooring poles, gondolas, a bridge of sighs, a teahouse, cascades, sculpture by A. Stirling Calder, obelisks, potted trees and an Empire bedroom from Malmaison completed the jumble of resort elegance. Unfortunately taste of this sort was abetted by historians like Rexford Newcomb whose book *The Spanish House for America*, published at Philadelphia in 1927, offered illustrations of many houses of Spanish flavor to be seen in California, Florida, New Mexico and Arizona.

Meanwhile the Southwest was spawning a regional architecture derived from rural buildings of Mediterranean countries. Winsor Soule's book, *Spanish Farmhouses and Minor Public Buildings* of 1924, provided the architects with plans of simple establishments, built around patios, surrounded by loggias and arcades that led to living and dining rooms. The houses were low, of one or two stories, with abundant porches; the floor levels and the roof lines could be varied picturesquely. Myron Hunt at Pasadena, Stacy-Judd at Los Angeles, Van Pelt and

Maybury at Pasadena and especially George Washington Smith at Santa Barbara and Ojai all designed ranch houses and villas, some of them tending mildly towards modern forms, by following and modifying the suggestions of the Spanish style. William Wilson Wurster opened his office at San Francisco in 1926 and his early ranch houses stemmed from the historical tradition of revivalism. The one-story grouping he did in the simplest vernacular for Mrs. Gregory in 1927, set in the Santa Cruz mountains, showed how fine such work might be when approached simply. But the romance was still there.

New Mexico recovered the adobe remains of the pueblos, and Texas's Governor's Palace at San Antonio was restored in 1931, concrete and wood replacing the mud walls. A writer in the *Architectual Record* of 1923, Rose Henderson, suggested "The Indians were the first cubists in this country," and she praised the modern cubist revival work of Carlos Vierra whose house at Santa Fé of 1922 was an imitation of the old pueblo buildings. Sante Fé's hotel La Fonda of 1925, the Museum of Art of 1917, and the Light and Water Company of 1920, all by Rapp and Rapp, were Indian pueblos. In 1926 the *Record* willingly went along with the joke by a full article entitled "The Southwest Develops Native Architecture." That joke was less funny in 1929 when it encouraged Albert Chase McArthur to build a pueblo village for the Arizona-Biltmore Hotel at Phoenix.

Except for the California work, the regional stylists most capable of outstanding performance worked in the vicinity of Philadelphia. Built in ledge stone, their houses were picturesque compositions, elementary in geometric form, based on rural French farm groups or the Cotswold cottages of England. Such compositions were not localized, as the Van Schweringen estate at Cleveland shows, but Philadelphia was their chief center. It had many French "villages" inspired by the farmhouses of Normandy that withstood scrutiny independent of the historical details because the brick and stone cylinders, conical roofs, high dormers, and long walls were admirably composed by such firms as Mellor, Meigs and Howe.

Most wealthy clients of a sentimental turn of mind, and this meant most wealthy clients, demanded historical copying and architects abounded to supply the copies. When Mrs. O. H. P. Belmont decided to plant a teahouse overlooking the ocean on her estate at Newport she readily enticed R. H. Hunt, a descendant of the famous Hunt, to design a green-tiled, wood-bracketed Japanese temple, and the *Architectural Record* of 1916 gave over thirteen pages to illustrate the sketches Hunt supplied. In an environment of that kind the creative artist had no place. Nor was he much better off in California where Packard dealer

Anthony had Bernard Maybeck do a Spanish castle complete with moat and portcullis, and William Randolph Hearst employed Julia Morgan, a graduate of M.I.T. and of the Beaux-Arts, to create at San Simeon a castle filled with rooms and furnishings brought over from Europe.

In all this America's greatest architect and his tradition were not quite forgotten. But it was generally asserted that Frank Lloyd Wright was finished. Even Henry-Russell Hitchcock tended to regard Wright's more ornamental work of the '20s as an unfortunate atavism. Paul Cret took the view that Wright and Sullivan had "struggled to open a trail to a barren country" and had survived their own influence. Fiske Kimball said they had been great masters "of a school which is now a thing of the past." Wright was moved to write Kimball: "I have been reading my obituaries to a considerable extent the past year or two, and think, with Mark Twain, the reports of my death greatly exaggerated."

There was no doubt that Wright was striking his own course in a nation that did not worship the artist-architect who worked poetically upon small residential problems, fitting each to his client, the site, the materials, the structure and the program. How far the excellence of Wright lay from the major animus of the times can be seen by comparing any of his work with the Empire State Building, regarded as the chief technical achievement of the period. Many of Wright's projects of the '20s remained in sketch form. Some were baroque fantasies like the project for the Doheny ranch in California of 1921. Others were progressive technically like the project for National Life Insurance Company of 1920-1925. His apartment projects of the late '20s were incredible accordions of concrete and glass forms, richly detailed, and planned to accommodate residents humanely. One of these, the St. Mark's Tower Project at New York, of 1929, was to be a tall tower carried upon a spine and four reinforced concrete vertical fins from which the floors and mezzanine inner floors would all be cantilevered. But none was built then.

Against Wright's eminently individual design, the Empire State diminishes in stature. A pedestrian work, its designer Richmond Shreve regarded it principally as a testament to advertising and economical office space. It rose in a series of setbacks at the twentieth, thirtieth and sixtieth floors to a great pinnacle. Charts of the building operation enabled the architects to accomplish a magnificent feat of planning: "Six months ago," Shreve wrote in 1930, "the working drawings . . . had not been begun; one year from now it will have been completed . . . fifty millions of dollars . . . 20,000 tenants . . . two million square feet . . . fifty thousand tons of steel . . . rising nearly a quarter mile

. . . in a brief eighteen months. Stone from Maine and Indiana, steel from Pittsburgh and Elmira, cement from Pennsylvania and New York, timber from Oregon or the Carolinas, brick from the Hudson River Valley or from the clay pits of Connecticut, glass from Ohio, marble from Vermont or Georgia or Italy . . . from all the world must come together and fit together with accuracy of measurement and precision of time. . . ." Plasterers finished the lower floors before the upper stories were framed, and the top floors were completed while drawings were still being made for the roof. Such standardized work required an enormous office staff of specialists, radically different from the atelier of a one-man designer. Even John Russell Pope, who never was an artist, felt the "commercialization of his profession" in 1931. It was a commercialization entirely unsuited to the kind of beauty Wright was creating and thus the times passed him by.

Yet in this period he built some of his best works. The Japanese called him to Tokyo to build the Imperial Hotel, unjustly more famous for its excessively low ceilings or for having withstood the great earthquake of 1924 than for its innovative plan and decoration. It was in reality one of his best combinations of interpenetrated spaces. Upon his return he created important houses, especially in Southern California and Oklahoma. Vertical and horizontal compositions were sympathetically related to the particular terrain, enriched with patterns molded in structural cement blocks. The Millards and Ennises and Barnsdalls of California resisted the prevailing fashion for Spanish Colonial and gave Wright a few commissions that carried him through this time.

But largely he was ignored and he turned inward at Taliesin East, Wisconsin, creating there a beautiful house and farm, where he surrounded himself, feudally, with young disciples, mostly from abroad where his reputation never faltered. It was a time for reflection, partly self-enforced by rebellion against society, prolonged by the rampant social urge toward standardization and advertising and extended still longer by the depression. But this does not mean that Wright's voice did not continue to be heard. *The Architectural Record* published a series of articles by him in 1927-1928 and there he proclaimed that the architect should be master of the machine and use it creatively, rather than falling victim to "standardization — the soul of the machine." He insisted that architecture begin with the "logic of the plan," and he fought against eclecticism, historical or modern. He insisted further that form develop solely from the personality of the designer, the materials, the site, the structure. To a generation dazzled by the gleaming products of machinery, he recalled the riches that were still latent in the quarry, the kiln, the sawmill. But this was not a message that looked backwards. He was foresighted about the possibilities of glass, concrete, and sheet metal. At Princeton in 1930 he delivered a set of lectures later published as *Modern Architecture*. He seemed then a man out of his time, against the modern style that was appearing in Europe, against almost everything except his own work. No one had an inkling that he, an acknowledged master, would live to see his dreams of the '20s appear in great buildings of the late '30s like Falling Water or the Johnson Wax Building. Certainly no one expected that the St. Mark's Tower project of 1929 would in the end be realized in 1955 as the Price Tower in Bartlesville, Oklahoma.

Wright's followers, unfortunately, failed to grow. Most of them modeled their work on his Prairie architecture of the first decade of the century, never creating anything so fine as the Robie House of 1908. The group was large enough so that it was written about and the world heard of Tallmadge and Watson, George W. Maher, Walter Burley Griffin, and William Drummond. Perhaps the best were Purcell and Elmslie, draftsmen under Louis Sullivan. Their work in Minneapolis was Sullivanesque. After the firm dissolved each designer became increasingly indebted to Wright, as we can see in the house Elmslie did for Bradley at Wood's Hole, Massachusetts, or in Purcell's own house at Rose Valley, Pennsylvania. Although the group emphasized horizontal lines and cubistic bracketing systems, it urged also careful adaptation of form to rural landscape. William Drummond's house in Chicago embraced the old trees on the site: "Because I love trees I bought this lot and snuggled my house among them, so that three big trees are growing through the front porch. I cut a hole in the eaves to make room for one."

Not all of Wright's apprentices stayed in the Middle West. One of them, R. M. Schindler, moved to California, where he built some interesting houses at La Jolla and Los Angeles, notably the Kings Road House of 1922. But the general attitude was against regional modernism. Both Schindler and Richard Neutra spent time with Wright at Taliesin East. Schindler had studied at Vienna under Otto Wagner and worked for Wright at Spring Green in 1918-1921. He supervised the Barnsdall House at Los Angeles and then remained there. In 1923 Neutra came to the United States and in 1925 formed a partnership with Schindler. Their designs showed more careful adaptation to rugged sites than the buildings of the international style, but it was no less mechanized. Schindler's house for Dr. Philip Lovell at Newport Beach of 1926 was a constructivist project in concrete, while Neutra's Lovell House in Griffith Park, Los Angeles, of 1927 was a white-ribboned, glass solarium, cubistic in inspiration. Their work picked up the cubism Irving Gill had used in the Los Angeles house of Mary Banning of

1911, which excited interest when it was belatedly published in the *Record* of 1929 and 1930, but still they received few commissions and these were minor.

The Architectural Forum of 1929 showed what was happening on the East Coast when it published a simplified, traditional house by Julius Gregory with the note, "We are gradually becoming accustomed to 'modern' architecture." The house was a plain version of Lindeberg's French eighteenth-century style and not modern at all but the remark was an admission that the public was being bombarded by modern design. In 1929-1930 *The Record* drew its readers' attention to the Europeans, Oud, Dudok, Brinckmann and Van der Vlugt in Holland, Le Corbusier, Perret, Bonnier, Roux-Spitz and Mallet-Stevens in France, Gropius, Neutra and Mies van der Rohe in Germany. At the same time the Museum of Modern Art rapidly became the propaganda center for the modern movement. The exhibition held there in 1929 and broadcast by Henry-Russell Hitchcock in a book *Modern Architecture, Romanticism and Reintegration* was succeeded by a second exhibition of 1932. Now Hitchcock and Philip Johnson wrote the descriptive and analytical text, *The International Style: Architecture Since 1922* which supplied a new and unfortunate tag to the movement, from which it has never quite been able to escape. The catalogue contained a foreword by Albert Barr. The new aesthetic, he asserted, was based on structure, materials and planning, in which volume was defined by planes as opposed to being enclosed by solids; regularity of repeated parts produced order in compositions that disregarded symmetry and tripartite division; compositions had the flexibility of asymmetrical balance; and the forms gained aesthetic worth through the technically perfect use of materials, without any ornament. The exhibition emphasized four founders of the international style: Gropius, Le Corbusier, Oud, and Mies van der Rohe, and it included Wright as the original inspiration.

The aroused interest in modern design had commercial implications. These were admitted by Norman Bel Geddes in his book *Horizons*, published in 1932. "Progressive business means new ideas, and new ideas invariably stimulate progress in design; progress in design brings technical progress. The three go hand in hand." In 1927 Bel Geddes broke from theater design when movies became popular to turn his attention to streamlined motorcars, ships, factories, and railways. His book revealed enormous excitement with air terminals, the Twentieth Century Limited of 1924, Sikorsky's amphibian plane, the S.S. *Bremen*, Malcolm Campbell's *Blue Bird* racing car of 1931, six plow blades laid side by side and strikingly photographed by Margaret Bourke-White.

"We are entering an era which, notably shall be characterized by design in the arts, painting, sculpture, music, literature and architecture that shall inspire the new era . . . in social structure to insure the organization of people, work, wealth, leisure . . . in machines that shall improve working conditions by eliminating drudgery . . . in all objects of daily use that shall make them economical, durable, convenient, congenial to everyone." Significantly Bel Geddes set a photograph of the Lycoming airplane motor, 1929, besides the Rheims rose window of 1212.

A little modernism appeared in a few East Coast houses at the end of the period. Many were designed by immigrant architects such as Kem Weber and Joseph Urban. William Lescaze from Switzerland teamed up with George Howe in Philadelphia and produced a number of houses including "Square Shadows," the residence of William Stix Wassermann at Whitemarsh, Pennsylvania, and the Speiser town house in Philadelphia. Raymond Hood moved into the modern camp with a house for Joseph Patterson, the owner of the New York *Daily News*, at Ossining, New York, in 1930. Such work was hardly representative of the residential work in America but the decade 1918-1929 did see domestic style go from the Colonial mansion and the Gothic manor to the central-masted Dymaxion House of R. Buckminster Fuller, though Gothic manors were much more common than "chicken coops on stilts" in 1933.

Thus it was a motley and unkempt architectural picture that America presented. European visitors could not comprehend what they saw, though they often found it fascinating enough so that they stayed. Erich Mendelsohn stayed though he could not reconcile the enormous contrasts between industrial products and domestic architecture; between organization in business and chaos on city streets. His book *Amerika*, published at Berlin in 1928, attempted to piece out this strange country across the Atlantic. America was first of all the New York skyline, the massive composite of the skyscrapers, the canyon running between them. He made a pointed emblem out of Trinity Church's dwarfed spire. Times Square was a blur of light and motion; the frothy elegance of Fifth Avenue and Park Avenue was seen behind a screen of Rolls Royces. Chicago was flour mills with grain elevator silos and conveyor ramps, and the harsh shapes of steel and buildings in the Loop. A long section of the book dealt with the symbols of money, from classic banks to Gothic skyscrapers. He contrasted these with the industrial architecture of cylinders, flutes and cubes. Our grotesque forms baffled his German sense of order: Broadway by night and by day; the subway; huge billboards; Chicago alleys. Then there was the

new and coming: Detroit's streamlined trolleys; the cage of a skyscraper still uncovered; the raw steel frame of a counterbalanced lift
bridge; the Monadnock slab; the Larkin Building and Unity Temple;
the Shelton Hotel, the Medical Center in New York, and the rear,
not the festooned front, the plain undecorated functional rear of the
Graybar. Neutra we recall had even more diffculty in interpreting the
United States in his book also called *Amerika*. But he too stayed.

I 7

NONE OF THESE LITTLE EFFORTS AT MODERNISM OR THE NUMBER OF ESSAYS
about them was of much interest to the Old Guard. The books gave the
impression that Americans were enormously addicted to utilitarianism
but covered it up with gross borrowing from Europe. That was the impression Jacques Gréber brought with him about 1918 when he left the
École des Beaux-Arts to go to America. One of his teachers had told
him that America was nothing but a forest of skyscrapers and factories,
that Americans with all their money multiplied the copies of the beautiful French monuments and tried to do with money what time alone
had permitted the French to accomplish: "Tell us about their machines,
but not about their works of art." Gréber was delighted to find his
teacher's opinion mistaken and remained to teach at the University of
Pennsylvania. His book, *L'Architecture aux États-Unis, Preuve de la
Force d'Expansion du Génie Français* of 1920 reveals the source of his
pleasure. He had found an architecture derived from France in Cass
Gilbert's Customs House, McKim's Penn Station, Burnham's Union
Station at Washington, the Cunard docks, M.I.T.'s new buildings, the
Morgan Library, the New York Public Library, the Widener Library at
Harvard, the Cleveland Museum, the Pan-American Building, the Har-
vard Club at New York, and large estates like the Rockefeller estate at
Pocantico Hills designed by Welles Bosworth.

Gréber's tribute to French architectural imperialism truthfully described the image of America desired by the majority of American
architects. Few would have disagreed with his selection of masterpieces
nor with those published by Edward Warren Hoak and Willis Humphry
Church in a folio edition of plates in 1930. All the buildings were in
the classical tradition derived from France. Paul Cret's introduction to
this book was "an Apology for Imitation." In it he suggested that the
Parthenon and Amiens represented "not the new but the perfected, not
the promise but the fulfillment." The emphasis on imitation was in
striking contrast to Guadet, who had earlier insisted upon functional

composition within a tradition. But the generation of the '20s tended to ignore the necessity to evolve differences in exterior forms, and were bent on imitation of examples they considered perfect. It was at this point that the Beaux-Arts camp followers became increasingly sterile, giving precedence to form over logic and structure and function while relying on historical paragons over which no improvement might be expected.

"The study of design — of proportion —" one teacher wrote in 1927, "resolves itself into a study of tradition." Books and foreign travel, museum collections and drawings were the tools and objects of an architect's study; he examined history not to understand the society and the emotions that had called for the buildings but to indenture him to a library of forms evolved for past problems of societies long dead. The whole history of architecture was now put on record for this ignoble purpose.

Systematic quarrying brought Georgian tradition to the surface and handsome books of plates described *The Great Georgian Houses of America*, while after 1916 the Association of Northern Pine Manufacturers published a series of twenty-six volumes of photographs, descriptions, plans, details and measured drawings of early American buildings; their *White Pine Series of Architectural Monographs* sired many Georgian houses in the suburbs. There were many other fine examples that a skillful copyist could now find to imitate.

No doubt the Beaux-Arts education had encouraged an enormous proficiency in drawing, audacity in composition, exact knowledge of materials, form and details and a keen sense of the kinds of space and finish that accompanied the good life. In all this the Beaux-Arts had supplied discipline. In none of it was there any implication of a sterile reliance on literal and established solutions. But in the '20s, absolute standards for good design were rigidly established by contemporary books written by teachers in American schools.

There was for example Nathaniel Cortlandt Curtis's *Architectural Composition*, published in 1923; nothing in the book would indicate that industrial America existed, nor was there any reflection of the challenges Le Corbusier and Gropius had already given to Europe. Perhaps the most thorough work was written by a much-beloved teacher at the University of Pennsylvania, John F. Harbeson; his book, *The Study of Architectural Design*, had special reference to the program of the Beaux-Arts Institute of Design, a national organization founded in 1916 at New York, which issued programs for the separate architectural schools. The level of proficiency expected of drawings was announced by the frontispiece, a skillful water color of the Tarpeian Rock at Rome by

Jacques Carlu. The architectural student was advised to follow a disciplined procedure: first, learning the grammar of architecture, taught through the *analytique,* a study in proportion and in the elements of architectures. All studies were initiated by *esquisses,* preliminary sketches done in a fixed time, usually nine hours spent *"en loge,"* that is, isolated in a box or booth. Proportions of the *esquisse* might later be varied, but the elements shown in the sketch had to appear in the final *analytique.* All drawing should be done "by the axes," the vertical planes separating the halves of symmetrical structures, and proportions of big masses were studied at small scale before they were enlarged to the proper size. It was at this introductory stage that the architectural student mastered the orders and the great monuments recorded in books. Next he learned how to make an effective and clear composition on the sheet that would present his final drawings. Those would be drawn in pencil before the architect "passed to ink," Chinese ink laboriously ground, strained through a wick, and etched into the parchment-like paper with ruling pens. Last came rendering, which modeled the forms by showing shadows cast by a sun conventionally indicated at an angle of forty-five degrees to the horizontal. Armories and prisons were fortresses to be built in Romanesque or Gothic style; banks should reveal their strength but also be inviting through Roman character. Everywhere the strong hand of tradition developed a reliance upon precedent. This shackle was coupled with another: an interest in geometry of form regardless of use or cost. There was a tendency to award prizes to the design that showed the most developed garnishing of form through the mosiac of moldings, steps, furnishings, reticulated walls, and elaborate landscape entourage, including terraces, gardens, fountains and loggias. Such encouragement led students to create prize plans that looked like magnifications of snowflake crystals, and it was this unrealistic version of paper architecture that marked the worst of the American Beaux-Arts work.

The unreality of the late Beaux-Arts was not incompatible with American ambitions so long as wealthy clients wanted Old World magnificence. The crazy prosperity of the postwar Harding, Coolidge and Hoover era gave the Beaux-Arts student his last ready clientele. He could ignore social reform, slum problems, traffic problems; he could turn his back on all industrial problems, and he generally left them to the safe if insensitive hands of engineers who had not cracked a book of antique orders. He fancied himself enormously audacious if his school, in a moment of academic adventuresomeness, permitted him to try his hand at an airport, skyscraper or gasoline station. The coming building types were factories and office buildings and public schools. Meanwhile the architectural student studied the central motif for a garden wall, a fountain to end a vista, a temple of love, a problem in superimposed orders, a municipal art gallery, an establishment at a mineral springs, a casino for the Mediterranean, a French embassy in the Far East, the palace of a president in the capital of a great republic. Nowhere was there an indication of the industrial basis of the prosperity, and the implications of a modern civilization based upon the revelations of Albert Einstein, Niels Bohr and Max Planck never appeared in the programs.

At no time was American architectural thought more dominated by a foreign school. Francophilism ran to inordinate devotion, and no architectural school thought itself complete without its *patron*. In the importation M.I.T., the oldest school, had led the way when its founder, William R. Ware, had brought Eugène Létang from France; he was succeeded in 1892 by Désiré Despradelle who stayed there for twenty years and was succeeded in turn by a parade of Frenchmen, Duquesne, Le Monnier, Ferrand and Jacques Carlu. Paul Cret came to the United States in 1903 and taught at Pennsylvania from that time until 1937, aided after 1918 by Gréber. Carnegie Institute of Technology had Ferrand and Grapin; Columbia, Prévot and Arnal; Cornell had a galaxy including Hébrard, Manxion and Prévot; Harvard had Duquesne and Haffner; Princeton drew Jean Labatut in 1928. Michigan had Albert Rousseau; Washington University had Abella and Ferrand; and Minnesota had Léon Arnal beginning in 1919. Many of these men were serious teachers; a few like Cret and Despradelle were excellent designers; but one and all were oriented towards classical architecture built on the grand axis; they understood very little about the social and intellectual ferment in America and they cared less. Their prescription for the ills of the city was the City Beautiful; their idea for a cultural institution was the grandiose classical monument, and America happily bought their ideas, in one last fling.

At its worst, what America bought was dreadful. There was, for example, John Russell Pope's ugly Temple of the Scottish Rite at Washington, built in 1916. The headquarters for the Supreme Council of the Scottish Rite of Freemasonry of the South, its ceremonial chambers and temple room were encased within a reconstruction of the mausoleum built by Queen Artemisia at Halicarnassus for the tomb of King Mausolus. Nor were the Beaux-Arts men successful in inventing a new style. Few buildings have been so abortively contrived as the Báhai Temple of Peace on the shore of Lake Michigan north of Chicago. Louis Bourgeois its designer, spotted nine piers upon a star-plan radiating to nine towers from which concave buttresses rose to a dome. In spite of its structural chaos and flagrant mishandling of materials, it caught the eye of juror

Henry Van Buren Magonigle who said, "It is the first new idea in architecture since the thirteenth century; I want to see it erected." It was novel enough, but its structure violated its plan and its ornament violated its structure, and the circle of violations had nothing whatever to do with architecture. Aberrations of that kind were excoriated by the good Beaux-Arts critics; but their formulas for good design could not summon genius, and few designers avoided Pope's commonplace or Bourgeois' fantasy.

1 8

THE CONSERVATIVE TRADITION WAS AT ITS BEST IN THE CITY BEAUTIFUL movement, particularly in the commemorative monument. Even here good taste did not intervene against having the mausoleum of Halicarnassus erected again as a War Memorial at Indianapolis in 1923-1933; nor was inspiration forthcoming at the Memorial Amphitheatre for Washington's Arlington National Cemetery or at San Francisco's Palace of the Legion of Honor of 1924. Those have no magic to move men's affections. Yet that magic did appear in Henry Bacon's Lincoln Memorial at Washington. A physical description fails to convey any sense of majesty. It is a Greek temple with a Roman attic. The temple contains four features: the statue of a man; two halls, one a memorial to the Gettysburg Address, the second to the Second Inaugural Address; and the naos itself. Thirty-six columns represent the number of states at the time of the Civil War; the frieze has wreaths with the names of forty-eight states and the dates of their entry into the Union. Not everything is successful. The iconography of columns and frieze is contrived. The two halls screened by Ionic colonnades are not memorable; Jules Guérin's allegorical paintings fail to convey the symbolism they intended. These must be dismissed, and they *are* in a flash when we confront the majestic statue of Lincoln, the work of Daniel Chester French, which in scale, in bearing, in expression, brings to life the real and mythical meaning of Lincoln's statesmanship. Here, building remains subservient to sculpture, but appropriately provides a resonating void for the statue, a platform for illuminating it, a colonnade that crowns it as laurel. The setting adds to the effectiveness as the great axis leads from the Capitol over a mile to the Washington obelisk and then past a long reflecting pool to the Memorial at the bank of the Potomac. The monumentality of the Lincoln Memorial is a matter of composition, refinement and sculptural art, not of Greek and Roman forms.

Another capable designer, Magonigle, recognized the true origins of monumentality in 1928 when he built the Liberty Memorial at Kansas City. Dedicated to the unnamed dead of World War I, the monument could have no sculpture so clearly themed as Lincoln was for Henry Bacon. Yet the composition of elemental forms conveyed a similar feeling. Two small block-like buildings were placed at the flanks of a cylindrical shaft 216 feet tall, with clusters of piers and buttresses hewn from the cylinder. A stylized frieze depicted the Progress of Civilization toward Peace, in a composition that had more meaning as patterns of light and shadow than as symbolism. The work of the Sculptor Robert Aitken, it fails upon close scrutiny to live up to the architectural setting, which gains its effect through massive cubistic masonry walls, the outdoor memorial court, the long axis, and most of all by the buttresses and piers, which soar aloft in unbroken lines to the altar of sacrifice at the top of the shaft.

In spite of a few such successes, the most finicky classicism prevailed in city, state and federal architecture. As governmental agencies grew in size and number, the glacier of classicism pushed across the land, grinding down the pockets of regionalism. Most cities acquired additional post offices, courthouses, office buildings and federal banks. Denver looked like a Western province of Washington. White, pilastered and domed buildings stood on axes at the perimeter of great malls, like those developed at Harrisburg, Pennsylvania. Guy Lowell's New York County Court House of 1926 was typical: hexagonal in plan with a central rotunda and fronted by a Roman temple portico. State capitols were similar, whether at Olympia, Washington, or at Madison, Wisconsin. When given a government commission, Cass Gilbert forsook the Gothic style of the Woolworth Building to build the Minnesota Capitol in 1925; he paid no attention to regional differences and willingly carried a similar classical form to the Capitol of West Virginia in 1931. The domed capitol was increasingly a *tour de force*; the enlarged number of offices required a block larger than the legislative chambers; but symbolism overrode function, and the classical designers simply increased the base for offices and enlarged the domes for the legislature.

A direct attack upon the problem was seldom made. One notable exception was the Capitol at Bismarck, North Dakota, which frankly admitted the changed relationship between the places of assembly and places of work. The offices stood in a modern slab skyscraper, while the legislature was in a separate, low cylinder. This work of Holabird and Root of 1932 might have opened the way towards modern government buildings, but it failed to convey a sense of government; and modernism, speciously identified with economy, was avoided wherever columns and domes were financially possible.

Yet even in the conservative camp, there was a movement towards modernized classical government buildings. Goodhue's first study for the Capitol at Lincoln, Nebraska, was entirely classical. His design of 1919 was a skyscraper, but it was later made more vertical, better organized and simpler in form when, in 1920, he studied the work of Eliel Saarinen, particularly his Finnish Parliament House at Helsinki of 1908. Goodhue's later design of 1920 solved the problem of the offices by spreading them out horizontally with one story under the terrace and one above it. Four interior courts, open to the sky, admitted light to four blocks of offices and provided natural ventilation. The Senate and House occupied large, beautifully paneled chambers right and left of a central hall. Out of the center of the terrace, Goodhue shot his tower skyward, and it rose in a series of strong steps to support a small polychromed dome on which the figure of The Sower was mounted. Thick corner piers rose to buttresses capped by human figures carved by Lee Lawrie. All decorative sculpture was carved into the structural form and made integral with them; so were the capitals of corn, wheat and sunflowers on the interior columns. The plan coordinated varied spaces upon axes, a triumphant demonstration of Beaux-Arts skill, and the elevations were progressive modern developments, only occasionally reminiscent of historical architecture.

Goodhue's building seemed to indicate the possibilities of a new American style, one that harmonized well with sculpture and painting, one that was in the great tradition of classic monumentality. He had abandoned his Gothicism after he broke away from Cram in 1914 at the end of a medieval brotherhood that had lasted twenty years. He thought that the common heritage of Western civilization had come in a direct line starting in the very beginning of Aryan civilization. He felt that the Nebraska State Capitol was a sort of classic. With time America might develop its own version of that tradition, Goodhue thought, much as Jefferson and Latrobe had thought earlier. But though Goodhue scored another if partial success in the National Academy of Arts and Sciences at Washington, nothing came of this attempt at a new classic. Indeed it was too easy for it to stray into the mere appropriation of historical detail as when Goodhue himself covered his California buildings with Spanish baroque ornament. The State Capitol at Lincoln might have contained the seed of a new national idiom but if so it fell on stony ground although Paul Cret cultivated it handsomely in one last example, the Folger Shakespeare Library at Washington of 1929-1932. Here the major walls rise smoothly to a rounded attic story, and the windows are set in simplified classic frames. Imitations of the Nebraska Capitol, often enriched by Lee Lawrie's sculptured buttresses, appeared over and over again in post offices, banks, and regional government agencies; it was seldom ugly but it was often pedestrian and insipid.

Meanwhile the Beaux-Arts architects continued to case their libraries and museums in the monumental classic envelope, emphasizing grand staircases and overly large public spaces, shunting functional areas to the side. But the spirit of the Boston Public Library was seldom recaptured by Trumbauer, Gilbert, Hunt, Goodhue as they built for Philadelphia, Detroit, Pasadena, or Los Angeles. Even Paul Cret's Indianapolis Public Library of 1917 was scarcely an exception although often called the best classic building in America. Its axial plan was dramatic but not serviceable. Greater attention was paid to the exteriors. Two tall pavilions terminate the Doric colonnade, a fine scheme for a scenic building to head a civic square. The difficult problem of arranging a single envelope to unify the vast spaces of reading rooms and the multiple smaller spaces was solved masterfully by changes in elevations which ranged from one story at the south to two on the east and west and to five on the north where a new rhythm and scale marked the fenestration of the bookstacks. Less effective was Cass Gilbert's Detroit Public Library of 1921. Its plan was simply too cumbersome and the excellent proportions of the front arcade were marred by gross details. One left the façade readily to appreciate the rear elevation where a nobly frank expression of the stacks is unsullied by classic monumentality.

Museums were no better, whether they were the archeological temples of Philadelphia or the more conventional and equally awkward palaces of Cleveland and Minneapolis, the less institutional Frick Mansion Museum at New York or Washington's Freer Gallery which Charles Platt arranged as a series of galleries around a central court. Cret's Detroit Institute of Arts of 1929 set a better precedent by abandoning the monumental staircase and corridors; its lighting came directly through walls rather than skylights, and the plan circulated spectators through galleries arranged chronologically with all the arts of each period assembled in appropriate architectural settings, but it seems unimaginative now.

19

CHURCHES CONTINUED TO REMAIN OUTSIDE THE CLASSICAL TRADITION AND to look away from modern suggestions. The triumph of the Gothic was clear by 1917 when Goodhue wrote an article in the *Architectural Review* (U.S.) in which he complained about the increasing absence of architectural, liturgical and ideological differences among churches.

Even Unitarians adopted the liturgical Episcopal architecture to which Presbyterians had previously succumbed. Princeton's Chapel was a striking indication of how architecture had betrayed the presbytery. Many of the buildings by men like Goodhue and Cram were pleasant enough, as Goodhue's St. Bartholomew's or St. Vincent Ferrer in New York reveal; in minor ways they were steps from archeological and academic Gothic; but they were not giant steps, any more than was the colorful bell tower which Magonigle and MacLaughlin provided for the First Plymouth Congregational Church at Lincoln, Nebraska. They were cheerful, comfortable, pretty — and unimportant. They were not more important when they were gargantuan like the major cathedrals at Washington and New York which, undaunted by modern commerce and industry, attempted to rival Amiens and Bourges, not only in form and size but in their slow handicraft construction. For anyone who knew the real thing they were as pale as old Quebec is compared to a real French city.

If few church architects and clients followed the mild leads of Goodhue or Magonigle, almost none encouraged greater change. They were quite uninterested in the modern church movement in Germany and Switzerland where an encyclical broadcast by Pope Pius X had encouraged Catholic architects to move toward a vigorously modern church architecture. In the United States even Catholics like the lively Charles D. Maginnis, the architect of many less lively Catholic churches, remained arch-conservative. In 1929 he wrote, "The self-conscious persuasion of such an architecture [modern] to the secular thought of the day would be impertinent and incalculably mischievous." Joseph Hudnut, writing in the *American Architect* of 1932, commented favorably about the modern spirit of church architecture in Europe; but his praise did not shake the general love for the Gothic. "Probably the safest method," wrote architect Hobart Upjohn in 1929, "is the following of established styles."

Educational institutions were as usual even less curious or courageous. The Harvard Business School Competition of 1925 resulted in an emasculated campus of red-brick Georgian buildings. Harvard's excellent system of undergraduate residence elicited no architecture to match it. If anything the situation was worse at Yale where the Gothic colleges by James Gamble Rogers affected Oxonian diversity inside a modern city; picturesqueness forfeited land and use. The form of one quadrangle was warped to include a tower based on one at Wrexham, Wales, a town where a president of Yale had died during a summer holiday; its Welsh Gothic, barbaric though it sounds, was not worse than the architecture of another quad which boasted an inner court of Georgian while the street façade was Gothic, a lesson of some sort to Yale undergraduates who would work on Madison Avenue.

Money poured forth for the Fogg Museum at Harvard with its inner court derived from an Italian palace; but scientific departments remained in poorly appointed quarters constructed during the '50s and '80s of the preceding century and the humanists of today might remember how much better off they were only a quarter century ago. Institutes of technology like the Carnegie Institute were comprehensively planned by Beaux-Arts men like Henry Hornbostel. Of these the new Massachusetts Institute of Technology revealed the best application of the City Beautiful movement to campus planning. Following the lead of Jefferson at the University of Virginia, Welles Bosworth placed a library in a rotunda at the summit of the plan, while a great lawn open to Boston across the wide Charles River Basin was framed by connected blocks of court-lighted buildings all connected by interior passageways. The plan itself offered flexibilities which were uncommon on traditional campuses whose individually separated buildings served to constrict the growth of the departments they housed while assisting to maintain departmental barriers. In the new M.I.T. all space was essentially interchangeable as to function (classroom, office, laboratory, library) and casual interdepartmental exchanges of ideas were common. If the neo-classic exterior belied the brilliance of Bosworth's plan, developed on strictly Beaux-Arts lines, the building was nevertheless ahead of its day, following industrial practice more than that of the universities.

At the University of Colorado, Day and Klauder avoided the Roman classic, Georgian and Gothic by developing a modest version of rural Spanish architecture. The result was far more successful than a more delicate example of dependence upon Spain like Myron Hunt's Occidental College at Los Angeles of 1914 or than Cram and Ferguson's pitiful variation upon Spanish Renaissance at Rice Institute in Houston. Architects could not long forego trying the skyscraper form for urban universities, but those who did usually forgot that greater building height should free more ground area, a mistake James Gamble Rogers made at Chicago's Northwestern University; and the skyscraper solution could not be shaken free of Gothic detail, as Klauder unfortunately proved in the Cathedral of Learning at Pittsburgh of 1933. The tower blatantly confused education, advertisement, religion; and its Gothic crypt was no palliative — with the changing patterns of college life it housed student activities and its absurdity in the service of student newspapers, quizzes, and booths, or in the presence of modern American student attire showed how little Gothic sentimentality accorded with the realities of American undergraduate life.

Under the leadership of Howard Myers, the *Architectural Forum* stumped for modern design. There is now, it said, "an opportunity for the newer colleges to erect thoroughly modern buildings, but few have availed themselves of this opportunity." A student at Yale in 1931 thought that "colleges are likely to become museums of gilt and glory rather than workplaces of simplicity and directness." Nowhere was architectural taste more banal, architectural daring more restrained, than in America's seats of learning in the age of Coolidge.

2 0

YET LITTLE CRITICISM WAS IN THE AIR SO LONG AS PROSPERITY CONtinued to mount. Nowhere was there more prosperity than in Chicago. In 1928 no American city felt more secure in her attainments. So she looked forward to celebrating the city's Centennial with an expenditure of twelve million dollars. Chicago had much to celebrate. Since 1833 she had become a city of steel and stone, the second largest city in America, the fourth in the world. A million people came daily to her bustling Loop. Thirty-three trunk lines served her livestock market and packing center. She was also cultured. The Old South might still look down on her; the New Yorker and the Bostonian might still notice a rawness of speech and manner and attitude; but she had gone beyond the condescension of a McKim or a McAllister even if she had not fulfilled the hopes of Sullivan and Wright. In 1928 she could proudly point to a tradition; the former Fair, the Chicago school of architects, John Dewey and his instrumentalism, Jane Addams, a thriving University, 1200 churches, 6000 acres of parks, 35,000 acres of forest preserves. She had six large libraries, a fine Art Institute, the Field Museum of Anthropology, the Shedd Aquarium, the Opera House and one of the leading opera companies, Orchestra Hall and one of the best symphony orchestras, the Museum of Science and Industry and the Adler Planetarium. She might have Studs Lonigan in the Loop and Scarface Al Capone ruling Cook County from adjacent Cicero but in 1928 she was ready to celebrate her progress in a great fiesta. Despite the deep depression that followed 1929 she carried through and in 1933 opened her Century of Progress Exhibition which was intended to look towards the future.

On the shores of Lake Michigan south of the Art Institute, 424 acres of land attempted to give the visitor a glimpse into the progress of science and industry. The major buildings were boldly angular, with planes of asbestos and gypsum board and plywood on light steel frames, standing on a lagoon bisected by the Skyride, an aerial railway carried on cables suspended from two steel towers. "Modernism" prevailed. "It would be incongruous to house exhibits showing man's progress in the past century in a Greek temple of the age of Pericles, or a Roman villa of the time of Hadrian," said members of the architectural commission. "We are trying to show the world not what has happened in the past, because that has already been effectively done, but what is being done in the present, and what may happen in the future." The display of what was possible architecturally was as feeble as the display of what was to come in science.

The buildings were vigorous, sometimes strident, displays of factory-made parts, prefabrication, steel frames and clips, new compositions; windowless, they assured people of advancements in interior lighting and filtered ventilation; gaily colored, they were "ultra-modern" and glorified mercury and sodium tube lighting. The Hall of Science Building by Paul Cret had a circular arc of pylons drawing the visitor to a U-shaped, cubicle structure relieved by rectilinear ornament. The Federal Building by E. H. Bennett was a dome with three tall flanking parallelepipeds. Some national exhibits were historical, a Chinese temple, a Mayan temple, but these were subordinate to the modern General Motors (Albert Kahn), Chrysler, and Travel and Transport Buildings. The latter, designed by Holabird, Bennett and Burnham, had a dome suspended on cables from twelve steel towers. The structural principle was displayed realistically, but the cables and towers had a sloppy, unfinished appearance, like motley derricks, and they were an incongruous match with the radiator-like grillwork of the lower portion of the building. The Fair was stridently, boisterously, self-consciously modern, and its "styling" could be seen in the exhibits. One showed how the modern family of 1933 lived: a city apartment, a radio, a refrigerator, electric range, shelves filled with sleek cans of prepared foods. There were the "new" houses, Stran-steel, Ferro-Enamel, Masonite, "The House of Tomorrow" — a circular glass house by George Fred Keck. The implication was that men living modern lived better, and the symbol was anything new, shiny and styled. For architecture perhaps the most important achievement of The Century of Progress was that it started Louis Skidmore, its director, on his way; but it was in any event an appropriate architectural end to the period of complacency.

It had been a period of superlatives, this twenty years of prosperity. Everything was on a colossal scale. Mass production engendered mass distribution, and these were dependent upon a huge market with an appetite for material possessions. That appetite salesmanship whetted and often created, always regardless of taste or social responsibility and always by means of superlatives — the fastest train, the tallest building, the most efficient kitchen, the quickest times for construction, the most lavish country clubs and country houses. If, at the other extreme, there were blighted slums and poverty amid the progress, they might be ignored, or eradicated by increased production and lowered costs. Charity might have to be forthcoming, but nothing seemed so mawkish to the "intellectuals" of the '20s as the idea that a man could not rise from original distress by his own bootstraps. It seemed mawkish because it belied "facts"; the areas where optimism and *laissez faire* failed to improve the welfare of the whole society were remote from the business office and the comfortable houses on manicured lawns in wooded neighborhoods. In such a society, architecture might move along without any social objective. It could drift complacently with the fashion of styles, with advertising, with increased demands for improved physical comfort.

When Woodrow Wilson illuminated the Woolworth Tower, he presciently forecast the temper of carefree prosperity that rapidly moved the country's sentiments away from the reforming zeal stirred up by Roosevelt and Taft. His idealism was renounced under Harding, Coolidge and Hoover during the inflated '20s, when a frenzied quest for spendthrift "normalcy" and a rampant inflation spiraled the nation into an optimistic materialism which the Great Depression proved to be unwarranted. The depression hit no professional group harder than it did those architects whose only training wedded them to the whims of an inflationary economy. In 1928 the total buildings by architects amounted to over 3½ billion dollars; in 1932 the figure was half a billion. The number of participating firms dropped from 9000 to 5000; the average volume of business done in each office was reduced from $400,000 to less than $100,000. Almost 4000 firms failed to weather the storm. Some limped back on housing schemes, road construction and public works projects, supported by state and federal governments.

They lived to see the end of an era of plenty. They were forced to reflect upon a wider social basis for architecture. The tower, the suburb, the monument, the country house had been the symbols of superlatively prosperous times. Between them lay acres of busy factories and hours of stop-and-go traffic. The electric light shortened the night; the telephone compressed time and distance; the automobile beguiled the observer of congestion into the belief that the whole nation could take to the woods on wheels. What the factory produced, the tower sold. Some of the proceeds went to the monument; but more went into the great general spectacle of luxury. What the tower distributed, the suburb bought. The outward form of each was a testimonial to advertising.

The works of Wright, the Philadelphia Saving Fund Society by

George Howe, Rockefeller Center and the McGraw-Hill Building by Raymond Hood, and a scattering of modern houses showed the way to the future. But they were neither typical nor much desired. The buildings that American architects liked to build in these years and the buildings that the informed American public most admired were Lindeberg's houses, Bacon's Lincoln Memorial, Goodhue's Nebraska State Capitol. These at least were buildings whose architects were competent if not contemporary; their taste good, if not forward-looking. To even more people the Paramount Building, the Chrysler and Empire State towers, the United States Supreme Court, the Minnesota Capitol and the phony Spanish revival of Santa Barbara seemed marvelous.

American architecture rested in complacency unable to justify itself by espousing a liberal social objective or by making a vigorous aesthetic statement. The Beaux-Arts had nothing more to say to modern America; the American modernists were merely dabblers playing with another foreign style; the regionalists could not long withstand the assaults of a universal technology or escape their own romantic historicism; Frank Lloyd Wright worked alone. Where other times had yielded Latrobe, Hunt and Richardson, McKim and Sullivan, these could yield only Goodhue and Hood. Avoiding the only compelling purposes of their art, the architects sat far out on a shaky limb that any social, political or economic storm might amputate. It remained to be seen whether they could rally and regain a respected position.

V

1933-1960

V

1933-1960

THE SELF-SATISFIED SOMNOLENCE OF THE COOL-
idge era was broken by the events of the Hoover administration.
In the quarter-century that followed the inauguration of Franklin
Roosevelt jolts were frequent, each more violent than the preceding. By
1960 it was obvious that the details of the American world differed
greatly from those of 1930, while many thought the principles had
shifted as well. American architectural attitudes went through a similar,
if transient, shift. It was now agreed that the architect could not be
cavalier about his social responsibility. There was no place for a vestigial
Stanford White. In the cause of a new and "functional" aesthetic, an
important junta of American designers and critics, reinforced by powerful immigrants from Europe, set out to convert the majority of Americans to a modern architecture, "expressive of the times," which that
majority was perfectly sure it did not want.

This small body of ardent protagonists arrayed themselves in active
opposition to the taste of men placed in the highest quarters of finance,
government, education, criticism, religion and the organized architectural profession. They assumed a polemical role; their aesthetic and
social protests were rebellious, bitter, and (as must be the case with all
successful revolutionaries) much exaggerated. In the end the aesthetic,
if not the civic, victory was complete. Sir John Summerson says that
architectural taste runs through cycles of about thirty years. Even if this
is a sound generalization, the drastic changes of this thirty, at least in the
United States, must be adduced as an extraordinary example. By 1960
there were hardly even enclaves of the old eclecticism. The early European leaders of the revolution, with the exception of Henry Van der
Velde all still living, were now enshrined as demigods in the new architectural Parnassus. So was the American, Frank Lloyd Wright. A new

crop of young modernists was pressing them for laurels, and this group had never known rebellion or failure. Even the eclectics worked with modern motifs. The painful question now was whether "modern motifs" did "express the times."

I

ALL THIS HAD COME ABOUT IN AN AGE OF GREAT TENSIONS AND UNCERtainties. For Americans there were first the problems caused by the general realization that their society, as constituted in the age of Coolidge and Hoover, had failed to be true to long-professed American theories; had failed to solve its own internal problems; and that the failure could not be corrected merely by the reaffirmation of some platitude, the repair of some minor part, the invention of some small modernizing component. The impulsive and gigantic inventions of the New Deal, some successful, some not, all caused strains. The strains were still to be felt in 1960 even though many of the revolutionary and equalitarian economic, social and political changes had by then come to be accepted.

Just as a breather seemed to have come, the second and heavier jolt was imposed by the dictators and the ensuing war. It laid new strains on the economy, evoked new and more powerful techniques of production and control. These inevitably remained to influence the uneasy peace. The power balance of the whole world was changed. Power passed from those most experienced in its use to those least experienced. The United States struggled with its problem of finding a position of responsibility consonant with its power. The old European nations had to learn to accommodate themselves to lower status. Russia openly reveled in her power. The potential power of what seemed to be an irresponsible and primitive China loomed as a threat. Another force of unpredictable influence could be seen in the drive of the old colonial areas to achieve parity in every respect, economic, political, social, aesthetic, and that overnight. The game to be played was for very high stakes and the ancient rules seemed to have no accepted validity. The new rules, if there were any, seemed elusive and the West was trying to understand them while its optimism about civilized "progress" had been shaken, if not dispelled, by Belsen and Dachau. Uncertainties and disquiet were inevitably bred in the United States where even the sophisticated could find scant comfort in the certainty that the other side was surely also suffering from uncertainty and disquietude.

The third jolt had been implicit for a long time but it was sensed by many only after the atomic destruction of Hiroshima and Nagasaki. For most it was, perhaps, confined to the glimmerings of comprehension about the razor edge most of the world's people were now walking between life and annihilation. This comprehension was, in itself, enough to drive many men to intense activity, or to despair. Most people seemed either to want not to know the facts, or to forget them as soon as known, since they appeared altogether too troublesome to manage. But it was a hard world for those who rejected this Byzantine solution.

It became still harder if one tried to look ahead with a provisional optimism about a *détente* in arms control, about some resolution of the economic competition between the two antagonistic ideologies; for beyond the crevasses of the present troubles, one did not see a terrain of greater safety and repose, however exciting and adventuresome it might be. Modern science and technology were expanding at such a rate as to pose majestic questions, not to be answered by crude and unenforceable measures such as moratoria on science. How were men to understand science, how were they to control technology lest it control them? Where were men who needed belief to sustain them against the events of life to find it as the works of the intellect steadily gnawed away at the foundations of their old belief? Much as it might have disturbed and still does disturb fundamentalists, Darwinism had been an optimistic doctrine. It could be read as the irreversible story of progress from ape, through man to superman, perfectly master of his environment, his destiny, perhaps even of himself. It had accepted as self-evident that progress was a meaningful word — and that its rate was roughly linear, so that human accommodation was possible.

But the new science, whether or not denying Darwinism, offered no such optimistic interpretations. The advances in knowledge, it turned out, were going to be geometric rather than linear. What Henry Adams had foreboded in isolation in 1905 was apparent to many in public in 1960. The new science provided no Spencer, offered no easy analogies to social Darwinism, either in relativity or in uncertainty. But along with it went a sort of geometric doubt among those who were not scientists or engineers as to whether all this necessarily meant progress at all, save in the most literal senses that the pool of knowledge in technical matters was obviously increasing, and that ever more daring and incredible machines could be designed and put to work.

For all human beings able to sense it, including the scientists as much as any, this situation engendered the deepest apprehensions. Some scientists could dismiss theirs in the pursuit of their science. Humanistic scholars struck out blindly and usually wildly. Artists became aware that their antennae, hitherto always the most sensitive of men's predictors, were no longer tuned sharply enough and this led to an uncertainty in

painting and sculpture. Theologians wriggled to adjust their theology
to more and more obdurate facts and hypotheses of science. Historians
found themselves in an incredible position. The cyclical theory which
had briefly displaced the theory of linear progress now gave way to views
such as those E. H. Carr delivered in his 1951 lectures, a view of cultural relativism. This, in the end, might lead to the conclusion that
there is no objective pattern in history and hence that history might no
longer be worth studying at all! To this, men like Louis J. Halle could
only answer, "the theories of yesterday are like the grass we cut down
this morning. They will be back again to-morrow." Philosophers saw
much of their ancient domain occupied by scientists and social scientists. Engineers looked beyond their engineering to its social consequences. In all this intellectual turmoil, could architects go unmoved, no
matter how little they, themselves, were disposed to be intellectual?

2

THE ARCHITECTURE OF AMERICA, IF IT WERE TO REFLECT THE LIFE OF
America, had somehow to respond to all these powerful thrusts, and this
in a time when an aesthetic conflict was being waged almost on independent terms. We say "independent" because even a slight examination of the theories of the conflict will reveal how inconsistent they
really were, how erratically related to the truths of the times.

For example, it is true that the genesis of the modern movement in
architecture rested on theories of Le Corbusier, Mies van der Rohe,
Gropius and Wright who all recognized that the machine was here to
stay and that architecture must seek to use it affirmatively, not to deny
it. But this was almost their only point of agreement, basic as it might
be. From it Wright deduced his theory of individuality, and Gropius his
theory of group-work and these notions were not the same thing, but, in
fact, antipodal. From the same premise Mies worked to his continuous
refinement of parts and Le Corbusier to his primitivism. These conclusions were again antipodal. The refinement of machine-made parts
was naturally plausible to American industrial technology so that the
greatest examples of Miesiana are in the United States; the primitive
theory was implausible to Americans who have no first-rate example
even of adulterated Corbusiana although few other important countries
of the world can boast so dubious a distinction.

Neither a common philosophy about the machine nor a common
philosophy about society drove these four great men to common conclusions about aesthetic solutions. They were no more in agreement

about aesthetics than they were about the logical use of the machine. Thus the road from a belief in the "organic," through the elevation of structure and mechanism, to worship of the primitive was perhaps both straight and circular but it was never communal. From all of the premises, some, though not many, of the actual expressions seemed to derive a common validity. It was perhaps only about 1955 that architects and critics alike began to see what their common banner had been, the banner which concealed their fundamental differences. It had been that of toppling the traditional and the eclectic from the seats of power. As soon as this triumph had been won, the four leaders emerged, each really on a separate throne. Acolytes surrounded each. While a new eclecticism was being prepared in those schools which sat admittedly at the foot of a single leader, a new catholicity of innovation was being brewed in the rest.

Thus in the success of "modern architecture" of 1960 there was a massive irony. The public now accepted modern architecture but the modern architects were not quite sure what modern architecture was, and even those who seemed sure did not agree. It had been born as one evidence of social reform but the new modern architects were not often individually identified with social reform. Nor was it really possible for anyone but a self-convinced zealot to insist that a geometrical design for a housing project à la Mies, or a romantic "human" design à la Wurster struck the greater blow in the cause of reform. Indeed, to the idea of reform, most of the great buildings were neutral.

Again, modern architecture had been born in the study of structure and in the felt necessity that this structure should be clearly, "honestly" revealed; it had moved to a classical expression of this necessity in the works of Mies van der Rohe and Pier Luigi Nervi but this necessity now seemed less universally urgent; on the one hand it was being concealed by the integuments of the neo-classicism of Minoru Yamasaki, Gordon Bunshaft, Paul Rudolph, Ieoh-ming Pei, Edward Stone and Walter Gropius's team, The Architects Collaborative; on the other hand it was being stretched into structural *tours de force*, structure for structure's sake, by Eero Saarinen, Felix Candela, Oscar Niemeyer, Victor Lundy and all the young men who were now fascinated by the form if not the analysis of conic sections.

Modern architecture had never been unconscious of aesthetics. But in its infancy it had played down aesthetic necessity, had seldom talked of art for art's sake, had defended its arbitrary aesthetic conclusions with appeals to the rationale of social need and structural necessity, rationally advanced even when garbed in explosively irrational polemic. But, with success, most of the architectural discussion became frankly aesthetic. This was nowhere more evident than in the position taken by the partisans of Wright in the Guggenheim dispute of 1959-1960 or in the endless arguments of the leading Continental and British architectural magazines of 1960. The same arguments could be heard over the cocktails of American architectural meetings. In 1958, an artist-architect, Minoru Yamasaki, said, "The social function of the architect is to create a work of art."

Perhaps we can perceive the ultimate ironies only dimly. What is clear is that the impact of New Deal reform and social unrest conditioned the pattern of American architectural thought, willy nilly. It joined with the aesthetic revolution to make our contemporary approaches to architecture possible. The war then extended American architectural horizons, increased the influence of exotic forms on American thinking, greatly widened the area of the world into which American designs would obtrude themselves from London to Accra to New Delhi. To all of these influences some direct responses were possible. The direction of these responses was, on the whole, favorable.

At this level of discourse one could say that the struggle had availed; that the architectural appearance of America had been improved. There were many notable new buildings. Alas, there were perhaps fewer than the occasion had provided and demanded. The postwar atmosphere was one of an apparently abundant prosperity with increasing inflation. Certainly one of the difficulties of the '50s was that the world was engaged in an unprecedented building boom, demanding more architectural attention than all the architects, brilliant and dull, sound and unsound, impulsive and reflective, could possibly provide, so that even reflective men were tempted to design without enough reflection. You were as likely to meet Gropius in Baghdad, or on an airstrip in the Pacific, as in the Harvard Yard; and so it went for all men of reputation. It was embarrassing for any American architect of any pretensions not to have at least one job in Hong Kong, Manila or Nairobi. Throughout the world exciting buildings were good for but a moment's discussion on a local street corner, almost never slated for reflective reconsideration. Many were exciting, perhaps enough were excellent.

But when one turned from the individual building to the city it was at once clear that things were out of hand. The city was falling apart in many ways, socially, politically, economically. All this was so trite that it was almost embarrassing to repeat it. But the city was falling apart aesthetically too for all its brave new architectural ornaments. Engineering czars like Robert Moses with strongly defined but not necessarily good hierarchies of values accomplished much, but not enough: aesthetic czars as brilliant as Le Corbusier at Chandigarh or Niemeyer at

Brasilia did some things much better but left other important questions quite unanswered; collections of stars on teams such as were assembled for New York's Lincoln Center project seemed to have their troubles and Lincoln Center was not a big enough test of the team anyway; great urban redevelopment schemes seemed either not to get under way or to end as sterile aesthetic, even human achievements. Many were led to wonder whether architects could learn, in time, to deal with the new and enormous scales, and time was pressing. It was not clear that they would have the chance even if they could learn. It was by no means certain that all the brilliant gains in personal architectural aesthetics of the past twenty-five years would not now be negated by the crushing, irresistible and insensitive Juggernaut of economic and political forces generated by urban expansion.

Behind this, for a few to ponder, lay the much larger philosophical questions of what the world of 1960 was really like, and whether anyone could understand it by the intellect or by the intuition or by both. Could anyone who did understand it begin to interpret it in architectural terms? Or would all this come about automatically? The confusion of the painters in these matters was painfully apparent to anyone who sampled the modern galleries. Was there perhaps the same confusion among the architects?

At the most elementary levels there was cause for comfort. The society *had* at long last reached some agreements as to what was architecturally important. Commerce and manufacturing *were* valuable and could now, and without remorse, be provided with dignified and beautiful architectural domiciles. Business could be a legitimate patron of the arts, perhaps might even become the most important patron. Social architecture, especially housing, *was* to be recognized as essential and important. The more ancient subjects of design, museums, libraries, universities and churches, were still to have as good architecture as they could get, often very good, but they must at least share the bench in the sun and probably give way even more than that. As to the private house, it remained interesting only as a point of relief from conformity. Although Americans clung to the idea of the private dwelling it was no longer quite such an important architectural problem; indeed few leading architects could afford to design modest private dwellings any more, unless like Neutra they chose to do one occasionally as an Antaean stimulus.

All this was accomplished. Perhaps it was enough. At any rate the details of this amount of progress and the relatively prosaic history of how it came about are all we can usefully venture here. In the end we will surely need to reflect more on the larger significances, on the

accommodation of architecture to philosophy. But in the meantime
there is a less complicated and happier story to be told; in one sense, at
least, a success story.

3

ALMOST EVERYONE WHO READS THIS STUDY CARRIES HIS OWN VIVID IM-
pressions of the first hundred days of the New Deal — and, if he has
none, countless texts have rehearsed them. Like the days of the Second
World War, they are too near at hand to require a detailed recall here.

They stopped the flood of failure, abated the financial crisis, repaired
the financial and commercial machinery. The president and his ebullient
advisers experimented with youth through the Civilian Conservation
Corps (CCC), with farming through the Agricultural Adjustment Administration (AAA), with the ecology of a valley through the Tennessee Valley Authority (TVA); they provided greater security for buyers
of stocks, for borrowers and lenders, for old and young. Relief, recovery and reform danced together in a complicated but exuberant ballet.

From it all the industrial labor force perhaps profited most. Industrial unions wrested leadership from the older and traditionally larger
craft unions; they pulverized the resistance of such industrial powers
as General Motors and United States Steel. After 1937 the Supreme
Court quite steadily supported legislation favorable to labor. The 40-
hour week, not yet attained in Russia, was taken for granted. A movement which in 1932 had accounted for only about 5 per cent of the
labor force by 1950 embraced fifteen million unionists or more than 20
per cent of all employed labor. The power of American labor had not
yet been fully measured but it was already time to begin to wonder
whether labor leaders could discard the bloody shirt, begin to prove
adequate to the different problems that came to them, begin to measure to the responsibility that was demanded by the new power.

Farmers, now less than an eighth of the population, kept pace with
labor under the largess of the New Deal. They were in trouble, more
even than usual. In October 1933 prices were so low that they tried a
farm strike in the middle western states. In November the penalty for
years of careless plowing and soil erosion was laid on the land. A great
dust storm swept across South Dakota. Two days later it was choking
the air of New York. Now began the dismal five-year trek of the
350,000 Okies and Arkies, braving the desert in their boiling jalopies to
cross to an inhospitable California which even tried, unconstitutionally,
to set up its own immigration laws. It was not the kind of disaster to
which the nation was accustomed. Countermeasures were prompt and

numerous, involving crop quotas, postponement of mortgage collections, easy loans, regulated grazing on the public lands, a Resettlement
Administration to move farmers from poor lands to better ones; and
new measures for rural electrification.

The labor measures of the New Deal had only indirect effects on
American architecture. The long-range improvement of labor's purchasing power brought a larger market for private houses, but the market
was largely preëmpted by real-estate developers and building contractors, though many architects attempted to supply designs for better
houses at comparable costs. If the site planning that the best architects
insisted upon had been allowed to govern the speculative developments,
the resulting communities, even those with amateur-designed and traditional houses, would have made American residences the boast of the
world, but unfortunately the developers and builders took the course
that gave immediate financial ease, ignoring the long-term benefits of
sound design. The improved lot of labor, made possible by higher
wages, forced the prices of building materials and construction to move
upward, thereby nearly removing traditional hand-tooled materials like
stone from the architect's palette. Mass-produced, standardized, cheaper,
but not always substantial materials replaced more architecturally satisfying ones such as wood or plaster. Some well-standardized materials like
brick became relatively more costly to put in place than they had once
been — not because they cost more to make but because unions restricted the number of bricks a man might lay for a day's wage, even
with a brick-laying machine in his hand. Though each trade was union-
ized, all the men involved in producing and assembling materials were
not in the same union. This helped in that buildings with concrete or
wooden structures might still rise during steel strikes. But it hindered,
for the absence of a single building union meant that it was practically
impossible to launch a full attack on new ways of fabricating buildings
since the responsibilities for individual traditional functions were atomized and zealously guarded. In the end trivial economies were effected
by eliminating ornament and by some modular standardization. But
the principal brake on the rising cost of the house was the steady shrink-
age of the amount of space it offered.

The farm measures bore more directly on architecture, stimulating
some model towns and farm workers' housing, creating a few new communities through rural electrification and power projects, even new types
of community. The Farm Security Administration (FSA) provided suggestive if financially unsuccessful demonstrations with its three Greenbelt towns. On another front, Yuba City, California, offered an example
of a well-planned housing scheme for 284 migrant families and 84 farm

families. Firebaugh and Woodville in California, and Chandler Farms in Arizona, offered notable chances to study low-cost housing, perhaps to make fruitful experiments in inexpensive amenity. At Chandler, Vernon De Mars provided houses whose site planning was imaginative although their architectural quality was minimal. Indeed, this was the general description of all the architecture supported by the depression agencies.

But these efforts still left too many Americans unemployed so that in January of 1935 Roosevelt had to announce to a joint session of Congress, "We must quit this business of relief." He asked that 3,500,000 jobs be created. In May his executive order established the Works Progress Administration.

It is easy enough to caricature the WPA projects — the inevitable waste and folly, given a hastily invented task, and direction by a strange mixture of theorists, idealists, and hardheaded ward politicians.

But the WPA, the other relief measures and the pump-priming reforms did temporarily end the disasters of unemployment. The WPA has even something to its credit in the arts. There was, for example the 1935 WPA painting project. Its effective director was Holger Cahill who had collected Williamsburg objects for Mrs. John D. Rockefeller, Jr., and who had been a pioneer in uncovering and overpraising the American popular arts. Whether the feeble quality of most of the WPA murals in federal post offices and banks was because of the conditions of the work, or because the artists were not competent, or because murals were no longer actually resonant with the times may not matter now. The murals were sentimental about national or local history, sentimental about regions, sentimental about underdogs. They tried for pointed social criticism and were usually only funny; they tried to be contemporary, aping what seemed to them the principal determinant of "contemporary" art, to wit, bad drawing. Even the murals by the most competent men like Boardman Robinson, Henry Varnum Poor, William Gropper, John Steuart Curry, Ben Shahn and Frank Mechau were not often good and perhaps never represented their best work. It can be said, though, for the "creative" side of the WPA program that it bridged a bad time for many painters who have since become well known. But it is an open question whether it would not have been better simply to buy whatever the painters wanted to paint than to go in for this mass-produced mural moralizing. Unfortunately, the directors wanted employment and social messages, not art. The Society of Abstract Artists, founded at New York in 1936, could hardly be a part of WPA, which from Roosevelt through Mrs. Roosevelt to Hopkins to Cahill was suffused with sentiment about the noble peasant and rural

America and the "humble" thing; the promoters of the WPA were bet-
ter fitted by taste and training to admire Grandma Moses than John
Marin, Thomas Hart Benton than Lyonel Feininger, John Steuart
Curry than Stuart Davis.

In the final assessment much the same things must be said of the
housing efforts of the New Deal. Here pump-priming became mixed
up with reform. The housing arrangements ran across a wide range.
The Federal Housing Administration (FHA) intended to help realtors
and bankers and builders, assisted in financing projects which would be
commercially justifiable, limited in dividends and developed to a
minimum standard. The Public Works Administration (PWA) built
a number of "low-cost" housing projects which, whatever they cost,
were to be low-rent. Finally there was the more important effort of the
United States Housing Authority (USHA), established by the Wagner-
Steagall Act to remedy the housing shortage among the lower-income
groups by subsidies administered through the states.

Each of the ventures scored some successes on its own terms. The
Home Owners Loan Corporation (HOLC), conceived at a time when
there were a thousand house foreclosures a day, purchased more than
a million mortgages and by 1950 was certain that it could liquidate its
investment of three and a half billion dollars without loss to the
government. FHA's home loan insurance bolstered the private housing
market and yielded a few exemplary projects, such as Baldwin Hills
Village, Los Angeles, by Clarence Stein and Robert Alexander. By 1949
the USHA had succeeded in working in forty-three states and at the
end of the war had accounted for 191,000 low-rent public housing units.

PWA produced 21,800 dwelling units in fifty-one low-rental developments spanning thirty-seven cities. Architect Robert Kohn was director, Architect Frederick L. Ackerman was in charge of slum clearance;
both had high ideals and fair experience in housing. But neither had
the aesthetic imagination or talent of the Europeans who were building houses in Europe. Kohn surrounded himself with a staff of young
Americans possessed of enormous enthusiasm and considerable critical
judgment, but inexperienced, better with words than with bricks and
mortar. PWA produced no better project than its first one, Lakewood
in Cleveland, designed by Walter McCornack. Its three-story apartments covered only 32 per cent of the slum-cleared land; there were
many playgrounds and some variety in the groupings. Despite readily
available and notable European example, the New Deal seldom did
much better. The general level of its architecture was almost as low as
the level of its painting, and considerably less amusing.

In quantity all the public-housing efforts together did not scratch the surface if, as the housers consistently alleged, one third of the nation was ill-housed. As soon as there were harbingers of prosperity they dispelled the vision of extensive well-ordered American public housing comparable to the communities of Sweden, Denmark, Holland, Switzerland or Germany. When it was all over it was clear that the American people did not covet the planned way of life, was unwilling to make its own plans and did not trust anybody else with them either. Left to themselves, the private builders soon forgot Baldwin Hills Village. The housing effort did not add much to the elegance of the American architectural scene. But it did create some sense of habit under which the citizens would no longer repudiate any and all public aid to housing, regardless of conditions of adversity or shortage, especially as private industry continued to fail to find a good antidote to subsidy.

In the absence of industrial advance, architects experimented with house construction though with less *élan* than they had displayed in the '20s. George Fred Keck advocated a solar house. Konrad Wachsmann, Gropius and Mies van der Rohe worked on problems of mass-produced standards with no really important results. Architects like William Wurster applied their minds briefly to the problem of the minimum house, still well designed. Many of these efforts were possibly frustrated by the fact that the shell of the house, on which the architect does so much of his work, costs but a small fraction of the whole and that changes made in the shell do not materially affect the cost of the land or the basic equipment. Planning alternatives that considered communal heating, cooking, or even clothes-washing facilities which were standard practice in Europe were simply rejected by American householders. When good houses were designed they were never purchased on a suitably large scale. There were again exceptions like Skidmore's houses at Oak Ridge, Tennessee, or the TVA demountable houses of 1944. The best of these may have been the Acorn House of 1950 and the Techbuilt House of 1952, each a pre-fabricated shed designed with considerable imagination by architect Carl Koch who collaborated with John Bemis. But even in 1960 America had not really applied factory production methods of mass housing. The largest single producer of houses made and sold the trivial number of 25,000 houses a year; its houses, practical enough, were banal even in their conventionality; and this isolated success really had no important industrial competitor. The field of the small individual house remained in the hands of speculative builders whose towns degraded even the occasional good house plan by their bad site planning and their mediocre architecture. Factory-made housing to be successful had to

come from mobilized industrial power, not from the dreams of architects. The industrial power never chose to mobilize for this purpose. At
best it geared up to produce elaborate trailers which by 1960 were
almost as big as a small house, were becoming less mobile, were
housing many other Americans besides the few gypsies and the many
Florida-bound gaffers who first took to them. Trailer parks might some
day develop the amenities of a well-planned residential area but
this was more a possibility than a likelihood. If trailers were to be the
total answer of industry, it had to be admitted that the New Deal
housing had at least sought something better.

To the record of architectural mediocrity, the New Deal offered one
distinguished exception. It was in the valley of the Tennessee. We do
not speak here of the politico-economic triumphs over private power
interests or the merit of the controversy. Cheap electricity, flood control and soil improvement were, in any event, brought to 40,000 square
miles in seven Southern states. It may even have marked the beginning
of the South's recovery. There in the valley great dams stimulated the
growth of industries and towns and the improvement of farms. The artificial lakes served recreation too. Buildings and parks were pleasing.
TVA architects and engineers under the direction of Roland Wank set
up a model organization for co-ordinated architectural-engineering
work. Their powerhouse at Pickwick Landing housed giant turbines
in beautiful elemental forms that were triumphs of functional design.
Their Watts Bar steam plant of 1942 provided an elegant display of a
few balanced elements. Kenneth Reid, writing in *Pencil Points* in 1939,
said that the TVA had demonstrated how beautiful works of engineering might be. The "engineering" demonstration had been made by
architects like Wank and his able designer, Mario Bianculli. No other
landmark could stand so well as the architectural monument to the
New Deal. None was so often visited by foreigners.

The New Deal established tax scales, corporate and private, which
were far from confiscatory, which did not, as so many people claimed,
destroy American initiative, but which nonetheless did level incomes
and reduce the power of individual wealth. When the tax schedules
were combined with the new power of labor, the relatively great gains
in workingmen's wage scales, the disappearance of domestic servants,
it became fashionable to declaim about America that it had become one
vast middle class. But it took some myopia to believe this. Like the
myth that Americans had become much more nomadic, it did not
stand the scrutiny of numbers. Thus between 1947 and 1954 it was
still true of America that the poorest tenth of our people enjoyed only
one one-hundredth of the national income while the richest tenth had

nearly a third. The figures shifted slightly through the decade in favor of an averaging down but the progress towards anything like even incomes was not really impressive. There were still rich men and stable and prosperous private enterprises. Both of these conditions, let us make no doubt, affected the future of American architecture. The private enterprise whose corporation felt a public responsibility held the promise of a fine industrial and commercial architecture. The great shift in distribution of wealth offered less promise, for though ultra-rich individuals might have built crazy things like P. T. Barnum's Iranistan in Connecticut, or the Victorian palaces on San Francisco's Nob Hill, they also provided brilliant things like J. P. Morgan's library. If more of architecture were to be built in America by government instead of by individuals, it was important that there be great changes from earlier cautious and bad expressions of the public taste. There was not much indication that the changes were being prepared. Moreover no record of history suggested that a vast middle class bereft of really wealthy patrons, operating on the decisions of a middle-class bureaucratic central government, was likely to encourage or produce any important art at all. Most great art seems to come from the poles of a society, not from its equator.

The ultimate disappointment of the New Deal to an architectural or art historian must be that its aesthetic aspirations were muffled in its social ideals. New Dealers were quite as content with shoddy aesthetics as Coolidge or Hoover might have been. Social reformers need not, of course, be identified with architectural reform; when they were so identified, they did not always fight for architecture with the same vigor as they fought for legislation. Nor need we blame them for this. One can tilt at too many windmills at the same time. Among the legions of reform there were surely many aesthetically conservative or even ignorant troops. Not one could safely be alienated for the sake of art. But beyond that it is regrettably clear that few of the leading New Dealers cared about the arts at all. Roosevelt himself may have cared as much as anyone. He was interested in architecture and even liked to design it on the back of envelopes. But he had an impulsive, dogmatic, sentimental and impeccably mediocre judgment in aesthetic matters.

4

WAR IS SOMETIMES IRRELEVANT TO ARCHITECTURAL HISTORY. IT MAY stop the course of building briefly. It may damage or destroy some admirable historical monuments. It may change the balance of world power and thus send a new colonial architecture coursing through the world. It may modify the taste of the winners or losers. It is too early to speak of the long-term effects of World War II on the architecture of the West or of the East.

Any war tends to establish a hiatus in arts which are not directly useful for fighting it, or serve it well as propaganda or escape. Modern was is less lenient about this than the war of the ancients. Whatever the Athenians may have accomplished on their Acropolis during the Peloponnesian War, our Seabees built no Parthenons in the Pacific during the years from 1940 to 1945, nor were important palaces erected at home. At the war's end the deficit in needed building was large, so that architecture not only recovered quickly but gained by the delay the war had imposed. The eclectic conservatives were five years older and wearier; new leaders had come to industry and the universities, and these men feared the new architecture less.

At the highest level of response, architecture could find no fitting answer to the times. The mood of the West was strange, unreal, almost trancelike. It felt doom yet was unready to concede it. It went about seeking peaceful uses of the new powers yet saw that these must be so delayed that they could not immediately affect architecture. Not even the palpable presence of rockets, aircraft, radar, television and automation could be immediately or obviously expressed.

On philosophical grounds, men with a doom sense might have declined to build at all, on the thesis that to build was meaningless; they might have built fantasies and luxuries in one grand final fling, a sort of architectural dance of death; they might have frantically sought to build underground cities for survival and this would not have been above their powers had they really believed that demolition was near or survival important; or they might have tried, as the Byzantines had tried unsuccessfully, to create new shrines and to mob them with feverish appeals to God to spare them from all the consequences of their inconsequence.

In the event they did none of these things. Instead, for the most part they went about their ordinary ways in an atmosphere of dream in which perhaps many hoped that they might wake to find that all the clouds had somehow rolled away into the night, or as Churchill had put it in 1949 that the Mongol armies and their leaders had mounted their ponies and all trooped home.

Historians trying to generalize from our buildings may develop elaborate hypotheses to explain the metal and glass cages as an expression of the feeling of a society with a sense of death, "ephemera, ephemera, all is ephemera," in which building for permanence was obviously futile and for which there was something symbolic in using fragile and transitory materials; or as the desire of the same society to catch all the physical light there was since so much of the spiritual world was dark. These would be no more far-fetched than interpretations that have sometimes been proposed for other architectures by people who like to read into works of art more than is there.

The scars laid on the conscience of the West, the uncertainty as to whether man had really become human during the long centuries of his alleged rise; all such philosophical questionings, heavy as they might lie on the hearts of individual architects, could find no outlet in the symbols of a society which, no doubt rightly, set out to try to get along with the daily act of living. There was little or nothing in the words or the lives of the people who were making the buildings of 1950 or 1960 to indicate any morbidity, conscious or subconscious. Unless the symbolism were clearer one was prone to conclude that the architectural results depended upon far more immediate and practical situations arising in an attitude of "let us do the best we can, so long as we can."

For each nation this posed a different problem. For those countries of Europe which had borne the brunt of the bombing and the shelling and the fires, and for equally devastated Japan, it meant an opportunity like that of the phoenix, a new day of chance to replace obsolete buildings, to revivify the city plan. But like the phoenix most of the reborn cities looked much like the old, save for some details of the plumage. The story of opportunities gloriously grasped, as at Coventry, England or at least partially enjoyed, as at Osaka and Nagoya, was outweighed by the story of opportunities muffed as at London and Tokyo. It is an important story of contemporary architecture but not this story, for the demolition passed America by. The problem was different for the newly developing nations, often building from scratch, having little worth saving, but this too varied from culturally mature India or aggressive Brazil to the newest and most naïve and most artificially constructed African tribal nation, seeking to create architectural symbols of status overnight. This too is an important story yet to be told, but again it is not our story. Nor is the still different and more conservative story of France or Scandinavia.

If America gained no chances to rebuild by the destruction of war, its soldier-architects did voyage afar and were influenced by what they saw, notably in Japan and Korea. The rise of the dictators forced a flow of brilliant architects from Europe to America and these were a major force both in the controversy and the subsequent victory. America's new world position asked her to do much more building abroad so that American architects were now called upon to design for foreign sites;

while in a sort of unofficial reciprocity many foreigners designed buildings or parts of buildings for America. It was a world in which, by 1960, and with the notable exception of the Soviet Union and Red China, architectural ideas were a free item of international exchange. But all of these consequences can best be dealt with later. Here we should pause, if only for a moment, on the drab details of the local efforts during the war and in America.

In this time private building stopped and architects sought to work for defense. In 1940, a report issued by Columbia University found William Lescaze urging that all architects, engineers and contractors be organized into self-reliant units to prepare for building the plants, shops, factories, garages, barracks, administration buildings, airports and workers' houses that were obviously going to be needed. It was a good war cry but little more.

In the hysteria close on the heels of Pearl Harbor, Americans had a short orgy of blackouts, bomb shelters and camouflage. Briefly and abortively they tried to use architects in these unnecessary tasks. Large firms such as Voorhees, Walker, Foley and Smith could be used effectively to supervise construction of new and major military installations, for their training included the kind of competence Shreve had displayed in erecting the Empire State Building. Of the service construction agencies, the Navy's Bureau of Yards and Docks, commanded by the colorful Admiral Ben Moreell, had the most sympathy with architecture and sometimes found reason to encourage a little of it at the bases. But for the most part Americans acted more like Spartans than Athenians during the war and there was little architectural "nonsense."

A few factories, a few light oil-refining plants were suggestive. The Main Reception Building at the Great Lakes Naval Training Station, by Skidmore, Owings and Merrill, and the United States Merchant Marine Cadet Basic School at San Mateo, California by Gardner Dailey, were beacons in the murk but the whole list of such exercises in imagination was short. A few aircraft hangars gave the engineers, Ammann and Whitney, some experience with concrete vaults but the Fascists were doing more exciting things at Orvieto. All this was outweighed by the miles of temporary barracks erected at places like Fort Dix, March Field or Fort Meade. These were understandably dull and homely temporary affairs. It might even have been argued that a comfortable and imaginative environment was precisely not the thing to provide a young man as you prepared him for battle. But buildings expected to outlast the war were not much better. They were either frankly efficient engineering, or, less happily, were swathed in mediocre Georgian details.

The war housing, military or civilian, was not much better; a dreary array of two-story row houses and apartment buildings, crowding too many people on small sites even when the specifications of the USHA were observed. The pressure of time rushed the schedules; bureaucratic redtape limited the quality of study. There were notable exceptions, to emphasize what might have been, by the Saarinens at Center Line, Michigan; by Gropius and Breuer at New Kensington, Pennsylvania; by Oscar Stonorov at Carver Court in Coatesville, Pennsylvania; by Wurster at Valencia Gardens, San Francisco. An outstanding example was provided by Richard Neutra for the Channel Heights project at San Pedro, California. Here pairs of low-cost, one-story houses were built on *cul-de-sac* access roads, well sited on landscaped terraces. All these showed was what might have been. In the end the war did not provide explicit and important examples for American architectural history; on the other hand it defaced a great deal of land with "temporary" buildings which have turned out to be remarkably permanent even in the heart of the capital city. If it had any benign influence at all, it was a remote one.

5

ALWAYS THE CENTER OF POPULATION CONTINUED TO MOVE RELENTLESSLY westwards, clinging firmly to the 39th Parallel, now crossing the Indiana line into Illinois. The West Coast became as culturally important as it had long wished to be. More people still lived in the South Atlantic states, for example, but too many of them were backward people and not influential culturally. The great power still rested in the Middle Atlantic states and the industrial Middle West. Each of these regions held a fifth of the population and a vastly bigger fraction of the national productive capacity and wealth. The South seemed to be beginning a renascence if it could abandon the race struggle. The agrarian Middle West was declining slightly. The prairie was still culturally cold and dry. The Mountain and Desert states were beginning to open up. But it was still true that most of the best education and the innovation came from New England or nearby; most of the lively arts and the ancient ones as well were centered around New York; there was still a preponderance of money in the East despite the blatant claims by individual Texas oil men; the Middle West was still the heartland whence came the new battalions of ambitious young men. But the Pacific Coast and Texas were roaring ahead, developing their enigmatic cultures. That there was more than one could be learned from even the briefest visit, say, to Portland, San Francisco, Los Angeles and

Houston. But the anthropologists were not speaking of a civilized city like San Francisco when they said that the new West contained the inevitable future culture of America. To much of the rest of the country, it might have seemed interesting to be recast in the mold of the Golden Gate but there might be less aspiration to emerge in the costume of Hollywood and Vine.

While the cultural dominance of New York was still felt in the world of publishing, the theater and painting, New York no longer had even a semblance of a monopoly on first-class architects. Men like Frank Lloyd Wright had of course never lived there but they were mavericks. In 1960 if you set out to stick pins in a map of the country to indicate the place of business of notable and imaginative architects, you would notice no heavy concentration, not even on Manhattan Island. Indeed, it was not certain that a list of the best five would have to include any New Yorkers. Important men could be found in Chicago, Detroit, San Francisco, Los Angeles, New Haven, and Boston; and good men almost everywhere.

The population, too, was less identifiable on grounds of racial or national origin. No new massive immigrations were permitted. Ill-conceived national quotas insured that the new immigrants would add little to the variety of America. The earlier immigrants were well established and the cultural pluralism that was developing was not drawn along particularly nationalistic lines. The small but influential immigration of the artistic and intellectual refugees of the '30s had been fully assimilated.

It was a population blessed with an enormous increase in the energy at its disposal. In 1930 Americans had had 24 thousand trillion BTU's to use, while by 1950 this had increased a half, to 36 thousand trillion; meantime the population had grown only a fifth. Water still supplied only a few per cent of the energy but coal which had furnished two thirds of it in 1930 yielded only one third in 1955. Petroleum had moved from one third to two thirds in the same period. Most of it was still consumed in the form of oil but natural gas was gaining steadily.

Though all might wonder what the nucleus would ultimately do to challenge the older sources of energy, even the change from coal to petroleum had many implications for architecture. It established new centers of wealth, often on virgin land and among culturally virgin people, and it offered to the people of Texas, Oklahoma and Louisiana or the Williston Basin an opportunity to forego the mistakes of their ancestors and to build a finer urban environment. This was just a chance and not a promise, and by 1960 it looked as though it might not be taken up.

Decentralization of plants became easier because oil, gas and electricity could be conveyed easily; railroad locations became less significant for industries whose primary problem was fuel. Petroleum combustion offered the opportunity for cleaner cities although these had been technically possible with coal and were not automatic with petroleum, as the smog-laden airs of California were demonstrating.

Consumers now used much more electricity in their homes. The per capita consumption of 550 kilowatt hours in 1930 was stretched five times by 1955. The total electric power used throughout the country was tripled.

The energies available merely increased the size of the problems of urban transportation without introducing new modes. The demands of transportation were positive and clear, but still they were not taken seriously until almost too late. Meanwhile the architects cultivated the gardens of their individual buildings. Individual residents abandoned public transportation for their private cars and drove in long lines to work, one rider per car; then public transportation abandoned them. And thus it was that the new buildings thrust their sharp and elegant faces among the burdock and thistles of the highways and the streets, proudly ignoring the life they would have to live among the deep-cutting canyons of the new roads, the exhausts and klaxons of a desecrated city, the constant flow of the lines of motors, more deadly to urban aesthetic when parked than when moving, so that all seemed to be asking whether man was not really the servant of this machine rather than its master.

After the peak of activity, in 1944, the decline of railway passenger traffic was precipitate. Despite the fantastic improvement in the speed, safety and comfort of air travel, which by 1960 had helped to obliterate comfortable and convenient rail travel, the big losses suffered by the rails were not to the air lanes but to the highways. Three million passenger cars were made in 1930; eight million were produced in 1955. The 24 million registered autos became 52 million; and each one averaged more than 10,000 miles in 1955. The trucks and buses grew bigger as well as more numerous. Despite frenetic road construction, which widened the highways and increased the safe speed on which they could be coursed, no important measures were taken to improve the conditions at the termini. Practically nothing was done to take account of the changes the highways were imposing on the cities themselves and in 1958 the President of the United States tolerated, even encouraged a highway building program conceived in a vacuum and in which those in the federal government responsible for the future of the American cities were scarcely consulted.

A few superhighways were built, a few new expressways were cut through the cities with as little concern for what they did as the railways and the rapid transit lines had previously shown. New lines of blight were gleefully created. Buildings continued to rise to increase the traffic densities without being required to contribute anything to reduce the mounting deficit of parking facilities. Even the few buildings which were designed to take account of this problem were not required to pay any attention to the problem of time and space and the new garages like the new bridges poured the flood of cars, highly concentrated in time, onto city streets that could not accommodate the ordinary flow. As the rails had once split cities and left devastation along their routes, now the great expressways were allowed to provide new and greater channels for erosion. The flight to the unfinished suburb which had only houses and none of the other requirements of a sound community accelerated while the centers of the cities continued to dwindle and to decay. In all this rush to the new desolation there were voices of protest, none stronger than that of Lewis Mumford. But they had as little influence as the ill-starred Cassandra. Even those contemporary architects who were most aware of the problem and most vociferous about the misdeeds of others were prone to forget when they themselves had interesting buildings to create, as irresponsible in their way as the City Beautiful men had been before them. For the city of 1960, public indifference and the automobile were greater enemies than the H-bomb. As between slow decay and demolition there was no significant choice. Though not solely responsible, the automobile became the symbol of the fall of the city.

6

CHANGES IN TECHNIQUES BURGEONED EVERYWHERE AFTER THE WAR. IN 1950, eight million television sets and forty-five million radio receivers raised their antennae over American roofs. The telephone became commonplace, its extraordinary technical advances taken for granted. Electricity served so many functions in a building as to go uncounted. Electric lights were so common and current so cheap that many were allowed to burn night and day. The first commercial fluorescent lamp was marketed in 1938 and this was soon followed by the circular fluorescent tube. Serving many important building purposes, the "neon" lights had an important visual impact, notably as their use in advertising changed the nocturnal aspect of cities. A great deal of variety was possible as a night visit to Broadway, Tokyo's Ginza, and Boston's

Charles River Basin would quickly show. Neon was not a trivial potential factor in urban design but no one knew how to control it.

Other inventions changed the living habits of the typical American
family. The deep-freeze had been prepared for household use by 1935
but it took the food rationing, the victory gardening, and the home
canning of the war, with the subsequent rise of the nation to Texan
standards of living, to make it a generally coveted device. In 1952 when
Betty Furness was selling appliances between the acts of the televised
national conventions, she plugged mostly the dishwashers and the
refrigerators. But garbage disposers, clotheswashers and dryers, and air
conditioners had all been designed, and by 1960 they were common
elements of American domestic life and an important determinant of
the layout and the cost of residential units. Space could be constricted,
architectural amenity could be absent in the mind of the typical family
if only the kitchen and the bathroom were efficient and well-stocked
with modern domestic machinery.

The great European architects had long vaunted the opportunities
that were present for architects who would use technology to the hilt.
American architects were a little slower in rallying to this gonfalon but
by the end of the war they were more than ready. Some of the older
architects had scorned technology, admitting that it was a necessary
evil but seeking to conceal it through art. They of course could not get
along without their copies of *Sweet's Catalog*, the compendium of building equipment that was begun in 1906. But the standardized hardware, plumbing and woodwork they could find there would go un-
specified if money were available for tailoring a gold bathtub, forging
a wrought-iron hinge, or carving a mantelpiece. On the other hand
Sweet's enchanted the immigrant architects. To them American industrial products offered a stockpile of inexpensive parts and their ideology
insisted that the stockpile was charming. "*Sweet's Catalogue*," the
Viennese Neutra wrote in 1937, "looked to me . . . as inspiring as a
healthy forest to a Norwegian carpenter."

Further contact with industrial products excited more general interest
in mechanical equipment and its possibilities in architecture although
the ancient concern with structure was still dominant. Rigid frames of
steel were conceived. There were new ideas about wind-bracing to reduce
vibration and eliminate distortion particularly in towers. Continuous
glass sash could be pivoted vertically or horizontally. The covering for
steel frames was drawn thinner as veneers of metal and glass replaced
brick and stone. Better floor finishes were found, better ways of conceal-
ing duct systems. More parts came prefabricated to the big buildings.
Thin concrete shells on the Zweis-Dywidag system began to be used as in

the Wrigley Building at Chicago. Such construction, however, made little headway in America until Amman and Whitney followed European and South American engineers in parting from the steel frames which had been so strongly entrenched by the successes of Albert Kahn. The timber industry sought new markets with its new timber connectors, glued laminates, lamellar diamond-trussed roofs all of which opened up wide spans to timber. These and other technical innovations occupied the thought of architects and engineers as much as design and history had occupied the man of the Beaux-Arts. Engineering became almost a fetish and the interest was inevitably reflected in the appearance as well as the working of the architecture.

The greatest lag was in the exploitation of the structural, plastic and textural potentials of reinforced concrete. It was not that American engineers were intellectually incapable of designing in the ways of Freyssinet, Maillart or Nervi but rather that their clients were more accustomed to steel. American building economies *seemed* adverse to brilliant uses of concrete, and the role of the engineer in America was clearly limited by the architects if he essayed to be an artist. Moreover the coarse textures that Le Corbusier and his Japanese disciples cultivated did not seem refined enough to the always polishing Americans, so when concrete structures were made they were often overrefined. The leadership that America had shown in the days of Roebling and Eads had moved to Italy and Spain and Mexico and Japan and it had not returned by 1960.

Architecture is sometimes modified imperceptibly by the accumulation of small inventions — a new closure material, a new connector, a new joint or calking compound, a new way of washing a window. The years teemed with such changes, with new minor products, with improvements in old ones but no one can be identified as having been crucially important, not even the more frequently present plastics.

Beyond the novelty of materials and the experiments with structure lay the rules set down by the demands of equipment. Not only did the equipment require more and more of the volumetric space of a building but it began to ask for strategic location as well. Air-conditioning plants could not push the air efficiently more than a few stories and intermediate units sometimes needed to be placed in high buildings. For almost all buildings the penthouse was a technical necessity which most architects continued to deal with as an afterthought. The machinery was beginning to set down some conditions for design itself and these conditions were not so well understood as the limitations of structure, which themselves were often misinterpreted. On the far horizon might loom the computing machines. For if these were to come to play the role in business operations that many predicted, they too might become conditioners of design; they might for example lead to a re-evaluation of the masses of an urban commercial building, ask for a return to the old broad blocks which had been abandoned for thin-slab buildings when it seemed that every office worker needed a chance for a daily look at the sun while sitting at his desk. The computers would have no such aspirations.

But if this forecast of the implications of technological development were far-fetched, it was evident that many other effects were not. New ways of doing things, such as air travel, called for new ideas of terminals and the ideas had difficulty keeping pace with the changes in the transport. Urban decentralization by the automobile reopened the discussion of the relative advantages of horizontal and vertical buildings. Incessant movement of peoples changed the rate at which an innovation here would be learned about there. Indeed the whole admiration of change, in knowledge, in speed, in space reinforced established American philosophy, now applied to the arts as well as to technology, even perhaps to economics and politics. This held that change was, in itself, a good; that innovation was desirable for its own sake; it helped to build a feeling in architect and client alike that each building must offer a new and dramatic adventure in which the newness was the most important thing. Thus each designer and each client was tempted to seek his own moment of euphoric collaboration to provide a building, poised like a butterfly, on the edge of the ephemeral.

It was in this atmosphere of technological change, large and small, real and fancied, beneficial and not, that the other influences on design were felt — felt by a prosperous and fickle clientele ready, even eager, for what was new and therefore choice.

The influences were of many kinds: the trends of commerce, of literature, of painting; the social attitudes of the architects; the critical preparation, the impact of the work of the great European pioneers and the one American, Wright, now suddenly appreciated in many quarters; the preaching of the Congrés Internationaux d'Architecture Moderne (CIAM) and its early American admirers; the actions of the opposition and finally the finishing touches applied by the taste-makers. We need now to examine these.

7

THE OTHER ARTS, AS THEY WERE BEING PRACTICED IN AMERICA, SEEMED to have little to say to the art of architecture. American literature was no doubt providing a true response to the times. In the last half of the '30s there were angry social comments from Anderson, Odets, Wolfe, Dos Passos, Steinbeck and Hemingway. After some romantic excursions with the folksy sentiments of the New Deal, MacLeish showed his poetic genius in such a dramatic poem as *The Fall of the City* (1937). There were somber undertones in such work when MacLeish's masterless men found their master and this was equated with the city's fall. Nevertheless MacLeish seemed the most typically American, standing squarely with affection for the people and abhorrence of despotism, following in his life as in his works the general development of liberal thought and action throughout the quarter-century. "Democracy," he said in 1941, "is never a thing done. Democracy is always something that a nation must be doing."

Then it was the time for Faulkner to be recognized as the strongest of the American novelists, with or without the benefit of labored interpretation. Directly, or suggestively, American literature was expressing concern about its twentieth-century life, even a rejection of it; sometimes the rejection was only of the secular development, sometimes of the very philosophical underpinning. Most of the writers chose still to try to communicate, troubled themselves about perfecting their craft, developed their symbols out of ancient and well-recognized forms or used their invented new ones often enough so that they too became recognizable. Then the èlan of the '30s died away. The beatniks following Kerouac, who emulated the painters in obscurity, never acquired so large a claque save among the young, and even there their status was not secure. This was demonstrated in 1959 when a wave of emotion swept the American colleges following the sudden death of Camus, who had offered hope to many.

Not many of the painters offered more hope; and if they did it might be hard to make it out in the obscure messages of men like de Kooning, Pollock, Baziotes, Callahan, Rothko, Tobey and Motherwell. Whether obscure or clarion, the message echoed endlessly in what they wrote to explain their painting. The age or at least the painter was sick, sick of mechanization, sick of human degeneracy, sick of "progress," sick of order, sick of old values, sick of science.

American painters had, on the whole, clung to realism longer than the Europeans, perhaps because American postures in the arts so consistently lagged behind the postures of Europe. Or it may have been because America still gave the painters some reason for confidence in the idea that criticism and calls for reform might be heeded, that reform was still possible. At least up to Hiroshima it may have been that American painters did not judge their world as a place in which personal refuge was of primary import.

During this earlier time they still vigorously sought for messages and for ways to send them. Many of them loved the American scene, even the ugly parts. Charles Burchfield found things to love in the small Midwestern towns that Mencken had found so depressing; Stuart Davis cast America in crudely drawn diagrams that were still loving, so that *Garage Lights* (1931) incorporated barns, gas pumps, booms, masts, coal elevators, excursion steamers, fish piers and floodlights into semi-abstractions which were not flights from reality, denials of America or even bitter criticism; Edward Hopper, the most typical and the most faithful to his love, worked with the ordinary, never glamorizing it, never prettifying it, but never satirizing it or wallowing in its meanness either unless the reality was satire enough. The characteristic *Early Sunday Morning* (1930) was a deadpan portrayal of a deserted Main Street of two-storied, gaunt-windowed, monotonous brick buildings, their awnings raised, shades prominent, accentuating the lonely barber pole and fire hydrant. If people invaded such streets, as in *Night Hawks* (1942), for Hopper they were even less individualized than the buildings.

By 1933 social-satiric painting was also direct and common. Reginald Marsh showed it in his Hogarthian girls; Philip Evergood in *My Forebears Were Pioneers* (1940) exclaimed as some of the novelists did against the betrayal of the American dream. But by 1954 in *American Shrimp Girl* Evergood, like others of the fiery WPA days, had said farewell to satire and to protest which was either no longer necessary or no longer any use. The same thing happened to the still more critical Ben Shahn, who had said earlier, "You paint something because you like it a lot or else because you hate it." In the end there was more love than hate although there was still an abhorrence of sentimentality: "All the wheels of business and advertising are turning night and day to prove the colossal falsehood that America is smiling. And they want me to add my two per cent. Hell, no!"

Jack Levine began with what was little more than caricature of back streets and moved to become a powerful painter. In his work there was a suggestion of some deep-lying evil and good, more significant than the good or bad motions a society might make in any moment. The sensuous, thick-lipped, heavy-lidded Old Testament faces were universal. Sometimes the paintings were comments on social actions such as those of a banqueting American brigadier general, of courts or elections, sometimes, as in *King Saul* (1952), footnotes on the human race in general. However, he did not abandon satire and protest as fully as some of the others and his painting of 1954, *Election Night*, with its evening-dressed frumps with funny hats and its forlorn cigarette girl in can-can costume, suggests the fundamental inconsequence with which some types of Americans approach even an election.

But if Evergood, Shahn and Levine were in the way of being painters of distinction and not quite like anybody in Europe, they were unlikely to be of much direct service to the cause of architecture. Their methods of composition, their concepts of space were not calculated to provoke a new or better architectural understanding. Their choice of subject matter was not calculated, either, to appeal as murals, for it was too often revolutionary, critical, sardonic, sinister, or at best somber.

It would have been silly to expect that the most powerful protests in paint should have come from America. Here, despite all difficulties, the protests were inevitably minor; and in the face of the Kremlin, the Brown Shirts, the Spanish Civil War, the difficulties of America were actually trivial. Thus it is not surprising that the Spanish Picasso, working in France, should produce the great monument of protest in *Guernica*, where fractured planes of black, white and gray held the macabre finale of a bullfight, in which the triumphant brute surveyed his slaughter by the light from one naked, shimmering bulb. If made to condemn the atrocities of the Spanish Civil War, it managed somehow to expand into a bitter and universal indictment of man's inhumanity.

The painting of the Mexicans Rivera and Orozco was not only more palatable as to style but the messages also were less insistent and for a time almost unrealized. This set the stage for the lusty comedy produced when Dartmouth College commissioned murals by José Clemente Orozco and Rockefeller Center ordered paintings by Diego Rivera and the two Socialist-Communists were invited to speak their pieces in the halls of capitalism. Ever since 1921 Rivera had been creating large murals exhibiting Mexico's social problems, and his trip to Soviet Russia in 1927-1928 had reaffirmed his social convictions. It was naïve to commission him; not surprising that the frescoes in the RCA Building at Rockefeller Center raised a storm of protest. The east wall panels depicted the American Revolution, westward expansion, slavery, the Mexican war, and the Civil War leading to the First International under Marx. The west wall showed imperialism, farmers' revolts, hunger marchers, strikers, the New Deal, unemployment. The labor fights during the '90s were against Big Business, symbolized by Rockefeller who was shown with a maimed face; Wilson's World War stood alongside a "trial by prejudice" in which President Lowell of Harvard was shown rendering his committee's recommendation about Sacco and Vanzetti, who cowered in front of the Statue of Liberty. Imperialism, Cuban sugar, Wall Street, bananas, oil — all came in for abuse. The Pope was shown blessing Mussolini, and Hitler was seen watching police brutalize a woman with her head shaved and a sign attached to her, "I have given myself to a Jew." A serene moment extolled Stalin, Trotsky and Marx: "Workers of the World Unite." Shortly after they were completed, the frescoes were covered with plaster, and in February 1934 workmen chipped them from the walls amid voluble protests, especially from Communists, but also from painters like Leon Kroll who thought the Rockefellers had no moral right to destroy the paintings although the morality of Rivera himself to destroy a Rockefeller patron's society went unchallenged. Such murals did not affect architecture, which soon afforded few walls for artists, anyway.

Where painting could affect architecture in this time it seemed to do so from the works of the abstractionists more than from the works of the very competent realists. There had been notable immigrants in the '30s and many of them, though not all, were abstractionists. Grosz and Zerbe were not, but there were many others like Feininger, Tchelitchev, Berman, Ozenfant, Mondriaan, Koerner, Albers, Moholy-Nagy and Kepes. Now there was a spate of American abstraction typified at its best by de Kooning and Pollock. But it was the older Mondriaan and Doesburg or the meticulous Albers more than the slovenly Motherwell who had anything to say to the new American architecture; and it was the constructivist Gabo rather than Calder the maker of mobiles who furnished useful architectural suggestions, at least for the moment, though the work of the latter was among the gayest and most original of all the American efforts of the time, and well fitted to cooperate with architecture. But even the ideas of Doesburg and Mondriaan and Gabo found their way to American architecture indirectly through the influence they may have first had on the European proposals of the great elder statesmen of the modern architectural movement.

The abstract expressionists often supplied their own criticism even if unconsciously. What was one to think of painting which consisted of an "unknown adventure into an unknown space"? Rothko assembled his brushes, pails, spoons, toothpaste tubes and brooms and insisted that people find expressions of emotions in the movements of the painting. But what movement? And whose emotions? The emotions of the individual painters, of course. It had to be taken for granted that the emotions of every dauber were by some mysterious process important to someone besides himself; it had to be accepted that de Kooning was saying something profound and not something silly when he declared that the world of the atoms was beginning to bore him. As time went on, the vanguard of the school seemed to depart further and further from any will to craftsmanship or communication. At best, many were producing only intricate and colorful or bold and rough ornaments for the large blank walls and empty spaces of neutral office buildings.

In the same time there were potential new stimuli from Europe. There was the matured Mondriaan's *Composition in Black, White, and Red* of 1936, the humorous Miró, the frightening Picasso, the ebullient Léger, a modern man who still knew how to paint on a wall, and perhaps most prescient for the future of an architecture that might someday break the cage, Arp's *Human Concretion* of 1935, Brancusi's sleek shapes, and the interpenetrated work of Henry Moore.

American architects were well enough aware of these artists in the general sense and, if they were modern, architects tended to accept them all quite indiscriminately as fellow revolutionaries who were also "progressive" and "men of our time." But who were the men of the time? The range took you from Dali's *Portrait of Gala* of 1935 to Siqueiros' *Echo of a Scream* of 1937, from Matisse's *Girl on a Red Background* of 1936, through Rouault's *Christ* to Bonnard's *Le Cannet* (1940) and so to the geometrical abstractionists and the "action" painters. This range was so great that no one architect followed the lines of many while at the same time he tended to esteem them all collectively since they, like himself, were "modern" even though they beckoned down altogether too many mutually contradictory roads.

8

IF THE ESTABLISHED AND SERIOUS ARTS OF AMERICA SEEMED TO HAVE little to say that might influence architecture, it was still possible that the new "lively" mass arts might have something to offer. The question might have been shouted into the void but few echoes came back. The Broadway theater was a mass art on Manhattan at least, pandering to the low taste of expense-account men from all over America. It often provided dramatic excitement, particularly in ballet, sometimes a social message, but little visual imagination which might have influenced architecture, while as costs mounted scenery became ever more wispy.

The radio said little and the television showed less that might have been worth listening to or looking at; but they were specially mute or inept when it came to the visual arts. They made few significant experiments in vision. When they approached the arts descriptively or critically it was on tiptoe and with hushed voice. Even in 1960 NBC's hour program about architecture was both dull and misinformative. When, and rarely, they took the arts in their stride, they caused them to suffer from the same banality, vulgarity, triviality, or outright deception that suffused so many other things they did, thinking it significant for example that a jockey collected paintings. It was not often different with the movies and Hollywood. Occasional "art" films scored minor successes. But at the end of the period the movies and television were depressing.

Music, painting, architecture, sculpture had found some assistance in technology, much new subject matter, and architecture at least had found new problems, but for all the ancient so-called "fine arts" the role of technology as a helper was marginal. The new arts of the movies and television owed their existence to technology. They had had a long chance to justify this existence, to develop their own unities. In this they seemed to have failed. That they were a powerful cultural force could not be denied; that they were a good one could not be asserted. For architecture neither really had anything to say though there were a few anxious years when it seemed as though American domestic taste might be formed by the taste of the Hollywood stars; then we learned that the stars were just American peasants whose taste was quite like our own. Perhaps we may be thankful that the movies and television felt no need to conduct an architectural crusade. What architectural taste might have been like in America had it been ministered to by Sam Goldwyn, Cecil B. De Mille, John Gunther, Lowell Thomas, Gabriel Heatter, Bishop Fulton J. Sheen, Arthur Godfrey, and even Steve Allen is something better not to contemplate.

Things were more promising on the industrial front. Industrial advertising occasionally approached a level of communication appealing even to sophisticated taste. Designers at Chicago's Institute of Design made a mark with their layouts for posters, advertising, photo-montages and photography. In adopting these, progressive businessmen like the late Walter Paepcke, Chairman of the Container Corporation of America, led the way, employing artists like Herbert Bayer, Herbert Matter, Leo Lionni and Gyorgy Kepes to design advertisements. Some of their work was put together in a folder; more appeared in Kepes's study of visual communication, *The Language of Vision*, published in 1944. Here he tried to apply Gestalt psychology to optical communication. His first sentence revealed the social objectives of these visual studies: "Today we experience chaos . . . our common life has lost its coherency. . . ." His examples of new typography and paintings, his analyses of texture, focus and spatial patterns revealed an open desire to relate manifold discrete aspects of modern thought. Still in 1960 the problem of communicating ideas visually was not as near solution as it had been in the Middle Ages or the Renaissance. The old common symbols had been discarded but there were no new and common ones. The real and lasting symbols earn meaning only through much use and nothing was used long enough in commerce to gain much meaning.

In advertising there lay another and rather obscure commentary on the American architectural scene or at least on the American advertisers' appraisal of the American architect to whom they wished to appeal. European architectural magazines were consistently gay with advertisements of building products, designed by good artists, laid before architect-readers in an abstract way but quite in keeping with the art manners the architects were known to approve. The advertising pages were thereby quite as interesting as the text. No such nonsense reached the pages of the American architectural magazines, whose advertisers regularly advanced dreary sets of facts or claims aimed at the most pedestrian instincts of the profession. Of course it is also true that no industrial Olivetti (other than Paepcke) arose to subsidize architectural and art magazines so that they could afford to be bold, critical and gay. It was almost inevitable that advanced American architects and especially architectural students should seek their stimulus in magazines of Italy, England, Germany and France and not in those of their own country.

Developments in industrial design had a more direct and not always benign effect, at least upon the public taste. To this day, architects and probably people in general have not been able to establish clear-cut and logical attitudes about the role of industrial design in an industrial society. Primitive societies do not entertain such doubts. The maker of the utensil, the craftsman, and the maker of magic, the artist, have different roles but the question of status does not arise. But the primitive craftsman makes his utensil for use and does not try to make it more salable through design. Eastern societies generally do not make the distinction between the minor arts or "crafts" and the major arts such as we make in the West; particularly they do not assign to useful things a necessarily lower status.

But sometime in Western history, and for us it does not matter when, this schism arose. It persists. We think there is something nobler about the useless arts (or theoretical physics) than is to be found in useful tools (or engineering). Time and again from William Morris, through the German Bauhaus, to the Institute of Design in Chicago, first-class talents have asserted that the problems of industrial design are genuine problems of contemporary art, deserving first-class attention. Time and again but with varying success they have applied that attention. New York's Museum of Modern Art has made notable displays of the products of industrial design. The chances are that the ordinary objects in daily use in a conventional contemporary American house have never been more efficient or more lovely in any other time; and it is ten to one that they are more lovely than any objects of art the same household has collected. Yet the stigma remains.

Industrial designers are sometimes very prosperous and influential in these days. Men like Walter Dorwin Teague, Raymond Loewy, Henry Dreyfuss are men of considerable talent. Yet they act embarrassed when they get involved in an architectural job, apologizing in advance to architects. No leading architectural school in America is willing to house a school of industrial design despite the brilliant example in Dessau.

We need not attempt here to follow all the implications of this curious position. Industrial design may have deserved its lowly status because industrial designers have not consistently been incorruptible. The hucksters perhaps call too many of their tunes. For every fine bowl, mixer or gas stove in an American kitchen there is a vulgar automobile in an American garage.

Industrial design at its highest seeks to improve both the performance of the product and the attractiveness of the package. In this it has some similarity to architecture. Like architecture it becomes corrupt if it is concerned only with the package. At its lowest level industrial design cares only about selling a product. During the hectic days after 1933 American architecture began to be affected by the corruption of packaging, sometimes became itself a package and more blatantly than Woolworth's terra cotta had been. At its worst this meant substituting a series of modern clichés for the old crockets of Victorian products.

Industrial products became "streamlined" about 1934. The 1933 Ford, blocky, with large useful square windshield, was changed to a V-motif in 1937 mainly for reasons of style quite divorced from the aerodynamic reasons which had caused the clumsy strut-winged Condor biplane also of 1933 to give way to the Boeing Clipper of 1938.

Now Raymond Loewy's Pennsylvania locomotive, his familiar Greyhound buses, and his Coca-Cola bottle became national emblems. The styling and packaging were similar, no matter what the object. Thus Walter Dorwin Teague's Ford Exposition Building at San Diego bore a family resemblance to his Brownie camera, dynamos, and Texaco gas stations, all emanating from a standard solution with trade-mark value in a variety of geographic, social, operating and competitive conditions. As Edgar Kaufmann, Jr., pointed out in the London *Architectural Review* of 1948 in an article called "Borax, or the Chromium-Plated Calf," form followed sales.

The most popular form in the '30s, the teardrop, became a symbol of machine production. It perverted functional design and became a sell-

ing trick applied indiscriminately. Now vivid colors, shiny textures and
horizontal or vertical stripes culminated in the ubiquitous cult of "three
little lines." This was not the kind of modern display any good architect wanted, but rather what industrial designers called "Borax," the
jargon for flashy, bulbous, mendacious, tawdry, modernistic design. By
1950 it was difficult to purchase anything else, while the obscenities of
the rear fenders were yet to come. For a moment in Dessau it had
seemed that architecture and industrial design might achieve a common
destiny but this hope was blown away by the men of sales and advertising who were less dangerous when they knew they had no taste than
when they all began to aspire to it. The momentary influence on architecture of a few industrially inspired shapes did not last. The useful
residue lay, on the one hand, in chairs, lamps, and other items of furniture or fabrics with whose design leading architects liked to play from
time to time; or in utensils with which the architect had seldom anything to do professionally save when, and rarely, he involved himself in
the liturgical properties of a church. The great threat that industrial
design might ruin architecture went away; the great hope that it might
ally itself with architecture went away as well.

9

THUS, OUT OF ALL THE MESSAGES THE OTHER ARTS OF AMERICA MIGHT BE
sending to its architects, only the message of the painters had meaning.
But their rebellious and accusing roads could not lead directly to a new
rebellious and accusing architecture. The communistic and revolutionary ideology of much of the bitterest European and Mexican painting
was not entrancing to the American architect and he was unlikely to lay
down an indictment comparable to Rivera's. But, in less radical form,
and for a short time, the most striking fact about the new generation of
architects was their social idealism. This generation would not listen
seriously to Cram's orisons for a return to the Middle Ages. Even
Geoffrey Scott's apostrophe to the Renaissance seemed to be a useless
delight in form enjoyed independently of social purpose. There were
new gods: the sociologists, men like Lewis Mumford, women like Catherine Bauer, who kept the architect mindful of his practical, social mission. Established and well-connected architects like Wallace Harrison
concurred with social liberalism: "As a builder . . . [the architect]
must take his place as the originator of both better buildings and a better society to control those buildings." No one seemed very sure about
how the architect would acquire such controls or handle them once he

got them. Yet the architect was to be the emergent leader, as Mumford spurred him to "organize the forces of society, discipline them for humane ends" and "express them in plastic-utilitarian building." A similar faith in the pedagogical magic of architecture excited educators like Joseph Hudnut, Harvard's Dean of Architecture, who renounced for a time the poetry of his Georgian Revival youth and brought Walter Gropius and Marcel Breuer to his faculty: "The young architect must leave our halls . . . resolute to use his technology for the reconstruction of our human environment."

His social awakening prompted the young architect of the '30s and '40s to swallow whole all that Sullivan and Wright had spoken about the architect as the man of faith, of emotion, the individual, the hero, the genius. He longed to become the great architect who would reconstruct the world along Utopian lines, fighting the bankers, the industrialists, the politicians, the conservative architects as he went. It was heady brew, rich with nineteenth-century faith in the morality of art, made stronger by the twentieth-century statement of a social ideal. A similar potion had nauseated old-time intellectuals of Mencken's coterie. Now it seemed mawkish to Robert Anderson, writing in *Pencil Points* of 1937; the new thesis, he thought, was ridiculous; he longed to return to the tradition wherein the architect was merely a "masterbuilder of buildings," not ideals.

In defense of Anderson, it must be admitted that the new social emphasis tended to obscure the need even for technical competence, let alone good design. It might seem praiseworthy merely to have a scheme that voiced a strong and parochially popular social conviction. The word "beauty" had become suspect.

The new books, too, tended to discuss buildings primarily in relation to their technology and their social history. Talbot Hamlin's *Architecture Through the Ages* (1940) attempted hazily to relate design to general psychology. Students no longer took out texts on composition or books of theory such as Guadet's *Elements*, as the library circulation cards reveal. Meanwhile catchily phrased psychological interpretations of architecture, lightheaded and often in bad taste, became dog-eared. More serious treatises, such as Le Corbusier's *Towards a New Architecture*, and books by sociologists, even confused and amateurish ones like Buckminister Fuller with his *Nine Chains to the Moon*, were read extensively and heavily underlined. As in architecture itself, social analysis was often one-sided and naïve; valued any form, however inept, mediocre or ugly, provided that it expressed social ideals or claimed to.

Ironically, the architects who were inclined towards new forms as well as social liberalism received little support from liberal governments, here or abroad. There was little difference between Fascist taste, Communist taste, and democratic taste at least as expressed through official channels. It was abnormal that Niemeyer, admittedly a Communist, and extreme in the freedom of his designs, remained influential in Brazilian governmental circles; that Le Corbusier, with strong ideas for collective social action, was able to build in Marseilles even admitting that the city had always been a notorious breeder of revolution.

But the Russian experience was no doubt the most traumatic. Here Bruno Taut, Oud, Mendelsohn, Le Corbusier and others had hoped to work freely. After a decade of supporting modern work, including city planning which was praised by Wright on his visit of 1937, the Soviet climate changed and the modern artists were expelled. The competition for the Palace of the Soviets at Moscow, open to international architects, had included Le Corbusier, Gropius and Mendelsohn, who were invited to make submissions. None of the principal modern architects won a prize. The highest awards went to two Russians, including Iofan, and to G. O. Hamilton of New Jersey, who submitted a building wrapped in Paul Cret's version of classic. The publication of all the entries announced Russia's intention to favor an eclectic architecture springing particularly from Greece and Rome. Maxim Gorki was quoted in his paraphrase of Cicero to the effect that he who does not know about the past cannot work in the future. Zorach's commentary was pungent; he called it a "reactionary form of architecture wholly unsuited to revolutionary ideas . . . It goes back to the most decadent pseudo-Roman development." Things had not changed in the USSR by 1953 when Rudnev designed the monstrous caricature of the Wrigley Building for Lomonosov State University which quickly became the pride of Moscow.

For the best modernists, except Le Corbusier, America became for the moment the remaining land of opportunity. But even the New Deal liberals, notably Roosevelt, preferred John Russell Pope's classic for the Jefferson Memorial and National Gallery of Art or the Georgian of Hyde Park to any modern architecture, and the new American embassy in Moscow was built in a "truly American style," American Colonial, by Harrie Lindeberg, while Australian Canberra's Californian terrain and climate received a pathetic recollection of Williamsburg.

Indeed, the progressive architect could not look to any governmental or cultural institution for a sponsor in 1933. Even the private individual became less important after 1940 as the Revenue Act of 1935 proved the most voracious income-reducing measure to date, and restricted the architectural expenditures of private citizens. Industrial corporations became increasingly dominant, joined later by governments, while privately supported churches and colleges followed their lead. The architect saw a nation of increasingly similar people whose dominant locale was the managerial office, the salesroom, the secretarial room — no longer the vividly individual farmer or mechanic, seldom Maecenas. He saw a nation responding almost unanimously to similar advertisements and sharing the uniform products of nation-wide technology and communication. It was a nation of city and suburb dwellers whose folkways and regional ways were disappearing. Though the great deserts and great mountains and the sea coasts still marked their peoples, the marks were not so clear as they once had been. Despite revolts from the consequences of this change, decisions were national and this called for an architecture that reflected a nation-wide technology.

In these conditions it was not surprising that the large architectural firm practicing on a national basis was a unique American development. Leading architects of the rest of the world had always worked in small and highly personalized groups, and this was particularly true of the leading modernists. It was also generally true of the men who were leading the revolution in America. Most of the large firms doing large work were conservative by the very nature of their responsibilities and their clientele. From this it was an easy jump to the *non sequitur* that no large firm could ever do much in the way of innovation, could ever be capable of distinction even in its imitations. For many of America's largest firms the allegations were true, for some the further allegation that they were better salesmen than artists may have been valid, but for at least one, Skidmore, Owings and Merrill, the evidence was that the generalization would not stick. When brilliant young men left architectural schools they shunned employment with most of the large firms but they flocked to and were welcomed by this firm. Thus the whole question of what you thought about the big firm became more a matter of your prejudices than of the truth. It was true beyond doubt that some large firms seemed to turn out potboilers as they became larger, but the truism could not fairly be applied indiscriminately to all giant firms. Skidmore, who recognized the importance of research and organization in the handling of large commissions for the growing corporate clientele, together with design partners like Gordon Bunshaft and Walter Netsch, seized upon the Miesian idiom and employed it skillfully. Like other big firms, this one did not often aim to produce innovations but it did expect to undertake major commissions, and give them thorough and honest study. Moreover such firms were not necessarily monolithic. The Chicago office of Skidmore, Owings and Merrill seemed more interested in experiment; the New York office in perfection; and as time went on sophisticated observers could note the difference and find the Chicago work more interesting though the range of difference continued to seem smaller to outside observers than it did to the partners.

European-born architects largely remained outside the new arrangement. Like Wright, they preferred to keep small offices, gaining their reputation on the basis of innovation and quality and preserving in their work the sense of an individual who can make mistakes. The European attitude toward the big firm was expressed by Giedion in 1951: "Even today almost all the more important buildings [in America] are exclusively in the hands of huge architectural firms with hundreds of employees. In this environment the backbone and the creative impulse of the young architect are effectively crushed. Those architects who have refused to bow to whatever the customer has believed he wanted have been able to find a limited field in the construction of single family houses and an occasional workers' housing project or a group of shops." The statement was not only overdrawn but it also ignored the fact that by 1952 some though not all of the big firms were often doing the most professional work while amateurish failures in performance and aesthetics were being eliminated. It also ignored the new kind of corporate client, frequently a steward of other people's money, who thought it had to place commissions in firms that were tested and reliable, that could meet production schedules, that had the staff to design and supervise the building and guarantee work. Finally, it ignored the great volume of work that was coming to men like Eero Saarinen and Minoru Yamasaki and even younger ones.

Thus the sheer size and institutionalism of the new American business and industrial client insisted upon having a type of firm that, by its very nature, would perfect types of building but not be expected to make radical innovations in design. At their best, as in the case of Skidmore, Owings and Merrill, such firms might do some of the finest architecture of the day. Some other big firms did some of the worst. It was perhaps no worse than some of the small work but it was unfortunately more noticeable. And bigness had other perils. There were firms whose commercial instincts exceeded their architectural desires and from their boards came little but blight. Architecture is not something to be sold like cosmetics over a counter, and Wright was one of the first to declaim this axiom. If supersalesmanship were to overcome conscience then the fear of the big firm might prove more than justified. By 1960 it was not clear what the outcome would be. There were good small firms and mediocre small firms and a few, hardly firms at all, who nurtured a single genius. There were brilliant large firms but not many and some large firms were stodgy or worse.

What such firms might do could not even be predicted any more as the San Francisco competition of 1960 showed that a large firm like that of Welton Becket might suggest a more sensitive and human solution than some of the small independents had done. But large firms, brilliant or stodgy, were anyhow an inevitable response to our industrial growth. Indeed, had they not existed the architects might have lost the game to the "package builders" altogether, become only artists on salary. As it was they carried out large contracts with enough distinction and enough responsibility so that the more innovative Saarinens and Yamasakis had their chance at the same sort of big game. Moreover their own rigid patterns were crumbling. In 1960 Bunshaft's proposals for the Lambert building in Brussels, Netsch's Air Force Academy Chapel and Owings's building for the John Hancock Mutual Life Company in San Francisco denied that the big firm was frozen in a mold at the very same moment that another of their San Francisco buildings, the Crown-Zellerbach, seemed to reaffirm it.

The major question confronting designers, whether in a large or a small firm, was how to develop an architectural style. It seems almost impossible that the course of this development was not changed drastically by the European architects who came to the United States in the late '30s. Without them one suspects American architecture might have tried to remain eclectic, taking off from the classic of Cret and Goodhue, taking note of the functional work of Albert Kahn, following perhaps the modified "modern" of Ralph Walker or the cautious work of Pietro Belluschi of the Portland Museum, influenced certainly by the elder Saarinen and Dudok but by no one more drastic, rediscovering perhaps the ways of Magonigle and Myron Hunt.

I O

BUT WHETHER, IN THE END, AMERICAN ARCHITECTURE COULD HAVE RESISTED a world movement of which, as things turned out, it became a leader, it is certain that the immigration accelerated the American acceptance. The immigrants had the advantage of coming to America after there had been a wave of critical preparation; and of having been principals in establishing the gospel which they were now to preach to a new audience.

The social commitment of the newcomers had come largely from Freudian and Marxist sources. These diminished the luster of the old architectural formalism. They readily won favor among a generation which believed that art might, indeed ought to have important social consequences. The new belief was typified by Bruno Taut as we saw earlier. It was also advocated by the English critic, Herbert Read, whose early books, *Art Now* and *Art and Industry*, had passionately advocated modernism. In *Art and Society*, published in 1937, he announced a belief in the psychological and social function of art: "The only function which gives [the artist] . . . his unique faculties, is this capacity to materialize the instinctual life of the deepest levels of the mind. At that level we suppose the mind to be collective in its representations, and it is because the artist can give visual shape to these invisible phantasms that he has power to move us deeply." This drew Read so close to the notion of art as propaganda that he took special pains to point out the crimes Nazi Germany and Soviet Russia had perpetrated: ". . . in certain ages society has made the artisan an exponent of the moral and ideal emanations of the super-ego, and art has thus become the handmaid of religion or morality or social ideology. In that further process art, as art, has always suffered." This was a strange and untenable generalization in the face of the Virgin of Chartres but for a generation concerned about having indigenous art and alarmed about Rivera's Communist murals in Rockefeller Center, Read performed the service of insisting that the expressive content of art be a spontaneous, almost subconscious thing.

In his earlier book, *Art Now*, published in 1933, Read had not been so careful. He regretted that modern artists "are singularly devoid of ideological motivation." On that score he was wrong again. Neither Bruno Taut nor Gropius disagreed with social utilitarianism. If, like Gropius, they had been influenced by the ideas of William Morris and John Ruskin and some of the themes of Marx and Kropotkin, they could not help but have ideological motivation. "The Bauhaus," Gropius later wrote to D. D. Egbert "was more than an art institute. We were seeking to find a new way of life. The main tendency with which everyone was imbued was to stress the point that in this world of economic expediency the human being should be again the focus. That is to say, that all the economical and industrial issues are to be subordinated to the life requirements of men." Such notions were tinged with the kind of liberalism that was denounced later by the McCarthys and Jenners and Donderos in the American Congress following the 1948 election. Liberals then had to step carefully, moderating the social convictions they had so readily and safely voiced in the '30s. Thus Gropius felt impelled to add: "In consequence of this many of the members of the Bauhaus were interested in social improvements but the main tendency was very much anti-Marxist." Such a qualification was seldom made in the '30s and there was no reason to make it. Then the staff of the Bauhaus particularly wanted to find a way to make industry serve humanitarian problems like adequate housing for the masses. Their interest was drawn to the most pressing social problems of the day, and theirs became the increasingly dominant social orientation of American architectural schools after the depression.

Such a social objective implied a relationship between art and society that now became the arena of scholarship. Geoffrey Scott was no longer so popular. In 1949 his amoral interpretation of Renaissance architecture was challenged by Rudolph Wittkower, who showed that Renaissance central-type churches were intended to express neo-Platonic ideas of God and nature. Emile Mâle, Richard Krautheimer and Erwin Panofsky exhibited similar affinities between medieval art and religion. Mumford's trilogy, *Technics and Civilization*, *The Culture of Cities*, and *The Conduct of Life*, considered art not as form but as expressions of social, political and technical accomplishments. That had been the thesis of European historians, beginning with Max Dvorak and Jacob Burckhardt, whom Sigfried Giedion brilliantly followed in *Space, Time and Architecture* and *Mechanization Takes Command*. Following their lead, John P. Coolidge made a pioneering study of the related rise and decline of industry and architecture in the town of Lowell, Massachustts. Meanwhile, E. Baldwin Smith wrote a religious and social interpretation of Egyptian architecture in 1938, followed by *The Dome: A Study in the History of Ideas* (1950) and *Architectural Symbolism of Imperial Rome and the Middle Ages* (1956).

The most persistent social idea in America was "nationalism." What is truly "American" had long interested our scholars and architects. As we have repeatedly said, the interest defies the historical fact that no past civilization has had a great architecture that was purely national. Yet Americans persistently wanted to believe that they are different and that their uniqueness should appear in an indigenous style and, as we have shown, the belief was nurtured by Greenough, Sullivan and Wright, and sung by Emerson and Whitman. In the '20s and '30s many books claimed that qualities such as robustness, naturalness, standardization, informality and close affiliation with technology were typically "American." Some, like Hugh Morrison's *Louis Sullivan: Prophet of Functionalism*, revived interest in the Chicago school. This interest was much intensified by the publication in 1941 of Sigfried Giedion's *Space, Time and Architecture* which stressed America's development of functional forms like Windsor chairs and the balloon frame, culminating in the functionalism of the Chicago school in the '80s and '90s. This important book grew out of lectures which Giedion had delivered in 1938-1939 when, with unintentional irony, he was appointed Charles Eliot Norton lecturer at Harvard University. Periodically reissued with addenda, it remains a modern classic setting forth a number of important theses. Most durable, perhaps, is the insistence that the modern movement will attain no stature until it aims at monumental expression based on modern concepts of space. This idea became an important inspiration for much of the work done after 1952.

Other themes are perhaps more tenuous, such as the particular interpretation of Sullivan and Wright, the aggrandizement of the legend of the Chicago school, the overpraise of "anonymous architecture" or the illusion that using the words "space-time" establishes any firm analogy with relativity. The work is weakest in its failure to give any credit to the not always malign contributions of French academic architecture and its purblindness about living American architects other than Wright. But these shortcomings do not really diminish the luster of the work or destroy its long-range significance. They may even have enhanced its appeal to progressive architects. Over all it did well to counteract the notion that the best American work was a testimonial to French genius, a thesis that had been argued strongly in the '20s by men like Gréber, Réau, Hegemann and Peets and widely accepted, too.

Another influential source was the earlier thesis of Lewis Mumford, published as *Sticks and Stones* in 1924. This held that America, despite much blindness, *was* developing an architecture in the tradition of Greenough, Richardson, Sullivan and Wright. Mumford was no victim of any of the arguments of CIAM. He did not really admire science and the machine as Le Corbusier seemed to; perhaps he did not really accept the automobile and certainly he rejected the automobile-centered cities of the Swiss theorist. Moreover his social commitment to planning caused him to waver in the extent of his interest in aesthetic quality; in this he was unlike Montgomery Schuyler, the critic of the '90s whom he admired.

Mumford's book opened the floodgates. Hamlin's *The American Spirit in Architecture* (1926) was followed by books of American architectural history written in 1927 and 1928 by Tallmadge, Kimball and Edgell.

I I

BUT IN THE END THE VICTORY OWED ONLY MODEST THANKS TO THE preparation by the writers, to the propaganda of CIAM and the Bauhaus, to the brilliant theoretical and polemical writing of Le Corbusier, or to the later acclaim of the American taste-makers bringing up the rear. All of these influences helped, may even have been necessary, but the central influence was the solid architectural accomplishment on the European scene, beginning to be clearly evident, as we have noted before, as early as 1923. Of course one can go endlessly back into sources before that date but it was in 1923 that the Dutch *de Stijl* exhibited models and plans in the Leonce Rosenberg gallery at Paris to make the new aesthetics widely known. Just as analytic cubism had created a new organization of space on a flat surface by dissection of a massive object, revealed also as transparent, so van Doesburg and van Eesteren divided the volumes of their houses, creating rectangular spaces defined by transparent and opaque planes. Le Corbusier recalled his early concept of space more vividly in the La Roche house in 1923 and followed it with the definitive Villa Savoye at Poissy-sur-Seine in 1929-1931. Mies van der Rohe worked with the same sort of space, describing one single internal volume by hovering, overhanging horizontal planes and subdividing it by discontinuous vertical planes of glass, marble and stucco. Such ideas appeared in his brick country house of 1923, his Tugendhat house at Brno of 1930 and especially in his German Pavilion at Barcelona of 1929.

Concurrently with the new statements about space there were experiments with materials. The traditionally dominant ones were replaced by white stucco, glass and fine metals and stones, emphasizing the quality of surface rather than mass. Construction was exposed or featured, particularly when a metal or reinforced concrete skeleton allowed thin closing walls to be cut by broad bands of windows or large areas of glass. Transparency and interpenetration of spaces (what came to be called "the flow of space") were confined largely to rectilinear compositions, and the continuous spaces were shaped by discontinuous rectilinear planes. There was some cultism in the direction of sparseness and austerity, sun and light worship, and the machined qualities of materials. Thus all ornament was banished as being unsuited to machine production, which was presumed to produce precise edges and machine-smooth surfaces. It was good doctrine to repeat uniform, factory-made parts, but not with much solicitude for the phrasing of older architecture. Composition, satisfied often by a brutal silhouette, was derived from programmatic planning and frank, even forced, exhibition of functions. Envelopes for buildings were the forms needed to enclose distinct spaces containing distinct functions. There was a rational, even an irrational, attention to problems of function and construction and insistence that these be expressed in design, even if it were necessary to exaggerate them. It was this kind of architecture that some Americans began to see in the '20s, as the Austrian Neutra brought it when he arrived in 1923, and as it was exhibited at the Museum of Modern Art in 1932. It was only a beginning, less sophisticated than it would become, and it shocked most American architects and observers who only looked at it without repeating or accepting the accompanying credo, both aesthetic and social.

The credo was based on mechanism, the belief that the world is best understood as a machine that operates efficiently in accordance with strict laws ultimately expressible in mathematical terms. Such a metaphysics placed high priority on natural science and on its extrapolations, even on false analogies drawn from it, on rigorously statistical methods of structural analysis, on physical efficiency, and on finding objective and durable laws underlying human behavior. Carefully balanced rectilinear compositions proclaimed new forms, new materials and new construction, and architects addressed new problems with the sense that modernity alone was compatible with mechanism. They admired industrial buildings, pure, funicular engineering, and those objects like airplanes and ships and bascule bridges whose clean lines, sheer planes, and simple surfaces were the results of careful adjustment of form to performance.

Consequently the new group espoused an extreme functionalism; Moholy-Nagy wrote in *The New Vision:* ". . . the artist pioneers . . . dared to proclaim the conception of 'functional rightness' even as applied to machine products." With this idealized functionalism went an aesthetic envelope related to the geometric art seen in paintings by Mondriaan and van Doesburg. It was a healthy and moderately tough-minded point of view; given the hypothesis, it was objective and teachable. There was no Wrightian glorification of the individual, nothing personal or anarchic, none of the elfishness of Alvar Aalto. Though Le Corbusier's Villa Savoye contained a roof terrace of forms that would later be developed into the most personal of buildings, Ronchamp, his theory during the '20s broadcast the functional house, *la machine à habiter*, which, as a product of technology, could operate in any place, regardless of terrain. It seemed then as if design might be analyzed and described and as if even the zeniths of architecture might be aspired to by teams, as Gropius insisted. "Not the single piece of work, nor the individual, highest attainment, has to be emphasized," Moholy-Nagy wrote, "but the creation of the commonly usable type, the development of the standard." Thus the objective was to have efficient planning and strictly geometric form and to realize these with mass-produced materials that could be economically assembled by modern industry.

Gropius consistently advocated mechanism. "We want to create a clear, organic architecture, whose inner logic will be radiant and naked,

unencumbered by lying façades and trickeries. . . . We want an architecture adapted to our world of machines, radios, and fast motor cars,"
he wrote in *Bauhaus*. Since fully functional architecture would require
it to be adaptable to new uses, it must be flexible, even temporary, he
thought, and proceeded to the questionable conclusion that nothing
permanent, nothing merely ornamental or monumental, is truly useful:
"The old monument was a symbol for a static conception of the world
now overruled. I believe, therefore, that the equivalent for monumental
expression is developing in the direction of a new physical pattern
for a higher form of civil life, a pattern characterized by *flexibility for
continuous growth and change*." But this belief, reminiscent of the
scientists in America during the '70s, notably Charles William Eliot,
save that it was not very clear about science, failed to recognize the
facts of economics, tradition, and beauty, even of evolution, or that
sentiment and affection are as often noble as foolish.

Intransigent mechanism had other strange consequences. If change
were to be the pervasive mood of American society, as Gropius suggested,
then there could be no immutable architectural laws, whether of composition or style. Rather than aiming at static and absolute values,
Gropius sought an architecture that served the needs of current society,
"for modern man has made the important discovery that there is no
such thing as finality or eternal truth." Consequently, Gropius tried to
explore architectural problems as if there had been no previously satisfactory solutions: "If the emphasis today is on the plain human being,
not on the Caesars, we have to study man's biological way of life, his
way of seeing, his perception of distance, in order to grasp what scale
will fit him." To the great detriment of architecture, history had little
part in his program: the goals of education are to "stimulate the student's mind towards his own creative thinking *according to laws of
nature*." Those laws were objective principles derived from mechanics
and psychology: ". . . a special language of shape . . . a scientific
knowledge of objectively valid optical facts." What those facts were,
Gropius never announced. None of the great men seems seriously to have
studied psychology. Gropius's glorification of science seemed strained to
a later generation which deplored his failure to make *space* the chief
objective of architecture or to those who knew he knew no science. They
regarded the functional road as a probable blind alley which the Bauhaus
had carefully dug through the steep grade of structures and the beautiful
landscape of formal design. It had been useful as an educational
discipline, but Eduardo Catalano or Paul Rudolph, both taught by
Gropius, later found it an empty way, failing to lead towards total
architecture.

The modern buildings of America that will gain a place on history's scene were seldom monuments to such extreme functionalism. To be sure, the awe-inspiring grandeur of the dams at Boulder, the Grand Coulee or the TVA, could be sensed at once; to be sure, much of Albert Kahn's mastery was obviously functional as it was revealed, for example, in the Dodge truck plant at Detroit. But the important buildings, though not unfunctional, were something more. They depended quite as much upon their sympathetic understanding of materials, their environment, their details as upon their functionalism. Perhaps they depended more. This was quite apparent in such different buildings as Neutra's Bell Experimental School at Los Angeles, Belluschi's Equitable Building at Portland, or Eliel Saarinen's Lutheran Church at Minneapolis. Modern world or not, science or not, architecture was still not a matter of the intellect alone. Great buildings continued to transcend their functional requirements.

I 2

UNIVERSALLY VALID OR NOT, THE WORK AND WRITING OF THE GREAT men had an irresistible impact. It is dangerous to try to write history of one's own times and about men whom one knows in life, and history can easily change to personal criticism. But with this much apology let us say that it now seems safe to conclude that in all the galaxy, the star of Le Corbusier was brightest. Of all the Europeans, he might most beneficially have influenced America by his presence. He had the best grasp of space and the most fertile imagination of any of the Europeans. His city plans, including the Voisin and the St. Dié, were the most influential urban proposals known to modern architects. But he remained in Europe, staying there even through the war. His book, *Vers une Architecture*, translated into English in 1927, contained important sections about American factories, skyscrapers and machinery. He made a trip to New York in 1935, sponsored by the Museum of Modern Art; he came again after the war to engage in what turned out to be an unhappy experiment in playing on the team, captained by Wallace Harrison, which produced the United Nations buildings, in an emasculated version of what seems clearly to have been his original idea. His impressions are recorded in his book, *When the Cathedrals Were White*. It bears the telling subtitle, *A Journey to the Country of Timid People*. He was at once fascinated by the drive and the opportunity of America and appalled by the American failure to exploit the opportunity to the hilt.

The influence of this Swiss on America was thus largely indirect and in print. It was enormous even upon those who professed to deny his teaching, even among the few who had the temerity to assert that their ideas had predated his. No young designer invited to prepare a scheme for a new urban complex could avoid the suggestions Le Corbusier had made as early as 1922 when he set tall sheer towers and lower functionally shaped buildings in large pedestrian plazas and parks; but sometimes his followers forgot that adequate space between the towers was a *sine qua non* of his proposals. Suggestions of the '50s by Ieoh Ming Pei for Philadelphia and Denver, of Belluschi and Gropius for Boston's Back Bay, of Ralph Walker for Chicago's Lake Meadows, and of Skidmore, Owings and Merrill for the later Fort Dearborn project, all owed their origin to Le Corbusier, whose ideas were most maturely expressed in the end in his unexecuted plan for reconstructing the war-leveled city of St. Dié in 1945.

On another front his *Unité d'Habitation,* a colossal apartment house for the workers of Marseille, 1952, was a modular slab in which two-story apartments and communal rooms, including a central floor devoted to shops and markets, were supported on sculptural *pilotis* and crowned by a roof-terrace of plastically modeled concrete "play sculpture." This again was an extension of ideas he had been proposing since the '20s.

Such sculptural freedom showed still more clearly in his planning for the new town of Chandigarh in India, beginning in 1952; it emerged to shape the space of the most original of all modern churches, Notre Dame du Haut at Ronchamp (1957), whose silhouette offers ever-changing lyrics as the three towers and the rolling overhanging roof present themselves in various combinations of architectural sculpture. The linearity of Marseille and the freedom of Ronchamp were combined in the brilliantly honeycombed cell-block and the sinuous ambulatory of the Dominican convent of La Tourette at Eveux-sur-Arbresle of 1959. Here too his theory of proportion, the modulor, was brought fully and obviously into play in the spacing of the columns of the cloister.

As Le Corbusier's ideas developed he become more of a complete artist, less of an architect as usually conceived; he needed no crutch, whether it was provided by his universal module, his universal geometry, or the resources of modern technology which, as a matter of fact, he very often did not or could not apply. His leap into poetry automatically released him from the prose written by too many commercial firms in America or by the sober functionalism of less commercial moderns. At the same time a general interest in the total city advanced along lines he had forecast in his exhibition at the Salon d'Automne of 1922.

It was the freedom and power that Le Corbusier exploited in concrete which most escaped Americans, whose ultra-refined desire to polish tended always to reject its honest coarseness of form and texture which was well recognized not only by the Swiss but by talented disciples in Italy and Japan. It was a gospel which could be found brilliantly displayed in almost every other part of the world from Brasilia to Ahmedabad to Tokyo and Kyoto and at the hands of men of quite different births who had either passed through the atelier on the Rue de Sévres or admired him from afar, knowing him only through his buildings and his works. Indeed, his ultimate modesty and retiring nature, concealed beneath a formidable masquerade of ego, and sharp comment, made him quite difficult to know on other terms. Between his executed and unexecuted projects he proposed most of the important individual ideas of modern architecture, including a great many of the most important details; to this he added the most thorough theory of the city. Lesser men rejoiced at the many times he lost commissions but could not take much comfort in the patent fact that even his unexecuted proposals were more influential than their completed work.

His Palace of the Soviets seems to have influenced even Gropius's project for auditoria at Tallahassee in 1957; his scheme for the League of Nations was mined by traditionalists and modernists alike. But this great man was never very happy in America, flitted through briefly, and it remained for others to try to work out American versions of his urban proposals; in this working out there was almost no reflection of the plasticity of architectural space that he had created beginning in the '30s. At the end of 1959 it was announced that he would design a new building for the fine arts at Harvard University — a bold and wise decision by this ancient seat of learning, but for America as a whole, and no matter how it came out, this was much too little and no doubt too late as well.

But even in 1960 most Americans were not at ease with the work of Le Corbusier. They hoped for something less disturbing. They found it in a thoroughgoing, uncapricious philosophy of design, tied to a social program, capable of being institutionalized so as to be partly independent of genius, achievable by groups who could assault problems collaboratively relying on a few mutually accepted axioms. Although in the end the most American demonstration of this has to be attached to the work of Mies van der Rohe and his acolytes, the revolutionary point of view of the Deutsches Bauhaus was at first the most influential. This brilliant school, as we have noted briefly before, was founded in Germany in 1919, under the direction of Walter Gropius who, for a brief span, had lived with Le Corbusier and Mies under the tutelage of Peter Behrens.

Gropius was a figure to comand respect. He had great natural dignity, restraint, surface modesty. He had unshakable convictions and steadfastness, even stubborness of purpose. If Le Corbusier was a scalpel, Gropius was a rock. He honestly believed in the social mission of architecture, in the beneficial potentials of the machine for all the arts, in the blessings to come from true standardization, in the genuine creative productivity of teams in which personal glories would be submerged.

It is perhaps even harder to assess Gropius than it is Le Corbusier, for the very reason that Gropius has been easier to know. The facts of his life seem clear enough although they may have been confused by over-adulatory biographers. From 1907 to 1914 he was primarily a promising young architect; from 1919 to 1928 at the Bauhaus he was primarily an educator; in 1934-1937 as an exile he practiced in England; from 1937 to 1952 he was again an educator, this time at Harvard. In this period he was surely the most influential single man in planting modern architecture firmly in America. At the end of this long and distinguished career he retired from the university in 1952, surrounded himself with younger associates and under the name of The Architects Collaborative (TAC) had more important commissions than had come to him in all the rest of his life.

In the beginning Gropius provided some of the best and most influential buildings of the early modern movement, notably the Fagus Works of 1911, the office buildings of the Cologne Workbund Exhibition of 1914 (with Adolf Meyer) and of course the Bauhaus itself. Although in the long verdict of history he will probably not stand as one of the greatest artists of the modern development, and surely not as its greatest theorist, his contributions always had elements of distinction, even of innovation, while there can be no doubt that he was the greatest teacher of the day.

The early German Bauhaus may have witnessed Gropius's finest days. Of the ideas then followed, he now says he would change only details. He held that the machine was the modern executant of design; its terms could not be avoided. All designers had to recognize this and this meant that new aesthetic criteria would have to be established. He asserted a "common citizenship of all forms of creative work and their logical interdependence on one another." To him the scale and complexity of the modern world made the necessity for collaboration self-

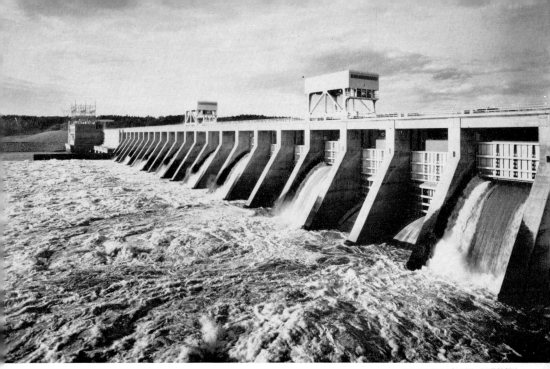

TENNESSEE VALLEY AUTHORITY

Tennessee Valley Authority, Pickwick Landing Dam, 1935-1938

Chicago, Illinois Institute of Technology, Crown Hall, 1955,
Ludwig Mies van der Rohe, arch.

BILL ENGDAHL, HEDRICH-BLESSING

VICTOR GRUEN ASSOCIAT

Fort Worth, Texas, model showing the city of 1970,
Victor Gruen Associates, archs., 1956

BILL HEDRICH, HEDRICH-BLESSING

Colorado Springs, Colorado, U. S. Air Force Academy, Academic Building,
Cadet Library, Cadet Quarters and Social Hall, 1957-1960,
Skidmore, Owings and Merrill, archs.

Wellesley, Massachusetts, Wellesley College, Jewett Art Center, 1959,
Paul Rudolph, with Anderson, Beckwith and Haible, archs.

CREATIVE PHOTOGRAPHERS, INC.

New York, Lever House, 1952,
Skidmore, Owings and
Merrill, archs.

EZRA STOLLER

New York, Lever House, 1952, court, Skidmore, Owings and Merrill, archs.

EZRA STOLL

MORLEY BAER

Palo Alto, California, Center for Advanced Study in the Behavioral
Sciences, 1955, Wurster, Bernardi and Emmons, archs.

Cottage Grove, Oregon, First Presbyterian Church, 1951,
Pietro Belluschi, arch.

PRESBYTERIAN LIFE, MARY SETH

EZRA STOLLE

Detroit, Michigan, General Motors Technical Center, Styling Buildings, 1955,
Eero Saarinen, arch.

Detroit, Michigan, General Motors Technical Center, Research Laboratories
Administration Building, lobby, 1955, Eero Saarinen, arch.

EZRA STOLLER

BILL HEDRICH, HEDRICH-BLESSING

Bear Run, Pennsylvania, "Falling Water,"
residence of E. J. Kaufmann, 1936,
Frank Lloyd Wright, arch.

Racine, Wisconsin, S. C. Johnson Company,
Administration Building, lobby, 1939,
Frank Lloyd Wright, arch.

S. C. JOHNSON COMPANY

H. C. PRICE COMPANY

Bartlesville, Oklahoma, H. C. Price
Tower, 1954, Frank Lloyd Wright, arch.

BALTAZAR KORAB

Detroit, Michigan,
Reynolds Aluminum Building,
1959, Minoru Yamasaki, arch.

BALTAZAR KORA

evident; and so was the need for manual training of a very practical sort coupled with theoretical instruction in the laws of design. It was in the manual exercises that the transplantation to Harvard was least effective — for American universities, of which Harvard was the arch-type, have for a long time had scant affection for any work save that of the mind. Were these theories of Gropius silly or romantic? Are they obsolete? Does any current architectural school face its problems as squarely as the Bauhaus did? These were questions which James Marston Fitch asked rhetorically in the *Architectural Forum* in May of 1960. The answer was almost certainly No.

Under Gropius's direction, the early German Bauhaus became the leading school of modern architectural design in the whole world. In the halcyon years, first at Weimar but mostly at Dessau, the Bauhaus steadily stretched its influence. Its scope included all the visual arts; urban planning, architecture, furniture, painting, sculpture, typography, photography, industrial design, ballet, theater, film. It insisted that these should originate in a common modern understanding, including an acceptance of the machine as a tool for modern artists. It aimed at perfecting an elastic method of working that would produce a total environment, untrammeled by traditons of style. It stimulated design-ers to be mindful of industrial processes and of the social consequences of design. It sought for quality in quantity production. It brought together more artists of eminent talent than any other art school of the day. Its building at Dessau of 1925-1926 was the most forward-looking building on any campus. It grappled with real social problems such as that of low-cost housing. Its spokesmen were strong and per-suasive. They had a flair for dramatizing their ideas throughout the world. And they had courage. But a number of the individuals were Jews; a number were inclined to the political left; their designs could not possibly appeal to the ideological purposes or the low-bourgeois taste of the Nazi leaders. As the latter grew powerful they first put shackles on the Bauhaus, then truncated it and moved it to Berlin, and finally abolished it altogether. After that the hegira was inevitable. It was America's good fortune that the hegira went westwards, begin-ning about 1937.

Despite all its doctrine the Bauhaus was less rigid than might be imagined. It could not be hospitable to an artist who rejected the machine or who sought to see nature in a nineteenth-century romantic light. It could not have been indiscriminately palatable to all leaders of modernism and it is hard to imagine that Wright, Le Corbusier, Aalto or Léger could have thrived there. But it could accommodate people of such different purposes and tastes as Albers, Bayer, Breuer,

Kandinsky, Klee, Feininger and Schlemmer, to say nothing of Moholy-Nagy. As Mies van der Rohe said at a Chicago dinner in honor of Gropius in 1953: "The Bauhaus was not an institution with a clear program — it was an idea, and Gropius formulated this idea with great precision. . . . The fact that it was an idea, I think, is the cause of this enormous influence the Bauhaus has had on every progressive school around the globe. You cannot do that with organization, you cannot do that with propaganda. Only an idea spreads so far."

After the first buildings of the pre-Bauhaus day, Gropius's own architectural work was less influential than the work of others — less influential than his theories, his writing, his teaching. It is not easy to see any very enormous development from Fagus of 1911 to Harvard Graduate Center of 1950. Many of his late buildings have been said to be clichés of his earlier ones; the Berlin apartments, the embassy at Athens, the buildings at Brandeis University, the Baghdad University project cannot be simply credited to or blamed upon him.

But Gropius also gave his students an example of character, and this may be the thing that students least often see. Unlike Wright or Mies he was driven always to consider the social setting, just as Le Corbusier was so driven. He was not always sophisticated about social problems; but at least he chose what he deemed the principled, not the expedient position. Suffering many early defeats did not discourage him and he proved himself a brilliant architectural politician and statesman in the negotiations which finally placed the designs for Unesco House, Paris, in the hands of Breuer, Zehrfuss and Nervi. Nothing in his principles was hospitable to Marxism. He always insisted that solutions depended on "a change in the individual's attitude toward his work, not on the betterment of his outward circumstances." But, if not Marxist, he was certainly Utopian, even Transcendental. These traits were endearing to Americans, as the sharp wit of Le Corbusier was not. To Americans he was and will remain the great Puritan of the modern movement.

Very late in his life he visited Japan for the first time. Like all other modern architects he was moved by the architecture of Japan. This was not surprising since it had contributed so much to the early modern thinking through the pollen-bearing activities of Taut and Wright. He noted that Japanese architecture was capable of an endless variety within a fundamental unity and remarked, "For the first time in my life I felt myself with the majority." Wright died without having or at least admitting to such an experience. But whether there is any great consolation in an ultimate acceptance may depend on temperament. It is hard for front-line fighters to forget the glorious days on the barricades. It is not every Cincinnatus who can return happily to the plow.

Other Europeans, also men of major talents, had their influence on American thinking. Mies van der Rohe continued to move inexorably towards universal space, always simpler, thoroughly interchangeable, subdivided by admittedly temporary partitions, urging the paradox, "Less is more." In the end he had an enormous effect on at least one aspect of American architecture. But this effect did not become strong until he moved to the United States in 1939. In the meanwhile there was much to be said.

In his glass-skyscraper project of the '20s he had made an important statement to the effect that it was not light and shade that mattered but the play of reflections on the wall. In his 1923 project for a country house he had mixed the planes of Doesburg with a free-standing wall. This, Philip Johnson discovered, broke "the traditional box by sliding out from beneath the roof and extending into the landscape." From that point to the masterpieces of Seagram's or Lafayette Park in Detroit was nothing but a steady, undeviating, long evolution of strongly contrasted forms, precisely articulated structures and decisive details. For many architects it had the advantage over the work of Le Corbusier or Wright that the Miesian order was one that could be learned and then repeated. This was shown in good time by such talented imitators as Gordon Bunshaft, Ieoh Ming Pei and Philip Johnson, and for a time even by such talented innovators as Paul Rudolph and Eero Saarinen. By 1960 Bunshaft and Johnson and Pei were also trying to erase the debt but it remained to be seen whether they would succeed. Meanwhile as the *Architectural Record* justly said in its tribute of April 1960, ". . . some less able architects have been released from the imperatives of originality and architecture is the better for it."

But as early as 1960 Mies, himself, rejected so easy an imitation when he reminded an audience at the Illinois Institute of Technology, "I hope you will understand that architecture has nothing to do with the invention of forms. It is not a playground for children, young or old." The great influence of Mies in America, which probably reached its peak a little before 1960, also owed much to the fact that the results seemed clear to American clients, a reasonable expression of the American machine and of American organization in a way that the freedoms and even primitivisms of Le Corbusier and Wright never could.

There were others, less influential. The great humanity and the

poetic manipulations of brick by Alvar Aalto were much admired
though not much emulated save perhaps now and again by Eero Saarinen. The muscular concrete engineering of the Italian Pier Luigi Nervi
was also much admired but even less often emulated. In the end the
big influences remain those of Le Corbusier and Gropius and Mies, and
of these Gropius and Le Corbusier will in the end be seen to have
cast the longest shadows. There was, of course, one other who cast
long shadows — the American Wright.

For a while it was not apparent to most observers that Wright's architecture was actually quite different from the Europeans' both in theory and in realization. His early exhibitions in Europe had moved
the European revolutionaries and they had adopted him, though he
proved to be an unwilling foster-member of the family. He was
included, along with them, in the book, unhappily named *The International Style*, published at the time of an important exhibition of
contemporary architecture at the Museum of Modern Art in 1932. His
Larkin Building at Buffalo and the Robie House of 1908 at Chicago
seemed to be progenitors of European modernism of the Saarinen-
Dudok persuasion. But this was not the line of the Germans, and his
course was in fact set against the functional and mechanized forms and
materials Gropius and Mies employed and the "houses on stilts" of
Le Corbusier. His diatribes against the other leaders of the modern
movement which became more virulent as he aged were not mere
perverse exhibitions of displeasure that some other architect had a place
in the sun.

Wright's buildings found their geometric themes in the contours of
the land; his space was plastic; his lighting was soft and chiaroscuro;
he preferred natural rough textures; his colors were autumnal, not
primary. His architecture grew like an organism by adaptation to
specific sites, materials, structures. Scholars like Henry-Russell Hitchcock were noting this clearly enough as early as 1942 when Hitchcock
published his important monograph on Wright's work, *In the Nature of
Materials*. This book awakened renewed interest in our native titan.

But even if Wright had been generally recognized as the author of
an American architecture (and he was not), it is doubtful that any
other designer could have attained his inimitable personal style. Some
tried but even the best of them, Alden Dow, Harris Armstrong, Paul
Schweikher and Bruce Goff, somehow failed fully to capture his spirit.
Others who by the '50s had come to accept him were often, like
Ralph Walker, perhaps a little more sympathetic to his forms than
they were to the European forms which they castigated; but principally,
one suspects, they liked the doctrine of individuality which Wright

proclaimed for himself and presumably extended to others even if he did not admire their talents. Wright's statements could not be otherwise than personal. They did not conform to a national technology or to any classifiable national sentiment.

In 1948 a portfolio of the *Architectural Forum* showed a decade of his work. His imagination bounded like a lamb in spring. His exhibition held at Gimbel's in Philadelphia in 1950 was taken later to Europe where it had almost as great an effect as his earlier show of 1910. Now many new buildings showed his unsurpassable skill in handling volumes and especially planes. This appeared in great variety at "Eaglefeather" in the hills of Santa Monica, in a Sports Club for Hollywood Hills, in some of the buildings at Florida Southern College, in the Johnson Wax Administration Building, in the Pauson House, in Falling Water. Moreover his long career was reaching an epitome in his thinking about the city.

His book, *The Disappearing City*, of 1932, had announced an agrarian, almost Populist, denunciation of contemporary urban life, and it set him upon the problem of developing a new form for communities. That emerged in Broadacre City, a plan first exhibited at Rockefeller Center in 1935 and again at the Museum of Modern Art in 1940. The model of Broadacre City showed how four square miles of land might be developed as a country seat with residences, civic buildings, cultural buildings, industries and farms. Here we find quotations from a lifetime of work: the Gordon Strong Planetarium of 1925, the Steel Cathedral of 1926, apartment houses like St. Mark's Tower and another for Elizabeth Noble of 1929; the gasoline and service stations of 1928; farm units and market units of 1932; small industries, a theater, a college, schools, hospital, airports, hotels, art schools, stores, an administrative center; there were many types of house, large and expensive houses like the House on the Mesa, as well as minimal dwellings like the Usonian houses Wright invented. Each was to stand on a large lot of landscaped ground, connected with special highways and bridges for automobiles. It was obvious that Wright here anticipated the tremendous exodus from the city and prepared a plan for suburbia and the rural communities, facing a problem which was largely ignored at the most crucial time by planners, American and European alike. Broadacre City was more a compilation of Wrightiana, to be sure, than a great and serious solution of the urban problem. It did not have the same complete logic and understanding of the automobile that Le Corbusier had shown in his earlier proposals. Wright's solutions were at once less efficient and more humane. Taken literally they could set no pattern for the future as the ideas of Le Corbusier did. But they had in them a consideration for personal life that was most missing in Le Corbusier when he was most logical. And it was this that the planners threw away. If Wright was ignored, no other comparable American voice was there to be heard. His influence was more to be sensed than explained; and more often indirectly through the voices of Europeans than through his own voice. Moreover many more professed to admire him than chose to try to walk in his footsteps; and even after his death there were many American architects, picking away at his genius, who hardly had enough genius themselves to be fit to man his pencil-sharpener.

It is hard to realize now that, in 1933, there was still a question whether the American public would recognize the messages of modern architecture coming from abroad and the few harbingers built here; whether it would accept them without further architectural miscarriages such as the Jefferson Memorial in Washington. Indeed, there was every reason for apprehension that the infant American modern movement might die in a backwater built around the enthusiasm which had greeted Eliel Saarinen when he came from Finland to head the new Cranbrook Academy at Bloomfield Hills, Michigan. Saarinen had done notable modern work in Finland and had achieved fame here, we will recall, by his design for the Chicago *Tribune* competition. But now the modern movement somehow began to pass him by, as it also did Dudok. His new school, though eclectic in a special Scandinavian way, still struck a note for innovation in the use of ornament, rich materials, and good design. He encouraged sculptors like the Swede Carl Milles, who visited America in 1929. Milles returned to become a citizen in 1932 and to provide monumental yet whimsical sculptural arrangements, usually not of such great quality as those he had made for the squares of Stockholm and Göteborg. There were fountains at Cranbrook, at the Metropolitan Museum, New York, and the one before the Union Station at St. Louis where sportive Mississippi catfish (or exotic sharks) sprayed water on Missouri nereids, all looking more Nordic than Southern, to celebrate the great meeting of the waters.

The Saarinen-Milles combination offered a new but momentary note of distinction to America. Their popularity was brief as the irresistible wave of mechanistic dogma swept the land. In 1960 it seemed less certain than it had in 1952 that these bones, too, might not rise again. Meanwhile there was the distinguished and reverent church architecture of the elder Saarinen, and the emerging products of the Cranbrook school in the shape of such men as Harry Weese or Charles Eames or Eliel's own son Eero.

There was nothing stark or brutal about the buildings Saarinen designed for Cranbrook. They showed the kind of empathy that suffused

Ragnar Östberg's Town Hall on the canals of Stockholm. This building was much more to American taste than the projects of Le Corbusier, Gropius or Mies. It was prominently displayed in America and won for Östberg the gold medal from the A.I.A. in 1934, long before it was conferred on Gropius or Mies, to say nothing of Le Corbusier who got the honor only in 1961, while Mies received his award in 1960. The work of Dudok at Hilversum, Holland, also gained enough popularity to win him an early medal as a modernist.

The early A.I.A. awards may now seem to have been applauding mostly the laggards of the modern movement. This simply reflected general American taste which hoped that the American architectural revolution could be gentle, even unnoticeable.

The work that was most easily accepted sought to develop a modern idiom in ornament and shape without ignoring or discarding ancient principles of composition. It exposed a desire for rich craftsmanship in architectural accessories such as tiles, lamps, and textiles, not inevitably products of the machine. The question was whether this was enough or whether America needed the wholesale shock of a revolution. Would Americans adopt the revolutionary notions that had already been so clearly set forth in Europe? Would they develop something comparable of their own? Would they ignore the new altogether? Or would they follow their traditional course of a reluctant cultural importation? If that were to be the way, American modern might have to wait a long time, for the modern movement was not really firmly established in the European seats of power.

But, as the *Architectural Review* pointed out in 1960, Wright, Mies, Le Corbusier and Gropius had each to fashion a modern world in terms they could build. Each cast the world in his own image, one organic, one structural, one primitive, one mechanistic. Together they offered the generations to come both ideas and choice and this would have been enough. In fact, a major share of what they contributed was to make "the gift of their worlds."

1 3

SOME OF THESE GIFTS NEEDED FURTHER EXPOSITION. READY AT HAND WAS the Congrès Internationaux d'Architecture Moderne (CIAM) which propagated the faith from its founding at Sarraz in Switzerland in 1928 to its official demise at Dubrovnik in 1956 and the failure to resuscitate it at Otterloo in 1959. CIAM was for a long time the most effective spokesman for modern principles, notably those of Le Cor-

busier and the Bauhaus, but also of Wright. The Europeans accepted its
support with as much enthusiasm as Wright repudiated it. The first congress at Sarraz was succeeded by others at Frankfurt (1929), Brussels
(1930), Athens (1933), Paris (1937), Bridgewater, England (1947),
Bergamo (1949), Hoddesdon, England (1951), Aix-en-Provence (1953).
By this time much of the élan, indeed much of the purpose had evapo-
rated. At the Congress of Dubrovnik in 1956 the leaders of CIAM
officially declared its mission accomplished. But a few of those who
owed much to CIAM and who had faith in the continuing vitality of
its principles, including the Italian, Ernesto Rogers, were determined to
revive it at the 1959 meeting, held symbolically at Otterloo, the site of
Henry van der Velde's greatest work. Rogers provided a personal farewell in his magazine, *Casabella:* "The CIAM represents the moment of
greatest commitment and solidarity in modern architecture; a commitment still more valid today and more and more necessary if we are not
to abandon the debate and our hope for a progressive architecture."

But the young English, who by 1960 were finding themselves powerful propagandists and critics, if not interesting architects, mustered the
strength of other Europeans who felt as they did. John Voelcker drew
the significant contrasts which supported the *coup de grâce* of CIAM.
In 1930 CIAM, he said, espoused a frame-building and multi-level high-
rise urban image containing a complete urban system, but by 1950 its
image was random, drawn from many sources, made up of single ideas,
which one by one contributed to change and extended the experience
of space. The prototype buildings and master plans of 1930 were didac-
tically charged with a full international program while by 1950 the
buildings related to unique situations. How could there longer be a
program for such an organization? The critics were no doubt right but
were they aware that their picture of CIAM was really a portrait of the
whole modern movement, old or new?

CIAM had never been a group which one could join at will. It was
self-selecting and in the beginning most of the selections were brilliantly
made. Its architects came together for a purpose expressed by Le Corbusier: "In CIAM we do only what the individual can't do alone."
It was, in a way, an effort to establish a common vocabulary for a group
of very individual individualists. It was not a group which could be
expected to march indefinitely in harness — the poetic and mercurial
Aalto, the poetic and polemical Le Corbusier, the patient, stubborn and
prosy Gropius and Markelius. There were other threats to ultimate unity
such as the mounting menace of closed borders and contradictory
national ideologies. But for a time and very likely under the relentless
prodding of the distinguished Swiss historian-critic Sigfried Giedion,

this group of Pegasuses did act as a team. They prepared presentations to a common theme sometimes even with standardized format and symbols. They discussed the presentations in their congresses, agreed upon resolutions which are more a part of European than of American habit, published several of the congresses in influential books of which we need cite only two which placed major emphasis on problems of housing and city planning: *Dwellings for the Lowest Classes*, 1930, and *Can Our Cities Survive?*, the latter written by José Luis Sert in 1942.

The CIAM broadcast the modern movement influentially for many years but outlived its maximum effectiveness and by the mid-'50s it was saddening to see some of the members poking in the embers, as indeed they also did about the Bauhaus, hoping for a phoenix in Berlin in 1957, which seemed unlikely. The individuals remained friends long after their personal successes and the differences of their temperaments had no longer seemed to make it desirable for many of them to continue to try to work in carefully structured group efforts. These men had found a common bond in CIAM in their difficult years and had hoed together a row which isolated individual Americans were trying to hoe alone. Thus they had forged a durable bond. So, as the point of CIAM grew duller, the peripheral men still did not resign, did not withdraw in a display of acrimonious pyrotechnics aimed at each other, but simply kept their names on the roster without participating. In the end CIAM was mostly the shadow of Giedion. But before that it had burned with a brilliant flame and everyone who had helped to stoke it could be proud of his part.

Many national action groups sprang from CIAM, such as GATEPAC in Spain and MARS in England, but the ways of CIAM and the dogmatic approach of Giedion were not calculated to make it appealing to Americans. In 1939 Giedion tried to organize a more effective American wing of CIAM, with no great success. Americans were characteristically unenchanted by joint theoretical projects, characteristically uninterested in writing manifestoes or passing resolutions, characteristically unwilling to regard K. Lönberg-Holm and Serge Chermayeff as typifying American attitudes. CIAM's leadership in America had to be of a different sort, principally through its publications.

But even in its best days there were disturbing things about the CIAM line. The opinions of an individual critic may be admired or detested, accepted or rejected, in whole or in part. When these are expressed as organizational doctrine the color is different. There seems to have been in the organization or among its leaders a penchant for the doctrinaire which tolerated only its own heresies. Stringent adaptation to function was applauded and the cult of sparse austerity dominated its aesthetic canons. Thus the work of Markelius in Sweden was denounced in 1951 when Giedion published *CIAM: A Decade of New Architecture:* the new empiricism ". . . under cover of 'humanising' architecture leads it only into another cul-de-sac." Though the book contained the work of such Americans as Eames, Lescaze, Schweikher, Wurster, Harris, Soriano and Catalano, many of whom were not members of CIAM, America was generally castigated with very little sensitivity as to what America was really like. CIAM remained a group of aging fighters meeting after the fight was over; and somehow it never found a new Theseus or a new cause for him to lead. Yet in its day it provided a beacon for Americans, especially for young Americans, and especially for architectural students of the new generation.

14

BUT ANOTHER PUSH WAS NEEDED, ONE THAT HAD TO COME FROM A GROUP of tough-minded aggressive designers located in America, men who would be spokesmen for the technological, universal architecture, who would ask all to take sides for or against their buildings, who would be stubbornly, even passionately, dedicated to radical design. They needed also a plausible philosophy and sociology to defend it. Later on there would be efforts to trace the genesis farther back, for example to men like the Gills in Southern California. But that was historical afterthought. In the meantime there were transplanted European candidates.

R. M. Schindler thought that his Beach House of 1926 in California with *pilotis* of concrete was the earliest fully modern house in the United States. As early as 1922 he had built his own house, one story high, cellarless, with a full-height wall of glass and sliding doors that opened to a patio; but in spite of his prescience Schindler was neither a top-flight designer nor a convincing protagonist.

Richard J. Neutra, the Austrian import, was a stronger character in every way but he never managed to gain a point of vantage in governmental or educational circles where he might have been fully influential until the victory was won and he was clearly an elder statesman. William Lescaze, like Eliel Saarinen, had little revolutionary impetus. Erich Mendelsohn quickly became identified with Jewish communities but his American work displayed a tendency to compromise that had not been so clearly forecast when he was in Europe. Thus though his Maimonides Hospital in San Francisco and his much less refined synagogues at Cleveland, St. Louis and St. Paul gave some life to Jewish architecture, he was not prepared to affect the national scene. The influence of Antonin Raymond was felt more in Japan than in America, while Oskar Stonorov's was localized in Philadelphia. Far too many of the European architects were too extreme to be given jobs even at educational institutions. Typical was Frederick Kiesler, who came to the United States in 1926 after a European career that had begun in the office of Adolf Loos. His Space House of 1934 was of continuous shell construction with continuous windows opening upon a single space tenuously subdivided into fourteen living areas. In 1942 he opened the Peggy Guggenheim Gallery with paintings at different eye levels and without benefit of frames, floating upon unseen supports from a curved wooden background; other paintings, suspended on strings stretched between floor and ceiling, floated in space. This supplied spectacular staging. So did his sets for the Juilliard School of Music, but neither his talents nor his personality was directed toward those agencies that could effect a major change in American environment.

Thus no positive turning point, no indigenous movement can be clearly perceived. If there was a turning point, it came at about 1937 when the great Germans and Central Europeans came to the United States, generally after a sojourn in England. Walter Gropius and Marcel Breuer joined the faculty of design at Harvard, headed by Joseph Hudnut. Lazlo Moholy-Nagy went to Chicago, where he established the New Bauhaus in 1937. This attracted other Bauhaus men like Gyorgy Kepes. In 1939 Mies van der Rohe, Gropius's successor in Germany, accepted appointment as head of the architectural school at the Armour Institute, later joined with the Lewis Institute to become the Illinois Institute of Technology. Josef and Anni Albers joined the faculty at Black Mountain College in North Carolina. Those who started a new life at experimental and progressive institutions such as Black Mountain had years of uncertainty, turmoil, internal dissensions and financial difficulties. Despite some staunch support from industrialists of Chicago, the New Bauhaus was launched and maintained only with the greatest difficulty and self-sacrifice on the part of Moholy, his wife and the staff. Their commitment to modern art was not casual; it was a religion, all-demanding and all-consuming. Life was easier at older institutions like IIT where Mies, almost from the first, became king. But at Harvard there was steady friction, even though Gropius prevailed, and his fifteen years as chairman of the School of Design ended in a clash between urgency and patience and an unhappy dispute between Hudnut and him which helped neither. But by then the heroic, historic, role of Gropius and the solid acceptance of his cause made this more a matter for personal regret than of any deeper significance. In the end, the appointment of José Luis Sert as Gropius's successor guaranteed that Harvard would see a continuity of principle, if not of detail. Moreover the modern cause was so thoroughly accepted throughout America that a reaction at Harvard would have done more harm to the University than to architecture.

Much the same thing could be said of the dénouement at IIT. Here the instruction was very rigorously laid out by Mies and brooked no deviation from the principles he was espousing in his own work as he went inexorably towards universal space. Whenever it was inconvenient to attend the functional efficiency of space he disregarded it. Though he worked on proportions and on the details of materials with the greatest care and refinement even his structure might be symbolic. This was clearly admitted in the steel beams he set vertically outside the skeleton of 860 Lake Shore Drive of 1951, which he carefully terminated above the ground so no one could imagine they were columns. The German Pavilion at Barcelona of 1929 had not been functional in any purely utilitarian sense and, in the end, this is what you had to say of 860 Lake Shore Drive, nearly a quarter-century later.

But such freedom from function was delayed by the depression. In the meantime, and until after the war, Mies worked out his proportions with great care and refinement which came to fruition in such buildings as Crown Hall at IIT of 1955 or the Seagram's Building at New York City in 1957.

Such refined study of proportions and of scale controlled both the design of the buildings he made for IIT and the training he gave its students. But when his retirement came in 1958 there was another unhappy crisis. The rumor that he would not continue to do the buildings for IIT proved true and was the occasion for a good deal of acrimonious comment. But in the end everyone realized that IIT had valued physical comfort more than the privilege of being wholly designed by one of the great men of the twentieth century. The decision could not seriously arrest the course of modern architecture though it would not add to the reputation of IIT. It was also clear that architectural training at IIT might change as well. But again, and as in the case of Gropius and Harvard, this could not reverse the course of history. The impress of Gropius and Mies had been laid ineradicably on their times.

But in the years between 1937 and 1960 the outcome was not always so predictable.

15

DURING THE STRUGGLES FOR ACCEPTANCE, MIES VAN DER ROHE WAS RE-
fused permission to practice alone in New York and Aalto had to be
joined with another and lesser man in Boston. Even when a modern
firm, the Saarinens, won a competition to design the new Smithsonian
Institution at Washington, the best efforts of Joseph Hudnut and others on his handpicked jury could not persuade Washington to rally to its
support and the prize design was left to languish unbuilt until, many
years later, a new director, Leonard Carmichael, settled for a banal
design.

Even the social aims of the Bauhaus group and other modernists
were disliked. Gropius's appointment to Harvard in 1937 excited de-
rision among many older architects, such as Charles Killam, Professor
of Architecture Emeritus at Harvard, who wrote bitterly against the
appointment of "social reformers," "mere critics," "specialists in domestic work of low-cost housing," "extreme modernists." Others were
suspicious of what Gropius called "a new way of life." Conservative
communities such as Lexington, Massachusetts, thought that all the
modernists who were settling on Six Moon Hill or in nearby Lincoln
in modern houses must be liberals, even radicals, probably intent on
violent reform.

The most outspoken critic was Ralph Adams Cram. His autobiography, *My Life in Architecture*, of 1936, bristled with Gothic fury
against the sacrileges of modernism. If industry and commerce were
modern, they might have a new architecture, he thought, but only because they were ephemeral and culturally unimportant. "The cubist,
'dimaxion.' 'functional' house . . . the work of M. Le Corbusier . . .
or the new type of apartment house . . . seem to me to be a betrayal
of trust, a vicious though unintentional assault on the basic principles
of a sane and wholesome society." Of modern religious sculpture, he
said "while they have their place in the New York Museum of Modern
Art or in the showrooms of the Carnegie Institute in Pittsburgh, they
adapt themselves with scant sympathy to the purposes of any religion
other than that of Voodooism, fetishism, and similar psychopathic
manifestations." There was much folly that Cram could point to in
the modern movement. Dadaism, surrealism, futurism, each had its lunatic fringe. An exhibitionist like Salvador Dali did not help matters
when, on his arrival in New York in 1936, he announced his desire to
live in a "fur-lined uterus."

Essentially a Ruskinian, Cram did not object to the social purposes of architecture, but he did disagree with Gropius's relativism and attacked the anti-individual and irreligious positions of the mechanistic functionalists: "For my own part," he wrote, "I cannot conceive of an adequate training in art which does not involve the element of worship . . . All good art in the past has developed from organized religion." His religious beliefs buttressed his notion of aristocracy. He disliked the current "perilous condition of fictitious social equality."

Cram, of course, was not a spokesman for the whole architectural profession, but his ideas about modernism reflected those of many who were still active when he died in 1941. Believing that medieval art had been the finest, Cram called functionalism "the Pentecost of ugliness" and insisted that industry should not be the dominating influence in society or its architecture.

Others who were not conservatives still had strong reservations about the new European architecture. The most eminent of these was Wright. He never forgot that the art of architecture has many sides for which function and economy are no measure. He always insisted that the architect makes the image of his age, is not merely a reflector for it. He called the modern European housing "the slum of the future." Others like Eliel Saarinen consistently avoided extremes, remained apart from the rigorous functionalists much as Aalto, Fisker and Markelius were doing in Scandinavia, achieved performance and harmony in modest, attractive ways. Still others, like Edward Stone, converted by the immigrant architects, came late to mechanistic architecture, only to have another change of heart later. Other latecomers, like Pietro Belluschi and William Wurster, never succumbed to the Bauhaus, and kept their designs sensitive to regional landscape, materials, history and institutions.

As in other times, many architects escaped the challenges altogether. There were lingering classicists, like Cass Gilbert, John Russell Pope and Otto Eggers, who kept on grinding out classic monuments at Washington; the Supreme Court and the National Gallery of Art — buildings of a hollow and pompous cast, despite materials so rich that any modernist envied them the opportunity. There were tattered remnants of medieval piety, still visible in the unfinished Episcopal Cathedral at New York and the Episcopal and Roman Catholic Cathedrals at Washington, which kept to their handicraft, pseudo-Gothic ways. Nor was Georgian languishing: heavy, elephantine and clumsy, badly sited, feebly composed, it appeared in public schools and town halls and churches throughout the nation, and it received official sanction from Franklin Roosevelt when he designed his own library at

Hyde Park. Sometimes a New England architect like Robert Dean, once a devotee of Williamsburg and then of Dudok's Town Hall, combined the incompatible two in an extraordinary if not otherwise notable high school, as at Wellesley, or in a downtown department store for Boston.

Courageous men of an earlier day, such as Ralph Walker, tried to make their own personal compromise between the old and the new, "*sans dogme, sans monotonie*," but, perhaps because of their admitted strength, they were too weak to concede anything to the new prophets and hence unable to learn anything either. Some of these men might have played majestic roles in an earlier American day. It was their misfortune to live in a different age; and though many of them continued to have many clients, they had to reconcile themselves in the privacy of their libraries to the fact that their buildings would seldom be published, seldom praised by any knowing critic and that their position as middle of the roaders was no better than that of the "black reactionaries." By the '50s no competent revivalists remained. When the wistful Henry Hope Reed, Jr., the lonesome piping voice of the Renaissance revival, needed to find a designer for propaganda purposes for San Francisco, he had to turn to an obscure friend "over the bay in Berkeley" who was ready to come forward if called. No call was heard.

One might have expected the traditionalists to fall under the demands for functional and economical performance during the depression. But aesthetics really remained the crucial issue. "Modern" came to be identified in the popular mind with something unusual, blatant, ugly. When the public spoke scathingly of modern designs it thought of the extreme, even the experimental ones. Those who disliked flat roofs and "chicken coops" in the landscape had little that was good to say for architectural experimentation, on the ground that architecture needed no further study or research. Soleri's glass dome for a desert house in California seemed to be a flagrant defiance of nature. There were aesthetic shortcomings in Buckminster Fuller's Dymaxion House and in Bruce Goff's Umbrella House at Aurora, Illinois, of 1950. But even those who did not perceive these criticized the structural exhibitionism and the obviously capricious subdivision of internal space. Philip Johnson's early house on Ash Street in Cambridge, with its solid plywood wall around the front garden, provoked the curious to kneel on the sidewalk to peer through the small crack beneath the front door to see how a privacy-loving bachelor lived. Polevitzky's Bird Cage house built in Florida in 1950 seemed to be nothing but the work of a *flâneur*, despite the sophistication of its spaces; Charles Eames's experiment in assembling standard materials for his case-study house in California of 1950 suggested to the conventional a box kite, filled arbitrarily with a clutter of materials. Few laymen were able to see past Paul Nelson's hung stairs and rooms and ramps to appreciate the graceful spaces and stately rhythms for the model of the Suspended House he showed in 1939.

The critics were not always wrong. Some of the modern buildings were atrocious. Some were cheaply commercial like Wright's store in San Francisco, or belligerently harsh and crude, like the dormitories at Clemson, South Carolina. More were boringly monotonous, with flat roofs, crude juxtapositions of planes of glass and masonry; many were ruled by an inexorable and unimaginative geometry that was insistently rectilinear in plan, elevation and section. The new clichés were turned out endlessly. Many designers flunked the problems of transition as others had before them but the failure was perhaps more nakedly apparent. Intent upon the grail of functionalism, many forgot the determinants of great design. Hypnotized by the mysteries of the right angle, some ignored the exciting spaces that might have been created with modern materials and structures. Clichés like the tapered corridor, the corner window, the shed roof, the open house-stair were seized avidly, consumed voraciously.

But if the first phase of the modern movement was troubled by the rigors of doctrinaire and uncouth rectangularity, it was succeeded by the even more destructive notion that the cliché must be avoided at all costs. Now many architects, and not always only the younger ones with the lesser names, became obsessed with the ambition to be original. They thought they must always create startling forms, even new religious symbols out of whole cloth. You could see this in Arthur Brown's First Lutheran Church at Tucson, or Lloyd Wright's Swedenborgian crystal at Palos Verdes, California. Even the master Wright succumbed at times. Abandoning the poetic integration of space and structure he had achieved in the much earlier Unity Temple of 1901, he provided the Unitarian Church at Madison, Wisconsin, with an attention-getting roof in 1950. It pitched towards a steeple that rose obliquely from the ground. Harrison and Abramovitz scored some kind of high mark in this direction when they lunged into the eye-catching First Presbyterian Church at Stamford, Connecticut, erected in 1958, while the skillful Eero Saarinen seemed to be fighting himself on this issue all through the last part of the '50s.

This aim to be unique was a strange bedfellow for functionalism. Innovation tended to stop any effort to perfect interesting types of structure, plans, elevations. In 1938-1940 many architects were critical of Anderson and Beckwith's elegant design for the Alumni Swimming

Pool at M.I.T. because it leaned on an excellent Swedish precedent; yet its performance and the improvements the architects introduced clearly justified the study. They had improved greatly upon a good precedent. But individuality seemed to be more highly valued than perfection among the *avant garde* and until they learned to produce at least some charming spaces and forms the public could easily rest its antagonism toward change on the most bizarre products of the cult of originality.

Those who resented even modest and thoroughly legitimate experiments in space and structure were delighted when they could find functional inadequacies in the modern buildings. This was often easy to do. Suddenly all the Colonial gutters whose paint was peeling were forgotten and so were the tiring stairs and the dark reading-rooms of the public libraries. The opposition gloated when it learned that a hurricane had caused some difficulties for Neutra's glass-enclosed house for John Nicholas Brown on Fisher's Island, New York. It never forgot that Frank Lloyd Wright's roofs leaked or that one of Gropius's clients had not been given the book-lined living room she had expressly demanded of her "functional architect." Far too many modern buildings were cheap and looked it. Their artificial materials soon became shabby, their flimsy construction fell apart. Wright had never been secure against physical failure. The houses of younger modernists, eager to try their wings even in the face of lean budgets, were no match for the excellent construction and careful detailing that Goodhue, Magonigle or Lindeberg provided for their usually wealthier clients. Too much of the modern work was amateurish. There were strong suggestions that the houses of Mies were notoriously awkward to live in; they were far from cheap, their white walls and pristine furnishings responded badly to grimy-fingered children or to disorder. They were unsuitable for a mother with three children, "one girl in bed, one girl in school" and a recalcitrant boy pounding his way into the Czerny exercises; she might pray for the return of partitions that were now so old hat. It was said that the students living in Gropius's Graduate Center at Harvard could not study for the corridor noise and that they cared little about using its common rooms. The plate glass in the main cafeteria at Eero Saarinen's General Motors Technical Center was so strongly affected by wind that post-construction bracing had to be added even though it marred the proportions of the building; and there were anxious days at his Kresge Auditorium at M.I.T. when the concrete shell refused to stop creeping as soon as it was supposed to. At the very end of our saga James Johnson Sweeney, director of the Guggenheim Museum introduced strenuous alterations into Wright's wonderful new space in order to hang pictures at all and thereby launched another international controversy on art versus use. There was enough truth in all such accusations, or most of them, so that the public, already suspicious about the aesthetics of modern design, doubted also its claims to economy and performance, even when penitents of the modern movement, examining more conservative buildings, showed that they, too, seldom stood the same tests.

These demurrers had some justification as long as the members of the new movement acted like *enfants terribles* suddenly discovering architecture for the good of the world. The modernists undoubtedly claimed too much for their social and functional achievements and underplayed their aesthetics. No one could question their sincerity, but their work was still often ungainly, awkward, contrived, and filled with an infantile urgency.

The vigor may have suffused the work and sustained it against any merely aesthetic or practical judgment. But however expressive such vigor might be, expression alone could not constitute great architecture and the public sensed what the younger modernists later had to discover. It was a point which had been impressively made by Geoffrey Scott in 1914. To an entire generation befuddled by Ruskin's desire for moral expression, Scott had declared that the basic value of architecture lay solely in its capacity to give pleasurable sensuous experience, quite independent of any ethical or social undertones. This formalism buttressed the inclinations of architects of the '20s like Hood, Corbett and Goodhue who cheerfully ignored or denied social and moral programs. But in the revolt the new generation could not accept the art-for-art's-sake mentality as anything but an irresponsible anachronism. In the face of housing problems and those of war production Henri Focillon's romanticism of 1942 seemed incredible: ". . . form, guided by the play and interplay of metamorphoses, go[es] forever forward, by its own necessity, toward its own liberty." Formalism could not weather the storms of demand that architecture be bound to social purpose; and it was only at the end of the '50s that modern architects began to read Scott again and to suggest that art might be first and foremost a matter of visible spaces and physical forms, not social beliefs.

Meanwhile the opponents of the new movement had almost everything on their side; the schools suppressed it and sneered at it even while the students sought it; the bankers denied it in their loans and the realtors in their projects; journalists like Mencken tried to kill it with bitter ridicule; the public did not understand it, did not really like it, were more content with things to which they were accustomed; the public wish, if this were represented by the opinions of legislators and governors and presidents, would have none of it in public buildings; university trustees were assiduous in keeping it off the campus and were fully supported by the few alumni who were observant and articulate about the architecture of Alma Mater which they inevitably venerated more for its memories than for its distinction. Even in 1958 most Bostonians who wrote to the newspapers hoped that their new city center would be 22-story Georgian, or at least theirs were the letters the editors cared to print. People who had never gone near Beacon Hill now feared its degradation.

16

SLOWLY CONSERVATISM MODIFIED THE MODERN MOVEMENT. DURING THE '50s, younger architects like Rudolph, Yamasaki and Nowicki sought solutions undominated by the stringent original mechanical aims of the Bauhaus group. Older converts like Howe, Belluschi and Wurster reserved their admiration for Le Corbusier's imagination, Wright's masterly sensitivity, and Mies's patiently studied proportions. The resulting humanization of modern architecture was most apparent first on the West Coast where the Bauhaus group had never planted one of its dogged pioneers. It appeared in a number of houses by Wurster, Soriano, Henry Hill, Neutra, Harwell Harris, Mario Corbett and Belluschi. Each respected its terrain, used natural materials so as to emphasize their textures and colors, and seemed to be free of clichès in their windows, plans, roof lines or compositions. Planned picturesquely, they achieved unity through balance, often occult, and the counterpoise of masses and spaces. Above all, these Western houses seemed to stand in a long line of development out of the Spanish ranch houses and not to owe so much to the inventions of a few European innovators. It was even possible to imagine that they were in the line of the earlier Maybeck, and the brothers Gill and Greene. Many a client who would have recoiled at the thought of commissioning Breuer or Lescaze now became a client of one of these exponents of a more gentle modernism.

For some time, modern architecture was not publicized in the United States with a thorough and convincing attack, such as the Chicago Fair of 1893 had led for classicism, but after the '30s, exhibitions began to spearhead the modern propaganda. In 1931 the New York Architectural League staged a show organized by men who had designed New York's skyscrapers with an eye to the decoration they had seen at the Paris Exposition of Decorative Arts in 1925; they excluded all truly modern work, and so the show was picketed by the progressives. In 1940 the League reversed itself in a new show. Called *Versus*, it led visitors past a simple and conventional display of old buildings like the Boston Public Library and Harvard's Lowell House, while upstairs all the tricks of contemporary display technique helped to glamorize modern work.

Expositions also turned modern. The International Exposition at Paris in 1937 showed modernized classical buildings. Le Corbusier and his followers, excluded from the exhibition, created their own tent at the Porte Maillot where they exhibited a convincing model of an ideal city. This caught the favor of some American architects who had already essayed the tepid and misconceived modernism of Chicago's 1933 Fair.

Thus the major expositions at New York and San Francisco in 1939 were filled with efforts at modern design. California had buildings by Pflueger, Born, and Wurster; New York's trylon and perisphere were the work of Harrison and Fouilhoux, while Albert Kahn, Lescaze, Howe, Teague, and Stonorov designed some of the buildings. Most of them derived from European work of the '20s in the manner of Loos and Hoffman; long planes of white plaster, incised by strip windows, frequently at the corners, were topped by flat roofs and terraces.

But among this conventional unconventionality, two small and winning exhibits were more important than all the display of established modernism. Both were from Scandinavia, the Swedish Pavilion by Sven Markelius and the Finnish Pavilion by Alvar Aalto. There, modern architects learned from Markelius the strength of continuous space, from Aalto the interest of sinuosity and that old materials like wood could be handled freshly and beautifully. They were reminded that the articulation of small structural parts might offer a way to give scale to buildings. Overall, Markelius and Aalto taught a lesson in the plastic manipulation of form and space, offering American architects the first clear path away from the rigid plans and the hard materials of the Bauhaus. This might lead merely to a romantic and charming architecture or provide a truly rich environment where structures were sympathetic to materials. No American, Russian, British, French or Italian building at the fair was memorable for its architecture even though the evening scene was enlivened by the fountains and fireworks of Jean Labatut. In the end, and except for the magnificent gastronomy possible on Flushing Meadows, only the Swede and the Finn prevailed.

It was possible to look to a few museums for leadership in the new taste. Despite the excellence of their collections of earlier art, the National Gallery of Washington and the new Nelson Gallery of 1933 in Kansas City were set against such excursions. This was the usual view among the directors of the older museums of the country who had generally been hostile to contemporary painting as well. But several communities were more fortunate. In Pittsburgh the Carnegie Institute held important shows and began to praise modern artists; at Hartford, Connecticut, the Avery Memorial of the Wadsworth Athenaeum acquired a new building with modern galleries for modern paintings; at Boston the Institute of Contemporary Art became a modestly important center, while the Boston Museum of Fine Arts continued to suggest up to 1956 that art had stopped with Monet. But the outstanding center was in New York. Even the Metropolitan Museum organized a series of exhibitions of contemporary American industrial art beginning in 1929 with a series of generally unsuccessful rooms designed by Hood, Urban, Albert Kahn, Walker, Eliel Saarinen and Root. A second show opened in 1934 and now the rooms, especially the striking one by Eliel Saarinen, showed a tremendous advance in the handling of space and the quality of the modern furnishings. Farther to the left, the Whitney and Guggenheim collections, very well selected, stimulated a limited but scarcely a popular audience.

Indeed, the story of American education in modern design is almost completely the story of New York's Museum of Modern Art. In 1929, when the Museum opened, an important exhibition was organized by Philip Johnson. It gave Americans their first large look at the work of Le Corbusier, Mies, Gropius, Oud, even of Frank Lloyd Wright. This exhibition spawned an important book, *Modern Architecture*, published in 1929, with essays by Henry-Russell Hitchcock, Johnson, Mumford and Alfred Barr. In 1931, Johnson and Hitchcock began to collect photographs of modern architecture, and in 1932 there was a second major exhibition, held in the Museum's quarters in the Heckscher Building. This show gave the modern European movement the inappropriate name "International Style," widely broadcast by the book of the same title, written largely by Hitchcock. The latter was a scholarly critic of enormous vigor and a keen nose for the future. He anticipated and nourished professional and even popular interest in Wright, Richardson, Victorian architecture, Gaudi and the European modernists. As a consultant to the Museum, he became one of the most important spokesmen for the new movement in America.

In 1935, the Museum brought Le Corbusier to the United States and organized an extensive lecture tour for him. The preceding year had seen Johnson's Machine Art Exhibition, which showed furnishings designed by modern architects, such as a desk lamp, inkstand and calendar by Howe and Lescaze; these were placed alongside industrial products: a flush valve, a caliper, a propeller, the section of a wire rope, self-aligning ball-bearings, a burglar-proof chest and a brass plumb bob. The first choice of the judges was the section of a steel spring, a product of the American Steel and Wire Company. Such awards and exhibits attempted to end the old fight between art and the machine, and tried to improve the state of industrial design by insisting for example, that wallboard cease to imitate marble through application of decalcomania, and asbestos shingles no longer imitate the rough grain of wood. Some derived the naïve notion from these exhibitions that machinery could become the source for architectural design, and the idea was reinforced in 1939 when the Museum held the Bauhaus exhibit, strongly emphasizing the mechanistic approach of many members of that school.

Meanwhile the Museum acquired its present building, the design of Goodwin and Stone, erected in 1939. Refusing to concede anything to its inconspicuous site and the nearby St. Thomas's Church, the building had a glass-enclosed lobby that invited the public to visit the galleries behind the grid of its bold façade. Dramatic exhibition techniques, notably René d'Harnoncourt's open vista grouping, pioneered in the South Seas exhibit, lured the public to study paintings in the Museum's growing collection as well as special shows such as that of the engineering of Robert Maillart in 1947, the sculpture of Henry Moore in 1946 or of Gabo and Pevsner in 1948. Lively discussions about modern art and architecture, notably one held in 1948 to address the question "What's Happening in Modern Architecture?" kept the Museum in the forefront as a promoter of modern design. Against this skillful and insistent presentation of work that was gaining in stature, the protesting books of Robsjohn-Gibbings or the more scholarly ones of Francis Henry Taylor had no real chance. The battle was long and tiring but it did not have many ups and downs. The Museum really paved the way for the advent of Gropius.

Now architectural magazines joined in the taste-making. None aimed consistently at a sophisticated audience and none boasted a critic comparable to the earlier Montgomery Schuyler. For some time they essayed their own eclecticism, publishing the architecture they thought best, regardless of style. For example in January, 1934, the *Architectural Forum* spent many pages on two houses. One was in Regency style; the other was a very modern design by Frederick Kiesler: ". . . both are excellent examples of their respective kinds," said the *Forum*. A typical issue of that day contained William Templeton Johnson's Music Auditorium at Claremont College, California, which was North Italian Renaissance; a group of Philadelphia houses by McCaskey which were in the regional style that had been popularized locally by

Mellor, Meigs and Howe; a Master Detail Series showing a Georgian Colonial house by Philip Goodwin and a Regency house by Verna Cook Salomonsky; and eight unfortunate model houses designed by New York's skyscraper architects, Walker, Hood, Corbett, Van Alen, Kahn, Harmon, White and Schultze, all of whom were attempting to be modern in a halfhearted way.

In defense of this weak and catholic editorial policy we must recall that there was little modern architecture of any quality to publish and that the older experienced anti-moderns were often producing better buildings than the modernists. Thus, the *Forum* devoted an issue of Master Design Series of 1934 to California Spanish architecture as it was being designed by Wallace Neff, Reginald Johnson, Gordon B. Kaufmann and H. Roy Kelley. The houses were charming and much more than competent. Beginning with their cool and comfortable patios, filled with moist air and rich plants, they were consistently graceful and comfortable. Simple exterior façades were formed by broad, white stucco walls, covered by low-pitched tile roofs. Wrought-iron balconies, sequestered views, varied vistas and luxuriant foliage created a wealth of textures, color, patterns of light and shade, and a gracious ease of movement through space; the buildings were professionally finished, yet never dull, as delightful quirks and unexpected deviations from a rigorous scheme featured a statue, a potted shrub, a pool, a fireplace or window. In 1934, outside of Wright's work, which the editors generally championed, no other American architecture had comparable warmth.

The problem faced by the editors was a knotty one; namely how to encourage modern design and its adventurous advocates while being mindful of their faults. Unfortunately the educational problem became mired in questions of how to maintain circulation and advertising copy. For a time magazines like the *Architectural Record* seemed to ignore this question as they followed the direction of Mumford and Stein and others who had a liberal social mission, freely praising the fine planning of towns like Radburn, New Jersey, while conveniently neglecting to criticize their undistinguished architecture.

But as modern work became better and more acceptable, the editorial direction of magazines followed the leaders. After the war traditional work found little sympathy even when it was praiseworthy. The hinterlands and the architectural centers were still full of traditionalists, but their work reached the eye of the magazine reader only when it came in for abusive attack such as was properly leveled at Pope's National Gallery of Art. There were fewer and fewer philosophical articles in the magazines. No strong stands were taken on major questions of research, social philosophy or design. Criticism almost disappeared. A student seeking aid in distinguishing between good and bad designs in 1950 received scant help from editors or publishers. In part this was a reflection of the uncritical basis for modern design which tended to favor innovation rather than excellence; in part it stemmed from fear that modernism was so tender a plant that it might wither if abused; in part it was a result of increased reliance on advertising which inexorably forced each magazine to seek a headline, an exclusive masterpiece of the month, a scoop. Naturally there were not enough scoops to go around, especially when the more influential popular news magazines joined in the competition.

But illustrations in magazines did offer a noncommittal, reportorial, apparently objective way to help modern design to gain ground. Long before any advertisements were showing modern buildings, the *Architectural Forum* and the *Architectural Record* occasionally devoted sections to architecture done abroad. Factory buildings at Avellaneda, Argentina, by Luciano Chersanaz, and the work of Pier Luigi Nervi and Ernesto Rogers in Italy were suddenly presented about 1941. They dazzled architects and engineers who had thought that Albert Kahn's preoccupation with the steel frame had placed America in the forefront of industrial architecture.

There was naturally still a great deal of noisy opposition from influential traditionalists. But the temper of the times had set against them as early as 1937. What the young wanted was clearly shown at the Princeton Architectural Round Table of that June. A. Lawrence Kocher, editor of the *Architectural Record* and himself a modern designer, stood firmly for functionalism. Clarence Stein exhorted the Princeton graduate students to believe that architecture should start "with the social life in which we live."

Such ideas left no place for the vacillations of Ely Jacques Kahn, whose style was only skin-deep. "Is not the ultimate function of the architect to please the client?" he seemed to ask. "Why go into all this frenzy of cantilevered buildings and insist on doing something stunty . . . ? Why can't we take it for granted that we are different people, liking different things?" At one point he made the error of asking the group assembled in Cram's Gothic college whether, if Princeton were destroyed overnight, they would like to see it rebuilt by Le Corbusier; the students' "yeas" were overwhelming. But university trustees and especially Princeton trustees were the last to agree with the students. They have not really agreed yet. And in another decade the students might have changed their minds as they aged into being alumni.

Few of them had any aesthetic convictions. By 1960 the magazines, newspapers, museums, and all other sources of influence had so unanimously mounted the bandwagon that if there were to be a Salon des Refusés it would have to be for any architects who tried to design in the older ways. Institutional buying of something that could at least be called contemporary design was so confirmed that the institution which bought conventionally bought modern, while the one which tried to buy Georgian or Gothic seemed only eccentric. But the progression to this dénouement was not without travail; the beginnings were tentative and meager.

17

INDIVIDUAL CLIENTS FOLLOWED CONVICTIONS ABOUT THE NEW IDEAS LONG before anybody else did. But still they moved slowly. In 1939, the *Architectural Forum* was disappointed to note that thirty years after Wright's Coonley House and fourteen after Le Corbusier's Pavillon d'Esprit Nouveau and Mies's Tugendhat House the new houses in the 1939 landscape were still predominantly traditional. But this was not surprising. Individuals continued to have leanings towards sentimentally rustic primitivism. These were nurtured by charming books about old New England village life such as Samuel Chamberlain's beautifully sympathetic drawings and photographs of Old Sturbridge or Deerfield, which seemed to reflect the American longing for a past that seemed less vexatious than the present was known to be. This was fortified in 1933 when the Historic American Building Survey was inaugurated in an effort to provide useful relief for unemployed architects and draftsmen. In the summer of 1938 architects and art historians began to plan a Society of Architectural Historians which made its debut in 1940. Their *Journal* frequently dealt with the Colonial and Georgian scene, and for a long time it published less and less about ancient and medieval architecture, or foreign buildings generally, while it also contained few pieces about modern American building or city planning. In this the editors reflected the mood of many Americans.

The mood was pampered by the restoration of Colonial Williamsburg, a village that could not possibly suggest any solutions to modern problems, even in its reconstruction, which began in 1927. Some applauded the idea on the ground that America should own a few choice restorations as documents of civic art. This was the defensible position of city planners like Kevin Lynch. Others like Gropius questioned whether the expenditures of the Rockefellers were justified in such projects in view of the social needs of the American people — a far-fetched view. A more serious criticism came from historians who knew how often the restoration ignored historical evidence and this is what bothered men like Lawrence Kocher and Marcus Whiffen. Others like Frank Lloyd Wright never ceased to ridicule the "Williamsburg Wigs" and the "Codfish Colonial" sentimentalists for fear of the damage they might do to American taste. Their fears were justified. The American public listened to no intellectual explanations, cared for no carping criticism. One and all, they were charmed by the gardens, houses and costumed guides, quite as much as by the buildings Perry, Shaw and Hepburn invented or restored. Since 1937, when Williamsburg acquired an Inn, invented out of whole cloth, the annual pilgrimage has been heavy. The question of motor cars among the Colonial precincts, of streets paved whose traces had once been deep in mud, of overelaborate collections of furniture, all this paled beside the sense of pilgrimage Americans felt while journeying to an ancient provincial capital whose minor significance in American history they understood but faintly if at all. What they could understand was the privilege of photographing their children in the stocks.

Such pilgrimages stimulated support for preserving other villages. Money poured in for Colonial, Georgian and Federalist buildings, for the Rappite colony at Economy, Pennsylvania; for ghost towns of the Gold Rush and Spanish missions; and later for a few Victorian arks. Meanwhile, the Larkin Building and the Marshall Field Wholesale Warehouse fell to the wrecker's bar and swinging ball. Wright's Robie House was threatened with demolition in 1958 at a moment when Congress willingly prepared to spend vast moneys for adding a completely useless and dome-diminishing classic façade to the National Capitol in Washington. Such a view was not of course exclusively American. In the same time Horta's work in Belgium and some of Le Corbusier's in France were equally threatened by time and "progress."

But even when the choice of what to preserve was, as in the case of Williamsburg, a reasonable one, the effect was to slow down the acceptance of modern designs. In 1939, the architectural magazines of America could show a few white-stuccoed cubist boxes such as Howe, Lescaze and Kenneth Day occasionally built around Philadelphia, or a little, still European work by Gropius and Breuer around Boston. Edward Stone's vigorous house for A. Conger Goodyear in Old Westbury, Long Island, was a rarity in 1940. After the war, however, acceptance was rapid. By 1952, the F. W. Dodge Corporation could publish a book displaying eighty-two modern houses, many of which were good. Few had been designed by architects of international or even national reputation, for by 1952, economics had made the house the province of competent young designers or small firms.

At this point there was, perhaps, not much originality. The work fol-

lowed the style of one or another major man. Among these the influence of Mies van der Rohe was strong though few emulated his purity;
no one handled volumes, for example, as austerely as he had in his
Barcelona Pavilion. But still many aspired to the Miesian brilliance with
materials, with hovering planes, with modulated space. They were given
a striking example of ultimate purity in 1950 when the Farnsworth
House was completed at Plano, Illinois. It was limited to the most basic
elements: two rectangular floor and roof planes suspended on eight
steel columns, walled solely by glass, and interrupted only by a utility
core of kitchen, bathrooms, heating unit and fireplace near one end of
the single room. A year earlier Philip Johnson completed a similar house
for himself at New Canaan, Connecticut. The ultimate in purist, even
self-conscious simplicity, it contained a single space defined by the brick
floor, the roof, steel columns, and glazed walls. The space was subdivided only by furniture, a painting, plants and a brick cylinder containing the bathroom. Its classical, measured spirit reappeared in the
symmetrical house Johnson, collaborating with Landis Gores, designed
in 1951 for Richard Hodgson at New Canaan. An interior patio, full of
foliage, was the focus for all major rooms in the house, and it provided a
strong contrast to the planar walls of pale gray, glazed brick.

Another leading inspiration for house design was the work of Gropius
and Breuer. Somewhat angular and awkward in their early attempts at
fitting houses into the landscape of Lincoln, Massachusetts — although
from the beginning impressed with the quality of New England's characteristic white-painted wood siding — they became increasingly less addicted to unblended machined parts, like the Lally columns in Gropius's own house. Their house for Henry G. Chamberlain at Wayland,
Massachusetts, of 1940, notwithstanding some awkward moments in
the disposition of doors and windows, showed a greater appreciation of
native materials like rough fieldstone and wooden siding, and its rectangular module admitted their greater concern for proportion. Gropius's
pupils carried similar domestic designs to various parts of the United
States and even to Australia.

In California, Neutra's style was changing rapidly in the direction of
greater sympathy with the landscape. The Tremaine House at Mon-
tecito of 1949 was a series of planes interrupted by wide windows. The
center of the plan was devoted to living and dining and the remainder
branched outward like the spokes of a pinwheel, with a wing for the
servants' quarters, another for family bedrooms, another for guests and
a fourth for the outdoor terrace. The whole still contrasted its precise
lines to the rocky slope and gnarled trees, but its openness created an
informality sympathetic to the site.

The architect who displayed the most remarkable genius for America's broad terrain continued to be Wright, whose houses consistently developed themes compatible to their sites. Boulders and hills near the Friedman house at Pleasantville, New York, suggested the great disks covering the house and carport. A huge boulder near a lake in Quasqueton, Iowa, became the theme for the massive oblongs of a boathouse, while the bluff above demanded the stroke of the long, low-lying silhouette of the Walter House, with its unexpected quirk in the roof. Cacti and desert rock suggested the battered walls and angular cantilevers of the Pauson House at Phoenix, Arizona, while the bunker of a hillside shaped a modern sod-house in Wisconsin. Each of these was Wright's original creation, quoting no one, not even his own prairie houses. Falling Water, the country lodge at Bear Run, Pennsylvania, belonging to Edgar Kaufmann, became the most celebrated of the houses. Inseparably related to its unique site, the house took its theme from the waterfall, where a massive rock was the spillway for a brook. Cantilevered balconies repeated the theme, as the upper balcony overlapped the space created by the lower one and the pools seemed to run in and out of the building. Sun terraces and masonry walls echoed the stratified split ledge stone in the hillside. Diffused light within the interlocking spaces of the interior reflected the foliage around the brook. The theme appeared also in the bastion of the small bridge, but now in stone, where space was enclosed by intermeshed L-shaped masses like those of the balconies, but no longer cantilevered since stone, unlike reinforced concrete, is brittle. Falling Water, built in 1936, never failed to look fresh and intriguing; its breath-taking leap over water and ground excited admiration, and its dark, penetrated spaces provided recesses that seemed inviting, comfortable and harmonious with their purpose, as a weekend retreat in a Pennsylvania woodland.

This quality of site expression extrapolated to a regional level was sought by many architects especially in the Western states. In California, William Wurster's houses, like the Clark House at Aptos and the early house for the Gregorys in the Santa Cruz Mountains, used native wood and made prominent use of enclosed courtyards. Other designers, like Soriano, Dinwiddie, Hill, Dailey, Langhorst and John Funk, produced attractive houses of wood, with open plans. Mario Corbett tended towards classical elegance, as in his house for Moritz Thomsen at Vina, in 1952; but Harwell Harris seemed to have studied the Japanese villas and the romantic work of earlier architects like Greene and Greene always leaning to the purer austerity of Nippon. His Johnson House at Los Angeles of 1951 and his earlier house at Fellowship Park, Los Angeles, of 1935, masterfully adapted pitched roofs, wooden structure and open plans to romantic topography. Around San Francisco, there was so much of that kind of design that it seemed briefly as though a new style had emerged. The *Architectural Record* published a series of articles in 1949 on the question, "Is there a Bay Area Style?"

The Californians were sure they had something different. Even as late as 1960 Wurster wrote about it in *Casabella*. Their attitude, he said, was relaxed and undogmatic, not bound to accede to a machine aesthetic but also not bound by tradition, genuinely bound however by the regional conditions. Socially he thought the houses reflected two conditions, the taste for outdoor activities and the natural landscape and the lack of domestic servants. The California architects wanted to achieve their results simply and did not care about labels. Of this northern California architecture he concluded, "It is therefore a truly popular architecture, in a sense that much of the internationalists' work is not, it is an architecture of *everyday use* rather than form or intellectual theory. Viewed as sculpture, it may disappoint, but if in a democratic society architecture is a social art, it may have some validity."

To all this it was possible to agree without conceding that it was an exclusively Californian phenomenon. In the Pacific Northwest the Watzek House by John Yeon and Pietro Belluschi offered a particularly beautiful instance of regional expression. Built around an interior garden, its wooden walls and columns and its ledge-stone piers and chimneys were sensitively detailed; above all, the roofs were grouped into picturesque compositions which subtly echoed the distant view of the sometimes visible Mount Hood. Others appropriate to their terrain could be found in Florida and Massachusetts. Houses of this kind were major influences in producing a general appreciation of modern design. They were neither bizarre not austere. They did not require a change in a way of life; they did not lug the machine or the washbasin into the living room; they were comfortable for children as well as adults; they could tolerate a little mess; and they needed neither manifestoes nor exhibitions to explain themselves.

Modern furniture and decoration did much to provide general acceptance. Many people who could not build new houses or who might have built conventional ones if they could, nonetheless were attracted by the new utensils, the new fabrics, the new chairs. Of these, most found the Scandinavian work of Wegner, the Dane, Mathsson, the Swede, and Aalto, the Finn, more ingratiating than Le Corbusier's severe structural logic or his witty reclining chairs. Not very many could afford the opulent steel-and-leather Barcelona chair by Mies van der Rohe. But there were American designers too, such as the younger Saarinen and Eames.

Altogether one could find many a modern interior in a house whose
façade was reminiscent only of the cartoons of Charles Addams. Much
of the acceptance was, of course, based on fashion rather than on merit,
but regardless of motive it paved the way to familiarity with modern interiors and thence to acceptance of the full range of modern design.

Similar influences were imposed by the new gardens, which abandoned formal parterres and meandering English Romantic types in
favor of outdoor spaces intended to serve as centers for recreation,
shaped by informal architectural elements, using new types of peren-
nials and shrubs that were both hardy and easily tended but also provided some sense of the exotic. In California and the Far West during
the '40s and '50s, Thomas Church and Garrett Eckbo invented exciting
ways to compose the new shapes, colors and textures. In all these
changes the formal informality and the subtle restraint of Japanese gardens were clearly influential, notably in layouts by such men as Isamo
Noguchi, Minoru Yamasaki and Hideo Sasaki. All of these had too much
sense, most of the time, to import Japanese treatments of the most ab-
struse type such as the Zen stone garden at Ryoanji. Such treatments
would have been most appropriate to the austere designs of the house-
builders, but would also have been mannered and inappropriate in
America. The gardens were therefore things that could be appreciated at
once and by many and they, too, helped modern architecture in its struggle for acceptance.

1 8

IT IS NOT SURPRISING THAT THE FIRST INROADS SHOULD HAVE BEEN MADE IN
the domestic field, for here all that was needed was to convince a single
human being or at most a couple, especially if they had enough money
so that a banker, too, need not be convinced. It is not surprising either
that the first committee-accepted architecture to come into the modern
tent was industrial. Industry had new problems as it moved from ancient sites to new ones, on the periphery of the old cities or even into
new regions; it had a chance to try a new horizontality. The plants on
the great highways offered a chance for architecture to serve public
relations. Industrialists like General Robert Johnson became advocates
of beautiful factory architecture. The Ligature Building of his Johnson and Johnson Company on Route 1, near New Brunswick, New
Jersey, offered one of the earliest displays of the new factory symbol.
Designed by R. W. Cory, it took full advantage of its highway location.
From their cars, speeding motorists saw the long white planes, ribbon
windows and clear signs. These were twenty-four-hour advertisements,

lighted by searchlights at night. The whole effect was a convincing suggestion of the integrity of the firm's products. But one of the ironies was that as each new highway unclogged the traffic for a year or so, the decentralizing industry drawn by the highway and served by it clogged it up again. Often you could drive fastest through the old factory areas although the cobbles were rough and the views unsightly.

In some instances functional design produced strong and telling forms. The Hortonspheroids on the shores of Texas and Louisiana and the refineries at Baton Rouge or Bayonne with their intricate diagrams of steel lighted by flaming gas, were near to being wonderful if unconscious sculpture. The Willow Run Bomber Plant spoke clearly of the traffic of personnel and materials, the assembly lines, traveling cranes, bridge cranes and chain conveyors it housed. The solid glass-block walls of a rayon factory at Painesville, Ohio, of 1939, told of the need for thoroughly controlled environment in the manufacturing of synthetic fibers. A new throwing mill at Winston-Salem, North Carolina, dipped and rose over the vats and racks where the nylon was processed. At the Pulp Mill of the Weyerhaeuser Timber Company at Everett, Washington, designed by Schoenwerk, an engineer, the concrete tanks and acid vats were powerful cylinders. They stood in rhythmic array against the sulphur storage bins. Conveyors leading to the chipping room dramatically brought the eye to climactic steel digesters turning timber to pulp.

Functional architecture for the mass-production industries still remained the domain of Albert Kahn, but there were notable competitors like Boston's Stone and Webster and Cleveland's Austin Company, who made frank and logical statements of arc-welded rigid frames, as in the Allen Corporation factory at Detroit. But the pre-eminent design staff was Kahn's, to whom the *Architectural Forum* devoted an entire issue in 1938. When his buildings expressed a long span roof with trussed butterfly monitors, as in the Ohio Steel foundry, the results were elegant. Never tied to a single form, Kahn also scored successes with the glass cage suspended beneath giant trusses as in the press shop of the De Soto Plant at the Chrysler Corporation. His occasional "Borax" jobs, like the factory for Lady Esther, Limited, at Clearing, Illinois, were naturally less admirable, for he worked in earnest only on such realistic problems as transforming the giant cranes and rollers of the hot and cold strip mills at Cleveland, of 1938, into fantasies Piranesi might have dreamed. His grain elevators at Battle Creek, Michigan, and his Assembly Building for the Glenn Martin airplane plant at Baltimore showed that architectural quality might be evoked by industrial necessity.

We did not learn of a more beautiful architecture created out of reinforced concrete until after the war, when Nervi's work in Italy was
generally discovered by American architects. The initial work of Freyssinet had been ignored by Kahn. The usual explanation, that high labor
costs and low steel costs prevented our exercises in concrete, ignores the
fact that Americans have purchased anything they really wanted; the
truth is that until recently Americans did not understand concrete well
enough to design in it and did not want the forms enough to wish to
study the methods. Until the war's restrictions upon steel, neither Ammann and Whitney, nor Roberts and Schaefer gained many commissions for thin-shell designs, and American industry remained content
with the steel buildings the Kahns erected.

Satisfaction with the works of Kahn encouraged industries to employ
architects for industrial buildings. There were early successes like the
B. B. Chemical Company at Cambridge, Massachusetts, of 1939, a surprising display of modernism on the part of the then traditionalist firm,
Coolidge, Shepley, Bulfinch and Abbott. The Forest Products Laboratory at Madison, Wisconsin, by Holabird and Root in 1933, used fins of
cypress and vertical mullions to advantage. In 1950 Ford planned to
build a huge administrative center, and hired Skidmore, Owings and
Merrill to make the design. The Corning Glass Works employed Harrison and Abramovitz to design a new plant and exhibition gallery expressive of its sophisticated products. Lever Brothers hired the Bechtel
Corporation and Welton Becket to lay out a factory in Los Angeles with
strong industrial forms, tanks and piping systems all displayed as architectural elements. At Corpus Christi, Texas, in 1949 the Bluebonnet
Plant of the Corn Products Refining Company, designed by Frank J.
Whitney of H. K. Ferguson Company, brilliantly exposed the manufacturing processes in its Mill House and Steep House, covering them only
with platforms, a roof, and some sunshades. Alden Dow created distinguished work for his family's Chemical Company at Midland, Michigan,
while William Lescaze designed the new Kimball Glass Company at
Vineland, New Jersey.

But the most ambitious and successful was the General Motors Technical Center on which the Saarinens began work in 1945, though it was
not completed until 1956. The Center, a vast project, was conceived by
Alfred Sloan as a long-term reminder to his successor executives of General Motors that their successes were founded not on law, but on mer-
chandising, not on financial plans or super-service but on technology.
In the end Eero Saarinen contrived one of his finest groupings to provide the symbol. The buildings were low, of great simplicity and dignity,
skillfully placed on a technological campus, embracing reflecting pools,

fountains, plazas and modern sculpture by Alexander Calder. Colored glazed bricks were used on the end walls. The design building contained a handsome open stair hung on wires of stainless steel, hovering over a graceful pool. A punctuation was provided by the circular display conference room, which served as the secret kiva in which the design executives would first see the new car models. All this excellence, even that serving the mumbo-jumbo of design secrecy, might have influenced the designers to make better designs, but the hope that architecture may improve society escaped the promoters of swept-finned automobiles.

By 1960 there was even more provocative industrial architecture to ponder. The architecture of General Motors was refined, acceptable, and a great improvement even though it contained little of experiment. It was quite otherwise when O'Neil Ford set out to provide a plant near Dallas, Texas, for Texas Instruments, Incorporated, in 1958. This company, manufacturing transistors, was growing rapidly in a business where freedom to change was fundamental. The management was adventurous in every direction and naturally demanded efficient flexibility. In particular, it needed enormous areas of unencumbered floor space, while at the same time it needed a complex of water or gas pipes, electric tables and other manufacturing resources, which might be required on any square foot of the building, at any time, and on short notice. To solve the problem, Ford provided an intermediate service story which acted as skeleton, circulatory and nervous system for the working floors above and below it. This story consisted of one great space frame of precast concrete struts and tension members running along the edges of what would have been pyramids had they been solid. Between the tetrahedal arches thus formed, stretching in both directions, supporting the ceiling of the story below and the floor of the story above, electricians, plumbers, steam-fitters and other bringers-of-service could walk and work at ease, channel their wires and pipes at will, drop them through the ceiling or push them up through the floor to any desired point. To permit unencumbered floor space at the top, the roof of the building was a set of hyperbolic paraboloid concrete shells. The structure itself was novel and daring; but it was even more daring that the architects should have decided to let the intermediate structure show through glass walls. As they saw the possibilities in this, so they saw the Léger-like nature of the great machinery room which they emphasized in the use of various colors of paint on variously functioning units.

This building was done hastily and with élan. It had many mistakes of detail that were not to be found in the refined works of Bunshaft or Saarinen when either was in his Miesian phase. The lighting problems were not fully solved; the fire escapes which made a good part of the daylight architecture, cast ugly shadows at night; most of all the enormous parking lots destroyed much of the dignity of the ensemble. But this they were doing on every other important decentralized factory lot in the country, denying, for example, the purity of the buildings Bunshaft had erected for the Connecticut General in Hartford. Nevertheless the principles of Ford's design were valuable, the results exciting; given more projects and more time, the refinement into a great design might easily come.

<h1 style="text-align:center">1 9</h1>

New office buildings seldom lived up to the new factories in the early days of the modern movement. With few exceptions their designers ignored the lessons of the McGraw-Hill and PSFS buildings, following, instead, the older Metropolitan Tower; even when they were more adventurous, they tended to produce downright dull exhibits of functional clothing on skeletal structures. Supplied with an overabundance of office space, the new clients did not vie for height and no building reached toward the Empire State Building. Some of the new buildings like Philadelphia's Penn Mutual Life Building of 1934 mocked the style of nearby Independence Hall, disregarding the great difference in scale which made the contemporary application ludicrous. The New England Mutual Life Building at Boston by Cram and Ferguson would have been equally laughable had it not been the first flagrant vandalism of the distinguished and discreet low Boston skyline. The building was a Roman temple between two wings flanking a tall tower that supported a ridiculous lantern, a far cry from the competence of the departed Gothic man whose reputation the firm still wore by title. The equally absurd Provident Mutual Life Insurance building at Philadelphia borrowed its façade from Bulfinch's State House at Boston but added a tower and lantern for good measure. Such thinking led to the climactic John Hancock Building in Boston of 1947 which completed the ruin of the scale of Boston's skyline, failed to retain any portion of its block for open plazas for pedestrians, and created a traffic and parking problem at an already busy corner, however comfortable the occupants may have been, however rentable the space.

Removing the ornament from such buildings or changing their sheathing to expose a grid of windows did not improve the architectural quality. The boom in office and commercial construction that followed the war produced monotonous bores like the Mellon Bank and United States Steel Building in Pittsburgh; 477 Madison Avenue in

New York belabored the standard clichés: the first story, set on posts, supported nine stories of vertical mullions over recessed spandrels, then six stories of ungainly setbacks turned horizontal — without any reason for the changes. These proved that architecture is never a matter of style, for the horrors appeared in all styles; sometimes the worst were modern, as many of the office buildings erected around St. Thomas's in New York later revealed.

There were fortunately a few notable exceptions. William Wurster's office buildings for the Schuckl Canning Company at Sunnyvale, California, of 1942 used a rural site and warm climate and restricted wartime materials to advantage. It afforded sheltered parking space for automobiles; outdoor recreation decks found a functional use for the flat roofs; asymmetry revealed the functional layout of offices, the cafeteria and reception area. Decisively horizontal windows admitted light, and the brown-stained vertical boarding and louvers gave scale. Somewhat earlier, William Lescaze had used white planes of stucco and ribbons of glass to house the NBC Studio at Los Angeles (1938) and his Longfellow Building at Washington (1941), with its balconies that acted as louvers for the lower windows, brought a dated modernism to the classical city, briefly earning him the sobriquet "Balcony Bill."

Of all the office buildings of that day the only one that contained spaces and forms fine enough to be compared with the Gothic and Roman masterpieces of the past was the group Administration Building and Research Tower for the Johnson Wax Company of 1936-1938 and 1950. These buildings in Racine, Wisconsin, revealed Frank Lloyd Wright's undisputed mastery over new materials like plexiglass tubing and new engineering forms. The beautiful dendriform columns made of concrete reinforced with wire mesh turned the heavy and utilitarian mushroom column into a thing of grace. They were America's first major architectural demonstration of concrete used plastically, not as wood or steel or as chunky cantilevered slabs like those in Wright's early Unity Temple. Wright's drawing of the column labeled the major parts "stem," "calyx" and "petal." He had developed his column upon the analogy of a plant, much as Paxton had used the Victoria Regia when he invented the structure for the Crystal Palace.

This organic theme exfoliated in the sculptural masses and spaces of the two buildings at Racine. The Research Tower of 1950 was a tall stack in which the floors were slabs, branched off a single reinforced concrete trunk. Alternate cantilevers were narrow mezzanines that increased the laboratory space within and enabled Wright to treat the tower with a larger sequence of bays to give it greater apparent scale, though there were those who thought the organization might not be favorable for research. The theme of the cathedral-like main office space in the Administration Building was similar; dendriform columns were clustered to form a forested canopy over the secretaries' desks. It was pedantic to carp about the fact that these powerful and beautiful columns actually supported only a light roof and glass tubing. Their function was to be beautiful, and that function was magnificently performed and brought an environment of rare loveliness to people who were involved in routine tasks. The balconies and walls surrounding the space and the red brick walls of the foyer and exterior flowed in curves that further developed the theme of the columns. In the foyer one felt that Wright no longer worked with palpable concrete and brick, but rather with space itself, kneading it, grasping it, letting it go, pinching it down here, releasing it there.

Ignoring the spatial lessons Wright offered, other architects moved towards the planar aesthetics of rectilinear grid walls patterned in Mondriaanesque ways. The search was on for an elegant covering for the steel or concrete structural frame. The Woolworth's terra cotta had to give way to less expensive materials like porcelain enamel, glass and metal. Bulk alone made millions of bricks impossible, and increased costs for labor made any kind of masonry uneconomical. The ideal sheathing, as Robert McLaughlin defined it, would be a curtain wall pre-assembled in panels capable of lasting a hundred years, no more than two inches thick, light, insulating, fire-resistant, withstanding winds up to 150 miles per hour, weatherproof and vaporproof, ventilated and drained, and allowing flexibility of application. Such a hung wall would have to be made of glass and metal or possibly of new materials like plastics. It would be the ideal envelope architects had aimed at in earlier buildings like Polk's Hallidie, Gropius's Fagus Factory and Bauhaus, Despradelle's Berkeley Building and Mies's unexecuted project for a glass skyscraper.

Pietro Belluschi's glass and aluminum sheathing on the sparkling Equitable Building in Portland, Oregon, of 1948, opened architects' eyes to the aesthetic possibilities of transparency, mirroring, exposure of structure, and sheer finish in a wall that projected no more than seven eights of an inch. It was not a curtain wall in the technical sense since the bays were not filled with pre-packaged panels. But it carried forward the movement towards a sheer plane of glass and spandrels, which had been given separated and horizontal expression in the Philadelphia Savings Fund Society and the McGraw-Hill buildings. The rich Italian heritage of Belluschi added another brilliant element in the marbles at the base but this kind of arbitrary elegance disappeared in the buildings to come as the theme was simplified, and all was turned to glass.

The United Nations Secretariat of 1950 by Wallace Harrison was the first of the stronger statements of the new office building form. Its thirty-nine stories were wrapped with green-tinted glass subdivided by thin aluminum mullions and spandrels to create a non-directional geometric grid. Three bands of aluminum screens marked the floors devoted to mechanical equipment; an aluminum grille, enclosing the equipment on the roof, effectively brought the rhythm of glass and mullion to a stop against the sky. A narrow southern wall entirely of marble protected that side against the sun although the north wall was a concession to formalism with a juncture at the glazed sides that was ill considered. The great glass walls of the east and west façades were exciting. One photographed brilliantly from across the East River; the other was a magnificent mirror catching the clouds and the sunsets and tranforming the skyscrapers of Manhattan into pictures for those outside the building; meanwhile the people inside shrank from the trying western sun.

The advertising value of such walls caught on quickly. Lever Brothers, the manufacturers of soap and edible oils, commissioned Skidmore, Owings and Merrill to design their new office building on Park Avenue, New York, in 1950-1952 and out of this commission Gordon Bunshaft, a designing partner, created one of the important buildings of our day. On a low box of glass supported on pilotis he threw a sheer shaft of glass reaching heavenward. The curtain wall contained mullion, panel frame and spandrel all in one unit. Its green-colored glass offered a new note to austere Park Avenue while it helped a little to reduce the effects of insolation on the occupants. For the first time since Rockefeller Center, New Yorkers found a little building space given to them as they wandered in and out among the plants that adorned the outdoor space that the firm had left open on the ground floor. Even the window-washing trolley was skillfully incorporated into the design. Until Mies van der Rohe built the Seagram Building on a diagonal corner, Lever House was the finest new building in New York.

Different curtains were less successful. One such was attempted by Harrison and Abramovitz in their Alcoa Building, Pittsburgh, 1952. Made up of small railroad-like windows set in aluminum frames and inflated tubular rubber gaskets, it appeared almost windowless as the aluminum panels were deformed to add rigidity, create shadows and attempt to produce scale. Despite a pleasant lobby and some good interior spaces, the dull mass of the building and the superficiality of its metal panels displeased most architectural critics.

Mies van der Rohe and his temporary acolyte Philip Johnson achieved the purest of the new buildings in 1957-1958, the House of Seagram on Park Avenue, whose amber glass and warm sheathing rose sheer from a portion of its large platform. *Time* and *Life* added another plaza and tower to Rockefeller Center, while Socony-Mobil, in a new building at 150 East Forty-second Street, offered a massive and dizzily patterned stainless steel block. The most sought after firm seemed to be Skidmore, Owings and Merrill who followed their success in Lever House with a new building for the H. J. Heinz Company, and a glass bowl for the Manufacturers Trust Company at New York. By now the curtain wall was a formula, and Skidmore, Owings and Merrill employed landscaped gardens and sculpture to enhance it. A more sculptural effect within the building itself was achieved by the Chicago office of the same firm whose designers, Walter Netsch and Bruce Graham, completed the Inland Steel Building at the corner of Dearborn and Monroe Streets, in Chicago, in 1958. Here interior space unencumbered by columns was obtained by putting the columns outside the exterior wall and putting all elevators and service elements in a blank-walled ancillary shaft, adjacent to the office building. The massive columns of the main structure, clad in stainless steel, rose outside the floors and the cage of glass and thinner mullions which they supported. The entrance lobby was inadequate, without doubt, but otherwise the whole building was one magnificent and chaste icicle and the executive offices on the nineteenth floor and the lounge on the thirteenth were among the finest sustained modern interiors, just as the building as a whole found few peers anywhere.

Meanwhile Frank Lloyd Wright was enabled by the H. C. Price Company, manufacturers of oil-well pipe, to consummate in Bartlesville, Oklahoma, the design he had conceived for the St. Mark's Tower twenty-five years before. The Price Tower, built in 1953-1956, consolidated offices and apartments within a multi-faceted concrete-and-copper-sheathed building. Angular living spaces were cantilevered from a central stem or core in a composition of amazing visual charm, though it was not free from troublesome interior constrictions. Like Sullivan's bank in Owatonna, the Price Tower brought permanent distinction to a city which had never had any before.

The best among these office buildings, such as Seagram's or the Inland Steel, firmly established modern design as the emblem of national business concerns. America had finally achieved an architecture compatible with her industrial might. The successes scored with such architecture after 1952, particularly as it became more refined, even more classic, confirmed the achievement; the only pity was that so many of the copies were crude and insensitive. But then that had always been the way of copies of any style, made by incompetents, detrimental to the cityscape. If the style were too personal such as that of Gaudi or Wright the copyist might flinch or his failure be too apparent. But the Miesian classic was open to sensitive repetition and modest organic variation by those with any appreciation at all. This was shown not only by great disciples such as Bunshaft and Netsch but by many others; unfortunately there were still too many crows in the architectural nest, and the list of bad versions outran the list of good.

2 0

THE NEW WAS GRADUALLY ACCEPTED EVEN FOR CHURCHES, WHICH IN THE beginning resisted modern design in this country. Resistance to new architecture had never been the problem of the Roman Catholic Church which, since the fifth century, had shown an adaptability to the basilica, the Romanesque, the Byzantine, the classic, the Renaissance and the baroque, and it had the same adaptability to any new form — though its Irish wing was reactionary. The more recent denominations had no such history. Protestant parishioners were used to churches of the kind they had been brought up in, whether Romanesque or Tudor or New England meetinghouse, and change seemed to border on sacrilege. Thus innovations were opposed on grounds of tradition, symbolism or mere personal notions of reverence and beauty. The clients were naturally enough not convinced that what was to be done in a contemporary church was so new as to require new space; or that the old spaces had failed them in any consequential way. As long as modernism was thought to be crude exhibitionism, such resistances were not easily overcome. Neither Gropius nor Breuer built a church before 1957. Mies's chapel for IIT in Chicago was a hollow box which seemed to most observers to be cold and uninspired; devotionally uninspiring. It only reinforced the idea that modern architecture had little range and could produce no church that did not resemble a shoebox. Meanwhile Georgian and Gothic chapels were built in Atlanta, Philadelphia, Boston and Chicago throughout the '30s and '40s. Most were obviously dull; they lacked any spiritual quality beyond that lent to them by literary symbolism.

Writing in 1940, Talbot Hamlin discussed the causes of the poor state of church architecture. He had to turn to Europe for noteworthy contemporary examples. America offered little except an occasional piece by Paul Schweikher or O'Neil Ford such as the former's brick and wood Third Unitarian church at Chicago and the latter's brick-vaulted church at the Texas State College for Women. These, outstanding for their rarity, were mere glimmerings of the vigorous modern church architecture then being produced in Germany, Finland, France, Switzerland, the Scandinavian countries, and even in Japan where Antonin Raymond erected his Church of St. Paul at Karuizaw in 1936. The European churches awakened Roman Catholics to the possibility of realizing the encyclical letter Pope Pius X had written about the necessity of developing an art form compatible with the modern period and the Catholic service. An American Catholic magazine, *The Liturgical Arts Quarterly*, under its intelligent editor, Maurice Lavanoux, became a strong advocate of good contemporary design in the furnishings, art and architecture of American churches. In the end, great Protestant theologians like Paul Tillich took up the same cudgels. Only the Mormons and the Christian Scientists seemed to stand immune.

The most successful American churches started on modest premises. They tried to offer spaces that had repose and quiet dignity rather than awe. This was no doubt a commentary on the religious psychology of the time that sought security and serenity and comradeship. It did not take long to learn that such spaces would not arise from designing with fixed symbols in mind. Barry Byrne's St. Francis Xavier Church at Kansas City, which had a plan abstracted from the shape of a fish, as a symbol for Christ, was an artifice in which the imposed form gave no very distinguished architectural results. It was better to start with the requirements for a beautiful auditorium or liturgical space. This approach resulted in the strikingly handsome though perhaps melodramatic Corpus Christi Roman Catholic Church at San Francisco by Mario Ciampi where raw colored glass squares were dominant. Eliel Saarinen's Tabernacle Church of Christ at Columbus, Indiana, spread out in several wings, its offices in the south, the Sunday Schools at the southwest; its main block contained the auditorium and stately nave which were beautifully related to the ground by reflections in the large pool on the west, while the whole was held together by a dignified and simple rectangular tower. He followed this by one of his finest works at Christ Lutheran Church in Minneapolis (1949) whose simple brick and wood interior never fails to move the visitor. In the Northwest, Pietro Belluschi also used brick and wood to make warm and lovely churches, with atria that suggested Japanese courts, and with eloquent experiments in small light sources. Such buildings as his First Presbyterian at Cottage Grove, Oregon, won many more people to modern church architecture.

Thus the period saw a steady improvement in American church design which can best be epitomized by the serene and modest interiors by Belluschi. The spaces were good but not more, the structures conventional, most of the effect came from the play of colored abstract light.

These were fine enough and in terms of their aspiration first class. Were the aspirations too low or was it explanatory of America that more vigorous efforts, whether made by Harrison or Lloyd Wright or Joseph Murphy or Marcel Breuer, in Stamford, at Palos Verdes, in St. Louis or at Northfield, Minnesota, did somehow not seem to hit the mark? The notable experiments in modern church architecture had to be sought elsewhere — at Assy, Vence, Ronchamp, Milan, Blumenau in Brazil, Francavilla-a-Mare, Helsinki, or Zurich, and the architects were Swiss, French, Italian, German or Finnish — not American.

2 1

THOUGH THE CHURCHES WERE MODEST AND FOUND THEIR WAY QUICKLY TO small communities many of the littler places got their first taste of modern design with their school buildings. The oppressive multi-story barracks of brick, filled with box-like classrooms that WPA had fostered in the '30s now gave way to the new demands for project-type teaching, laboratories, exhibitions. Under John Dewey's influence, Dwight Perkins, Reginald Johnson and Myron Hunt had essayed early designs that aimed to facilitate object-teaching and problem-solving. Now this was good official doctrine. Howe and Lescaze designed low, one-story buildings filled with sunlight and flexible classrooms for the Oak Lane Country Day School at Philadelphia and Hessian Hills at Croton-on-Hudson; Lescaze followed this with another model in his High School for Ansonia, Connecticut. Neutra's experimental school on Bell Avenue, Los Angeles, of 1935-1937 was outstanding. A covered passageway on the east ran past five one-story classrooms with sliding doors on the west, opening to outdoor classrooms. A light wood-framed building, the structure, with its movable partitions, allowed flexibility and permitted quick alteration of classroom size. The long glass walls were protected by deeply overhung roofs and canvas blinds supplied good lighting. The Midwest achieved its exemplary modern school in 1940 when the younger Dwight Perkins with Philip Will built the Crow Island School at Winnetka, Illinois. Here different age-groups were separated in four wings, each with its outdoor play area. The one-story wings were composed of model classroom units. Each unit was L-shaped with a work area in the short side and a well-lighted classroom with movable furniture on the long. Though some of the detail was heavy, bright colors created a gay atmosphere, and the flat chimney-clock tower at the entrance later became an emblem of many modern schools.

The new buildings hugged the ground and spread along it. They were seldom more than two stories high and usually one. They discharged children quickly into the open and were thus both more pleasant and safer as they reduced the threat of fire or of accidents on stairs. They sought natural light and orientation, ventilation from the prevailing breezes, courted flexibility, removed the barriers between outside and indoors, tore down the earlier sense of confinement and restraint which had been the hallmark of the old school buildings. Campus-type plans were almost inevitable, there was gaiety and color. So it came to pass that the finest living and aesthetic experience in the life of many American children came to them in their schools. It was not hard to see that American taste might be much altered after they had grown up. There were those like Dorothy Thompson who remembered with pleasure the rigors of confinement of their school days, who deprecated the lack of educational discipline in the new school world and who, associating the two, concluded with the *non sequitur* that the buildings were to blame, while also inappropriately extravagant. But most Americans had more sense.

Thus the dreary stacked-up school of the '20s and '30s gave way to the finger-plans of the '30s and '40s. Individual classrooms sprang from the spine of a central corridor, while landscaped courts and gardens separated the individual units. Such plans were revealed by schools like Franklin and Kump's Acalanes Union High School at Lafayette, California, of 1940-1941. Here the dispersed plan with an outlying gymnasium and cafeteria made handsome yet functional use of a large rural site. Maynard Lyndon's Elementary School at Vista, California, combined the finger-plan with clerestory lighting and well-made covered walkways scaled to the dimensions of a child. Ernest Kump's High School at San José of 1952 had a denser finger-plan but its concrete framed buildings had a crisp Miesian appearance that created a mature environment suitable for additional use as a community center.

As the applications of the theories matured, the schools became steadily more attractive. In the early '50s John Lyon Reid in California, one of the very best of the school designers, provided the Garfield Elementary School at Carmichael, California, where classrooms were arranged about grass and paved courts, and where covered walkways, low eaves, color, and small detail gave a strong sense of shelter. Skidmore, Owings and Merrill did comparable work for the Grout Park Elementary School at Schenectady. One of the best of these schools was Donald Barthelme's elementary school at West Columbia, Texas, built in 1952. A tall block at the center contained a theater, library, arts studio, washrooms and clinic; two-storied wings east and west of the central block contained classrooms opening to an interior court. The structural details of the girders and bar joists in the steel frame were exposed for their decorative value, while colored panels enlivened the top-lighted classrooms.

In 1955 Reid invented a loft-plan high school with fluctuating room sizes to encompass the flexibility demanded by shifting departmental boundaries and the changing community of San Mateo, California. About 1953, the cluster plan became popular. In this there were separate pavilions of one to eight rooms, without corridors, with students separated into "age neighborhoods" and a chance to isolate disparate activities. Perhaps the most publicized of these was Perkins and Will's Heathcote School at Scarsdale, New York, 1952, which had a core surrounded by little schoolhouses containing hexagonal classrooms with natural light on all four sides. An auditorium for a theater-in-the-round, a cheerful library and a central hall for each group of four classrooms completed this attractive school which also demonstrated that school problems, managed with more ease in the favorable climate of California and the Southwest, could also be solved under the more stringent conditions of the East. In 1959 the long and effective pioneering work of William Caudill in the Southwest, made up of excellent propaganda pieces and fine and always progressive buildings, was capped by his school at San Angelo, Texas. Throughout the country choice modern schools could now be seen and there seemed little doubt that America led the world in this kind of architecture.

2 2

UNHAPPILY, THE QUALITY OF PRIMARY AND SECONDARY SCHOOL BUILDINGS was seldom matched by the buildings for American higher education. If some school boards were forward-looking, most university trustees kept their eyes on the rear-view mirror. Before the war there were few advanced college buildings to match M.I.T.'s Swimming Pool by Anderson and Beckwith (1938) or the University of California's Stern Hall which William Wurster designed for Harvey Wiley Corbett, who had the commission. The Museum of Modern Art and *Architectural Forum* sponsored modern design for college campuses as an aftermath to the ill-fated competition of 1938 for a new art center at Wheaton College, but little came of it. Although the Saarinens won a second prize in the competition for Goucher College in 1938, the award went to a firm of modified traditionalists whose campus site plan gave birth to a set of homely buildings. Colleges and universities generally remained impervious to modern architecture until after the war and resistant after that, often belying by the new buildings they acquired the principles of what they were teaching in their own architectural schools. After 1957 the wave of acceptance could be seen to be sweeping over all but the most adamant. A modern building on an ancient campus was no longer noteworthy and the *Architectural Record* could devote a whole issue to successful contemporary college and university designs. But this came to pass only a long time after modernism was firmly in the saddle elsewhere.

Trustees at universities and colleges who were becoming bold with respect to their corporate architecture or even their personal houses remained naïvely traditional when they were acting as custodians of education. For a time they were supported in this by their own architectural schools. There men like Everett Meeks, Leopold Arnaud, William Emerson and Paul Cret, at Yale, Columbia, M.I.T. and Pennsylvania, all traditionalists, wielded strong influence through the '30s and '40s. To be sure, leading young American moderns often emerged from these conservative schools. But, characteristically, their contact with modern design had come through magazines and visiting lecturers or travel. As faculties were renovated, some schools offered strong support for modern design. When William Wurster became dean at M.I.T. in 1944 he found already installed a force for modernism centering around Professors Lawrence Anderson, John Lyon Reid, and Herbert Beckwith, products of the older ways but navigators of their own revolution, and this encouraged M.I.T.'s continued experimentation with contemporary design which had begun with the Swimming Pool of 1938 and now was continued with additional works by Anderson and Beckwith and others by Aalto, Saarinen, Rapson, Koch, de Mars, Stubbins, Bunshaft and Pei with only occasional backsliding into more conventional hands. A few other architectural faculties assumed some leadership in addition to the obvious excitement at Harvard and IIT. Yale, North Carolina, Minnesota and Oklahoma were examples, but they were not followed by Cornell, Columbia, Princeton or California until much later.

Meanwhile, even where the faculties had at least some interest in contemporary principles it was rare that presidents and trustees did. At Wheaton College in 1946 a new president, disliking modern architecture, appointed a traditional firm despite strong protest from members of the faculty, notably the head of the art department who resigned. Thus execution of the building along the lines of the modern entry by Richard M. Bennett and Caleb Hornbostel which had won the competition of 1938 was first postponed and then abandoned. It was even rumored that its public success had led to the downfall of the president who sponsored it. This was unhappily a typical story. In the end the arch-

citadel of reaction remained at Princeton, cozy in its Gothic. The relatively modern Firestone Library was encased in a pseudo-Gothic stone
cloak. Even as late as 1960 the distinguished Italian modern architect
Enrico Peressutti, after years of patience, resigned publicly from the architectural faculty as a reproach to the archaic architectural policy of
Princeton's trustees. They and the president took this in haughty stride
and the freeze continued. But there was a thaw almost everywhere else.

Even before the war a few colleges had tentatively opened their gates
to the new design. They were likely however to be experimental places
such as Black Mountain College. Here the students and faculty collaborated to erect a new building designed by A. Lawrence Kocher, who was
professor of architecture there. About 1938 Florida Southern College at
Lakeland offered Wright his first opportunity to work for an institution
of higher learning when it commissioned him to plan eighteen units
for its West Campus, of which ten were built. It was his largest commission since the Imperial Hotel in Tokyo but was not, unfortunately,
one of his most successful jobs. A handful of other newly founded colleges toyed with modernism. But in many cases inadequate finances, ill-
defined curricula, internecine disputes thwarted the efforts at obtaining
fine new campuses.

Meanwhile the famous old institutions clung to the old terrain. In
1934 John Russell Pope designed Calhoun College at Yale, the seventh
residential unit on that campus. Intended for about two hundred undergraduates, the college centered on quadrangles and the buildings
formed walls to baffle the street noise from the interior rooms. The college construction was a modern steel frame. This was covered with random ashlar in full Tudor Gothic detailing. The planning had come
from English precedent. Its virtues were attested by centuries of use, at
least in England and at least in earlier centuries. It occurred to no one to
introduce a new way of life by a new architecture; perhaps the question
did not even arise whether Yale undergraduates were any longer living
the life of medieval Oxonians or had any intention even of trying to
live such a life; if it did the faculty and trustees answered the question
with a resounding "Yes" or thought that the manifest masquerade in
architecture did not matter for a university which obviously did not encourage masquerade in the more serious matter of scholarship.

A notable example of compromise that lacked conviction appeared
at Princeton in 1960, where Douglas Orr, the University's Consulting
Architect, sought to placate young demands for a modern architecture
while assuring old tigers that their house was safe from "chaos and a jumble of new and daring styles, each screaming for a place in the magazines." Admittedly, Orr's was no easy task. It was not so simple as saying

merely that Le Corbusier or Gropius or Mies might be retained to design a new building; for they had sometimes shown a disregard for the harmony, the coherence, the recessive, muted background buildings, and the pervasive landscape that made Princeton's one of the finest American campuses. But several younger men, including Paul Rudolph in his Jewett Art Center at Wellesley (1959) and TAC in their buildings for Brandeis, had demonstrated that they might tackle the problem of coherence with modern conviction. The firms actually chosen by Princeton, including the vestigial McKim, Mead and White, produced weak boxes studded with mean windows, flimsy joints, overbearing cornices, and dull rhythms. Gothic was gone, but its replacement, a weak set of reminiscent compromises, was worse, however much it tried to be all things to all men.

Other universities did not fare much better, perhaps worse, when they timidly attempted a modern appearance produced by men who had no real affection for modern aesthetic or any respects for and belief in the convictions it asserted. In fact these pseudo-modern buildings may have helped to ruin fine campuses of another day. You could see them at Kresge Hall at Harvard, at the Woodrow Wilson School at Princeton, at Buckland Hall at Mount Holyoke College and many other places where the results would have been better had there been no attempt at modernism at all.

Some outstandingly successful college buildings were badly needed to break the grip of traditionalist and vapid architecture as the colleges began to build after the war. The Saarinens' Cranbrook School and their work for Wayne University and Stephens College offered examples of modest design well appointed to give good performance but did not crystallize the issue.

Aalto's Baker House dormitory at M.I.T. of 1948, whose serpentine plan offered views of the Charles River, dramatized some of the difficulties in producing modern architecture in an environment that was only partly friendly. The difficulties did not arise from the trustees or the senior administration but rather from the general building climate in Boston which required the Finn to be associated with a local firm whose affection for his skills was at best tepid. Aalto started with the premise that every room should have sun in the morning or the afternoon, that every room should have a view of the river. M.I.T. stipulated against multiple entries. The number of rooms required combined with the small size of the lot dictated that the rooms must look up and down the river and not straight across. The choice was then between a regimented set of chevroned pavilions set diagonally to the street which might have been most functional and the freer serpentine form which had always been part of Aalto's palette. He elected the latter. Rooms were thereby less standardized, many had to be pie-shaped, some were less convenient and certainly less conventional than they would have been on an orthodox plan. But the built-in furniture and the far greater interest of the building outweighed the inconveniences. Any reasonable person had finally to admit that the combination of reason and intuitive caprice had produced something fine. Student affection for the building, despite its defects, supported the view. By 1960, acclaimed from Zurich to Tokyo as one of Aalto's greatest buildings, Baker House remains a landmark in American university architecture.

An influential version of college architecture appeared on Chicago's South Side when Mies van der Rohe was appointed to develop the campus of IIT. He began there with the Metals and Minerals Building of 1943, and on this campus worked out his style. The whole was a formal group of precisely designed research buildings, classrooms, chapel, boiler plant and dormitories. Steel frames, buff-colored filler bricks between the columns and beams, defined the prisms. The result was a somewhat cold but precision-calibrated campus, homogeneous, meticulously detailed. As time went on Mies steadily refined the details. No doubt he failed, as we have suggested, with the chapel which seems almost an afterthought. As of 1960 the handsomest of the buildings was Crown Hall built for the Department of Architecture. It was here that Mies was able to follow his own theories most closely, to accept the fewest limitations by permanent partitions or other encroachments on free and flexible space. His attitude, formalism, necessarily involved a lessened attention, some thought an irresponsibility, toward utility, especially as regards privacy, noise, storage, control of light, and circulation. It remained to be seen whether the Miesian flexibility would work out well for a library and administration building. Those who admired purity of design excused the faults; those who disliked the forms were able to recount only the troubles. But Illinois Tech offered a first-class foretaste of things to come for town and gown. The main lines were soon recapitulated by Saarinen at Drake, and at General Motors, and by Skidmore, Owings and Merrill at Connecticut General, at Smith College, at M.I.T., at the Air Force Academy in Colorado Springs, and by many others in less excellent demonstrations. These later buildings were often more colorful, better planted, even more agreeable, but the principle of their designs was set forth unequivocally and first by Mies. Thus IIT attained almost overnight an internationally famous campus.

Such ultra-modern university buildings were naturally viewed with mixed emotions. It took considerable courage for old institutions to break with tradition for any building that had to be financed by alumni subscriptions. Led by President James B. Conant, Provost Paul Buck and Dean Erwin Griswold, Harvard, for example, erected modern dormitories for law and other graduate students in 1950. The site plan by The Architects Collaborative was masterful; eight buildings were arranged to form three well-shaped quadrangles with good planting, interesting vistas and changes of level, all reminiscent in modern terms of the scale and surprise of the old Harvard Yard and suggested by it. The dormitories had concrete frames enclosed with buff-colored brick and artificial limestone trim. The Commons was a separate building with lounges on the first floor and a large, subdivided dining room opening off the cafeteria in the second story. There and in the lounges of one dormitory, modern artists, Miró, Arp, Kepes, Albers, and Bayer made murals while Lippold provided sculpture for the focal point in the sunken quadrangle in front of the curved wall of the Commons. The best features of the Graduate Center were unsurpassed even by the buildings in the Yard. The scale of buildings and spaces was fine, the color of brick brought the Harvard campus to excellent conclusion at the north, the site plan was excellent. But even the admirers of those matters could not approve all the details. The brick walls carrying the murals in the dining rooms were arbitrarily placed within the window frames; many of the interiors were dark and somber; the connections between the dormitories and the roofs over the paths were awkward, and the columns, running up through rectangular holes in those roofs, impressed some as clumsy. Nor had there been enough study of the dormitories. Cramped and squeezed quarters were not adequate for students, no provisions had been made for book storage; corridor lights bothered students trying to sleep; and economical cinder-block partitions combined with paired top-hinged windows to conduct noise from one part of the building to the next. Students accustomed to living in dormitories like Harvard's houses complained about the poor performance of the bedrooms and lounges, and ultimately in 1956 when the University tried to raise money for a new house, an official pamphlet admitted the functional shortcomings of the Graduate Center.

It was a disappointment to the friends of modern architecture; so much had been accomplished there, but those who were predisposed to dislike the design never forgave lapses in performance which they took for granted in conventional work. Hence they were heartened to see a resurgence of pastiche Georgian at Radcliffe and the Harvard Business School, where misscaled buildings, bad site planning, and even plywood pilasters (which would soon raise maintenance problems) were readily overlooked, as sentimental eyes melted at the sight of red brick, white trim and multi-paned windows.

Contrasted to these the Graduate Center was fresh and alive, strong in its convictions, able to rest its case on having provided the strongest community among modern buildings yet achieved. Until Wurster completed his picturesque retreat, the Center for Advanced Study in the Behavioral Sciences at Palo Alto, there was no better example of modern collegiate design than the Graduate Center, which was courageously pioneered under the administration of a college president who rose above his own predilections in the arts and set an example that other presidents of many kinds of institutions might profitably follow.

Thereafter the college and university afforded more frequent bright spots. Brandeis, a new institution, sought to house itself in an almost completely new and modern campus. Settling on only a fair campus plan, it acquired a collection of fair to undistinguished buildings, though the three chapels for separate faiths, designed by Abramovitz in 1955, made a noble effort to cover and express the needs of diverse rituals; and the latest buildings by TAC and Stubbins were beginning to tie things together. Oberlin acquired a new auditorium as early as 1943, also designed by Harrison and Abramovitz, but its funnel-shaped walls lacked the scale that should have subordinated this "Moby Dick," as the students called it, to the old green. By 1959 this college was commissioning other buildings by Yamasaki and Bunshaft. In 1951 Marcel Breuer completed his Cooperative Dormitory at Vassar College. In 1954 Saarinen produced the distinguished and much discussed auditorium and chapel at M.I.T., a move in the direction of circular freedom. At Detroit, Minoru Yamasaki produced a new site plan for Wayne State University, and his jewel-like McGregor Memorial of 1958 provided a monumental yet personal glass-roofed central court, a highly sculptured building set above a Japanese-like garden with pools. Attempting to avoid the rigor of a single idiom, such as had dominated IIT, Yamasaki retained control over the site plan but embarked on a stated policy of encouraging the administration to invite other architects to design some of the individual pieces.

Other efforts to free the forms were made by Paul Rudolph at Wellesley College and Eero Saarinen at Yale University. Rudolph, associated with Anderson and Beckwith, produced the Jewett Art Center at Wellesley in 1957. Here he had to deal with a dominant existing Gothic architecture. He carried the bay-and-gable theme of a neighboring Gothic quadrangle into a programmatic building housing galleries, an auditorium, work spaces and offices and achieved a bold yet sympathetic transition of appearances though at some cost to the lighting of the gallery. Saarinen's Ingalls Ice Rink at Yale, in 1958, was not dominated by the old campus. Here he provided one of the most spectacular forms of present times, a great parabolic central rib swelling like the inverted keel of a Viking ship, supporting a roof which fell away from it in a modified catenary. There was no doubt about the elegance of the space once the occupant was in his seat at a hockey game or on his runners on the ice, but entrances, washrooms, and the appearance from the back were perhaps a little casual. There were in this building moments of drama and moments of failure and the ultimate judgment would have to be postponed. What it did say resoundingly was that when universities did succumb, they succumbed wholeheartedly. Nowhere in the whole range of modern American architectural experiment were so many fantastic buildings now to be found as on the campuses of the land.

Still, up to 1960, the steel-framed cage dominated the college field. This was most dramatically exposed in Netsch's complete campus for the United States Air Force Academy at Colorado Springs. Here whole hills were bulldozed down and new mesas graded up to provide the platforms against which the Miesian idiom, now at massive scale, could be displayed against the backdrop of even more massive mountains. Here the architects had to yield convictions obtained in other systems of education. That group marching must influence the design might perhaps be taken for granted by anyone who had visited Gothic West Point or Beaux-Arts Annapolis. But that all the cadets must eat in a common mess hall and at one time to achieve "togetherness," instead of aiming for it as they would in the intimate commons of the halls of ivy, was a new idea. From it came one of the most interesting buildings, perhaps the only one that was very differentiated, save the chapel which began to rise in 1960. The dining hall was one great free space, enclosed by glass, covered by a massive and projecting roof and referred to by English critics as possibly the Parthenon of a new Acropolis. In any event the Air Force Academy uttered a stentorian shout to the effect that modern design had won the battle of the campuses as it had earlier won the battle of the residence, of the factory, of the office building, of the church, of the school. In 1960 Saarinen was to do the new colleges at Yale, Harvard had commissioned Le Corbusier to design its Fine Arts Building. Pei and Stubbins were designing for M.I.T. But the pockets of resistance remained, particularly at distinguished Old Nassau where the trustees resolutely covered their ears and their eyes that they might hear and see no evil.

2 3

THE FEDERAL GOVERNMENT PROVED A HARDER NUT THAN THE UNIVERSITIES.
The competition for the Federal Reserve Board Building at Washington in 1935 was closed to any except conservative firms. The prize-
winners, Cret, Pope and Rogers, were all classically disposed. In 1937
Pope's proposal for the Jefferson Memorial raised a stormy discussion.
Critics balked at the proposed destruction of cherry trees, at the secrecy
surrounding the selection of the architect. They might have balked at
more important things. Pope's Roman rotunda, absurd as it was, was defended by Harvey Corbett and by McKim, Mead and White. Senator
William Borah and Frank Lloyd Wright spoke against the whole idea of
spending three million dollars on a monument but Wright's reasons
were aesthetic and Borah's economic. Wright called it "an arrogrant
insult" to the memory of Jefferson — which was probably true, though
Jefferson might have liked it. It memorialized his lesser side. Educators
protested against it, led by Columbia's faculty of architecture including
Hudnut, Bauer and Mumford. It was a waste of breath. The rotunda
went through and no doubt pleased the taste of those legislators who
ever looked at it. As we have already pointed out, the winning modern
design for the Smithsonian was laid on the shelf until nineteen years
later it could be replaced by a dull compromise.

Once in a while a modern post office or fire station could be found in
some small community such as Orchard Heights, Washington. Yeon's
Tourist Center at Portland, Oregon, of 1949 was a sophisticated sign
for the city. Brazos County Courthouse in Texas was built by Caudill in
1958 as an excellent adaptation of school-campus planning to a county
political complex. But all this was spotty and things certainly moved
faster at the local than at the federal level.

In fact, despite an occasional military building such as Skidmore's Reception Building at the Great Lakes Naval Training Station of 1942
there was almost no good federal architecture. Among the states there
had even been some retrogression since the Capitol at Bismarck, North
Dakota, had suggested that future state buildings might at least head in
the direction of such modest work as Dudok's Town Hall at Hilversum or the city halls of Oslo and Stockholm, if not so far as the new
prefectural halls being built in Japan by men like Kenzo Tange and
Kunio Maekawa. But the later Oregon State Capitol was a curious misscaled miscegenation of classic and modern genes. Cret's Federal Reserve Bank of 1937 still seemed progressive to most official Washing-

tonians who admired the Supreme Court and the National Archives Buildings. It might have been hoped that a new National Gallery would lead the way; but Pope's confection of 1939-1941 was an outdated extravaganza of multiple-returned cornices, pilasters and entablatures intended to provide genteel backgrounds for fine Italian primitives but not really well suited for the exhibition of any art, architecture or sculpture, ancient or modern. Buildings for the Army and Navy were bombastic assertions of crude forms: the Pentagon in Washington had an efficient plan, less bewildering than it was sometimes accused of being, easy for a familiar to use and much less complicated than any comparable arrangement of the integrated housing of so many offices might have been; but it lacked all other distinction. The earlier War Department Building, later to serve the State Department, verged on the German neo-classic so much beloved by Adolf Hitler.

European urban and national governments especially in Scandinavia had long supported excellent modern design; Communist Russia, Nazi Germany, Fascist Italy and Democratic America remained the most ardent supporters of classicism. The American symbol of government threatened to house the United Nations in a sterile and monumental package. In 1946, when the United Nations was expected to rise upon a site at Flushing Meadows Park, architects in New York made a design in which a dome for the General Assembly was raised on a slab platform, and it was fronted by a long mall of courts approached between a row of pylons. The pompous quality in the scheme prompted the *Architectural Forum*'s editors to emerge from an anonymous objectivity; the pylons standing knee-deep in a moat-like reflecting pool seemed "to introduce the *memento mori* note," and the hollow, formal group was "a guileless admiration for pageantry." A reasonably clear form did not emerge until the Rockefellers had given land for the UN, and an international commission of architects had been set up, chaired by Wallace Harrison. For the architects it was not a very happy experience. The Russian representative engineer Bassov had little to offer; Markelius was so bored with the procedure that he took to making master plans for Manhattan; Le Corbusier almost certainly provided the main elements of the ultimate design but in the end he, and his friends, asserted that he had been deprived of influence and his design emasculated beyond recognition by Harrison. Certainly it did not have the powerful connotations of buildings the Swiss had done alone. To some of those quite oblivious to this smoldering controversy the slab of the Secretariat and the funnel of the General Assembly seemed to lack symbolism or beauty and this view was not confined to traditionalists. But the combination of forms was unique; and in the end it became an emblem for the United Nations that no one ever mistook.

Solely American governmental work continued to limp at home, but farther away from the cynosure of Senatorial eyes it might be bolder. By a fortunate chance, in 1954, and responding to much persuasion, the Foreign Buildings Operations of the Department of State wisely appointed the statesmanlike architects Shepley, Walker and Belluschi to give advice about government buildings abroad, where America's classical embassies had often denoted imperialism, perhaps more than conversatism. The advisers encouraged the State Department to appoint outstanding modern architects, sometimes on the basis of competitions, as in the case of the London Chancellery, 1956, but more successfully without competitions, and the architects were encouraged to seek regional expressions appropriate to the countries in which the new embassies, chancelleries, consulates, information centers and staff quarters would be built. In a marked turn from the few examples of International Style architecture Harrison and Abramovitz had pioneered at Havana and Rio de Janeiro, and Rapson and Vandermeulen had built at Neuilly, Stockholm and Copenhagen, the designs for new buildings tended to develop modern interpretations of regional motifs. Financed by foreign debts from Lend Lease, sales of surplus property, and Marshall Plan funds, the buildings broadcast the work of Ketchum, Gina and Sharp (Morocco), Kump (Korea), Raymond and Rado (Indonesia), Warnecke (Thailand), Neutra and Robert Alexander (Pakistan), Yamasaki (Kobe), Saarinen (England and Norway), Rudolph (Amman, Jordan) and Harry Weese (Ghana). Of all these designs, the leaders were Edward Stone's Embassy for New Delhi, Warnecke's for Bangkok, Sert's for Baghdad and Gropius's for Athens. These were unities, attentive to scale and local forms though none had the boldness of Le Corbusier's Chandigarh and they suffered by comparison. They should have encouraged better work for governmental architecture at home even though they did not escape criticism from modernists who found them too "pretty."

Indeed, none of these buildings transcended criticism. Rapson's were thought to be too indifferent to the mores of Stockholm. Saarinen's London building was badly castigated for its vulgar use of metal. Of Breuer's new one for The Hague, J. J. Vriend wrote in *Bouw:* "We see here a once truly functional architect losing himself in modern '*l'art pour l'art*' in a fashionable dressing up of essentially elementary space and form."

All this criticism was no doubt justified. It was an expression of the concern that was mounting as to the trend of American contemporary work in 1960. But to those who brought a less apprehensive eye the whole foreign program could look only admirable in the light of what might so easily have been a proliferation of Williamsburg all around the world.

Thus it seemed that real strides were being taken and this was endorsed by Hugh Stubbins's dramatic Conference Hall for the Berlin Exposition of 1955 and Stone's American pavilion at Brussels of 1958. But it was easy to underestimate the strength of tradition, particularly in this field. Perhaps Henry Hope Reed, Jr., was not very important as he preached a return to classic forms, displaying drawings by his New York associate John Barrington Bayley to convince New York that it would be improved by tall classic and baroque skyscrapers topped by statues of Minerva. But behind these patent absurdities there were other and quieter people who shared Bayley's hope that the classical architectural idioms might find an appropriate use in the twentieth century city. Even more felt that what might do for commerce was not worthy of the dignity of the government.

Some of these broke their silence at the first sight of the designs for the chapel for the Air Force Academy, prepared by Walter Netsch in the Chicago office of Skidmore, Owings and Merrill. Now the halls of Congress resounded to the denunciations of Representative Fogarty and others; and of their special witness, Frank Lloyd Wright, who denounced the advisory commission of Saarinen, Belluschi and Becket as a team of a small boy, a schoolteacher and a man who had done a great deal of harm to American architecture. Congressman Hardy of Virginia thought the Academy looked like a cigarette factory. Senator Flanders was not alone in calling the chapel sacrilegious. President Eisenhower, whose sophistication and taste in architecture were not great, is said to have "flushed with anger" when he learned that the proposed design of the chapel was seriously advanced. In spite of this, it appeared the chapel would be built.

In 1957 the Eighty-fifth Congress, under the stimulus of men like Representative Frank Thompson of New Jersey, entertained proposals for creating some form of legislation fostering the arts. Representative Thompson cannot be held responsible for the tenor of the discussions that followed. On September 8, 1957, the New York Times printed a rendering of "A National Theater Project for Washington, D. C.," a fully Roman building, much like the Supreme Court, only more massive and gross, the proposal of Eggers and Higgins, stalwart and thriving survivors of the Beaux-Arts days. Even when the will was there, it was too common that funds were not adequate to build good government buildings and the will for good contemporary work was seldom there; and when present, was neither strong nor solid. Government buildings still required appropriations and members of Congress still liked to make speeches exhibiting the poverty of their aesthetic judgments. Most of these indicated ominously enough the village mind that still prevailed in the Capitol, but it was not different at the other end of the Avenue.

The staggering confirmation of bad federal taste came on May 1, 1960, when President Eisenhower proposed to Congress a project for a $24,000,000 monument, the Freedom Shrine, to be built on federal park land overlooking the Potomac River, adjoining Arlington National Cemetery. Designed by Eric Gugler, the colossal structure was an innocuous fascist version of classic tombs and temples, intended to enclose a pompous court, approximately 327 feet long and 24 feet wide, shielded by walls 68 feet high decorated with historic reliefs and inscriptions carved by Paul Manship. In 1953 Gugler had proposed to erect a Hall of History in Central Georgia, but was unsuccessful; a year later, the National Monument Commission was established by Congress to secure designs for a *useful* monument symbolizing democratic faith in the freedoms; five years later, on April 15, 1960, the Commission reported its selection of a design for the Freedom Monument — Mr. Gugler's Hall of History. The reactionary consultants to the Commission were John Harbeson — whose early intelligence as a Beaux-Arts theorist foundered when he served as adviser for the ruinous remodeling of the East Front of the Capitol — Gilmore D. Clarke, landscape architect for the proposed memorial, and Gugler himself. Thus the Commission, aided by its consultants, seemed to have spent five years merely to give official ratification to Gugler's antiquated inconsequence. The secrecy that surrounded the deliberations never offered qualified critics opportunity to ask whether a monument was necessary, whether a monument costing federal funds at least $12,000,000 should receive public scrutiny, whether the best architects and sculptors should be invited to suggest alternatives, whether "consultants" should be allowed to be eligible for undertaking the work. The building might in the end not be approved. But the contrast between the public going-over imposed on the Air Force Academy chapel and the under-the-rug treatment of this proposal was glaring.

The *New York Times* permitted Ada Louise Huxtable to criticize the project and the procedure for obtaining it. But even with public criticism there was no assurance that the arts could survive federal patronage. This was discouraging to sincere men who entered the competition for a memorial to F.D.R., announced in May, 1960; even if the excellent jury should award a modern design the prize, a Commission, a Congress, a President might still impose a third-rate village taste, accepting only watered-down tradition as has always been the tendency where art lies under the domination of conservative but uninformed laymen.

2 4

MEANWHILE THE FACE OF THE AMERICAN CITY SEEMED LIKELY TO BE DEtermined more by the appearance of its housing than by the elegance or the mediocrity of its new monuments which were drowned in the flood of residential building. This was particularly evident on the urban peripheries where monuments were scarce but the expanding population pressed everywhere as the urban core degenerated and failed to offer the income needed for metropolitan services. The overlapping of independent municipal units no longer dealt effectively with sprawling metropolitan regions, particularly where the suburbs straddled state lines or clung like leeches to the dying city. All these problems could be seen clearly in the physical form of urban environment. No architect could escape them, but many tried to forget.

The short supply of housing in the postwar period brought a boom in large urban housing projects. There had been some good precedents for apartment towers like George Fred Pelham's Castle Village, Manhattan, of 1939, which developed a superb site north of 181st Street on Riverside Drive with five cross-shaped towers twelve stories tall. Much improvement might have been made upon its judicious planting and the plastic grouping of the towers. But, more typically, developers like the Metropolitan Life Insurance Company built gargantuan projects with colossal buildings that overcrowded the land. Even so vast a project as the Peter Cooper Village contained a whole city of people without adequate areas for shopping, schools, playgrounds and entertainment. Metropolitan's Stuyvesant Town became the classic pedagogical warning against the speculator-built project. Built in 1947 on seventy-five acres of land between 14th and 20th Streets on the East River, it was a housing colossus of eighteen blocks with 8759 apartments that were intended for 24,000 persons. The buildings were towers raised upon a cross-plan; their staggered alignment on the site was so dull and mechanical that the three-acre park and ten small playgrounds did little to alleviate it. The city had given a twenty-five-year partial tax exemption to the insurance company to help finance the project; still, it contained no schools, forced the high density of 390 persons per acre, and did not include a shopping or cultural center.

But it was not impossible to treat such projects considerately. William Ballard showed this in the community center, auditorium, shop and nursery schools at the Queensbridge Houses, New York, where the residential buildings were sited so as to provide central parks and play areas. The James Weldon Johnson Houses in New York presented fifteen-story apartment buildings, severely simple in their lines, serving to accent vistas, define open areas and parks, and to supply a neutral background for sensitive planting. Smaller buildings were even more successful. The Fort Dupont housing at Washington was an excellent community with its variety, its domestic scale and its communal parks. Two-story row housing was handled well at Arthur Brown's Holly Courts at San Francisco in which low, cubic buildings with sensitive fenestration were set on terraces so that changes in level separated playgrounds and planting areas and sunlit courts were attractive and homelike. Some of the projects were further enriched as by the sculpture in the Jane Addams Housing Project in Chicago (John A. Holabird, Chief Architect), which brought life and scale to the buildings.

About 1950 considerable interest was awakened in the field of elegant high-cost apartments. Two of the most interesting buildings in that field were done in Cambridge, Massachusetts, and Chicago. The Cambridge building was the apartment house at 100 Memorial Drive, designed by Robert Kennedy, Carl Koch, Vernon DeMars, Ralph Rapson and William Brown of the M.I.T. faculty. Sited so that its entrance and bedrooms stood on a relatively traffic-free and quiet street, the building was an eleven-story slab with two wings projected southward to form a large open court on the side that overlooked the Charles River and the skyline of Boston. Apartments were entered from a corridor on every third floor from which vestibules and private stairs led to upper or lower apartments. The skip-floor elevator system reduced corridor space, provided cross-ventilation to apartments and enabled them to have large living rooms with glass walls and large balconies overlooking the court and the river. The traffic and living pattern was faithfully displayed in the exterior form, whose strip windows indicated the corridors. Strongly varied colors adorned the balcony ends; a somewhat gross *porte cochère* designated the entrance, while balconies, bathroom windows, living room windows and bedroom windows exhibited the dwelling functions in an unabashed way. The functional display later caused some to criticize the building for being a jumble of many different forms, telling enough, but cluttered and awkward. But the "clutter" was orderly; it was enhanced rather than disturbed by the individual idiosyncrasies of apartment dwellers whose varied interior decorations, Christmas trees, lighting, and personal vagaries regarding curtains and blinds strengthened the design, rather than producing the customary disruption. Such an approach permitted charming over-all effects without regimenting the tenant. It was one of the few modern buildings with gaiety.

The opposite approach was attempted by Mies van der Rohe at 860 Lake Shore Drive, Chicago, of 1951. There, two tall glass prisms, abstract enough to look like drawings, announced a radical departure from functional expression. To keep the glass façades uniform in color, reflection, and pattern, all apartments were equipped with gray curtains. Tenants were permitted to install their own curtains behind those. At most, their effect upon the buildings' appearance was to create varied Mondriaanesque patterns within the grid of windows as the gray curtains were drawn or opened. Thus the variety of apartment interiors was denied expression on the exterior. A further turn away from functionalism appeared in the sheathing. Both buildings were steel frames embedded in concrete, but the concrete was not expressed on the exterior. Steel I-beams painted black were applied to the façades to serve as window mullions and to provide vertical accents. These two towers were the closest approximation America had yet made to Le Corbusier's city schemes of the '20s. They formed an impressive group on the shore of Lake Michigan, prophesying a formalism which became increasingly dominant after 1952. The open spaces beneath them gave free views to the lake; the high style of the fenestration pattern made them supreme examples of Miesian doctrine. The tenants suffered some discomforts not to be met in more traditional quarters and felt some exultations that were simply not possible in the older buildings. If you prized average convenience more than exultation perhaps you moved out. But few of the critics of the apartments were themselves tenants and whether for snobbish or other reasons there was always a waiting list even for the new units that were not completed.

The ultimate in this approach to design was reached by Mies in his layout for Lafayette Park, Detroit, of 1960. Here a twenty-one-story apartment slab was connected with twenty-one sets of row houses numbering 186 in all. Their lawns were set three and one-half feet above the street line to "digest" the inevitable motorcars. Downtown, cooperative, interracial, the project half-completed was generally acclaimed as the epitome of what might be achieved in conscious refinement. But in the very day of its success it was threatened; new developers seemed content with or even set upon compromise. Late in 1959 its promoter, Herbert S. Greenwald, died in a plane crash. Long an admirer and supporter of Mies, this entrepreneur would be missed. For architecture requires talented clients as well as talented architects.

Whether cities could be talented clients for their own redevelopment was about to be tested in San Francisco in 1960. If ever the test might be made on favorable terms it was in that ethereal city.

Directed by Justin Herman and the San Francisco Redevelopment Authority, the Golden Gateway Project drew nine competing proposals from syndicates of developers and architects, who submitted plans for turning twenty of an eventual forty acres of the city's blighted produce district into a park with 2200 apartment units, parking garages, landscaped malls, and an office or apartment tower. Exceptionally fine schemes were the hierarchically scaled submittal by the team of Wurster, Bernardi and Emmons and DeMars and Reay (with Perini-San Francisco Associates) and the monumental project proposing three curved twenty-two-story apartment slabs, the work of Skidmore, Owings and Merrill (Golden Gateway Center Corporation); one exceptionally refreshing series of terraced apartments was submitted by Jan Lubicz-Nycz, a Polish designer (collaborating with John Collier, Philip Langley, Sidney Leiken Enterprises and Theodore G. Meyer and Sons). The competition established an important principle: that intense and prolonged public scrutiny should be given the plans, which were well published in advance of the judgment, while in April, 1960, the Authority retained an advisory panel of distinguished architects, planners, critics and evaluators, including Mario Ciampi, Lawrence Anderson, Henry Churchill, Louis Kahn, Morris Ketchum, Minoru Yamasaki, and the Chicago mortgage banker, Fred Kramer. The intention was to enlist public enthusiasm for an imaginative proposal that would go beyond financial returns to investors. In contrast, the contemporaneous near-secrecy that surrounded plans for the Prudential Center at Boston revealed that the matter of private profit versus commonwealth had not been worked out on the East Coast, even though those who proposed to build the Center requested stabilizing tax concessions from the city.

Between the Lafayette Park demonstration of Miesian order and the "human" romance of the San Francisco proposals of Wurster, Warnecke or Becket there was a considerable gap of theory. But each showed, if in a polar way, that architects were able to come to grips with the problem of middle-sized housing groups just as they could and had come to grips with the problem of grouping a few large buildings as in Rockefeller Center. The question remained whether they knew how to deal with the problem when it was presented at still larger scale. It was not obvious that they did.

2 5

WHATEVER ELSE THEY MIGHT FAIL TO DO, LOCAL AND NATIONAL GOVERN-
ments were interested in providing still larger channels for the flow of
automobiles. As an effort to solve the traffic problems within cities, decayed areas were redeveloped as freeways beginning with the urban
expressway that opened in St. Louis in 1936. Interurban and interstate
transportation improved with the building of great turnpikes like the
Pennsylvania which opened in 1940. Many graceful bridges appeared
as the suspension spans became longer. Daring engineering produced
new vehicular tunnels without always providing easy egress at bridge or
tunnel head. Some improved small railroad stations were built, but it
was a last gasp. Except for their observation towers, the first big air
terminals, like La Guardia, did not suggest flight in the sense that the
old railroad sheds had caught the adventure of travel by steam on the
rails. The architecture of flight remained tentative and flimsy even in
attempts at new plans such as Boston's Logan Airport, and it was usually
obsolete before it was occupied.

More hope for the future of the airport as a gateway to the city began
to appear about 1954 when dramatic shells leaped across spaces with
some of the enthusiasm an air traveler might expect. The earliest to be
admired was Hellmuth, Yamasaki and Leinweber's terminal at St. Louis
where three pairs of intersecting concrete barrel vaults of 120-foot spans
sprang from small point supports. The new Idlewild Airport proposed in
December 1957 to erect even more dramatic terminals for United Airlines by Skidmore, Owings and Merrill, for American Airlines by Kahn
and Jacobs, for Pan-American Airlines by Tippetts, and for Trans-World
Airlines for which Saarinen proposed a thin shell, almost birdlike in its
wingspread. But on the scale of Idlewild there was doubt whether
the experience could ever be that of a gateway but only that of arriving
at a sort of elegant way station, to be hoisted by bus to mid-Manhattan as soon as possible. It was not yet clear in 1960 whether airports
would in the end, and quite consistently, develop a fine architecture.
Even if they should, they would be peripheral to the central city or
independent of it. Meanwhile the central city was being eaten alive by
the ubiquitous and proliferating automobile.

2 6

INDEED, NO OTHER INSTRUMENT SO AFFECTED THE AMERICAN LANDSCAPE. It spawned highway architecture from Maine to California and all the architecture was alike. Highway strips soon became the scene of the worst imaginable visual abuse. Roads once attractive and safe became hazards under the acts of *laissez-faire* development. New highways built by local, state and federal money were quickly exploited as sites for diners, stores, factories, nurseries, hardware shops, car washers, gas stations, garages, doughnut stands, for hubcap salesmen. National concerns worked with iconographic emblems such as Howard-Johnson's standard orange-tiled roofs; but even these did not always shout loudly enough above the clashing signs and colors that vied to catch the motorist's eye. The sincere efforts of national gasoline companies to provide respectable, clean stations, designed by Teague, Loewy or Bel Geddes, did not often survive the housekeeping of the proprietors or the sales efforts of the local offices who flooded the buildings with flapping pennants, gas-war signs, tire bargains, and gadget-filled windows that weakened the architectural lines and efficiency of the plans. Car-hop restaurants, flourishing in Los Angeles before the war, adopted futuristic and exhibitionistic roofs to attract the hot-rod crowd that flashed its headlights for service and ate in cars from trays brought by girls in cowboy boots or on roller skates. Roadside diners and drive-ins, begun in the early '20s, appeared as architectural problems at schools in 1934, and even the Beaux-Arts Institute of Design assigned the problem of a refreshment stand for a highway in 1939. Motels sprouted rapidly. Originally called roadside cabins, auto camps or auto courts, they made their initial architectural appearance in the *Architectural Record* of 1933, and 30,000 were estimated to be in the United States in 1952. They steadily grew in size, comfort and cost and by 1957 some had pushed the in-town hotels in most matters of convenience and comfort at tariffs, which were also nearing those of downtown, while also beginning to acquire the inconvenience as well. Indeed, the motels themselves began to appear on downtown sites and perhaps the hotel of the future might be a new type, developed by a merger of the advantages of a Ritz-Carlton and a Holiday Inn, now that the travails of the city were reducing the value of downtown land so that it was economical to run a motor park on it and thus a downtown builder might begin after a century to think again in horizontal rather than vertical terms.

Trailer occupancy flourished as migratory farm workers followed har-

vests, industrial workers moved among defense projects, and drifters followed the sun southward to Florida and California as whole trailer
towns developed to reveal a low standard of American living. The craze
for a mobile house prompted Buckminster Fuller to design a unit that
could be slid upon a trailer and transported easily. In 1934 the first
drive-in theater was built at Camden, New Jersey, in accordance with a
design patented by R. M. Hollingshead, Jr. They became increasingly
frequent appendages to the highway as young people acquired cars in
which they lived most of the day and, until television became general,
married couples found that they could have entertainment without leaving their children at home with a baby sitter. Very little of this highway
architecture was as beautiful as Raphael Soriano's attractive Garden
Center for the Hallawell Seed Company on Sloat Boulevard in San
Francisco of 1942. Few states attempted to control it, and even Connecticut's magnificent Merritt Parkway, with clean, official service stations, attractive landscaping and borders zoned against the commercial
development, did not encourage neighboring states like Massachusetts
to develop similar parkways, until toll turnpikes were created to take the
driver from Boston to New York to Chicago with never a grade crossing,
a stop light or even a toll-house from entrance to final exit. Occasionally
a pretzel or giant cloverleaf on the ramped approaches to Triborough
Bridge afforded almost futurist vistas that were powerful sculptures,
and nowhere were these more brilliant than in automobile cities like
Detroit or Los Angeles. Indeed, the freeways of the latter may have become its noblest architecture, until they, too, choked with cars.

The planned shopping center was potentially a most important development in highway architecture. Initial ideas for such centers began
with studies like one of neighborhood shopping facilities that Clarence
Stein and Catherine Bauer published in the Architectural Record of
1934. The biggest incentive to the planned shopping center came during the war, when new communities like Orchard Heights, Washington, acquired well-planned shopping facilities. One of the best of these,
Belluschi's shopping center for the FPHA war housing project at
McLoughlin Heights, Vancouver, Washington, of 1942, provided
parking, covered passageways and a group of low wooden stores around
a landscaped court. One of the earliest building-type studies of the
shopping center appeared in the Architectural Record of 1940. Its examples emphasized the mall-type plan in which buildings were arranged
around the sides of an open court. This plan appeared in the Shopper's
World at Framingham, Massachusetts, designed by Ketchum, Gina and
Sharp, who specialized in this sort of complex. An attractive variation
upon the mall-type was that in the shopping center for Linda Vista,

California, of 1944. Neatly tailored store fronts with discreet signs surrounded a central landscaped area in which one side was enclosed by an arc of shops. The small space devoted to recreational use within that arc became an increasingly larger element in later centers, signalized by Victor Gruen's article in *Progressive Architecture* of 1952 in which he wrote that the ideal shopping center would also be a cultural center containing an auditorium, governmental offices, lecture halls, exhibition rooms, reading rooms, theaters, restaurants and lounges. Even without all these some of the new shopping centers had distinctly cultural implications. Perhaps the most famous was Gruen's Northland Shopping Center at Detroit of 1952, a commercial center for pedestrians. Its plan contained a series of connected open courts, walks and small stores that were clustered around Hudson's large department store. Its 165 acres housed eighty-one stores with a total rentable area of more than a million square feet. Sixty-eight acres were reserved for auto-parking areas, strategically located to reduce the walk from car door to store door. Generous colonnades, fourteen feet wide, connected the malls and courts. These had sculpture by many artists, fountains and planting of rhododendron, azaleas, flowering cherries and magnolias laid out by landscape architect Edward Eichstedt in patterns unparalleled in many other public spaces of the land. Here commercial enterprise offered an environment of distinction, which Gruen achieved again at Eastland. It was possible that they might offer clues for a new and good urbanism. But they were slow in coming and the usual shopping center had none of this scale, none of this taste, none of this pleasure, offering another somber example of the termite that the real estate developer had become.

Fine shopping centers, extended in purpose and sophistication, might indeed become the patterns for new central cities but before that could happen some other problems needed to be solved. Few of these were architectural. It was becoming banal to say that cities were dead. Yet it seemed to be true, if urbanity were to be the measure of the city. Measured on other terms the city was very much alive even if it were changing drastically. The amorphous structure and unprecedented size of the new metropolitan areas, increasing as populations were drawn to the cities and as the urban birth rate mounted, accentuated problems of cost, management and democratic government; they suggested the creation of political super-authorities such as those organized for the ports in New York and New Jersey or for the power of the Tennessee Valley; but they did not answer how these new and larger authorities would be understood or supported by a people which had been apathetic about smaller, more intimate and more comprehensible units. Technological change had removed the necessity for some of the things that had determined the earlier city: poor communications, conditions of defense, strategic or economic location, diversity of occupational opportunity, the necessity that populations be concentrated in centers of mass production and mass distribution. But not all kinds of production or distribution could get along without such concentrations, unless television, for example, were to be a satisfactory substitute for all other aspects of the visual arts and hi-fi to replace live music.

So, as some of the earlier forces for urban living were weakened they opened opportunity for those who had, perforce, dwelt in cities, but had never cared for urbane living, to leave the city and thus free the urban scene for those who really admired it, for those who craved what it had to offer. What it had to offer, if it could be realized, was that the metropolis was uniquely fitted to facilitate the free interchange of ideas among people of diverse temperaments, vocations and habits. The communication might be in matters of sports, of food, of the arts as well as in matters of the intellect. Those who sought no such interchanges were better off on the periphery with their small plots of anemic grass and their thin patches of personal sky; those who craved the urbanity might look forward to a time when it too could be combined with a way of life that permitted quiet conversation, sauntering, the song of birds even in the heart of the metropolis. Thus many urban projects, notably those for convention centers, arts centers, entertainment centers, and office groups, proposed after mid-century, were intended to capitalize on this need for civilized communication without the intervening censorship of uncivilized radio and television monitors. It was what lay at the bottom of Victor Gruen's proposal for the center of Fort Worth which would have kept private transportation out of the hub altogether and put the public transportation below the surface, thus restoring the land to people. All this would have been admirable and attainable had enough people wanted it enough, just as in Boston the Public Garden and the Boston Common stood as a daily challenge to the lethargy of the citizens and the selfishness of the abutters. But no such plan could be complete unless enough people wanted it enough. It had also to presuppose that many of those who craved the urbane life, would come back to live in the city, that they need be of a number of different income levels and not just all rich or all poor. The formula for such a combination of living had not been well developed in America, as it had for example in such a subcenter as Vållingby at the end of the Stockholm subway.

Furthermore while the truck and automobile weakened the tie of the manufacturing plant to the urban area and its tracks and waterfronts, and industrial plants began to cluster on the peripheries in belts of almost autonomous factories, the high cost of transporting retail goods over long distances coincided with the growth of the large peripheral populations and large local markets capable of supplying at least most of the needs of the peripheral men. Thus national companies were encouraged to establish satellite plants close to the large cities, particularly on circumferential highways which all too often had originally been planned for recreation but over which adequate controls had not been placed. Thus while manufacturing generally tended to quit the center of cities, businesses that offered services had either to be nucleated so as to serve a substantial number of automobile-borne customers or remain in the central city itself. The only services that could be different in the central city were those which met the extraordinary need. It no longer required an urbane center to support a complete Rexall store; but it might be different for some specialized commodities.

What this meant in logical terms was beginning to become clear as 1960 approached. Logically it suggested that the peripheral family, all of whose aspirations were met by the mass supermarket, the mass drive-in movie, the mass television set, need never incur any of the "disadvantages" of the city but instead could live out its conforming yet peripheral life sleeping in a peripheral suburb, working in a peripheral factory, shopping in a peripheral market and never penetrating to the center at all. Indeed this was becoming the lot of many suburbanites and, so far as it was the lot they wished and enjoyed, it seemed absurd for sociologists and social philosophers to go on viewing suburbia with alarm. Suburbs did indeed offer political problems and economic problems and even problems of the national tone if, as some thought, a nation mostly of conformists was inevitably a weak nation. But had not all nations been made up mostly of conformists and was this on the whole a bad thing?

The problem was actually a different one, the problem of Gresham's Law. Perhaps the massive conformity of the periphery would make it impossible to have vital diversity at the center. For the individuals with individuality the center might be a mecca if it could ever arise. But as it was, the central city was not rising in this form. Instead it was becoming a place for a few very rich people who sent their children out of town to grow up, and a great many very poor who were far from urbane and would escape to the periphery as soon as their personal economics permitted. If they could be poured out of the central city and the non-suburbanites who lived in the suburbs be brought back to town there might yet be an elegant and urbane civilization in some American cities which would lift the level of the whole civilization. But it was much

easier to speculate about it and to write about it and even to draw about
it than it was to make serious and effective efforts to bring it about.
Whether Lincoln Center was or was not to be a fine achievement for the
performing arts of New York City when it was ready in the '60s might
not matter much if the problems of uptown Manhattan were not solved.
Nor would a high office building on top of Grand Central Terminal automatically lure more commuters back to the waning commuter services.

Major civic surgery was needed, surgery and grafting; fantastic cooperation between financial powers; brilliant new political machinery and
courageous and foresighted politicians; in the end it surely meant abandonment of much private interest in favor of a greater and communal
urban interest.

But any such major efforts could hardly be made until there was more
agreement as to what was wanted. If it was true that architects could no
longer think of cities as collections of independently designed buildings
with spaces between them but had also to inject the dimension of time
and the dimension of the motor car, it was also true that no one knew
what to do about the automobile which Americans loved so much. And
it was not only Americans who were seduced. The automobile was as
disruptive to Rome and to Tokyo as it was to New York. No one really
liked what was happening; but no one really wanted to give up anything
either. Reyner Banham of the *Architectural Review* probably summarized the general attitude when he said in 1960: "Yet most citizens —
including those called upon to plan — are determined to have the best
of both worlds. They expect to be able to drive straight down an
Autoroute de l'Ouest, straight through the Arc de Triomphe, and into a
Champs Elysées that still has the urbanity of a sequence from *Gigi*."

Such a possibility was remote and it was not even a possibility save
through some drastic action such as making the automobile a public
utility or excluding it from large areas of human life. Yet any drastic
action required either dictatorial powers or democratic unselfishness at
a pitch the democracy had never displayed save in moments of obvious
local catastrophe or national crisis. The catastrophe of the automobile
was just enough short of disaster so that it did not insist upon unselfishness. In such circumstances one could have only a limited enthusiasm
for a single brilliant achievement in architecture. The gnawing question
remained whether the Americans were prepared to abandon private interest in favor of a greater communal urban interest. It did not seem
likely.

This was the more frightening for the growth of the problem had
been so fast as to outrun even the doomsayers. Time had seemed to be

available until the recovery of 1935 and perhaps even until the population explosion that followed World War II.

Having sprawled into the country with their quaint Colonials and Garrisons and later with their ranch houses, the population now drained the metropolis for services, and congested the transportation lines leading into shopping districts and business centers. The site planning of office buildings gained increasing importance as the density of tall structures diminished the well-lighted open spaces on city streets. Unfortunately building codes were not amended to prescribe limited land coverage as well as limited height and setback. Rockefeller Center remained the single example of excellent site planning. Even that was marred after 1935 when additional buildings like Number 11, Time and Life and International crowded the area to the west of the main plaza. Major skyscrapers like Chicago's Field Building of 1935 and Boston's John Hancock preserved no unbuilt land. To have left a portion of their sites open would not necessarily have been altruism. In areas of dense commercialism lower-story office and store space became increasingly difficult to rent at figures that brought in adequate revenue. That fact was an increment to be added to the obvious advertising advantages to be gained by having people swarm around the symbol of a national concern. This may have been some of the justification for Lever House, which rose from only a fraction of its land squarely in the middle of opulent and costly mid-Manhattan.

This site plan and others like the plazas of the Alcoa Building were pale reflections of the proposals Le Corbusier and city planners had advocated for many years. No city in America passed legislation or established the agencies that would have guided the future growth of industries, commerce and residences along lines that the elder Saarinen or Le Corbusier had proposed during the '20s. Even in the hardest hour of the climb back from the depression, urban and federal governments failed to grasp the opportunity for planned decentralization and urban renewal. The city planning proposals of men like Hilberseimer and Stein were consistently ignored in Washington. There were exemplary instances of metropolitan planning such as Robert Moses's Port Authority and recreational program at New York, and there were even some outstanding instances of interstate action in the preservation of areas like Bear Mountain Park and the Palisades. But they were exceptional, and comparably felicitous opportunities for similar work would not occur again — unless bombs leveled the urban cores or the centers withered to the point where drastic surgery became essential and economic. The appalling fact was that so little interest seemed to be aroused in the possibilities of reform. A brilliant exhibit in Philadelphia in 1947, designed by Oscar Stonorov and Edmund Bacon, was one of the few attempts at alerting citizens, and its educational power was attested when Penn Center and other projects gave Philadelphia a new face in 1955-1957.

27

IF ONE WANTED TO GAIN SOME IDEA ABOUT WHAT THE CITY MIGHT BE-come, he might go to Penn Center, begun in 1955, to Denver's Mile High Center (1955), or to Pittsburgh's Golden Triangle Gateway Center (begun in 1953). There he would find much to like in the reservation of space for pedestrians, in clean buildings, but he would still be disheartened by the failure of modern architects to build harmoniously with each other, to create fine spaces, to use sculpture and painting effectively, to gain a scale that was personal and to control large areas of the metropolis, or to lure people to their new plazas as they came naturally to those of Venice, Paris or Göteborg. For visions of what might have been, he would turn to unexecuted projects: Wright's baroque cylinder for the Golden Triangle, his Ninth Symphony, which remains only a great drawing on sheets of rice paper, or Boston's Back Bay Center as proposed by Belluschi, Gropius and a group of Boston architects. For each of these a banal design was substituted, often because it seemed more "practical," more functional; and even the fine designs seemed to disclaim the fountain and the trees.

But if the architect of the '50s had learned anything about art, it was surely to take a maturer view of functionalism. The best designers now recognized what had been formerly neglected in doctrinaire modernism, that an essential function of architecture is to be a work of art. Hence the purely programmatic expression of a building's function no longer dominated the artist. Beginning about 1948, architects and critics began to search for a new artistic and monumental expression. In that year London's *Architectural Review* predicted that the future of modern architecture would be a broadening of functionalism to include a building's emotional functions; Hitchcock spoke of our needs for durability, solidity, dignity, testimonials, fundamental emotional impact; and Giedion wanted a monumental architecture "representing . . . social, ceremonial and community life . . . more than a functional fulfillment . . . the expression of . . . aspirations for joy, for luxury and for excitement." In 1951 Mumford decried the mechanical solution and "self-imposed poverty" and applauded subjective impressions and expressions, even the willful, the capricious and those deficient in common sense. Rudolph, Yamasaki and other architects joined the critics, and their point of view was best summarized in Matthew Nowicki's dictum, "Form follows form," in which he meant to suggest that functions arise because of form if the form is expressive and commanding.

Such ideas led designers toward two contrasting viewpoints: the first was the single-form, single-space composition achieved through the use of monumental thin shells and curved geometry, as in Nowicki's Stock Pavilion at Raleigh, Saarinen's Auditorium at M.I.T. and Hockey Rink at Yale, or Yamasaki's Airport at St. Louis. Sometimes the space might be rectilinear and universal, as in Mies's Crown Hall at IIT, and sometimes it might be associated with separate service cores as in Louis Kahn's Art Gallery at Yale. The opposite approach was to try to unify a composition by using fine over-all patterns such as decorative screens, either to envelop a classically composed building as a single unit with well-defined base, terminations and cornice, as in Stone's embassy at New Delhi, or to provide a mantle across the face of a building whose interior was subdivided programmatically, as in Rudolph's Art Gallery at Wellesley. Each of these promised a future for art in modern architecture so that Yamasaki, for example, created the McGregor Memorial Building at Wayne State University employing features of the single-form building, the decorative sculptural roof and column, and the screen. "If we stop at function," he had said in 1955, "and function only, we have not even commenced with architecture." And those who saw his buildings frequently were convinced that a full art had now blossomed; nor were they surprised that this modernist should have sat before so venerable a building as the Taj Mahal, drinking in its proportions, its symphony of consonances, its development of beautiful detail amidst perfect concept and proclaimed, "I believe it is without peer . . . pure joy to behold."

Outside such classicizing tendencies stood an opposing point of view, held by architects who were less concerned with the serene monument or climax of a composition than with creating vigorous background architecture, but free of the Miesian idiom. Again, much of the lead was European, and not only from Le Corbusier's Ronchamp and La Tourette, but from buildings that seemed urgent, even violent, like those of Vittoriano Vigano in Italy, André Wogensky in France, and Alison and Peter Smithson in England, who wanted to make strong structures legible, expose rough concrete, and gain abruptly ruptured silhouettes by faceting their buildings into coarse blocks that were randomly projected, recessed, raised and lowered.

In his less classic moments, Paul Rudolph seemed to be well on the way toward such syncopated rhythms, hurtling horizontals and rocketing verticals, as his gallery at Wellesley and high school at Sarasota, Florida, suggested. They were an architecture intended to stand with the classic, unified building, indeed to be its foil; any campus or city needed both. Thus Louis Kahn drew international attention for his work in Philadelphia. After a long and quiet and studious career in which he had been much appreciated by a few architects and critics for his adventurous theory of served and servant spaces and his insistence upon accommodating mechanical equipment usefully and handsomely, Louis Kahn capped his work at Philadelphia's CIO Medical Center, Trenton's Jewish Community Center, and Yale's Art Gallery, with a great lunge toward boldness, the Richards Medical Research Building at the University of Pennsylvania, completed in 1960. Its clusters of jagged towers were built in brick and treated as salient masses, over-sized and stark, brazenly offering unflinching contrasts to the irregular voids exposed by Vierendeel trusses. It was the one architectural experience on a campus where the bland monument or the banal historicism had stifled space.

So an important bridge was already being crossed by 1960 — but only one; there remained a second and more difficult one. Every previous important architecture had used sculpture and painting profusely — and integrally. Modern architects had not tried very often and had almost never really succeeded to do more than add casual if charming punctuation marks. Gropius had not really achieved what he dreamed in the Harvard Graduate Center; nor had Breuer come out much better in his more elaborate experiment for the new Unesco Building in Paris. Noguchi's stones for Bunshaft's Connecticut General seemed almost an irrelevancy; Lippold's wires in the Inland Steel lobby were inadequate in a lobby that was itself inadequate; the fountains of Seagram's were trivial. Indeed some architects, like Mies van der Rohe, formally thought the attempt to use artists was undesirable. Work like Rudolph's denied the other arts. Some few like Le Corbusier were sculptor, painter and architect rolled into one, and all too many architects who were not such complete artists tried to be. But it was clear for all the effort that the other arts were not playing the role they had in Athens, Byzantium, India, Cambodia, Rome, Burgundy, the Île de France, Tuscany or Guatemala. Was it the fault of a time which was too much concerned with words to care for visual messages? Was it the fault of artists who had so divorced themselves from life that they had nothing to say to the public? Was it the fault of the architects who had become so arrogant that they could ignore art? Or was it all unimportant anyway since whatever history might say about other times it had nothing whatsoever to say about ours? You could hear many different answers. What was clear was that the merger did not exist.

28

SO THE PERIOD 1933 TO 1960 SAW AMERICA DEVELOP A MODERN ARCHI-tecture by assimilating still another immigrant art form and gradually modifying it to its characteristic institutions and thereby making it as American as any architecture was likely ever to be. The art was not so pure as when it had arrived; it was nothing like what Wright would have had it; it had not learned enough from Le Corbusier or even from Aalto; but it was assuredly an art of and for the times. It could be designed and built with some conviction, perhaps best when it was in a state of hectic uncertainty and change — for that, too, was the spirit of the times. Though the areas of agreement among the most talented architects seemed to be growing smaller, it was true that many individually excit-ing and even beautiful buildings were being made for an age which had lost its critical anchors. But these fine buildings accounted for a minuscule fraction of everything that was being built. A great many of the others caused American as well as foreign observers to think that the American landscape was getting worse, not better. The highway-scape was wretched, the urban approaches were worse, the cityscape deteriorating. Few Americans should have taken offense at the long photographic essay which appeared in 1952 in London's *Architectural Review* showing "the mess that is man-made America" or been consoled that an equally damning essay with fewer good contemporary allevia-tions could have been photographed in England.

The tragedy lay in the fact that things could have been so much bet-ter. The architects and planners awaited a franchise, one that would come not only from local and national governments but from bankers and school treasurers and university trustees, most of all from subdivi-sion speculators and the merchants of the highway strips. We had too long postponed a mature answer to the question of how to control our visual environment. We had too long cowered at the suggestion that beauty was an expensive frill, and repose or silence a threat to a way of life built on the consumption of gasoline.

But there was one encouraging thing in the scene of 1960 that had not been visible fifty years before. This was that Americans could now see superior examples of what good building could be and in any part of the land. There was enough brilliant architecture and it was widely enough distributed so that Americans could easily learn what they would be able to do if they ever got around to wanting to do it.

They could see this, at least, in individual buildings and in small collections of buildings. They might not be so readily able to see it if they could peer into the minds of architects. For there uncertainties were prominent; modern architecture had triumphed but what, now, was modern architecture? Was it being atomized along with the rest of society? Must architects follow the lonesome path of the painters? In the end would each talented man go his solitary way to the confusion of cities and societies and ultimately of himself? Could architecture continue to get along without other artists? But these were almost the trivial questions. There were others that cut deeper.

How could an architect now be educated so that, retaining his aesthetic intuitions unblunted, he would know enough to plan wisely or to coordinate those who, as specialists, must advise him? Could he really trust his personal intuition in matters of complex social behavior? If not, could he ever learn to be a good enough economist, sociologist, psychologist, engineer, political scientist, even demagogue — and remain an artist at all? If not, could he as artist survive, much less remain as the coordinator of building? Was he, was any team, capable really of dealing with urban enterprises of the size they now seemed to demand without losing all contact with human reality? The good architects knew they were not ready in 1960; the question they had to ask was whether they could ever be ready or must lose the game to the package builder who was even less ready but was more prepared to sell his gilt as gold.

Mountaineers know the annoying moment when, after hours of toil on an unknown terrain, they triumphantly reach the top — of the false summit. This was the predicament of the architects of 1960, all over the world. The problem was evident in Italy and Scandinavia and England and Japan — and it would have been evident in the USSR too had there been any architecture there. The men who stood on the false summit seemed to have won an architectural victory. Far below lay the crevasses they had crossed. But the true summit seemed perhaps farther away than the false summit had thirty years ago. Could they whip their energies again, or find new resources and new and younger talents for the next assault? Even when they reached the goal would it yet be the true summit? These would be interesting things for someone to report in 2007, when the American Institute of Architects would meet for its 150th celebration. If meanwhile the architects had not learned how to manage enormous affairs, if the public had not come to want a great architecture, there might be little to celebrate. One might call, then, for a return to Shirley Center. But Shirley Center would not be there.

Acknowledgments

First of all, we are indebted to The American Institute of Architects. In June 1955 a committee on the Centennial observance was planning the celebration which was to take place on May 12-17, 1957. Dean Burchard was approached by a subcommittee appointed to deal with the problem of a history for the Centennial observance and he agreed to develop such a book, subject to two important reservations: first, that it would be quite impossible to do a respectable job in the time before the Centennial date, and secondly that he wished Professor Bush-Brown as co-author. Both of these were agreed to and the A.I.A. then made a grant in support of research leading up to the book, in return for which they took title to the manuscript.

During all the intervening years we have been much indebted to the friendly and patient understanding and help of some members of the A.I.A. Notably, these were William Wilson Wurster and the two other members of his subcommittee on the book, Frederick T. Hannaford and David T. Witmer; Alexander S. Cochran, chairman of the parallel committee on the Centennial Exhibition; Alexander C. Robinson, III, chairman of the parent committee on the Centennial observance. In the Octagon itself we owe special thanks to Philip Will, Jr., President of the A.I.A.; to J. Roy Carroll, Jr., Secretary; to Edmund R. Purves, Executive Director; to Arthur B. Holmes, Director of Convention Activities; to Joseph Watterson, Editor of the A.I.A. *Journal*; and to Henry H. Saylor, beloved Editor Emeritus of the *Journal*.

Next we are indebted to a group of influential advisers. As soon as the work was undertaken we wrote to some thirty friends and colleagues who have in their own work dealt with the whole of our subject or a significant part of it or with relevant historical materials in other fields. It speaks well for the camaraderie of the academic community that more than half of them provided suggestions of real importance and we have pleasure in listing them here and thanking them for their early aid: James S. Ackerman, Catherine Bauer (Wurster), John M. Blum, Julian P. Boyd, J. Bronowski, Carvel Collins, John P. Coolidge, Thomas H. Creighton, Donald D. Egbert, Naum Gabo, Sigfried Giedion, Frederick Gutheim, Oscar Handlin, Douglas Haskell, Henry-Russell Hitchcock, Richard Hofstadter, Stephen W. Jacobs, Howard Mumford Jones, Robert W. Kennedy, Elting E. Morison, Stephen C. Pepper, J. M. Richards, David Riesman, the late John Knox Shear, the late E. Baldwin Smith, James Johnson Sweeney. They are obviously not responsible for any interpretation we have made of their suggestions.

Next, we are indebted to a large number of architects scattered throughout the country. In the early stages of the study Dean Burchard traveled for months visiting architectural monuments in all parts of the United States to supplement the knowledge he already had. This involved looking at a great many buildings that would generally be called obscure. To do this he solicited the aid of individual architects in many communities. Almost every one of these people devoted a good deal of time to preparing for the visit in such a way that the work could be done efficiently, and usually acted as guides and advisers as well. This was an indispensable part of the preparation which in the end meant that the authors had seen the buildings of every state in the union, and we wish to thank here the extensive list of architects and a few others who assisted us in this endeavor: Ray Alderson, San Diego; Robert E. Alexander, Los Angeles; Harris Armstrong, St. Louis; Silvio L. Barovetto, Sacramento; Rex L. Becker, St. Louis; Robert L. Bliss, Minneapolis; J. Palmer Boggs, Norman; Ernest O. Brostrom, Kansas City, Missouri; John Albury Bryan, St. Louis; Harold E. Burket, Ventura; G. M. Cameron, Stockton; Georgius Cannon, Salt Lake City; Norman Chrisman, Jr., Lexington; Grady Clay, Louisville; Colonel Harry F. Cunningham, Lincoln; George R. Eckel, St. Joseph; William H. Hartmann, Chicago; Roger Hayward, Pasadena; Maurice Hefley, Oklahoma City; Earl T. Heitschmidt, Los Angeles; George F. Hellmuth, St. Louis; Frank J. Hoffman, Racine; Edward D. James, Indianapolis; Perry B. Johanson, Seattle; Roy W. Jones, Minneapolis; Edgar Kaufmann, Jr., Pittsburgh; W. J. Keenan, Columbia, South Carolina; Frank Latenser, Omaha; Samuel E. Lunden, Los Angeles; Edwin H. Lundie, St. Paul; W. G. Lyles, Columbia, South Carolina; Harlan E. McClure, Clemson; Fred T. Meyer, Sainte Genevieve; R. G. Miller, Oklahoma City; Joseph D. Murphy, St. Louis; Walter A. Netsch, Jr., Chicago; Gyo Obata, St. Louis; Louise M. Pedersen, Tacoma; W. F. Petty, Columbia, South Carolina; Buford L. Pickens, St.

Louis; Charles S. Pope, San Francisco; W. H. Porter, La Jolla; Lutah M. Riggs, Santa Barbara; Marion D. Ross, Eugene; Paul Rossiter, Dubuque; W. F. Ruck, Los Angeles; Eero Saarinen, Detroit; Robert W. Schmertz, Pittsburgh; Albert Simons, Charleston, South Carolina; Sven Skaar, Nevada City, California; Whitney R. Smith, Pasadena; Clifford C. Sommer, Owatonna; Philip Souers, Eugene; Henry P. Staats, Charleston, South Carolina; Glenn Stanton, Portland, Oregon; Donald J. Stewart, Portland, Oregon; Charles R. Strong, Cincinnati; John Sullivan, Jr., Dayton; Paul Thiry, Seattle; Charles Truax, Dayton; Robert J. Upshur, Columbia, South Carolina; Walter K. Vivrett, Minneapolis; Grant W. Voorhees, Des Moines; James E. Webb, Oklahoma City; Harry Weese, Chicago; Harry C. Weller, Pullman, Washington; Ronald Whiteley, Manhattan, Kansas; Wayne R. Williams, Pasadena; Henry Withey, Sherman Oaks; Muriel H. Wright, Oklahoma City; William Wilson Wurster, Berkeley; Minoru Yamasaki, Detroit.

Every book of this sort requires extensive library reference and every scholar knows the debt he owes to librarians in time of need. This book is no exception. We cannot list all the librarians who helped us but we had an unusual amount of help from Irma Y. Johnson, Reference Librarian, Massachusetts Institute of Technology; H. Katherine McNamara, Librarian, Graduate School of Design, Harvard University; and Caroline Shillaber, Librarian, Rotch Library, Massachusetts Institute of Technology.

We are grateful to Emily Morison Beck and Peter H. Davison of the Atlantic Monthly Press for steady and imaginative reading and editing of the manuscript. John Rackliffe did wonderful service with his sympathetic and helpful editing of copy.

On the home front, Margaret C. Hopkins did an enormous amount of work at all stages, including a great deal of redaction, and saved us from many errors.

Finally, every work of this sort owes a considerable debt to the previous writings of others. We are grateful to the many people who have contributed to our thinking by what they have written and published in the past. Of these special note should be made of Donald D. Egbert, Sigfried Giedion, Henry-Russell Hitchcock, and Lewis Mumford.

General Bibliography

We have made no attempt to list every work of every kind we have consulted in preparing this book. The scholar will wish to make his own general bibliography and the other readers will not care. Aside from works dealing with broad phases of American history, the young student will perhaps wish to consult the leading European periodicals, notably *Zodiak*, *Casabella* and the *Architectural Review* (London), and for earlier times *L'Architecture d'Aujourd'hui* as well. The various Skira books of paintings are valuable. All the works of Le Corbusier are worth studying. There are monographs, and sometimes several, about almost every one of the leading modern architects and these bear examining though few are thorough or reliable. Naturally, the files of the leading American magazines are useful, notably *Architectural Record*, *Architectural Forum*, *Progressive Architecture* and the *Journal of the A.I.A.* Earlier journals, now disappeared, have been sources for us and hence will be found in the Notes. Many inclusive compilations of photographs and drawings of historical America are useful.

The Notes (page 519) contain specific reference to everything we have quoted. As a result, almost all the classics of the field will be found in that section. It remains to list a few other titles we have found helpful. Not all of them are about architecture.

Andrews, Wayne, *Architecture, Ambition and Americans*, New York, Harper, 1955.

Bannister, Turpin, *The Architect at Mid Century: Evolution and Achievement*, New York, Reinhold, 1954, 2 vols.

Barr, Alfred (ed.), *Art in Our Time*, New York, Museum of Modern Art, 1939.

Baur, John I. H., *Revolution and Tradition in Modern American Art*, Cambridge, Harvard, 1951.

Behrendt, Walter C., *Modern Building*, New York, Harcourt, Brace, 1937.

Bellamy, Francis R. (ed.), *The Architect at Mid-Century: Conversations across the Nation*, New York, Reinhold, 1954.

Brooks, Van Wyck, *The Writer in America*, New York, Dutton, 1953. (*Aficionados* may also wish to read his famous Flowering and Coming of Age books.)

Bush-Brown, Albert, *Image of a University: A Study of Architecture as an Expression of Education at Colleges and Universities in the United States*, Ph. D. Thesis, Princeton University, 1958.

Cahill, Holger (ed.), *American Folk Art: The Art of the Common Man*, New York, Museum of Modern Art, 1932.

Commager, Henry Steele, *The American Mind*, New Haven, Yale, 1950.

Le Corbusier, *The City of Tomorrow*, trans. from *Urbanisme*, by Frederick Etchells, New York, Payson and Clarke, n.d.

Creese, Walter Littlefield, *American Architecture from 1918 to 1933 with special emphasis on European Influence*, Ph. D. Thesis Harvard University, 1950.

Croly, Herbert D., *The Promise of American Life*, New York, Macmillan, 1911.

Curti, Merle, *Probing Our Past*, New York, Harper, 1955.

Davidson, Marshall B., *Life in America*, Boston, Houghton Mifflin, 1951, 2 vols.

Dreier, Katherine S., with Gabo, Naum, and Sweeney, James J., *Three Lectures on Modern Art*, New York, Philosophical Library, 1949.

Early, James, *Romantic Thought and Architecture in the United States*, Ph. D. Thesis, Harvard University, 1953.

Geddes, Patrick, *Cities in Evolution*, New York, Oxford, 1950.

Giedion-Welcker, Carola, *Contemporary Sculpture*, New York, Wittenborn, 1955.

Handlin, Oscar (ed.), *This Was America*, Cambridge, Harvard, 1949.

Handlin, Oscar, *The Uprooted*, Boston, Little, Brown, 1951.

Hauser, Arnold, *The Social History of Art*, New York, Knopf, 1951, 2 vols.

Hitchcock, Henry-Russell, and Drexler, Arthur, *Built in USA — Post-War Architecture*, New York, Museum of Modern Art, 1952.

Hitchcock, Henry-Russell, *The Architecture of H. H. Richardson and His Time*, New York, Museum of Modern Art, 1936.

Hitchcock, Henry-Russell, *Painting toward Architecture*, New York, Duell, Sloan, 1948.

Hitchcock, Henry-Russell, *Architecture, Nineteenth and Twentieth Centuries*, Baltimore, Penguin, 1958.

Howard, John T., *Our American Music: Three Hundred Years of It*, 3rd ed., New York, Crowell, 1946.

Joedicke, Juergen, *A History of Modern Architecture*, London, The Architectural Press, 1959.

Jones, Howard Mumford, *Guide to American Literature and to Its Backgrounds Since 1890*, Cambridge, Harvard, 1953.

Kaufmann, Emil, *Von Ledoux bis Le Corbusier*, Vienna, Verlag Rolf Passer, 1933.

Kazin, Alfred, *On Native Grounds*, New York, Reynal and Hitchcock, 1942.

Kepes, Gyorgy, *The New Landscape in Art and Science*, Chicago, Theobald, 1956.

Kimball, Fiske, *American Architecture*, Indianapolis, Bobbs, Merrill, 1928.

Larkin, Oliver W., *Art and Life in America*, New York, Rinehart, 1949.

Lavedan, Pierre, *Histoire de l'Urbanisme*, Paris, Laurens, 1926-1952, 3 vols.

Lee, Rose Hum, *The City: Urbanism and Urbanization in Major World Regions*, Philadelphia, Lippincott, 1955.

Lewis, R. W. B., *The American Adam — Innocence, Tragedy and Tradition in the 19th Century*, Chicago, 1955.

Madsen, S. T., *Sources of Art Nouveau*, Oslo, Aschehoug, New York, Wittenborn, 1956.

Mumford, Lewis, *Roots of Contemporary Architecture*, New York, Reinhold, 1956 (c.1952).

Nelson, Paul, *Cité Hospitalière de Lille*, Paris, Cahiers d'Art, 1933.

Nervi, Pier Luigi, *Structures*, trans. from *Costruire Corettamente*. Milano, 1955, by Giuseppina and Mario Salvadori, New York, Dodge, 1956.

Nevins, Allan (ed.), *America through British Eyes*, New York, Oxford, 1948; 1st ed., 1923.

Owen, Wilfred, *Cities in the Motor Age*, New York, Viking, 1959.

Parrington, Vernon L., *Main Currents of American Thought*, New York, Harcourt, Brace, 1930.

Pevsner, Nikolaus, *Pioneers of Modern Design*, New York, Museum of Modern Art, 1949.

Rasmussen, Steen, *Experiencing Architecture*, Cambridge, Technology, 1959.

Read, Herbert, *The Art of Sculpture*, New York, Pantheon, 1956.

Richards, J. M., *An Introduction to Modern Architecture*, Harmondsworth, Penguin, 1940.

Richardson, E. P., *Painting in America*, New York, Crowell, 1956.

Riemer, Svend, *The Modern City*, New York, Prentice Hall, 1952.

Riesman, David, *The Lonely Crowd*, New Haven, Yale, 1950.

Roth, Alfred, *The New Architecture*, Zurich, Girsberger, 1940.

Saarinen, Eliel, *The City*, New York, Reinhold, 1943.

Schlesinger, Arthur Meier, *The Rise of Modern America: 1865-1951*, R. ed., New York, Macmillan, 1951.

Schuyler, Montgomery, *American Architecture*, New York, Harper, 1892.

Scully, Vincent J., *The Shingle Style*, New Haven, Yale, 1955.

Shaffer, Robert B., *Charles Eliot Norton and Architecture*, Ph. D. Thesis, Harvard University, 1951.

Spiller, Robert E., *The Cycle of American Literature*, New York, Macmillan, 1955.

Steinman, D. B., *Builders of the Bridge*, New York, Harcourt, Brace, 1945.

Summerson, John N., *Heavenly Mansions*, New York, Scribner's, 1950.

Tunnard, Christopher, with Reed, Henry Hope, *American Skyline*, Boston, Houghton Mifflin, 1955.

Ulanov, Barry, *A History of Jazz in America*, New York, Viking, 1952.

Weatherhead, Arthur Clason, *The History of Collegiate Education in Architecture in the United States*, Los Angeles, n.p. 1941 (Ph. D. Thesis, Columbia University).

Wecter, Dixon, *The Hero in America*, New York, Scribner's, 1941.

White, Morton G., *Social Thought in America: The Revolt against Formalism*, New York, Viking, 1949.

Wright, Frank Lloyd, *Autobiography*, New York, Longmans, 1932.

Zucker, Paul, *Town and Square*, New York, Columbia, 1959.

In addition to the biographies cited in the individual parts, almost every American artist and architect of past repute has been written about, sometimes by scholars, sometimes by friends or relatives. The following are among the better works:

Bulfinch. Place, C. A., *Charles Bulfinch, Architect and Citizen*, Boston, Houghton Mifflin, 1925.

Burnham. Moore, Charles, *Daniel H. Burnham, Architect, Planner of Cities*, Boston, Houghton Mifflin, 1921, 2 vols.

Goodhue. Whitaker, C. H. (ed.), *Bertram Grosvenor Goodhue, Architect and Master of Many Arts*, New York, American Institute of Architects, 1925.

Harrison. Bridenbaugh, Carl, *Peter Harrison, First American Architect*, Chapel Hill, University of North Carolina, 1949.

Hunt.   Knowlton, Helen M., *Art-Life of William Morris Hunt*, Boston, Little, Brown, 1899.

La Farge.   Cortissoz, Royal, *John La Farge: A Memoir and a Study*, Boston, Houghton Mifflin, 1911.

McIntire.   Cousins, Frank, and Riley, P. M., *The Woodcarver of Salem*, Boston, Little, Brown, 1916.

Mills.   Wilson, C. C., *Robert Mills, Architect*, Bull. 77, University of South Carolina, Columbia, S. C., 1919.

Gallagher, Helen Mar (Pierce), *Robert Mills, Architect of the Washington Monument*, 1781-1855, New York, Columbia, 1935.

Olmsted.   Mitchell, Broadus, *Frederick Law Olmsted: A Critique of the Old South*, Baltimore, Johns Hopkins, 1924.

White.   Baldwin, C. C., *Stanford White*, New York, Dodd, Mead, 1931.

Notes

The text page to which each note refers is
shown by the number preceding the note.

vii   *Procopius*, with an English translation by H. B. Dewing (Loeb
Classical Library), Vol. VII (translated with the collaboration
of Glanville Downey), Cambridge, Harvard, 1940, p. 3.

vii   Thucydides, *The History of the Peloponnesian War*, edited in translation by Sir R. W. Livingstone (World's Classics), London,
Oxford, 1943, p. 38.

45   Wright, Frank Lloyd, *Frank Lloyd Wright on Architecture*, Gutheim,
F. (ed.), New York, Duell, Sloan, 1941, p. 192.

45   De Voto, Bernard, *The Course of Empire*, Boston, Houghton Mifflin,
1952, p. 44.

46   Webb, Walter Prescott, "The American West, Perpetual Mirage,"
Harper's Magazine, CCXIV (May 1957), pp. 25 f.

46   King, Clarence, *Mountaineering in the Sierra Nevada*, Boston, James
R. Osgood, 1872, p. 24.

48   Stuart, Jesse, "America's Last Carbon Copy," *Saturday Review*, XL 52
(Dec. 28, 1957), p. 5.

48   de Crèvecoeur, Michel-Guillaume Jean, (*John Hector St. John*),
Letters from an American Farmer, "What Is an American?"
London, Chatto, 1908, reprint from original of 1782, p. 51.

48   de Tocqueville, Alexis, *Democracy in America*, Bradley, P. (ed.), New
York, Knopf, 1945, Vol. II, p. 74.

48-49   Whitbeck, Ray H., and Thomas, Olive J., *The Geographic Factor*,
New York, Century, 1932, pp. 4 f.

50   de Crèvecoeur, M.-G.J., *op. cit.* (see note to page 48), p. 55.

50   Adams, Henry, *The Education of Henry Adams*, Boston, Houghton
Mifflin, 1918, 25th impression, February 1924, pp. 466 f.

50   Mencken, Henry L., "The Libido for the Ugly," originally published

in *Prejudices,* 6th series, 1927, and reprinted in *The Vintage Mencken,* ed. Alistair Cooke, New York, Vintage, 1955, pp. 177 f.

52 de Tocqueville, Alexis, *op. cit.* (see note to page 48), Vol. I, p. 355.

55 Adams, James Truslow, *The Epic of America,* Boston, Little, Brown, 1932, Preface, viii.

55 Latrobe, Benjamin Henry, inscription on Virginia prison recorded in his ms. Journal for July 24, 1947, and published by Talbot Hamlin in *Benjamin Henry Latrobe,* New York, Oxford, 1955, p. 124.

56 Carpenter, Frederic I., *American Literature and the Dream,* New York, Philosophical Library, 1955.

58 Kirker, Harold C. Generally helpful in connection with California history was his then unpublished thesis, "A Social History of California Architecture in the Nineteenth Century," 1957, University of California Library; now revised and published as *California's Architectural Frontier: Style and Tradition in the Nineteenth Century,* San Marino, Huntington Library, 1960.

62 Mumford, Lewis, *Sticks and Stones,* 2nd rev. ed., New York, Dover, 1955, p. 23.

64 Jefferson, Thomas, letter to Hugh L. White, Thomas M'Corry, *et al.,* May 6, 1810, in *The Writings of Thomas Jefferson,* Lipscomb, A., and Bergh, A. E. (ed.), Washington, Jefferson Memorial Association, 1903, XII, pp. 387 f.

67 Latrobe, Benjamin Henry, *The Journal of Latrobe,* Latrobe, J. H. B. (ed.), New York, Appleton, 1905, p. 51.

69 Mumford, Lewis, *op. cit.* (see note to page 62), p. 62.

70 Kouwenhoven, John A., *Made in America,* Garden City, Doubleday, 1948.

70 Wheeler, Gervase, *Homes for the People, in suburb and country; the villa, the mansion, and the cottage, adapted to American climate,* New York, Scribner's, 1855.

70 Vaux, Calvert, on balloon frames, in Kouwenhoven, *op. cit.,* p. 65.

71 Kouwenhoven, John, *op. cit.* (see note to page 70), pp. 84 f.

71 Latrobe, Benjamin Henry, *Impressions Respecting New Orleans,* New York, Columbia, 1951, p. 42.

72 Emerson, Ralph Waldo, *Journals of Ralph Waldo Emerson,* Boston, Houghton Mifflin, 1914, Vol. X, p. 197.

83 Mills, Robert, quoted in Gallagher, Helen Mar (Pierce), *Robert Mills,* New York, Columbia, 1935, Appendix.

83 Cabot, James E., "Notes on Domestic Architecture," *Atlantic Monthly,* I, 3, 1858, pp. 259 and 262.

84 L'Enfant, Pierre Charles, *L'Enfant and Washington, 1791-92, Published and Unpublished Documents . . . ,* Kite, Elizabeth S. (ed.), Baltimore, Johns Hopkins, 1929, p. 62.

85 Jarves, James Jackson; see *The Art-Idea: Sculpture, Painting and*

Architecture in America, New York, Hurd and Houghton, 1864.

85 Lodoli, Carlo, quoted, Algarotti, Francesco Conte, "Saggio sopra l'architettura" (1756) in *Opere*, Leghorn, 1764, II, 62, trans. by Kaufmann, Emil, *Architecture in the Age of Reason*, Cambridge, Harvard, 1955, p. 96.

86 Alison, Archibald, *Essay on the Nature and Principles of Taste*, 1790, 2nd American ed., Hartford, Goodwin, 1821, pp. 281 f.

88 Latrobe, Benjamin Henry, *The Journal of Latrobe, op. cit.* (see note to page 67), p. 140.

88 Latrobe, Benjamin Henry, *ibid.*, p. 139.

90 Mumford, Lewis, *The South in Architecture*, New York, Harcourt, Brace, 1941, p. 59.

90 Latrobe, Benjamin Henry, *The Journal of Latrobe, op. cit.* (see note to page 67), p. 140.

91 Hume, David, quoted in Knight, Richard Payne, *An Analytical Enquiry into the Principles of Taste*, 2nd ed., London, Payne, 1805, p. 16.

92 Knight, Richard Payne, quoted in Pevsner, Nikolaus, "Richard Payne Knight," *Art Bulletin*, XXXI, 1949, pp. 293-320.

93 Latrobe, Benjamin Henry, *The Journal of Latrobe, op. cit.* (see note to page 67), p. 139.

93 Walter, Thomas U., "Architecture," *Journal of the Franklin Institute*, XXXII, 3rd series, 1 (Jan. 1, 1841), p. 12.

94 Hone, Philip, *The Diary of Philip Hone*, Nevins, Allan (ed.), New York, Dodd, Mead, 1927, p. 302.

94 Hamlin, Talbot, *Greek Revival Architecture in America*, New York, Oxford, 1944, p. 331.

94 Biddle, Nicholas, "Diary," January 1839, published in *Pennsylvania Magazine of History and Biography*, XVIII, 1894, pp. 354 f., and quoted by Agnes Addison Gilchrist in "Girard College: An Example of the Layman's Influence on Architecture," *Journal of the Society of Architectural Historians*, XVI, 2, 1957, p. 23.

94 Chandler, Joseph R., "Address Delivered on the Occasion of the Placing of the Crowning Stone, August 29, 1846," printed, Davis, John C., *Final Report of the Building Committee of the Girard College for Orphans*, Philadelphia, L. R. Bailey, 1848, pp. 76 f.

97 Cleveland, Henry R., "American Architecture," *North American Review*, XLIII, 1836, pp. 379 f.

97 Pugin, Augustus Welby, *True Principles of Pointed or Christian Architecture*, London, Bohn, 1853.

98 Upjohn, Richard, quoted in Upjohn, E., *Richard Upjohn, Architect and Churchman*, New York, Columbia, 1939, p. 82.

99 Walter, Thomas U., eulogy of Upjohn, in *Richard Upjohn, op. cit.*, p. 192.

100   Owen, Robert D., *Hints on Public Architecture*, New York, Putnam, 1849, p. 44.

100   Downing, Andrew Jackson, *The Architecture of Country Houses . . .* (*1850*), New York, Appleton, 1861, p. 30.

100   Downing, Andrew Jackson, *Cottage Residences . . .* , New York, Wiley and Putnam, 1844.

100-101   Davis, Alexander Jackson, quoted in Hamlin, Talbot, *op. cit.*, (see note to page 94), pp. 290 f.

101   Allen, Lewis F., *Rural Architecture*, 1852, quoted by Russell Lynes in *The Tastemakers*, New York, Harper, 1954, pp. 26 f.

101   Fowler, O. S., *A Home for All*, quoted by Lynes, *ibid.*, p. 36.

101   Cleaveland, Henry W., and Backus, William, *Village and Farm Cottages*, New York, Appleton, 1856.

101   Downing, Andrew Jackson, *The Architecture of Country Houses, op. cit.* (see note to page 100), Preface, p. v.

101   —— *Cottage Residences, op. cit.* (see note to page 100), p. iii.

102   —— *The Architecture of Country Houses, op. cit.* (see note to page 100), pp. 24 f.

102   Gilmor, Robert, Jr., letter to Thomas Cole, 1826, printed by Miller, Lillian Beresnack, "Patronage, Patriotism and Taste in Mid-19th-Century America," *Magazine of Art*, XLV, 7, 1952, p. 322.

102   Cooper, James Fenimore, quoted from *Home as Found* by Howard Mumford Jones, in "James Fenimore Cooper and the Hudson River School," *Magazine of Art*, XLV, 6, 1950, p. 245.

103   Henry, Joseph, "Address to the American Association for the Advancement of Science," *Scientific American*, May 1854, reprinted, *ibid.*, CXC, 5, 1954, p. 14.

103   Emerson, Ralph Waldo, "Thoughts on Art," *The Dial*, I, 3, 1841, p. 369.

103   Griffiths, John Willis, *Treatise on Marine and Naval Architecture*, New York, Appleton, 1851, p. 49.

104   Paxton, Joseph, quoted by Markham, Violet, *Paxton and the Bachelor Duke*, London, Hodder and Stoughton, Ltd., 1935, p. 182.

104   Emerson, Ralph Waldo, *op. cit.* (see note to page 103), p. 369.

105   Greenough, Horatio, "American Architecture," *A Memorial of Horatio Greenough*, Tuckerman, Henry (ed.), New York, Putnam, 1853, p. 125.

105   *Ibid.*

105   —— Letter to Charles Sumner, November 16, 1839, Florence, in papers of Charles Sumner, Houghton Library, Harvard University.

105   —— "American Architecture," *op. cit.* (see note to page 105), p. 127 and p. 128.

105-106   —— Letter to Emerson, *The Dial*, 1841, quoted by Theodore M. Brown in "Greenough, Paine, Emerson, and the Organic

Aesthetic," *Journal of Aesthetics and Art Criticism*, XIV, 3, 1956, p. 304.

106 —— "Aesthetics at Washington," in *A Memorial of Horatio Greenough, op. cit.* (see note to page 105), p. 90.

106 —— *A Memorial of Horatio Greenough, op. cit.* (see note to page 105), p. 78 and p. 125.

106 Coleridge, Samuel Taylor, *Lectures on Shakespeare and Other Poets and Dramatists*, Everyman's Library, London, J. M. Dent and Co., 1907, reprinted 1909, p. 46.

106 Emerson, Ralph Waldo, *op. cit.* (see note to page 103), p. 369.

107 Ward, Samuel Gray, "Notes on Art and Architecture," *The Dial*, IV, 1843, p. 109.

107 Vaux, Calvert, *Villas and Cottages*, New York, Harper, 1857, pp. 15 f.

107 Thoreau, Henry D., *Walden*, Boston, World's Classics Edition, 1854, p. 31.

109 Van Brunt, Henry, "Cast Iron in Decorative Architecture," *The Crayon*, VI, 1, 1859, pp. 17 f.

110-111 Greenough, Horatio, *A Memorial of Horatio Greenough, op. cit.* (see note to page 105), p. 63.

111 Norton, Charles Eliot, "Dwellings and Schools for the Poor," *North American Review*, LXXIV, 1852, p. 465.

111-112 Vaux, Calvert, *Villas and Cottages, op. cit.* (see note to page 107), pp. 17 f.

116-117 Jarves, James Jackson, *op. cit.* (see note to page 85), pp. 286 f.

117 —— *Ibid.*, p. 287.

117 Adams, Henry, *op. cit.* (see note to page 50), pp. 7 f.

118 MacLean, Kenneth, *Agrarian Age*, New Haven, Yale, 1950. A good essay on the subject of this page.

118 Hofstadter, Richard, *The Age of Reform*, New York, Knopf, 1955. An excellent general source which we have used freely.

118-119 —— *Ibid.*, p. 43.

125 —— *Social Darwinism in American Thought*, Philadelphia, Pennsylvania, 1944. An excellent general reference on its topic.

126 Rogers, Henry, Letter, 1849, printed, *William Barton Rogers, Life and Letters*, Rogers, Emma Savage (ed.), Boston, Houghton Mifflin, 1896, 2 vols., Vol. I, p. 311.

130 Gilman, Daniel Coit, *The Sheffield Scientific School of Yale University*, New Haven, Sheffield, 1897, p. 7.

131 Schlesinger, Arthur Meier, *The Rise of the City: 1878-1898*, New York, Macmillan, 1933. A fine general reference on the period.

133 Anon., Editorial, *American Architect and Building News*, I, 1, 1876, p. 9.

136-137 Hyatt, Thaddeus, review of his work in *American Architect and Building News*, III, 107, 1878, p. 13.

137 Rockefeller, John D., Jr., quoted in Hofstadter, *Social Darwinism, op. cit.* (see note to page 125), p. 31.

137 Carnegie, Andrew, *Autobiography of Andrew Carnegie,* Boston, Houghton Mifflin, 1920, p. 339.

138 Bascom, John, *Aesthetics; or, The Science of Beauty,* Boston, Crosby and Nichols, 1862, p. 199.

139 Mumford, Lewis, *The Brown Decades: A Study of the Arts in America, 1865-1895,* New York, Dover, 2nd revised ed., 1955, p. 49 (Harcourt, Brace, 1931).

140 Anon., "The Labor Troubles," *American Architect and Building News,* II; "Class Organization," III, 110, 1878, p. 39; III, "Communism," III, 113, 1878, p. 63.

143 Kirkland, Edward Chase, *Dream and Thought in the Business Community, 1860-1900,* Ithaca, Cornell, 1956, p. 3.

143 Clemens, Samuel, letter to Andrew Lang, 1889.

144 Whitman, Walt, "Plate Glass Notes, St. Louis, Missouri, Nov. '79" in *Prose Works,* Philadelphia, David McKay, n.d. (1888?), p. 415.

145 Fergusson, James, *History of the Modern Styles of Architecture,* London, John Murray, 1862, pp. 482 f.

145 Anon., *Examples of the Architecture of the Victorian Age,* 1862, quoted by Peter F. R. Donner in "A Harris Florilegium," *Architectural Review* (London), XCIII, 554, 1943, p. 51.

145 Harris, Thomas, *Three Periods of English Architecture,* (1894), quoted by Donner, Peter F. R., *op. cit.,* p. 51.

147 Moholy-Nagy, Sibyl, *Native Genius in Anonymous Architecture,* New York, Horizon, 1957. With Giedion and Richards, a leading exponent of the virtues of anonymous architecture.

147 Richards, J. M., *The Functional Tradition,* London, Architectural Press, 1958. With Giedion and Sibyl Moholy-Nagy, a leading exponent of the virtues of anonymous architecture.

150 Anon., *New York Times,* August 29, 1859. Quoted by Kouwenhoven, John A., *The Columbia Historical Portrait of New York,* Garden City, Doubleday, 1953, p. 283.

150 Fryer, William John, Jr., "Iron Store-Fronts," *The Architectural Review and American Builders' Journal,* I, 1869, p. 621.

156-157 Anon., three quotations from *Cleveland Leader,* Feb. 7, 1860; July 18, 1860; Mar. 5, 1861; all cited by Chapman, Edmund H., "City Planning under Industrialization: The Case of Cleveland," *Journal of the Society of Architectural Historians,* XII, 2, 1953, p. 24.

157 Carnegie, Andrew, *Autobiography, op. cit.* (see note to page 137), p. 137 and pp. 93 f.

160 Anon., "Our Homeless Poor," *Frank Leslie's Illustrated Newspaper,* series, 1872.

162-163 Brown, Mark H., and Felton, W. R., *The Frontier Years*, New York, Holt, 1955. An interesting general source.

166-167 Meeks, Carroll L. V., *The Railroad Station*, New Haven, Yale, 1956. A valuable monograph.

169 Scully, Vincent J., *The Shingle Style*, New Haven, Yale, 1955. A valuable monograph.

171 Kirkland, Edward Chase, *Dream and Thought*, *op. cit.* (see note to page 143), p. 30.

172 Moore, Charles H., "Ruskin as a Critic of Architecture," *Architectural Record*, LVI, 2, 1924, pp. 117 f. The quotation is paraphrased.

173 Ruskin, John, *Stones of Venice*, Collected Works, Cook, E. T., and Wedderburn, A., ed., London, 1904, XI, p. 227.

173 Wight, Peter Bonnett, *The National Academy of Design*, New York, S. P. Avery, 1866, n.p. A description of the National Academy of Design serving as introduction to book of photos of the Academy.

173 Norton, Charles Eliot, "The National Academy of Design," *North American Review*, CIII, 1866, p. 586.

174 ———— "A Criticism of Harvard Architecture Made to the Board of Overseers," *Harvard Graduates' Magazine*, XII, 1903-1904, pp. 359 f.

175 Freeman, E. A., "The Architecture of American Cities," *American Architect and Building News*, XIII, 374, 1883, p. 91.

175 Root, John W., In Monroe, Harriet R., *John Wellborn Root, A Study of His Life and Work*, Boston, Houghton Mifflin, 1896, pp. 128 f. (Uncertain from text whether quote from Root or Montgomery Schuyler.)

177 Keim, DeBonneville Randolph, *Washington and Its Environs*, Washington, for the Compiler, 1874.

178 Moser, John, "Key to a Design Entitled 'Suggestion of a Façade for the A.I.A. Building, New York City,' by Mr. John Moser, Architect, Anniston, Alabama," *American Architect and Building News*, XV, 421, 1884, p. 31.

178 ———— "The Search for an American Style," *American Architect and Building News*, XXI, 576, 1887, p. 17.

179 Cook, Clarence, "Architecture in America," *North American Review*, CXXXV, 310, 1882, pp. 247 f., pp. 249 f.

179 Gilman, Daniel Coit, "Hand-craft and Rede-craft," *Launching of a University*, New York, Dodd, Mead, 1906, p. 286, p. 287.

180 ———— Letter, Oct. 3, 1875, to the President of the Board of Trustees, in Franklin, Fabian, *The Life of Daniel Coit Gilman*, New York, Dodd, Mead, 1910, p. 210.

180 Huxley, Thomas Henry, "Address at the Inauguration of Daniel Coit Gilman as President of the Johns Hopkins University," printed by Fabian Franklin in *The Life of Daniel Coit Gilman*, *op. cit.*, pp. 223-224.

181   Hopkins, Johns, letter, 1873, printed, Billings, John Shaw, *Description of the Johns Hopkins Hospital*, Baltimore, Friedenwald, 1890, p. 12.

182   Woodworth, Dr. John M., *Annual Report of the Supervising Surgeon-General*, Washington, U.S. Marine Hospital Service, 1873, cited by Brown, Francis Henry, in "General Principles of Hospital Construction," in Buck, Albert H., ed., *A Treatise on Hygiene and Public Health*, New York, Wood, 1879, p. 745.

182   Billings, John Shaw, *Barracks and Hospitals*, Circular 4, Publication of the Surgeon-General's Office, U. S. Government Printing Office, 1870, p. 3.

182   Eliot, Charles William, letter, printed in James, Henry, *Charles William Eliot*, Boston, Houghton Mifflin, 1930, I, pp. 125 f., p. 134.

182   Ruskin, John, "The Poetry of Architecture" (1837), *The Crayon*, I, 1854, p. 83.

182   Eidlitz, Leopold, *The Nature and Functions of Art*, New York, 1881, quoted in book review, *American Architect and Building News*, XI, 329, 1882, p. 173.

182   Greenough, Horatio, *A Memorial of Horatio Greenough*, *op. cit.* (see note to page 105), p. 63.

183   Hall, G. Stanley, letter, 1888, printed, *Letters of G. Stanley Hall to Jonas Gilman Clark*, Rush, N. O. (ed.), Worcester, Clark University Library, 1948, pp. 8 f.

183   Eliot, Charles William, letter, printed, James, Henry, *op. cit.* (see note to page 182), p. 133.

183   Agassiz, Louis, *Report*, 1868, quoted *Harvard Book*, Vaille, F. O. (ed.), Cambridge, Welch, Bigelow, 1875, I, p. 336.

183   Wallace, Alfred Russel, "American Museums," *Fortnightly Review*, XLII N.S., CCXLIX, 1887, p. 355.

184   Norton, Charles Eliot, book review of *The Oxford Museum* by Henry W. Acland and John Ruskin, in *Atlantic Monthly*, IV, XXVI, 1859, pp. 767 f.

187   Richardson, Henry Hobson, quoted, Van Rensselaer, Mrs. Schuyler, *Henry Hobson Richardson and His Works*, Boston, Houghton Mifflin, 1888, p. 57.

187-188   ——— *Ibid.*, p. 119.

189   Van Brunt, Henry, "Henry Hobson Richardson," *Atlantic Monthly*, LVIII, CCCXLIX, 1886, p. 692.

190   Richardson, Henry Hobson, quoted in Van Rensselaer, *op. cit.* (see note to page 187), p. 23.

190   ——— *Ibid.*, p. 38.

190   Brooks, Phillips, *Ibid.*, p. 37.

190   Van Brunt, Henry, *op. cit.* (see note to page 189), p. 691.

190   ——— "On the Present Condition and Prospects of Architecture," *Atlantic Monthly*, LVII, CCCXLI, 1886, p. 382.

198 Santayana, George, "The Genteel Tradition in American Philosophy," from *Winds of Doctrine*, New York, Scribner's, 1912, pp. 187 f.

199 Turner, Frederick Jackson, "The Significance of the Frontier in American History," in *Annual Report of the American Historical Association*, Washington, Government Printing Office, 1894, pp. 199-227.

201 Sullivan, Louis Henri, unpublished manuscript (1908), "A Man-Search," in Burnham Library, Chicago, p. 43.

202 de Tocqueville, Alexis, *op. cit.* (see note to page 48), p. 59; p. 58.

202-203 Root, John Wellborn, quoted in Monroe, *op. cit.* (see note to page 175), p. 192.

203 ———— *Ibid.*, p. 62.

204 Sullivan, Louis Henri, *Kindergarten Chats*, Washington, Scarab Fraternity Press, 1934, p. 83.

205-206 Corser, Frederick G., "The Northern View," *Transactions of the Architectural Association of Minnesota*, 1885, pp. 78-80, cited by Donald R. Torbert in "The Advent of Modern Architecture in Minnesota," *Journal of the Society of Architectural Historians*, XIII, 1, 1954, p. 18.

206 Wright, Frank Lloyd, *Frank Lloyd Wright on Architecture*, *op. cit.* (see note to page 45), p. 33.

206 ———— *Ibid.*, p. 36.

206 Ferree, Barr, "An American Style of Architecture," *Architectural Record*, I, 1, 1891-1892, p. 39.

207 Root, John Wellborn, quoted in Monroe, *op. cit.* (see note to page 175), p. 69.

207 ———— Report of meeting of Illinois State Association, March 5, 1887, *Inland Architect*, IX and X, 1887-1888, March 1887, p. 23.

208 Kipling, Rudyard, quoted by Ferris Greenslet in *The Life of Thomas Bailey Aldrich*, Boston, Houghton Mifflin, 1908, p. 169.

209 Strong, Josiah, *The Twentieth Century City*, New York, 1898, cited in Hofstadter, *The Age of Reform*, *op. cit.* (see note to page 118), p. 175.

209 Hofstadter, Richard, *The Age of Reform*, *op. cit.* (see note to page 118), pp. 178-179.

209 Donnelly, Ignatius, *ibid.*, p. 87 (from *The Golden Bottle*, pp. 202 f.).

209-210 Ross, Edward A., *ibid.*, pp. 178, 179.

216 Baker, Sir Benjamin, November 27, 1890, lecture at Edinburgh Literary Society.

216 Schuyler, Montgomery, "Modern Architecture," Butterfield Lecture at Union College, March 9, 1894, *Architectural Record*, IV, 1, 1894, p. 13.

216 Veblen, Thorstein, *The Theory of the Leisure Class*, New York, Macmillan, 1899; the New American Library, Mentor edition, 1953, p. 226.

216   Fitch, James Marston, *American Building*, Boston, Houghton Mifflin, 1948, p. 108.

217   McKinley, William, third Annual Message.

218   Roosevelt, Theodore, "The New Nationalism," Address at Ossawatonie, Kansas, August 31, 1901.

218   Wilson, Woodrow, address to Commercial Club of Chicago, January 11, 1913.

218   Brandeis, Louis D., *Other People's Money*, New York, Stokes, 1932, 8th printing, p. 33.

219   Tarbell, Ida M., "John D. Rockefeller: A Character Study," *McClure's* magazine, XXV, July-August 1905, pp. 249, 387.

219   Lloyd, Henry Demarest, *Wealth against Commonwealth*, New York, Harper, 1894, p. 510.

219-220   Godkin, E. L., "The Duty of Educated Men in a Democracy," *Forum*, XVII, 1894, p. 43.

220   Perkins, Charles Elliott, letter to Edward Atkinson, June 7, 1881, quoted from Atkinson Papers in Massachusetts Historical Society by Kirkland, *op. cit.* (see note to page 143), pp. 23 f.

221   Beveridge, Senator Albert J., April 1898, cited in Hofstadter, Miller and Aron, *The United States*, Englewood Cliffs, Prentice-Hall, 1957, p. 556.

221   Clark, Senator Champ, February 14, 1911, *ibid.*

223   Baer, George F., statement of July 17, 1902.

225-226   Wright, Frank Lloyd, Hull House Address, 1901. Revised and published in *Modern Architecture*, Princeton, Princeton, 1931 (the Kohn Lectures for 1930), p. 8.

226   ——— *Ibid.*, p. 13.

229-230   Rideout, Walter B., *The Radical Novel in the United States*, Cambridge, Harvard, 1956. A valuable source on this subject.

230   James, Henry, quoted in Hofstadter, Miller and Aron, *The United States*, *op. cit.* (see note to page 221), p. 522.

232   Roosevelt, Theodore, "A Layman's Views of an Art Exhibition," *The Outlook*, 103, March 29, 1913, pp. 718 f.

238   Meakin, Budgett, *Model Factories and Villages: Ideal Conditions of Labour and Housing*, Philadelphia, Jacobs, 1905, p. 23.

239   ——— *Ibid.*, p. 71.

239   Anon., editorial, appended to Kohn, Robert D., "Architecture and Factories," *Architectural Record*, XXV, 2, 1909, p. 136.

241   Sturgis, Russell, "The Warehouse and the Factory in Architecture," *Architectural Record*, XV, 1, 1904, p. 14, p. 133.

244   Schuyler, Montgomery, "The Sky-line of New York," *Harper's Weekly*, 41, March 20, 1897, p. 295.

245   Condit, Carl W., *The Rise of the Skyscraper*, Chicago, Chicago, 1952. One of the most thorough treatments of the successes of the "Chicago School."

245 Ericsson, Henry, *Sixty Years a Builder,* autobiography of Henry Erics-
     son written with Myers, Lewis E., Chicago, Kroch, 1942. An
     illuminating account of what it was like to be a builder in Chicago
     in the eighties and nineties (and later).

246 Viollet-le-Duc, Eugene E., *Discourses on Architecture,* New York,
     Grove Press, 1959, I, p. 448.

247 Sullivan, Louis Henri, *Autobiography of an Idea,* New York, A.I.A.,
     1924, pp. 254 f.

247 Semper, Gottfried, "Development of Architectural Style," trans.,
     J. W. Root, *Inland Architect and News Record,* XIV, 7, 1889,
     p. 76.

247 Wright, Frank Lloyd, *Frank Lloyd Wright on Architecture, op. cit.*
     (see note to page 45), p. 35, p. 42.

248 ———— *Ibid.,* pp. 31 f.

248 Guadet, Julien, *Elements et Theorie d'Architecture,* Paris, Librairie
     de la Construction Moderne, n.d. [1901], p. 134.

250 ———— *Ibid.,* p. 135.

252 Blackall, C. H., "Notes of Travel — Chicago," *American Architect
     and Building News,* XXIII, 635, 1888, pp. 90 f.

252 Anon., "Architectural Aberrations, No. 7 — The Fagin Building, St.
     Louis," *Architectural Record,* II, 4, 1892-1893, p. 470.

253 Monroe, Harriet R., *op. cit.* (see note to page 175), p. 248.

254 Adams, Henry, *op. cit.* (see note to page 50), pp. 340 f.

254 Fitch, James Marston, *op. cit.* (see note to page 216), caption to
     Fig. 91.

255 Kouwenhoven, John A., *op. cit.* (see note to page 70), p. 95.

255 Cret, Paul Philippe, "The Ecole des Beaux Arts: What Its Archi-
     tectural Teaching Means," *Architectural Record,* XXIII, 5, 1908,
     p. 369.

256 Sullivan, Louis Henri, "The Tall Office Building Artistically Con-
     sidered," *Lippincott's Magazine,* LVII, 1896, parts reprinted in
     Kimball, Fiske, "Louis Sullivan — An Old Master," *Architectural
     Record,* LVII, 4, 1925, p. 301.

257 ———— *Ibid.,* pp. 301-302.

258 ———— *Ibid.,* p. 302.

259 Desmond, H. W., "Rationalizing the Skyscraper," *Architectural
     Record,* XVII, 5, 1905, p. 423.

260 ———— *Ibid.,* p. 423.

260-261 Anon., editorial, *Architectural Review* (U.S.) XIV, 7, 1907,
     p. 184.

261 Sturgis, Russell, "The Larkin Building in Buffalo," *Architectural
     Record,* XXIII, 4, 1908, pp. 311, 319, and 321.

262 Wright, Frank Lloyd, "In the Cause of Architecture," *Architectural
     Record,* XXIII, 3, 1908, p. 167.

262 McKim, Charles Follen, quoted in Moore, Charles, *The Life and*

Times of Charles Follen McKim, Boston, Houghton Mifflin, 1929, pp. 167 f.

266-267 ——— *Ibid.*, pp. 281 f.

269 Riis, Jacob, *How the Other Half Lives*, New York, Scribner's, 1890, p. 69.

272 Meakin, Budgett, *op. cit.* (see note to page 238), p. 412.

274 Bragdon, Claude, "Architecture and Democracy," *Architectural Record*, XLIV, 1, 1918, p. 77.

275 Burnham, Daniel H. This famous quotation is now doubted. See Saylor, Henry H., " 'Make No Little Plans' Daniel Burnham Thought It But Did He Say It?" *Journal of the American Institute of Architects*, XXVII, 3, 1957, pp. 95 f.

276 Burnham, Carrère and Brunner, "Report of Group Plan Commission," 1902, quoted in Hegemann, Werner, and Peets, Elbert, *The American Vitruvius: An Architects' Handbook of Civic Art*, New York, Architectural Book Pub. Co., 1922, p. 139.

278 Bragdon, Claude, *op. cit.* (see note to page 274), p. 83.

283 Cram, Ralph Adams, *The Significance of Gothic Art*, Boston, Marshall Jones, 1918, p. 23.

284 Shinn, George W., "The American Cathedral," *American Architect and Building News*, XXXVI, 860, 1892, p. 178.

285 Wight, Peter Bonnett, "Condition of Architecture in the Western States," *American Architect and Building News*, VII, 221, 1880, p. 118.

286 Oakey, A. F., "Notes on Modern Church Building," *American Architect and Building News*, VIII, 243, 1880, p. 88.

287 Maybeck, Ralph Bernard, *Blue and Gold of 1900*, quoted in Cardwell, Kenneth, and Hays, William C., "Fifty Years from Now," *California Monthly*, XLIV, 8, 1954, p. 22.

288 Junghaendel, Max, quoted, *San Francisco Bulletin*, in Cardwell and Hays, *op. cit.*, p. 22.

290 Cram, Ralph Adams, *The Gothic Quest*, New York, Baker and Taylor, 1907, p. 217.

290 ——— *My Life in Architecture*, Boston, Little, Brown, 1936, p. 275.

290 ——— *The Gothic Quest*, *op. cit.*, p. 158.

290-291 West, Andrew Fleming, quoted in Egbert, Donald Drew, "The Architecture and the Setting," *The Modern Princeton*, Princeton, Princeton, 1947, pp. 93 f.

291 Collins, V. Lansing, *Princeton Past and Present*, Princeton, Princeton, 1945, Sections 84 f.

311 Schlesinger, Arthur M., Jr., *The Crisis of the Old Order*, Boston, Houghton Mifflin, 1957. The most informative single work on the period although other valuable comments are provided by Ride-

out, *op. cit.* (see note to page 229), Hofstadter, *op. cit.* (see note to page 118), and Wecter (cited below).

312 Wecter, Dixon, *The Age of the Great Depression: 1929-1941*, New York, Macmillan, 1948.

315 Kennan, George F., *Russia Leaves the War*, Princeton, Princeton, 1956.

315-316 Mencken, Henry L., "Theodore Dreiser," *A Book of Prefaces*, 1916, reprinted in *The Vintage Mencken, op. cit.* (see note to page 50), p. 37.

317 Bridgman, Percy, quoted from *Harper's Magazine*, CLVIII, March 1929, pp. 443-451, by John Van Vleck in "The Uncertainty Principle," *Encyclopaedia Britannica*, 1960, Vol. 22, p. 681.

325 Jones, Howard Mumford, private communication.

327 Mikkelsen, Michael A., "Two Problems of Architecture," *Architectural Record*, 65, 1, 1929, p. 65.

328 Atterbury, Grosvenor, quoted in Bemis, Albert Farwell, and Burchard, John E., *The Evolving House*, Vol. III, *Rational Design*, Cambridge, Technology, 1936, p. 351.

330 Creighton, Thomas H., private communication.

332 Dos Passos, John, quoted by Rideout, Walter B., *op. cit.* (see note to page 229), p. 165.

333 Gold, Michael, "Towards Proletarian Art," in *Liberator*, IV (February 1921), 20-24, p. 23, quoted by Rideout, Walter B., *op. cit.* (see note to page 229), p. 124, p. 125.

333 Mencken, Henry L. This statement and comparable ones by others (Nathan, Hergesheimer, Cabell) are cited in Schlesinger, *The Crisis of the Old Order, op. cit.* (see note to page 311), p. 145.

334 Eliot, T. S., *The Waste Land and Other Poems*, London, Faber and Faber, 1949.

340 Mencken, Henry L., "The New Architecture," *American Mercury*, February 1931, reprinted in *The Vintage Mencken, op. cit.* (see note to page 50), p. 202, p. 203.

341 Nimmons, George C., "Modern Industrial Plants," *Architectural Record*, XLIV, 5, 1918, pp. 414 f.; 533 f.; XLV, 4, 1919, p. 343.

341 Schuyler, Montgomery, "A New Departure in 'Big Business'," *Architectural Record*, XXXV, VI, 1914, p. 507.

341 Dempsey, Florence, "Nela Park: A Novelty in the Architectural Grouping of Industrial Buildings," *Architectural Record*, XXXV, VI, 1914, p. 501.

341 Price, George M., *The Modern Factory: Safety, Sanitation and Welfare*, New York, Wiley, 1914.

342 Wallis, Frank E., "Is American Architecture a Live Art? Does It Stand the Factory Test?" *Architectural Review* (U. S.), XX, 7, 1915, pp. 81, 82, 88.

343 Gilbert, Cass, "Industrial Architecture in Concrete," *Architectural Forum*, XXXIX, 3, 1923, p. 84.

344 Corbett, Harvey Wiley, "Annual Exhibition of the Architectural League, New York," *Architectural Record*, LXV, 1, 1929, p. 97.

344 Anon., editorial, *Architecture*, XLI, 4, 1920, p. 107.

345 Hood, Raymond M., *Raymond M. Hood*, New York, McGraw-Hill, 1931, p. 16.

345 Corbett, Harvey Wiley, "The American Radiator Building, New York City, Raymond M. Hood, Architect," *Architectural Record*, LV, 5, 1924, p. 473.

345 Kimball, Fiske, "Louis Sullivan — An Old Master," *Architectural Record*, LVII, 4, 1925, pp. 289 f.

348 Kent, H. Harold, "The Chicago Tribune Competition," *Architectural Record*, LIII, 4, 1923, p. 379.

348 Sullivan, Louis Henri, "The Chicago Tribune Competition," *Architectural Record*, LIII, 2, 1923, pp. 153 f.

349 Solon, Leon V., "The Passing of the Skyscraper Formula for Design," *Architectural Record*, LV, 2, 1924, p. 137.

349-350 Corbett, Harvey Wiley, "Zoning and the Envelope of the Building," *Pencil Points*, IV, 4, 1923, pp. 15 f.

351 Bossom, Alfred C., *Building to the Skies*, London, Studio, 1934, p. 18.

351 Stacy-Judd, Robert B., "Wanted — All-American Architecture with Ancient Maya Motifs as a Background," *Architect and Engineer*, CXV, 1, 1933, p. 11.

352 Kahn, Ely Jacques, *Ely Jacques Kahn: Contemporary American Architects*, New York, Whittlesey, 1931, p. 10.

353 Polk, Willis, *Hallidie Building* illustrated in *Architectural Record*, XLIV, 4, 1918, p. 381; LXIX, 2, 1931, p. 131.

354 Anon., "Answers to Criticisms of Radio City published in the New York Times and Herald-Tribune," *Pencil Points*, XII, 5, 1931, p. 387.

355 Croly, Herbert, "Architectural Response to Social Change," *Architectural Record*, LVIII, 2, 1925, pp. 186 f.

356-357 Garnier, Tony, *Une Cité Industriellé*, Paris, Vinceul, n.d. [1901?].

357 Le Corbusier, *Vers une Architecture*, Paris, Crès (préf. 1928) rév. et aug. (first published 1923).

357 —— *Towards a New Architecture*, trans. by Frederick Etchells, London, Architectural Press, 1948.

357 Sitte, Camillo, *Der Städtebau nach seinen Kunstlerischen Grundsatzen*, (1889) Vienna, Graeser, 1922.

357 Hegemann, Werner, and Peets, Elbert, *The American Vitruvius: An Architects' Handbook of Civic Art*, New York, Architectural Book Publishing Co., 1922.

357-358 Corbett, Harvey Wiley, "The Problem of Traffic Congestion, and a Solution," *Architectural Forum*, XLVI, 3, 1927, p. 204.

358   Ferriss, Hugh, *Metropolis of Tomorrow*, New York, Ives Washburn, 1929, p. 124.

358   Corbett, Harvey Wiley, "New Stones for Old: America's Architectural Supremacy," *Saturday Evening Post*, CXCVIII, March 27, 1926, p. 7.

359   Ferriss, Hugh, *op. cit.* (see note to page 358), p. 71.

359   Hood, Raymond M., "A City under a Single Roof," *Nation's Business*, XVII, 12, 1929, p. 20.

360-361   Taut, Bruno, *Modern Architecture*, London, Studio, 1929, pp. 9, 89, and 97.

361   Scott, Geoffrey, *The Architecture of Humanism*, New York, Scribner's, 1914, 2nd ed. 1924. Paper version of 2nd ed., New York, Doubleday, 1954.

361-362   Taut, Bruno, *op. cit.* (see note to page 360), pp. 140 f.

362   Price, C. Matlack, quotes Goodhue in "The Panama-California Exposition," *Architectural Record*, XXXVII, 3, 1915, p. 234.

363   Sorokin, Pitirim, *Principles of Rural-Urban Sociology*, New York, Holt, 1929.

363   Weber, Adna F., *The Growth of Cities in the Nineteenth Century: A Study in Statistics*, Columbia University Studies in History, Economics and Public Law, Vol. XI, New York, Macmillan, 1899.

364   Perry, Clarence A., "The Neighborhood Unit," *Neighborhood and Community Planning, Regional Plan of New York and Its Environs*, Vol. VII, New York, 1929, p. 59.

366   Kocher, A. Lawrence, "The American Country House," *Architectural Record*, LVIII, 5, 1925, pp. 402 f.

366   Newcomb, Rexford, *The Spanish House for America*, Philadelphia, Lippincott, 1927.

366   Soule, Winsor, *Spanish Farm Houses and Minor Public Buildings*, New York, Architectural Book Publishing Co., 1924.

367   Henderson, Rose, "A Primitive Basis for Modern Architecture," *Architectural Record*, LIV, 2, 1923, p. 189.

367   Cassidy, Louise Lowber, "The Southwest Develops Native Architecture," *Architectural Record*, LIX, 4, 1926, p. 395.

367   Fessenden, DeWitt H., "Mrs. O. H. P. Belmont's Tea House, Newport, R. I.," *Architectural Record*, XXXIX, 6, 1916, p. 499.

368   Cret, Paul Philippe, Kimball, Fiske, and Wright, Frank Lloyd, "Correspondence of Walter Pach, Paul Cret, Frank Lloyd Wright and Erich Mendelsohn with Fiske Kimball," *Architectural Record*, LXV, 5, 1929, p. 431, p. 434.

368-369   Shreve, Richmond H., "The Economic Design of Office Buildings," *Architectural Record*, LXVII, 4, 1930, p. 341.

369   Pope, John Russell, "Office Manual of John Russell Pope, Architect," *Architectural Record*, LXIX, 2, 1931, p. 177.

369   Wright, Frank Lloyd, "In the Cause of Architecture," *Architectural*

Record, LXI, 5, 1927, pp. 394 f., pp. 478 f.; LXIII, 1, 1928, pp. 49 f., pp. 145 f., p. 337, p. 350, pp. 555 f.; LXIV, 1, 1928, p. 11, p. 99, p. 334, p. 507.

370 —— Modern Architecture, op. cit. (see note to page 225).

370 Drummond, William, quoted in Wight, Peter Bonnett, "Country House Architecture in the Middle West," Architectural Record, XL, 4, 1916, p. 292.

370 Schindler, R. M., Architectural Record, LXVI, 3, 1929, p. 257.

370 Gill, Irving, Architectural Record, LXVIII, 5, 1930, p. 439.

371 Sexton, R. W., "And Now — A 'Modern' House," Architectural Forum, LI, 5, 1929, p. 537.

371 Oud, Dudok, et al, Architectural Record, LXV, 4, 1929, pp. 329 f.; LXVIII, 4, 1930, passim.

371 Hitchcock, Henry-Russell, Modern Architecture, Romanticism and Reintegration, New York, Harcourt, Brace, 1929.

371 Hitchcock, Henry-Russell, and Johnson, Philip, The International Style: Architecture since 1922, New York, Norton, 1932.

371-372 Geddes, Norman Bel, Horizons, Boston, Little, Brown, 1932, pp. 4 f.

373 Neutra, Richard J., Amerika, Vienna, Schroll, 1930.

373 Mendelsohn, Erich, Amerika, Berlin, Mosse, 1928.

373 Gréber, Jacques, L'Architecture aux États-Unis, Preuve de la Force d'Expansion du Génie Français, Paris, Payot, 1920, p. 13.

373-374 Cret, Paul Philippe, Introduction to Hoak, Edward Warren, and Church, Willis Humphry, Masterpieces of Architecture in the United States, New York, Scribner's, 1930, p. 3.

374 Harbeson, John F., The Study of Architectural Design with special reference to the program of the Beaux-Arts Institute of Design, New York, Pencil Points Press, 1927, p. 27.

374 Architects' Emergency Committee, Great Georgian Houses of America, New York, printed by Scribner press, 1937, 2 vols.

374 Whitehead, Russell F., White Pine Series of Architectural Monographs, New York, 26 vols., 1915-1928.

374 Curtis, Nathaniel Cortlandt, Architectural Composition, Cleveland, Jansen, 1923.

375 Harbeson, John F., op. cit. (see note to page 374).

377 Magonigle, H. Van Buren, quoted in Reid, J. R., "The Model for the Bahai Temple, Chicago, Louis J. Bourgeois, Architect," Architectural Record, XLVII, 6, 1920, p. 501.

380 Goodhue, Bertram Grosvenor, "Church Architecture in the United States," Architectural Review (U. S.), XXII, 11, 1917, p. 251.

381 Maginnis, Charles D., "Architectural Modernism and the Church," Architectural Forum, 50, 2, 1929, p. 424.

381 Hudnut, Joseph, "The Modern Spirit Enters Contemporary Church Architecture," American Architect, CXLII, 2614, 1932, pp. 12 f.

381   Upjohn, Hobart B., "Is Gothic a Dead Style?" *Architectural Forum*,
        L, 3, 1929, p. 367.

383   Stowell, Kenneth K., "The Editor's Forum," *Architectural Forum*,
        LIV, 6, 1931, p. 689.

383   Hale, William Harlan, "Old Castles for New Colleges," *Architectural
        Forum*, LIV, 6, 1931, p. 729.

384   Quoted, members of architectural commission, *Official Guide, Book of
        the Fair*, 1933, Chicago, A Century of Progress, 1933, p. 22.

392   Halle, Louis J., "Does History Have a Future?" *Saturday Review*,
        April 23, 1960, p. 18.

401   Reid, Kenneth, "Design in TVA Structures," *Pencil Points*, XX, 11,
        1939, pp. 691-719.

403   Churchill, Winston S., quoted in *Mid-Century: The Social Implica-
        tions of Scientific Progress*, ed. Burchard, John E., Cambridge,
        Technology and Wiley, 1950, p. 72.

405   Lescaze, William, "AIA Sets up Defense-Aid Program," *Architectural
        Record*, 88, 2, 1940, p. 10.

410   Neutra, Richard J., "Richard J. Neutra," by Henry Robert Harrison,
        Pencil Points, XVIII, 7, 1937, p. 411.

414   Shahn, Ben, quoted by Eliot, Alexander, *Three Hundred Years of
        American Painting*, New York, Time Inc., 1957, p. 239, p. 241.

418   Kepes, Gyorgy, *The Language of Vision*, Chicago, Paul Theobald,
        1944, p. 12.

420   Kaufmann, Edgar, Jr., "Borax, or the Chromium-Plated Calf," *Archi-
        tectural Review* (London), CIV, 620, 1949, p. 88.

421   Cram, Ralph Adams, *The Gothic Quest, op. cit.* (see note to page
        290).

421   —— *My Life in Architecture, op. cit.* (see note to page 290).

421   Scott, Geoffrey, *op. cit.* (see note to page 361).

422   Anderson, Robert, "Road to the Future," *Pencil Points*, XVIII, 10,
        1937, p. 650.

422   Hudnut, Joseph, quoted in Anderson, "Road to the Future," *supra*,
        p. 650.

422   Anderson, Robert, "The Religion of Art," *Pencil Points*, XVIII, 12,
        1937, pp. 777-778.

422   Hamlin, Talbot, *Architecture through the Ages*, New York, Putnam,
        1940.

422   Guadet, Julien, *op. cit.* (see note to page 248).

422   Le Corbusier, *Towards a New Architecture, op. cit.* (see note to page
        357).

422   Fuller, R. Buckminster, *Nine Chains to the Moon*, Philadelphia,
        Lippincott, 1938.

423   Wright, Frank Lloyd, "Architecture and Life in the U.S.S.R.," *Archi-
        tectural Record*, 82, 4, 1937, pp. 57-63.

425 Giedion, Sigfried, ed., *A Decade of New Architecture*, Zurich, Editions Girsberger, 1951, p. 3.

427 Read, Herbert, *Art and Society*, New York, Macmillan, 1937, p. 203.

427 —— *Art Now*, New York, Pitman, 1948 (1933), p. 12.

427 Gropius, Walter, letter to Donald Drew Egbert quoted in Egbert, Donald Drew, and Persons, Stow, ed., *Socialism and American Life*, Princeton, Princeton, 1952, Vol. I, p. 662.

428 Mâle, Emile, *L'Art Religieux en France*, Paris, Colin, 3 vols., 1924-1925.

428 Wittkower, Rudolf, *Architectural Principles in the Age of Humanism*, Studies of the Warburg Institute, London, Vol. 19, 1950.

428 Panofsky, Erwin, *Gothic Architecture and Scholasticism*, Latrobe, Pa., Archabbey Press, 1951.

428 Mumford, Lewis, *Technics and Civilization*, New York, Harcourt, Brace, 1934.

428 —— *The Culture of Cities*, New York, Harcourt, Brace, 1938.

428 —— *The Conduct of Life*, New York, Harcourt, Brace, 1951.

428 Giedion, Sigfried, *Space, Time and Architecture*, Cambridge, Harvard, 1941.

428 —— *Mechanization Takes Command*, New York, Oxford, 1948.

428 Coolidge, John P., *Mill and Mansion*, New York, Columbia, 1942.

428 Smith, E. Baldwin, *The Dome: A Study in the History of Ideas*, Princeton, Princeton, 1950.

428 Morrison, Hugh, *Louis Sullivan, Prophet of Functionalism*, New York, Norton, 1935.

429 Mumford, Lewis, *Sticks and Stones, op. cit.* (see note to page 62).

429 Hamlin, Talbot, *The American Spirit in Architecture*, New Haven, Yale, 1926.

429 Edgell, George H., *The American Architecture of To-day*, New York, Scribner's, 1928.

429 Tallmadge, Thomas Eddy, *The Story of Architecture in America*, New York, Norton, 1927.

429 Kimball, Fiske, *American Architecture*, Indianapolis, Bobbs-Merrill, 1928.

431 Moholy-Nagy, Laszlo, *The New Vision*, New York, Norton, 1938, p. 19.

431-432 Gropius, Walter, with Bayer, Herbert, and Gropius, Ise, *Bauhaus, 1919-1928*, New York, Museum of Modern Art, 1938, p. 29.

432 Gropius, Walter, "In Search of a New Monumentality: A Symposium," by Gregor Paulson, Henry-Russell Hitchcock, William Holford, Sigfried Giedion, Walter Gropius, Lucio Costa, and Alfred Roth, *Architectural Review* (London), 104, 621, 1948, pp. 117-128.

432 —— "Building and Biology," *Planning Man's Physical Environment*, Princeton University Bicentennial Conference, Series 2, Conference 5, p. 18.

432 ——— "Essentials for Architectural Education," *PM* (Magazine), IV, 5, 1938, n.p.

433 Le Corbusier, *Towards a New Architecture, op. cit.* (see note to page 357).

433 ——— *When the Cathedrals Were White: A Journey to the Country of Timid People*, New York, Reynal, 1947.

437 Fitch, James Marston, "Three Levers of Walter Gropius," *Architectural Forum*, 112, 5, 1960, pp. 128-133, pp. 203-204.

438 Giedion, Sigfried, *Walter Gropius: Work and Teamwork*, New York, Reinhold. Copyright 1954, Neuenschwander, Zurich, p. 27.

438 Gropius, Walter, quoted by Fitch, James Marston, *op. cit.* (see note to page 437), p. 204.

438 ——— *Ibid.*

439 Johnson, Philip, quoted, anon., *Architectural Record*, 127, 4, 1960, p. 166, from Johnson, Philip, *Mies van der Rohe*, New York, Museum of Modern Art, 2nd ed. rev., 1953.

439 Anon., *Architectural Record*, 127, 4, 1960, p. 165, quoted from Johnson, Philip, *Mies van der Rohe*, New York, Museum of Modern Art, 2nd ed. rev., 1953.

440 Hitchcock, Henry-Russell, *In the Nature of Materials: The Buildings of Frank Lloyd Wright, 1887-1941*, New York, Duell, Sloan, 1942.

440 ——— *Architectural Forum*, 88, 1, 1948, pp. 65-157.

441 Wright, Frank Lloyd, *The Disappearing City*, New York, Payson, 1932.

443 Jordy, William H., "The Formal Image: USA," *Architectural Review* (London), Vol. 127, No. 757, p. 168.

444 Rogers, Ernesto, on CIAM. In *Casabella*, 232 (October), 1959, quoted in *Architectural Review* (London), 127, 756, 1960, p. 79.

444 Voelcker, John, paraphrased in *Architectural Review* (London) 127, 756, 1960, p. 78.

445 CIAM, *Dwellings for the Lowest Income Classes*, Stuttgart, Julius Hoffman, 1930.

445 Sert, José Luis, *Can Our Cities Survive?* Cambridge, Harvard, 1942.

446 Giedion, Sigfried, *A Decade, op. cit.* (see note to page 425), p. 2.

449 Killam, Charles W., "School Training for Architecture," *Pencil Points*, XVIII, 7, 1937, p. 441.

449 Cram, Ralph Adams, *My Life in Architecture, op. cit.* (see note to page 290), p. 272, p. 281.

449 Dali, Salvador, quoted in Lescaze, *On Being an Architect*, New York, Putnam, 1942, p. 79.

450 Cram, Ralph Adams, *The Gothic Quest, op. cit.* (see note to page 290), p. 343, p. 23.

454 Scott, Geoffrey, *op. cit.* (see note to page 361).

454 Focillon, Henri, *The Life of Forms in Art*, New Haven, Yale, 1942, p. 76.

457   Hitchcock, Henry-Russell, *et al*, *Modern Architecture: Romanticism and Reintegration*, New York, Payson, 1929.

460   Kocher, A. Lawrence, Stein, Clarence, *et al*, quoted by Barney, W. Pope, "The Princeton Architectural Round Table, June, 1937," *Architectural Record*, 82, 3, 1937, p. 57.

462   Mason, Joseph B., ed., *82 Distinctive Houses from Architectural Record*, New York, F. W. Dodge Corp., 1952.

465   Wurster, William W., *et al*, "Is There a Bay Area Style?" *Architectural Record*, 105, 5, May 1949, pp. 92-97. (See also *Architectural Review*, London, 104, 622, 1948, p. 164.)

465   Wurster, William W., *Casabella*, 238, 1960, English trans. p. v.

481   Orr, Douglas W., "Princeton Builds," *Princeton Alumni Weekly*, LX, May 20, 1960, p. 8.

488   Anon., *Architectural Forum*, 85, 5, 1946, pp. 116-120.

489   Vriend, J. J., *Bouw*, 30, 1959, article on Breuer's Embassy for The Hague, cited in *Architectural Review* (London), CXXVII, 755, 1960, p. 7.

491   Huxtable, Ada Louise, "Critique of Project Questions Its Style," *New York Times*, June 3, 1960, p. 1.

498   Stein, Clarence, and Bauer, Catherine, "Store Buildings and Neighborhood Shopping Centers," *Architectural Record*, 75, 2, 1934, pp. 175-187.

498   "Building type-study," *Architectural Record*, 87, 6, 1940, pp. 99-120.

499   Gruen, Victor, and Smith, Lawrence P., "Shopping Centers," *Progressive Architecture*, XXXIII, 6, 1952, pp. 67-109.

502   Banham, Reyner, "1960: Stocktaking," *Architectural Review* (London), 127, 756, 1960, p. 100.

504   Giedion, Sigfried, "In Search of a New Monumentality," *op. cit.* (see note to page 432), pp. 117 f.

505   Yamasaki, Minoru, "Toward an Architecture for Enjoyment," *Architectural Record*, 118, 2, 1955, pp. 142 f.

505   ——— *Architectural Review* (London), 108, special number, 1950, on "Man Made America."

Index

A Note About the Indexes

For the convenience of the user, what would otherwise be a bulky single index has been divided into five sections.

The first lists architects, planners and landscape architects, American and foreign. From it the reader can readily find what we have said about any individual as well as those of his works which we have discussed.

The second lists American buildings cited in the book. They are classified by building types and are alphabetized by name under each building type. This index also includes the location of each building and usually its architect.

The third is an international list of cities. From this the reader can, for example, compose a summary of all the buildings in a given city which we have mentioned in the text.

The fourth index contains all the items which do not fit readily into one of the three rubrics described above.

The fifth is an index of illustrations. These have been chosen as representative of types and do not attempt to provide all the photographic information that would be desirable in a reference book or atlas of architecture, which, incidentally, would be a very good volume for somebody to produce.

INDEX I

Architects, Engineers, and Planners

Buildings of the U.S.A.

For brevity, only one architect's name is listed in the reference to any building. This is usually the first name to appear in the title of the principal firm, but may in special instances, for example, Shepley, be the name of the most active partner. For large firms like Skidmore, Owings and Merrill we have used the name Skidmore, rather than the designers Bunshaft or Netsch. For firms whose names have been perpetuated, such as McKim, Mead and White, or Cram and Ferguson, we have used McKim or Cram even though the principals were long deceased when the building was designed.

INDEX III

Cities

INDEX IV

General

INDEX V

Illustrations

Illustrations appear in six eight-page inserts, one in each section of the text. Page numbers below refer to the text page immediately preceding the insert in which the illustration appears.